FIFTH EDITION

PRINCIPLES OF

MACROECONOMICS

FIFTH EDITION

PRINCIPLES OF
MACROECONOMICS

Karl E. Case
WELLESLEY COLLEGE

Ray C. Fair
YALE UNIVERSITY

Prentice Hall, Upper Saddle River, New Jersey 07458

Acquisitions Editor:	Rod Banister
Developmental Editor:	Michael Elia
Assistant Editor:	Gladys Soto
Editorial Assistant:	William Becher
Editor-in-Chief:	James Boyd
Marketing Manager:	Patrick Lynch
Associate Managing Editor:	David Salierno
Permissions Coordinator:	Monica Stipanov
Managing Editor:	Dee Josephson
Manufacturing Supervisor:	Arnold Vila
Manufacturing Manager:	Vincent Scelta
Electronic Artist:	Warren Fischbach
Senior Production Manager:	Lorraine Patsco
Designer:	Ann France
Design Manager:	Patricia Smythe
Photo Research Supervisor:	Melinda Lee Reo
Image Permission Supervisor:	Kay Dellosa
Photo Researcher:	Melinda Alexander
Cover Illustration:	Theo Rudnak
Project Management/Composition:	TSI Graphics

Library of Congress Cataloging-in-Publication Data

Case, Karl E.
    Principles of macroeconomics / Karl E. Case, Ray C. Fair. — 5th
  ed.
      p. cm.
    Includes bibliographical references and index.
    ISBN 0-13-095733-X (alk. paper)
    1. Macroeconomics.   I. Fair, Ray C.   II. Title.
  HB172.5.C375   1999
  339—dc21

98-23825
CIP

Prentice-Hall International (UK) Limited, London
Prentice-Hall of Australia Pty. Limited, Sydney
Prentice-Hall Canada, Inc., Toronto
Prentice-Hall Hispanoamericana, S.A., Mexico
Prentice-Hall of India Private Limited, New Delhi
Prentice-Hall of Japan, Inc., Tokyo
Simon & Schuster Asia Pte. Ltd., Singapore
Editora Prentice-Hall do Brasil, Ltda., Rio de Janeiro

Printed in the United States of America

10 9 8 7 6 5 4 3 2 1

To
Professor Richard A. Musgrave
and
Professor Robert M. Solow

BRIEF CONTENTS

CONTENTS

MACROECONOMICS

PART 2: Concepts and Problems in Macroeconomics 113

GLOBAL COVERAGE

Because the study of macroeconomics crosses national boundaries, this book includes international examples in almost every chapter. The following list is a summary of global examples and discussions in the text.

PREFACE

THIS TEXTBOOK CONTAINS the five introductory chapters, fifteen microeconomics chapters, and four international chapters from our hardbound *Principles of Economics* textbook. It has been specially prepared for microeconomics courses where professors prefer to assign a paperback "split" rather than a single volume containing coverage of both microeconomics and macroeconomics.

So that users of this book and its companion volume, *Principles of Microeconomics,* can fully understand our methodology in preparing the fourth edition, what follows is an adaption of the preface as it appears in our single hardbound volume.

As this fifth edition is being prepared to go on press: We are into the 28th consecutive quarter of expansion in the U.S. economy. Unemployment is at its lowest in nearly 30 years. A number of Asian economies, including Korea, Thailand, and Indonesia, have suffered sharp economic downturns, and even Japan, the world's second largest economy, is suffering through recession and slow growth. Much of Europe is set to adopt a common currency. Hong Kong has become part of China. Congress passed the Taxpayer Relief Act and welfare reform has become reality. The Russian economy has begun to grow. (When our first edition was published in 1989, the Berlin Wall had not yet fallen, the Cold War still chilled internationalial relations, and Iraq had not yet invaded Kuwait.)

How rapidly the world is changing!

The degree to which the economic landscape has changed since our fourth edition was published, has led to hundreds of changes—some large, some not so large, some you might expect, some not—in this revision. One way of reflecting many of those changes in the landscape, is through the new Fast Facts feature we added to every chapter. Each Fast Fact contains some additional data or a current example, describing a significant change in the economy, adding depth to the text, while not adding bulk because they are concise, written to fit briefly in the margin column.

Revising a book involves adding new material, and there is a tendency for text books to grow in volume over time. But student time is a scarce resource, and longer books are more costly to produce. So our goal throughout was to update, refine and add material where needed but to end up cutting excess baggage and obsolete material wherever possible. The bottom line is that the fifth edition is a shorter book.

All tables and figures have been updated with the most recent data available, and the case studies (with accompanying videos) that end each part are completely new. And while we continue to cover the core of economic theory, we have added new material on important topics that have only recently emerged as major economic issues. These include the Fed's anti-inflationary responses to a growing economy, stock market volatility, the economic crisis in Asia, the European common currency, several countries' recent problems with currency debasement and volatile exchange rates, the new trade treaties, and the experiences of transitional economies.

In addition, the fifth edition contains more international material than any previous edition. Almost every chapter contains a global application or example. (A complete list of global examples follows the detailed table of contents.) We've also added additional problems to the end of each chapter and included solutions to the even-numbered problems at the end of the text.

To date, more than 300,000 students and professors have used *Principles of Economics* or one of its split volumes. In this new edition, we have made every effort to be responsive to our readers' suggestions while maintaining the book's basic focus and pedagogical organization. To make the book accessible to a wider range of students, we have cut a great deal of extraneous material, simplified several of the more analytical sections, and redrawn many of the more technical graphs using real numbers rather than variable names. And, to make the book more appealing to today's visual learners, we've completely revised the art, photo, and illustration program. The result, we hope, is a principles book that students will keep on their shelves and use throughout college and beyond.

THE PLAN OF *PRINCIPLES* OF *MACROECONOMICS*

Despite major revisions and new features, the themes of the fifth edition are the same themes of the first four editions. The purpose of this book is to introduce the discipline of economics and to provide a basic understanding of how economies function. This requires a blend of economic theory, institutional material, and real-world applications. We have tried to maintain a reasonable balance between these ingredients in every chapter in this book. Like the first four editions, the fifth edition also attempts to present different theoretical views in an evenhanded way.

Several new textbooks have shifted the emphasis in the presentation of macroeconomics from short run income determination to long run growth while deemphasizing business cycles, the role of countercyclical policy and the problems of unemployment and inflation. While we agree that growth deserves more attention in macroeconomics, we have chose *not* to follow their lead. We remain convinced that the basic structure of aggregate supply and aggregate demand provides a very powerful pedagogical framework within which students can come to understand the nature of the debates that now permeate the professional literature, including the efficacy of monetary and fiscal policy, the role of the Fed, and the factors that determine growth and the cyclical behavior of the economy. We are also convinced that unemployment and inflation remain serious potential problems for economies in the U.S. and across the world.

As in the fourth edition, we remain committed to the view that it is a mistake simply to throw aggregate demand and aggregate supply curves at students in the first few chapters of a principles book. To understand the AS and AD curves, one needs to know about the functioning of the goods market and the money market. The logic behind the simple demand curve is simply wrong when applied to the relationship between aggregate demand and the price level. Similarly, the logic behind the simple supply curve is wrong when applied to the relationship between aggregate supply and the price level.

Part of teaching economics is teaching economic reasoning. Our discipline is built around deductive logic. Once we teach students a pattern of logic, we want and expect them to apply it to new circumstances. When they apply the logic of a simple demand curve or simple supply curve to the aggregate demand or aggregate supply curve, the logic does not fit. We believe the best way to teach the reasoning embodied in the aggregate demand and aggregate supply curves without creating serious confusion is to build up to them carefully.

Organization   Like the fourth edition of *Principles of Macroeconomics,* the macroeconomics section begins with three introductory chapters (6–8) that introduce students to macroeconomic tools, national income accounting, and inflation and unemployment (both in the United States and abroad). These chapters are followed by two chapters that present the basic functioning of the goods market (chapters 9 and 10) and two chapters that present the basic functioning of the money market (chapters 11 and 12). It is in these four chapters that students are introduced to the concepts of fiscal and monetary policy. These chapters are followed by a chapter that brings the two markets together. This chapter, chapter 13, does in essence a very simplified version of *IS/LM* analysis verbally. (The *IS* and *LM* curves are included in an appendix to chapter 13 for those instructors who are interested in teaching them.)

Given the groundwork that has been laid in chapter 13, chapter 14 proceeds directly to derive the aggregate demand curve and then put together to determine the aggregate price level and to discuss the various theories of inflation.

Following the development of the *AD* and *AS* curves, we turn to a more detailed look at the labor market in chapter 15 and discuss various theories of unemployment. By the end of chapter 15, students have put the goods market, the money market, and the labor market together, and they have analyzed inflation, unemployment, and monetary and fiscal policy. Chapter 16 uses the material learned earlier to analyze a number of current macroeconomic issues, including proposed balanced-budget legislation and business cycles in Europe and Asia.

In chapter 17, we take a closer look at the behavior of households and firms in the macroeconomy. It can be skipped without losing the flow of the material. We close the macro section of the book by looking at some current debates in macroeconomics (chapter 18) and economic growth and productivity (chapter 19). We then consider international economics in more detail in chapters 20–23.

Content   In preparing the fifth edition, we have maintained the two innovations we introduced in the second edition. The first is the treatment of aggregate supply. Clearly, there is strong disagreement among economists and across economics textbooks on the exact nature of the aggregate supply curve. All economists agree that if input prices rise at the same rate as output prices, the aggregate supply curve is vertical; firms have no incentive to change output if their costs and revenues change at the same rate. For the *AS* curve to have a positive slope in the short run, input prices must either be constant or there must be some lag in their adjustment.

Some textbooks assume that input prices are constant when the overall price level changes, essentially treating the aggregate supply curve as if it were the sum of individual market supply curves. This assumption of constant input prices is obviously unrealistic, and in the second edition we changed our description of the short-run *AS* curve to one that assumes some lag in input price adjustment when the overall price level changes. In addition, we clarified and expanded our description of the long-run aggregate supply curve, incorporating the concept of potential GDP.

Second, we continue to distinguish between inflation (a change in the overall price level) and *sustained* inflation (an increase in the overall price level that continues for some period of time). There can be confusion in students' minds as to what inflation is and whether or not it is a purely monetary phenomenon, and we think that this distinction helps to clarify our discussions.

THE PLAN OF *PRINCIPLES* OF *MICROECONOMICS*

For professors who are teaching macroeconomics, a new version of *Principles of Microeconomics* is also available.

Market research and comments from users of the fourth edition convinced us that the organization of the microeconomic material is pedagogically sound. For this reason, we have not altered the presentation drastically in the fifth edition of *Principles of Microeconomics*.

The organization of the microeconomic material continues to reflect our belief that the best way to understand how market economies operate—and the best way to understand basic economic theory—is to work through the perfectly competitive model first, including discussions of output *and* input markets and the connections between them, before turning to noncompetitive market structures. When students understand how a simple competitive system works, they can start thinking about how the pieces of the economy "fit together." We think this is a better approach to teaching economics than some of the more traditional approaches, which encourage students to think of economics as a series of disconnected alternative market models.

Doing competition first also allows students to see the power of the market system. It is impossible to discuss the things that markets do well until students have seen how a simple system determines the allocation of resources. This is our purpose in chapters 6–11. Chapter 12 remains a pivotal chapter that links the world of perfect competition with the imperfect world of noncompetitive markets, externalities, imperfect information, and poverty, all of which we discuss in chapters 13–17. In chapters 18–20 students use everything they've learned in chapters 6–17 to take a closer look at some of the fields of applied microeconomics (the economics of taxation, labor economics, and the economics of health-care reform, immigration, and urban problems). Finally, in chapters 21–24, we examine some topics in international economics. Although we've chosen to place these chapters at the end of the book, professors can integrate them into their course at any time they feel is appropriate.

We do microeconomics first in the combined volume but have crafted the fifth edition so that professors can proceed directly to either microeconomics or macroeconomics after teaching the five introductory chapters.

HIGHLIGHTS OF THE FIFTH EDITION OF *PRINCIPLES* OF *MACROECONOMICS*

NEW FAST FACTS IN EVERY CHAPTER

An important new feature of the fifth edition is that between 2 and 4 Fast Facts have been added to every chapter. Each one is a new table of data, an additional example, a research result, or simply an illustration of a point made in the text. While brief and not as involved as a Box, we believe these will add depth and richness to the material. As an example, in the discussion of elasticity, we obtained some current estimates of price elasticity of demand for a number of common goods from Regional Financial Associates, a first rate forecasting and modelling firm in Philadelphia. Other examples include a brief discussion of the Three Gorges Dam under construction in China, the current U.S. dollar exchange rates against several currencies, and a table showing the cumulative effects of alternative growth rates over 10 and 20 year time periods.

RECENT DATA, EXAMPLES, EVENTS, AND TOPICS

Every chart, table, and graph in the book has been revised with the most recent data available. In addition, we have integrated topics that have generated a great deal of attention over the last few years—the recent experiences of Russia and the economies of Eastern Europe, the continuing economic problems of Asia, the adoption of a common currency in Europe, the debate about shifting to a consumption tax, and stock market volatility, to name just a few.

THE BEA'S NEW PROCEDURE

The Bureau of Economic Analysis (BEA) made a major change at the end of 1995 in its presentation of the national income and product accounts. The focus is no longer on constant-dollar magnitudes and on implicit price deflators, but instead on "chain-type annual weights" quantity and price indexes. This change is much more important than the BEA's change in focus a few years ago from GNP to GDP.

Unfortunately, our enthusiasm to get the description of the new and complex chain index into the fourth edition led us to pitch the discussion too high. We heard from many students and instructors that the presentation was too hard. We have completely rewritten that section and lowered the level of the discussion. The topic remains a difficult one for students to understand, however, and some may wish to skip it altogether.

INCREASED COVERAGE OF INTERNATIONAL MATERIAL

We have increased our coverage of international material in three ways. First, we have added many new "Global Perspective" boxes throughout the text. These boxes are designed to illustrate economic logic with global examples and to emphasize today's global economy. Second,

we introduce imports and exports into the simple goods market model early in macroeconomics. (We do, however, continue to believe that a complete treatment of open market macroeconomics should not be taught until students have mastered the logic of a simple closed macroeconomy. For this reason, we have chosen to place the "open-economy macro" chapter in International Economics, the final section of the book.) Finally, we have integrated international examples directly into the text whenever appropriate. All international examples are listed in a table following the book's detailed table of contents.

OPTIONAL CHAPTERS

We have tried to keep uppermost in our minds that time is always tight in a principles course. For this reason, we have made sure that certain chapters can be skipped without losing the flow of the material.

In macroeconomics, chapters 17–19 are optional. The chapters in the international section, with the exception of chapter 21 can be taught at any time that the instructor deems appropriate.

STUDENT LEARNING AIDS

Each chapter begins with a brief overview of what the student has learned in the previous chapter and ends with a brief "look ahead" to the following chapter. To help students study, key terms have been printed in boldface and glossed to the margins. Each chapter ends with a point-by-point summary of the chapter, a list of review terms and concepts (cross-referenced to text page), and a problem set.

Because many believe that economics must be relevant to be interesting, we have created three types of boxes for the fifth edition. *Global Perspective* boxes provide economic examples from around the world. *Application* boxes apply the theory learned in the text to real-world events and situations. *Issues and Debates* boxes examine many of the economic issues currently under debate.

In addition, we have set the major principles of economics off from the text in such a way as to highlight their importance. These highlights flow logically from the preceding text and into the text that follows. Students tell us that they find these very useful as a way of reviewing the key points in each chapter to prepare for exams.

PROBLEM SETS AND SOLUTIONS

Each chapter and appendix ends with a problem set that asks students to think about what they've learned in the chapter. These problems are not simple memorization questions. Rather, they ask students to perform graphical analysis or to apply economics to a real-world situation or policy decision. Approximately 40 percent of the problems are new to this edition. More challenging problems are indicated by an asterisk. The solutions to all even-numbered problems appear at the back of the book. The solutions to all odd-numbered problems, as well as additional problem sets, are available in the instructor's resource manual.

CASE STUDIES

The end-of-part case studies continue to be quite popular. The fifth edition features nine new case studies on topics ranging from the spotted owl and new homes to making your own money. Each case study is accompanied with questions for analytical thinking. The cases are not simply additional problems, and they are not simple extensions of the text material. They are meant to be applications of some of the *ideas* that the part was designed to teach and are designed to foster critical thinking and "thinking like an economist." They might be used as assignments or for class discussion.

TEACHING AND LEARNING TOOLS

The ancillary package for the fifth edition reflects changes in technology and utilizes new ways of disseminating information. A customized Web site links with Prentice Hall Learning on the Internet Partnership (PHLIP) to offer a comprehensive Internet package for the student and the instructor. An integrated package of software, printed supplements, videos, and reference guides completes the total teaching and learning package. Please contact your Prentice Hall sales representative for information on any of the Case and Fair supplements.

INTERNET RESOURCES (WWW.PRENHALL.COM/CASEFAIR)

The Case and Fair Web site offers students another opportunity to sharpen their problem-solving skills and to assess their understanding of the text material. Just go to the Case and Fair site and click on the Online Study Guide for additional true/false, multiple-choice, fill-in-the-blanks, and essay questions. The site also connects the student to the Take It to the Net Web-destination exercises cited at the end of each chapter in the text. The online study guide has a built-in grading feature; students take the exams and receive immediate feedback.

From the Case and Fair Web site, the student and the instructor can link to PHLIP. Developed by Dan Cooper at Marist College, PHLIP provides academic support for faculty and students using the fifth edition. The student section of PHLIP offers some downloadable supplements as well as PHLIPing through the News, a review of current-events articles keyed to topics in the text. Scott Simkins (North Carolina A&T State University) and Jim Barbour (Elon College) update the articles biweekly and provide summaries with discussion questions and research idea. The faculty section of PHLIP requires a user-name and password—please contact your Prentice Hall sales representative.

ECONOMICS EXPLORER RUNTIME MULTIMEDIA

The *Economics Explorer* CD-ROM, developed by Prentice Hall and Logal Software, Inc., combines video, animation, and spreadsheet capabilities to bring economics to live. Logal has taken the basic economic models from the textbook and created a series of dynamic, interactive simulations that help students visualize how math, graphs, and economic intuition are connected.

Once students have learned to use the simulation, they can design their own experiments and test their own conjectures. Using *Economics Explorer*, students can test the limits of economic models, input their own data to recreate events from economic history, and (using spreadsheet capabilities) record the results and display them in graphs like those from their textbook.

The fifth edition instructor's manual provides tips for integrating *Economics Explorer* into the course. The Study Guide alerts the students to relevant exercises tied to topics in the text.

STUDY GUIDES

A comprehensive study guide has been prepared by Thomas Beveridge of North Carolina State University. This study aid reinforces the textbook and provide students with additional applications and exercises. Each chapter contains the following elements:

- *Point-by-Point Objectives*. A list of learning goals for the chapter, along with a brief summary of the material, helpful study hints, practice questions with solutions, and page references to the text.
- *Practice Tests*. Approximately 20 multiple-choice questions and their answers.
- *Application Questions*. A series of multiple-choice questions that require the use of graphic or numerical analysis to solve economic problems.
- *Solutions*. Worked-out solutions to all questions in the Study Guide, complete with page references to the text.
- *Comprehensive Part Exams*. Nine part exams to test the students' overall comprehension consisting of up to 25 multiple-choice questions, extended examples, and problem questions where appropriate.

The study Guide also references the Take It to the Net Web exercises from the text and alerts the student to relevant applications in the *Economics Explorer* software.

INSTRUCTOR'S MANUAL

An innovative instructor's manual for *Principles of Macroeconomics* was written by Mary Lesser at Iona College. The manual is designed to help the instructor incorporate applicable elements of the fifth edition supplement package. The manual includes:

- Detailed chapter outlines with key terminology, teaching notes, and lecture suggestions.
- Video Guide for the 1998/99 Economics Video Library.
- Class Tips from Students, which feature real-world ideas from the students' point of view.
- Teaching Tips on incorporating the Take It to the Net Web exercises and *Economics Explorer* software.
- Additional Problems with solutions.
- Extended Applications, which include exercises, activities, and experiments to help make economics relevant to students.
- Solutions to all odd-numbered problems from the text.
- Case Study Solutions for the analytical thinking questions that accompany cases from the fifth edition text.

TEST ITEM FILE

The fifth edition test bank for *Principles of Macroeconomics* completely revised and updated by Timothy Duy of the University of Oregon, contains almost 4,000 true/false, multiple-choice, short-answer, and essay questions. Also included are Problem Sets, a series of questions based on a scenario or graph. Each question in the test bank is page-referenced and coded for level of difficulty (easy, moderate, challenging, and honors). Questions are also classified as fact, definition, single, and multi. Questions classified as single require the student to use a single-step analytical process to answer, whereas the questions classified as multi require the student to perform numerous steps in the analytical process.

A test item file is available for both microeconomics and macroeconomics, in printed form or in a computerized version.

PH CUSTOM TESTS

Available for Windows and Macintosh, PH Custom is the computerized version of the test item files. The test program allows professors to edit, add or delete questions from the test item file, edit existing graphics and create new graphics, and export files to word processing programs.

POWERPOINT LECTURE PRESENTATION

An all-new PowerPoint presentation, by Mark Karscig of Central Missouri State University, offers summaries and necessary reinforcement of important text material. Many important graphs "build" over a sequencing of slides so that students may see the step-by-step process involved in economic analysis. The package will allow for instructors to make full-color, professional-looking presentations while at the same time providing the ability for custom handouts to be provided to the students.

COLOR TRANSPARENCIES

All figures and tables from the text are reproduced as full-page, four-color acetates.

ABC NEWS/PRENTICE HALL VIDEO LIBRARY   **ABCNEWS**

ABC News and Prentice Hall combine their individual expertise in academic publishing and global reporting to provide a comprehensive video ancillary to the fifth edition. The 1998/99 Economics Video Library contains 23 news clips from *Nightline*, *World News Tonight*, *Wall Street Journal Report*, and *20/20*. Each clip illustrates the vital, ongoing connections between what is learned in the classroom and what is happening in the world around us. All the videos are timely or timeless, and many can be used at different points in the course. The instructor's manual provides suggestions on where and how to integrate each video.

THE NEW YORK TIMES "THEMES OF THE TIMES"

The New York Times, Inc., and Prentice Hall collaborate to offer *Economic Themes of the Times*—12 newspaper pages full of current articles on public policy, business, finance and other issues that expose the real-world, everyday relevance of economics. "Themes of the Times" is available for both Spring and Fall quarters.

The New York Times offers a reduced subscription rate for students and professors. For more information, call 1-800-631-1222.

SURFING FOR SUCCESS INTERNET GUIDE

Surfing for Success in Economics 1998/99 is an invaluable guide on using Internet resources. Scott Simkins and Jim Barbour join Andrew Stull in creating a reference that not only helps beginning students learn his/her way around the Internet, but lists economics-related sites and Your Turn Web-destination exercises to make surfing the Internet a natural part of the economics classroom.

THE SECOND YEAR SUPPLEMENT PACKAGE

A new wave of supplements will be available to help the instructor in the second year of using the fifth edition textbook:

- A brand new Test Item File, written by Mary Lesser, Iona College.
- 1999/2000 Economics Video Library and Video Guide.
- Presentation Manager.

ACKNOWLEDGMENTS

We are grateful to many people for help on the fifth edition. We are most grateful to Mike Elia, Senior Developmental Editor for Business Publishing at Prentice Hall, for stepping in to oversee the entire project. The quality of the book owes much to his guidance, and we owe much to his good humor. Gladys Soto, Assistant Editor, indefatigibility marshalled the extensive array of supplements to accompany this text.

We also owe much to Rod Banister, Executive Editor for Economics at Prentice Hall, for his help and enthusiasm.

We are also indebted to Elena Ranguelova, David Lindauer, Jack Triplett of the BEA, and Susan Skeath. We want to thank Peter Scott and Elizabeth Gill for their research assistance and proofreading of the entire manuscript.

We also owe a debt of gratitude to those who reviewed the fifth edition and provided us with a valuable insight as we prepared the new edition:

- Alex Anas, SUNY at Buffalo
- Charles A. Bennett, Gannon University
- Minh Quang Dao, Eastern Illinois University
- Douglas A. Greenley, Moorhead State University
- Cynthia S. McCarty, Jacksonville State Univerity
- James J. McLain, University of New Orleans
- Martha L. Olney, University of California-Berkeley
- Ben Young, University of Missouri-Kansas City
- Darrel Young, University of Texas

We are extremely indebted to James Shope and Michael Krause for reviewing the entire manuscript for this revision.

Last but not least, the following individuals were of immense help in reviewing all or part of this book and the teaching/learning package in various stages of development:

Lew Abernathy, University of North Texas • Jack Adams, University of Maryland • Doulas Agbetsiafa, Indiana University at South Bend • Sam Alapati, Rutgers University • Polly Allen, University of Connecticut • Stuart Allen, University of North Carolina at Greensboro • Jim Angresano, Hampton-Sydney College • Kenneth S. Arakelian, University of Rhode Island • Harvey Arnold, Indian River Community College • Nick Apergis, Fordham University • Kidane Asmeron, Pennsylvania State University • James Aylesworth, Lakeland Community College • Kari Battaglia, University of North Texas • Daniel K. Benjamin, Clemson University • Bruce Bolnick, Northeastern University • G. E. Breger, University of South Carolina • Dennis Brennan, William Rainey Harper Junior College • Lindsay Caulkins, John Carroll University • Atreya Chakraborty, Boston College • Harold Christensen, Centenary College • Daniel Christiansen, Albion College • Samuel Kim-Liang Chuah, Walla Walla College • David Colander, Middlebury College • Daniel Condon, University of Illinois at Chicago; Moraine Valley Community College • David Cowen, University of Texas at Austin • Michael Donihue, Colby College • Robert Driskill, Ohio State University • Gary Dymski, University of Southern California •

Jay Egger, Towson State University • Noel J. J. Farley, Bryn Mawr College • Mosin Farminesh, Temple University • Dan Feaster, Miami University of Ohio • Susan Feiner, Virginia Commonwealth University • Getachew Felleke, Albright College • Lois Fenske, South Puget Sound Community College • William Field, DePauw University • Bill Foeller, State University of New York at Fredonia • Roger Nils Folsom, San Jose State University • Sean Fraley, College of Mount Saint Joseph • N. Galloro, Chabot College • Tom Gausman, Northern Illinois University, DeKalb • Shirley J. Gedeon, University of Vermont • Gary Gigliotti, Rutgers University • Lynn Gillette, Texas A&M University • Sarah L. Glavin, Boston College • Devra Golbe, Hunter College • Roger Goldberg, Ohio Northern University • Douglas Greenley, Moorhead State University • Lisa M. Grobar, California State University at Long Beach • Benjamin Gutierrez, Indiana University at Bloomington • A. R. Gutowsky, California State University at Sacramento • David R. Hakes, University of Missouri at St. Louis • Stephen Happel, Arizona State University • Mitchell Harwitz, State University of New York at Buffalo • David Hoaas, Centenary College • Harry Holzer, Michigan State University • Bobbie Horn, University of Tulsa • John Horowitz, Ball State University • Janet Hunt, University of Georgia • Fred Inaba, Washington State University • Richard Inman, Boston College • Shirley Johnson, Vassar College • Farhoud Kafi, Babson College • R. Kallen, Roosevelt University • Arthur E. Kartman, San Diego State University • Hirshel Kasper, Oberlin College • Bruce Kaufman, Georgia State University • Dominique Khactu, The University of North Dakota • Phillip King, San Francisco State University • Barbara Kneeshaw, Wayne County Community College • Barry Kotlove, Elmira College • David Kraybill, University of Georgia at Athens • Rosung Kwak, University of Texas at Austin • Melissa Lam, Wellesley College • Jim Lee, Fort Hays State University • Judy Lee, Leeward Community College • Gary Lemon, DePauw University • Alan Leonard, Northern Illinois University • George Lieu, Tuskegee University • Stephen E. Lile, Western Kentucky University • Jane Lillydahl, University of Colorado at Boulder • Al Link, University of North Carolina at Greensboro • Robert Litro, U. S. Air Force Academy, Wallingford, CT • Burl F. Long, University of Florida • Gerald Lynch, Purdue University • Karla Lynch, University of North Texas • Michael Magura, University of Toledo • Don Maxwell, Central State University • Nan Maxwell, California State University at Hayward • J. Harold McClure, Jr., Villanova University • Rick McIntyre, University of Rhode Island • K. Mehtaboin, College of St. Rose • Shahruz Mohtadi, Suffolk University • Joe L. Moore, Arkansas Technical University • Robert Moore, Occidental College • Doug Morgan, University of California at Santa Barbara • Norma C. Morgan, Curry College • John Murphy, North Shore Community College, Massachusetts • Veena Nayak, State University of New York at Buffalo • Randy Nelson, Colby College • David Nickerson, University of British Columbia •

Rachel Nugent, Pacific Lutheran University • Akorlie A. Nyatepe-Coo, University of Wisconsin at LaCrosse • Norman P. Obst, Michigan State University • William C. O'Connor, Western Montana College • Kent Olson, Oklahoma State University • Carl Parker, Fort Hays State University • Spirog Patton, Neumann College • Tony Pizelo, Spokane Community College • Michael Rendich, Westchester Community College • Lynn Rittenoure, University of Tulsa • David C. Rose, University of Missouri at St. Louis • Richard Rosenberg, Pennsylvania State University • Mark Rush, University of Florida at Gainesville • Dereka Rushbrook, Ripon College • David L. Schaffer, Haverford College • Gary Sellers, University of Akron • Jean Shackleford, Bucknell University • Linda Shaffer, California State University at Fresno • Geoff Shepherd, University of Massachusetts at Amherst • Bih-Hay Sheu, University of Texas at Austin • Alden Shiers, California Polytechnic State University • Sue Skeath, Wellesley College • Paula Smith, Central State University, Oklahoma • John Solow, University of Iowa at Iowa City • Susan Stojanovic, Washington University, St. Louis • Ernst W. Stromsdorfer, Washington State University • Michael Taussig, Rutgers University • Timothy Taylor, Stanford University • Sister Beth Anne Tercek, SND, Notre Dame College of Ohio • Jack Trierweler, Northern State University • Brian M. Trinque, University of Texas at Austin • Ann Velenchik, Wellesley College • Chris Waller, Indiana University at Bloomington • Walter Wessels, North Carolina State University • Joan Whalen-Ayyappan, DeVry Institute of Technology • Robert Whaples, Wake Forest University • Leonard A. White, University of Arkansas • Abera Zeyege, Ball State University • James Ziliak, Indiana University at Bloomington

We welcome comments about the fifth edition. Please write to us care of Economics Editor, Prentice Hall Higher Education Division, One Lake Street, Upper Saddle River, N.J. 07458.

Karl E. Case
Ray C. Fair

Save a Tree!
Many of the components of the teaching and learning package are available in electronic format. Disk-based supplements conserve paper and allow you to select and print only the material you plan to use. For more information, please ask your Prentice Hall sales representative.

ABOUT THE AUTHORS

Karl E. Case

is the Marion Butler McLean Professor in the History of Ideas and Professor of Economics at Wellesley College. He also lectures on economics and tax policy in the International Tax Program at Harvard Law School and is a visiting scholar at the Federal Reserve Bank of Boston. He received his B.A. from Miami University in 1968, spent 3 years in the army, and received his M.A. and Ph.D. from Harvard University. In 1980 and 1981, he was Fellow in Law and Economics at Harvard Law School.

Professor Case's research has been in the areas of public finance, taxation, and housing. He is the author or coauthor of four other books, including *Economics and Tax Policy* and *Property Taxation: The Need for Reform*, as well as numerous articles in professional journals.

For the past 21 years, he has taught at Wellesley College. Before coming to Wellesley, he served as Head Tutor (director of undergraduate studies) at Harvard, where he won the Allyn Young Teaching Prize. He has been a member of the AEA's Committee on Economic Education and was Associate Editor of the *Journal of Economic Education*, responsible for the section on innovations in teaching. He teaches at least one section of the principles course every year.

Ray C. Fair

is Professor of Economics at Yale University. He is a member of the Cowles Foundation at Yale and a Fellow of the Econometric Society. He received a B.A. in economics from Fresno State College in 1964 and a Ph.D. in economics from M.I.T. in 1968. He taught at Princeton University from 1968 to 1974 and has been at Yale since 1974.

Professor Fair's research has primarily been in the areas of macroeconomics and econometrics, with particular emphasis on macroeconometric model building. His publications include *Specification, Estimation, and Analysis of Macroeconometric Models* (Harvard Press, 1984) and *Testing Macroeconometric Models* (Harvard Press, 1994).

Professor Fair has taught introductory and intermediate economics at Yale. He has also taught graduate courses in macroeconomic theory and macroeconometrics.

Professor Fair's United States and multicountry models are available for use on the Internet free of charge. The address is **http://fairmodel.econ.yale.edu.** Many teachers have found that having students work with the United States model on the Internet is a useful complement to even an introductory macroeconomics course.

INTRODUCTION

PART ONE

INTRODUCTION TO ECONOMICS

THE SCOPE AND METHOD OF ECONOMICS

THE STUDY OF ECONOMICS should begin with a sense of wonder. Pause for a moment and consider a typical day in your life. For breakfast you might have bread made in a local bakery with flour produced in Minnesota from wheat grown in Kansas and bacon from pigs raised in Ohio packaged in plastic made in New Jersey. You spill coffee from Colombia on your shirt made in Texas from textiles shipped from South Carolina.

After class you drive with a friend in a Japanese car on an interstate highway system that took 20 years and billions of dollars to build. You stop for gasoline refined in Louisiana from Saudi Arabian crude oil brought to the United States on a supertanker that took three years to build at a shipyard in Maine.

At night you call your brother in Mexico City. The call travels over fiber-optic cable to a powerful antenna that sends it to a transponder on one of over 1,000 communications satellites orbiting the earth.

You use or consume tens of thousands of things, both tangible and intangible, every day: buildings, the music of a rock band, the compact disc it is recorded on, telephone services, staples, paper, toothpaste, tweezers, soap, a digital watch, fire protection, antacid tablets, banks, electricity, eggs, insurance, football fields, computers, buses, rugs, subways, health services, sidewalks, and so forth. Somebody made all these things. Somebody decided to organize men and women and materials to produce them and distribute them. Thousands of decisions went into their completion. Somehow they got to you.

One hundred thirty-one million people in the United States—almost half the total population—work at hundreds of thousands of different jobs producing over $8 trillion worth of goods and services every year. Some cannot find work; some choose not to work. Some are rich; others are poor.

The United States imports over $140 billion worth of automobiles and parts and about $70 billion worth of petroleum and petroleum products each year; it exports around $55 billion worth of agricultural products, including food. High-rise office buildings go up in central cities. Condominiums and homes are built in the suburbs. In other places homes are abandoned and boarded up.

Some countries are wealthy. Others are impoverished. Some are growing. Some are stagnating. Some businesses are doing well. Others are going bankrupt.

At any moment in time every society faces constraints imposed by nature and by previous generations. Some societies are handsomely endowed by nature with fertile land, water, sunshine, and natural resources. Others have deserts and few mineral resources. Some societies receive much from previous generations—art, music, technical knowledge, beautiful buildings, and productive factories. Others are left with overgrazed, eroded land, cities leveled by war, or polluted natural environments. *All* societies face limits.

economics *The study of how individuals and societies choose to use the scarce resources that nature and previous generations have provided.*

Economics is the study of how individuals and societies choose to use the scarce resources that nature and previous generations have provided. The key word in this definition is *choose*. Economics is a behavioral, or social, science. In large measure it is the study of how people make choices. The choices that people make, when added up, translate into societal choices.

The purpose of this chapter and the next is to elaborate on this definition and to introduce the subject matter of economics. What is produced? How is it produced? Who gets it? Why? Is the result good or bad? Can it be improved?

WHY STUDY ECONOMICS?

There are four main reasons to study economics: to learn a way of thinking, to understand society, to understand global affairs, and to be an informed voter.

TO LEARN A WAY OF THINKING

Probably the most important reason for studying economics is to learn a way of thinking. A good way to introduce economics is to review three of its most fundamental concepts: *opportunity cost*, *marginalism*, and *efficient markets*. If your study of economics is successful, you will use these concepts every day in making decisions.

➤ **Opportunity Cost** What happens in an economy is the outcome of thousands of individual decisions. Households must decide how to divide their incomes among all the goods and services available in the marketplace. People must decide whether to work or not to work, whether to go to school, and how much to save. Businesses must decide what to produce, how much to produce, how much to charge, and where to locate. It is not surprising that economic analysis focuses on the process of decision making.

Nearly all decisions involve trade-offs. A key concept that recurs in analyzing the decision-making process is the notion of *opportunity cost*. The full "cost" of making a specific choice includes what we give up by not making the alternative choice. That which we forgo, or give up, when we make a choice or a decision is called the **opportunity cost** of that decision.

opportunity cost *That which we forgo, or give up, when we make a choice or a decision.*

This concept applies to individuals, businesses, and entire societies. The opportunity cost of going to a movie is the value of the other things you could have done with the same money and time. If you decide to take time off from work, the opportunity cost of your leisure is the pay that you would have earned had you worked. Part of the cost of a college education is the income you could have earned by working full time instead of going to school. If a firm purchases a new piece of equipment for $3,000, it does so because it expects that equipment to generate more profit. There is an opportunity cost, however, because that $3,000 could have been deposited in an interest-earning account. To a society, the opportunity cost of using resources to put astronauts on the moon is the value of the private/civilian goods that could have been produced with the same resources.

Opportunity costs arise because resources are scarce. *Scarce* simply means "limited." Consider one of our most important resources—time. There are only 24 hours in a day, and we must live our lives under this constraint. A farmer in rural Brazil must decide whether it is better to continue to farm or to go to the city and look for a job. A hockey player at the University of Vermont must decide whether she will play on the varsity team or spend more time improving her academic work.

▶ **Marginalism and Sunk Costs**   A second key concept used in analyzing choices is the notion of *marginalism*. In weighing the costs and benefits of a decision, it is important to weigh only the costs and benefits that arise from the decision. Suppose, for example, that you live in New Orleans and that you are weighing the costs and benefits of visiting your mother in Iowa. If business required that you travel to Kansas City, the cost of visiting Mom would be only the additional, or *marginal*, time and money cost of getting to Iowa from Kansas City.

Consider the cost of producing this book. Assume that 10,000 copies are produced. The total cost of producing the copies includes the cost of the authors' time in writing the book, the cost of editing, the cost of making the plates for printing, and the cost of the paper and ink. If the total cost were $600,000, then the average cost of one copy would be $60, which is simply $600,000 divided by 10,000.

Although average cost is an important concept, a book publisher must know more than simply the average cost of a book. For example, suppose a second printing is being debated. That is, should another 10,000 copies be produced? In deciding whether to proceed, the costs of writing, editing, making plates, and so forth are irrelevant. Why? Because they have already been incurred—they are *sunk costs*. **Sunk costs** are costs that cannot be avoided, regardless of what is done in the future, because they have already been incurred. All that matters are the costs associated with the additional, or marginal, books to be printed. Technically, *marginal cost* is the cost of producing one more unit of output.

There are numerous examples in which the concept of marginal cost is useful. For an airplane that is about to take off with empty seats, the marginal cost of an extra passenger is essentially zero; the total cost of the trip is essentially unchanged by the addition of an extra passenger. Thus, setting aside a few seats to be sold at big discounts can be profitable even if the fare for those seats is far below the average cost per seat of making the trip. As long as the airline succeeds in filling seats that would otherwise have been empty, doing so is profitable.

▶ **Efficient Markets—No Free Lunch**   Suppose you are driving on a three-lane highway and you come upon a toll plaza with six toll booths. Three toll booths are straight ahead in the three lanes of traffic, and the three other booths are off to the right. Which lane should you choose? It is usually the case that the wait time is approximately the same no matter what you do. If one line is much shorter than the others, cars will quickly move into it until the lines are equalized.

As you will see later, the term *profit* in economics has a very precise meaning. Economists, however, often loosely refer to "good deals" or risk-free ventures as *profit opportunities*. Using the term loosely, a profit opportunity exists at the toll booths if one line is shorter than the others. In general, such profit opportunities are rare. At any one time there are many people searching for them, and, as a consequence, few exist. Markets like this, where any profit opportunities are eliminated almost instantaneously, are said to be **efficient markets**. (We discuss *markets*, the institutions through which buyers and sellers interact and engage in exchange, in detail in chapter 2.)

The common way of expressing the efficient markets concept is "there's no such thing as a free lunch." How should you react when a stockbroker calls up with a hot tip on the stock market? With skepticism. There are thousands of individuals each day looking for hot tips in the market, and if a particular tip about a stock is valid there will be an immediate rush to buy the stock, which will quickly drive its price up.

FAST FACTS

NASA, which coordinates the U.S. space program, has spent an average of $15 billion per year over the last several years. It employs about 25,000 people.

Source: Statistical Abstract of the United States, 1997.

sunk costs *Costs that cannot be avoided, regardless of what is done in the future, because they have already been incurred.*

efficient market *A market in which profit opportunities are eliminated almost instantaneously.*

This economists' view that very few profit opportunities exist can, of course, be carried too far. There is a story about two people walking along, one an economist and one not. The noneconomist sees a twenty-dollar bill on the sidewalk and says, "There's a twenty-dollar bill on the sidewalk." The economist replies, "That is not possible. If there were, somebody would already have picked it up."

There are clearly times when profit opportunities exist. Someone has to be first to get the news, and some people have quicker insights than others. Nevertheless, news travels fast, and there are thousands of people with quick insights. The general view that profit opportunities are rare is close to the mark.

> The study of economics teaches us a way of thinking and helps us make decisions.

TO UNDERSTAND SOCIETY

Another reason for studying economics is to understand society better. Clearly, past and present economic decisions have an enormous influence on the character of life in a society. The current state of the physical environment, the level of material well-being, and the nature and number of jobs are all products of the economic system.

To get a sense of the ways in which economic decisions have shaped our environment, imagine looking out of a top-floor window of a high-rise office building in any large city. The workday is about to begin. All around you are other tall glass and steel buildings full of workers. In the distance you see the smoke of factories. Looking down, you see thousands of commuters pouring off trains and buses, and cars backed up on freeway exit ramps. You see trucks carrying goods from one place to another. You also see the face of urban poverty: Just beyond the freeway is a large public housing project and, beyond that, burned-out and boarded-up buildings.

What you see before you is the product of millions of economic decisions made over hundreds of years. People at some point decided to spend time and money building those buildings and factories. Somebody cleared the land, laid the tracks, built the roads, and produced the cars and buses.

Not only have economic decisions shaped the physical environment, they have determined the character of society as well. At no time has the impact of economic change on a society been more evident than in England during the late eighteenth and early nineteenth centuries, a period that we now call the **Industrial Revolution**. Increases in the productivity of agriculture, new manufacturing technologies, and the development of more efficient forms of transportation led to a massive movement of the British population from the countryside to the city. At the beginning of the eighteenth century, approximately two out of three people in Great Britain worked in agriculture. By 1812, only one in three remained in agriculture, and by 1900 the figure was fewer than one in ten. People jammed into overcrowded cities and worked long hours in factories. The world had changed completely in two centuries—a period that, in the run of history, was nothing more than the blink of an eye.

It is not surprising that the discipline of economics began to take shape during this period. Social critics and philosophers looked around them and knew that their philosophies must expand to accommodate the changes. Adam Smith's *Wealth of Nations* appeared in 1776. It was followed by the writings of David Ricardo, Karl Marx, Thomas Malthus, and others. Each tried to make sense out of what was happening. Who was building the factories? Why? What determined the level of wages paid to workers or the price of food? What would happen in the future, and what *should* happen? The people who asked these questions were the first economists.

Similar changes continue to affect the character of life today. In 1997 the number of jobs in the United States increased by more than 3 million, but nearly 7 million people who wanted a job could not find one. While the economy was growing, the wages of many workers were falling relative to the cost of living. While the Mexican economy

Industrial Revolution *The period in England during the late eighteenth and early nineteenth centuries in which new manufacturing technologies and improved transportation gave rise to the modern factory system and a massive movement of the population from the countryside to the cities.*

has been growing since the United States and Mexico signed a trade treaty in 1993, thousands of Mexicans continue to pour into the United States. How does one make sense of all of this? Why do we have unemployment? What forces determine wages? What are the ramifications of continued immigration into the United States?

> The study of economics is an essential part of the study of society.

TO UNDERSTAND GLOBAL AFFAIRS

A third reason for studying economics is to understand global affairs. News headlines are filled with economic stories. Great Britain and the rest of the European Union (a European trading bloc) struggle with the implications of their agreement to adopt a common currency, the Euro. The nations of the former Soviet Union are wrestling with a new phenomenon that clouds their efforts to "privatize" state-owned industries: organized crime. A new government in the Democratic Republic of Congo, formerly Zaire, is trying to reverse decades of stagnation.

All countries are part of a world economy, and understanding international relations begins with a basic knowledge of the economic links among countries. For centuries countries have attempted to protect their industries and workers from foreign competition by taxing and limiting the number of imports. Most economists argue, however, that unrestricted trade is in the long-run interest of all countries. Just after World War II many countries signed the General Agreement on Tariffs and Trade (GATT), in which they committed to lowering trade barriers. The process continues today as the Congress debates the most recent version of the GATT. The issue is a passionate one. French farmers, fearing the effects of cheap imports on their livelihood, protested strongly when France committed to signing the new GATT. Labor unions in the United States vowed to defeat any politicians who voted to ratify the North American Free Trade Agreement (NAFTA) with Mexico in 1993 and the new GATT in 1995.

Americans are investing heavily in industries in countries like Indonesia and China. During the 1980s the Japanese bought billions of dollars' worth of U.S. real estate, shares of corporate stocks, and government bonds. In recent years the Japanese, suffering economic problems at home, have pulled back, with important consequences for the United States. The end of the apartheid laws that legally separated the races in South Africa has created a new climate for international investment in that country. Meanwhile, the countries of Eastern Europe are struggling to create from the ground up economic and social institutions that took centuries to build in the West.

Another important issue in today's world is the widening gap between rich and poor nations. In 1998, world population was about 6 billion. Of that number, 4.5 billion lived in less-developed countries and 1.5 billion lived in more-developed countries.

WORRIES THAT FREE TRADE POLICIES WILL COST JOBS OFTEN BRING PROTESTS BY WORKERS.

The 75 percent of the world's population that lives in the less-developed countries receives less than 20 percent of the world's income. In dozens of countries, per capita income is only a few hundred dollars a year.

An understanding of economics is essential to an understanding of global affairs.

TO BE AN INFORMED VOTER

A knowledge of economics is essential to be an informed voter. During the last 25 years, the U.S. economy has been on a roller coaster. In 1973–1974, the Organization of Petroleum Exporting Countries (OPEC) succeeded in raising the price of crude oil by 400 percent. Simultaneously, a sequence of events in the world food market drove food prices up by 25 percent. By mid-1974, prices in the United States were rising across the board at a very rapid rate. Partially as a result of government policy to fight runaway inflation, the economy went into a recession in 1975. (An *inflation* is an increase in the overall price level in the economy; a *recession* is a period of decreasing output and rising unemployment.) The recession succeeded in slowing price increases, but in the process millions found themselves unemployed.

From 1979 through 1983, it happened all over again. Prices rose rapidly, the government reacted with more policies designed to stop prices from rising, and the United States ended up with an even worse recession in 1982. By the end of that year, 10.8 percent of the workforce was unemployed. Then, in mid-1990—after almost eight years of strong economic performance—the U.S. economy went into another recession. During the third and fourth quarters of 1990 and the first quarter of 1991, gross domestic product (GDP, a measure of the total output of the U.S. economy) fell, and unemployment again increased sharply. The recession of 1990–1991 was followed by a very slow recovery, which became the key issue in the 1992 presidential election. The 1994 congressional elections and the 1996 contest between Bob Dole and Bill Clinton focused on deficit reduction, tax reform, and welfare reform. The economic viability of "entitlement" programs, such as Social Security and Medicare, were also big issues. In 1997, the British election was dominated by the debate over Britain's full participation in the scheduled conversion to a common European currency. In the United States and throughout the world, economic issues continue to play a major role in the political process.

When we participate in the political process, we are voting on issues that require a basic understanding of economics.

THE SCOPE OF ECONOMICS

Most students taking economics for the first time are surprised by the breadth of what they study. Some think that economics will teach them about the stock market or what to do with their money. Others think that economics deals exclusively with problems like inflation and unemployment. In fact, it deals with all these subjects, but they are pieces of a much larger puzzle.

Economics has deep roots in, and close ties to, social philosophy. An issue of great importance to philosophers, for example, is distributional justice. Why are some people rich and others poor, and, whatever the answer, is this fair? A number of nineteenth-century social philosophers wrestled with these questions, and out of their musings economics as a separate discipline was born.

The easiest way to get a feel for the breadth and depth of what you will be studying is to explore briefly the way economics is organized. First of all, there are two major divisions of economics: microeconomics and macroeconomics.

MICROECONOMICS AND MACROECONOMICS

Microeconomics deals with the functioning of individual industries and the behavior of individual economic decision-making units: business firms and households. Firms' choices about what to produce and how much to charge, and households' choices about what and how much to buy, help to explain why the economy produces the things it does.

Another big question addressed by microeconomics is who gets the things that are produced. Wealthy households get more than poor households, and the forces that determine this distribution of output are the province of microeconomics. Why does poverty exist? Who is poor? Why do some jobs pay more than others?

Think again about all the things you consume in a day, and then think back to that view over a big city. Somebody decided to build those factories. Somebody decided to construct the roads, build the housing, produce the cars, and smoke the bacon. Why? What is going on in all those buildings? It is easy to see that understanding individual micro decisions is very important to any understanding of society.

Macroeconomics looks at the economy as a whole. Instead of trying to understand what determines the output of a single firm or industry or the consumption patterns of a single household or group of households, macroeconomics examines the factors that determine national output, or national product. Microeconomics is concerned with *household* income; macroeconomics deals with *national* income.

Whereas microeconomics focuses on individual product prices and relative prices, macroeconomics looks at the overall price level and how quickly (or slowly) it is rising (or falling). Microeconomics questions how many people will be hired (or fired) this year in a particular industry or in a certain geographical area, and the factors that determine how much labor a firm or industry will hire. Macroeconomics deals with *aggregate* employment and unemployment: how many jobs exist in the economy as a whole, and how many people who are willing to work are not able to find work.

To summarize:

> Microeconomics looks at the individual unit—the household, the firm, the industry. It sees and examines the "trees." Macroeconomics looks at the whole, the aggregate. It sees and analyzes the "forest."

Table 1.1 summarizes these divisions and some of the subjects with which they are concerned.

microeconomics *The branch of economics that examines the functioning of individual industries and the behavior of individual decision-making units—that is, business firms and households.*

macroeconomics *The branch of economics that examines the economic behavior of aggregates—income, employment, output, and so on—on a national scale.*

TABLE 1.1 EXAMPLES OF MICROECONOMIC AND MACROECONOMIC CONCERNS

DIVISION OF ECONOMICS	PRODUCTION	PRICES	INCOME	EMPLOYMENT
Microeconomics	*Production/Output in individual industries and businesses* How much steel How much office space How many cars	*Price of individual goods and services* Price of medical care Price of gasoline Food prices Apartment rents	*Distribution of income and wealth* Wages in the auto industry Minimum wage Executive salaries Poverty	*Employment by individual businesses and industries* Jobs in the steel industry Number of employees in a firm Number of accountants
Macroeconomics	*National Production/Output* Total industrial output Gross domestic product Growth of output	*Aggregate price level* Consumer prices Producer prices Rate of inflation	*National income* Total wages and salaries Total corporate profits	*Employment and unemployment in the economy* Total number of jobs Unemployment rate

THE DIVERSE FIELDS OF ECONOMICS

Individual economists focus their research and study in many diverse areas. Many of these specialized fields are reflected in the advanced courses offered at most colleges and universities. Some are concerned with economic history or the history of economic thought. Others focus on international economics or growth in less-developed countries. Still others study the economics of cities (urban economics) or the relationship between economics and law. (See the Application box titled "The Fields of Economics" for more details.)

Economists also differ in the emphasis they place on theory. Some economists specialize in developing new theories, whereas others spend their time testing the theories of others. Some economists hope to expand the frontiers of knowledge, whereas others are more interested in applying what is already known to the formulation of public policies.

As you begin your study of economics, look through your school's course catalog and talk to the faculty about their interests. You will discover that economics encompasses a broad range of inquiry and is linked to many other disciplines.

THE METHOD OF ECONOMICS

Economics asks and attempts to answer two kinds of questions, positive and normative. **Positive economics** attempts to understand behavior and the operation of economic systems *without making judgments* about whether the outcomes are good or bad. It strives to describe what exists and how it works. What determines the wage rate for unskilled workers? What would happen if we abolished the corporate income tax? The answers to such questions are the subject of positive economics.

In contrast, **normative economics** looks at the outcomes of economic behavior and asks if they are good or bad and whether they can be made better. Normative economics involves judgments and prescriptions for courses of action. Should the government subsidize or regulate the cost of higher education? Should medical benefits to the elderly under Medicare be available to those with incomes below some threshold? Should the United States allow importers to sell foreign-produced goods that compete with U.S.-produced products? Should we reduce inheritance taxes? Normative economics is often called *policy economics*.

Of course, most normative questions involve positive questions. To know whether the government *should* take a particular action, we must know first if it *can* and second what the consequences are likely to be. (For example, if we lower import fees, will there be more competition and lower prices?)

Some claim that positive, value-free economic analysis is impossible. They argue that analysts come to problems with biases that cannot help but influence their work. Furthermore, even in choosing what questions to ask or what problems to analyze, economists are influenced by political, ideological, and moral views.

Although this argument has some merit, it is nevertheless important to distinguish between analyses that attempt to be positive and those that are intentionally and explicitly normative. Economists who ask explicitly normative questions should be forced to specify their grounds for judging one outcome superior to another.

▶ **Descriptive Economics and Economic Theory** Positive economics is often divided into descriptive economics and economic theory. **Descriptive economics** is simply the compilation of data that describe phenomena and facts. Examples of such data appear in the *Statistical Abstract of the United States*, a large volume of data published by the Department of Commerce every year that describes many features of the U.S. economy. Massive volumes of data can now also be found on the World Wide Web.

positive economics *An approach to economics that seeks to understand behavior and the operation of systems without making judgments. It describes what exists and how it works.*

normative economics *An approach to economics that analyzes outcomes of economic behavior, evaluates them as good or bad, and may prescribe courses of action. Also called* policy economics.

descriptive economics *The compilation of data that describe phenomena and facts.*

THE FIELDS OF ECONOMICS

A good way to convey the diversity of economics is to describe some of its major fields of study and the issues that economists address.

■ INDUSTRIAL ORGANIZATION looks carefully at the structure and performance of industries and firms within an economy. How do businesses compete? Who gains and who loses?

■ URBAN AND REGIONAL ECONOMICS studies the spatial arrangement of economic activity. Why do we have cities? Why are manufacturing firms locating farther and farther from the center of urban areas?

■ ECONOMETRICS applies statistical techniques and data to economic problems in an effort to test hypotheses and theories. Most schools require economics majors to take at least one course in statistics or econometrics.

■ COMPARATIVE ECONOMIC SYSTEMS examines the ways alternative economic systems function. What are the advantages and disadvantages of different systems? What is the best way to convert the planned economies of the former Soviet Union to market systems?

■ ECONOMIC DEVELOPMENT focuses on the problems of poor countries. What can be done to promote development in these nations? Important concerns of development economists include population growth and control, provision for basic needs, and strategies for international trade.

■ LABOR ECONOMICS deals with the factors that determine wage rates,

employment, and unemployment. How do people decide whether to work, how much to work, and at what kind of job? How have the roles of unions and management changed in recent years?

■ FINANCE examines the ways in which households and firms actually pay for, or finance, their purchases. It involves the study of capital markets (including the stock and bond markets), futures and options, capital budgeting, and asset valuation.

■ INTERNATIONAL ECONOMICS studies trade flows among countries and international financial institutions. What are the advantages and disadvantages for a country that allows its citizens to buy and sell freely in world markets? Why is the dollar strong or weak?

■ PUBLIC ECONOMICS examines the role of government in the economy. What are the economic functions of government, and what should they be? How should the government finance the services that it provides? What kinds of government programs should confront the problems of poverty, unemployment, and pollution?

■ ECONOMIC HISTORY traces the development of the modern economy. What economic and political events and scientific advances caused the Industrial Revolution? What explains the tremendous growth and progress of post-World War II Japan? What caused the Great Depression of the 1930s?

SEVERAL OF THE FIELDS OF ECONOMICS ARE CONCERNED WITH POVERTY IN DEVELOPING COUNTRIES.

■ LAW AND ECONOMICS analyzes the economic function of legal rules and institutions. How does the law change the behavior of individuals and businesses? Do different liability rules make accidents and injuries more, or less, likely? What are the economic costs of crime?

■ THE HISTORY OF ECONOMIC THOUGHT, which is grounded in philosophy, studies the development of economic ideas and theories over time, from Adam Smith in the eighteenth century to the works of economists such as Thomas Malthus, Karl Marx, and John Maynard Keynes. Because economic theory is constantly developing and changing, studying the history of ideas helps give meaning to modern theory and puts it in perspective.

For more on the fields of economics, see the Case and Fair Web page at
http://www.prenhall.com/casefair.

Where do all these data come from? The Census Bureau produces an enormous amount of raw data every year, as do the Bureau of Labor Statistics, the Bureau of Economic Analysis, and nongovernment agencies such as the University of Michigan Survey

Research Center. One important study now published annually is the *Survey of Consumer Expenditure*, which asks individual households to keep careful records of all their expenditures over a long period of time. Another is the *National Longitudinal Survey of Labor Force Behavior*, conducted over many years by the Center for Human Resource Development at Ohio State University.

Economic theory attempts to generalize about data and interpret them. An **economic theory** is a statement or set of related statements about cause and effect, action and reaction. One of the first theories you will encounter in this text is the *law of demand*, which was most clearly stated by Alfred Marshall in 1890: When the price of a product rises, people tend to buy less of it; when the price of a product falls, they tend to buy more.

Theories do not always arise out of formal numerical data. All of us have been collecting observations of people's behavior and their responses to economic stimuli for most of our lives. We may have observed our parents' reaction to a sudden increase—or decrease—in income or to the loss of a job or the acquisition of a new one. We all have seen people standing in line waiting for a bargain. And, of course, our own actions and reactions are another important source of data.

THEORIES AND MODELS

In many disciplines, including physics, chemistry, meteorology, political science, and economics, theorists build formal models of behavior. A **model** is a formal statement of a theory. It is usually a mathematical statement of a presumed relationship between two or more variables.

A **variable** is a measure that can change from time to time or from observation to observation. Income is a variable—it has different values for different people, and different values for the same person at different times. The rental price of a movie on a videocassette is a variable; it has different values at different stores and at different times. There are countless other examples.

Because all models simplify reality by stripping part of it away, they are abstractions. Critics of economics often point to abstraction as a weakness. Most economists, however, see abstraction as a real strength.

The easiest way to see how abstraction can be helpful is to think of a map. A map is a representation of reality that is simplified and abstract. A city or state appears on a piece of paper as a series of lines and colors. The amount of reality that the map maker can strip away before the map loses something essential depends on what the map will be used for. If I want to drive from St. Louis to Phoenix, I need to know only the major interstate highways and roads. I lose absolutely nothing and gain clarity by cutting out the local streets and roads. However, if I need to get around in Phoenix, I may need to see every street and alley.

Most maps are two-dimensional representations of a three-dimensional world; they show where roads and highways go but do not show hills and valleys along the way. Trail maps for hikers, however, have "contour lines" that represent changes in elevation. When you are in a car, changes in elevation matter very little; they would make a map needlessly complex and much more difficult to read. But if you are on foot carrying a 50-pound pack, a knowledge of elevation is crucial.

Like maps, economic models are abstractions that strip away detail to expose only those aspects of behavior that are important to the question being asked. The principle that irrelevant detail should be cut away is called the principle of **Ockham's razor** after the fourteenth-century philosopher William of Ockham.

But be careful. Although abstraction is a powerful tool for exposing and analyzing specific aspects of behavior, it is possible to oversimplify. Economic models often strip away a good deal of social and political reality to get at underlying concepts. When an economic theory is used to help formulate actual government or institutional policy, political and social reality must often be reintroduced if the policy is to have a chance of working.

---

economic theory *A statement or set of related statements about cause and effect, action and reaction.*

model *A formal statement of a theory. Usually a mathematical statement of a presumed relationship between two or more variables.*

variable *A measure that can change from time to time or from observation to observation.*

MAPS ARE USEFUL ABSTRACT REPRESENTATIONS OF REALITY.

Ockham's razor *The principle that irrelevant detail should be cut away.*

The key here is that the appropriate amount of simplification and abstraction depends upon the use to which the model will be put. To return to the map example: You don't want to walk around San Francisco with a map made for drivers—there are too many very steep hills!

▶ **All Else Equal: *Ceteris Paribus*** It is almost always true that whatever you want to explain with a model depends on more than one factor. Suppose, for example, that you want to explain the total number of miles driven by automobile owners in the United States. The number of miles driven will change from year to year or month to month; it is a variable. The issue, if we want to understand and explain changes that occur, is what factors cause those changes.

Obviously, many things might affect total miles driven. First, more or fewer people may be driving. This number, in turn, can be affected by changes in the driving age, by population growth, or by changes in state laws. Other factors might include the price of gasoline, the household's income, the number and age of children in the household, the distance from home to work, the location of shopping facilities, and the availability and quality of public transport. When any of these variables change, the members of the household may drive more or less. If changes in any of these variables affect large numbers of households across the country, the total number of miles driven will change.

Very often we need to isolate or separate out these effects. For example, suppose we want to know the impact on driving of a higher tax on gasoline. This change would raise the price of gasoline at the pump, but would not (at least in the short run) affect income, workplace location, number of children, and so forth.

To isolate the impact of one single factor, we use the device of ***ceteris paribus***, or **all else equal**. We ask: What is the impact of a change in gasoline price on driving behavior, *ceteris paribus*, or assuming that nothing else changes? If gasoline prices rise by 10 percent, how much less driving will there be, assuming no simultaneous change in anything else—that is, assuming that income, number of children, population, laws, and so on all remain constant?

> **ceteris paribus,** or **all else equal**
> *A device used to analyze the relationship between two variables while the values of other variables are held unchanged.*

> Using the device of *ceteris paribus* is one part of the process of abstraction. In formulating economic theory, the concept helps us simplify reality in order to focus on the relationships that we are interested in.

▶ **Expressing Models in Words, Graphs, and Equations** Consider the following statements: "Lower airline ticket prices cause people to fly more frequently." "Higher interest rates slow the rate of home sales." "When firms produce more output, employment increases." "Higher gasoline prices cause people to drive less and to buy more fuel-efficient cars."

Each of these statements expresses a relationship between two variables that can be quantified. In each case there is a stimulus and a response, a cause and an effect. Quantitative relationships can be expressed in a variety of ways. Sometimes words are sufficient to express the essence of a theory, but often it is necessary to be more specific about the nature of a relationship or about the size of a response. The most common method of expressing the quantitative relationship between two variables is *graphing* that relationship on a two-dimensional plane. In fact, we will use graphical analysis extensively in chapter 2 and beyond. Because it is essential that you be familiar with the basics of graphing, the appendix to this chapter presents a careful review of graphing techniques.

Quantitative relationships between variables can also be presented through *equations*. For example, suppose we discovered that over time, U.S. households collectively spend, or consume, 90 percent of their income and save 10 percent of their income. We could then write:

$$C = .90Y \text{ and } S = .10Y$$

where C is consumption spending, Y is income, and S is saving. Writing explicit algebraic expressions like these helps us understand the nature of the underlying process of decision making. Understanding this process is what economics is all about.

▶ **Cautions and Pitfalls**   In formulating theories and models, it is especially important to avoid two pitfalls: the post hoc fallacy and the fallacy of composition.

The Post Hoc Fallacy   Theories often make statements, or sets of statements, about cause and effect. It can be quite tempting to look at two events that happen in sequence and assume that the first caused the second to happen. Clearly, this is not always the case. This common error is called the **post hoc, ergo propter hoc** (or "after this, therefore because of this") fallacy.

There are thousands of examples. The Colorado Rockies have won seven games in a row. Last night, I went to the game and they lost. I must have "jinxed" them. They lost *because* I went to the game.

Stock market analysts indulge in what is perhaps the most striking example of the post hoc fallacy in action. Every day the stock market goes up or down, and every day some analyst on some national news program singles out one or two of the day's events as *the* cause of some change in the market: "Today the Dow Jones industrial average rose five points on heavy trading; analysts say that the increase was due to progress in talks between the United States and Cuba." Research has shown that daily changes in stock market averages are very largely random. While major news events clearly have a direct influence on certain stock prices, most daily changes cannot be directly linked to specific news stories.

Very closely related to the post hoc fallacy is the often erroneous link between correlation and causation. Two variables are said to be *correlated* if one variable changes when the other variable changes. But correlation does not imply causation. Cities that have high crime rates also have lots of automobiles, so there is a very high degree of correlation between number of cars and crime rates. Can we argue, then, that cars *cause* crime? No. The reason for the correlation may have nothing to do with cause and effect. Big cities have lots of people, lots of people have lots of cars, and therefore big cities have lots of cars. Big cities also have high crime rates for many reasons—crowding, poverty, anonymity, unequal distribution of wealth, and the ready availability of drugs, to mention only a few. But the presence of cars is probably not one of them.

This caution must also be viewed in reverse. Sometimes events that seem entirely unconnected actually *are* connected. In 1978 Governor Michael Dukakis of Massachusetts ran for reelection. Still quite popular, Dukakis was nevertheless defeated in the Democratic primary that year by a razor-thin margin. The weekend before, the Boston Red Sox, in the thick of the division championship race, had been badly beaten by the New York Yankees in four straight games. Some very respectable political analysts believe that hundreds of thousands of Boston sports fans vented their anger on the incumbent governor the following Tuesday.

The Fallacy of Composition   To conclude that what is true for a part is necessarily true for the whole is to fall into the **fallacy of composition**. Suppose that a large group of cattle ranchers graze their cattle on the same range. To an individual rancher, more cattle and more grazing mean a higher income. But because its capacity is limited, the land can support only so many cattle. If every cattle rancher increased the number of cattle sent out to graze, the land would become overgrazed and barren, and everyone's income would fall. In short:

> Theories that seem to work well when applied to individuals or households often break down when they are applied to the whole.

---

post hoc, ergo propter hoc *Literally, "after this (in time), therefore because of this." A common error made in thinking about causation: If Event A happens before Event B, it is not necessarily true that A caused B.*

fallacy of composition *The erroneous belief that what is true for a part is necessarily true for the whole.*

▶ **Testing Theories and Models: Empirical Economics** In science, a theory is rejected when it fails to explain what is observed or when another theory better explains what is observed. Prior to the sixteenth century almost everyone believed that the earth was the center of the universe and that the sun and stars rotated around it. The astronomer Ptolemy (A.D. 127–151) built a model that explained and predicted the movements of the heavenly bodies in a geocentric (earth-centered) universe. Early in the sixteenth century, however, the Polish astronomer Nicholas Copernicus found himself dissatisfied with the Ptolemaic model and proposed an alternative theory or model, placing the sun at the center of the known universe and relegating the earth to the status of one planet among many. The battle between the competing models was waged, at least in part, with data based on observations—actual measurements of planetary movements. The new model ultimately predicted much better than the old, and in time it came to be accepted.

In the seventeenth century, building on the works of Copernicus and others, Sir Isaac Newton constructed yet another body of theory that seemed to predict planetary motion with still more accuracy. Newtonian physics became the accepted body of theory, relied on for almost 300 years. Then Albert Einstein's theory of relativity replaced Newtonian physics because it was able to explain some things that earlier theories could not.

Economic theories are also confronted with new and often conflicting data from time to time. The collection and use of data to test economic theories is called **empirical economics**.

Numerous large data sets are available to facilitate economic research. For example, economists studying the labor market can now test behavioral theories against the actual working experiences of thousands of randomly selected people who have been surveyed continuously since the 1960s by economists at Ohio State University. Macroeconomists continuously monitoring and studying the behavior of the national economy pass thousands of items of data, collected by both government agencies and private companies, back and forth on diskettes and over the Internet. Housing market analysts analyze data tapes containing observations recorded in connection with millions of home sales.

All scientific research needs to isolate and measure the responsiveness of one variable to a change in another variable *ceteris paribus*. Physical scientists, such as physicists and geologists, can often impose the condition of *ceteris paribus* by conducting controlled experiments. They can, for example, measure the effect of one chemical on another while literally holding all else constant in an environment that they control completely. Social scientists, who study people, rarely have this luxury.

Although controlled experiments are difficult in economics and other social sciences, they are not impossible. Researchers can isolate and measure the effect of one variable on another. There are a number of ways to do this. One way is to observe the behavior of groups of similar people under different circumstances. For example, suppose you wanted to estimate the effect of the tax rate increases enacted by Congress in 1993 on the amount that households save, an important tax policy issue. Of course, you could look at household saving before and after the change. But who's to say that what you observe is not due to changes in income that occurred at the same time? To isolate the tax effect, you could look at a set of households whose income did not change. Sophisticated computer programs are now allowing economists to isolate such effects more easily than ever before.

empirical economics *The collection and use of data to test economic theories.*

ECONOMIC POLICY

Economic theory helps us understand how the world works, but the formulation of *economic policy* requires a second step. We must have objectives. What do we want to change? Why? What is good and what is bad about the way the system is operating? Can we make it better?

Such questions force us to be specific about the grounds for judging one outcome superior to another. What does it mean to be better? Four criteria are frequently applied in making these judgments:

Criteria for Judging Economic Outcomes: 1. Efficiency
                                          2. Equity
                                          3. Growth
                                          4. Stability

► Efficiency In physics, "efficiency" refers to the ratio of useful energy delivered by a system to the energy supplied to it. An efficient automobile engine, for example, is one that uses up a small amount of fuel per mile for a given level of power.

In economics, **efficiency** means *allocative efficiency*. An efficient economy is one that produces what people want at the least possible cost. If the system allocates resources to the production of things that nobody wants, it is inefficient. If all members of a particular society were vegetarian and somehow half of all that society's resources were used to produce meat, the result would be inefficient. It is inefficient when steel beams lie in the rain and rust because somebody fouled up a shipping schedule. If a firm could produce its product using 25 percent less labor and energy without sacrificing quality, it too is inefficient.

The clearest example of an efficient change is a voluntary exchange. If you and I each want something that the other has and we agree to exchange, we are both better off, and no one loses. When a company reorganizes its production or adopts a new technology that enables it to produce more of its product with fewer resources, without sacrificing quality, it has made an efficient change. At least potentially, the resources saved could be used to produce more of something.

Inefficiencies can arise in numerous ways. Sometimes they are caused by government regulations or tax laws that distort otherwise sound economic decisions. Suppose that land in Ohio is best suited for corn production and that land in Kansas is best suited for wheat production. Clearly, a law that requires Kansas to produce only corn and Ohio to produce only wheat would be inefficient. If firms that cause environmental damage are not held accountable for their actions, the incentive to minimize those damages is lost, and the result is inefficient.

Because most changes that can be made in an economy will leave some people better off and others worse off, we must have a way of comparing the gains and losses that may result. Most often we simply compare their sizes in dollar terms. A change is efficient if the value of the resulting gains exceeds the value of the resulting losses. In this case the winners can potentially compensate the losers, and they would still be better off.

► Equity While efficiency has a fairly precise definition that can be applied with some degree of rigor, **equity** (fairness) lies in the eye of the beholder. To many, fairness implies a more equal distribution of income and wealth. Fairness may imply alleviating poverty, but the extent to which the poor should receive cash benefits from the government is the subject of enormous disagreement. For thousands of years philosophers have wrestled with the principles of justice that should guide social decisions. They will probably wrestle with such questions for thousands of years to come.

Despite the impossibility of defining equity or fairness universally, public policy makers judge the fairness of economic outcomes all the time. Rent control laws were passed because some legislators thought that landlords treated low-income tenants unfairly. Certainly most social welfare programs are created in the name of equity.

efficiency *In economics, allocative efficiency. An efficient economy is one that produces what people want at the least possible cost.*

In 1997, Tiger Woods signed on as a spokesman for American Express for a reported $18 million over five years. He has contracts worth $40 million with Nike and $20 million with Titleist.[a] The median annual money income of U.S. families and individuals in 1996 was about $42,000.[b]

Sources: [a]*New York Times,* May 20, 1997, p. 1; [b]*Economic Report of the President,* 1998, p. 320.

equity *Fairness.*

➤ **Growth** As the result of technological change, the building of machinery, and the acquisition of knowledge, societies learn to produce new things and to produce old things better. In the early days of the U.S. economy, it took nearly half the population to produce the required food supply. Today less than 2.5 percent of the country's population works in agriculture.

When we devise new and better ways of producing the things we use now and develop new products and services, the total amount of production in the economy increases. **Economic growth** is an increase in the total output of an economy. If output grows faster than the population, output per capita rises and standards of living increase. Presumably, when an economy grows there is more of what people want. Rural and agrarian societies become modern industrial societies as a result of economic growth and rising per capita output.

economic growth An increase in the total output of an economy.

Some policies discourage economic growth and others encourage it. Tax laws, for example, can be designed to encourage the development and application of new production techniques. Research and development in some societies are subsidized by the government. Building roads, highways, bridges, and transport systems in developing countries may speed up the process of economic growth. If businesses and wealthy people invest their wealth outside their country rather than in its own industries, growth in their home country may be slowed.

➤ **Stability** Economic **stability** refers to the condition in which national output is steady or growing, with low inflation and full employment of resources. An economy may at times be unstable. During the 1950s and 1960s, the U.S. economy experienced a long period of relatively steady growth, stable prices, and low unemployment. Between 1951 and 1969, consumer prices never rose more than 5 percent in a single year, and in only two years did the number of unemployed exceed 6 percent of the labor force. The decades of the 1970s and 1980s, however, were unstable. The United States experienced two periods of rapid price inflation (over 10 percent) and two periods of severe unemployment. In 1982, for example, 12 million people (10.8 percent of the workforce) were looking for work. The beginning of the 1990s was another period of instability, with a recession occurring in 1990–1991. In 1997 the economy was growing at a large enough rate that fears of inflation began to arise. In response, the Federal Reserve System (the U.S. central bank) acted to raise interest rates with a goal of slowing the country's growth rate. The causes of instability and the ways in which governments have attempted to stabilize the economy are the subject matter of macroeconomics.

stability A condition in which output is steady or growing, with low inflation and full employment of resources.

AN INVITATION

This chapter is meant to prepare you for what is to come. The first part of the chapter invited you into an exciting discipline that deals with important issues and questions. You cannot begin to understand how a society functions without knowing something about its economic history and its economic system.

The second part of the chapter introduced the method of reasoning that economics requires and some of the tools that economics uses. We believe that learning to think in this very powerful way will help you better understand the world.

As you proceed, it is important that you keep track of what you've learned in earlier chapters. This book has a plan; it proceeds step by step, each section building on the last. It would be a good idea to read through each chapter's table of contents and flip through each chapter before you read it to be sure you understand where it fits in the big picture.

SUMMARY

1. *Economics* is the study of how individuals and societies choose to use the scarce resources that nature and previous generations have provided.

WHY STUDY ECONOMICS?

2. There are many reasons to study economics, including (a) to learn a way of thinking, (b) to understand society, (c) to understand global affairs, and (d) to be an informed voter.

3. That which we forgo when we make a choice or a decision is the *opportunity cost* of that decision.

THE SCOPE OF ECONOMICS

4. *Microeconomics* deals with the functioning of individual markets and industries and with the behavior of individual decision-making units: firms and households.

5. *Macroeconomics* looks at the economy as a whole. It deals with the economic behavior of aggregates—national output, national income, the overall price level, and the general rate of inflation.

6. Economics is a broad and diverse discipline with many special fields of inquiry. These include economic history, international economics, and urban economics.

THE METHOD OF ECONOMICS

7. Economics asks and attempts to answer two kinds of questions: positive and normative. *Positive economics* attempts to understand behavior and the operation of economies without making judgments about whether the outcomes are good or bad. *Normative economics* looks at the results

of economic behavior and asks if they are good or bad and whether they can be improved.

8. Positive economics is often divided into two parts. *Descriptive economics* involves the compilation of data that accurately describe economic facts and events. *Economic theory* attempts to generalize and explain what is observed. It involves statements of cause and effect—of action and reaction.

9. An economic *model* is a formal statement of an economic theory. Models simplify and abstract from reality.

10. It is often useful to isolate the effects of one variable or another while holding "all else constant." This is the device of *ceteris paribus*.

11. Models and theories can be expressed in many ways. The most common ways are in words, in graphs, and in equations.

12. Because one event happens before another, the second event does not necessarily happen as a result of the first. To assume that "after" implies "because" is to commit the fallacy of *post hoc, ergo propter hoc*. The erroneous belief that what is true for a part is necessarily true for the whole is the *fallacy of composition*.

13. *Empirical economics* involves the collection and use of data to test economic theories. In principle, the best model is the one that yields the most accurate predictions.

14. To make policy, one must be careful to specify criteria for making judgments. Four specific criteria are used most often in economics: *efficiency*, *equity*, *growth*, and *stability*.

REVIEW TERMS AND CONCEPTS

ceteris paribus, 11
descriptive economics, 8
economic growth, 15
economic theory, 10
economics, 2
efficiency, 14
efficient market, 3
empirical economics, 13

equity, 14
fallacy of composition, 12
Industrial Revolution, 4
macroeconomics, 7
microeconomics, 7
model, 10
normative economics, 8

Ockham's razor, 10
opportunity cost, 2
positive economics, 8
post hoc, ergo propter hoc, 12
stability, 15
sunk costs, 3
variable, 10

PROBLEM SET

1. One of the scarce resources that constrain our behavior is time. Each of us has only 24 hours in a day. How do you go about allocating your time in a given day among competing alternatives? How do you go about weighing the alternatives? Once you choose a most important use of time, why do you

not spend all your time on it? Use the notion of opportunity cost in your answer.

2. Which of the following statements are examples of positive economic analysis? Which are examples of normative analysis?

a. The 1997 cut in the federal inheritance tax is likely to cause a moderate increase in saving by higher-income households and a decline in donations to charity.

b. The inheritance tax should be repealed because it is unfair.

c. President Clinton proposed allowing Chile to join the North American Free Trade Agreement (NAFTA) in 1998. (NAFTA is an agreement signed by the United States, Mexico, and Canada in which the countries agreed to establish all of North America as a free-trade zone.) Admission of Chile should not be allowed because Chile's environmental standards are not up to those in the United States, which would give Chilean firms a cost advantage in competing with U.S. firms.

d. Allowing Chile to join NAFTA would cause wine prices in the United States to drop.

e. The establishment of a new political regime in the Democratic Republic of Congo (DRC, formerly Zaire) in 1997 will cause the world price of diamonds to drop because the supply of diamonds from the DRC to world markets will increase.

f. The first priorities of the new regime in the Democratic Republic of Congo should be to rebuild schools and highways and to provide basic health care.

3. Selwyn signed up with an Internet provider for a fixed fee of $19.95 per month. For this fee he gets unlimited access to the World Wide Web. During the average month in 1998, he was logged onto the Web for 17 hours. What is the average cost of an hour of Web time to Selwyn? What is the marginal cost of an additional hour?

4. Describe one of the major economic issues facing the government of your city or your state. (*Hint:* You might look at a local newspaper. Most issues that make it into the paper will have an impact on people's lives.) Who will be affected by the resolution of this issue? What alternative actions have been proposed? Who will be the winners? The losers?

5. Suppose that all of the 10,000 voting-age citizens of Lumpland are required to register to vote every year. Suppose also that the citizens of Lumpland are fully employed and that they each value their time at $10 per hour. In addition, assume that nonvoting high-school students in Lumpland are willing to work for $5 per hour. The government has two choices: (1) It can hire 200 students to work at registration locations for 5 hours per day for 10 days, or (2) it can hire 400 students for 5 hours per day for 10 days. If the government hires 200 students, each of the 10,000 citizens will have to wait in line for an hour to register. If the government hires 400 students, there will be no waiting time.

Assume that the cost of paying the students is obtained by taxing each voting-age citizen equally. The current government is very conservative and has decided to hold taxes down by hiring only 200 students. Do you agree with this decision? Why or why not? Is it efficient? Is it fair?

6. Suppose that a city is considering building a bridge across a river. The bridge will be financed by tax dollars. The city gets these revenues from a sales tax imposed on things sold in the city. The bridge would provide more direct access for commuters and shoppers. It would also alleviate the huge traffic jam that occurs every morning at the bridge down the river in another city.

a. Who would gain if the bridge were built? Could those gains be measured? How?

b. Who would be hurt if the bridge were built? Could those costs be measured? How?

c. How would you determine if it were efficient to build the bridge?

7. A question facing many U.S. states is whether to allow casino gambling. States with casino gambling have seen a substantial increase in tax revenue flowing to state government. This revenue can be used to finance schools, repair roads, maintain social programs, or reduce other taxes.

a. Recall that efficiency means producing what people want at least cost. Can you make an efficiency argument in favor of allowing casinos to operate?

b. What nonmonetary costs might be associated with gambling? Would these costs have an impact on the efficiency argument you presented in part a?

c. Using the concept of equity, argue for or against the legalization of casino gambling.

8. For each of the following situations, identify the full cost (opportunity costs) involved:

a. A worker earning an hourly wage of $8.50 decides to cut back to half time in order to attend Houston Community College.

b. Sue decides to drive to Los Angeles from San Francisco to visit her son, who attends UCLA.

c. Tom decides to go to a wild fraternity party and stays out all night before his physics exam.

d. Annie spends $200 on a new dress.

e. The Confab Company spends $1 million to build a new branch plant that will probably be in operation for at least 10 years.

f. Alex's father owns a small grocery store in town. Alex works 40 hours a week in the store but receives no compensation.

TAKE IT TO THE NET

We invite you to visit the Case and Fair page on the Prentice Hall Web site:

http://www.prenhall.com/casefair

for this chapter's World Wide Web exercise.

HOW TO READ AND UNDERSTAND GRAPHS

Economics is the most quantitative of the social sciences. If you flip through the pages of this or any other economics text, you will see countless tables and graphs. These serve a number of purposes. First, they illustrate important economic relationships. Second, they make difficult problems easier to understand and analyze. Finally, patterns and regularities that may not be discernible in simple lists of numbers can often be seen when those numbers are laid out in a table or on a graph.

A **graph** is a two-dimensional representation of a set of numbers, or data. There are many ways that numbers can be illustrated by a graph.

TIME SERIES GRAPHS

It is often useful to see how a single measure or variable changes over time. One way to present this information is to plot the values of the variable on a graph, with each value corresponding to a different time period. A graph of this kind is called a **time series graph**. On a time series graph, time is measured along the horizontal scale and the variable being graphed is measured along the vertical scale. Figure 1A.1 is a time series graph that presents the total disposable income in the U.S. economy for each year between 1975 and 1997.[1] This graph is based on the data found in Table 1A.1. By displaying these data graphically, we can see clearly that (1) total personal disposable income has been increasing steadily since 1975, and (2) during certain periods, disposable income was increasing at a faster rate than during other periods.

GRAPHING TWO VARIABLES ON A CARTESIAN COORDINATE SYSTEM

More important than simple graphs of one variable are graphs that contain information on two variables at the same time. The most common method of graphing two variables is the **Cartesian coordinate system**. This system is constructed by simply drawing two perpendicular lines: a horizontal line, or **X axis**, and a vertical

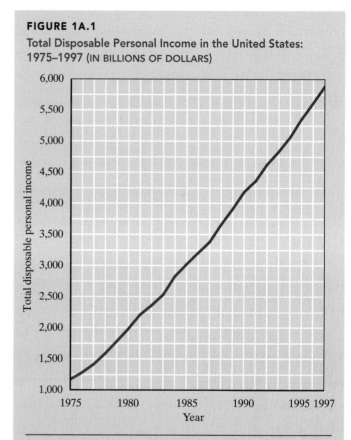

FIGURE 1A.1

Total Disposable Personal Income in the United States: 1975–1997 (IN BILLIONS OF DOLLARS)

Source: Economic Report of the President, 1998, p. 317.

line, or **Y axis**. The axes contain measurement scales that intersect at 0 (zero). This point is called the **origin**. On the vertical scale, positive numbers lie above the horizontal axis (that is, above the origin) and negative numbers lie below it. On the horizontal scale, positive numbers lie to the right of the vertical axis (to the right of the origin) and negative numbers lie to the left of it. The point at which the graph intersects the Y axis is called the **Y-intercept**.

When two variables are plotted on a single graph, each point represents a *pair* of numbers. The first number is measured on the X axis and the second number is measured on the Y axis. For example, the following points

---

[1]The measure of income presented in Table 1A.1 and in Figure 1A.1 is disposable income in billions of dollars. It is the total personal income received by all households in the United States minus the taxes that they pay.

TABLE 1A.1

TOTAL DISPOSABLE PERSONAL INCOME IN THE UNITED STATES, 1975–1997 (IN BILLIONS OF DOLLARS)

YEAR	TOTAL DISPOSABLE PERSONAL INCOME
1975	1,162.6
1976	1,277.1
1977	1,406.1
1978	1,585.8
1979	1,775.7
1980	1,980.5
1981	2,208.3
1982	2,355.8
1983	2,531.5
1984	2,819.8
1985	3,012.1
1986	3,198.5
1987	3,374.6
1988	3,652.6
1989	3,906.1
1990	4,179.4
1991	4,356.8
1992	4,626.7
1993	4,829.2
1994	5,052.7
1995	5,355.7
1996	5,608.3
1997	5,886.6

Source: Economic Report of the President, 1998, p. 317.

FIGURE 1A.2

A Cartesian Coordinate System

A Cartesian coordinate system is constructed by drawing two perpendicular lines: a vertical axis (the Y axis) and a horizontal axis (the X axis). Each axis is a measuring scale.

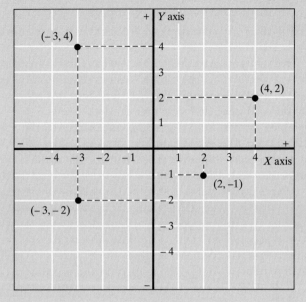

those households, ranked by income. For example, the average income for the top fifth (20 percent) of the households was $76,660. The average spending for the top 20 percent was $55,411.

TABLE 1A.2

CONSUMPTION EXPENDITURES AND INCOME, 1990[a]

	AVERAGE INCOME	AVERAGE CONSUMPTION EXPENDITURES
Bottom fifth	$ 5,637	$12,908
2nd fifth	14,115	17,924
3rd fifth	24,500	24,673
4th fifth	38,376	34,247
Top fifth	76,660	55,411

[a]Income and consumption data are for consumer units. Consumer units are defined as (1) all members of a particular household related by blood, marriage, adoption, or other legal arrangements, (2) a person living alone or sharing a household with others, but who is financially independent, or (3) two or more persons living together who pool their incomes.

Source: Statistical Abstract of the United States, 1992, p. 442.

(X, Y) are plotted on the set of axes drawn in figure 1A.2: (4, 2), (2, –1), (–3, 4), (–3, –2). Most, but not all, of the graphs in this book are plots of two variables where both values are positive numbers (such as [4, 2] in Figure 1A.2). On these graphs, only the upper right quadrant of the coordinate system (i.e., the quadrant in which all X and Y values are positive) will be drawn.

PLOTTING INCOME AND CONSUMPTION DATA FOR HOUSEHOLDS

Table 1A.2 presents some data collected by the Bureau of Labor Statistics (BLS). In a recent survey, 5,000 households were asked to keep careful track of all their expenditures. The table shows average income and average spending for

Figure 1A.3 presents the numbers from Table 1A.2 graphically using the Cartesian coordinate system. Along the horizontal scale, the *X* axis, we measure average income. Along the vertical scale, the *Y* axis, we measure average consumption spending. Each of the five pairs of numbers from the table is represented by a point on the graph. Because all numbers are positive numbers, we need to show only the upper right quadrant of the coordinate system.

To help you read this graph, we have drawn a dotted line connecting all the points where consumption and income would be equal. *This 45° line does not represent any data.* Rather, it represents the line along which all variables on the *X* axis correspond exactly to the variables on the *Y* axis (for example, [1, 1], [2, 2], [3.7, 3.7], etc.). The heavy blue line traces out the data; the dotted line is only to help you read the graph.

There are several things to look for when reading a graph. The first thing you should notice is whether the line slopes upward or downward as you move from left to right. The blue line in Figure 1A.3 slopes upward, indicating that there seems to be a **positive relationship** between income and spending: The higher a household's income, the more a household tends to consume. If we had graphed the percentage of each group receiving welfare payments along the *Y* axis, the line would presumably slope downward, indicating that welfare payments are lower at higher income levels. The income level/welfare payment relationship is thus a **negative** one.

SLOPE

The **slope** of a line or curve is a measure that indicates whether the relationship between the variables is positive or negative and how much of a response there is in *Y* (the variable on the vertical axis) when *X* (the variable on the horizontal axis) changes. The slope of a line between two points is the change in the quantity measured on the *Y* axis divided by the change in the quantity measured on the *X* axis. We will normally use Δ (the Greek letter *delta*) to refer to a change in a variable. In Figure 1A.4, the slope of the line between points *A* and *B* is ΔY divided by ΔX. Sometimes it's easy to remember slope as "the rise over the run," indicating the vertical change over the horizontal change.

To be precise, ΔX between two points on a graph is simply X_2 minus X_1, where X_2 is the *X* value for the second point and X_1 is the *X* value for the first point. Similarly, ΔY is defined as Y_2 minus Y_1, where Y_2 is the *Y* value for the second point and Y_1 is the *Y* value for the first point. Slope is equal to

$$\frac{\Delta Y}{\Delta X} = \frac{Y_2 - Y_1}{X_2 - X_1}.$$

As we move from *A* to *B* in Figure 1A.4(a), both *X* and *Y* increase; the slope is thus a positive number. However, as we move from *A* to *B* in Figure 1A.4(b), *X* increases [$(X_2 - X_1)$ is a positive number], but *Y* decreases [$(Y_2 - Y_1)$ is a negative number]. The slope in Figure 1A.4(b) is thus a negative number, as a negative number divided by a positive number gives a negative quotient.

To calculate the numerical value of the slope between points *A* and *B* in Figure 1A.4, we need to calculate ΔY and ΔX. Since consumption is measured on the *Y* axis, ΔY is 5,016 [$(Y_2 - Y_1) = (17,924 - 12,908)$]. Because income is measured along the *X* axis, ΔX is 8,478 [$(X_2 - X_1) = (14,115 - 5,637)$]. The slope between *A* and *B* is $\Delta Y/\Delta X = 5,016/8,478 = +.592$.

FIGURE 1A.3

Household Consumption and Income

A graph is a simple two-dimensional geometric representation of data. This graph displays the data from Table 1A.2. Along the horizontal scale (*X* axis), we measure household income. Along the vertical scale (*Y* axis), we measure household consumption. *Note:* At point *A,* consumption equals $12,908 and income equals $5,637. At point *B*, consumption equals $17,924 and income equals $14,115.

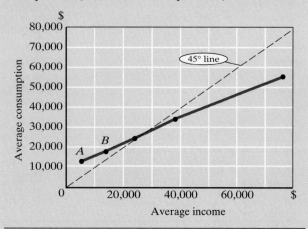

Source: *Statistical Abstract of the United States*, 1992, p. 442.

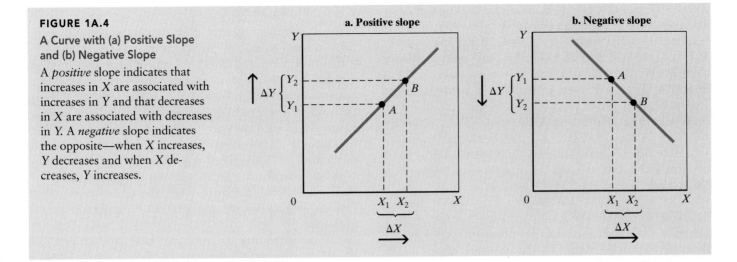

FIGURE 1A.4

A Curve with (a) Positive Slope and (b) Negative Slope

A *positive* slope indicates that increases in X are associated with increases in Y and that decreases in X are associated with decreases in Y. A *negative* slope indicates the opposite—when X increases, Y decreases and when X decreases, Y increases.

a. Positive slope

b. Negative slope

Another interesting thing to note about the data graphed in Figure 1A.3 is that all the points lie roughly along a straight line. (If you look very closely, however, you can see that the slope declines as one moves from left to right; the line becomes slightly less steep.) A straight line has a constant slope. That is, if you pick any two points along it and calculate the slope, you will always get the same number. A horizontal line has a zero slope (ΔY is zero); a vertical line has an "infinite" slope, because ΔY is too big to be measured.

Unlike the slope of a straight line, the slope of a *curve* is continually changing. Consider, for example, the curves in Figure 1A.5. Figure 1A.5(a) shows a curve with a positive slope that decreases as you move from left

FIGURE 1A.5

Changing Slopes Along Curves

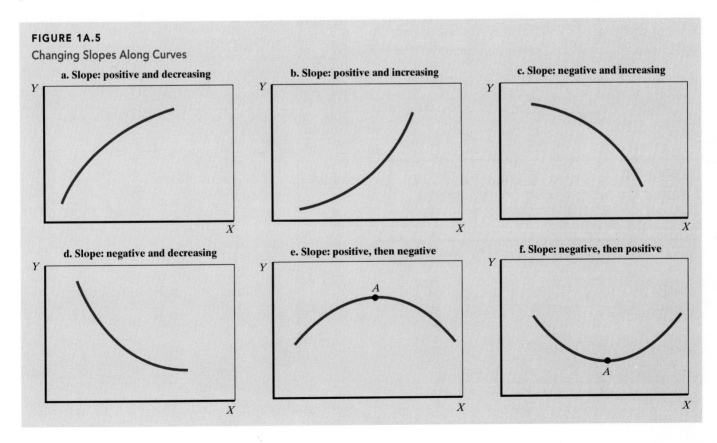

a. Slope: positive and decreasing

b. Slope: positive and increasing

c. Slope: negative and increasing

d. Slope: negative and decreasing

e. Slope: positive, then negative

f. Slope: negative, then positive

to right. The easiest way to think about the concept of increasing or decreasing slope is to imagine what it is like walking up a hill from left to right. If the hill is steep, as it is in the first part of Figure 1A.5(a), you are moving a lot in the Y direction for each step you take in the X direction. If the hill is less steep, as it is further along in Figure 1A.5(a), you are moving less in the Y direction for every step you take in the X direction. Thus, when the hill is steep, slope ($\Delta Y/\Delta X$) is a larger number than it is when the hill is flatter. The curve in Figure 1A.5(b) has a positive slope, but its slope *increases* as you move from left to right.

The same analogy holds for curves that have a negative slope. Figure 1A.5(c) shows a curve with a negative slope that increases (in absolute value) as you move from left to right. This time think about skiing down a hill. At first, the descent in Figure 1A.5(c) is gradual (low slope), but as you proceed down the hill (to the right), you descend more quickly (high slope). Figure 1A.5(d) shows a curve with a negative slope that *decreases* in absolute value as you move from left to right.

In Figure 1A.5(e), the slope goes from positive to negative as X increases. In 1A.5(f), the slope goes from negative to positive. At point A in both, the slope is zero. (Remember, slope is defined as $\Delta Y/\Delta X$. At point A, Y is not changing [$\Delta Y = 0$]. Therefore slope at point A is zero.)

SOME PRECAUTIONS

When you read a graph, it is important to think carefully about what the points in the space defined by the axes represent. Table 1A.3 and Figure 1A.6 present a graph of consumption and income that is very different from the one in Table 1A.2 and Figure 1A.3. First, each point in Figure 1A.6 represents a different year; in Figure 1A.3, each point represented a different group of households at the *same* point in time (1990). Second, the points in Figure 1A.6 represent *aggregate* consumption and income for the whole nation measured in *billions* of dollars; in Figure 1A.3, the points represented average *household* income and consumption measured in dollars.

It is interesting to compare these two graphs. All points on the aggregate consumption curve in Figure 1A.6 lie below the 45° line, which means that aggregate consumption is always less than aggregate income. However, the graph of average household income and consumption in Figure 1A.3 crosses the 45° line, implying that for some households consumption is larger than income.

TABLE 1A.3

AGGREGATE INCOME AND CONSUMPTION FOR THE ENTIRE UNITED STATES, 1930–1990
(IN BILLIONS OF DOLLARS)

	AGGREGATE NATIONAL INCOME	AGGREGATE CONSUMPTION
1930	75.3	70.2
1940	81.1	71.2
1950	241.7	192.7
1960	429.8	332.2
1970	840.6	648.1
1980	2,244.5	1,760.4
1990	4,652.1	3,839.3

Source: U.S. Department of Commerce, *Survey of Current Business,* August 1997, pp. 148, 164.

FIGURE 1A.6

National Income and Consumption

It is important to think carefully about what is represented by points in the space defined by the axes of a graph. In this graph, we have income graphed with consumption, as in Figure 1A.3, but here each observation point is national income and aggregate consumption in *different years,* measured in billions of dollars.

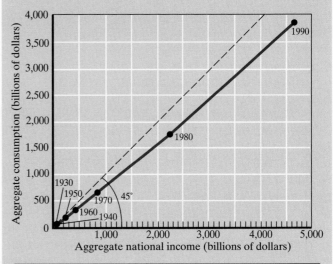

Source: See Table 1A.3.

SUMMARY

1. A *graph* is a two-dimensional representation of a set of numbers, or data. A *time series graph* illustrates how a single variable changes over time.

2. The most common method of graphing two variables on one graph is the *Cartesian coordinate system*, which includes an *X* (horizontal) *axis* and a *Y* (vertical) *axis*. The points at which the two axes intersect is called the *origin*. The point at which a graph intersects the *Y* axis is called the *Y-intercept*.

3. The *slope* of a line or curve indicates whether the relationship between the two variables graphed on a Cartesian coordinate system is positive or negative and how much of a response there is in *Y* (the variable on the vertical axis) when *X* (the variable on the horizontal axis) changes. The slope of a line between two points is the change in the quantity measured on the *Y* axis divided by the change in the quantity measured on the *X* axis.

REVIEW TERMS AND CONCEPTS

Cartesian coordinate system A common method of graphing two variables that makes use of two perpendicular lines against which the variables are plotted.   18

graph A two-dimensional representation of a set of numbers, or data.   18

negative relationship A relationship between two variables, *X* and *Y*, in which a decrease in *X* is associated with an increase in *Y*, and an increase in *X* is associated with a decrease in *Y*.   20

origin On a Cartesian coordinate system, the point at which the horizontal and vertical axes intersect.   18

positive relationship A relationship between two variables, *X* and *Y*, in which a decrease in *X* is associated with a decrease in *Y*, and an increase in *X* is associated with an increase in *Y*.   20

slope A measurement that indicates whether the relationship between variables is positive or negative and how much of a response there is in *Y* (the variable on the vertical axis)

when *X* (the variable on the horizontal axis) changes.   20

times series graph A graph illustrating how a variable changes over time.   18

X axis On a Cartesian coordinate system, the horizontal line against which a variable is plotted.   18

Y axis On a Cartesian coordinate system, the vertical line against which a variable is plotted.   18

Y-intercept The point at which a graph intersects the *Y* axis.   18

PROBLEM SET

1. Graph each of the following sets of numbers. Draw a line through the points and calculate the slope of each line.

1		2		3		4		5		6	
X	Y	X	Y	X	Y	X	Y	X	Y	X	Y
1	5	1	25	0	0	0	40	0	0	0.1	100
2	10	2	20	10	10	10	30	10	10	0.2	75
3	15	3	15	20	20	20	20	20	20	0.3	50
4	20	4	10	30	30	30	10	30	10	0.4	25
5	25	5	5	40	40	40	0	40	0	0.5	0

2. For each of the graphs in Figure 1 on page 24, say whether the curve has a positive or negative slope. Give an intuitive explanation for the slope of each curve.

3. For each of the following equations, graph the line and calculate its slope.
   a. $P = 10 - 2q_D$ (Put q_D on the *X* axis)
   b. $P = 100 - 4q_D$ (Put q_D on the *X* axis)
   c. $P = 50 + 6q_S$ (Put q_S on the *X* axis)
   d. $I = 10,000 - 500r$ (Put *I* on the *X* axis)

FIGURE 1

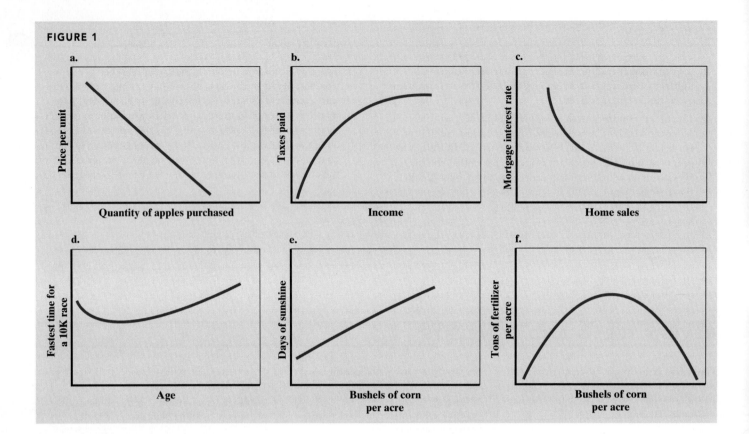

THE ECONOMIC PROBLEM: SCARCITY AND CHOICE

CHAPTER 1 BEGAN with a broad definition of economics. As you saw there, every society has some system or mechanism that transforms what nature and previous generations provide into useful form. Economics is the study of that process and its outcomes. Economists attempt to answer these questions: What gets produced? How is it produced? Who gets it? Why? Is it good or bad? Can it be improved?

This chapter explores these questions further. In a sense, this entire chapter *is* the definition of economics. It lays out the central problems addressed by the discipline and provides the framework that will guide you through the rest of the book.

Human wants are unlimited, but resources are not. Limited, or scarce, resources force individuals and societies to choose. The central function of any economy, no matter how simple or how complex, is to transform resources into useful form in accordance with those choices. The process by which this transformation takes place is called **production**.

The term **resources** is very broad. Some resources are the product of nature: land, wildlife, minerals, timber, energy, even the rain and the wind. At any given time, the resources, or **inputs**, available to a society also include those things that have been produced by previous generations, such as buildings and equipment. Things that are produced and then used to produce other valuable goods or services later on are called *capital resources*, or simply **capital**. Buildings, machinery, equipment, tables, roads, bridges, desks, and so forth are part of the nation's capital stock. *Human resources*—labor, skills, and knowledge—are also an important part of a nation's resources.

Producers are those who take resources and transform them into usable products, or **outputs**. Private manufacturing firms purchase resources and produce products for the market. Governments do so as well. National defense, the justice system, police and fire protection, and sewer services are all examples of outputs produced by the government, which is sometimes called the *public sector*.

Individual households often produce products for themselves. A household that owns its own home is in essence using land and a structure (capital)

production *The process by which resources are transformed into useful forms.*

resources or **inputs** *Anything provided by nature or previous generations that can be used directly or indirectly to satisfy human wants.*

capital *Things that have already been produced that are in turn used to produce other goods and services.*

producers *Those people or groups of people, whether private or public, who transform resources into usable products.*

outputs *Usable products.*

to produce "housing services" that it consumes itself. The Chicago Symphony Orchestra is no less a producer than General Motors. An orchestra takes capital resources—a building, musical instruments, lighting fixtures, musical scores, and so on—and combines them with land and highly skilled labor to produce performances.

SCARCITY, CHOICE, AND OPPORTUNITY COST

In the second half of this chapter, we discuss the global economic landscape. But before you can understand the different types of economic systems, it is important to understand the basic economic concepts of scarcity, choice, and opportunity cost.

THE THREE BASIC QUESTIONS

three basic questions
The questions that all societies must answer: (1) What will be produced? (2) How will it be produced? (3) Who will get what is produced?

All societies must answer **three basic questions:**

> 1. What will be produced?
> 2. How will it be produced?
> 3. Who will get what is produced?

Stated a slightly different way, the economic system must determine the *mix of output*, the *allocation of scarce resources* among producers, and the *distribution of that output* (Figure 2.1).

➤ **Scarcity and Choice in a One-Person Economy** The simplest economy is one in which a single person lives alone on an island. Consider Bill, the survivor of a plane crash, who finds himself cast ashore in such a place. Here, individual and society are one; there is no distinction between social and private. *Nonetheless, nearly all of the basic decisions that characterize complex economies must be made.* That is, although Bill himself will get whatever he produces, he still must decide how to allocate the island's resources, what to produce, and how and when to produce it.

First, Bill must decide *what* he wants to produce. Notice that the word *needs* does not appear here. Needs are absolute requirements, but beyond just enough water, basic nutrition, and shelter to survive, they are very difficult to define. What is an "absolute necessity" for one person may not be for another. In any case, Bill must put his wants in some order of priority and make some choices.

Next he must look at the *possibilities*. What can he do to satisfy his wants, given the limits of the island? In every society, no matter how simple or complex, people are constrained in what they can do. In this society of one, Bill is constrained by time, his physical condition, his knowledge, his skills, and the resources and climate of the island.

FIGURE 2.1

The Three Basic Questions

The three basic questions: 1. What will be produced?   2. How will it be produced?   3. Who will get what is produced?

Mix of output

Resources

Producers

Households

Allocation of resources

Distribution of output

Given that resources are limited, Bill must decide *how* to use them best to satisfy his hierarchy of wants. Food would probably come close to the top of his list. Should he spend his time simply gathering fruits and berries? Should he hunt for game? Should he clear a field and plant seeds? Clearly, the answers to these questions depend on the character of the island, its climate, its flora and fauna (*are* there any fruits and berries?), the extent of his skills and knowledge (does he know anything about farming?), and his preferences (he may be a vegetarian).

➤ **Opportunity Cost** The concepts of *constrained choice* and *scarcity* are central to the discipline of economics. They can be applied when discussing the behavior of individuals like Bill and when analyzing the behavior of large groups of people in complex societies.

Given the scarcity of time and resources, Bill has less time to gather fruits and berries if he chooses to hunt—he trades more meat for less fruit. There is a trade-off between food and shelter, too. If Bill likes to be comfortable, he may work on building a nice place to live, but that may require giving up the food he might have produced. As we noted in chapter 1, that which we forgo when we make a choice is the **opportunity cost** of that choice.

opportunity cost *That which we give up, or forgo, when we make a choice or a decision.*

Bill may occasionally decide to rest, to lie on the beach and enjoy the sun. In one sense, that benefit is free—he doesn't have to pay for the privilege. In reality, however, it does have an opportunity cost. The true cost of that leisure is the value of the other things Bill could have produced, but did not, during the time he spent on the beach.

In the 1960s, the United States decided to put a human being on the moon. To do so required devoting enormous resources to the space program, resources that could have been used to produce other things. Among other possibilities, taxes might have been lower. That would have meant more income for all of us to spend on goods and services. Those same resources could also have been used for medical research, to improve education, to repair roads and bridges, to aid the poor, or to support the arts.

In making everyday decisions it is often helpful to think about opportunity costs. Should I go to the dorm party or not? First, it costs $4 to get in. When I pay money for anything, I give up the other things that I could have bought with that money. Second, it costs two or three hours. Clearly, time is a valuable commodity for a college student. I have exams next week and I need to study. I could go to a movie instead of the party. I could go to another party. I could sleep. Just as Bill must weigh the value of sunning on the beach against more food or better housing, so I must weigh the value of the fun I may have at the party against everything else I might otherwise do with the time and money.

➤ **Scarcity and Choice in an Economy of Two or More** Now suppose that another survivor of the crash, Colleen, appears on the island. Now that Bill is not alone things are more complex, and some new decisions must be made. Bill's and Colleen's preferences about what things to produce are likely to be different. They will probably not have the same knowledge or skills. Perhaps Colleen is very good at tracking animals, and Bill has a knack for building things. How should they split the work that needs to be done? Once things are produced, they must decide how to divide them. How should their products be distributed?

The mechanism for answering these fundamental questions is clear when Bill is alone on the island. The "central plan" is his; he simply decides what he wants and what to do about it. The minute someone else appears, however, a number of decision-making arrangements immediately become possible. One or the other may take charge, in which case that person will decide for both of them. The two may agree to cooperate, with each having an equal say, and come up with a joint plan. Or they may agree to split the planning, as well as the production duties. Finally, they may go off to live alone at opposite ends of the island. Even if they live apart, however, they may take advantage of each other's presence by specializing and trading.

Modern industrial societies must answer exactly the same questions that Colleen and Bill must answer, but the mechanics of larger economies are naturally more complex. Instead of two people living together, the United States has over 268 million. Still decisions must be made about what to produce, how to produce it, and who gets it.

> **Specialization, Exchange, and Comparative Advantage** The idea that members of society benefit by specializing in what they do best has a long history and is one of the most important and powerful ideas in all of economics. David Ricardo, a major nineteenth-century British economist, formalized the point precisely. According to Ricardo's **theory of comparative advantage**, specialization and free trade will benefit all trading parties, even when some are "absolutely" more efficient producers than others. Ricardo's basic point applies just as much to Colleen and Bill as it does to different nations.

theory of comparative advantage *Ricardo's theory that specialization and free trade will benefit all trading parties, even those that may be absolutely more efficient producers.*

To keep things simple, suppose that Colleen and Bill have only two tasks to accomplish each week: gathering food to eat and cutting logs to be used in constructing a house. If Colleen could cut more logs than Bill in one day, and Bill could gather more nuts and berries than Colleen could, specialization would clearly lead to more total production. Both would benefit if Colleen only cuts logs and Bill only gathers nuts and berries. But suppose that Bill is slow and somewhat clumsy in his nut-gathering and that Colleen is better at both cutting logs *and* gathering food. Ricardo points out that it still pays for them to specialize and exchange.

Suppose that Colleen can cut 10 logs per day and that Bill can cut only 5. Also suppose that Colleen can gather 10 bushels of food per day and that Bill can gather only 8 (see table embedded in Figure 2.2). Assume also that Bill and Colleen value bushels of food and logs equally. How then can the two gain from specialization and exchange? Think of opportunity costs. When Colleen gives up a day of food production to work on the house, she cuts 10 logs and sacrifices 10 bushels of food. The opportunity cost of 10 logs is thus 10 bushels of food if Colleen switches from food to logs. But because Bill can cut only 5 logs in a day, he has to work for 2 days to cut 10 logs. In 2 days, Bill could have produced 16 bushels of food (2 days × 8 bushels per day). The opportunity cost of 10 logs is thus 16 bushels of food if Bill switches from food to logs.

As Figure 2.2 makes clear, even though Colleen is *absolutely* more efficient at food production than Bill, she should specialize in logs and Bill should specialize in food. This way, the maximum number of logs and bushels are produced. A person or a country is said to have a comparative advantage in producing a good or service if it is *relatively* more efficient than a trading partner at doing so.

Looking at the same situation from the standpoint of food production leads to exactly the same conclusion. If Colleen were to switch from cutting logs to gathering food, she would sacrifice 10 logs to produce only 10 bushels of food. But if Bill were to switch from cutting logs to gathering food, he would sacrifice 10 logs to produce a full 16 bushels! Even though Colleen has an *absolute advantage* in both cutting logs and producing food, Bill has a *comparative advantage* producing food because, for the same sacrifice of logs, Bill produces much more food.

The theory of comparative advantage shows that trade and specialization work to raise productivity. But specialization may also lead to the development of skills that enhance productivity even further. By specializing in log cutting, Colleen will get even stronger shoulders. By spending more time at gathering food, Bill will refine his food-finding skills. The same applies to countries that engage in international trade.

The degree of specialization in modern industrial societies is breathtaking. Once again let your mind wander over the range of products and services available or under development today. As knowledge expands, specialization becomes a necessity. This is true not only for scientists and doctors but also in every career from tree surgeon to

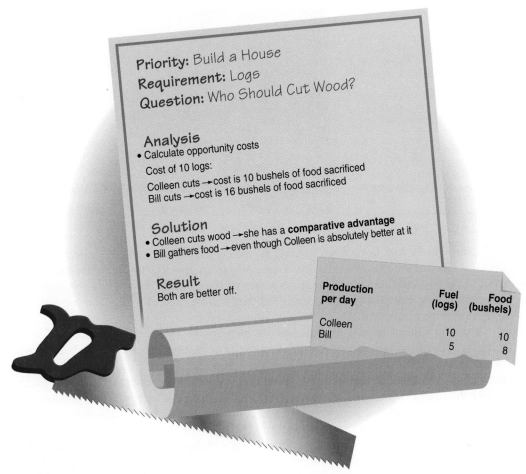

FIGURE 2.2
Comparative Advantage and Opportunity Costs

The content of the figure:

Priority: Build a House
Requirement: Logs
Question: Who Should Cut Wood?

Analysis
• Calculate opportunity costs
Cost of 10 logs:
Colleen cuts → cost is 10 bushels of food sacrificed
Bill cuts → cost is 16 bushels of food sacrificed

Solution
• Colleen cuts wood → she has a **comparative advantage**
• Bill gathers food → even though Colleen is absolutely better at it

Result
Both are better off.

Production per day	Fuel (logs)	Food (bushels)
Colleen	10	10
Bill	5	8

divorce lawyers. Understanding specialization and trade will help you to explain much of what goes on in today's global economy.

> **Weighing Present and Expected Future Costs and Benefits**   Very often we find ourselves weighing benefits available today against benefits available tomorrow. Here too the notion of opportunity cost is helpful.

While alone on the island, Bill had to choose between cultivating a field and just gathering wild nuts and berries. Gathering nuts and berries provides food now; gathering seeds and clearing a field for planting will yield food tomorrow, if all goes well. Using today's time to farm may well be worth the effort if doing so will yield more food than Bill would otherwise have in the future. By planting, Bill is trading present value for future values.

The simplest example of trading present for future benefits is the act of saving. When I put income aside today for use in the future, I give up some things that I could have had today in exchange for something tomorrow. Because nothing is certain, some judgment about future events and expected values must be made. What will my income be in 10 years? How long am I likely to live?

We trade off present and future benefits in small ways all the time. If you decide to study rather than go to the dorm party, you are trading present fun for the expected future benefits of higher grades. If you decide to go outside on a very cold day and run five miles, you are trading discomfort in the present for being in better shape later on.

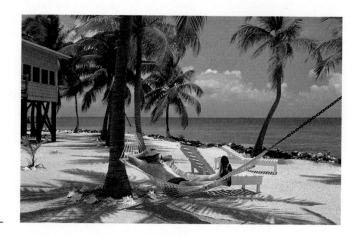

LEISURE IS NOT "COSTLESS." IT HAS AN OPPORTUNITY COST. LYING IN A HAMMOCK USES TIME THAT COULD HAVE BEEN USED TO DO OTHER THINGS.

▶ **Capital Goods and Consumer Goods** A society trades present for expected future benefits when it devotes a portion of its resources to research and development or to investment in capital. As we said earlier in this chapter, *capital* in its broadest definition is anything that has already been produced that will be used to produce other valuable goods or services over time.

Building capital means trading present benefits for future ones. Bill and Colleen might trade gathering berries or lying in the sun for cutting logs to build a nicer house in the future. In a modern society, resources used to produce capital goods could have been used to produce **consumer goods**—that is, goods for present consumption. Heavy industrial machinery does not directly satisfy the wants of anyone, but producing it requires resources that could instead have gone into producing things that do satisfy wants directly—food, clothing, toys, or golf clubs.

consumer goods *Goods produced for present consumption.*

Capital is everywhere. A road is capital. Once built, we can drive on it or transport goods and services over it for many years to come. A house is also capital. Before a new manufacturing firm can start up, it must put some capital in place. The buildings, equipment, and inventories that it uses are its capital. As it contributes to the production process, this capital yields valuable services through time.

In chapter 1 we talked about the enormous amount of capital—buildings, factories, housing, cars, trucks, telephone lines, and so forth—that you might see from a window high in a skyscraper. Much of it was put in place by previous generations, yet it continues to provide valuable services today; it is part of this generation's endowment of resources. To build every building, every road, every factory, every house, every car or truck, society must forgo using resources to produce consumer goods today. To get an education, I pay tuition and put off joining the workforce for a while.

Capital need not be tangible. When you spend time and resources developing skills or getting an education, you are investing in human capital—your own human capital. This capital will continue to exist and yield benefits to you for years to come. A computer program produced by a software company may come on a tangible disk that costs 75¢ to make, but its true intangible value comes from the ideas embodied in the program itself, which will drive computers to do valuable, time-saving tasks over time. It too is capital.

investment *The process of using resources to produce new capital.*

The process of using resources to produce new capital is called **investment**. (In everyday language, the term *investment* often refers to the act of buying a share of stock or a bond, as in "I invested in some Treasury bonds." In economics, however, investment *always* refers to the creation of capital: the purchase or putting in place of buildings, equipment, roads, houses, and the like.) A wise investment in capital is one that yields future benefits that are more valuable than the present cost. When you spend money for a house, for example, presumably you value its future benefits. That is, you expect to gain more from living in it than you would from the things you could buy today with the same money.

Because resources are scarce, the opportunity cost of every investment in capital is forgone present consumption.

THE PRODUCTION POSSIBILITY FRONTIER

A simple graphical device called the **production possibility frontier (ppf)** illustrates the principles of constrained choice, opportunity cost, and scarcity. The ppf is a graph that shows all the combinations of goods and services that can be produced if all of society's resources are used efficiently. Figure 2.3 shows a ppf for a hypothetical economy.

On the *Y* axis we measure the quantity of capital goods produced, and on the *X* axis, the quantity of consumer goods. All points below and to the left of the curve (the shaded area) represent combinations of capital and consumer goods that are possible for the society given the resources available and existing technology. Points above and to the right of the curve, such as point *G*, represent combinations that cannot be reached. If an economy were to end up at point *A* on the graph, it would be producing no consumer goods at all; all resources would be used for the production of capital. If an economy were to end up at point *B*, it would be devoting all of its resources to the production of consumer goods and none of its resources to the formation of capital.

While all economies produce some of each kind of good, different economies emphasize different things. About 16 percent of gross output in the United States in 1995 was new capital. In Japan, capital accounted for about 29 percent of gross output in 1995, while in Haiti the figure was 2 percent. Japan is closer to point *A* on its ppf, Haiti closer to *B*, and the United States is somewhere in between.

Points that are actually on the production possibility frontier are points of both full resource employment and production efficiency. (Recall from chapter 1 that an efficient economy is one that produces the things that people want at least cost. *Production efficiency* is a state in which a given mix of outputs is produced at least cost.) Resources are not going unused, and there is no waste. Points that lie within the shaded area, but that are not on the frontier, represent either unemployment of resources or production inefficiency. An economy producing at point *D* in Figure 2.3 can produce

production possibility frontier (ppf) *A graph that shows all the combinations of goods and services that can be produced if all of society's resources are used efficiently.*

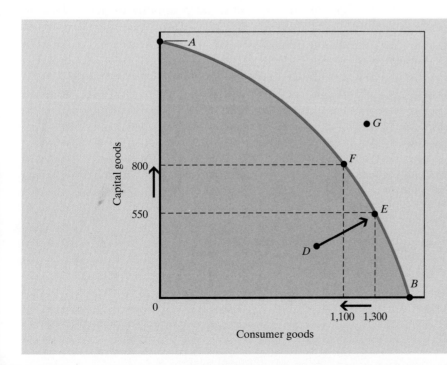

FIGURE 2.3

Production Possibility Frontier
The production possibility frontier illustrates a number of economic concepts. One of the most important is *opportunity cost*. The opportunity cost of producing more capital goods is fewer consumer goods. Moving from *E* to *F*, the number of capital goods increases from 550 to 800. But the number of consumer goods decreases from 1,300 to 1,100.

FAST FACTS

During the recession of 1975, only 72.9% of U.S. manufacturing plant capacity was being used. In the recession of 1982, only 71.8% was used. In contrast, at the end of 1997, 82.5% of U.S. manufacturing capacity was in use. The highest rate since World War II was 91.1% in 1966.

Source: Economic Report of the President, 1998, p. 343.

more capital goods and more consumer goods, for example, by moving to point *E*. This is possible because resources are not fully employed at point *D* or are not being used efficiently.

➤ **Unemployment** During the Great Depression of the 1930s, the U.S. economy experienced prolonged unemployment. Millions of workers found themselves without jobs. In 1933, 25 percent of the civilian labor force was unemployed. This figure stayed above 14 percent until 1940, when increased defense spending by the United States created millions of jobs. In June of 1975, the unemployment rate went over 9 percent for the first time since the 1930s. In December of 1982, when the unemployment rate hit 10.8 percent, nearly 12 million were out looking for work. In June of 1992, the number of unemployed rose to just under 10 million.

In addition to the hardship that falls on the unemployed themselves, unemployment of labor means unemployment of capital. During downturns or recessions, industrial plants run at less than their total capacity. Clearly, when there is unemployment of labor and capital, we are not producing all that we can.

Periods of unemployment correspond to points inside the production possibility frontier, points like *D* in Figure 2.3. Moving onto the frontier from a point like *D* means achieving full employment of resources.

➤ **Inefficiency** Although an economy may be operating with full employment of its land, labor, and capital resources, it may still be operating inside its production possibility frontier (at a point like *D* in Figure 2.3). It could be using those resources *inefficiently*.

Clearly, waste and mismanagement are the results of a firm operating below its potential. If I am the owner of a bakery and I forget to order flour, my workers and ovens stand idle while I figure out what to do. In 1997, Great Lakes Airways had to shut down operations for several weeks because its maintenance staff had been improperly trained.

Sometimes, inefficiency results from mismanagement of the economy rather than mismanagement of individual private firms. Suppose, for example, that the land and climate in Ohio are best suited for corn production, and the land and climate in Kansas are best suited for wheat production. If Congress passes a law forcing Ohio farmers to plant 50 percent of their acreage in wheat and Kansas farmers to plant 50 percent in corn, neither corn nor wheat production will be up to potential. The economy will be at a point like *A* in Figure 2.4—inside the production possibility frontier. Allowing

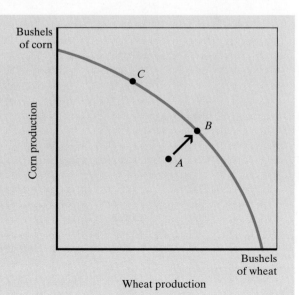

FIGURE 2.4

Inefficiency from Misallocation of Land in Farming

Society can end up inside its production possibility frontier at a point like *A* by using its resources inefficiently. If, for example, Ohio's climate and soil were best suited for corn production and those of Kansas were best suited for wheat production, a law forcing Kansas farmers to produce corn and Ohio farmers to produce wheat would result in less of both. In such a case, society might be at point *A* rather than point *B*.

each state to specialize in producing the crop that it produces best increases the production of both crops and moves the economy to a point like *B* in Figure 2.4.

> **The Efficient Mix of Output**   To be efficient, an economy must produce what people want. This means that, in addition to operating *on* the ppf, the economy must be operating at the *right point* on the ppf. Suppose that an economy devotes 100 percent of its resources to beef production and that the beef industry runs efficiently, using the most modern techniques. But also suppose that everyone in the society is a vegetarian. The result is a total waste of resources (assuming that the society cannot trade its beef for vegetables produced in another country.)

Both points *B* and *C* in Figure 2.4 are points of production efficiency and full employment. Whether *B* is more or less efficient than *C*, however, depends on the preferences of members of society.

> **Negative Slope and Opportunity Cost**   As we've seen, points that lie on the production possibility frontier represent points of full resource employment and production efficiency. But society can choose only one point on the curve. Because a society's choices are constrained by available resources and existing technology, when those resources are fully and efficiently employed it can produce more capital goods only by reducing production of consumer goods. The opportunity cost of the additional capital is the forgone production of consumer goods.

The fact that scarcity exists is illustrated by the negative slope of the production possibility frontier. (If you need a review of slope, see the appendix to chapter 1.) In moving from point *E* to point *F* in Figure 2.3, capital production *increases* by $800 - 550 = 250$ units (a positive change), but that increase in capital can be achieved only by shifting resources out of the production of consumer goods. Thus, in moving from point *E* to point *F* in Figure 2.3, consumer good production *decreases* by $1300 - 1100 = 200$ units of the consumer good (a negative change). The slope of the curve, the ratio of the change in capital goods to the change in consumer goods, is negative.[1]

> **The Law of Increasing Opportunity Costs**   The negative slope of the ppf indicates the trade-off that a society faces between two goods. We can learn something further about the shape of the frontier and the terms of this trade-off. Let us look at the trade-off between corn and wheat production in Ohio and Kansas. In a recent year Ohio and Kansas together produced 510 million bushels of corn and 380 million bushels of wheat. Table 2.1 presents these two numbers, plus some hypothetical combinations of corn and wheat production that might exist for Ohio and Kansas together. Figure 2.5 graphs the data from Table 2.1.

TABLE 2.1	PRODUCTION POSSIBILITY SCHEDULE FOR TOTAL CORN AND WHEAT PRODUCTION IN OHIO AND KANSAS	
POINT ON PPF	TOTAL CORN PRODUCTION (MILLIONS OF BUSHELS PER YEAR)	TOTAL WHEAT PRODUCTION (MILLIONS OF BUSHELS PER YEAR)
A	700	100
B	650	200
C	510	380
D	400	500
E	300	550

---

[1]The value of the slope of a society's production possibility frontier is called the *marginal rate of transformation (MRT)*. In Figure 2.3, the MRT between point *E* and point *F* is simply the ratio of the change in capital goods (a positive number) to the change in consumer goods (a negative number).

FIGURE 2.5

Corn and Wheat Production in Ohio and Kansas

The ppf illustrates that the opportunity cost of corn production increases as we shift resources from wheat production to corn production. Moving from *E* to *D*, we get an additional 100 million bushels of corn at a cost of 50 million bushels of wheat. Moving from *B* to *A*, we get only 50 million bushels of corn at a cost of 100 million bushels of wheat. The cost *per bushel* of corn—measured in lost wheat—has increased.

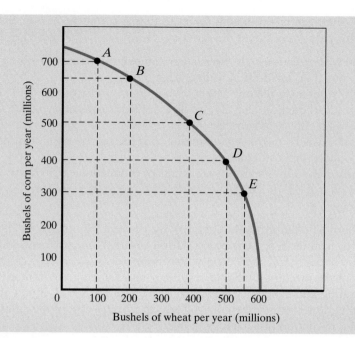

Suppose that society's demand for corn dramatically increases. If this happens, farmers would probably shift some of their acreage from wheat production to corn production. Such a shift is represented by a move from point *C* (where corn = 510, and wheat = 380) up and to the left along the ppf toward points *A* and *B* in Figure 2.5. As this happens, it becomes more and more difficult to produce additional corn. The best land for corn production was presumably already in corn, and the best land for wheat production already in wheat. As we try to produce more and more corn, the land is less and less well suited to that crop. And as we take more and more land out of wheat production, we will be taking increasingly better wheat-producing land. All of this is to say that the opportunity cost of more corn, measured in terms of wheat, increases.

Moving from *E* to *D*, Table 2.1 shows that we can get 100 million bushels of corn (400 − 300) by sacrificing only 50 million bushels of wheat (550 − 500)—that is, we get two bushels of corn for every bushel of wheat.[2] However, when we are already stretching the ability of the land to produce corn, it becomes more difficult to produce more, and the opportunity cost goes up. Moving from *B* to *A*, we can get only 50 million bushels of corn (700 − 650) by sacrificing 100 million bushels of wheat (200 − 100). For every bushel of wheat, we now get only half a bushel of corn. However, if the demand for *wheat* were to increase substantially and we were to move down and to the right along the production possibility frontier, it would become increasingly difficult to produce wheat, and the opportunity cost of wheat, in terms of corn, would rise. This is the *law of increasing opportunity cost.*

It is important to remember that the ppf represents choices available within the constraints imposed by the current state of agricultural technology. In the long run, technology may improve, and when that happens we have *growth*.

▶ **Economic Growth**   Economic growth is characterized by an increase in the total output of an economy. It occurs when a society acquires new resources or when society learns to produce more with existing resources. New resources may mean a larger

economic growth *An increase in the total output of an economy. It occurs when a society acquires new resources or when it learns to produce more using existing resources.*

[2]This implies that the marginal rate of transformation is −2 between *D* and *E*. Change in corn = +100; change in wheat = −50. MRT = +100/−50 = −2.

TABLE 2.2 INCREASING PRODUCTIVITY IN CORN AND WHEAT
PRODUCTION IN THE UNITED STATES, 1935–1995

	CORN		WHEAT	
	Yield Per Acre (Bushels)	Labor Hours Per 100 Bushels	Yield Per Acre (Bushels)	Labor Hours Per 100 Bushels
1935–1939	26.1	108	13.2	67
1945–1949	36.1	53	16.9	34
1955–1959	48.7	20	22.3	17
1965–1969	78.5	7	27.5	11
1975–1979	95.3	4	31.3	9
1981–1985	107.2	3	36.9	7
1985–1990	112.8	NA*	38.0	NA*
1990–1995	120.6	NA*	38.1	NA*

*Data not available.

Sources: U.S. Department of Agriculture, Economic Research Service, Agricultural Statistics, 1992; Statistical Abstract of the United States, 1996, Table 1105, p. 675.

labor force or an increased capital stock. The production and use of new machinery and equipment (capital) increases workers' productivity. (Give a man a shovel and he can dig a bigger hole; give him a steam shovel and wow!) Improved productivity also comes from technological change and *innovation*, the discovery and application of new, efficient production techniques.

The last 30 years have seen dramatic increases in the productivity of U.S. agriculture. Based on data compiled by the Department of Agriculture, Table 2.2 shows that yield per acre in corn production has increased fivefold since the late 1930s, while the labor required to produce it has dropped dramatically. Productivity in wheat production has also increased, at only a slightly less remarkable rate: Output per acre has almost tripled, while labor requirements are down nearly 90 percent. These increases are the result of more efficient farming techniques, more and better capital (tractors, combines, and other equipment), and advances in scientific knowledge and technological change (hybrid seeds, fertilizers, and so forth). As you can see in Figure 2.6, increases such as these shift the ppf up and to the right.

> **Sources of Growth and the Dilemma of the Poor Countries** Economic growth arises from many sources, the two most important of which, over the years, have been the accumulation of capital and technological advances. For poor countries, capital is essential; they must build the communication networks and transportation systems necessary to develop industries that function efficiently. They also need capital goods to develop their agricultural sectors.

Recall that capital goods are produced only at a sacrifice of consumer goods. The same can be said for technological advances. Technological advances come from research and development that uses resources; thus they too must be paid for. The resources used to produce capital goods—to build a road, a tractor, or a manufacturing plant—*and* to develop new technologies could have been used to produce consumer goods.

When a large part of a country's population is very poor, taking resources out of the production of consumer goods (such as food and clothing) is very difficult. In addition, in some countries those wealthy enough to invest in domestic industries choose instead to invest abroad because of political turmoil at home. As a result, it often falls to the governments of poor countries to generate revenues for capital production and research out of tax collections.

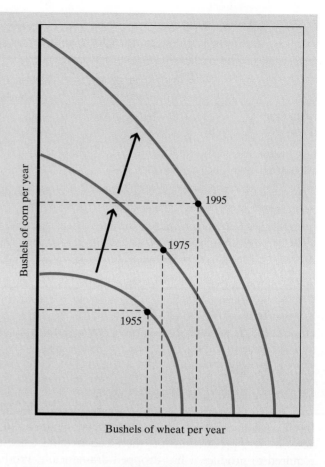

FIGURE 2.6

Economic Growth Shifts the ppf Up and to the Right

Productivity increases have enhanced the ability of the United States to produce both corn and wheat. As Table 2.2 shows, productivity increases were more dramatic for corn than for wheat. The shifts in the ppf were thus not parallel.

Note: The ppf also shifts if the amount of land or labor in corn and wheat production changes. Although we emphasize productivity increases here, the actual shifts between years were in part due to land and labor changes.

All these factors have contributed to the growing gap between some poor and rich nations. Figure 2.7 graphs the result, using production possibility frontiers. On the left, the rich country devotes a larger portion of its production to capital, while the poor country produces mostly consumer goods. On the right, you see the result: The ppf of the rich country shifts up and out farther and faster.

> Although it exists only as an abstraction, the production possibility frontier illustrates a number of very important concepts that we shall use throughout the rest of this book: scarcity, unemployment, inefficiency, opportunity cost, the law of increasing opportunity cost, and economic growth.

THE ECONOMIC PROBLEM

Recall the three basic questions facing all economic systems: (1) What will be produced? (2) How will it be produced? and (3) Who will get it?

When Bill was alone on the island, the mechanism for answering these questions was simple: He thought about his own wants and preferences, looked at the constraints imposed by the resources of the island and his own skills and time, and made his decisions. As he set about his work, he allocated available resources quite simply, more or less by dividing up his available time. Distribution of the output was irrelevant. Because Bill was the society, he got it all.

Introducing even one more person into the economy—in this case, Colleen—changed all that. With Colleen on the island, resource allocation involves deciding not only how each person spends time but also who does what; and now there are two sets of wants and preferences. If Bill and Colleen go off on their own and form two completely

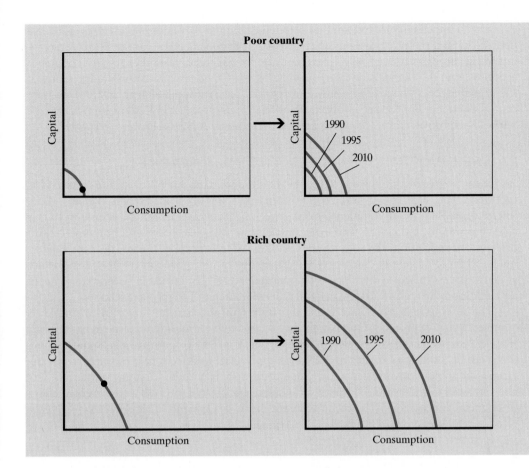

FIGURE 2.7

Capital Goods and Growth in Poor and Rich Countries
Rich countries find it easier to devote resources to the production of capital than poor countries do. But the more resources that flow into capital production, the faster the rate of economic growth. Thus the gap between poor and rich countries has grown over time.

separate self-sufficient economies, there will be lost potential. Clearly, two people can do many more things together than one person can do alone. They may use their comparative advantages in different skills to specialize. Cooperation and coordination may give rise to gains that would otherwise not be possible.

When a society consists of millions of people, the problem of coordination and cooperation becomes enormous, but so does the potential for gain. In large, complex economies, specialization can go wild, with people working in jobs as different in their detail as an impressionist painting is from a blank page. The range of products available in a modern industrial society is beyond anything that could have been imagined a hundred years ago, and so is the range of jobs.

The amount of coordination and cooperation in a modern industrial society is almost impossible to imagine. Yet something seems to drive economic systems, if sometimes clumsily and inefficiently, toward producing the things that people want. Given scarce resources, how, exactly, do large, complex societies go about answering the three basic economic questions? This is the **economic problem**, and this is what this text is about.

ECONOMIC SYSTEMS

Now that you understand the economic problem, we can explore how different economic systems go about answering the three basic questions.

COMMAND ECONOMIES

In a pure **command economy**, the basic economic questions are answered by a central government. Through a combination of government ownership of state enterprises and central planning, the government, either directly or indirectly, sets output targets, incomes, and prices.

economic problem *Given scarce resources, how exactly do large, complex societies go about answering the three basic economic questions?*

command economy *An economy in which a central government either directly or indirectly sets output targets, incomes, and prices.*

It is an understatement to say that planned economies have not fared well over the last decade. In fact, the planned economies of Eastern Europe and the former Soviet Union—including the Russian Republic—have completely collapsed. (Another former command economy, that of Poland, is doing somewhat better.) China remains committed to many of the principles of a planned economy, but reforms have moved it sharply away from pure central planning. For further information on the recent progress in Eastern Europe, see the Global Perspective feature, "Eastern Europe and Russia: A Mixed Progress Report."

LAISSEZ-FAIRE ECONOMIES: THE FREE MARKET

At the opposite end of the spectrum from the command economy is the **laissez-faire economy**. The term *laissez faire*, which, translated literally from French, means "allow [them] to do," implies a complete lack of government involvement in the economy. In this type of economy, individuals and firms pursue their own self-interest without any central direction or regulation; the sum total of millions of individual decisions ultimately determines all basic economic outcomes. The central institution through which a laissez-faire system answers the basic questions is the **market**, a term that is used in economics to mean an institution through which buyers and sellers interact and engage in exchange.

The interactions between buyers and sellers in any market range from simple to complex. Early explorers of the North American Midwest who wished to exchange with Native Americans did so simply by bringing their goods to a central place and trading them. Today, a jewelry maker in Maine may sell gold necklaces to a buyer through the Home Shopping Network that shows the product on television—customers call in orders and pay with a credit card. Ultimately, funds are transferred through a complicated chain of financial transactions. The result is that a buyer in Oakland, California, buys a necklace from an unseen jewelry producer in Maine.

In short:

> Some markets are simple and others are complex, but they all involve buyers and sellers engaging in exchange. The behavior of buyers and sellers in a laissez-faire economy determines what gets produced, how it is produced, and who gets it.

The following chapters explore market systems in great depth. A quick preview is worthwhile here, however.

▶ **Consumer Sovereignty** In a free, unregulated market, goods and services are produced and sold only if the supplier can make a profit. In simple terms, making a *profit* means selling goods or services for more than it costs to produce them. Clearly, you can't make a profit unless someone wants the product that you are selling. This logic leads to the notion of **consumer sovereignty**: The mix of output found in any free market system is dictated ultimately by the tastes and preferences of consumers, who "vote" by buying or not buying. Businesses rise and fall in response to consumer demands. No central directive or plan is necessary.

▶ **Individual Production Decisions: Free Enterprise** Under a free market system, individual producers must also figure out how to organize and coordinate the actual production of their products or services. The owner of a small shoe repair shop must buy the equipment and tools that she needs, hang signs, and set prices by herself. In a big corporation, so many people are involved in planning the production process that in many ways corporate planning resembles the planning in a command economy. In a free market economy, producers may be small or large. One person who hand paints eggshells may start to sell them as a business; a woman who has been showing her poodle may start handling other people's dogs in the show ring. On a larger scale, a group of furniture designers may put together a large portfolio of sketches, raise several million dollars, and start a bigger business. At the extreme are huge corporations like

laissez-faire economy *Literally from the French: "allow [them] to do." An economy in which individual people and firms pursue their own self-interests without any central direction or regulation.*

market *The institution through which buyers and sellers interact and engage in exchange.*

consumer sovereignty *The idea that consumers ultimately dictate what will be produced (or not produced) by choosing what to purchase (and what not to purchase).*

EASTERN EUROPE AND RUSSIA: A MIXED PROGRESS REPORT

During the late 1980s, the command economies of Eastern Europe collapsed like a row of dominoes. The process began in November 1989, when the Berlin Wall, which had separated the communist East from the capitalist West for nearly 30 years, was torn down. Finally, in 1991, the once mighty Soviet Union disintegrated, ending 75 years of communism and nearly a half century of Cold War with the West.

A decade has passed, and the transition to a set of independent economies oriented to the market is nearly complete. But the road to prosperity has been uneven and quite rocky. Some countries, including Poland, Hungary, and the Czech Republic, are doing quite well. Poland, which was the first of the group to begin recording positive growth (in 1992), was growing at an annual rate of 7.3 percent in early 1997. However, poorer countries like Albania, Bulgaria, and Romania were still waiting for the first signs of growth:

With fading memories of the jubilation at the collapse of Communism seven years ago, there is a new divide—some call it the latter-day iron curtain—between have and have-not nations of Central and Eastern Europe. Only in the former does the joy remain.

The 1996 economic data show the division clearly. Foreign investment and rising buying power have transformed the larger cities of Hungary, the Czech Republic and Poland into places with many of the accouterments of the West: fast-food restaurants, self-service gas stations, Benetton stores and apartment complexes outfitted with satellite dishes.

More than $15 billion in foreign investment has poured into Hungary since 1990. In neighboring Romania, which has more than twice the people, only $2 billion has come in, and in Bulgaria, a paltry $700 million.

The average monthly wage in Poland is now well over $300, and people have access to adequate and cheap medical care. In chaotic Bulgaria . . . many hospitals lack even such basics as X-ray film.[a]

The biggest country making the transition was, of course, Russia. While slumping through the early and mid-1990s, Russia showed signs of life for the first time in 1997 when aggregate output rose. But deep problems and much uncertainty remain:

The officially recorded economy has been contracting for eight years in a row, leaving it at the end of 1996 at about half its size in 1989—a steeper fall than in America at the time of the Great Depression (though the black economy has expanded).

Meanwhile prices, unemployment and the tally of unpaid wages have been rising.

[Russia's] is now a market economy, whatever its imperfections. Moreover, much of the pain necessary to achieve such an economy may at last be over. In particular, inflation—enemy of the poor and destroyer of social stability— has dropped from 2,505% in 1992 to an annual rate of 15% in April this year.

Even more notable is the transfer of property into private hands—the biggest in history. In just three years after 1991, 120,000 enterprises changed from state to private ownership.

What all this adds up to is that 22% of Russians, or 32m people, are living below the official poverty line (defined as a minimum subsistence level of 394,000 rubles— $70—a month). Among other things, as Communists like to point out, this means falling meat and milk consumption: the average salary buys only about two-thirds as much meat as in Soviet days, and only about one-third as much milk.[b]

Sources: [a]Jane Perlez, "New Bricks, Same Old Walls for Europe's Poor Nations," *The New York Times*, Jan. 24, 1997, p. 1. Copyright © 1997 by The New York Times Co. Reprinted by permission. [b]"A Survey of Russia," *The Economist*, July 12, 1997, pp. 1–19.

For more on the economies of Eastern Europe and Russia, see the Case and Fair Web page at http://www.prenhall.com/casefair.

IBM, Mitsubishi, and Exxon, each of which sells tens of billions of dollars' worth of products every year. Whether the firms are large or small, however, production decisions in a market economy are made by separate private organizations acting in what they perceive to be their own interests.

In a market economy, individuals seeking profits are free to start new businesses. Because new businesses require capital investment before they can begin operation, starting a new business involves risk. A well-run business that produces a product for which demand exists will succeed; a poorly run business or one that produces a product for which little demand exists is likely to fail. It is through *free enterprise* that new products and new production techniques find their way into use.

CHAPTER TWO
The Economic Problem: Scarcity and Choice

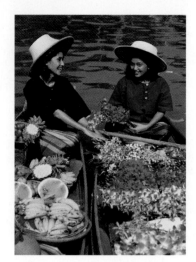

FREE ENTERPRISE "AFLOAT" IN
SOUTHEAST ASIA.

price *The amount that a product
sells for per unit. It reflects what
society is willing to pay.*

Proponents of free market systems argue that free enterprise leads to more efficient production and better response to diverse and changing consumer preferences. If a producer produces inefficiently, competitors will come along, fight for the business, and eventually take it away. Thus in a free market economy, competition forces producers to use efficient techniques of production. It is competition, then, that ultimately dictates how outputs are produced.

▶ **Distribution of Output** In a free market system, the distribution of output—who gets what—is also determined in a decentralized way. The amount that any one household gets depends on its income and wealth. *Income* is the amount that a household earns each year. It comes in a number of forms: wages, salaries, interest, and the like. *Wealth* is the amount that households have accumulated out of past income through saving or inheritance.

To the extent that income comes from working for a wage, it is at least in part determined by individual choice. You will work for the wages available in the market only if these wages (and the things they can buy) are sufficient to compensate you for what you give up by working. Your leisure certainly has a value also. You may discover that you can increase your income by getting more education or training. You *can't* increase your income, however, if you acquire a skill that no one wants.

▶ **Price Theory** The basic coordinating mechanism in a free market system is price. A **price** is the amount that a product sells for per unit, and it reflects what society is willing to pay. Prices of inputs—labor, land, capital—determine how much it costs to produce a product. Prices of various kinds of labor, or *wage rates*, determine the rewards for working in different jobs and professions. Many of the independent decisions made in a market economy involve the weighing of prices and costs, so it is not surprising that much of economic theory focuses on the factors that influence and determine prices. This is why microeconomic theory is often simply called *price theory*.

In sum:

> In a free market system, the basic economic questions are answered without the help of a central government plan or directives. This is what the "free" in free market means—the system is left to operate on its own, with no outside interference. Individuals pursuing their own self-interest will go into business and produce the products and services that people want; others will decide whether to acquire skills or not, whether to work or not, and whether to buy, sell, invest, or save the income that they earn. The basic coordinating mechanism is price.

MIXED SYSTEMS, MARKETS, AND GOVERNMENTS

The differences between command economies and laissez-faire economies in their pure forms are enormous. But in fact these pure forms do not exist in the world; all real systems are in some sense "mixed." That is, individual enterprise exists and independent choice is exercised even in economies in which the government plays the major role.

Conversely, no market economies exist without government involvement and government regulation. The United States has basically a free market economy, but government purchases accounted for about 18 percent of its total production in 1997. The U.S. government directly employs about 16 percent of all workers, and taxes are about a third of the total income of the economy. The government also redistributes income by means of taxation and social welfare expenditures, and it regulates many economic activities.

One of the major themes in this book, and indeed in economics, is the tension between the advantages of free, unregulated markets and the need for government involvement. Advocates of free markets argue that such markets work best when left to themselves. They produce only what people want; without buyers, sellers go out of business. Competition forces firms to adopt efficient production techniques. Wage differentials lead people to acquire needed skills. Competition also leads to innovation in both production techniques and products. The result is quality and variety. But market systems have problems too.

> Even staunch defenders of the free enterprise system recognize that market systems are not perfect. First, they do not always produce what people want at lowest cost—there are inefficiencies. Second, rewards (income) may be unfairly distributed, and some groups may be left out. Third, periods of unemployment and inflation recur with some regularity.

Many people point to these problems as reasons for government involvement. Indeed, for some problems government involvement may be the only solution. But government decisions are made by people who presumably, like the rest of us, act in their own self-interest. While governments may indeed be called upon to improve the functioning of the economy, there is no guarantee that they will do so. Just as markets may fail to produce an allocation of resources that is perfectly efficient and fair, governments may fail to improve matters. We return to this debate many times throughout this text.

LOOKING AHEAD

This chapter has described the economic problem in broad terms. We have outlined the questions that all economic systems must answer. We also discussed very broadly the two kinds of economic systems. In the next chapter we turn from the general to the specific. There we discuss in some detail the institutions of U.S. capitalism: how the private sector is organized, what the government actually does, and how the international sector operates. Chapters 4 and 5 then begin the task of analyzing the way market systems work.

SUMMARY

1. Every society has some system or mechanism for transforming what nature and previous generations have provided into useful form. Economics is the study of that process and its outcomes.

2. *Producers* are those who take resources and transform them into usable products, or *outputs*. Private firms, households, and governments all produce something.

SCARCITY, CHOICE, AND OPPORTUNITY COST

3. All societies must answer *three basic questions:* What will be produced? How will it be produced? Who will get what is produced? These three questions make up the *economic problem.*

4. One person alone on an island must make the same basic decisions that complex societies make. When a society consists of more than one person, questions of distribution, cooperation, and specialization arise.

5. Because resources are scarce relative to human wants in all societies, using resources to produce one good or service implies *not* using them to produce something else. This

concept of *opportunity cost* is central to an understanding of economics.

6. Using resources to produce *capital* that will in turn produce benefits in the future implies *not* using those resources to produce consumer goods in the present.

7. Even if one individual or nation is absolutely more efficient at producing goods than another, all parties will gain if they specialize in producing goods in which they have a *comparative advantage.*

8. A *production possibility frontier* (ppf) is a graph that shows all the combinations of goods and services that can be produced if all of society's resources are used efficiently. The production possibility frontier illustrates a number of important economic concepts: scarcity, unemployment, inefficiency, increasing opportunity cost, and economic growth.

9. *Economic growth* occurs when society produces more, either by acquiring more resources or by learning to produce more with existing resources. Improved productivity may come from additional capital, or from the discovery and application of new, more efficient, techniques of production.

ECONOMIC SYSTEMS

10. In some modern societies, government plays a big role in answering the three basic questions. In pure *command economies*, a central authority directly or indirectly sets output targets, incomes, and prices.

11. A *laissez-faire economy* is one in which individuals independently pursue their own self-interest, without any central direction or regulation and ultimately determine all basic economic outcomes.

12. A *market* is an institution through which buyers and sellers interact and engage in exchange. Some markets involve simple face-to-face exchange; others involve a complex series of transactions, often over great distance or electronically.

13. There are no purely planned economies and no pure laissez-faire economies; all economies are mixed. Individual enterprise, independent choice, and relatively free markets exist in centrally planned economies, and there is significant government involvement in market economies such as that of the United States.

14. One of the great debates in economics revolves around the tension between the advantages of free, unregulated markets and the need for government involvement in the economy. Free markets produce what people want, and competition forces firms to adopt efficient production techniques. The need for government intervention arises because free markets are characterized by inefficiencies and an unequal distribution of income and experience regular periods of inflation and unemployment.

REVIEW TERMS AND CONCEPTS

PROBLEM SET

1. Define *capital*. What distinguishes land from capital? Is a tree capital?

2. "Studying economics instead of going to town and partying is like building a boat instead of lying on the beach." Explain this statement carefully, using the concepts of capital and opportunity cost.

3. Kristen and Anna live in the beach town of Santa Monica. They own a small business in which they make wristbands and potholders and sell them to people on the beach. Kristen can make 15 wristbands per hour, but only 3 potholders. Anna is a bit slower and can make only 12 wristbands or 2 potholders in an hour.

	OUTPUT PER HOUR	
	KRISTEN	**ANNA**
Wristbands	15	12
Potholders	3	2

a. For Kristen, what is the opportunity cost of a potholder? For Anna? Who has a comparative advantage in the production of potholders? Explain.

b. Who has a comparative advantage in the production of wristbands? Explain.

c. Assume that Kristen works 20 hours per week in the business. If Kristen were in business on her own, graph the possible combinations of potholders and wristbands that she could produce in a week. Do the same for Anna.

d. If Kristen devoted half of her time (10 out of 20 hours) to wristbands and half of her time to potholders, how many of each would she produce in a week? If Anna did the same thing, how many of each would she produce? How many wristbands and potholders would be produced in total?

e. Suppose that Anna spent all 20 hours of her time on wristbands and Kristen spent 17 hours on potholders and 3 hours on wristbands. How many of each would be produced?

f. Suppose that Kristen and Anna can sell all their wristbands for $1 each and all their potholders for $5.50 each. If each of them worked 20 hours per week, how should they split their time between wristbands and potholders? What is their maximum joint revenue?

4. Briefly describe the trade-offs involved in each of the following decisions. Specifically, list some of the opportunity costs associated with the decision, paying particular attention to the trade-offs between present and future consumption.
   a. After a stressful senior year in high school, Sherice decides to take the summer off rather than work before going on to college.
   b. Frank is overweight and decides to work out every day and to go on a diet.
   c. Mei is very diligent about taking her car in for routine maintenance, even though it takes two hours of her time and costs $100 four times each year.
   d. Jim is in a big hurry. He runs a red light on the way to work.

5. "If an economy is operating at a point inside its production possibility frontier, it must be the case that resources are unemployed." Do you agree or disagree?

6. Suppose that a simple society has an economy with only one resource, labor. Labor can be used to produce only two commodities—X, a necessity good (food), and Y, a luxury good (music and merriment). Suppose that the labor force consists of 100 workers. One laborer can produce either 5 units of necessity per month (by hunting and gathering) or 10 units of luxury per month (by writing songs, playing the guitar, dancing, and so on).
   a. On a graph, draw the economy's production possibility frontier. Where does the ppf intersect the Y axis? Where

does it intersect the X axis? What meaning do those points have?
   b. Suppose the economy ended up producing at a point *inside* the ppf. Give at least two reasons why this could occur. What could be done to move the economy to a point *on* the ppf?
   c. Suppose you succeeded in lifting your economy to a point on its ppf. What point would you choose? How might your small society decide the point at which it wanted to be?
   d. Once you have chosen a point on the ppf, you still need to decide how your society's product will be divided up. If you were a dictator, how would you decide? What would happen if you left product distribution to the free market?

7. What progress has been made during the last year in Eastern Europe? Which countries are growing? Which are in decline? What factors seem to have contributed to the differences in success across countries?

*8. Match each diagram in Figure 1 with its description. Assume that the economy is producing or attempting to produce at point A, and most members of society like meat and not fish. Some descriptions apply to more than one diagram, and some diagrams have more than one description.

_____
*Throughout the book, an asterisk designates a more challenging problem, as explained in the Preface.

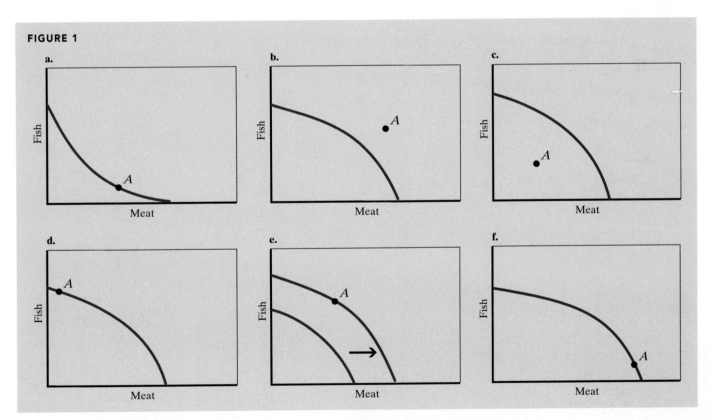

FIGURE 1

a. Inefficient production of meat and fish.
b. Productive efficiency.
c. An inefficient mix of output.
d. Technological advances in the production of meat and fish.
e. The law of increasing opportunity costs.
f. An impossible combination of meat and fish.

9. A nation with fixed quantities of resources is able to produce any of the following combinations of bread and ovens:

LOAVES OF BREAD (MILLIONS)	OVENS (THOUSANDS)
75	0
60	12
45	22
30	30
15	36
0	40

These figures assume that a certain number of previously produced ovens are available in the current period for baking bread.

a. Using the data in the table, graph the production possibilities frontier (with ovens on the vertical axis).

b. Does the principle of "increasing opportunity cost" hold in this nation? Explain briefly. (*Hint*: What happens to the opportunity cost of bread—measured in number of ovens—as bread production increases?)

c. If this country chooses to produce both ovens and bread, what will happen to the production possibilities frontier over time? Why?

d. A politician running for national office wants to reallocate resources to produce the maximum possible quantity of bread, with no production of ovens. His slogan is: "You can't eat ovens!" If this politician is successful, explain what will happen to the production possibilities curve over time. Why?

Now suppose that a new technology is discovered that allows twice as many loaves of bread to be baked in each existing oven.

e. Illustrate (on your original graph) the effect of this new technology on the production possibilities curve.

f. Suppose that before the new technology is introduced, the nation produces 22 ovens. After the new technology is introduced, the nation produces 30 ovens. What is the effect of the new technology on the production of bread? (Give the number of loaves before and after the change.)

TAKE IT TO THE NET

We invite you to visit the Case and Fair page on the Prentice Hall Web site:

http://www.prenhall.com/casefair

for this chapter's World Wide Web exercise.

Chapter 3

THE STRUCTURE OF THE U.S. ECONOMY: THE PRIVATE, PUBLIC, AND INTERNATIONAL SECTORS

THE PREVIOUS CHAPTER described the economic problem. All societies are endowed by nature and by previous generations with scarce resources. The production process combines and transforms these resources into goods and services that are demanded by the members of society.

At the end of chapter 2, we briefly described the economic systems that exist in the world today. This chapter describes the basic institutional structure of the U.S. economy in more detail. Because most production is undertaken by private individuals and organizations, we first look at the private sector. The **private sector** is made up of independently owned firms that exist to make a profit, nonprofit organizations, and individual households. It includes Chrysler Corporation, Occidental College, the Catholic Church, soybean farms in Iowa, the corner drugstore, and the babysitter down the street. The private sector is defined by independent ownership and control. In essence, it includes all the decision-making units within the economy that are not part of the government.

Next, we turn to a discussion of the public sector. The **public sector** is the government and its agencies at all levels—federal, state, and local. Government employees—tax assessors, public school teachers, post office workers, colonels in the army, Supreme Court justices, and the president—work in the public sector. Just as the Ford Motor Company uses land, labor, and capital to produce automobiles, the public sector uses land, labor, and capital to produce goods and services such as police and fire protection, education, and national defense. The public sector in the United States also produces some things that are simultaneously produced by the private sector. The post office provides overnight express-mail service that competes directly with similar services provided by private firms such as

private sector *Includes all independently owned profit-making firms, nonprofit organizations, and households; all the decision-making units in the economy that are not part of the government.*

public sector *Includes all agencies at all levels of government—federal, state, and local.*

45

FedEx and United Parcel Service. The University of Michigan, part of the public sector, directly competes for "buyers" of its "product" with private sector schools such as Northwestern University and Colorado College.

Finally, we provide a brief introduction to the **international sector** and discuss the importance of imports and exports to the U.S. economy. From any one country's perspective, the international sector consists of the economies of the rest of the world. Over the last several decades, the U.S. economy has become increasingly influenced by events abroad. The adoption of a common currency in Europe, the transfer of Hong Kong to the People's Republic of China, the elimination of farm subsidies in France, the end of a recession in Japan, and other global events all have important implications for the functioning of the U.S. economy. In a very real sense there is only one economy: the world economy.

Recall the distinction drawn in chapter 1 between descriptive economics and economic theory, and then notice what this chapter is not. We do not analyze behavior in this chapter. Here we describe institutions only as they exist. We also avoid normative distinctions. We do not talk about proper or improper roles of government in the economy, for example, or the things that governments might do to make the economy more efficient or fair.

THE PRIVATE SECTOR: U.S. BUSINESS AND INDUSTRIAL ORGANIZATION

How is business organized in the United States? Let us see first how the law permits *individual firms* to be organized. Then we can talk about the different ways that *industries* are structured. An individual firm's behavior depends on both its own legal structure and its relationship to other firms in its industry.

THE LEGAL ORGANIZATION OF FIRMS

Most private sector activity takes place within business firms that exist to make a profit. Some other private sector organizations that exist for reasons other than profit—clubs, cooperatives, and nonprofit organizations, for example—do produce goods or services. But because these organizations represent a small fraction of private sector activity, we focus here on profit-making firms.

> A business set up to make profits may be organized in one of three basic legal forms: (1) a proprietorship, (2) a partnership, or (3) a corporation. A single business may pass through more than one of these forms of organization during its development.

➤ **The Proprietorship**   The least complex and most common form a business can take is the simple **proprietorship**. There is no legal process involved in starting a proprietorship. You simply start operating. You must, however, keep records of revenues and costs and pay personal income taxes on your profit.

A professor who does consulting on the side, for example, receives fees and has costs (computer expenses, research materials, and so forth). This consulting business is a proprietorship, even though the proprietor is the only employee and the business is very limited. A large restaurant that employs hundreds of people may also be a proprietorship if it is owned by a single person. Many doctors and lawyers in private practice report their incomes and expenses as proprietors.

In a proprietorship, one person owns the firm. In a sense, that person *is* the firm. If the firm owes money, the proprietor owes the money; if the firm earns a profit, the proprietor earns a profit. There is no wall of protection between a proprietor and her business, as we will see there is between corporations and their owners.

international sector *From any one country's perspective, the economies of the rest of the world.*

proprietorship *A form of business organization in which a person simply sets up a business to provide goods or services at a profit. In a proprietorship, the proprietor (or owner) is the firm. The assets and liabilities of the firm are the owner's assets and liabilities.*

TABLE 3.1   NUMBER OF FIRMS AND SALES BY TYPE OF BUSINESS, 1993

	NUMBER OF FIRMS (THOUSANDS)	PERCENT OF TOTAL FIRMS	TOTAL SALES ($ BILLIONS)	PERCENT OF TOTAL SALES
Proprietorships	15,848	74.5	757	5.7
Partnerships	1,467	6.9	627	4.8
Corporations	3,965	18.6	11,814	89.5
Total	21,280	100.0	13,198	100.0

Source: Statistical Abstract of the United States, 1997, Table 833.

The Internal Revenue Service (IRS) estimates that there are over 15.8 million proprietorships in the United States. That is one for every 16 adults in the country. Most of these proprietorships are small; while they make up over 70 percent of all businesses, they account for only 5.7 percent of total sales (Table 3.1).

▶ **The Partnership**   A **partnership** is a proprietorship with more than one proprietor. When two or more people agree to share the responsibility for a business, they form a partnership. Although no formal legal process is required to start this kind of business, most partnerships are based on agreements signed by all the partners. These agreements detail who pays what part of the costs and how profits shall be divided. Because profits from partnerships are taxable, accurate records of receipts and expenditures must be kept and each party's profits must be reported to the Internal Revenue Service.

In a partnership, as in a proprietorship, there is no limit to the liability of the owners (that is, the partners) for the firm's debts. But with a partnership each partner is both *jointly* and *separately* liable for all the debts of the partnership. What does this mean? If you own one third of a partnership that goes out of business with a debt of $300,000, you owe your creditors $100,000, and so does each of your partners. But if your partners skip town, you owe the entire $300,000.

Just under 7 percent of all firms in the United States are partnerships, and they account for only 4.8 percent of total sales (see again Table 3.1).

▶ **The Corporation**   A **corporation** is a formally established legal entity that exists separately from those who establish it and those who own it. To establish a corporation, a corporate charter must be obtained from a state government. In most states this is quite easily accomplished. A lawyer simply fills out the appropriate paperwork and files it with the right state agency, along with certain fees. When a corporation is formed, **shares of stock** (certificates of partial ownership) are issued and either sold or assigned. A corporation is owned by its shareholders, who are in a sense partners in the firm's success or failure. Each share of stock entitles the holder to a portion of the corporation's profits. Shareholders differ from simple partners, however, in two important ways. First, the liability of shareholders is limited to the amount they paid for the stock. If the company goes out of business or bankrupt, the shareholders may lose what they have invested, but no more than that. They are *not* liable for the corporation's debts beyond the amount they invested. Second, the federal government and all but four states levy special taxes on corporations. These government bodies do not levy special taxes on proprietors and partners.

The federal corporate income tax is a tax on the **net income**, or profits, of corporations. The tax is 15 percent of net income on the first $50,000, but it rises to 25 percent for taxable income between $50,000 and $75,000 and to 34 percent after income exceeds $75,000. (In 1993, as part of President Clinton's deficit reduction package, the top rate was raised to 35 percent on taxable net income over $10 million.) Actually,

partnership *A form of business organization in which there is more than one proprietor. The owners are responsible jointly and separately for the firm's obligations.*

corporation *A form of business organization resting on a legal charter that establishes the corporation as an entity separate from its owners. Owners hold shares and are liable for the firm's debts only up to the limit of their investment, or share, in the firm.*

share of stock *A certificate of partial ownership of a corporation. Entitles the holder to a portion of the corporation's profits.*

net income *The profits of a firm.*

TABLE 3.2	THE DISTRIBUTION OF CORPORATE PROFITS IN 1997	
	BILLIONS OF DOLLARS	PERCENT OF BEFORE-TAX PROFIT
Profits before tax	729.8	100.0
Minus profits tax liability	−249.4	−34.2
Profits after tax	480.4	65.8
Minus dividends paid	−336.1	−46.1
Undistributed profits	144.3	19.7

Source: U.S. Department of Commerce, Bureau of Economic Analysis.

dividends *The portion of a corporation's profits that the firm pays out each period to shareholders. Also called* distributed profits.

99 percent of all corporate net income is taxed at the 35 percent rate. In essence, this means that tax is paid twice on corporate net income: once by the corporation when it pays tax on its profits, and again by the shareholders when they pay personal income tax on their **dividends**—that is, the share of profits they receive from the corporation each period.

The special privilege granted to corporations limiting their liability is often called a *franchise.* Some view the corporate tax as a payment to the government in exchange for limited liability status. In New York State, the state corporation tax is actually called the franchise tax.

Corporate net income is usually divided into three pieces. Some of it is paid to federal and state governments in the form of taxes. Some of it is paid out to shareholders as dividends (sometimes called *distributed profits*). And some of it usually stays within the corporation to be used for the purchase of capital assets. This part of corporate profits is called **retained earnings**, or *undistributed profits*.

retained earnings *The profits that a corporation keeps, usually for the purchase of capital assets. Also called* undistributed profits.

In 1997, U.S. corporations earned total profits of $729.8 billion. Out of this, $249.4 billion in taxes were paid, leaving $480.4 billion in after-tax profits. Of this amount, $336.1 billion was paid out to shareholders and the rest, $144.3 billion, was retained. In percentage terms, taxes accounted for 34.2 percent, while shareholders directly received 46.1 percent of total profits (Table 3.2). Turning again to Table 3.1, in 1993 there were about 4 million corporations, just under 20 percent of all firms. But these 4 million firms accounted for almost 90 percent of total sales.

Many corporations are very large. Each year *Fortune* magazine publishes a list of the 500 largest industrial corporations in the United States. Topping the *Fortune 500* in 1997 was General Motors. GM's total sales in 1996 were more than $168 billion. The company employed over 647,000 people that year!

The internal organization of a firm, whether it is a proprietorship, a partnership, or a corporation, affects its behavior and the behavior of potential investors. For example, because they are protected by a corporation's limited liability status, potential investors may be more likely to back high-risk but potentially high-payoff corporate ventures.

Although a firm's internal structure is important, it is less important to an understanding of a firm's behavior than the organization of the industry or the market in which the firm competes. For example, whether it is a proprietorship or a corporation, a firm with little or no competition is likely to behave differently from a firm facing stiff competition from many rivals. With this in mind, we now expand our focus from the individual firm to the industry.

THE ORGANIZATION OF INDUSTRIES

industry *A group of firms that produce a similar product. The boundaries of a "product" can be drawn very widely ("agricultural products"), less widely ("dairy products"), or very narrowly ("cheese"). The term* industry *can be used interchangeably with the term* market.

The term **industry** is used loosely to refer to groups of firms that produce similar products. Industries can be defined narrowly or broadly, depending on the issue being discussed. For example, a company that produces and packages cheese is a part of the cheese industry, the dairy products industry, the food products industry, and the agricultural products industry.[1]

Whether we define industries broadly or narrowly, how firms within any industry behave depends on how that industry is organized. When we speak of **market organization** we refer to the way an industry is structured: how many firms there are in an industry, whether products are virtually the same or differentiated, whether or not firms in the industry can control prices or wages, whether or not competing firms can freely enter and leave the industry, and so forth. The kind of industry—or *market*—in which a firm operates determines, in large part, how it will behave.

In the discussion that follows, we analyze industries as if their structures fit their definitions precisely. In reality, however, industries are not always easy to categorize. Nonetheless, these categories provide a useful and convenient framework.

> **Perfect Competition** At one end of the market-organization spectrum is the competitive industry, in which many relatively small firms produce nearly identical products. **Perfect competition** is a very precisely defined form of industry structure. (The word *perfect* here does not refer to virtue. It simply means "total," or "complete.") In a perfectly competitive industry, no single firm has any control over prices. That is, no single firm is large enough to affect the market price of its product or the prices of the inputs that it buys. This crucial observation follows from two characteristics of competitive industries. First, a competitive industry is composed of many firms, each small relative to the size of the industry. Second, every firm in a perfectly competitive industry produces exactly the same product; the output of one firm cannot be distinguished from the output of the others. Products in a perfectly competitive industry are said to be **homogeneous**.

These characteristics limit the decisions open to competitive firms and simplify the analysis of competitive behavior. Because all firms in a perfectly competitive industry produce virtually identical products, and because each firm is small relative to the market, perfectly competitive firms have no control over the prices at which they sell their output. Taking prices as a given, then, each firm can decide only how much output to produce and how to produce it.

Consider agriculture, the classic example of a perfectly competitive industry. A wheat farmer in South Dakota has absolutely no control over the price of wheat. Prices are determined not by the individual farmers but rather by the interaction of many suppliers and many demanders. The only decisions left to the wheat farmer are how much wheat to plant and when and how to produce the crop.

Another mark of perfectly competitive industries is ease of entry. *Ease of entry* means that new firms can easily enter a market and compete for profits. No barriers exist to prevent new firms from competing. New firms can, and do, frequently enter such industries in search of profits, whereas others go out of business when they suffer losses. For example, anyone who has been to Seattle, Washington, recently knows the importance of coffee. Several years ago, a firm called Starbucks opened a series of gourmet coffee shops in the city. Within a short while, business was booming, and Starbucks was making enormous profits. The success of Starbucks attracted competition, and hundreds of new firms entered the market during the 1990s. Entry was easy: After all, to sell coffee all you need is a place to do business, a coffee maker, perhaps an espresso machine, and some effort. Today, Seattle's landscape is filled with coffee and espresso signs; even McDonald's sells gourmet coffee there. Starbucks has expanded nationwide, and it is likely to attract competition wherever it goes because entry into the market is easy.

When a firm *exits* an industry, it simply stops producing a product. Sometimes an exiting firm goes out of business altogether. During the last 10 years, for example,

market organization *The way an industry is structured. Structure is defined by how many firms there are in an industry, whether products are differentiated or are virtually the same, whether or not firms in the industry can control prices or wages, and whether or not competing firms can enter and leave the industry freely.*

perfect competition *An industry structure in which there are many firms, each small relative to the industry, producing virtually identical products and in which no firm is large enough to have any control over prices. In perfectly competitive industries, new competitors can freely enter and exit the market.*

homogeneous products *Undifferentiated outputs; products that are identical to, or indistinguishable from, one another.*

FAST FACTS

The percentage of U.S. workers employed in agriculture has dropped steadily over the years. In 1840, the figure was above 68%. By 1997, it had dropped to 2.6%:

1840	68.6%
1870	53.0%
1900	37.5%
1940	20.1%
1950	12.2%
1960	8.3%
1970	4.4%
1980	3.4%
1990	2.7%
1997	2.6%

Sources: Historical Statistics of the United States, 1789–1945, Tables D1–10 (For 1840–1900 data); Economic Report of the President, 1998, p. 322 (For 1940–1997 data).

---

[1]The U.S. Department of Commerce has devised a code system, the Standard Industrial Classification (S.I.C.) System, which defines industries at various levels of detail.

In competitive markets, new firms can enter an industry with relative ease and compete for profits. Hundreds of new upscale coffee shops have entered the market to compete with Starbucks.

thousands of small farmers have gone out of business, sold off their assets, paid what bills they could, and disappeared.

To summarize:

> Perfectly competitive industries are made up of many firms, each small relative to the size of the total market. In these industries, individual firms do not distinguish or differentiate their products from those of their competitors. Product prices are determined by market forces and are virtually unaffected by decisions of any single firm. Entry into and exit from the market are relatively easy.

monopoly *An industry structure in which there is only one large firm that produces a product for which there are no close substitutes. Monopolists can set prices but are subject to market discipline. For a monopoly to continue to exist, something must prevent potential competitors from entering the industry and competing for profits.*

barrier to entry *Something that prevents new firms from entering and competing in an industry.*

▶ **Monopoly** At the other end of the spectrum is **monopoly**, a market or industry in which only one firm produces a product for which there are no close substitutes.

When there is only one firm in a market, that firm sets the price of its product. This does not mean, however, that monopolies can set any price they please. Even if a firm produces a product that everyone likes, the firm gains nothing if it charges a price so high that no one buys it. Thus, even a monopolist is subject to discipline imposed by the market.

For a monopoly to remain a monopoly, it must find some way to keep other firms from entering its market and competing for profits. Often governments erect such **barriers to entry**. Sometimes they grant an exclusive license to one producer. In Taiwan, for example, the national government licensed only one company to produce beer and prohibited beer imports until 1987. In the United States, public utilities—electric power and gas companies, for example, most of which are privately owned—have traditionally been shielded by the government from competition. For many years the American Telephone and Telegraph Company was essentially the exclusive producer of telephone services, both local and long distance. However, dramatic changes in the telecommunications industry, including the breakup of AT&T by the courts in 1983, have made that market much more competitive. In 1998, competition was even introduced into increasingly deregulated electricity and natural gas markets.

Sometimes monopolies are specific to a particular time and location. Professional sports teams sign exclusive vendor agreements for games. Most often, for example, a single vendor will be responsible for food and beverage sales at a pro football game. Because most stadiums do not permit you to bring food and beverages into a game, the vendor is providing a service for which there is no close substitute, and entry is blocked. Have you ever noticed the price of food and drinks at a pro ballgame?

In sum:

> A monopoly is a one-firm industry that produces a product for which there are no close substitutes. Such a firm can set price, but its pricing behavior is constrained by its market: It can sell a product only if people are willing to buy it. A monopolist is protected from competition by barriers to entry.

▶ **Monopolistic Competition** Somewhere between monopoly and competition, but much closer to competition, is a very common hybrid market organization called **monopolistic competition**. In a monopolistically competitive industry, many firms compete for essentially the same customers, but each firm produces a slightly different product. If these firms can *differentiate* their products successfully, they establish a *brand loyalty* that allows them to enjoy the benefits of a monopoly. Procter & Gamble is the only producer of Ivory Soap—it "monopolizes" the market for Ivory—but the soap business is still very competitive because many close substitutes are available. Prentice Hall is the only company that can sell this book, but there are many other economics texts.

Although individual firms in perfectly competitive markets have no control over price, monopolistic competitors do exercise some price-setting power. That control is quite limited, however, because of the many close substitutes available. Monopolistically competitive firms are thus subject to a great deal of "market discipline."

A good example of monopolistic competition can be found in the music industry. Every rock band has a unique style; each has its own name. Entry is relatively inexpensive; all you need are musicians, instruments, amplifiers, and a P.A. system. Thinking of each band as a small firm, management differentiates the product in an attempt to compete, and the competition is fierce. Very successful rock bands are more like monopolies, however; there are no "close" substitutes for R.E.M., U2, or the Rolling Stones.

In monopolistically competitive industries, there is both price and quality competition. Firms often enter these industries because they have an idea for a new product that represents a slight variation or improvement on an old one. Perhaps the purest example of a monopolistically competitive market is the restaurant industry. Every major city in the world contains hundreds and hundreds of restaurants, each producing a slightly differentiated product in a highly competitive way. The cosmetics and clothing industries are also monopolistically competitive. Firms in such industries must decide on output, price, and quality of product.

Free, or at least relatively easy, entry and exit characterize monopolistic competition. When a firm enjoys success in one of its product lines, its profits invite new firms to come into its market with new brands or styles. Many new restaurants are born every year and many unsuccessful ones quietly expire.

To summarize:

> Monopolistically competitive firms contain large numbers of relatively small firms. Unlike firms in perfectly competitive industries, monopolistically competitive firms differentiate their products. Individual firms produce unique products and thus, despite their small size, exercise some control over price. Entry and exit are relatively easy.

▶ **Oligopoly** An industry in which there are only a small number of firms is an **oligopoly**. For example, the automobile industry in the United States has only three major U.S. competitors and a few smaller ones. A total of eight firms produce 100 percent of all the primary copper produced in the United States, and four large firms control 87 percent of the breakfast cereal industry. Except for the fact that each contains only a few competitors, however, oligopolistic industries have little in common. In some, products are highly differentiated (automobiles and cereal, for example); in others,

monopolistic competition
An industry structure in which many firms compete, producing similar but slightly differentiated products. There are close substitutes for the product of any given firm. Monopolistic competitors have some control over price. Price and quality competition follows from product differentiation. Entry and exit are relatively easy, and success invites new competitors.

oligopoly *An industry structure with a small number of (usually) large firms producing products that range from highly differentiated (automobiles) to standardized (copper). In general, entry of new firms into an oligopolistic industry is difficult but possible.*

TABLE 3.3 CHARACTERISTICS OF DIFFERENT MARKET ORGANIZATIONS

	NUMBER OF FIRMS	PRODUCTS DIFFERENTIATED OR HOMOGENEOUS	FIRMS HAVE PRICE-SETTING POWER	EASY ENTRY	DISTINGUISHING CHARACTERISTICS	EXAMPLES
Perfect competition	Many	Homogeneous	No	Yes	Price competition only	Wheat farmer Textile firm
Monopolistic competition	Many	Differentiated	Yes, but limited	Yes	Price and quality competition	Restaurants Music industry
Oligopoly	Few	Either	Yes	Limited	Strategic behavior	Breakfast cereal Primary copper
Monopoly	One	A unique, single product	Yes	No	Still constrained by market demand	Public utility Beverage vendor at a pro football game

they are not (the steel industry, for example). In some, the industry is dominated by one very large firm; in others, the participating firms are of roughly equal size and have roughly equal power.

Oligopolies behave unpredictably. In markets where two or three large rivals compete head-on, the competing firms often execute strategies that anticipate counterstrategies. In setting price, for example, one firm must take into account how its competitors in the oligopoly are likely to react. One firm's action usually triggers a reaction from another, which in turn triggers still another reaction, and so on. The strategies and counterstrategies employed by these firms determine who gets the sales. As a result, oligopolies are characterized by a great deal of uncertainty, and it is difficult to generalize about their behavior.

Entry into an oligopolistic industry is usually possible, but difficult. Because firms in oligopolies are generally large, a large initial investment is usually required to break in.

In sum:

Oligopolies are industries with a few large firms, but beyond that it is hard to generalize. In some oligopolies, firms differentiate their products; in others, they do not. Individual firms do exercise control over prices and generally behave "strategically" with respect to one another.

The four main kinds of market organization in the United States are summarized in Table 3.3.

HOW COMPETITIVE IS THE U.S. ECONOMY?

In an article published in the early 1980s, William G. Shepherd provides some evidence on the extent of competition in the U.S. economy.[2] Shepherd defines four market types that correspond roughly to the categories we have just defined: (1) pure monopolies, (2) industries with dominant firms, (3) tight oligopolies, and (4) effectively competitive industries.

In Shepherd's classification scheme, monopolies are just as we described them. One firm accounts for 100 percent (or nearly 100 percent) of an industry's total sales. No close substitutes for its product exist and entry to the market is blocked. Industries with dominant firms are near monopolies. In such industries, the dominant firm accounts for 50 percent to 90 percent of total industry sales, no close

[2]William G. Shepherd, "Causes of Increased Competition in the U.S. Economy, 1939–1980," *Review of Economics and Statistics* LXIV (November 1982), 613–626.

TABLE 3.4 TRENDS IN COMPETITION IN THE U.S. ECONOMY, 1939–1980

	1939	1958	1980
Pure monopoly	6.2	3.1	2.5
Dominant firm	5.0	5.0	2.8
Tight oligopoly	36.4	35.6	18.0
Effectively competitive firms	52.4	56.3	76.7
Total	100.0	100.0	100.0

Note: Percentage share of national income by industry category.

Source: William G. Shepherd, "Causes of Increased Competition in the U.S. Economy, 1939–1980," *Review of Economics and Statistics* LXIV (November 1982), 613–626.

rivals exist, and entry to the market is difficult. Tight oligopolies are industries in which the top four firms account for over 60 percent of total sales and in which entry barriers are high. Shepherd lumps all other firms together in the "effectively competitive" category.

The classification "effectively competitive" signifies more than just perfect competition. It also includes all of what we described as monopolistic competition. In Shepherd's effectively competitive group, the top four firms control less than 40 percent of the market, and entry barriers are low.

Table 3.4, based on Shepherd's estimates, shows what happened to the level of competition in the U.S. economy between 1939 and 1980. Pure monopolies, a category that includes most public utilities and some patented goods, accounted for only 2.5 percent of total national income in 1980, down from 6.2 percent in 1939. In fact, purely monopolistic and dominant-firm industries together accounted for just a little over 5 percent of national income in 1980. In contrast, 76.7 percent of national income originated in sectors that Shepherd classifies as effectively competitive, up from 52.4 percent in 1939. The estimates indicate that the percentage of national income originating in tight oligopolies was cut in half between 1958 and 1980.

The U.S. economy has apparently become more competitive over the years. A number of factors may have contributed to this change. Without going into detail here, these factors include increased competition from imports, deregulation (particularly in the trucking, airline, and telecommunications industries), and enforcement of antimonopoly laws.

STRUCTURAL CHANGE SINCE 1970

Table 3.5 gives a breakdown of employment by major product type or industry. These data point to a number of important changes. First, the percentage of the total employment accounted for by manufacturing has been continuously shrinking for 30 years.

TABLE 3.5 PERCENTAGE OF NONAGRICULTURAL EMPLOYMENT BY SECTOR, 1970–1997

	MANUFACTURING	WHOLESALE AND RETAIL TRADE	SERVICES	GOVERNMENT	CONSTRUCTION	FINANCIAL INSURANCE AND REAL ESTATE	OTHER
1970	28.3	21.1	16.1	17.7	4.6	5.1	7.1
1980	23.1	22.5	19.3	18.0	4.6	5.6	6.9
1990	17.7	23.7	25.2	17.0	4.5	6.1	5.8
1997	15.3	23.7	28.8	16.4	4.3	5.9	5.6

Source: Department of Labor, Bureau of Labor Statistics, 1997 Benchmark Revisions; authors' tabulation.

The decline since 1970 has been due in part to increased competition from abroad: Americans buy a tremendous number of products, including automobiles, textiles, televisions, VCRs, cameras, and machine tools, from Korea, Japan, and Taiwan. One of the biggest-selling new manufactured items in the United States today is the fax machine. But even though the fax machine was invented in the United States, not a single machine is currently manufactured in the United States. By 1997, manufacturing had dropped to only 15.3 percent of U.S. nonagricultural jobs.

The fastest growing sector of the U.S. economy has been the service sector. Americans eat at restaurants, stay at hotels, and consume recreation, entertainment, and personal services at a far greater rate than ever before. In addition to personal services, business services are an important part of the service sector. Business services include consulting, software production, and legal services—all of which have been growing in recent years.

One frequently voiced concern is that "good" jobs are being lost and replaced by "bad" ones. Manufacturing in the United States has traditionally been a high-wage sector. Most people who work in plants receive substantial hourly wages. As manufacturing has declined, though, more and more jobs have opened up in the expanding service sector, where hourly wages have traditionally been lower. But recent data show that this situation is changing. The service sector is now generating more high-paying jobs. For more details, see the Application feature titled "The Changing Mix of Jobs in the United States."

Although some people are deeply concerned over this structural change in the U.S. economy, others see it as a natural consequence of continued economic growth and progress. As recently as 1870, agriculture accounted for 22 percent of national income and more than half of employment. But as farmers learned more and more productive farming methods, the need for farm labor declined, and so did food prices. With lower food prices, people could spend their incomes on other things—manufactured goods and services. Because agriculture needed fewer workers, labor was available for employment in the new expanding sectors. By 1997, fewer than 3 percent of American workers were in agriculture. Thus as the U.S. economy grew and developed, some sectors, such as agriculture, shrank in relative importance and others, such as manufacturing and services, grew in relative importance.

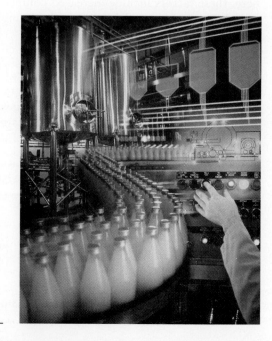

THE SERVICE SECTOR HAS BEEN GROWING FASTER THAN MANUFACTURING OVER THE LAST SEVERAL DECADES. HOWEVER, THE SERVICE SECTOR IS MORE THAN JUST FAST FOOD. SOFTWARE DEVELOPMENT IS PART OF THE SERVICE SECTOR, AND IT REQUIRES SKILLED WORKERS AND PAYS HIGH WAGES.

THE CHANGING MIX OF JOBS
IN THE UNITED STATES

As the following excerpt from a recent article from the *New York Times* points out, you shouldn't believe everything you hear about the current job situation in the United States:

The notion that Americans are working more for less pay is firmly embedded in public rhetoric. And it is practically gospel that the growing American economy cannot deliver the higher pay that American workers want.

No doubt many Americans are losing ground economically. But in fact most of the jobs the economy has added in the last [few] years are

in occupations that pay more, not less, than the average, which is now about $15.50 an hour.

[In 1994 alone], 72 percent of the 2.5 million new jobs [were] for managers, from the chief executive to the branch sales manager, and for professionals, from surgeons and nurses to software programmers, accountants and high school teachers. And despite its reputation for low wages, the service sector is adding most of the higher-wage jobs.

As a result, average hourly pay for all employees . . . is slowly rising, government data show, not falling as so many politicians and

commentators have been saying. Average hourly compensation, which includes health benefits, paid vacations, pensions and other benefits, is also rising. . . .

The source of much of the improvement is the service sector, which is supposed to have been producing only low-wage jobs like hamburger flipping and baby-sitting.

Source: Sylvia Nasar, "Statistics Reveal Bulk of New Jobs Pay Over Average," *The New York Times*, Oct. 17, 1994, p. A1. Copyright © 1994 by The New York Times Co. Reprinted by permission.

For more on the changing mix of jobs in the United States, see the Case and Fair Web page at
http://www.prenhall.com/casefair.

Modern economies are in a continuous state of change. Resources are always moving. In the process, the basic industrial structure changes. The purpose of this book is to help you understand this process. Why are new firms formed? Why do others go out of business? Why are some sectors expanding while others are contracting?

THE PUBLIC SECTOR: TAXES AND GOVERNMENT SPENDING

Thus far we have talked only about the sets of decisions facing private firms. But this is only part of the story. Although the U.S. economy is basically a market economy, it also has a public sector that plays a major role in determining the allocation of resources, the mix of output, and the distribution of rewards. To understand the workings of any economic system, it is necessary to understand the role of government—the public sector.

Government in the United States operates on three different levels—federal, state, and local. Each of these levels has assumed a different set of functions and responsibilities over the years, and although there is some overlap, each level derives its main revenues from different sources. How big is this public sector? What does it spend its money on, and where does it get its money?

THE SIZE OF THE PUBLIC SECTOR

An economy's **gross domestic product**, or **GDP**, is the total value of all goods and services produced in the economy in a given period of time, say, a year. The concept of GDP is used extensively in macroeconomics. Here it is enough to say that GDP is used as a measure of a nation's total annual output. As you can see from Figure 3.1, public expenditure at all levels, as a percentage of GDP, increased from 19.3 percent in 1940 to 34.8 percent in 1990, then dropping slightly to 33.8 percent in 1997. The federal portion of total expenditures increased more rapidly, more than doubling

gross domestic product (GDP)
The total value of all goods and services produced by a national economy within a given time period.

CHAPTER THREE
Private, Public, International Sectors
55

FIGURE 3.1

Total Government Expenditure as a Percentage of GDP, 1940–1997

Total government expenditures grew from 19.3% of GDP in 1940 to 34.8% in 1990. Since 1990, the percentage has fallen slightly. The share of state and local governments grew only slightly, but the federal share more than doubled.

Sources: U.S. Department of Commerce, Bureau of Economic Analysis. Grants to states and localities included in federal.

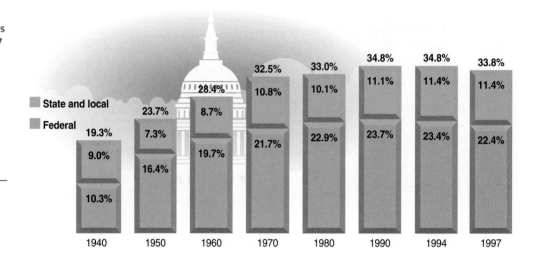

government consumption and investment *A category of government spending that includes the portion of national output that the government uses directly—ships for the navy, memo pads for the FBI, salaries for government employees.*

government transfer payments *Cash payments made by the government directly to households for which no current services are received in return. They include social security benefits, unemployment compensation, and welfare payments.*

government interest payments *Cash payments made by the government to those who own government bonds.*

since 1940, whereas the state and local share grew only from 9.0 percent of GDP to 11.4 percent in the same period.[3]

Government spending can be broken into three major categories: consumption and investment, goods and services, transfer payments to households, and interest payments. **Consumption and investment** make up that portion of national output that government actually uses, or "consumes," directly. They include the airplanes purchased from McDonnell Douglas by the air force, the new Senate office building (in the year that it was built), and the paper, books, and pens produced by private companies that are used by government employees. This category also includes the wages and salaries paid for the services of government employees. Table 3.6 shows that government nondefense consumption and investment as a percentage of GDP have remained roughly constant since 1970. Government defense consumption and investment as a percentage of GDP have decreased substantially since 1960.

Transfer payments are cash payments made directly to households—social security benefits, unemployment compensation payments, welfare payments, and so forth. The government receives no current services in return for these payments. **Interest payments** are also cash payments, but they are paid to those who own government bonds. Table 3.6 shows that both transfer payments and interest payments as a percentage of GDP have increased sharply since 1960.

The increase in the size of the social security system accounts for much of the increase in transfer payments. Social security is a self-financing system in which benefits are paid out of taxes contributed by workers and their employers. Some have argued that because workers who have contributed will ultimately be entitled to benefits, the system should be separated from other federal receipts and expenditures for accounting purposes, but this has not been done so far.

As Table 3.6 shows, interest payments in 1990 almost doubled as a percentage of GDP over the 1980 level. This is because of the huge deficits run up during the early 1980s. When the government spends more than it taxes, it must borrow. It does so by issuing bonds, and it must pay interest on the bonds. The percentage has dropped slightly since 1990.

Another way to look at the relative size of the public sector is to look at government employment as a percentage of total employment (see again Table 3.6). In 1997, federal government civilian employment was only 2.1 percent of total employment. In addition,

[3]Federal grants to state and local governments are included as a federal expenditure rather than a state and local expenditure because they are paid for out of federal tax revenues.

TABLE 3.6 THE SIZE OF THE PUBLIC SECTOR, 1940–1997

Government Expenditure as a Percentage of GDP

	1940	1950	1960	1970	1980	1990	1994	1997
Total	19.3	23.7	28.4	32.5	33.0	34.8	34.8	33.8
Consumption and investment, nondefense	12.3	9.2	11.1	14.0	14.3	14.0	13.9	13.6
Consumption and investment, defense	2.5	6.8	10.4	8.7	6.3	6.5	5.0	4.3
Transfer payments	2.7	6.1	5.6	8.1	11.4	11.8	13.6	13.7
Interest payments (net)	1.2	1.5	1.3	1.2	1.2	2.2	2.1	2.0

Government Employment as a Percentage of Total Employment (Excluding Military) in the Economy

	1950	1960	1970	1980	1990	1994	1997
Total	13.3	15.4	17.7	18.0	16.6	16.8	15.3
Federal	4.2	4.2	3.8	3.2	2.8	2.5	2.1
State and local	9.1	11.2	13.9	14.8	13.8	14.3	13.2

Sources: U.S. Department of Commerce, Bureau of Economic Analysis and Bureau of Labor Statistics.

federal civilian employment as a percentage of total employment in the United States has fallen steadily since 1950. State and local government employment grew steadily as a fraction of total employment in the economy through 1980. Since 1980, however, it has dropped back to about the 1970 level. Total government employment in 1997 was 15.3 percent of total employment in the economy, down from 18.0 percent in 1980.

How big is the public sector in the United States relative to the public sectors in other countries? Good statistics on employment and spending are not easy to find, but Figure 3.2 presents some international comparisons based on taxes collected. (Taxes

FIGURE 3.2

Taxes as a Percentage of Gross Domestic Product, 1980 and 1994

Source: Statistical Abstract of the United States, 1994, p. 867, 1997, p. 844.

57

are used as the basis of comparison because they support the public sector's activities, and tax data are easy to find.) The figure shows total national and local taxes as a percentage of gross domestic product (GDP).

In 1980, U.S. federal, state, and local taxes amounted to 26.9 percent of GDP. This placed the United States fifteenth among the 19 countries in the comparison. Between 1980 and 1994, taxes as a percentage of GDP increased in all 19 countries except the United Kingdom. The smallest increase for the 18 countries that had increases was registered in the United States, where taxes as a percentage of GDP rose only .7 percentage points. As of 1994, only Turkey, among this group of more developed countries, had lower taxes as a percentage of GDP than the United States.

GOVERNMENT EXPENDITURES

The detailed breakdown of federal expenditures for fiscal year 1997 in Table 3.7 shows that the top six categories account for over 88 percent of the total. National defense and social security alone account for nearly 40 percent of federal spending. Table 3.8 compares the same categories for 1985 and 1997. With the end of the Cold War, expenditures for national defense have been shrinking sharply. Expenditures for Medicare and health have been growing rapidly. The crisis in health-care costs that is such an important issue today is evident in these numbers. Medicare and health-care expenditures taken together rose from 10.5 percent of total expenditures in 1985 to 19.7 percent of total expenditures in 1997.

TABLE 3.7   FEDERAL EXPENDITURES BY FUNCTION, 1997

	BILLIONS OF DOLLARS	PERCENTAGE OF TOTAL
Social security	367.7	22.5
National defense	267.2	16.4
Net interest	247.4	15.2
Income security	238.9	14.6
Medicare	194.3	11.9
Health	127.6	7.8
Education, training, employment	51.3	3.1
Veterans benefits	39.7	2.4
Transportation	39.3	2.4
Natural resources environment	22.8	1.4
Administration of justice	20.8	1.3
Science, space, and technology	16.6	1.0
International affairs	14.8	.9
General governments	13.1	.8
Community and regional development	12.8	.8
Agriculture	10.3	.6
Miscellaneous and offsetting receipts	−53.6	−3.1
Total	1631.0	100.0

Source: Statistical Abstract of the United States, 1997, Table 520.

TABLE 3.8 FEDERAL EXPENDITURES BY FUNCTION: PERCENTAGE SHARES OF TOTAL COMPARED FOR 1985 AND 1997

	1985	1997	CHANGE IN SHARE
National defense	26.7	16.4	−10.3
Social security	19.9	22.5	+2.6
Net interest	13.7	15.2	+1.5
Income security	13.5	14.6	+1.1
Medicare	7.0	11.9	+4.9
Health	3.5	7.8	+4.3
All other	15.7	11.6	−4.1
Total	100.0	100.0	

Source: Statistical Abstract of the United States, 1997, Table 520, 1994, Table 509.

Table 3.9 shows state and local government spending by category in 1994. In that year, 32.9 percent of all state and local spending went for education—mostly public elementary and secondary education, although all states spend money on higher education as well. Since 1980, education and highways have contracted as a portion of total spending, while interest on debt, public welfare, and health and hospitals have assumed a significantly larger share.

SOURCES OF GOVERNMENT REVENUE

A breakdown of the sources of federal tax revenues appears in Table 3.10. The biggest single source of revenue for the federal government is the *individual income tax*, which accounted for 44.5 percent of total revenues in 1980. That figure dropped slightly to 43.7 percent in 1997. Federal income tax is withheld from most people's pay each week by their employers, who send it to the Internal Revenue Service. Self-employed people are responsible for sending in their own estimated taxes four times each year.

TABLE 3.9 STATE AND LOCAL EXPENDITURES BY FUNCTION, 1980 AND 1994

	PERCENTAGE OF TOTAL, 1980	PERCENTAGE OF TOTAL, 1994	BILLIONS OF DOLLARS, 1994
Education	36.3	32.9	353.3
Public welfare	12.4	16.7	179.8
Health and hospitals	8.8	9.3	100.4
Highways	9.1	6.7	72.1
Interest on debt	4.0	5.1	55.0
Police and fire	5.2	5.1	54.8
General administration	1.8	1.9	20.6
Other[a]	22.4	22.3	238.0
Total	100.0	100.0	1,074.0

[a]*Includes parks, sanitation, and housing, among other areas.*

Source: Statistical Abstract of the United States, 1997, p. 304.

TABLE 3.10 FEDERAL RECEIPTS BY SOURCE, 1980 AND 1997

	1980		1997	
	Billions of Dollars	*Percent*	*Billions of Dollars*	*Percent*
Individual income taxes	249.7	44.5	753.8	43.7
Corporate income taxes	70.3	12.5	211.9	12.3
Social insurance taxes	195.3	34.8	645.9	37.5
Excise taxes	32.5	5.8	71.6	4.2
Gift and estate taxes	6.5	1.2	20.6	1.2
Customs duties	7.2	1.2	19.7	1.1
Total	561.5	100.0	1,723.5	100.0

Source: U.S. Department of Commerce, Bureau of Economic Analysis.

social insurance, or payroll, taxes *Taxes levied at a flat rate on wages and salaries. Proceeds support various government-administrated social-benefit programs, including the social security system and the unemployment benefits system.*

Social insurance taxes are levied at a flat rate on wages and salaries up to a maximum amount. Because these taxes are figured as a percentage of wages and salaries and are levied on both employers and employees, they are also known as **payroll taxes**. The payroll tax is levied at a flat rate of 7.65 percent on employees and another 7.65 percent on employers. Self-employed persons pay between 12.8 percent and 14.2 percent depending on their income.

Social insurance taxes go into one of several trust funds that pay social security cash and health benefits to retirees, the disabled, and the survivors of workers who paid into the system. Payroll taxes also fund the unemployment compensation system.

Payroll taxes now account for a much larger portion of federal revenues than they have in the past. In 1997, they brought in 37.5 percent of total federal revenues, up from 34.8 percent in 1980. In 1965, they brought in only 21 percent of total revenues (not shown in Table 3.10). The payroll tax rate has been increased steadily because of worries about the future solvency of the system. A huge number of people will reach retirement age soon after the year 2000. At the same time, the labor force will be smaller. Because the tax rate required to support the increasing number of elderly then would be intolerable, the rate was sharply increased during the 1970s. It continues to increase now, in order to generate a surplus in the social security trust funds that should prevent the system's collapse in the future.

corporate income taxes *Taxes levied on the net incomes of corporations.*

Corporate income taxes are levied on the net income of corporations only, not on the profits of other forms of business organization (proprietorships and partnerships), which are taxed directly as ordinary personal income to the owners. Although payroll taxes have been increasing as a share of total tax revenues, corporate income taxes have had their ups and downs. In 1960, they accounted for about 22 percent of federal revenues. Table 3.10 shows that they accounted for 12.5 percent in 1980 and 12.3 percent in 1997. Big cuts came in 1981 when Congress enacted the Economic Recovery Tax Act, designed to stimulate business investment. The Tax Reform Act of 1986 sharply reduced personal income taxes and partly offset the lost revenues by increasing the corporation tax. The net effect is that the share of corporate taxes was about the same in 1997 as in 1980.

excise taxes *Taxes on specific commodities.*

Excise taxes make up only about 4.2 percent of the federal total. These are taxes on specific commodities like cigarettes, alcoholic beverages, gasoline, tires and tubes, and telephone service.

The sources of state and local revenues in 1997 appear in Table 3.11. Sales taxes, levied primarily by states, account for 23.6 percent of the total. Property taxes, 19.1

TABLE 3.11	STATE AND LOCAL TAX RECEIPTS, 1997	
	BILLIONS OF DOLLARS	**PERCENT OF TOTAL TAXES**
Sales taxes	257.4	23.6
Property taxes	208.8	19.1
Personal income taxes	159.8	14.7
Social insurance taxes	86.2	7.9
Corporate taxes	37.6	3.4
Federal grants	224.2	20.6
Other	116.5	10.7
Total	1,090.5	100.0

Sources: U.S. Department of Commerce, Bureau of Economic Analysis.

percent of the total, are levied primarily by local governments (such as counties, cities, and towns) on the estimated, or "assessed," value of commercial, industrial, and residential property. Personal income taxes account for 14.7 percent of state and local revenues, social insurance taxes 7.9 percent and corporate taxes 3.4 percent. Of total state and local revenue, 20.6 percent comes in the form of federal grants.

THE INTERNATIONAL SECTOR: IMPORTS AND EXPORTS

One of the great economic lessons of the 1970s and 1980s was that all economies, regardless of their size, depend to some extent on other economies and are affected by events outside their borders. Ask anyone in Iowa about the impact of foreign trade on farm prices and, therefore, on the well-being of U.S. farmers. Or ask steel-workers in Pittsburgh and Youngstown about the effect of cheap German and Japanese steel on the economies of those towns. One of the most controversial trade issues in recent years was the North American Free Trade Agreement (NAFTA), which was signed by President Bush in December 1992, and approved by the Congress in 1993. The purpose of NAFTA is to reduce trade barriers between the United States, Canada, and Mexico. In 1995, the Congress ratified the General Agreement on Tariffs and Trade (GATT), also designed to reduce trade barriers, after extended and often bitter debate.

The U.S. economy is by no means "closed." Thousands of transactions between the United States and virtually every country in the world take place daily. In 1997 the United States sold $51.3 billion in agricultural products to the rest of the world and bought about $70.8 billion in petroleum products from other countries. Overall, the United States imported $1,058.8 billion worth of goods and services in 1997, 13.1 percent of its GDP.

The growth of the international sector of the U.S. economy is a relatively recent phenomenon. Prior to 1970, imports and exports of goods and services accounted for a relatively small and stable fraction of U.S. GDP. Table 3.12 shows imports and exports for selected years since 1929. Between 1929 and 1970, imports were less than 6 percent of GDP. During the Depression and immediately following World War II, imports were even below 4 percent of GDP.

FAST FACTS

The following numbers are total exports as a percentage of total national output in 1995 for selected countries:

Ireland	75%
Belgium	74
United Arab Emirates	70
Namibia	53
Thailand	42
Korea	33
Chile	29
Germany	23
India	12
United States	11
Japan	9
Brazil	7
Haiti	4

Source: World Bank, *World Development Indicators, 1997,* Table 4.12.

TABLE 3.12 U.S. IMPORTS AND EXPORTS OF GOODS AND SERVICES, 1929–1997

	EXPORTS OF GOODS AND SERVICES		IMPORTS OF GOODS AND SERVICES	
	Billions of Dollars	Percentage of GDP	Billions of Dollars	Percentage of GDP
1929	5.9	5.7	5.6	5.4
1933	2.0	3.6	1.9	3.4
1945	6.7	3.0	7.5	3.4
1955	17.6	4.2	17.2	4.1
1960	25.3	4.8	22.8	4.3
1965	35.4	4.9	31.5	4.4
1970	57.0	5.5	55.8	5.4
1974	124.3	8.3	127.5	8.5
1976	148.9	8.2	151.1	8.3
1978	186.1	8.1	212.3	9.3
1980	278.9	10.0	293.8	10.6
1981	302.8	9.7	317.8	10.2
1982	282.6	8.7	303.2	9.4
1983	277.0	7.9	328.6	9.3
1984	303.1	7.8	405.1	10.4
1985	303.0	7.2	417.2	10.0
1986	320.7	7.3	452.2	10.2
1987	365.7	7.8	507.9	10.8
1988	447.2	8.9	553.2	11.0
1989	509.3	9.4	589.7	10.8
1990	557.3	9.7	628.6	10.9
1991	601.8	10.2	622.3	10.5
1992	639.4	10.2	669.0	10.7
1993	658.6	10.0	719.3	11.0
1994	721.2	10.4	812.1	11.7
1995	818.4	11.3	904.5	12.4
1996	870.9	11.4	965.7	12.6
1997	958.0	11.9	1,058.8	13.1

Source: U.S. Department of Commerce, Bureau of Economic Analysis.

Beginning in 1970, however, the volume of international trade increased significantly. Imports and exports doubled as a percentage of GDP by the end of the 1970s. Imports reached more than 10 percent by 1980. Exports dropped to 7.2 percent in 1985, but rebounded to 10 percent by 1991. There has been a substantial increase in both exports and imports since 1994.

➤ **The Composition of U.S. Trade**   Table 3.13 lists the types of merchandise the United States imported and exported in 1997. Perhaps the most surprising thing about this merchandise is its tremendous diversity.

The largest category—42.9 percent of U.S. exports and 28.6 percent of U.S. imports—is capital goods except automotive, a very broad category that includes many specialized and diverse products. The second most important category of U.S. exports is industrial supplies and materials—$152.7 billion in 1997. In third place is consumer goods except automotive, followed in fourth place by automobiles.

TABLE 3.13 MAJOR CATEGORIES OF MERCHANDISE IMPORTS AND EXPORTS BY THE UNITED STATES, 1997

EXPORTS	BILLIONS OF DOLLARS	PERCENTAGE OF TOTAL
Agricultural products	58.3	8.5
Nonagricultural products	628.2	91.5
Total	686.5	100.0
Food, feeds, and beverages	51.0	7.4
Industrial supplies and materials	152.7	22.2
Capital goods except automotive (machinery, aircraft, etc.)	294.5	42.9
Automobiles, vehicles, parts, and engines	73.7	10.8
Consumer goods except automotive	77.5	11.3
All other	37.1	5.4
Total	686.5	100.0

IMPORTS	BILLIONS OF DOLLARS	PERCENTAGE OF TOTAL
Petroleum and petroleum products	72.1	8.1
Nonpetroleum products	816.6	91.9
Total	888.7	100.0
Petroleum and petroleum products	72.1	8.1
Food, feeds, and beverages	39.7	4.5
Industrial supplies and materials	135.1	15.2
Capital goods except automotive (machinery, aircraft, etc.)	254.1	28.6
Automobiles, vehicles, parts, and engines	141.3	15.9
Consumer goods except automotive	192.9	21.7
All other	53.5	6.0
Total	888.7	100.0

Sources: U.S. Department of Commerce, Bureau of Economic Analysis.

Prior to 1970, imports of petroleum and petroleum products never amounted to more than $3 billion annually and were never more than 10 percent of total imports. The rapid increase in oil prices in 1973 to 1974 changed all this. By 1980 crude oil accounted for nearly a third of total imports. But in the early 1980s the United States began to cut its consumption of petroleum. By 1988, petroleum and natural gas accounted for only 8.8 percent of total imports. With the 1990 invasion of Kuwait, oil prices rose and the dollar volume of imports jumped back to over 12 percent of the total. After the Persian Gulf War, prices again fell and the figure dropped back to 8.1 percent in 1997.

Another important category of imports that has received a great deal of attention because of its impact on major U.S. industries is automobiles. In 1997 imports of automobiles and parts totaled $141.3 billion.

FROM INSTITUTIONS TO THEORY

This chapter has sketched the institutional structure of the U.S. economy. As we turn to economic theory, both positive and normative, you should reflect on the basic realities of economic life in the United States presented here. Why is the service sector expanding and the manufacturing sector contracting? Why is the public sector as large as it is? What economic functions does it perform? What determines the level of imports and exports? What effects do cheap foreign products have on the U.S. economy?

One of the most important questions in economics concerns the relative merits of public sector involvement in the economy. Should the government be involved in the economy, or should the market be left to its own devices? Before we can confront these and other important issues, we need to establish a theoretical framework. Our study of the economy and its operation begins in chapter 4 with the behavior of suppliers and demanders in private markets.

SUMMARY

1. The *private sector* is made up of privately owned firms that exist to make a profit, nonprofit organizations, and individual households. The *public sector* is the government and its agencies at all levels—federal, state, and local. The *international sector* is the global economy. From any one country's perspective, the international sector consists of the economies of the rest of the world.

THE PRIVATE SECTOR: U.S. BUSINESS AND INDUSTRIAL ORGANIZATION

2. A *proprietorship* is a firm with a single owner. A *partnership* has two or more owners. Proprietors and partners are fully liable for all the debts of the business. A *corporation* is a formally established legal entity that limits the liability of its owners. The owners are not responsible for the debts of the firm beyond what they invest.

3. The term *industry* is used loosely to refer to groups of firms that produce similar products. Industries can be broadly or narrowly defined. A company that produces cheese belongs to the cheese industry, the dairy industry, the food products industry, and the agricultural products industry.

4. In *perfect competition*, no single firm has any control over prices. This follows from two characteristics of this industry structure: (1) Perfectly competitive industries are composed of many firms, each small relative to the size of the industry, and (2) each firm in a perfectly competitive industry produces exactly the same product—that is, products are *homogeneous*.

5. A *monopoly* is an industry structure in which only one firm produces a product for which there are no close substitutes. To remain a monopoly in a profitable industry, a firm must be able to block the entry of competing firms.

6. In *monopolistic competition*, many firms compete, but each firm produces a slightly different product. Although each firm's product is unique, there are many close substitutes. Entering and exiting monopolistically competitive industries are relatively easy.

7. An *oligopoly* is an industry with a small number of firms. In general, entry of new firms into an oligopolistic industry is difficult but possible.

THE PUBLIC SECTOR: TAXES AND GOVERNMENT SPENDING

8. Public expenditures at all levels increased from 19.3 percent of GDP in 1940 to 33.8 percent in 1997. The federal portion of total expenditures grew more rapidly than the state and local portion, more than doubling since 1940.

9. Other measures of the size of the public sector have not increased as rapidly. Government employment increased slightly, from 13.3 percent of total employment in 1950 to 15.3 percent in 1997.

10. National defense and social security account for nearly 40 percent of federal spending. The top four categories of state and local spending are education, public welfare, health and hospitals, and highways.

11. Individual income taxes and social insurance taxes together accounted for about 81 percent of federal revenues in 1997. Over the last quarter century, social insurance taxes have increased dramatically as a portion of total federal revenues. Sales taxes and property taxes accounted for about 43 percent of state and local revenues in 1997.

THE INTERNATIONAL SECTOR: IMPORTS AND EXPORTS

12. Thousands of transactions between the United States and virtually every other country in the world take place daily. This has led to the increased importance of the international sector in the U.S. economy. In 1997, the United States imported $1,058.8 billion worth of goods and services, 13.1 percent of its GDP.

REVIEW TERMS AND CONCEPTS

barrier to entry, 50

corporate income taxes, 60

corporation, 47

dividends, 48

excise taxes, 60

government interest payments, 56

government consumption and
   investment, 56

government transfer payments, 56

gross domestic product (GDP), 55

homogeneous products, 49

industry, 48

international sector, 46

market organization, 49

monopolistic competition, 51

monopoly, 50

net income, 47

oligopoly, 51

partnership, 47

perfect competition, 49

private sector, 45

proprietorship, 46

public sector, 45

retained earnings, 48

share of stock, 47

social insurance, or payroll, taxes, 60

PROBLEM SET

1. Health care continues to be a major issue in U.S. society. Look up the latest figures on health-care expenditures as a percentage of GDP. What share of total government expenditure (federal, state, and local) is devoted to health care?

2. The figures presented in Table 3.4 suggest that the U.S. economy is becoming more competitive. Does your experience over the last few years seem to support this conclusion? Can you think of specific industries or markets that have become or are becoming more competitive?

3. Do a short research project on one of the following large government programs. What does the program accomplish or hope to accomplish? What is the basic logic for government involvement? How much was spent on the program in 1998 compared to 1980?
   a. Medicare
   b. Medicaid
   c. Social security
   d. State colleges and universities
   e. Student financial aid
   f. Aid to Families with Dependent Children (AFDC)
   g. Food stamps
   h. Interstate highways

4. The Congress debated the GATT in 1994 and approved it in 1995. What groups in the United States were opposed to its passage? Why? What are the basic arguments in favor of the GATT? The basic arguments against it?

5. State whether each of the following industries is essentially competitive, monopolistically competitive, oligopolistic, or monopolistic. Your answer should be based on your impressions as a buyer of goods or services or on what you know about the industry, not on research. Briefly explain your answer.
   a. The hotel/motel industry
   b. The cable television industry
   c. The shampoo industry
   d. The airline industry
   e. The hamburger industry
   f. The higher education (college and university) industry

6. The chapter contains conflicting evidence on whether the public sector has expanded relative to the rest of the economy in the last 20 to 30 years. What figures might be quoted in support of the proposition that it has expanded? Do they tell the whole story? Discuss.

7. What are the differences between a proprietorship and a corporation? If you were going to start a small business, which form of organization would you choose? What are the advantages and disadvantages of the two forms of organization?

8. "Most firms are corporations, but they account for a relatively small portion of total output in the United States." Do you agree or disagree with this statement? Explain your answer.

9. In 1997 shareholders directly received only 37.8 percent of total corporate profits. What happened to the rest?

10. Perfectly competitive industries are made up of large numbers of firms, each small relative to the size of the industry and each producing homogeneous products. What does this imply about an individual firm's ability to influence price? Explain your answer.

11. How is a monopolistically competitive industry like a monopoly? In what ways is it like a perfectly competitive industry?

12. How is it possible for government spending to increase as a percentage of GDP while taxes and government employment are both decreasing?

13. Why is the federal government spending much more on interest payments now than it was a decade ago? Explain.

14. Of the items that you buy frequently or services that you spend money on, which ones are produced in the United States and which are imported? Of the major industries in your home state, which produce products or services that are exported?

15. It is sometimes argued that the government's practice of awarding patents (exclusive rights) to inventors and producers of products creates monopoly power and deprives consumers of the advantages of free competition. The argument surfaces frequently in discussions about the prescription drug market. For example, if a researcher were to discover a cure for AIDS and procure a patent, she would be a monopolist, and she'd be able to charge a very high price for her product. Do you agree with this argument? What is the rationale for issuing patents? If you were to procure a patent on a new formula for a lovely new perfume, would you be a monopolist? Explain your answers.

TAKE IT TO THE NET

We invite you to visit the Case and Fair page on the Prentice Hall Web site:
http://www.prenhall.com/casefair
for this chapter's World Wide Web exercise.

EMAND, SUPPLY, AND MARKET EQUILIBRIUM

CHAPTERS 1 AND 2 INTRODUCED the discipline, methodology, and subject matter of economics. Chapter 3 described the institutional landscape of the U.S. economy—its private, public, and international sectors. We now begin the task of analyzing how a market economy actually works. This chapter and the next present an overview of the way individual markets work. They introduce some of the concepts needed to understand both microeconomics and macroeconomics.

As we proceed to define terms and make assumptions, it is important to keep in mind what we are doing. In chapter 1 we explained what economic theory attempts to do. Theories are abstract representations of reality, like a map that represents a city. We believe that the models presented here will help you understand the workings of the economy just as a map helps you find your way around a city. But just as a map presents one view of the world, so too does any given theory of the economy. Alternatives exist to the theory that we present. We believe, however, that the basic model presented here, while sometimes abstract, is useful in gaining an understanding of how the economy works.

In the simple island society discussed in chapter 2, Bill and Colleen solved the economic problem directly. They allocated their time and used the island's resources to satisfy their wants. Bill might be a farmer, Colleen a hunter and carpenter. He might be a civil engineer, she a doctor. Exchange occurred, but complex markets were not necessary.

In societies of many people, however, production must satisfy wide-ranging tastes and preferences. Producers therefore specialize. Farmers produce more food than they can eat in order to sell it to buy manufactured goods. Physicians are paid for specialized services, as are attorneys, construction workers, and editors. When there is specialization, there must be exchange, and *markets* are the institutions through which exchange takes place.

This chapter begins to explore the basic forces at work in market systems. The purpose of our discussion is to explain how the individual decisions of households and firms together, without any central planning or direction, answer the three basic questions: What will be produced, how will it be produced, and who will get what is produced? We begin with some definitions.

FIRMS AND HOUSEHOLDS: THE BASIC DECISION-MAKING UNITS

Throughout this book, we discuss and analyze the behavior of two fundamental decision-making units: *firms*—the primary producing units in an economy—and *households*—the consuming units in an economy. Both are made up of people performing different functions and playing different roles. In essence, then, what we are developing is a theory of human behavior.

A **firm** exists when a person or a group of people decides to produce a product or products by transforming *inputs* (that is, resources in the broadest sense) into *outputs* (the products that are sold in the market). Some firms produce goods; others produce services. Some are large, some are small, and some are in between. But all firms exist to transform resources into things that people want. The Colorado Symphony Orchestra takes labor, land, a building, musically talented people, electricity, and other inputs and combines them to produce concerts. The production process can be extremely complicated. For example, the first flutist in the orchestra uses training, talent, previous performance experience, a score, an instrument, the conductor's interpretation, and her own feelings about the music to produce just one contribution to an overall performance.

firm *An organization that transforms resources (inputs) into products (outputs). Firms are the primary producing units in a market economy.*

Most firms exist to make a profit for their owners, but some do not. Columbia University, for example, fits the description of a firm: It takes inputs in the form of labor, land, skills, books, and buildings and produces a service that we call education. Although it sells that service for a price, it does not exist to make a profit, but rather to provide education of the highest quality possible.

Still, most firms exist to make a profit. They engage in production because they can sell their product for more than it costs to produce it. The analysis of firm behavior that follows rests on the assumption that *firms make decisions in order to maximize profits.*

An **entrepreneur** is one who organizes, manages, and assumes the risks of a firm. When a new firm is created—whether a proprietorship, a partnership, or a corporation—someone must organize the new firm, arrange financing, hire employees, and take risks. That person is an entrepreneur. Sometimes existing companies introduce new products, and sometimes new firms develop or improve on an old idea, but at the root of it all is entrepreneurship, which some see as the core of the free enterprise system.

entrepreneur *A person who organizes, manages, and assumes the risks of a firm, taking a new idea or a new product and turning it into a successful business.*

At the root of the debate about the potential of free enterprise in formerly socialist Eastern Europe is the question of entrepreneurship. Does an entrepreneurial spirit exist in that part of the world? If not, can it be developed? Without it, the free enterprise system breaks down.

The consuming units in an economy are **households**. A household may consist of any number of people: a single person living alone, a married couple with four children, or 15 unrelated people sharing a house. Household decisions are presumably based on individual tastes and preferences. The household buys what it wants and can afford. In a large, heterogeneous, and open society such as the United States, wildly different tastes find expression in the marketplace. A six-block walk in any direction on any street in Manhattan or a drive from the Chicago Loop south into rural Illinois should be enough to convince anyone that it is difficult to generalize about what people like and do not like.

households *The consuming units in an economy.*

Even though households have wide-ranging preferences, they also have some things in common. All—even the very rich—have ultimately limited incomes, and all must pay in some way for the things they consume. Although households may have some control over their incomes—they can work more or less—they are also constrained by the availability of jobs, current wages, their own abilities, and their accumulated and inherited wealth (or lack thereof).

Input Markets and Output Markets: The Circular Flow

Households and firms interact in two basic kinds of markets: product (or output) markets and input (or factor) markets. Goods and services that are intended for use by households are exchanged in **product** or **output markets**. In output markets, firms *supply* and households *demand*.

To produce goods and services, firms must buy resources in **input** or **factor markets**. Firms buy inputs from households, which supply these inputs. When a firm decides how much to produce (supply) in output markets, it must simultaneously decide how much of each input it needs to produce the desired level of output. To produce automobiles, Chrysler Corporation must use many inputs, including tires, steel, complicated machinery, and many different kinds of labor.

Figure 4.1 shows the *circular flow* of economic activity through a simple market economy. Note that the flow reflects the direction in which goods and services flow through input and output markets. For example, goods and services flow from firms to households through output markets. Labor services flow from households to firms through input markets. Payment (most often in money form) for goods and services flows in the opposite direction.

In input markets, households *supply* resources. Most households earn their incomes by working—they supply their labor in the **labor market** to firms that demand labor and pay workers for their time and skills. Households may also loan their accumulated or inherited savings to firms for interest, or exchange those savings for claims to future profits, as when a household buys shares of stock in a corporation. In the **capital market**, households supply the funds that firms use to buy capital goods. Households may also supply land or other real property in exchange for rent in the **land market**.

Inputs into the production process are also called **factors of production**. Land, labor, and capital are the three key factors of production. Throughout this text, we use the terms *input* and *factor of production* interchangeably. Thus, input markets and factor markets mean the same thing.

product or **output markets**
The markets in which goods and services are exchanged.

input or **factor markets**
The markets in which the resources used to produce products are exchanged.

labor market *The input/factor market in which households supply work for wages to firms that demand labor.*

capital market *The input/factor market in which households supply their savings, for interest or for claims to future profits, to firms that demand funds in order to buy capital goods.*

land market *The input/factor market in which households supply land or other real property in exchange for rent.*

factors of production *The inputs into the production process. Land, labor, and capital are the three key factors of production.*

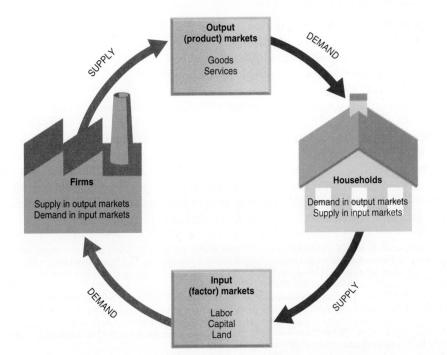

FIGURE 4.1

The Circular Flow of Economic Activity
Diagrams like this one show the circular flow of economic activity, hence the name *circular flow diagram*. Here, goods and services flow clockwise: Labor services supplied by households flow to firms, and goods and services produced by firms flow to households. Money (not pictured here) flows in the opposite (counterclockwise) direction: Payment for goods and services flows from households to firms, and payment for labor services flows from firms to households.

Note: Color Guide—In Figure 4.1 households are depicted in *blue* and firms are depicted in *red*. From now on all diagrams relating to the behavior of households will be blue or shades of blue, and all diagrams relating to the behavior of firms will be in red or shades of red.

Early economics texts included entrepreneurship as a type of input, just like land, labor, and capital. Treating entrepreneurship as a separate factor of production has fallen out of favor, however, partially because it is unmeasurable. Most economists today implicitly assume that it is in plentiful supply. That is, if profit opportunities exist, it is likely that entrepreneurs will crop up to take advantage of them. This assumption has turned out to be a good predictor of actual economic behavior and performance.

The supply of inputs and their prices ultimately determine households' income. The amount of income a household earns thus depends on the decisions it makes concerning what types of inputs it chooses to supply. Whether to stay in school, how much and what kind of training to get, whether to start a business, how many hours to work, whether to work at all, and how to invest savings are all household decisions that affect income.

As you can see, then:

> Input and output markets are connected through the behavior of both firms and households. Firms determine the quantities and character of outputs produced and the types of quantities of inputs demanded. Households determine the types and quantities of products demanded and the quantities and types of inputs supplied.[1]

The following analysis of demand and supply will lead up to a theory of how market prices are determined. Prices are determined by the interaction between demanders and suppliers. To understand this interaction, we first need to know how product prices influence the behavior of demanders and suppliers *separately*. We therefore discuss output markets by focusing first on demanders, then on suppliers, and then on the interaction.

DEMAND IN PRODUCT/OUTPUT MARKETS

In real life, households make many decisions at the same time. To see how the forces of demand and supply work, however, let us focus first on the amount of a *single* product that an *individual* household decides to consume within some given period of time, such as a month or a year.

> A household's decision about what quantity of a particular output, or product, to demand depends upon a number of factors:
>
> - The *price of the product* in question.
> - The *income available* to the household.
> - The household's *amount of accumulated wealth*.
> - The *prices of other products* available to the household.
> - The household's *tastes and preferences*.
> - The household's *expectations* about future income, wealth, and prices.

quantity demanded *The amount (number of units) of a product that a household would buy in a given period if it could buy all it wanted at the current market price.*

Quantity demanded is the amount (number of units) of a product that a household would buy in a given period *if it could buy all it wanted at the current market price.*

Of course, the amount of a product that households finally purchase depends on the amount of product actually available in the market. The phrase *if it could buy all it wanted* is critical to the definition of quantity demanded because it allows for the possibility that quantity supplied and quantity demanded are unequal.

---

[1] Our description of markets begins with the behavior of firms and households. Modern orthodox economic theory essentially combines two distinct but closely related theories of behavior. The "theory of household behavior," or "consumer behavior," has its roots in the works of nineteenth-century utilitarians such as Jeremy Bentham, William Jevons, Carl Menger, Leon Walras, Vilfredo Pareto, and F. Y. Edgeworth. The "theory of the firm" developed out of the earlier classical political economy of Adam Smith, David Ricardo, and Thomas Malthus. In 1890 Alfred Marshall published the first of many editions of his *Principles of Economics*. That volume pulled together the main themes of both the classical economists and the utilitarians into what is now called "neoclassical economics." While there have been many changes over the years, the basic structure of the model that we build can be found in Marshall's work.

> **Changes in Quantity Demanded versus Changes in Demand** The most important relationship in individual markets is that between market price and quantity demanded. For this reason, we need to begin our discussion by analyzing the likely response of households to changes in price using the device of *ceteris paribus*, or "all else equal." That is, we will attempt to derive a relationship between the quantity demanded of a good per time period and the price of that good, holding income, wealth, other prices, tastes, and expectations constant.

It is very important to distinguish between price changes, which affect the quantity of a good demanded, and changes in other factors (such as income), which change the entire relationship between price and quantity. For example, if a family begins earning a higher income, it might buy more of a good at every possible price. To be sure that we distinguish between changes in price and other changes that affect demand, we will throughout the rest of the text be very precise about terminology. Specifically:

Changes in the price of a product affect the *quantity demanded* per period. Changes in any other factor, such as income or preferences, affect *demand*. Thus we say that an increase in the price of Coca-Cola is likely to cause a decrease in the *quantity of Coca-Cola demanded*. However, we say that an increase in income is likely to cause an increase in the *demand* for most goods.

PRICE AND QUANTITY DEMANDED: THE LAW OF DEMAND

A **demand schedule** shows the quantities of a product that a household would be willing to buy at different prices. Table 4.1 presents a hypothetical demand schedule for Anna, a student who went off to college to study economics while her boyfriend went to art school. If telephone calls were free (a price of zero), Anna would call her boyfriend every day, or 30 times a month. At a price of $.50 per call, she makes 25 calls a month. When the price hits $3.50, she cuts back to seven calls a month. This same information presented graphically is called a **demand curve**. Anna's demand curve is presented in Figure 4.2.[2]

You will note in Figure 4.2 that *quantity* is measured along the horizontal axis, and *price* is measured along the vertical axis. This is the convention we follow throughout this book.

> **Demand Curves Slope Downward** The data in Table 4.1 show that at lower prices, Anna calls her boyfriend more frequently; at higher prices, she calls less frequently. There is thus a *negative, or inverse, relationship between quantity demanded and price*. When price rises, quantity demanded falls, and when price falls, quantity demanded rises. Thus demand curves always slope downward. This negative relationship between price and quantity demanded is often referred to as the **law of demand**, a term first used by economist Alfred Marshall in his 1890 textbook.

Some people are put off by the abstractness of demand curves. Of course, we don't actually draw our own demand curves for products. When we want to make a purchase, we usually face only a single price, and how much we would buy at other prices is irrelevant. But demand curves help analysts understand the kind of behavior that households are *likely* to exhibit if they are actually faced with a higher or lower price. We know, for example, that if the price of a good rises enough, the quantity demanded

---

[2]Drawing a smooth curve, as we do in Figure 4.2, suggests that Anna can make a quarter of a phone call or half of a phone call. For example, according to the graph, at a price of $12 per call, Anna would make half a call and at $9 per call, about a call and a half. While fractional purchases can be made for goods that are *divisible*, such as phone calls—you might talk for one minute instead of two minutes—and products sold by weight, they are impossible for large purchases, such as automobiles. We use the term *lumpy* to describe goods that cannot be divided. You would not draw a smooth, downward sloping curve of a household's demand for automobiles, for example, because there might be only one (or at most two) points, and any points in between would be meaningless. Whenever we draw a smooth demand curve, we are assuming divisibility.

TABLE 4.1

ANNA'S DEMAND SCHEDULE FOR TELEPHONE CALLS

PRICE (PER CALL)	QUANTITY DEMANDED (CALLS PER MONTH)
$ 0	30
.50	25
3.50	7
7.00	3
10.00	1
15.00	0

demand schedule *A table showing how much of a given product a household would be willing to buy at different prices.*

demand curve *A graph illustrating how much of a given product a household would be willing to buy at different prices.*

law of demand *The negative relationship between price and quantity demanded: As price rises, quantity demanded decreases. As price falls, quantity demanded increases.*

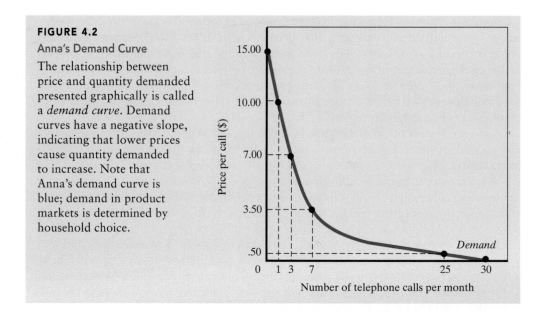

FIGURE 4.2

Anna's Demand Curve

The relationship between price and quantity demanded presented graphically is called a *demand curve*. Demand curves have a negative slope, indicating that lower prices cause quantity demanded to increase. Note that Anna's demand curve is blue; demand in product markets is determined by household choice.

must ultimately drop to zero. The demand curve is thus a tool that helps us explain economic behavior and predict reactions to possible price changes.

Marshall's definition of a social "law" captures the idea:

> The term "law" means nothing more than a general proposition or statement of tendencies, more or less certain, more or less definite . . . a *social law* is a statement of social tendencies; that is, that a certain course of action may be expected from the members of a social group under certain conditions.[3]

It seems reasonable to expect that consumers will demand more of a product at a lower price and less of it at a higher price. Households must divide their incomes over a wide range of goods and services. If I spend $4.50 for a pound of prime beef, I am sacrificing the other things that I might have bought with that $4.50. If the price of prime beef were to jump to $7 per pound, while chicken breasts remained at $1.99 (remember *ceteris paribus*—we are holding all else constant), I would have to give up more chicken and/or other items to buy that pound of beef. So I would probably eat more chicken and less beef. Anna calls her boyfriend three times when phone calls cost $7 each. A fourth call would mean sacrificing $7 worth of other purchases. At a price of $3.50, however, the opportunity cost of each call is lower, and she calls more frequently.

Another explanation behind the fact that demand curves are very likely to slope downward rests on the notion of *utility*. Economists use the concept of *utility* to mean happiness or satisfaction. Presumably we consume goods and services because they give us utility. But as we consume more of a product within a given period of time, it is likely that each additional unit consumed will yield successively less satisfaction. The utility I gain from a second ice cream cone is likely to be less than the utility I gained from the first; the third is worth even less, and so forth. This *law of diminishing marginal utility* is an important concept in economics. If each successive unit of a good is worth less to me, I am not going to be willing to pay as much for it. It is thus reasonable to expect a downward slope in the demand curve for that good.

The idea of diminishing marginal utility also helps to explain Anna's behavior. The demand curve is a way of representing what she is willing to pay per phone call. At a

[3]Alfred Marshall, *Principles of Economics*, 8th ed. (New York: Macmillan, 1948), p. 33. (The first edition was published in 1890.)

price of $7, she calls her boyfriend three times per month. A fourth call, however, is worth less than the third—that is, the fourth call is worth less than $7 to her, so she stops at three. If the price were only $3.50, however, she would keep right on calling. But even at $3.50, she would stop at seven calls per month. This behavior reveals that the eighth call has less value to Anna than the seventh.

Thinking about the ways that people are affected by price changes also helps us see what is behind the law of demand. Consider this example: Luis lives and works in Mexico City. His elderly mother lives in Santiago, Chile. Last year, the airlines servicing South America got into a price war, and the price of flying between Mexico City and Santiago dropped from 20,000 pesos to 10,000 pesos. How might Luis's behavior change?

First, he is better off. Last year he flew home to Chile three times at a total cost of 60,000 pesos. This year he can fly to Chile the same number of times, buy exactly the same combination of other goods and services that he bought last year, and have 30,000 pesos left over! Because he is better off—his income can buy more—he may fly home more frequently. Second, the opportunity cost of flying home has changed. Before the price war, Luis had to sacrifice 20,000 pesos worth of other goods and services each time he flew to Chile. After the price war he must sacrifice only 10,000 pesos worth of other goods and services for each trip. The trade-off has changed. Both of these effects are likely to lead to a higher quantity demanded in response to the lower price.

In sum:

> It is reasonable to expect quantity demanded to fall when price rises, *ceteris paribus*, and to expect quantity demanded to rise when price falls, *ceteris paribus*. Demand curves have a negative slope.

> **Other Properties of Demand Curves** Two additional things are notable about Anna's demand curve. First, it intersects the Y, or price, axis. This means that there is a price above which no calls will be made. In this case, Anna simply stops calling when the price reaches $15 per call.

> As long as households have limited incomes and wealth, all demand curves will intersect the price axis. For any commodity, there is always a price above which a household will not, or cannot, pay. Even if the good or service is very important, all households are ultimately constrained, or limited, by income and wealth.

Second, Anna's demand curve intersects the X, or quantity, axis. Even at a zero price, there is a limit to the number of phone calls Anna will make. If telephone calls were free, she would call 30 times a month, but not more.

> That demand curves intersect the quantity axis is a matter of common sense. Demands for most goods are limited, if only by time, even at a zero price.

To summarize what we know about the shape of demand curves:

1. They have a negative slope. An increase in price is likely to lead to a decrease in quantity demanded, and a decrease in price is likely to lead to an increase in quantity demanded.
2. They intersect the quantity (X) axis, a result of time limitations and diminishing marginal utility.
3. They intersect the price (Y) axis, a result of limited incomes and wealth.

But that's all we can say; it is not possible to generalize further. The actual shape of an individual household demand curve—whether it is steep or flat, whether it is bowed in or bowed out—depends on the unique tastes and preferences of the household and other factors. Some households may be very sensitive to price changes; other households may respond little to a change in price. In some cases, plentiful substitutes are available; in other cases they are not. Thus, to fully understand the shape and position of demand curves, we must turn to the other determinants of household demand.

OTHER DETERMINANTS OF HOUSEHOLD DEMAND

Of the many factors likely to influence a household's demand for a specific product, we have considered only the price of the product itself. Other determining factors include household income and wealth, the prices of other goods and services, tastes and preferences, and expectations.

➤ **Income and Wealth** Before we proceed, we need to define two terms that are often confused, *income* and *wealth*. A household's **income** is the sum of all the wages, salaries, profits, interest payments, rents, and other forms of earnings received by the household *in a given period of time*. Income is thus a *flow* measure: We must specify a time period for it—income *per month* or *per year*. You can spend or consume more or less than your income in any given period. If you consume less than your income, you save. To consume more than your income in a period, you must either borrow or draw on savings accumulated from previous periods.

Wealth is the total value of what a household owns less what it owes. Another word for wealth is **net worth**—the amount a household would have left if it sold off all its possessions and paid off all its debts. Wealth is a *stock* measure: It is measured at a given point in time. If, in a given period, you spend less than your income, you save; the amount that you save is added to your wealth. Saving is the flow that affects the stock of wealth. When you spend more than your income, you *dissave*—you reduce your wealth.

Clearly, households with higher incomes and higher accumulated savings or inherited wealth can afford to buy more things. In general, then, we would expect higher demand at higher levels of income/wealth and lower demand at lower levels of income/wealth. Goods for which demand goes up when income is higher and for which demand goes down when income is lower are called **normal goods**. Movie tickets, restaurant meals, telephone calls, and shirts are all normal goods.

But generalization in economics can be hazardous. Sometimes demand for a good falls when household income rises. Consider, for example, the various qualities of meat available. When a household's income rises, it is likely to buy higher quality meats—its demand for filet mignon is likely to rise—but its demand for lower quality meats—chuck steak, for example—is likely to fall. Transportation is another example. At higher incomes, people can afford to fly. People who can afford to fly are less likely to take the bus long distances. Thus higher income may reduce the number of times someone takes a bus. Goods for which demand tends to fall when income rises are called **inferior goods**.

➤ **Prices of Other Goods and Services** No consumer decides in isolation on the amount of any one commodity to buy. Rather, each decision is part of a larger set of decisions that are made simultaneously. Households must apportion their incomes over many different goods and services. As a result, the price of any one good can and does affect the demand for other goods.

This is most obviously the case when goods are substitutes for one another. To return to our lonesome first-year student: If the price of a telephone call rises to $10, Anna will call her boyfriend only once a month (see Table 4.1). But, of course, she can get in touch with him in other ways. Presumably she substitutes some other, less costly, form of communication, such as writing more letters or sending more E-mails.

When an *increase* in the price of one good causes demand for another good to *increase* (a positive relationship), we say that the goods are **substitutes**. A *fall* in the price of a good causes a *decline* in demand for its substitutes. Substitutes are goods that can serve as replacements for one another.

income *The sum of all a household's wages, salaries, profits, interest payments, rents, and other forms of earnings in a given period of time. It is a flow measure.*

wealth or **net worth** *The total value of what a household owns minus what it owes. It is a stock measure.*

A major portion of household wealth, one determinant of demand, is made up of financial assets. At the end of 1996, financial assets of households was about $23 trillion: 16% was held in bank deposits, 28% in pension funds, 21% in shares of stock, 9% in bonds and other fixed-income investments, 7% in mutual funds, and the remaining 19% in other forms.

Source: Flow of Funds Accounts of the United States.

normal goods *Goods for which demand goes up when income is higher and for which demand goes down when income is lower.*

inferior goods *Goods for which demand tends to fall when income rises.*

substitutes *Goods that can serve as replacements for one another; when the price of one increases, demand for the other goes up.*

To be substitutes, two products need not be identical. Identical products are called **perfect substitutes**. Japanese cars are not identical to American cars. Nonetheless, all have four wheels, are capable of carrying people, and run on gasoline. Thus, significant changes in the price of one country's cars can be expected to influence demand for the other country's cars. Compact discs are substitutes for records and tapes, restaurant meals are substitutes for meals eaten at home, and flying from New York to Washington is a substitute for taking the train.

perfect substitutes *Identical products.*

Often, two products "go together"—that is, they complement each other. Our lonesome letter writer, for example, will find her demand for stamps and stationery rising as she writes more letters, and her demand for Internet access rising as she sends more E-mails. Bacon and eggs are **complementary goods,** as are cars and gasoline, and cameras and film. During a price war among the airlines in the summer of 1994 when travel became less expensive, the demand for taxi service to and from airports and for luggage increased across the country. When two goods are complements, a *decrease* in the price of one results in *increase* in demand for the other, and vice versa.

complements, complementary goods *Goods that "go together"; a decrease in the price of one results in an increase in demand for the other, and vice versa.*

Because any one good may have many potential substitutes and complements at the same time, a single price change may affect a household's demands for many goods simultaneously; the demand for some of these products may rise while the demand for others may fall. For example, one of the newest technologies for personal computers is the CD-ROM. Massive amounts of data can now be stored digitally on compact disks that can be read by personal computers with a CD-ROM drive. When these drives first came on the market they were quite expensive, selling for several hundred dollars each. Now they are much less expensive, and most new computers have them built in. As a result, the demand for the CD-ROM disks (complementary goods) is soaring. As more and more students adopt the CD technology and the price of CDs and CD hardware falls, fewer people will be buying things like encyclopedias printed on paper (substitute goods).

▶ **Tastes and Preferences** Income, wealth, and the prices of things available are the three factors that determine the combinations of things that a household is *able* to buy. You know that you cannot afford to rent an apartment at $1,200 per month if your monthly income is only $400. But within these constraints, you are more or less free to choose what to buy. Your final choice depends on your individual tastes and preferences.

Changes in preferences can and do manifest themselves in market behavior. Twenty-five years ago the major big-city marathons drew only a few hundred runners. Now tens of thousands enter and run. The demand for running shoes, running suits, stopwatches, and other running items has greatly increased. For many years, people drank soda for refreshment. Today convenience stores are filled with a dizzying array of iced teas, fruit juices, natural beverages, and mineral waters.

Within the constraints of prices and incomes, it is preference that shapes the demand curve. But it is difficult to generalize about tastes and preferences. First of all, they are volatile: Five years ago, more people smoked cigarettes and fewer people had computers. Second, they are idiosyncratic: Some people like to talk on the telephone, while others prefer the written word; some people prefer dogs, while others are crazy about cats; some people like chicken wings, while others prefer legs. The diversity of individual demands is almost infinite.

PERFECT SUBSTITUTES? ON A HOT DAY IN THE DESERT, ONE BRAND IS AS GOOD AS ANOTHER.

▶ **Expectations** What you decide to buy today certainly depends on today's prices and your current income and wealth. But you also have expectations about what your position will be in the future. You may have expectations about future changes in prices, too, and these may affect your decisions today.

There are many examples of the ways expectations affect demand. When people buy a house or a car, they often must borrow part of the purchase price and pay it back over a number of years. In deciding what kind of house or car to buy, they presumably must think about their income today, as well as what their income is likely to be in the future.

As another example, consider a student in his final year of medical school living on a scholarship of $12,000. Compare him with another person earning $6 an hour at a full-time job, with no expectation of a significant change in income in the future. The two have virtually identical incomes. But even if they had the same tastes, the medical student is likely to demand different things, simply because he expects a major increase in income later on.

Increasingly, economic theory has come to recognize the importance of expectations. We will devote a good deal of time to discussing how expectations affect more than just demand. For the time being, however, it is important to understand that demand depends on more than just *current* incomes, prices, and tastes.

SHIFT OF DEMAND VERSUS MOVEMENT ALONG A DEMAND CURVE

Recall that a demand curve shows the relationship between quantity demanded and the price of a good. Such demand curves are derived while holding income, tastes, and other prices constant. If this condition of *ceteris paribus* were relaxed, we would have to derive an entirely new relationship between price and quantity.

Let us return once again to Anna (Table 4.1 and Figure 4.2). Suppose that when we derived the demand schedule in Table 4.1, Anna had a part-time job that paid $200 per month. Now suppose that her parents inherit some money and begin sending her an additional $200 per month. Assuming that she keeps her job, Anna's income is now $400 per month.[4]

With her higher income, Anna would probably call her boyfriend more frequently, regardless of the price of a call. Table 4.2 and Figure 4.3 present Anna's original-income schedule (D_1) and increased-income demand schedule (D_2). At $.50 per call, the frequency of her calls (the quantity she demands) increases from 25 to 33 calls per month; at $3.50 per call, frequency increases from 7 to 18 calls per month; at $10 per call, frequency increases from one to seven calls per month. (Note in Figure 4.3 that even if calls are free, Anna's income matters; at zero price, her demand increases. With a higher income, she may visit her boyfriend more, for example, and more visits might mean more phone calls to organize and plan.)

The conditions that were in place at the time we drew the original demand curve have now changed. In other words, a factor that affects Anna's demand for telephone calls

TABLE 4.2 SHIFT OF ANNA'S DEMAND SCHEDULE DUE TO INCREASE IN INCOME

Price (Per Call)	SCHEDULE D_1 Quantity Demanded (Calls Per Month at an Income of $200 Per Month)	SCHEDULE D_2 Quantity Demanded (Calls Per Month at an Income of $400 Per Month)
$ 0	30	35
.50	25	33
3.50	7	18
7.00	3	12
10.00	1	7
15.00	0	2
20.00	0	0

[4]The income from home may affect the amount of time Anna spends working. In the extreme, she may quit her job and her income will remain at $200. In essence, she would be spending the entire $200 on leisure. Here we assume that she keeps the job and that her income is higher. The point is that because labor supply decisions affect income, they are closely tied to output demand decisions. In a sense, the two decisions are made simultaneously.

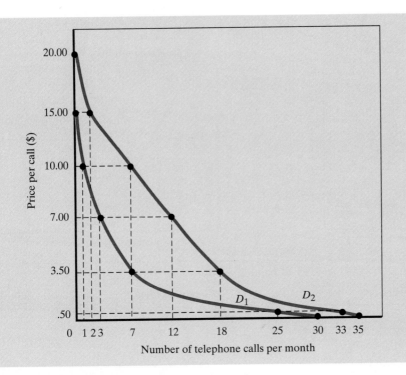

FIGURE 4.3
Shift of a Demand Curve
Following a Rise in Income
When the price of a good
changes, we move *along* the
demand curve for that good.
When any other factor that
influences demand changes
(income, tastes, etc.), the
relationship between price and
quantity is different; there is a
shift of the demand curve, in
this case from D_1 to D_2.

(in this case, her income) has changed, and there is now a new relationship between price and quantity demanded. Such a change is referred to as a **shift of the demand curve.**

It is very important to distinguish between a change in quantity demanded—that is, some movement *along* a demand curve—and a shift of demand. Demand schedules and demand curves show the relationship between the price of a good or service and the quantity demanded per period, *ceteris paribus.* If price changes, quantity demanded will change—this is a **movement along the demand curve.** When any of the *other* factors that influence demand change, however, a new relationship between price and quantity demanded is established—this is a *shift of the demand curve.* The result, then, is a *new* demand curve. Changes in income, preferences, or prices of other goods cause the demand curve to shift:

shift of a demand curve
The change that takes place in a demand curve corresponding to a new relationship between quantity demanded of a good and the price of that good. The shift is brought about by a change in the original conditions.

movement along a demand curve *The change in quantity demanded brought about by a change in price.*

Change in price of a good or service

> leads to
>
> ⟶ Change in *quantity demanded* (**Movement along the demand curve**).

Change in income, preferences, or prices of other goods or services

> leads to
>
> ⟶ Change in *demand* (**Shift of demand curve**).

Figure 4.4 illustrates the differences between movement along a demand curve and shifting demand curves. In Figure 4.4a, an increase in household income causes demand for hamburger (an inferior good) to decline, or shift to the left from D_1 to D_2. (Because quantity is measured on the horizontal axis, a decrease means a shift to the left.) In contrast, demand for steak (a normal good) increases, or shifts to the right, when income rises.

In Figure 4.4b, an increase in the price of hamburger from $1.49 to $3.09 a pound causes a household to buy less hamburger each month. In other words, the higher price causes the *quantity demanded* to decline from 10 pounds to 5 pounds per month. This change represents a movement *along* the demand curve for hamburger. In place

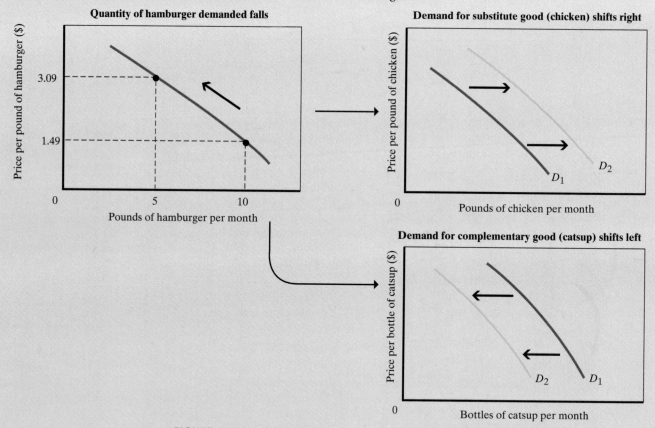

a. Income rises

Demand for inferior good shifts left

Price per pound of hamburger ($)

D_2 D_1

0   Pounds of hamburger per month

Demand for normal good shifts right

Price per pound of steak ($)

D_1 D_2

0   Pounds of steak per month

b. Price of hamburger rises

Quantity of hamburger demanded falls

Price per pound of hamburger ($)

3.09

1.49

0   5   10

Pounds of hamburger per month

Demand for substitute good (chicken) shifts right

Price per pound of chicken ($)

D_1 D_2

0   Pounds of chicken per month

Demand for complementary good (catsup) shifts left

Price per bottle of catsup ($)

D_2 D_1

0   Bottles of catsup per month

FIGURE 4.4

Shifts versus Movement along a Demand Curve

a. When income increases, the demand for inferior goods *shifts to the left* and the demand for normal goods *shifts to the right*. **b.** If the price of hamburger rises, the quantity of hamburger demanded declines—this is a movement along the demand curve. The same price rise for hamburger would shift the demand for chicken (a substitute for hamburger) to the right and the demand for catsup (a complement to hamburger) to the left.

of hamburger, the household buys more chicken. The household's demand for chicken (a substitute for hamburger) rises—the demand curve shifts to the right. At the same time, the demand for catsup (a good that complements hamburger) declines—its demand curve shifts to the left.

FROM HOUSEHOLD DEMAND TO MARKET DEMAND

Market demand is simply the sum of all the quantities of a good or service demanded per period by all the households buying in the market for that good or service. Figure 4.5 shows the derivation of a market demand curve from three individual demand curves. (Although this market demand curve is derived from the behavior of only three people, most markets have thousands or even millions of demanders.) As the table in Figure 4.5 shows, when the price of a pound of coffee is $3.50, both A and C would purchase 4 pounds per month, while B would buy none. At that price, presumably, B drinks tea. Market demand at $3.50 would thus be a total of 4 + 4 or 8 pounds. At a price of $1.50 per pound, however, A would purchase 8 pounds per month, B 3 pounds, and C 9 pounds. Thus, at $1.50 per pound, market demand would be 8 + 3 + 9, or 20 pounds of coffee per month.

The total quantity demanded in the marketplace at a given price, then, is simply the sum of all the quantities demanded by all the individual households shopping in the

> **market demand** *The sum of all the quantities of a good or service demanded per period by all the households buying in the market for that good or service.*

FIGURE 4.5
Deriving Market Demand from Individual Demand Curves
Total demand in the marketplace is simply the sum of the demands of all the households shopping in a particular market. It is the sum of all the individual demand curves—that is, the sum of all the individual quantities demanded at each price.

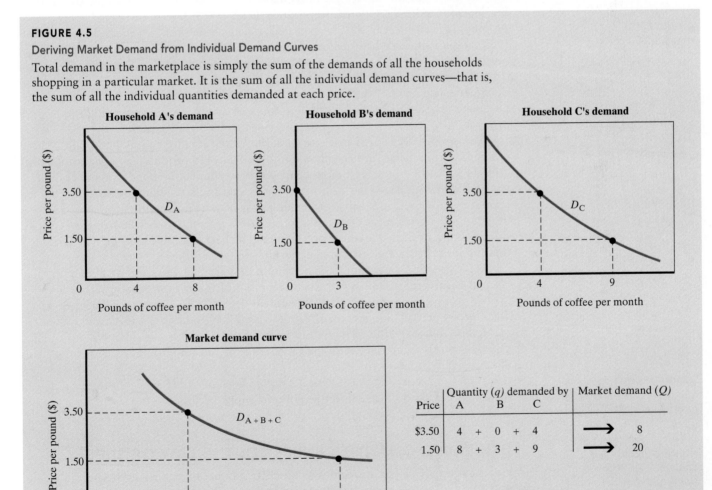

Price	Quantity (q) demanded by			Market demand (Q)
	A	B	C	
$3.50	4 +	0 +	4	→ 8
1.50	8 +	3 +	9	→ 20

market *at that price*. A market demand curve shows the total amount of a product that would be sold at each price if households could buy all they wanted at that price. As Figure 4.5 shows, the market demand curve is the sum of all the individual demand curves—that is, the sum of all the individual quantities demanded at each price. The market demand curve thus takes its shape and position from the shapes, positions, and number of individual demand curves. If more people decide to shop in a market, more demand curves must be added, and the market demand curve will shift to the right. Market demand curves may also shift as a result of preference changes, income changes, or changes in the number of demanders.

As a general rule throughout this book, capital letters refer to the entire market and lowercase letters refer to individual households or firms. Thus, in Figure 4.5, Q refers to total quantity demanded in the market, while q refers to the quantity demanded by individual households.

SUPPLY IN PRODUCT/OUTPUT MARKETS

In addition to dealing with households' demands for outputs, economic theory deals with the behavior of business firms, which supply in output markets and demand in input markets (see again Figure 4.1). Firms engage in production, and we assume that they do so for profit. Successful firms make profits because they are able to sell their products for more than it costs to produce them.

Supply decisions can thus be expected to depend on profit potential. Because **profit** is the simple difference between revenues and costs, supply is likely to react to changes in revenues and changes in production costs. The amount of revenue earned by a firm depends on the price of its product in the market and on how much it sells. Costs of production depend on many factors, the most important of which are (1) the kinds of inputs needed to produce the product, (2) the amount of each input required, and (3) the prices of inputs.

The supply decision is just one of several decisions that firms make in order to maximize profit. There are usually a number of ways to produce any given product. A golf course can be built by hundreds of workers with shovels and grass seed or by a few workers with heavy earth-moving equipment and sod blankets. Hamburgers can be individually fried by a short-order cook or grilled by the hundreds on a mechanized moving grill. Firms must choose the production technique most appropriate to their products and projected levels of production. The best method of production is the one that minimizes cost, thus maximizing profit.

Which production technique is best, in turn, depends on the prices of inputs. Where labor is cheap and machinery is expensive and difficult to transport, firms are likely to choose production techniques that use a great deal of labor. Where machines are available and labor is scarce or expensive, they are likely to choose more capital-intensive methods. Obviously, the technique ultimately chosen determines input requirements. Thus, by choosing an output supply target and the most appropriate technology, firms determine which inputs to demand.

With the caution that no decision exists in a vacuum, let us begin our examination of firm behavior by focusing on the output supply decision and the relationship between quantity supplied and output price, *ceteris paribus*.

PRICE AND QUANTITY SUPPLIED: THE LAW OF SUPPLY

Quantity supplied is the amount of a particular product that a firm would be willing and able to offer for sale at a particular price during a given time period. A **supply schedule** shows how much of a product a firm will supply at alternative prices. Table 4.3 itemizes the quantities of soybeans that an individual farmer such as Clarence Brown might

profit *The difference between revenues and costs.*

quantity supplied *The amount of a particular product that a firm would be willing and able to offer for sale at a particular price during a given time period.*

supply schedule *A table showing how much of a product firms will supply at different prices.*

supply at various prices. If the market paid $1.50 or less a bushel for soybeans, Brown would not supply any soybeans. For one thing, it costs more than $1.50 to produce a bushel of soybeans; for another, Brown can use his land more profitably to produce something else. At $1.75 per bushel, however, at least some soybean production takes place on Brown's farm, and a price increase from $1.75 to $2.25 per bushel causes the quantity supplied by Brown to increase from 10,000 to 20,000 bushels per year. The higher price may justify shifting land from wheat to soybean production or putting previously fallow land into soybeans. Or it may lead to more intensive farming of land already in soybeans, using expensive fertilizer or equipment that was not cost-justified at the lower price.

Generalizing from Farmer Brown's experience, we can reasonably expect an increase in market price, *ceteris paribus*, to lead to an increase in quantity supplied. In other words, there is a positive relationship between the quantity of a good supplied and price. This statement sums up the **law of supply**: An increase in market price will lead to an increase in quantity supplied, and a decrease in market price will lead to a decrease in quantity supplied.

The information in a supply schedule may be presented graphically in a **supply curve**. Supply curves slope upward. The upward, or positive, slope of Brown's curve in Figure 4.6 reflects this positive relationship between price and quantity supplied.

Note in Brown's supply schedule, however, that when price rises from $4 to $5, quantity supplied no longer increases. Often an individual firm's ability to respond to an increase in price is constrained by its existing scale of operations, or capacity, in the short run. For example, Brown's ability to produce more soybeans depends on the size of his farm, the fertility of his soil, and the types of equipment he has. The fact that output stays constant at 45,000 bushels per year suggests that he is running up against the limits imposed by the size of his farm, the quality of his soil, and his existing technology.

TABLE 4.3

CLARENCE BROWN'S SUPPLY SCHEDULE FOR SOYBEANS

PRICE (PER BUSHEL)	QUANTITY SUPPLIED (BUSHELS PER YEAR)
$1.50	0
1.75	10,000
2.25	20,000
3.00	30,000
4.00	45,000
5.00	45,000

law of supply *The positive relationship between price and quantity of a good supplied: An increase in market price will lead to an increase in quantity supplied, and a decrease in market price will lead to a decrease in quantity supplied.*

supply curve *A graph illustrating how much of a product a firm will supply at different prices.*

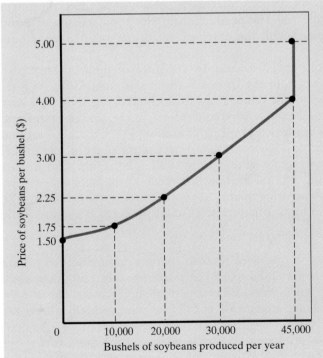

FIGURE 4.6

Clarence Brown's Individual Supply Curve

A producer will supply more when the price of output is higher. The slope of a supply curve is positive. Note that the supply curve is red: Supply is determined by choices made by firms.

In the longer run, however, Brown may acquire more land, or technology may change, allowing for more soybean production. The terms *short run* and *long run* have very precise meanings in economics; we will discuss them in detail later. Here it is important only to understand that time plays a critical role in supply decisions. When prices change, firms' immediate response may be different from what they are able to do after a month or a year. Short-run and long-run supply curves are often different.

OTHER DETERMINANTS OF FIRM SUPPLY

Of the factors we've listed that are likely to affect the quantity of output supplied by a given firm, we have thus far discussed only the price of output. Other factors that affect supply include the cost of producing the product and the prices of related products.

▶ **The Cost of Production** Regardless of the price that a firm can command for its product, price must exceed the cost of producing the output for the firm to make a profit. Thus, the supply decision is likely to change in response to changes in the cost of production. Cost of production depends on a number of factors, including the available technologies and the price of the inputs needed by the firm (labor, land, capital, energy, and so forth).

Technological change can have an enormous impact on the cost of production over time. Consider agriculture. The introduction of fertilizers, the development of complex farm machinery, and the use of bioengineering to increase the yield of individual crops have all powerfully affected the cost of producing agricultural products. Farm productivity in the United States has been increasing dramatically for decades. Yield per acre of corn production has increased fivefold since the late 1930s, and the amount of labor required to produce 100 bushels of corn has fallen from 108 hours in the late 1930s, to 20 hours in the late 1950s, to less than 3 hours today.

When a technological advance lowers the cost of production, output is likely to increase. When yield per acre increases, individual farmers can and do produce more. The output of the Ford Motor Company increased substantially after the introduction of assembly line techniques. The production of electronic calculators, and later personal computers, boomed with the development of inexpensive techniques to produce microprocessors.

Cost of production is also affected directly by the price of the factors of production. During 1994 timber prices in the United States rose dramatically. As a result, the cost of building new homes jumped significantly and the supply of new homes dropped. Also, in 1996, due to a very cold winter in the United States and Europe, demand pushed the world price of oil from around $17 a barrel to around $26. As a result, cab drivers faced higher gasoline prices, airlines faced higher fuel costs, and manufacturing firms faced higher heating bills. The result: Cab drivers probably spent less time driving around looking for fares, airlines cut a few low-profit routes, and some manufacturing plants stopped running extra shifts. The moral of this story: Increases in input prices raise costs of production and are likely to reduce supply.

▶ **The Prices of Related Products** Firms often react to changes in the prices of related products. For example, if land can be used for either corn or soybean production, an increase in soybean prices may cause individual farmers to shift acreage out of corn production and into soybeans. Thus, an increase in soybean prices actually affects the amount of corn supplied.

Similarly, if beef prices rise, producers may respond by raising more cattle. But leather comes from cowhide. Thus, an increase in beef prices may actually increase the supply of leather.

FAST FACTS

Technical change often leads to increased worker productivity and lower costs. A rough measure is "output per hour" of worker time. The total change in output per hour for workers in several industries between 1975 and 1994 was:

Telephone	+175%
Soft drinks	+167
Synthetic fibers	+155
Steel	+144
Air transport	+90
Concrete	+18
Bakery	+11
Lodging	+10
Dining	−11
Food stores	−13

Source: U.S. Bureau of Labor Statistics, *Productivity Measures for Selected Industries and Government Services*, June 1996.

To summarize:

> Assuming that its objective is to maximize profits, a firm's decision about what quantity of output, or product, to supply depends on
>
> 1. The price of the good or service
> 2. The cost of producing the product, which in turn depends on
>   - The price of required inputs (labor, capital, and land), and
>   - The technologies that can be used to produce the product
> 3. The prices of related products

SHIFT OF SUPPLY VERSUS MOVEMENT ALONG A SUPPLY CURVE

A supply curve shows the relationship between the quantity of a good or service supplied by a firm and the price that good or service brings in the market. Higher prices are likely to lead to an increase in quantity supplied, *ceteris paribus*. Remember: The supply curve is derived holding everything constant except price. When the price of a product changes *ceteris paribus*, a change in the quantity supplied follows—that is, a *movement along* the supply curve takes place. But, as you have seen, supply decisions are also influenced by factors other than price. New relationships between price and quantity supplied come about when factors other than price change, and the result is a *shift* of the supply curve. When factors other than price cause supply curves to shift, we say that there has been a *change in supply*.

Recall that the cost of production depends on the price of inputs and the technologies of production available. Now suppose that a major breakthrough in the production of soybeans has occurred: Genetic engineering has produced a superstrain of disease- and pest-resistant seed. Such a technological change would enable individual farmers to supply more soybeans at *any* market price. Table 4.4 and Figure 4.7 describe this change. At $3 a bushel, farmers would have produced 30,000 bushels from the old seed (schedule S_1 in Table 4.4); with the lower cost of production and higher yield resulting from the new seed, they produce 40,000 bushels (schedule S_2 in Table 4.4). At $1.75 per bushel, they would have produced 10,000 bushels from the old seed; but with the lower costs and higher yields, output rises to 23,000 bushels.

Increases in input prices may also cause supply curves to shift. If Farmer Brown faces higher fuel costs, for example, his supply curve will shift to the left—that is, he will produce less at any given market price. If Brown's soybean supply curve shifted far enough to the left, it would intersect the price axis at a higher point, meaning that it would take a higher market price to induce Brown to produce any soybeans at all.

TABLE 4.4 SHIFT OF SUPPLY SCHEDULE FOR SOYBEANS FOLLOWING DEVELOPMENT OF A NEW DISEASE-RESISTANT SEED STRAIN

Price (Per Bushel)	SCHEDULE S_1 Quantity Supplied (Bushels Per Year Using Old Seed)	SCHEDULE S_2 Quantity Supplied (Bushels Per Year Using New Seed)
$1.50	0	5,000
1.75	10,000	23,000
2.25	20,000	33,000
3.00	30,000	40,000
4.00	45,000	54,000
5.00	45,000	54,000

FIGURE 4.7

Shift of Supply Curve for Soybeans Following Development of a New Seed Strain

When the price of a product changes, we move *along* the supply curve for that product; the quantity supplied rises or falls. When any other factor affecting supply changes, the supply curve *shifts*.

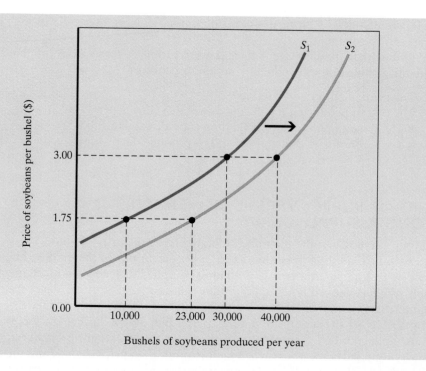

As with demand, it is very important to distinguish between *movements along* supply curves (changes in quantity supplied) and *shifts in* supply curves (changes in supply):

Change in price of a good or service

leads to

⟶ Change in *quantity supplied* (**Movement along a supply curve**).

Change in costs, input prices, technology, or prices of related goods and services

leads to

⟶ Change in *supply* (**Shift of supply curve**).

FROM INDIVIDUAL FIRM SUPPLY TO MARKET SUPPLY

market supply *The sum of all that is supplied each period by all producers of a single product.*

Market supply is determined in the same fashion as market demand. It is simply the sum of all that is supplied each period by all producers of a single product. Figure 4.8 derives a market supply curve from the supply curves of three individual firms. (In a market with more firms, total market supply would be the sum of the amounts produced by each of the firms in that market.) As the table in Figure 4.8 shows, at a price of $3 farm A supplies 30,000 bushels of soybeans, farm B supplies 10,000 bushels, and farm C supplies 25,000 bushels. At this price, the total amount supplied in the market is 30,000 + 10,000 + 25,000, or 65,000 bushels. At a price of $1.75, however, the total amount supplied is only 25,000 bushels (10,000 + 5,000 + 10,000). The market supply curve is thus the simple addition of the individual supply curves of all the firms in a particular market—that is, the sum of all the individual quantities supplied at each price.

The position and shape of the market supply curve depend on the positions and shapes of the individual firms' supply curves from which it is derived. But they also depend on the number of firms that produce in that market. If firms that produce for a particular market are earning high profits, other firms may be tempted to go into that line of business. When the technology to produce computers for home use became available,

Firm A's supply

Firm B's supply

Firm C's supply

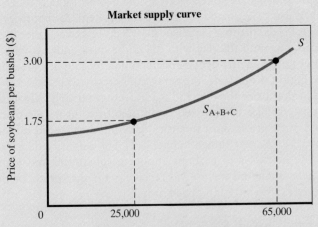

Market supply curve

Price	Quantity (q) supplied by			Market supply (Q)
	A	B	C	
$3.00	30,000 +	10,000 +	25,000	→ 65,000
1.75	10,000 +	5,000 +	10,000	→ 25,000

FIGURE 4.8

Deriving Market Supply from Individual Firm Supply Curves

Total supply in the marketplace is the sum of all the amounts supplied by all the firms selling in the market. It is the sum of all the individual quantities supplied at each price.

literally hundreds of new firms got into the act. The popularity and profitability of professional football has three times led to the formation of new leagues. When new firms enter an industry, the supply curve shifts to the right. When firms go out of business, or "exit" the market, the supply curve shifts to the left.

MARKET EQUILIBRIUM

So far we have identified a number of factors that influence the amount that households demand and the amount that firms supply in product (output) markets. The discussion has emphasized the role of market price as a determinant both of quantity demanded and quantity supplied. We are now ready to see how supply and demand in the market interact to determine the final market price.

We have been very careful in our discussions thus far to separate household decisions about how much to demand from firm decisions about how much to supply. The operation of the market, however, clearly depends on the interaction between suppliers and demanders. At any moment, one of three conditions prevails in every market: (1) The quantity demanded exceeds the quantity supplied at the current price, a situation called *excess demand*; (2) The quantity supplied exceeds the quantity demanded at the current price, a situation called *excess supply*; or (3) the quantity supplied equals the quantity demanded at the current price, a situation called **equilibrium**. At equilibrium, no tendency for price to change exists.

equilibrium *The condition that exists when quantity supplied and quantity demanded are equal. At equilibrium, there is no tendency for price to change.*

excess demand or **shortage** *The condition that exists when quantity demanded exceeds quantity supplied at the current price.*

EXCESS DEMAND

Excess demand, or a **shortage**, exists when quantity demanded is greater than quantity supplied at the current price. Figure 4.9, which plots both a supply curve and a demand curve on the same graph, illustrates such a situation. As you can see, market demand at $1.75 per bushel (50,000 bushels) exceeds the amount that farmers are currently supplying (25,000 bushels).

When excess demand occurs in an unregulated market, there is a tendency for price to rise as demanders compete against each other for the limited supply. The adjustment mechanisms may differ, but the outcome is always the same. For example, consider the mechanism of an auction. In an auction, items are sold directly to the highest bidder. When the auctioneer starts the bidding at a low price, many people bid for the item. At first there is a shortage: Quantity demanded exceeds quantity supplied. As would-be buyers offer higher and higher prices, bidders drop out, until the one who offers the most ends up with the item being auctioned. Price rises until quantity demanded and quantity supplied are equal.

At a price of $1.75 (see Figure 4.9 again), farmers produce soybeans at a rate of 25,000 bushels per year, but at that price the demand is for 50,000 bushels. Most farm products are sold to local dealers who in turn sell large quantities in major market centers, where bidding would push prices up if quantity demanded exceeded quantity supplied. As price rises above $1.75, two things happen: (1) The quantity demanded falls as buyers drop out of the market and perhaps choose a substitute, and (2) the quantity supplied increases as farmers find themselves receiving a higher price for their product and shift additional acres into soybean production.[5]

FIGURE 4.9

Excess Demand, or Shortage

At a price of $1.75 per bushel, quantity demanded exceeds quantity supplied. When *excess demand* arises, there is a tendency for price to rise. When quantity demanded equals quantity supplied, excess demand is eliminated and the market is in equilibrium. Here, the equilibrium price is $2.50, and the equilibrium quantity is 35,000 bushels.

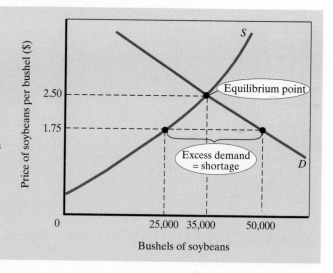

[5]Once farmers have produced in any given season, they cannot change their minds and produce more, of course. When we derived Clarence Brown's supply schedule in Table 4.3, we imagined him reacting to prices that existed at the time he decided how much land to plant in soybeans. In Figure 4.9, the upward slope shows that higher prices justify shifting land from other crops. Final price may not be determined until final production figures are in. For our purposes here, however, we have ignored this timing problem. The best way to think about it is that demand and supply are *flows*, or *rates*, of production—that is, we are talking about the number of bushels produced *per production period*. Adjustments in the rate of production may take place over a number of production periods.

BIDDING AT AN AUCTION IS ONE WAY TO QUICKLY ELIMINATE EXCESS DEMAND.

This process continues until the shortage is eliminated. In Figure 4.9, this occurs at $2.50, where quantity demanded has fallen from 50,000 to 35,000 bushels per year and quantity supplied has increased from 25,000 to 35,000 bushels per year. When quantity demanded and quantity supplied are equal and there is no further bidding, the process has achieved an equilibrium, a situation in which *there is no natural tendency for further adjustment*. Graphically, the point of equilibrium is the point at which the supply curve and the demand curve intersect.

The process through which excess demand leads to higher prices is different in different markets. Consider the market for houses in the hypothetical town of Boomville with a population of 25,000 people, most of whom live in single-family homes. Normally about 75 homes are sold in the Boomville market each year. But last year, a major business opened a plant in town, creating 1,500 new jobs that pay good wages. This attracted new residents to the area, and real estate agents now have more buyers than there are properties for sale. Quantity demanded now exceeds quantity supplied. In other words, there is a shortage.

Auctions are not unheard of in the housing market, but they are rare. This market usually works more subtly, but the outcome is the same. Properties are sold very quickly and housing prices begin to rise. Boomville sellers soon learn that there are more buyers than usual, and they begin to hold out for higher offers. As prices for Boomville houses rise, quantity demanded eventually drops off and quantity supplied increases. Quantity supplied increases in at least two ways: (1) Encouraged by the high prices, builders begin constructing new houses, and (2) some people, attracted by the higher prices their homes will fetch, put their houses on the market. Discouraged by higher prices, however, some potential buyers (demanders) may begin to look for housing in neighboring towns and settle on commuting. Eventually, equilibrium will be reestablished, with the quantity of houses demanded just equal to the quantity of houses supplied.

Although the mechanics of price adjustment in the housing market differ from the mechanics of an auction, the outcome is exactly the same:

When quantity demanded exceeds quantity supplied, price tends to rise. When the price in a market rises, quantity demanded falls and quantity supplied rises until an equilibrium is reached at which quantity demanded and quantity supplied are equal.

CHAPTER FOUR
*Demand, Supply,
and Market Equilibrium*   **87**

This process is called *price rationing*. When a shortage exists, some people will be satisfied and some will not. When the market operates without interference, price increases will distribute what is available to those who are willing and able to pay the most. As long as there is a way for buyers and sellers to interact, those who are willing to pay more will make that fact known somehow. (We discuss the nature of the price system as a rationing device in detail in chapter 5.)

EXCESS SUPPLY

excess supply or **surplus**
The condition that exists when quantity supplied exceeds quantity demanded at the current price.

Excess supply, or a **surplus,** exists when the quantity supplied exceeds the quantity demanded at the current price. As with a shortage, the mechanics of price adjustment in the face of a surplus can differ from market to market. For example, if automobile dealers find themselves with unsold cars in the fall when the new models are coming in, you can expect to see price cuts. Sometimes dealers offer discounts to encourage buyers; sometimes buyers themselves simply offer less than the price initially asked. In any event, products do no one any good sitting in dealers' lots or on warehouse shelves. The auction metaphor introduced earlier can also be applied here: If the initial asking price is too high, no one bids, and the auctioneer tries a lower price. It's almost always true, and 1997 was no exception, that certain items do not sell as well as anticipated during the Christmas holidays. After Christmas, most stores have big sales during which they lower the prices of overstocked items. Quantities supplied exceeded quantities demanded at the current prices, so stores cut prices.

Across the state from Boomville is Bustville, where last year a drug manufacturer shut down its operations and 1,500 people found themselves out of work. With no other prospects for work, many residents decided to pack up and move. They put their houses up for sale, but there were few buyers. The result was an excess supply, or surplus, of houses: The quantity of houses supplied exceeded the quantity demanded at the current prices.

As houses sit unsold on the market for months, sellers start to cut their asking prices. Potential buyers begin offering considerably less than sellers are asking. As prices fall, two things are likely to happen. First, the low housing prices may attract new buyers. People who might have bought in a neighboring town see that there are housing bargains to be had in Bustville, and quantity demanded rises in response to price decline. Second, some of those who put their houses on the market may be discouraged by the lower prices and decide to stay in Bustville. Developers are certainly not likely to be building new housing in town. Lower prices thus lead to a decline in quantity supplied as potential sellers pull their houses from the market. This was exactly the situation in New England and California in the early 1990s.

Figure 4.10 illustrates another excess supply/surplus situation. At a price of $3 per bushel, farmers are supplying soybeans at a rate of 40,000 bushels per year, but buyers demand only 20,000. With 20,000 (40,000 minus 20,000) bushels of soybeans going unsold, the market price falls. As price falls from $3 to $2.50, quantity supplied decreases from 40,000 bushels per year to 35,000. The lower price causes quantity demanded to rise from 20,000 to 35,000. At $2.50, quantity demanded and quantity supplied are equal. For the data shown here, then, $2.50 and 35,000 bushels are the equilibrium price and quantity.

Early in 1994, crude oil production worldwide exceeded the quantity demanded, and prices fell significantly as competing producer countries tried to maintain their share of world markets. Although the mechanism by which price is adjusted is different for automobiles, housing, soybeans, and crude oil, the outcome is the same:

When quantity supplied exceeds quantity demanded at the current price, the price tends to fall. When price falls, quantity supplied is likely to decrease and quantity demanded is likely to increase until an equilibrium price is reached where quantity supplied and quantity demanded are equal.

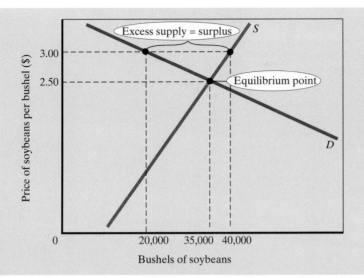

FIGURE 4.10

Excess Supply, or Surplus

At a price of $3, quantity supplied exceeds quantity demanded by 20,000 bushels. This excess supply will cause price to fall.

CHANGES IN EQUILIBRIUM

When supply and demand curves shift, the equilibrium price and quantity change. The following example will help to illustrate this point.

South America is a major producer of coffee beans. A cold snap there can reduce the coffee harvest enough to affect the world price of coffee beans. In the summer of 1994, a major freeze hit Brazil and Colombia and drove up the price of coffee on world markets to a record $2.40 per pound.

Figure 4.11 illustrates how the freeze pushed up coffee prices. Initially, the market was in equilibrium at a price of $1.20. At that price, the quantity demanded was equal to quantity supplied (13.2 billion pounds). At a price of $1.20 and a quantity of 13.2 billion pounds, the demand curve (labeled D) intersected the initial supply curve (labeled S_1). (Remember that equilibrium exists when quantity demanded equals quantity supplied—the point at which the supply and demand curves intersect.)

The freeze caused a decrease in the supply of coffee beans. That is, it caused the supply curve to shift to the left. In Figure 4.11, the new supply curve (the supply curve that shows the relationship between price and quantity supplied after the freeze) is labeled S_2.

At the initial equilibrium price, $1.20, there is now a shortage of coffee. If the price were to remain at $1.20, quantity demanded would not change; it would remain at 13.2 billion pounds. But at that price, quantity supplied would drop to 6.6 billion pounds. At a price of $1.20, quantity demanded is greater than quantity supplied.

When excess demand exists in a market, price can be expected to rise, and rise it did. As the figure shows, price rose to a new equilibrium at $2.40. At $2.40, quantity demanded is again equal to quantity supplied, this time at 9.9 billion pounds—the point at which the new supply curve (S_2) intersects the demand curve.

Notice that as the price of coffee rose from $1.20 to $2.40, two things happened. First, the quantity demanded declined (a movement along the demand curve) as people shifted to substitutes such as tea and hot cocoa. Second, the quantity supplied began to rise, but within the limits imposed by the damage from the freeze. (It might also be that some countries or areas with high costs of production, previously unprofitable, came into production and shipped to the world market at the higher price.) That is, the quantity supplied increased in response to the

FIGURE 4.11

The Coffee Market: A Shift of Supply and Subsequent Price Adjustment

Before the freeze, the coffee market was in equilibrium at a price of $1.20. At that price, quantity demanded equaled quantity supplied. The freeze shifted the supply curve to the left (from S_1 to S_2), increasing equilibrium price to $2.40.

higher price *along* the new supply curve, which lies to the left of the old supply curve. The final result was a higher price ($2.40), a smaller quantity finally exchanged in the market (9.9 billion pounds), and coffee bought only by those willing to pay $2.40 per pound.

Figure 4.12 presents 10 examples of supply and demand shifts and the resulting changes in equilibrium price and quantity. Be sure to go through each graph carefully and ensure that you understand each.

DEMAND AND SUPPLY IN PRODUCT MARKETS: A REVIEW

As you continue your study of economics, you will discover that it is a discipline full of controversy and debate. There is, however, little disagreement about the basic way that the forces of supply and demand operate in free markets. If you hear that a freeze in Florida has destroyed a good portion of the citrus crop, you can bet that the price of oranges will rise.[6] If you read that the weather in the Midwest has been good and a record corn crop is expected, you can bet that corn prices will fall. When fishermen in Massachusetts go on strike and stop bringing in the daily catch, you can bet that the price of fish will go up. For additional examples of how the forces of supply and demand work, see the Application feature titled "Supply and Demand in the News."

---

[6]In economics you have to think twice, however, even about a "safe" bet. If you bet that the price of frozen orange juice will rise after a freeze, you will lose your money. It turns out that much of the crop that is damaged by a freeze can be used, but for only one thing—to make frozen orange juice. Thus, a freeze actually *increases* the supply of frozen juice on the national market. Following the last two hard freezes in Florida, the price of oranges shot up, but the price of orange juice fell sharply!

A. DEMAND SHIFTS

1. Increase in income: X is a normal good

2. Increase in income: X is an inferior good

3. Decrease in income: X is a normal good

4. Decrease in income: X is an inferior good

5. Increase in the price of a substitute for X

6. Increase in the price of a complement for X

7. Decrease in the price of a substitute for X

8. Decrease in the price of a complement for X

B. SUPPLY SHIFTS

9. Increase in the cost of production of X

10. Decrease in the cost of production of X

FIGURE 4.12

Examples of Supply and Demand Shifts for Product X

SUPPLY AND DEMAND IN THE NEWS

The basic forces of supply and demand are at work all around us, as the following news articles illustrate.

1. Supply shifts to the right:

ORANGE JUICE HITS 4-YEAR LOW

Orange juice . . . prices sank yesterday to their lowest level in four years after the Government said a freeze last month would not reduce a record Florida orange crop. . . .

The Department of Agriculture's third forecast since October once again predicted that 220 million boxes of oranges would be harvested in Florida this year. Last year, the state yielded 203.2 million boxes.

The report surprised traders, who expected the agency to lower its forecast by as many as 15 million boxes after the freeze. The agency even raised its estimate for the amount of juice each box would yield, to 1.54 gallons from 1.53 last month.

"The crop is bigger and the yields are higher," said Walter Spilka, an analyst at Smith Barney in New York. "There's no problem in Florida. There's an ocean of orange juice and prices are going to go lower."[a]

2. Demand shifts to the right; supply is expected to shift to the left:

WHETHER CUP OF JOE OR GOURMET'S CAFÉ, ITS PRICE IS SOARING

From a cappuccino grande at Starbucks to a plain cup of black no-sugar at a street vendor's cart, from a pound of Swiss water-processed decaf beans at Zabar's to a can of ground Folgers at the grocery store, the price of coffee is going up. . . .

The price increase, caused in part by increased demand for good coffee and shortages in stockpiles, is the longest sustained price rise in 20 years, and its impact is being felt across the board by importers and roasters, as well as small specialty retailers and consumers. . . .

The price surge began when industry forecasters began projecting smaller crops in Central America during the current season, and in South America in the coming season.[b]

3. Demand shifts to the right, causing short-run inventories to fall; higher prices should increase quantity supplied:

COPPER PRICES MOVE HIGHER

Copper prices rose yesterday after a larger-than-expected drop in stockpiles renewed expectations that demand would keep supplies lean. . . .

Builders are the largest consumers of copper, and last week, the Commerce Department reported that American construction spending rose 2.3 percent in February, the second consecutive increase.

GOOD WEATHER IN FLORIDA MEANS A GOOD HARVEST. SUPPLY SHIFTS TO THE RIGHT AND CAUSES ORANGE PRICES TO DROP.

"Stockpiles are falling because demand in the U.S. is still fairly good and the recent economic data are very constructive," said William O'Neill, director of futures research at Merrill Lynch in New York.[c]

Sources: [a]"Orange Juice Hits 4-Year Low; Crude Oil Slips as Stocks Rise," *The New York Times,* Feb. 13, 1997, p. D15; [b]David Halbfinger, "Whether Cup of Joe or Gourmet's Café, Its Price is Soaring," *The New York Times,* May 13, 1997, p. A1; [c]"Copper Prices Move Higher As Drop in Supply Accelerates," *The New York Times,* April 9, 1997, p. D15. Copyright © 1997 by The New York Times Co. Reprinted by permission.

 For more on recent examples of supply and demand changes, see the Case and Fair Web page at http://www.prenhall.com/casefair.

Here are some important points to remember about the mechanics of supply and demand in product markets:

1. A demand curve shows how much of a product a household would buy if it could buy all it wanted at the given price. A supply curve shows how much of a product a firm would supply if it could sell all it wanted at the given price.
2. Quantity demanded and quantity supplied are always per time period—that is, per day, per month, or per year.

3. The demand for a good is determined by price, household income and wealth, the prices of other goods and services, tastes and preferences, and expectations.
4. The supply of a good is determined by price, costs of production, and the prices of related products. Costs of production are determined by available technologies of production and input prices.
5. Be careful to distinguish between movements along supply and demand curves and shifts of these curves. When the price of a good changes, the quantity of that good demanded or supplied changes—that is, a movement occurs along the curve. When any other factor changes, the curves shift, or change position.
6. Market equilibrium exists only when quantity supplied equals quantity demanded at the current price.

LOOKING AHEAD: MARKETS AND THE ALLOCATION OF RESOURCES

You can already begin to see how markets answer the basic economic questions of what is produced, how it is produced, and who gets what is produced. A firm will produce what is profitable to produce. If it can sell a product at a price that is sufficient to leave a profit after production costs are paid, it will in all likelihood produce that product. Resources will flow in the direction of profit opportunities.

■ Demand curves reflect what people are willing and able to pay for products; they are influenced by incomes, wealth, preferences, the prices of other goods, and expectations. Because product prices are determined by the interaction of supply and demand, prices reflect what people are willing to pay. If people's preferences or incomes change, resources will be allocated differently. Consider, for example, an increase in demand—a shift in the market demand curve. Beginning at an equilibrium, households simply begin buying more. At the equilibrium price, quantity demanded becomes greater than quantity supplied. When there is excess demand, prices will rise, and higher prices mean higher profits for firms in the industry. Higher profits, in turn, provide existing firms with an incentive to expand and new firms with an incentive to enter the industry. Thus, the decisions of independent private firms responding to prices and profit opportunities determine *what* will be produced. No central direction is necessary.

Adam Smith saw this self-regulating feature of markets more than 200 years ago:

> Every individual . . . by pursuing his own interest . . . promotes that of society. He is led . . . by an invisible hand to promote an end which was no part of his intention.[7]

The term Smith coined, the *invisible hand*, has passed into common parlance and is still used by economists to refer to the self-regulation of markets.

■ Firms in business to make a profit have a good reason to choose the best available technology—lower costs mean higher profits. Thus, individual firms determine *how* to produce their products, again with no central direction.
■ So far we have barely touched on the question of distribution—*who* gets what is produced? But you can see part of the answer in the simple supply and demand diagrams. When a good is in short supply, price rises. As it does, those who are willing and able to continue buying do so; others stop buying.

The next chapter begins with a more detailed discussion of these topics. How, exactly, is the final allocation of resources (the mix of output and the distribution of output) determined in a market system?

---

[7]Adam Smith, *The Wealth of Nations*, p. 456.

SUMMARY

1. In societies with many people, production must satisfy wide-ranging tastes and preferences, and producers must therefore specialize.

FIRMS AND HOUSEHOLDS: THE BASIC DECISION-MAKING UNITS

2. A *firm* exists when a person or a group of people decides to produce a product or products by transforming resources, or *inputs*, into *outputs*—the products that are sold in the market. Firms are the primary producing units in a market economy. We assume firms make decisions to maximize profits.

3. *Households* are the primary consuming units in an economy. All households' incomes are subject to constraints.

INPUT MARKETS AND OUTPUT MARKETS: THE CIRCULAR FLOW

4. Households and firms interact in two basic kinds of markets: *product* or *output markets* and *input* or *factor markets*. Goods and services intended for use by households are exchanged in output markets. In output markets, competing firms supply and competing households demand. In input markets, competing firms demand and competing households supply.

5. Ultimately, firms determine the quantities and character of outputs produced, the types and quantities of inputs demanded, and the technologies used in production. Households determine the types and quantities of products demanded and the types and quantities of inputs supplied.

DEMAND IN PRODUCT/OUTPUT MARKETS

6. The quantity demanded of an individual product by an individual household depends on (1) price, (2) income, (3) wealth, (4) the prices of other products, (5) tastes and preferences, and (6) expectations about the future.

7. Quantity demanded is the amount of a product that an individual household would buy in a given period if it could buy all it wanted at the current price.

8. A *demand schedule* shows the quantities of a product that a household would buy at different prices. The same information can be presented graphically in a *demand curve*.

9. The *law of demand* states that there is a negative relationship between price and quantity demanded: As price rises, quantity demanded decreases, and vice versa. Demand curves slope downward.

10. All demand curves eventually intersect the price axis because there is always a price above which a household cannot, or will not, pay. All demand curves also eventually intersect the quantity axis because demand for most goods is limited, if only by time, even at a zero price.

11. When an increase in income causes demand for a good to rise, that good is a *normal good*. When an increase in income causes demand for a good to fall, that good is an *inferior good*.

12. If a rise in the price of good X causes demand for good Y to increase, the goods are *substitutes*. If a rise in the price of X causes demand for Y to fall, the goods are *complements*.

13. Market demand is simply the sum of all the quantities of a good or service demanded per period by all the households buying in the market for that good or service. It is the sum of all the individual quantities demanded at each price.

SUPPLY IN PRODUCT/OUTPUT MARKETS

14. Quantity supplied by a firm depends on (1) the price of the good or service, (2) the cost of producing the product, which includes the prices of required inputs and the technologies that can be used to produce the product, and (3) the prices of related products.

15. Market supply is the sum of all that is supplied each period by all producers of a single product. It is the sum of all the individual quantities supplied at each price.

16. It is very important to distinguish between *movements* along demand and supply curves and *shifts* of demand and supply curves. The demand curve shows the relationship between price and quantity demanded. The supply curve shows the relationship between price and quantity supplied. A change in price is a movement along the curve. Changes in tastes, income, wealth, expectations, or prices of other goods and services cause demand curves to shift; changes in costs, input prices, technology, or prices of related goods and services cause supply curves to shift.

MARKET EQUILIBRIUM

17. When quantity demanded exceeds quantity supplied at the current price, *excess demand* (or a *shortage*) exists and the price tends to rise. When prices in a market rise, quantity demanded falls and quantity supplied rises until an equilibrium is reached at which quantity supplied and quantity demanded are equal. At *equilibrium*, there is no further tendency for price to change.

18. When quantity supplied exceeds quantity demanded at the current price, *excess supply* (or a *surplus*) exists and the price tends to fall. When price falls, quantity supplied decreases and quantity demanded increases until an equilibrium price is reached where quantity supplied and quantity demanded are equal.

REVIEW TERMS AND CONCEPTS

capital market, 69

complements, complementary goods, 75

demand curve, 71

demand schedule, 71

entrepreneur, 68

equilibrium, 86

excess demand or shortage, 86

excess supply or surplus, 88

factors of production, 69

firm, 68

households, 68

income, 74

inferior goods, 74

input or factor markets, 69

labor market, 69

land market, 69

law of demand, 71

law of supply, 81

market demand, 79

market supply, 84

movement along a demand curve, 77

normal goods, 74

perfect substitutes, 75

product or output markets, 69

profit, 80

quantity demanded, 70

quantity supplied, 80

shift of a demand curve, 77

substitutes, 74

supply curve, 81

supply schedule, 80

wealth or net worth, 74

PROBLEM SET

1. Illustrate the following with supply and demand curves:
   a. In 1997 and 1998, the economy expanded, increasing the demand for labor and pushing up wages.
   b. In the mid-1990s, more and more people decided to lease their cars rather than buy them. When leases expire, people usually turn in their cars and lease new ones. During 1997, there was a big increase in used cars available for sale, and the price of used cars dropped sharply.
   c. As more and more people bought home computers during the 1990s, the demand for access to the World Wide Web and the Internet increased sharply. At the same time, new companies like Erol's began to enter the Internet-access market, competing with older, more established services such as America Online. Despite a massive increase in demand, the price of access to the Web actually declined.
   d. Before economic reforms were implemented in the countries of Eastern Europe, regulation held the price of bread substantially below equilibrium. When reforms were implemented, prices were deregulated and they rose dramatically. As a result, the quantity of bread demanded fell and the quantity of bread supplied rose sharply.
   e. Good weather in the Midwest during 1997 produced a very large wheat crop and pushed wheat prices down to below $3.50 per bushel.

2. During the summer of 1997, the Baltimore Orioles and the New York Yankees were battling it out for first place in the American League East. Meanwhile, the Detroit Tigers were in last place. When the Yankees came to Baltimore on September 11 to play the Orioles at Camden Yard (the Baltimore stadium), all 48,000 tickets to the game were sold out months in advance, and many of the fans who wanted tickets couldn't get them. In contrast, a few weeks earlier, the Orioles had travelled to Detroit to play the Tigers in Tiger Stadium, and the game set a record for low attendance. In fact, only 15,000 went to the game in a stadium that holds 52,000. Assume for simplicity that all tickets to both games sold for $20 each.
   a. Draw supply and demand curves for tickets to each of the two games. Draw one graph for each game. Label the excess demand or excess supply, where appropriate. (*Hint*: Supply is fixed. It does not change with price.)
   b. Is there a pricing policy that would have filled Tiger Stadium for the Detroit game?
   c. The price system was not allowed to work to ration the Yankee tickets to those who would pay the most for them. How do you know this? What might have determined who got the tickets?

3. During 1997, Orlando, Florida was growing rapidly, with new jobs luring young people into the area. Despite increases in population and income growth that expanded demand for housing, the price of existing houses barely increased. Why? Illustrate your answer with supply and demand curves.

4. Do you agree or disagree with each of the following statements? Briefly explain your answers.
   a. The price of a good rises, causing the demand for another good to fall. The two goods are therefore substitutes.
   b. A shift in supply causes the price of a good to fall. The shift must have been an increase in supply.
   c. During 1997, incomes rose sharply for most Americans. This change would likely lead to an increase in the prices of both normal and inferior goods.
   d. Two normal goods cannot be substitutes for each other.
   e. If demand increases and supply increases at the same time, price will clearly rise.
   f. The price of Good A falls. This causes an increase in the price of Good B. Goods A and B are therefore complements.

5. The U.S. government administers two programs that affect the market for cigarettes. Media campaigns and labeling requirements are aimed at making the public aware of the health dangers of cigarettes. At the same time, the Department of Agriculture maintains price supports for

tobacco. Under this program, the supported price is above the market equilibrium price, and the government limits the amount of land that can be devoted to tobacco production. Are these two programs at odds with respect to the goal of reducing cigarette consumption? As a part of your answer, illustrate graphically the effects of both policies on the market for cigarettes.

6. Housing prices in Boston and Los Angeles have been on a roller coaster ride. Illustrate each of the following situations with supply and demand curves:
   a. In both cities an increase in income combined with expectations of a strong market shifted demand and caused prices to rise rapidly during the mid- to late 1980s.
   b. By 1990, the construction industry boomed as more and more developers started new residential projects. But those new projects expanded the supply of housing just as demand was shifting as a result of falling incomes and expectations during the 1990 to 1991 recession.
   c. In 1997, housing in higher-income towns in the Boston area was experiencing price increases at the same time as housing prices in lower income towns were experiencing price decreases. In part this effect was due to "trade-up" buyers selling houses in lower-income areas and buying houses in higher-income areas.
   d. Despite falling incomes, housing markets in lower-income areas in Los Angeles were actually experiencing some price increases in 1994 and 1995 as immigration of lower-income households continued.

7. The following two sets of statements contain common errors. Identify and explain each.
   a. Demand increases, causing prices to rise. Higher prices cause demand to fall. Therefore, prices fall back to their original levels.
   b. The supply of meat in Russia increases, causing meat prices to fall. Lower prices mean that Russian households spend more on meat.

8. For each of the following, draw a diagram that illustrates the likely effect on the market for eggs. Indicate in each case the impact on equilibrium price and equilibrium quantity.
   a. A surgeon general warning that high-cholesterol foods cause heart attacks.
   b. A decrease in the price of bacon, a complementary product.
   c. An increase in the price of chicken feed.
   d. Caesar salads become trendy at dinner parties. (The dressing is made with raw eggs.)
   e. A technological innovation that reduces egg breakage during packing.

9. "An increase in demand causes an increase in price. But an increase in price causes a decrease in demand. Increases in demand, therefore, largely cancel themselves out." Comment.

*10. Suppose the demand and supply curves for eggs in the United States are given by the following equations:

$$Q_d = 100 - 20P$$
$$Q_s = 10 + 40P$$

where Q_d = millions of dozens of eggs Americans would like to buy each year; Q_s = millions of dozens of eggs U.S. farms would like to sell each year; P = price per dozen eggs.
   a. Fill in the following table:

PRICE (PER DOZEN)	QUANTITY DEMANDED (Q_d)	QUANTITY SUPPLIED (Q_s)
$ .50	_____	_____
$1.00	_____	_____
$1.50	_____	_____
$2.00	_____	_____
$2.50	_____	_____

   b. Use the information in the table to find the equilibrium price and equilibrium quantity.
   c. Graph the demand and supply curves, and identify the equilibrium price and quantity.

*11. Housing policy analysts debate the best way to increase the number of housing units available to low-income households. One strategy—the demand-side strategy—is to provide people with housing "vouchers," paid for by the government, that can be used to rent housing supplied by the private market. Another—a supply-side strategy—is to have the government subsidize housing suppliers or to build public housing.
   a. Illustrate supply- and demand-side strategies using supply and demand curves. Which results in higher rents?
   b. Critics of housing vouchers (the demand-side strategy) argue that because the supply of housing to low-income households is limited and will not respond at all to higher rents, demand vouchers will serve only to drive up rents and make landlords better off. Illustrate their point with supply and demand curves.

*12. Suppose the market demand for pizza is given by $Q_d = 300 - 20P$ and the market supply for pizza is given by $Q_s = 20P - 100$, where P = price (per pizza).
   a. Graph the supply and demand schedules for pizza using $5 through $15 as the value of P.
   b. In equilibrium, how many pizzas would be sold and at what price?
   c. What would happen if suppliers set the price of pizza at $15? Explain the market adjustment process.
   d. Suppose the price of hamburgers, a substitute for pizza, doubles. This leads to a doubling of the demand for pizza (at each price consumers demand twice as much pizza as before). Write the equation for the new market demand for pizza.
   e. Find the new equilibrium price and quantity of pizza.

_____

*Note: Problems marked with an asterisk are more challenging.

TAKE IT TO THE NET

We invite you to visit the Case and Fair page on the Prentice Hall Web site:
http://www.prenhall.com/casefair
for this chapter's World Wide Web exercise.

Chapter

5

SUPPLY, DEMAND, AND THE PRICE SYSTEM

EVERY SOCIETY has a system of institutions that determines what is produced, how it is produced, and who gets what is produced. In some societies, these decisions are made centrally, through planning agencies or by government directive. But in every society many decisions are made in a *decentralized* way, through the operation of markets.

Markets exist in all societies, and chapter 4 provided a bare-bones description of how markets operate. In this chapter, we continue our examination of supply, demand, and the price system.

THE PRICE SYSTEM: RATIONING AND ALLOCATING RESOURCES

The market system, also called the *price system*, performs two important and closely related functions. First, it provides an automatic mechanism for distributing scarce goods and services. That is, it serves as a **price rationing** device for allocating goods and services to consumers when the quantity demanded exceeds the quantity supplied. Second, the price system ultimately determines both the allocation of resources among producers and the final mix of outputs.

price rationing *The process by which the market system allocates goods and services to consumers when quantity demanded exceeds quantity supplied.*

PRICE RATIONING

Consider first the simple process by which the price system eliminates a shortage. Figure 5.1 shows hypothetical supply and demand curves for lobsters caught off the coast of New England.

Lobsters are considered a delicacy. Maine produces most of the lobster catch in the United States, and anyone who drives up the Maine coast cannot avoid the hundreds of restaurants selling lobster rolls, steamed lobster, and baked stuffed lobster.

As Figure 5.1 shows, the equilibrium price of live New England lobsters was $3.27 per pound in 1998. At this price, lobster boats brought in lobsters at a rate of 47 million pounds per year—an amount that was just enough to satisfy demand.

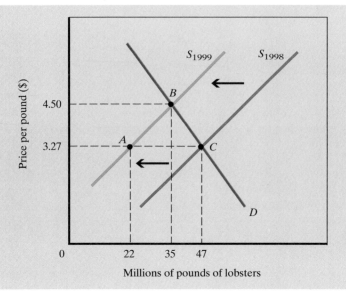

FIGURE 5.1

The Market for Lobsters

Suppose that in 1999, 20,000 square miles of lobstering waters off the coast of Maine are closed. The supply curve shifts to the left. Before the waters are closed, the lobster market is in equilibrium at the price of $3.27 and a quantity of 47 million pounds. The decreased supply of lobster leads to higher prices, and a new equilibrium is reached at $4.50 and 35 million pounds.

Market equilibrium existed at $3.27 per pound, because at that price quantity demanded was equal to quantity supplied. (Remember that equilibrium occurs at the point where the supply and demand curves intersect. In Figure 5.1, this occurs at point C.)

Now suppose that in 1999 the waters off a section of the Maine coast become contaminated with a poisonous parasite. As a result, the Department of Agriculture is forced to close 20,000 square miles of the most productive lobstering areas. Even though many of the lobster boats shift their trapping activities to other waters, there is a sharp reduction in the quantity of lobster supplied. The supply curve shifts to the left, from S_{1998} to S_{1999}. This shift in the supply curve creates a situation of excess demand at $3.27. At that price, the quantity demanded is 47 million pounds and the quantity supplied is 22 million pounds. Quantity demanded exceeds quantity supplied by 25 million pounds.

The reduced supply causes the price of lobster to rise sharply. As the price rises, the available supply is "rationed." Who gets it? Those who are willing and able to pay the most.

You can see the market's price rationing function clearly in Figure 5.1. As the price rises from $3.27, the quantity demanded declines along the demand curve, moving from point C (47 million pounds) toward point B (35 million pounds). The higher prices mean that restaurants must charge much more for lobster rolls and stuffed lobsters. As a result, many people simply stop buying lobster or order it less frequently when they dine out. Some restaurants drop it from the menu entirely, and some shoppers at the fish counter turn to lobster substitutes such as swordfish and salmon.

As the price rises, lobster trappers (suppliers) also change their behavior. They stay out longer and put out more traps than they did when the price was $3.27 per pound. Quantity supplied increases from 22 million pounds to 35 million pounds. This increase in price brings about a movement along the 1999 supply curve from point A to point B.

Finally, a new equilibrium is established at a price of $4.50 per pound and a total output of 35 million pounds. The market has determined who gets the lobsters: *The lower total supply is rationed to those who are willing and able to pay the higher price.*

This idea of "willingness to pay" is central to the distribution of available supply, and willingness depends on both desire (preferences) and income/wealth. Willingness to pay does not necessarily mean that only the very rich will continue to buy lobsters when the price increases. Lower-income people may continue to buy some lobster, but they will have to be willing to sacrifice more of other goods to do so.

In sum:

> The adjustment of price is the rationing mechanism in free markets. Price rationing means that whenever there is a need to ration a good—that is, when a shortage exists—in a free market, the price of the good will rise until quantity supplied equals quantity demanded—that is, until the market clears.

There is some price that will clear any market you can think of. Consider the market for a famous painting such as van Gogh's *Portrait of Dr. Gachet*, illustrated in Figure 5.2. At a low price, there would be an enormous excess demand for such an important painting. The price would be bid up until there was only one remaining demander. Presumably, that price would be very high. In fact, van Gogh's *Portrait of Dr. Gachet* sold for a record $82.5 million in 1990. If the product is in strictly scarce supply, as a single painting is, its price is said to be *demand determined*. That is, its price is determined solely and exclusively by the amount that the highest bidder or highest bidders are willing to pay.

One might interpret the statement that "there is some price that will clear any market" to mean "everything has its price." But that is not exactly what it means. Suppose you own a small silver bracelet that has been in your family for generations. It is quite possible that you wouldn't sell it for *any* amount of money. Does this mean that the market is not working, or that quantity supplied and quantity demanded are not equal? Not at all. It means simply that *you* are the highest bidder. By turning down all bids, you must be willing to forgo what anybody offers for it.

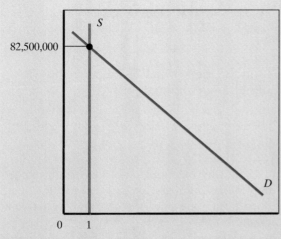

WHEN SUPPLY IS FIXED OR SOMETHING FOR SALE IS UNIQUE, ITS PRICE IS *DEMAND DETERMINED*. PRICE IS WHAT THE HIGHEST BIDDER IS WILLING TO PAY. IN 1990, THE HIGHEST BIDDER WAS WILLING TO PAY $82.5 MILLION FOR VAN GOGH'S *PORTRAIT OF DR. GACHET*.

CONSTRAINTS ON THE MARKET AND ALTERNATIVE RATIONING MECHANISMS

On occasion, both governments and private firms decide to use some mechanism other than the market system to ration an item for which there is excess demand at the current price. (This was often the case in the former Soviet Union and other Communist nations like China, Cuba, Poland, and East Germany. For more information, see the Global Perspective box titled "The Market Comes to China.") Policies designed to stop price rationing are commonly justified in a number of ways.

The rationale most often used is fairness. It is not "fair" to let landlords charge high rents, not "fair" for oil companies to run up the price of gasoline, not "fair" for insurance companies to charge enormous premiums, and so on. After all, the argument goes, we have no choice but to pay—housing and insurance are necessary, and one

FIGURE 5.2

Market for a Rare Painting

There is some price that will clear any market, even if supply is strictly limited. In an auction for a unique painting, the price (bid) will rise to eliminate excess demand until there is only one bidder willing to purchase the single available painting.

Quantity of Van Gogh's Portrait of Dr. Gachet

(Graph axis label: 82,500,000; curves labeled S and D; points 0 and 1 on horizontal axis)

THE MARKET COMES TO CHINA

Price rationing allocates goods and services to those who are willing and able to pay for them. One of the central premises of communism is that price rationing for basic necessities, such as food, is unfair; everyone should be able to afford such items as food and shelter. But regulating prices to "fair" levels below equilibrium means that quantity supplied will be less than quantity demanded.

In addition, preventing the price mechanism from operating requires that some device other than price be used to ration the available goods. Before the collapse of communism in the Soviet Union and Eastern Europe, people waited in long lines at state stores, which could not meet the citizens' demands. The stores were not well stocked in part because farmers could get a much better price for their goods on the illegal black market. The biggest problem with regulated prices, however, is that the incentive to produce is lost.

In 1997, China's paramount leader Deng Xiaoping died. More than any other leader in the communist world, Deng understood the importance of market prices as an incentive. In 1978, local officials associated with Deng began allowing poor rural peasants to grow grain on their own individual plots of land. The peasants could not own the land, and the government took a fixed amount of the grain they produced as a tax. But they were permitted to sell all surpluses in private markets at market prices. This policy had a dramatic effect on the level of output. As prices increased, so did the quantity supplied. Productivity soared, and Chinese agriculture began to grow dramatically.

Deng also knew that the industrial sector could not function without market prices playing a role. As of 1997, markets—not bureaucracies—determined the prices of nearly nine-tenths of all finished goods in China.

For the 75 percent of Chinese who make their living from the land, incomes have gone up over 200 percent since 1978, to $1,000 per year. Industrial incomes have risen even more. China's economy has grown at an average rate of over 9 percent since 1982. In 1997, it grew at an impressive 10 percent annual rate.

Source: "Deng's China," *The Economist,* February, 1997.

For more on recent changes in China, see the Case and Fair Web page at
http://www.prenhall.com/casefair.

needs gasoline to get to work. While it is not precisely true that price rationing allocates goods and services solely on the basis of income and wealth, income and wealth do constrain our wants. Why should all the gasoline or all the tickets to the World Series go just to the rich?

Various schemes to keep price from rising to equilibrium are based on several perceptions of injustice, among them (1) that price-gouging is bad, (2) that income is unfairly distributed, and (3) that some items are necessities, and everyone should be able to buy them at a "reasonable" price. Regardless of the rationale, the following examples will make two things clear:

1. Attempts to bypass price rationing in the market and to use alternative rationing devices are much more difficult and costly than they would seem at first glance.
2. Very often, such attempts distribute costs and benefits among households in unintended ways.

▶ **Oil, Gasoline, and OPEC**   In 1973 and 1974, the Organization of Petroleum Exporting Countries (OPEC) imposed an embargo on shipments of crude oil to the United States. What followed was a drastic reduction in the quantity of gasoline available at local gas pumps.

Had the market system been allowed to operate, refined gasoline prices would have increased dramatically until quantity supplied was equal to quantity demanded.

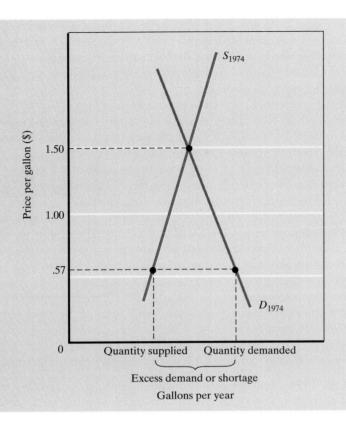

FIGURE 5.3

Excess Demand (Shortage) Created by a Price Ceiling

In 1974, a ceiling price of 57¢ per gallon of leaded regular gasoline was imposed. If the price had instead been set by the interaction of supply and demand, it would have increased to approximately $1.50 per gallon. At 57¢ per gallon, the quantity demanded exceeded the quantity supplied. Because the price system was not allowed to function, an alternative rationing system had to be found to distribute the available supply of gasoline.

But the government decided that rationing gasoline to only those who were willing and able to pay the most was unfair, and Congress imposed a **price ceiling**, or maximum price, of 57¢ per gallon of leaded regular gasoline. That price ceiling was intended to keep gasoline "affordable," but it also perpetuated the shortage. At the restricted price, quantity demanded remained greater than quantity supplied, and the available gasoline had to be divided up somehow among all potential demanders.

You can see the effects of the price ceiling by looking carefully at Figure 5.3. If the price had been set by the interaction of supply and demand, it would have increased to approximately $1.50 per gallon. Instead, Congress made it illegal to sell gasoline for more than 57¢ per gallon. At that price, quantity demanded exceeded quantity supplied and a shortage existed. Because the price system was not allowed to function, an alternative rationing system had to be found to distribute the available supply of gasoline.

Several devices were tried. The most common of all nonprice rationing systems is **queuing**, a term that simply means waiting in line. During 1974 very long lines began to appear at gas stations, starting as early as 5 A.M. Under this system, gasoline went to those who were willing to pay the most, but the sacrifice was measured in hours and aggravation rather than in dollars.[1]

price ceiling *A maximum price that sellers may charge for a good, usually set by government.*

queuing *Waiting in line as a means of distributing goods and services; a nonprice rationing mechanism.*

---

[1]You can also show formally that the result is inefficient—that there is a resulting net loss of total value to society. First, there is the cost of waiting in line. Time has a value. With price rationing, no one has to wait in line and the value of that time is saved. Second, there may be additional lost value if the gasoline ends up in the hands of someone who places a lower value on it than someone else who gets no gas. Suppose, for example, that the market price of gasoline if unconstrained would rise to $2, but that the government has it fixed at $1. There will be long lines to get gas. Imagine that to motorist A, ten gallons of gas is worth $35 but that she fails to get it because her time is too valuable to wait in line. To motorist B, ten gallons is worth only $15, but his time is worth much less, so he gets the gas. Clearly, in the end, A could pay B for the gas and both could be better off. If A pays B $30 for the gas, A is $5 better off and B is $15 better off. In addition, A doesn't have to wait in line. Thus, the allocation that results from nonprice rationing involves a net loss of value. Such losses are called dead weight losses.

favored customers *Those who receive special treatment from dealers during situations of excess demand.*

ration coupons *Tickets or coupons that entitle individuals to purchase a certain amount of a given product per month.*

black market *A market in which illegal trading takes place at market-determined prices.*

Gasoline prices were a major concern in the 1970s. Since 1980, however, gasoline prices have been remarkably stable:

	% Change in:	
	Prices in General	The Price of Gasoline
1980–85	+30.6%	+1.3%
1985–90	+21.5%	+2.5%
1990–95	+16.6%	−1.2%

A second nonprice rationing device used during the gasoline crisis was that of **favored customers**. Many gas station owners decided not to sell gasoline to the general public at all but to reserve their scarce supplies for friends and favored customers. Not surprisingly, many customers tried to become "favored" by offering side payments to gas station owners. Owners also charged high prices for service. By doing so, they increased the real price of gasoline but hid it in service overcharges to get around the ceiling.

Yet another method of dividing up available supply is the use of **ration coupons**. It was suggested in both 1974 and 1979 that families be given ration tickets, or coupons, that would entitle them to purchase a certain number of gallons of gasoline each month. That way, everyone would get the same amount, regardless of income. Such a system had been employed in the United States during the 1940s, when wartime price ceilings on meat, sugar, butter, tires, nylon stockings, and many other items were imposed.

When ration coupons are used with no prohibition against trading them, however, the result is almost identical to a system of price rationing. Those who are willing and able to pay the most simply buy up the coupons and use them to purchase gasoline, chocolate, fresh eggs, or anything else that is sold at a restricted price.[2] This means that the price of the restricted good will effectively rise to the market-clearing price. For instance, suppose that you decide not to sell your ration coupon. You are then forgoing what you would have received by selling the coupon. Thus the "real" price of the good you purchase will be higher (if only in opportunity cost) than the restricted price. Even when trading coupons is declared illegal, it is virtually impossible to stop black markets from developing. In a **black market**, illegal trading takes place at market-determined prices.

▶ **The World Cup, 1994** Another way to understand the price system's rationing function is to look at the ways in which tickets to popular sporting events and concerts are sold and distributed. One of the most interesting recent examples is the 1994 World Cup soccer tournament.

In the summer of 1994, the World Cup came to the United States. The matches took place in nine cities, including Boston, Washington, Chicago, and Los Angeles. A total of 52 games were played among qualifying teams representing 24 countries. The final game between Italy and Brazil was played on July 17 in the Rose Bowl in Pasadena, California. (Brazil won.)

A total of 3.6 million tickets were available for the games. Demand for soccer tickets was very high. Soccer is without question the most popular sport in the world, and it is literally true that wars have been fought because of the outcome of matches. With national pride at stake, tens of thousands of people flocked to the United States. In addition, the sport's growing popularity in the United States led to high ticket demand by U.S. residents. Rather than charging market-clearing prices, the event's organizers decided to charge "fair" prices and set the average ticket price at about $58.

This price was below equilibrium, and there was excess demand for the tickets almost from the time that they went on sale. Interestingly, organizers of similar high-interest sporting events (like the Super Bowl, the NBA playoffs, and the World Series) almost always price tickets below the level that would just fill the stadiums. Why? In their words, to do otherwise would be "unfair." As Alan Rothenberg, chairman of World Cup USA put it: "We definitely could have charged more. . . . Obviously we wanted to price the tickets high enough so we can pay for the event. . . . but at the same time not be unfair to the public."

We have seen, however, that if the price system is not going to be used to allocate the tickets among demanders, another method must be found. One method gives the tickets to certain favored customers. The *Washington Post* (December 25, 1993) reported that 25 percent to 30 percent of the tickets were committed to "corporate sponsors, city

[2]Of course, if you are assigned a number of tickets, and you sell them, you are better off than you would be with price rationing. Ration tickets thus serve as a way of redistributing income.

IF U.S. FANS WERE WILLING TO PAY $3,000 FOR A TICKET TO THE WORLD CUP IN LOS ANGELES IN 1994, WHAT DO YOU THINK THE MORE FRENZIED SOCCER FANS IN EUROPE WILL PAY FOR A TICKET TO THE 1998 FINALS AT THE NEWLY BUILT STADIA FRANCE JUST OUTSIDE OF PARIS?

officials, members of Congress, and other dignitaries." Another 15 percent were held for soccer's world governing body, and yet another 15 percent were held for the "U.S. soccer community"—coaches, officials, and players. The remaining tickets were sold through a mail lottery and, in some cities, by queuing.

The distribution of tickets was not really over until the final match was played. Consider the demand for tickets to the final match that were distributed to fans months earlier. The organizing body did charge more for final game tickets—the price of the cheapest ticket was $180 and the most expensive $475, with the average around $300. But consider the potential demand! As *Worth* magazine (May 1994) put it, "Foreign fans will be waving huge wads of bills near game day." Because the Rose Bowl holds only 91,794 people, by some estimates the equilibrium ticket price was in the vicinity of $3,000!

Figure 5.4 illustrates the situation. The supply curve is vertical at 91,794 tickets—the fixed number of seats available. As the demand curve shows, some people were willing to pay prices far in excess of $3,000—and many did. The *Los Angeles Times* reported that one man paid $250,000 for a set (unspecified number) of tickets. Even before tickets were issued, an extensive and complicated black market had begun operating.

Now consider someone who paid $180 for a final game ticket and went to the game. What price did she really pay to go to the game? The answer: A lot more than $180. By not selling her ticket, she revealed that going to the game was worth more to her than all the other things that $3,000 or $4,000 could buy.

What, then, can we conclude about alternatives to the price rationing system?

No matter how good the intentions of private organizations and governments, it is very difficult to prevent the price system from operating and to stop willingness to pay from asserting itself. Every time an alternative is tried, the price system seems to sneak in the back door. With favored customers and black markets, the final distribution may be even more unfair than that which would result from simple price rationing.

PRICES AND THE ALLOCATION OF RESOURCES

Thinking of the market system as a mechanism for allocating scarce goods and services among competing demanders is very revealing. But the market determines much more than just the distribution of final outputs. It also determines what gets produced and how resources are allocated among competing uses.

FIGURE 5.4

Supply of and Demand for World Cup Final Game Tickets

World Cup 1994 final game tickets were initially sold for an average face price of about $300. The Rose Bowl in Pasadena holds 91,794 people. Thus, the supply curve is vertical at 91,794 tickets. At $300, the quantity demanded far exceeded the quantity supplied. The result was enormous excess demand.

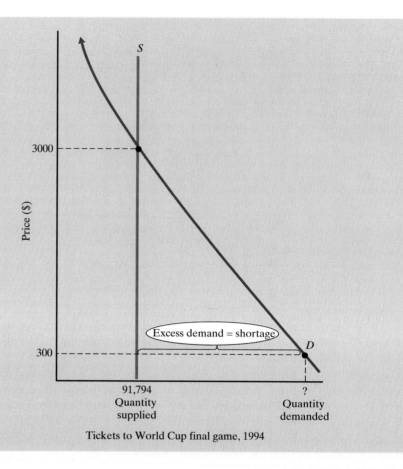

Tickets to World Cup final game, 1994

Consider a change in consumer preferences that leads to an increase in demand for a specific good or service. During the 1970s, for example, people began going to restaurants much more frequently than before. Researchers think that this trend, which continues today, is partially the result of social changes (such as a dramatic rise in the number of two-earner families) and partially the result of rising incomes. The market responded to this change in demand by shifting resources, both capital and labor, into more and better restaurants.

With the increase in demand for restaurant meals, the price of eating out rose, and the restaurant business became more profitable. The higher profits attracted new businesses and provided old restaurants with an incentive to expand. As new capital, seeking profits, flowed into the restaurant business, so too did labor. New restaurants need chefs. Chefs need training, and the higher wages that came with increased demand provided an incentive for them to get it. In response to the increase in demand for training, new cooking schools opened and existing schools began to offer courses in the culinary arts.

This story could run on and on, but the point is clear:

Price changes resulting from shifts of demand in output markets cause profits to rise or fall. Profits attract capital; losses lead to disinvestment. Higher wages attract labor and encourage workers to acquire skills. At the core of the system, supply, demand, and prices in input and output markets determine the allocation of resources and the ultimate combinations of things produced.

SUPPLY AND DEMAND ANALYSIS: AN OIL IMPORT FEE

The basic logic of supply and demand is a powerful tool of analysis. As an extended example of the power of this logic, we will consider a recent proposal to impose a tax on imported oil. The idea of raising the federal gasoline tax is hotly debated, with many arguing strongly for such a tax. Many economists, however, believe that a fee on imported crude oil, which is used to produce gasoline, would have better effects on the economy than would a gasoline tax.

Consider the facts. Between 1985 and 1989, the United States increased its dependence on oil imports dramatically. In 1989, total U.S. demand for crude oil was 13.6 million barrels per day. Of that amount, only 7.7 million barrels per day (57 percent) were supplied by U.S. producers, with the remaining 5.9 million barrels per day (43 percent) imported. The price of oil on world markets that year averaged about $18. This heavy dependence on foreign oil left the United States vulnerable to the price shock that followed the Iraqi invasion of Kuwait in August 1990. In the months following the invasion, the price of crude oil on world markets shot up to $40 per barrel.

Even before the invasion, many economists and some politicians had recommended a stiff oil import fee (or tax) that would, it was argued, reduce the U.S. dependence on foreign oil by (1) reducing overall consumption and (2) providing an incentive for increased domestic production. An added bonus would be improved air quality from the reduction in driving.

Supply and demand analysis makes the arguments of the import fee proponents easier to understand. Part a of Figure 5.5 shows the U.S. market for oil. The world price of oil is assumed to be $18, and the United States is assumed to be able to buy all the oil that it wants at this price. This means that domestic producers cannot get away with charging any more than $18 per barrel. The curve labeled $Supply_{US}$ shows the amount that domestic suppliers will produce at each price level. At a price of $18, domestic production is 7.7 million barrels. Stated somewhat differently, U.S. producers will produce at point A on the supply curve. The total quantity of oil demanded in the United States in 1989 was 13.6 million barrels per day. At a price of $18, the quantity demanded in the United States is point B on the demand curve.

The difference between the total quantity demanded (13.6 million barrels per day) and domestic production (7.7 million barrels per day) is total imports (5.9 million barrels per day).

Now suppose that the government levies a tax of 33 percent on imported oil. Because the import price is $18, a tax of $6 (or .33 × $18) per barrel means that importers of oil in the United States will pay a total of $24 per barrel ($18 + $6). This new higher price means that U.S. producers can also charge up to $24 for a barrel of crude. Note, however, that the tax is paid only on imported oil. Thus the entire $24 paid for domestic crude goes to domestic producers.

Figure 5.5b shows the result of the tax. First, because of higher price the quantity demanded drops to 12.2 million barrels per day. This is a movement *along* the demand curve from point B to point D. At the same time, the quantity supplied by domestic producers increases to 9.0 million barrels per day. This is a movement *along* the supply curve from point A to point C. With an increase in domestic quantity supplied and a decrease in domestic quantity demanded, imports decrease to 3.2 million barrels per day (12.2 − 9.0).[3]

---

[3]These figures were not chosen randomly. It is interesting to note that in 1985 the world price of crude oil averaged about $24 a barrel. Domestic production was 9.0 million barrels per day, and domestic consumption was 12.2 million barrels per day, with imports of only 3.2 million. The drop in the world price between 1985 and 1989 increased imports to 5.9 million, an 84% increase.

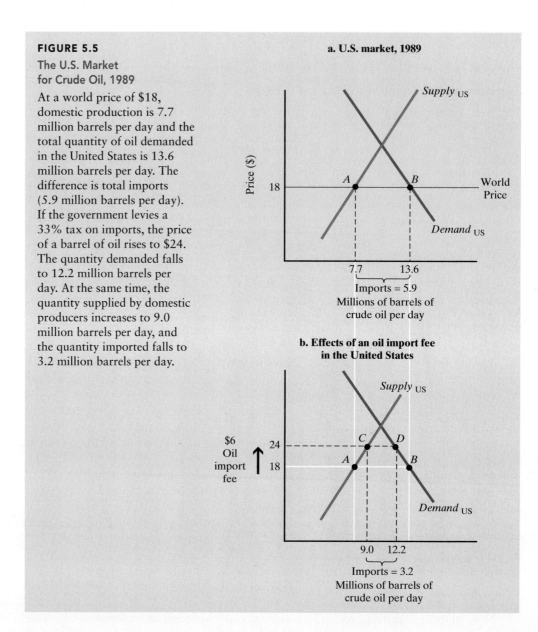

FIGURE 5.5

The U.S. Market for Crude Oil, 1989

At a world price of $18, domestic production is 7.7 million barrels per day and the total quantity of oil demanded in the United States is 13.6 million barrels per day. The difference is total imports (5.9 million barrels per day). If the government levies a 33% tax on imports, the price of a barrel of oil rises to $24. The quantity demanded falls to 12.2 million barrels per day. At the same time, the quantity supplied by domestic producers increases to 9.0 million barrels per day, and the quantity imported falls to 3.2 million barrels per day.

a. U.S. market, 1989

Price ($)

Supply US

18   A   B   World Price

Demand US

7.7   13.6

Imports = 5.9

Millions of barrels of crude oil per day

b. Effects of an oil import fee in the United States

Supply US

$6 Oil import fee   24   C   D

18   A   B

Demand US

9.0   12.2

Imports = 3.2

Millions of barrels of crude oil per day

The tax also generates revenues for the federal government. The total tax revenue collected is equal to the tax per barrel ($6) times the number of imported barrels. When the quantity imported is 3.2 million barrels per day, total revenue is $6 × 3.2 million, or $19.2 million *per day* (about $7 billion per year).

What does all of this mean? In the final analysis, an oil import fee would (1) increase domestic production and (2) reduce overall consumption. This would in turn help with the problem of air pollution and simultaneously reduce U.S. dependence on foreign oil.

LOOKING AHEAD

We have now examined the basic forces of supply and demand and discussed the market/price system. These basic concepts will serve as building blocks for what comes next. Whether you are studying microeconomics or macroeconomics, you will

TRAFFIC CONGESTION AND ORGAN DONATIONS

We can now use what we've learned about the price system to examine two topics of current interest: traffic congestion and organ donations.

TRAFFIC CONGESTION

Very few people in the United States have not had the frustrating experience of sitting in traffic. Indeed, traffic jams are by no means unique to the United States. Some of the worst traffic congestion in the world can be found in Bangkok (Thailand) and Taipei (Taiwan).

Traffic jams are costly. Clearly, time has a value, and the opportunity cost of sitting in traffic for two hours can be significant. A recent study estimated the cost of the morning rush hour in a major U.S. city at over $13 million.

You can think of congestion as "excess demand for road space." That is, at the current price, the quantity demanded exceeds the quantity supplied. The way we currently ration that shortage of space is by waiting in line to use it.

Can we use the price mechanism to help? While this idea goes back at least 100 years, most credit the late Nobel Prize-winning economist William Vickrey for pushing an idea whose time may have finally come. The idea is simple: Charge people a price to use highways . . . a price high enough to keep the traffic flowing. As the price is raised, those who live near public transportation and those who might be able to avoid travelling altogether would avoid the congested roads, at least during peak hours. In essence, quantity demanded will drop. Those who must continue to use the roads will pay, but they will not waste time waiting in traffic.

How might such a price be collected? One obvious answer is a toll. Many states impose tolls for the use of bridges, turnpikes, and thruways, but most prices are low enough that they have little impact on highway use. The city-state of Singapore requires car owners to purchase a very expensive license (mounted on the car's windshield) if they want to drive on downtown streets during peak hours. This system has helped Singapore's congestion problems greatly. Professor Vickrey proposed that every car be equipped with a radio signal that would ring up a charge every time the car passes a designated street corner. The charges could be changed depending on the time of day and the degree of congestion in the area.

With today's small powerful microprocessors, the necessary technology is already here; it is being used by a number of states to speed traffic through toll booths. Many are betting that the next few years will see a dramatic increase in road prices.[a]

ORGAN DONATIONS

Improved medical technology has led to a dramatic increase in the number of organ transplants performed in the United States and elsewhere in the world. The availability of organs is constraining the use of transplants, however. In simple terms, the quantity demanded is far greater than the quantity supplied. For example, there were about 10,000 kidney transplants in 1995 while over 30,000 people were awaiting the procedure.

The supply of available organs comes primarily from people who donate them for use in transplants after they die. Some states ask people to indicate on their driver's license whether they agree to the use of their organs after an accidental death, but so far (despite a recent campaign supported by Michael Jordan) persuasion hasn't solved the problem.

Can the market help? A recent proposal by Nobel Prize-winning economist Gary Becker argues that potential organ donors should be paid a price to induce them to register as a potential organ donor. Such a price, he argues, would increase the quantity supplied sharply, because today the price is zero![b]

Sources: [a]Kim Clark, "How to Make Traffic Jams a Thing of the Past," Fortune, March 31, 1997; William Vickrey, "Pricing as a Tool in Coordination of Local Transportation," in Transportation Economics (New York: National Bureau of Economic Research, 1965); and [b]Gary Becker, "How Uncle Sam Could Ease the Organ Shortage," Business Week, January 20, 1997.

For more on the use of the price system, see the Case and Fair Web page at
http://www.prenhall.com/casefair.

be studying the functions of markets and the behavior of market participants in more detail in the following chapters.

Because the concepts presented in the first five chapters are so important to your understanding of what is to come, this might be a good point for a brief review of part 1.

SUMMARY

THE PRICE SYSTEM: RATIONING AND ALLOCATING RESOURCES

1. In a market economy, the market system (or price system) serves two functions. It determines the allocation of resources among producers and the final mix of outputs. It also distributes goods and services on the basis of willingness and ability to pay. In this sense, it serves as a *price rationing* device.

2. Governments, as well as private firms, sometimes decide not to use the market system to ration an item for which there is excess demand. Examples of nonprice rationing systems include *queuing, favored customers,* and *ration coupons.* The most common rationale for such policies is "fairness."

3. Attempts to bypass the market and use alternative nonprice rationing devices are much more difficult and costly than it would seem at first glance. Schemes that open up opportunities for favored customers, black markets, and side payments often end up less "fair" than the free market.

SUPPLY AND DEMAND ANALYSIS: AN OIL IMPORT FEE

4. The basic logic of supply and demand is a powerful tool for analysis. For example, supply and demand analysis shows that an oil import tax will reduce quantity of oil demanded, increase domestic production, and generate revenues for the government.

REVIEW TERMS AND CONCEPTS

black market, 102

favored customers, 102

price ceiling, 101

price rationing, 97

queuing, 101

ration coupons, 102

PROBLEM SET

1. Illustrate the following with supply and/or demand curves:
   a. A situation of excess labor supply (unemployment) caused by a "minimum wage" law.
   b. The effect of a sharp increase in heating oil prices on the demand for insulation material.

2. The scalping of tickets to sporting events and concerts, which is illegal in most states, may in fact serve a useful function. Do you agree or disagree? Write an essay explaining your answer.

3. In an effort to "support" the price of some agricultural goods, the Department of Agriculture pays farmers a subsidy in cash for every acre that they leave *unplanted.* The Agriculture Department argues that the subsidy increases the "cost" of planting and that it will reduce supply and increase the price of competitively produced agricultural goods. Critics argue that because the subsidy is a payment to farmers, it will reduce costs and lead to lower prices. Which argument is correct? Explain.

4. Illustrate the following with supply and/or demand curves:
   a. The federal government "supports" the price of wheat by paying farmers not to plant wheat on some of their land.
   b. The impact of an increase in the price of chicken on the price of hamburger.
   c. Incomes rise, shifting the demand for gasoline. Crude oil prices rise, shifting the supply of gasoline. At the new equilibrium, the quantity of gasoline sold is less than it was before. (Crude oil is used to produce gasoline).

5. "The price of blue jeans has risen substantially in recent years. Demand for blue jeans has also been rising. This is hard to explain because the law of demand says that higher prices should lead to lower demand." Do you agree?

6. Illustrate the following with supply and demand curves:
   a. The economy was doing very well in 1997. Income was rising and the stock market hit new record highs. As a result, the price of housing rose.
   b. In 1996, several cows in Great Britain came down with "mad cow disease." As a result, the countries of the European Union banned the import of British beef. The result was higher beef prices in Continental Europe.
   c. In 1997, the mayor of New York City and the governor of New York State negotiated a slow phaseout of rent control in the city. Under rent control, rents are held by law below their equilibrium levels. The result will be higher rents.
   d. In 1998, a survey of plant stores indicated that the demand for houseplants was rising sharply. At the same time, dozens of low-cost producers started growing plants for sale. The net result was a decline in the average price of houseplants.

7. Suppose that the world price of oil is $16 per barrel, and suppose that the United States can buy all the oil it wants at this price.

Suppose also that the demand and supply schedules for oil in the United States only are as follows:

PRICE ($ PER BARREL)	U.S. QUANTITY DEMANDED	U.S. QUANTITY SUPPLIED
14	16	4
16	15	6
18	14	8
20	13	10
22	12	12

a. On graph paper, draw the supply and demand curves for the United States.

b. With free trade in oil, what price will Americans pay for their oil? What quantity will Americans buy? How much of this will be supplied by American producers? How much will be imported? Illustrate total imports on your graph of the U.S. oil market.

c. Suppose the United States imposes a tax of $4 per barrel on imported oil. What quantity would Americans buy? How much of this would be supplied by American producers? How much would be imported? How much tax would the government collect?

d. Briefly summarize the impact of an oil-import tax by explaining who is helped and who is hurt among the following groups: domestic oil consumers, domestic oil producers, foreign oil producers, the U.S. government.

8. Use the data in problem 7 to answer the following questions. But now suppose that the United States allows no oil imports.

a. What is the equilibrium price and quantity for oil in the United States?

b. If the United States imposed a price ceiling of $18 per barrel on the oil market, would there be an excess supply or an excess demand for oil? How much?

c. Under the price ceiling, quantity supplied and quantity demanded differ. Which of the two will determine how much oil is purchased? Briefly explain why.

TAKE IT TO THE NET

We invite you to visit the Case and Fair page on the Prentice Hall Web site:

http://www.prenhall.com/casefair

for this chapter's World Wide Web exercise.

THE SPOTTED OWL, THE LUMBER INDUSTRY, AND THE MARKET FOR NEW HOMES

The housing industry is an important sector of the U.S. economy. Federal Reserve officials monitor this industry because of the possible economy-wide effects of changes in housing market activity. Bank managers closely watch the housing market because bank lending can be affected by fluctuations in the number of housing sales. In the labor market, fluctuations in new home construction can cause similar fluctuations in the number of employed individuals in the home construction industry. A variety of local businesses can also be affected by changes in housing market conditions because new home owners buy, among other things, new appliances. And the spending of individuals can change as changes in housing prices affect individuals' wealth.

The price of newly constructed homes is determined by supply and demand in that market. The supply of new homes is affected by changes in labor costs in the construction industry, other construction costs (for example, lumber prices), and the price of land. The demand for new homes is determined by changes in income, interest rates (which determine the cost of financing the purchase of a new home), demographics, and, in some cases, prospective home buyers' expectations of future home prices. A change in any one of these determinants of supply and demand will cause changes in the price and number of new homes.

In the early 1990s, the market for new homes was affected by the impact of regulatory actions taken to protect the northern spotted owl. By 1990, an estimated 4,000 to 6,000 spotted owls were believed to exist in the old-growth forests of northern California, Oregon, and Washington; old-growth forests include trees that are 200 to more than 1,000 years old. Over time, the spotted owl had become dependent on the food species found in these forests and, therefore, could not exist elsewhere. On June 22, 1990, the U.S. Fish and Wildlife Service declared the northern spotted owl a threatened species, placing it under the protection of the Endangered Species Act.

One federal study indicated 8.4 million acres of old-growth forest were needed for the spotted owl's survival. With approximately 5.4 million acres already off limits to timber harvesting, this meant an additional 3 million acres would need to be removed from logging. The declaration of the spotted owl as a threatened species placed it in the middle of a debate between those concerned about the possible loss of a species and those concerned about the effects of logging restrictions on timber supplies and on the economies of the Pacific Northwest.

Logging restrictions on federal, state, and privately owned land were ordered in 1991, limiting the amount of timber that could be harvested. Critics of these restrictions cited a number of costs of protecting the spotted owl:

1. significant timber-related job losses (with some estimates of job losses in excess of 100,000).
2. the possible closure of local sawmills.
3. increased prices of wood products as a result of reductions in timber supply.
4. reductions in government revenues caused by reduced timber sales from federally owned land.
5. increased costs to the government in the form of, for example, increased unemployment claims in regions affected by harvesting restrictions.

Proponents of the policy to limit harvesting argued that endangered species must be protected from extinction. They also argued that the effects of restrictions on timber-dependent industries would not be nearly as severe as critics claimed because, for example, firms would respond to these restrictions by seeking alternative sources of timber. Some environmentalists even proposed a ban on the export of logs from federal and state lands. The sale of logs to foreign sawmills, it was argued, caused reductions in the number of jobs at local sawmills.

By 1991, these logging restrictions appeared to affect wood and lumber prices (see Figure 1). The prices of some wood products, such as two-by-fours and half-inch plywood, increased by nearly 20 percent over a two-week period in the spring of 1991. Although these logging restrictions caused layoffs and the closure of some sawmills, adversely affecting some communities in the Pacific Northwest, some firms benefited from the restrictions. For example, the Weyerhaeuser Corporation, a forest products company, owned 5.6 million acres of timber not affected by the logging restrictions. As timber prices increased because of the logging restrictions, Weyerhaeuser was able to harvest its own timber and sell logs and lumber at higher prices. Furthermore, as some timber mills closed, other "leaner," more efficient mills increased hiring during the period as they successfully made the transition to the harvesting of smaller trees.

Questions for Analytical Thinking

1. a. Using supply and demand curves, graphically illustrate and explain the effects of timber harvest restrictions on lumber prices. Explain how the lumber price effects of logging restrictions might change as logging companies have more time to respond to the effects of these restrictions.
b. In 1994, federal judge William Dwyer lifted the logging ban on some of the federally owned land. What effect, if any, do you think this action might have had on the supply of lumber and wood products and, therefore, on lumber product prices? Explain.
c. Are your conclusions in parts a and b consistent with the actual movements in lumber and wood product prices found in Figure 1? Explain.

2. A June 21, 1991, editorial in the *Wall Street Journal* referred to the possible effects of logging restrictions on new home prices as a "spotted owl surcharge."
a. Using supply and demand curves for new homes, graphically illustrate and explain the effects of logging restrictions on the market for new homes. Based on your analysis, what do you think happened to the demand for new homes as a result of these restrictions? Explain.
b. As the price of new homes changed due to logging restrictions, how might potential new home buyers have responded in their search for housing services?
c. New homes and existing homes are likely viewed as substitutes by

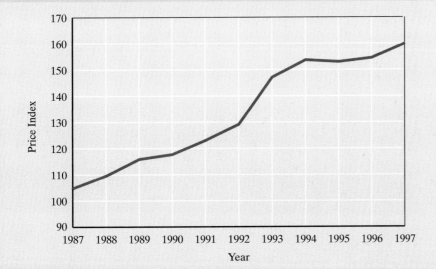

FIGURE 1

Producer Price Index for Lumber and Wood Products (excluding furniture)

Base Year: 1982

home buyers. Given your previous analysis, explain what effect, if any, these logging restrictions might have had on the market for existing homes. Use supply and demand curves in your analysis.
d. And finally, how might home builders (contractors) have changed their behavior as lumber prices increased? Explain.

3. Between 1990 and 1995, the median price of existing homes in the Hartford, Connecticut, area fell each year. During this same period, lumber and wood product prices increased each year. Are these two observations inconsistent with our understanding of the ability of the supply and demand model to explain the price of existing homes? Explain.

4. The share price of a company's stock generally reflects investors' expectations of the company's current and future profitability. When proposals to limit timber harvesting in the Pacific Northwest were being discussed in the spring of 1991, the price of Weyerhaeuser stock actually increased. Why do you think this occurred?

5. When policy makers examine proposals to protect a particular species (or some other natural resource), what costs and benefits do you think they should consider when making this decision?

Sources: Karl E. Case, "The Real Estate Cycle and the Economy: Consequences of the Massachusetts Boom of 1984–87," *New England Economic Review*, Federal Reserve Bank of Boston, Sept./Oct. 1991, pp. 37–46; Timothy Egan, "Oregon, Foiling Forecasters, Thrives as It Protects Owls," *New York Times*, October 11, 1994; Daniel A. Hagen, James W. Vincent, and Patrick B. Welle, "Benefits of Preserving Old-Growth Forests and the Spotted Owl," *Contemporary Policy Issues*, April 1992, pp. 13–26; Bill Richards, "Owls, of All Things, Help Weyerhaeuser Cash In on Timber," *Wall Street Journal*, June 24, 1992; David Schaefer and Sylvia Nogaki, "Threatened—Wildlife Agency Makes It Official on Spotted Owl," *Seattle Times*, June 22, 1990.

MACROECONOMICS

PART TWO

CONCEPTS AND PROBLEMS IN MACROECONOMICS

▐NTRODUCTION TO MACROECONOMICS

WE NOW BEGIN OUR STUDY of macroeconomics. We glimpsed the differences between microeconomics and macroeconomics in chapter 1. **Microeconomics** examines the functioning of individual industries and the behavior of individual decision-making units, typically business firms and households. With a few assumptions about how these units behave (firms maximize profits, households maximize utility), we can derive useful conclusions about how markets work, how resources are allocated, and so forth.

Macroeconomics, instead of focusing on the factors that influence the production of particular products and the behavior of individual industries, focuses on the determinants of total national output. Macroeconomics studies not household income but *national* income, not individual prices but the *overall* price level. It does not analyze the demand for labor in the automobile industry but rather total employment in the economy.

Both microeconomics and macroeconomics are concerned with the decisions of households and firms. Microeconomics deals with individual decisions, macroeconomics deals with the sum of these individual decisions. *Aggregate* is used in macroeconomics to refer to sums. When we speak of **aggregate behavior**, we mean the behavior of all households and firms together. We also speak of aggregate consumption and aggregate investment, which refer to total consumption and total investment in the economy.

Because microeconomists and macroeconomists look at the economy from different perspectives, you might expect they will reach somewhat different conclusions about the way the economy behaves. This is true to some extent. Microeconomists generally conclude that markets work well. They see prices as flexible, adjusting to maintain equality between quantity supplied and quantity demanded. Macroeconomists, however, observe that important prices in the economy—for example, the wage rate (or price of labor)—often seem "sticky." **Sticky prices** are prices that do not always adjust rapidly to maintain equality between quantity supplied and quantity demanded. Microeconomists do not expect to see the quantity of apples supplied exceeding the quantity of apples demanded, because the price of apples is not sticky. But macroeconomists—who analyze aggregate behavior—examine periods of high unemployment, where the quantity of labor

microeconomics *Deals with the functioning of individual industries and the behavior of individual decision-making units—business firms and households.*

macroeconomics *Deals with the economy as a whole. Macroeconomics focuses on the determinants of total national income, deals with aggregates such as aggregate consumption and investment, and looks at the overall level of prices rather than individual prices.*

aggregate behavior *The behavior of all households and firms together.*

sticky prices *Prices that do not always adjust rapidly to maintain equality between quantity supplied and quantity demanded.*

supplied appears to exceed the quantity of labor demanded. At such times, it appears that wage rates do not adjust fast enough to equate the quantity of labor supplied and the quantity of labor demanded.

Until recently, macroeconomists tended to be relatively uninterested in reconciling their analyses with the postulates and conclusions of microeconomic theory. The new trend among macroeconomists, however, is to try to make macroeconomic analysis consistent with microeconomic postulates—that is, with the idea that firms and households make their decisions along the lines suggested by microeconomic theory. If prices do not appear to adjust to equate the quantity supplied and the quantity demanded, for example, macroeconomists now look for solid microeconomic reasons why not. One of the aims of this book is to explain the **microeconomic foundations of macroeconomics.**

microeconomic foundations of macroeconomics *The microeconomic principles underlying macroeconomic analysis.*

THE ROOTS OF MACROECONOMICS

THE GREAT DEPRESSION

Great Depression *The period of severe economic contraction and high unemployment that began in 1929 and continued throughout the 1930s.*

Economic events of the 1930s, the decade of the **Great Depression**, spurred a great deal of thinking about macroeconomic issues. The 1920s had been prosperous years for the U.S. economy. Virtually everyone who wanted a job could get one, incomes rose substantially, and prices were stable. Beginning in late 1929, things took a sudden turn for the worse. In 1929, 1.5 million people were unemployed. By 1933, that had increased to 13 million out of a labor force of 51 million. In 1929, the United States produced $103 billion worth of new goods and services; by 1933, production had fallen to $55 billion, a drop of nearly 50 percent. In October of 1929, when stock prices collapsed on Wall Street, billions of dollars of personal wealth were lost. Unemployment remained above 14 percent of the labor force until 1940.

▶ **Classical Models** Before the Great Depression, economists applied microeconomic models, sometimes referred to as "classical models," to economy-wide problems. (The word *macroeconomics* was not invented until after World War II.) For example, classical supply and demand analysis assumed that an excess supply of labor would drive down wages to a new equilibrium level; as a result, unemployment would not persist.

In other words, classical economists believed that *recessions* (downturns in the economy) were self-correcting. As output falls and the demand for labor shifts to the left, the argument went, the wage rate will decline, thereby raising the quantity of labor demanded by firms who would want to hire more workers at the new lower wage rate. (Graph this movement along the new demand curve yourself.)

But, during the Great Depression unemployment levels remained very high for nearly 10 years. In large measure, the failure of simple classical models[1] to explain the prolonged existence of high unemployment provided the impetus for the development of macroeconomics. It is not surprising that what we now call macroeconomics was born in the 1930s.

▶ **The Keynesian Revolution** One of the most important works in the history of economics, *The General Theory of Employment, Interest and Money*, by John Maynard Keynes, was published in 1936. Building on what was already understood about markets and their behavior, Keynes set out to construct a theory that would explain the confusing economic events of his time.

---

[1]Classical models are also sometimes known as "market clearing" models because they emphasize that prices and wages adjust to ensure that markets always clear—that is, that the quantity supplied is equal to the quantity demanded.

Much of macroeconomics has roots in Keynes's work. According to Keynes, it is not prices and wages that determine the level of employment, as classical models had suggested, but rather the level of aggregate demand for goods and services. Keynes believed governments could intervene in the economy and affect the level of output and employment. The government's role during periods when private demand is low, Keynes argued, is to stimulate aggregate demand and, by so doing, to lift the economy out of recession. (See Application box, "The Great Depression and John Maynard Keynes.")

RECENT MACROECONOMIC HISTORY

After World War II, and especially in the 1950s, Keynes's views began to gain increasing influence over both professional economists and government policy makers. Governments came to believe they could intervene in their economies to attain specific employment and output goals, and they began to use their powers to tax and spend, as well as their ability to affect interest rates and the money supply, for the explicit purpose of controlling the economy's ups and downs. This view of government policy became firmly established in the United States with the passage of the Employment Act of 1946. This act established the President's Council of Economic Advisors, a group of economists who advise the president on economic issues. It also committed the federal government to intervening in the economy to prevent large declines in output and employment.

▶ **Fine Tuning in the 1960s** The notion that the government could, and should, act to stabilize the macroeconomy reached the height of its popularity in the 1960s. During these years, Walter Heller, the chairman of the Council of Economic Advisors under both President Kennedy and President Johnson, alluded to **fine tuning** as the government's role in regulating inflation and unemployment. During the 1960s, many economists believed the government could use the tools available to manipulate unemployment and inflation levels fairly precisely.

fine tuning *The phrase used by Walter Heller to refer to the government's role in regulating inflation and unemployment.*

▶ **Disillusionment Since the 1970s** Since 1970, the U.S. economy has been through a series of wide fluctuations in employment, output, and inflation. In 1974 to 1975 and again in 1980 to 1982, the United States experienced severe recessions. While not as catastrophic as the Great Depression of the 1930s, these recessions left millions without jobs and resulted in billions of dollars of lost output and income. In 1974 to 1975 and again in 1979 to 1981, the United States saw very high rates of inflation. The U.S. economy also experienced a moderate recession in 1990 to 1991 and very slow growth for about two years after the recession. (We discuss these events in more detail in later chapters.)

Moreover, the 1970s witnessed the birth of **stagflation** (stagnation + inflation). Stagflation occurs when the overall price level rises rapidly (inflation) during periods of recession or high and persistent unemployment (stagnation). Until the 1970s, rapidly rising prices had been observed only in periods when the economy was prospering and unemployment was low (or at least declining). The problem of stagflation was vexing, both for macroeconomic theorists and for policy makers concerned with the health of the economy.

stagflation *Occurs when the overall price level rises rapidly (inflation) during periods of recession or high and persistent unemployment (stagnation).*

It was clear by 1975 that the macroeconomy was more difficult to control than either Heller's words or textbook theory had led economists to believe. The events of the 1970s and afterward have had an important influence on macroeconomic theory. Much of the faith in the simple Keynesian model and the "conventional wisdom" of the 1960s has been lost. New ways of understanding the behavior of the macroeconomy have been proposed, but as yet there is no consensus as to which explanation is best. It is precisely this flux in macroeconomics, the sense that the discipline is wide open and that many of the most important issues have yet to be resolved, that makes it so exciting to study.

THE GREAT DEPRESSION AND JOHN MAYNARD KEYNES

Much of the framework of modern macroeconomics comes from the works of John Maynard Keynes, whose *General Theory of Employment, Interest and Money* was published in 1936. The following excerpt by Robert L. Heilbroner provides some insights into Keynes's life and work.

By 1933 the nation was virtually prostrate. On street corners, in homes, in Hoovervilles (communities of makeshift shacks), 14 million unemployed sat, haunting the land . . . .

It was the unemployment that was hardest to bear. The jobless millions were like an embolism in the nation's vital circulation; and while their indisputable existence argued more forcibly than any text that something was wrong with the system, the economists wrung their hands and racked their brains . . . . but could offer neither diagnosis nor remedy. Unemployment—this kind of unemployment—was simply not listed among the possible ills of the system: it was absurd, impossible,

unreasonable, and paradoxical. But it was there.

It would seem logical that the man who would seek to solve this impossible paradox of not enough production existing side by side with men fruitlessly seeking work would be a Left-winger, an economist with strong sympathies for the proletariat, an angry man. Nothing could be further from the fact. The man who tackled it was almost a dilettante with nothing like a chip on his shoulder. The simple truth was that his talents inclined in every direction. He had, for example, written a most recondite book on mathematical probability, a book that Bertrand Russell had declared "impossible to praise too highly"; then he had gone on to match his skill in abstruse logic with a flair for making money—he accumulated a fortune of £500,000 by way of the most treacherous of all roads to riches: dealing in international currencies and commodities. More impressive yet, he had written his mathematics treatise on the side, as it were, while engaged

JOHN MAYNARD KEYNES.

in Government service, and he piled up his private wealth by applying himself for only half an hour a day while still abed.

But this is only a sample of his many-sidedness. He was an economist, of course—a Cambridge don with all the dignity and erudition

MACROECONOMIC CONCERNS

Three of the major concerns of macroeconomics are *inflation*, *output growth*, and *unemployment*. Government policy makers would like to have low inflation, high output growth, and low unemployment. They may not be able to achieve these goals, but the goals themselves are clear. (The effectiveness of government policies is the subject of later chapters.)

One troublesome fact should be kept in mind throughout this discussion:

Almost all macroeconomic events are interrelated—making progress on one front often means making conditions worse on another.

For example, some economists believe the only way to cure inflation is to put the economy into a recession (increasing unemployment and lowering output). Not all the good things we want may be compatible with each other, alas. Macroeconomics is rife with trade-offs! One aim of the following chapters is to explore and explain the nature of these trade-offs.

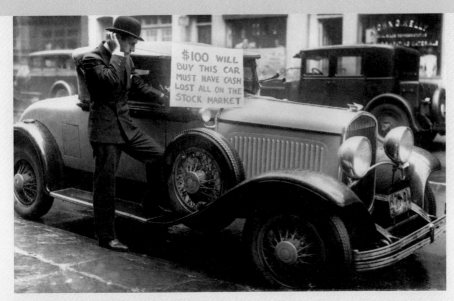
THE GREAT DEPRESSION PERSISTED LONG AFTER THE STOCK MARKET CRASH IN 1929.

that could be traced back to one William de Cahagnes and 1066. Keynes was a traditionalist; he liked to think that greatness ran in families, and it is true that his own father was John Neville Keynes, an illustrious enough economist in his own right. But it took more than the ordinary gifts of heritage to account for the son; it was as if the talents that would have sufficed half a dozen men were by happy accident crowded into one person.

By a coincidence he was born in 1883, in the very year that Karl Marx passed away. But the two economists who thus touched each other in time, although each was to exert the profoundest influence on the philosophy of the capitalist system, could hardly have differed from one another more. Marx was bitter, at bay, heavy and disappointed; as we know, he was the draftsman of Capitalism Doomed. Keynes loved life and sailed through it buoyant, at ease, and consummately successful to become the architect of Capitalism Viable.[a]

that go with such an appointment . . . . He managed to be simultaneously the darling of the Bloomsbury set, the cluster of Britain's most avant-garde intellectual brilliants, and also the chairman of a life insurance company, a niche in life rarely noted for its intellectual abandon. He was a pillar of stability in delicate matters of international diplomacy, but his official correctness did not prevent

him from acquiring a knowledge of other European politicians that included their . . . neuroses and financial prejudices . . . . He ran a theater, and he came to be a Director of the Bank of England. He knew Roosevelt and Churchill and also Bernard Shaw and Pablo Picasso. . . .

His name was John Maynard Keynes, an old British name (pronounced to rhyme with "rains")

Source: [a]Reprinted with the permission of Simon & Schuster from The Worldly Philosophers by Robert L. Heilbroner. Copyright © 1953, 1961, 1967, 1972, 1980, 1986 by Robert L. Heilbroner. Also reprinted with permission of Penguin Books Limited, U.K.

For more on John Maynard Keynes, Keynesian economics, and the Great Depression, see the Case and Fair Web page at **http://www.prenhall.com/casefair.**

INFLATION

Inflation is an increase in the overall price level. The reduction of inflation has long been a goal of government policy. Especially problematic are **hyperinflations,** or periods of very rapid increases in the overall price level.

Most Americans are unaware of what life is like under very high inflation. In some countries people are accustomed to prices rising by the day, by the hour, or even by the minute. During the hyperinflation in Bolivia in 1984 and 1985, the price of one egg rose from 3,000 pesos to 10,000 pesos in one week. In 1985, three bottles of aspirin sold for the same price as a luxury car had sold for in 1982. At the same time, the problem of handling money became a burden. Banks stopped counting deposits—a $500 deposit was equivalent to about 32 million pesos, and it just did not make sense to count a huge sack full of bills. Bolivia's currency, printed in West Germany and England, was the country's third biggest import in 1984, surpassed only by wheat and mining equipment.

Skyrocketing prices in Bolivia are a small part of the story. When inflation approaches rates of 2,000 percent per year, the economy, and the whole organization, of a country begin to break down. Workers may go on strike to demand wage increases in

inflation *An increase in the overall price level.*

hyperinflation *A period of very rapid increases in the overall price level.*

WITH THE MONEY YOU NEEDED TO BUY A LUXURY CAR SUCH AS THIS ONE IN 1982, YOU COULD BUY NO MORE THAN THREE BOTTLES OF HEADACHE PAINKILLER IN 1985—HYPERINFLATION IN BOLIVIA.

business cycle *The cycle of short-term ups and downs in the economy.*

aggregate output *The total quantity of goods and services produced in an economy in a given period.*

recession *A period during which aggregate output declines. Conventionally, a period in which aggregate output declines for two consecutive quarters.*

depression *A prolonged and deep recession.*

line with the high inflation rate, firms find it almost impossible to secure credit, and the economy grinds to a halt. Fortunately, hyperinflations usually end very abruptly. In a few months, Bolivia went from having the highest inflation rate in the world to one of the lowest inflation rates in the Western Hemisphere.

Hyperinflations are rare. Nonetheless, economists have devoted much effort to identifying the costs and consequences of even moderate inflation. Who gains from inflation? Who loses? What costs does inflation impose on society? How severe are they? What causes inflation? What is the best way to stop it? We will focus on some of these questions in chapters 8 and 14 where we will see that inflation is a major issue in macroeconomics.

OUTPUT GROWTH

Rather than grow at an even rate at all times, economies tend to experience short-term ups and downs in their performance. The technical name for these ups and downs is the **business cycle**. The main measure of how an economy is doing is **aggregate output**, the total quantity of goods and services produced in the economy in a given period. When less is produced (in other words, when aggregate output decreases), there are fewer goods and services to go around, and the average standard of living declines. When firms cut back on production, they also lay off workers, increasing the rate of unemployment.

Recessions are periods during which aggregate output declines. It has become conventional to classify an economic downturn as a "recession" when aggregate output declines for two consecutive quarters. A prolonged and deep recession is called a **depression**, although economists do not agree on when a recession becomes a depression. Since the beginning of the twentieth century, the United States has experienced one depression (during the 1930s), three severe recessions (1946, 1974 to 1975, and 1980 to 1982), and a number of less severe, shorter recessions (1954, 1958, 1970, and 1990 to 1991). Other countries have also experienced recessions in the twentieth century, some roughly coinciding with U.S. recessions, some not. In 1994, while the U.S. recovery was under way, Japan was still in a recession.

Devising explanations for and predicting the business cycle, macroeconomics tries to address: Why does the economy fluctuate so much? Why at times does it not seem to respond to the simple forces of supply and demand?

There is more to output than its up-and-down movements during business cycles. The size of the growth rate of output over a long period (longer, say, than the typical length of a business cycle) is also of concern to macroeconomists and policy makers. If the growth rate of output is greater than the growth rate of the population, there is a growing amount of goods and services produced per person. So, on average, people are becoming better off. Policy makers are thus concerned not only with smoothing fluctuations in output during a business cycle but also with policies that might increase the long-run growth rate. Long-run growth issues are taken up in chapters 8 and 19.

UNEMPLOYMENT

You cannot listen to the news or read a newspaper without noticing that data on the unemployment rate are released each month. The **unemployment rate**—the percentage of the labor force unemployed—is a key indicator of the economy's health. Because the unemployment rate is usually closely related to the economy's aggregate output, announcements of each month's new figure are followed with great interest by economists, politicians, and policy makers.

Although macroeconomists are interested in learning why the unemployment rate has risen or fallen in a given period, they also try to answer a more basic question: Why is there any unemployment at all? We do not expect to see zero unemployment. At any time, some firms may go bankrupt due to competition from rivals, bad management, or bad luck. Employees of such firms typically are not able to find new jobs immediately, and while they are looking for work, they will be unemployed. Also, workers entering the labor market for the first time may require a few weeks, or months, to find a job.

If we base our analysis on supply and demand, as we have in all our discussions so far, we would expect conditions to change in response to the existence of unemployed workers. Specifically, when there is unemployment beyond some minimum amount, there is an excess supply of workers—at the going wage rates, there are people who want to work who cannot find work. In microeconomic theory, the response to excess supply is a decrease in the price of the commodity in question and therefore an increase in the quantity demanded, a reduction in the quantity supplied, and the restoration of equilibrium. With the quantity supplied equal to the quantity demanded, the market clears.

The existence of unemployment seems to imply that the aggregate labor market is not in equilibrium—that something prevents the quantity supplied and the quantity demanded from equating. But why do labor markets not clear when other markets do? Or is it that labor markets are clearing and the unemployment data are reflecting something different? The implications of the unemployment data, a major puzzle in macroeconomics, are the focus of chapters 8 and 15.

unemployment rate *The percentage of the labor force that is unemployed.*

Unemployment rates vary from country to country. In 1997, 4.9% of the workforce in the United States was unemployed; the figure was 3.4% in Japan, 5.3% in Great Britain, 8.6% in Australia, 11.7% in Germany, 12.4% in Italy, and 20.8% in Spain. Unemployment is difficult to measure in the emerging economies.

Source: The Economist, October 11–17, 1997.

GOVERNMENT IN THE MACROECONOMY

Much of our discussion of macroeconomics concerns the potential role of government in influencing the economy. There are three kinds of policy that the government has used to influence the macroeconomy:

Government policies for influencing the macroeconomy	1. fiscal policy 2. monetary policy 3. growth or supply-side policies

▶ **Fiscal Policy** One way the federal government affects the economy is through its tax and expenditure decisions, or **fiscal policy**. The federal government collects taxes from households and firms and spends these funds on items ranging from missiles to parks to social security payments to interstate highways. Both the magnitude and composition of these taxes and expenditures have a major effect on the economy.

One of Keynes's main ideas in the 1930s was that fiscal policy could and should be used to stabilize the level of output and employment. Specifically, Keynes believed the government should cut taxes and/or raise spending—called *expansionary fiscal policies*—to get the economy out of a slump. Conversely, he held that the government should raise taxes and/or cut spending—called *contractionary fiscal policies*—to bring the economy out of an inflation.

fiscal policy *Government policies regarding taxes and expenditures.*

GRAFFITI SCULPTURE? NO, IT'S
WHAT REMAINS OF THE BERLIN
WALL, WHICH HAD SEPARATED
THE TWO HALVES OF BERLIN
BETWEEN 1961 AND 1989, WHEN
THE WALL WAS DISMANTLED.
SINCE THEN, THE REUNIFIED
GERMANY HAS FACED MANY
ECONOMIC CHALLENGES.
MACROECONOMICS STUDIES
NOT ONLY WHAT HAS HAPPENED
IN GERMANY SINCE 1989, BUT
ALSO HOW ECONOMIC EVENTS
IN GERMANY AFFECT THE REST
OF THE WORLD.

monetary policy *The tools used by the Federal Reserve to control the money supply.*

➤ **Monetary Policy**   Taxes and spending are not the only variables the government controls. Through the Federal Reserve, the nation's central bank,[2] the government can determine the quantity of money in the economy. The effects and proper role of **monetary policy** are among the most hotly debated subjects in macroeconomics. Most economists agree that the quantity of money supplied affects the overall price level, interest rates and exchange rates, the unemployment rate, and the level of output. The main controversies arise regarding how monetary policy manifests itself and exactly how large its effects are.

➤ **Growth Policies**   Many economists are skeptical about the government's ability to regulate the business cycle with any degree of precision using monetary and fiscal policy. Their view is that the focus of government policy should be to stimulate aggregate supply—to stimulate the potential growth of aggregate output and income. A host of policies have been aimed at increasing the rate of growth. Many of these are targeted at specific markets and are largely discussed in microeconomics. One major worry of macroeconomists is that government borrowing to finance excesses of spending over tax collections (the "deficit") is sopping up saving that would otherwise flow to businesses to be used for investment in capital. Another focus of pro-growth government policies has been the tax system. A major goal of tax reforms in 1981 and 1986 was to increase the incentive to work, save, and invest by lowering tax rates. In addition, the Taxpayer Relief Act of 1997 included a number of pro-growth measures that we will discuss later. These are sometimes referred to as **supply-side policies**. (See Application box, "Shift of Focus Toward Growth During the 1990s.")

supply-side policies
Government policies that focus on aggregate supply and increasing production rather than stimulating aggregate demand.

THE COMPONENTS OF THE MACROECONOMY

Macroeconomics focuses on four groups: *households* and *firms* (the private sector), the *government* (the public sector), and the *rest of the world* (the international sector). We provided data on each in chapter 3. These four groups interact in a variety of ways, many involving either the receipt or payment of income.

THE CIRCULAR FLOW DIAGRAM

circular flow *A diagram showing the income received and payments made by each sector of the economy.*

A useful way of seeing the economic interactions among the four sectors in the economy is a **circular flow** diagram, which shows the income received and payments made by each. A simple circular flow diagram is pictured in Figure 6.1.

[2]The Federal Reserve is a quasi-independent agency, and it does not always do what the president or Congress wants it to do. Nevertheless, because it is part of the government rather than part of the private sector, we consider it in this section.

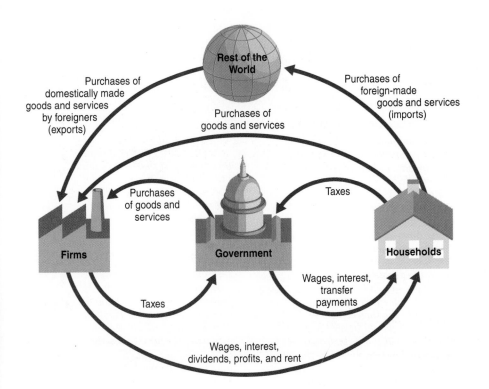

FIGURE 6.1

The Circular Flow of Payments
Households receive income from firms and the government, purchase goods and services from firms, and pay taxes to the government. They also purchase foreign-made goods and services (imports). Firms receive payments from households and the government for goods and services; they pay wages, dividends, interest, and rents to households, and taxes to the government. The government receives taxes from both firms and households, pays both firms and households for goods and services—including wages to government workers—and pays interest and transfers to households. Finally, people in other countries purchase goods and services produced domestically (exports). *Note:* Though not shown in this diagram, firms and governments also purchase imports.

Let's walk through the circular flow step by step. Households work for firms and the government, and they receive wages for their work. Our diagram shows a flow of wages *into* the household sector as payment for those services. Households also receive interest on corporate and government bonds and dividends from firms. Many households receive other payments from the government, such as social security benefits, veterans' benefits, and welfare payments. Economists call these kinds of payments from the government (for which the recipients do not supply goods, services, or labor) **transfer payments**. Together, all these receipts make up the total income received by the households.

Households spend by buying goods and services from firms and by paying taxes to the government. These items make up the total amount paid out by the households. The difference between the total receipts and the total payments of the households is the amount that the households save or dissave.[3] If households receive more than they spend, they *save* during the period. If they receive less than they spend, they *dissave*. A household can dissave by using up some of its previous savings or by borrowing. In the circular flow diagram, household spending is shown as a flow *out* of the household sector.

Firms sell goods and services to households and the government. These sales earn revenue, which shows up in the circular flow diagram as a flow *into* the firm sector. Firms pay wages, interest, and dividends to households, and they pay taxes to the government. These payments are shown flowing *out* of the firm sector.

The government collects taxes from households and firms. The government also makes payments. It buys goods and services from firms, pays wages and interest to households, and makes transfer payments to households. If the government's revenue is less than its payments, the government is dissaving.

Finally, households spend some of their income on *imports*—goods and services produced in the rest of the world. Similarly, people in foreign countries purchase *exports*—goods and services produced by domestic firms and sold to other countries.

transfer payments *Cash payments made by the government to people who do not supply goods, services, or labor in exchange for these payments. They include social security benefits, veterans' benefits, and welfare payments.*

---

[3]Saving by households is sometimes termed a "leakage" from the circular flow because it withdraws income, or current purchasing power, from the system.

SHIFT OF FOCUS TOWARD GROWTH DURING THE 1990s

The recession of 1990 to 1991 ended during the second quarter of 1991. Between 1991 and 1998 the U.S. economy experienced a period of relative stability—low inflation; and the lowest rates of unemployment in 25 years. This led policy makers to focus more attention on the growth of output/income. You can see the focus in the following excerpts from the 1997 *Economic Report of the President*:

The sources of economic growth can be grouped under three headings: increases in physical capital, improvements in human capital, and increases in the overall efficiency of the economy—the amount of output per unit of input. The Administration's economic agenda is based on strengthening each of these three pillars of economic growth.

INCREASING PHYSICAL CAPITAL

The first pillar of economic growth is increases in physical capital, which enables workers to produce more goods and services. Because it reduces the government's borrowing, deficit reduction will remain the key to how much of national saving is available for private investment in physical capital.

IMPROVING HUMAN CAPITAL

The second pillar of economic growth is improvements in what economists call human capital: the knowledge, experience, and skills of the workforce. As the economy has changed, the demands imposed on the brainpower of the American workforce have increased enormously. . . . the President has set ambitious goals for the Nation's education system: every 8-year-old should be able to read, every 12-year-old should be able to log onto the Internet, every 18-year-old should be able to go to college, and every classroom and library in America should be linked to the Internet.

An array of policies, current and proposed, are directed toward achieving these goals.

RESEARCH AND DEVELOPMENT

The third pillar of growth is greater economic efficiency—learning to produce more output with fewer inputs. Additions to the Nation's technological arsenal through research and development are an important contributor to efficiency: private industry invests over $100 billion in research and development each year. This is a huge sum, but it may not be enough: history and economic theory suggest that, left to their own devices, private firms will not invest sufficiently in improving technology, because they themselves do not realize the full benefit therefrom.

INCREASING COMPETITION

Improving the efficiency of the economy is not just a matter of improving technology. How the economy is organized plays just as important a role in creating incentives for firms to use their capital and labor as efficiently as possible. If the market economy is to deliver on its promise of growth and prosperity, markets have to be competitive, because it is competition that drives firms to be efficient and innovative.

EXPANDING TRADE

The third source of increasing efficiency in the economy is more-open markets abroad. Like the freeing up of domestic markets, opening of foreign markets shifts resources into relatively more productive areas.

For more on economic growth, see the Case and Fair Web page at http://www.prenhall.com/casefair.

One lesson of the circular flow diagram is that everyone's expenditure is someone else's receipt. If you buy a personal computer from IBM, you make a payment to IBM and IBM receives revenue. If IBM pays taxes to the government, it has made a payment and the government has received revenue.

> Everyone's expenditures go somewhere. It is impossible to sell something without there being a buyer, and it is impossible to make a payment without there being a recipient. Every transaction must have two sides.

THE THREE MARKET ARENAS

Another way of looking at the ways households, firms, the government, and the rest of the world relate to each other is to consider the markets in which they interact, as depicted in Figure 6.2.

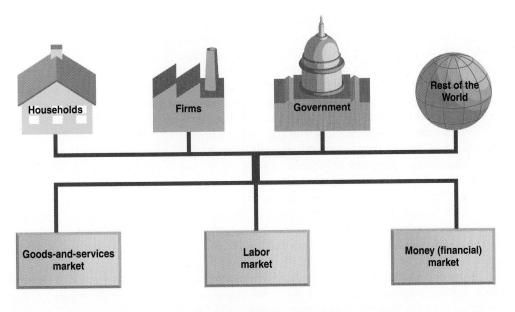

The Three Basic Markets
Households, firms, the
government, and the rest
of the world all interact in
the goods-and-services, labor,
and money markets.

The three market arenas	1. goods-and-services market 2. labor market 3. money (financial) market

> **Goods-and-Services Market** Households and the government purchase goods and services from firms in the *goods-and-services market*. In this market, firms also purchase goods and services from each other. For example, Levi Strauss buys denim from other firms to make its blue jeans. In addition, firms buy capital goods from other firms. If General Motors needs new robots on its assembly lines, it will probably buy them from another firm rather than make them itself.

Firms *supply* to the goods-and-services market. Households, the government, and firms *demand* from this market. Finally, the rest of the world both buys from and sells to the goods-and-services market. As we mentioned in chapter 3, the United States now imports hundreds of billions of dollars worth of automobiles, VCRs, oil, and other goods. At the same time, the United States exports hundreds of billions of dollars worth of computers, airplanes, and agricultural goods.

> **Labor Market** Interaction in the *labor market* takes place when firms and the government purchase labor from households. In this market, households *supply* labor, and firms and the government *demand* labor. In the U.S. economy, firms are the largest demanders of labor, although the government is also a substantial employer. The total supply of labor in the economy depends on the sum of decisions made by households. Individuals must decide whether to enter the labor force (whether to look for a job at all) and how many hours to work.

Labor is also supplied to and demanded from the rest of the world. In recent years, the labor market has become an international market. For example, vegetable and fruit farmers in California would find it very difficult to bring their product to market if it were not for the labor of migrant farm workers from Mexico. For years, Turkey has provided Germany with "guest workers" who are willing to take low-paying jobs that more prosperous German workers avoid.

> **Money Market** In the *money market*—sometimes called the *financial market*—households purchase stocks and bonds from firms. Households *supply* funds to this market in the expectation of earning income in the form of dividends on stocks and interest on bonds. Households also *demand* (borrow) funds from this market to finance various

CHAPTER SIX
*Introduction to
Macroeconomics*   **123**

purchases. Firms borrow to build new facilities in the hope of earning more in the future. The government borrows by issuing bonds. The rest of the world both borrows from and lends to the money market; every morning there are reports on TV and radio about the Japanese and British stock markets. Much of the borrowing and lending of households, firms, the government, and the international sector is coordinated by financial institutions—commercial banks, savings and loan associations, insurance companies, and the like. These institutions take deposits from one group and lend them to others.

When a firm, a household, or the government borrows to finance a purchase, it has an obligation to pay that loan back, usually at some specified time in the future. Most loans also involve payment of interest as a fee for the use of the borrowed funds. When a loan is made, the borrower nearly always signs a "promise to repay," or *promissory note*, and gives it to the lender. When the federal government borrows, it issues "promises" called **Treasury bonds, notes**, or **bills** in exchange for money. Corporations issue **corporate bonds**. A corporate bond might state, for example, "General Electric Corporation agrees to pay $5,000 to the holder of this bond on January 1, 2001, and interest thereon at 8.3 percent annually until that time."

Instead of issuing bonds to raise funds, firms can also issue shares of stock. A **share of stock** is a financial instrument that gives the holder a share in the firm's ownership and therefore the right to share in the firm's profits. If the firm does well, the value of the stock increases, and the stockholder receives a *capital gain*[4] on the initial purchase. In addition, the stock may pay **dividends**—that is, the firm may return some of its profits directly to its stockholders, rather than retain them to buy capital. If the firm does poorly, so does the stockholder. The capital value of the stock may fall, and dividends may not be paid.

Stocks and bonds are simply contracts, or agreements, between parties. I agree to loan you a certain amount, and you agree to repay me this amount plus something extra at some future date. Or I agree to buy part ownership in your firm, and you agree to give me a share of the firm's future profits.

A critical variable in the money market is the *interest rate*. Although we sometimes talk as if there were only one interest rate, there is never just one interest rate at any time. Rather, the interest rate on a given loan reflects the length of the loan and the perceived risk to the lender. A business that is just getting started will have to pay a higher rate than will General Motors. A 30-year mortgage has a different interest rate than a 90-day loan. Nevertheless, interest rates tend to move up and down together, and their movement reflects general conditions in the financial market. (We discuss interest rates in later chapters.)

Treasury bonds, notes, and bills *Promissory notes issued by the federal government when it borrows money.*

corporate bonds *Promissory notes issued by corporations when they borrow money.*

shares of stock *Financial instruments that give to the holder a share in the firm's ownership and therefore the right to share in the firm's profits.*

dividends *The portion of a corporation's profits that the firm pays out each period to its shareholders.*

THE METHODOLOGY OF MACROECONOMICS

Macroeconomists build models based on theories, and they test their models using data. In this sense, the methodology of macroeconomics is similar to the methodology of microeconomics.

CONNECTIONS TO MICROECONOMICS

How do macroeconomists try to explain aggregate behavior? One way assumes that the same factors that affect individual behavior also affect aggregate behavior. For example, we know from microeconomics that an individual's wage rate should affect her consumption habits and the amount of labor she is willing to supply. If we were to apply this microeconomic hypothesis to the aggregate data, we would say that the average wage rate in the economy should affect total consumption and total labor supply (which seems to be true).

---

[4]A *capital gain* occurs whenever the value of an asset increases. If you bought a stock for $1,000 and it is now worth $1,500, you have earned a capital gain of $500. A capital gain is "realized" when you sell the asset. Until you sell, the capital gain is *accrued* but not *realized*.

The reason for looking to microeconomics for help in explaining macroeconomic events is simple:

> Macroeconomic behavior is the sum of all the microeconomic decisions made by individual households and firms. If the movements of macroeconomic aggregates, such as total output or total employment, reflect decisions made by individual firms and households, we cannot understand the former without some knowledge of the factors that influence the latter.

Consider unemployment. The unemployment rate is the number of people unemployed as a fraction of the labor force. To be classified as "in the labor force," a person must either have a job or be seeking one actively. To understand aggregate unemployment, we need to understand individual household behavior in the labor market. Why do people choose to enter the labor force? Under what circumstances will they drop out? Why does unemployment exist even when the economy seems to be doing very well? A knowledge of microeconomic behavior is the logical starting point for macroeconomic analysis.

AGGREGATE DEMAND AND AGGREGATE SUPPLY

A major theme through the next few chapters is the behavior of aggregate demand and aggregate supply. **Aggregate demand** is the total demand for goods and services. **Aggregate supply** is the total supply of goods and services.

Figure 6.3 shows *aggregate demand* and *aggregate supply* curves. Measured on the horizontal axis is aggregate output. Measured on the vertical axis is the *overall price level*, not the price of a particular good or service—very important to keep it in mind. The economy is in equilibrium at the point at which these curves intersect.

As you will discover, aggregate demand and supply curves are much more complicated than the simple demand and supply curves we described in chapters 4 and 5. The simple logic of supply, demand, and equilibrium in individual markets does not explain what is depicted in Figure 6.3. It will take the entire next chapter for us to describe what is meant by "aggregate output" and the "overall price level." Furthermore, although we will look to the behavior of households and firms in individual markets for clues about how to analyze aggregate behavior, there are important differences when we move from the individual to the aggregate level.

aggregate demand *The total demand for goods and services in an economy.*

aggregate supply *The total supply of goods and services in an economy.*

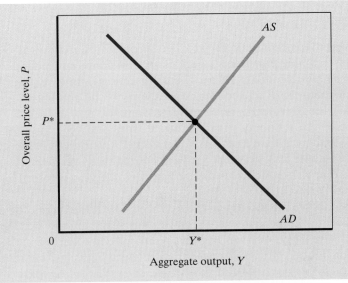

FIGURE 6.3

The Aggregate Demand and Aggregate Supply Curves

A major theme in macro-economics is the behavior of aggregate demand and aggregate supply. The logic behind the aggregate demand and aggregate supply curves is much more complex than the logic underlying the simple demand and supply curves described in chapters 4 and 5.

Consider, for example, *demand,* one of the most important concepts in economics. When the price of a specific good increases, perhaps the most important determinant of consumer response is the availability of other goods that can be substituted for the good whose price has increased. Part of the reason that an increase in the price of airline tickets causes a decline in the quantity of airline tickets demanded is that a higher price relative to other goods means that the opportunity cost of buying a ticket is higher: The sacrifice required in terms of other goods and services has increased. But when the overall price level changes, there may be no changes at all in relative prices. When analyzing the behavior of aggregate demand, the availability of substitutes is irrelevant.

Microeconomics teaches us that, *ceteris paribus,* the quantity demanded of a good falls when its price rises and rises when its price falls. (This is the microeconomic law of demand.) In other words, individual demand curves and market demand curves slope downward to the right. The reason the *aggregate* demand curve in Figure 6.3 slopes downward to the right is complex. As we will see later, the downward slope of the aggregate demand curve is related to what goes on in the money (financial) market.

The aggregate supply curve is very different from the supply curve of an individual firm or market. A firm's supply curve is derived under the assumption that all its input prices are fixed. In other words, the firm's input prices are assumed to remain unchanged as the price of the firm's output changes. When we derived Clarence Brown's soybean supply schedule in chapter 4, we took his input prices as fixed. A change in an input price leads to a shift in Brown's supply curve, not a movement along it. If we are examining changes in the overall price level, however, *all* prices are changing (including input prices), so the aggregate supply curve cannot be based on the assumption of fixed input prices. We will see that the aggregate supply curve is a source of controversy in macroeconomics.

Because of the complexity of the aggregate demand and aggregate supply curves, we will need to build our analysis piece by piece. In chapter 7, we discuss the methods of measuring economic activity and aggregate output. In chapter 8, we describe the key macroeconomic problems of business cycles, inflation, and unemployment. Chapters 9 through 14 present the material we need to understand the equilibrium levels of aggregate output and the overall price level. In these chapters, we discuss the behavior of households, firms, and the government in both the goods-and-services market and the money market. Chapter 15 brings the labor market into the picture. Later chapters elaborate on this material and discuss a number of macroeconomic policy issues.

THE U.S. ECONOMY IN THE TWENTIETH CENTURY: TRENDS AND CYCLES

As we said, most macroeconomic variables go through ups and downs over time, and the economy as a whole experiences periods of prosperity and periods of recession. The trend of the U.S. economy in the twentieth century, however, has been toward prosperity. One measure of an economy's prosperity is the amount of goods and services that it produces during a year, or its gross domestic product (GDP, the subject of the next chapter). An economy is said to grow from one year to another if GDP is larger in the second year than in the first. Between 1900 and 1997, the U.S. economy grew at an average rate of 3.4 percent per year. During those years the economy was on average 3.4 percent richer each year than it had been the year before. This is the economy's "long-run" growth rate.

Remember that we are discussing the average growth rate here. The economy did not actually grow by 3.4 percent every year. In some years, growth was less than 3 percent, and in some years growth was negative (GDP fell). In other years, the growth rate was greater than 3.4 percent. So, we need to distinguish between *long-term,* or *secular, trends* in economic performance and *short-term,* or *cyclical, variations.*

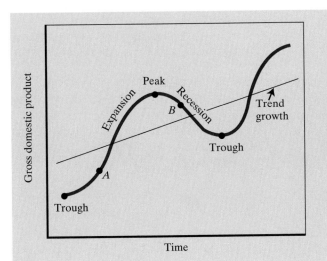

FIGURE 6.4

A Typical Business Cycle

In this business cycle, the economy is expanding as it moves through point A from the trough to the peak. When the economy moves from a peak down to a trough, through point B, the economy is in recession.

EXPANSION AND CONTRACTION: THE BUSINESS CYCLE

Macroeconomics is concerned both with long-run trends—Why has the U.S. economy done so well over the past 100 years while Great Britain's has done rather poorly?—and with short-run fluctuations in economic performance—Why did the world experience a severe recession in the early 1980s? Most of this part of the text focuses on short-run fluctuations, known as the *business cycle*, because they are somewhat better understood. A typical business cycle is illustrated in Figure 6.4.

Because the U.S. economy on average grows over time, the business cycle in Figure 6.4 shows a positive trend—the *peak* (the highest point) of a new business cycle is higher than the peak of the previous cycle. The period from a *trough*, or bottom of the cycle, to a peak is called an **expansion** or a **boom**. During an expansion, output and employment grow. The period from a peak to a trough is called a **contraction, recession,** or **slump,** when output and employment fall.

In judging whether an economy is expanding or contracting, note the difference between the level of economic activity and its rate of change. If the economy has just left a trough (point A in Figure 6.4), it will be growing (rate of change is positive), but its level of output will still be low. If the economy has just started to decline from a peak (point B), it will be contracting (rate of change is negative), but its level of output will still be high.

The business cycle in Figure 6.4 is symmetric, which means the length of an expansion is the same as the length of a contraction. All business cycles are not symmetric, however. It is possible, for example, for the expansion phase to be longer than the contraction phase. When contraction comes, it may be fast and sharp, while expansion may be slow and gradual. Moreover, the economy is not nearly as regular as the business cycle in Figure 6.4 indicates. While there are ups and downs in the economy, they tend to be erratic.

What do actual business cycles in the United States look like? See Figure 6.5, where the percentage deviation of U.S. GDP around its trend is plotted for 1900 to 1997. Although many business cycles have occurred in the last nine decades, each has been unique. The economy is not so simple that it has regular cycles.

The periods of the Great Depression and World War II are the low and high points of Figure 6.5, although other large contractions and expansions have taken place. Note the expansion in the 1960s and the recessions at the beginning of the 1980s and 1990s. Some of the cycles have been long, some have been very short. Note also that GDP actually increased between 1933 and 1937, even though at its peak in 1937 GDP was still quite low. The economy did not really come out of the Depression until the defense buildup prior to the start of World War II.

expansion or **boom** *The period in the business cycle from a trough up to a peak, during which output and employment rise.*

contraction, recession, or **slump** *The period in the business cycle from a peak down to a trough, during which output and employment fall.*

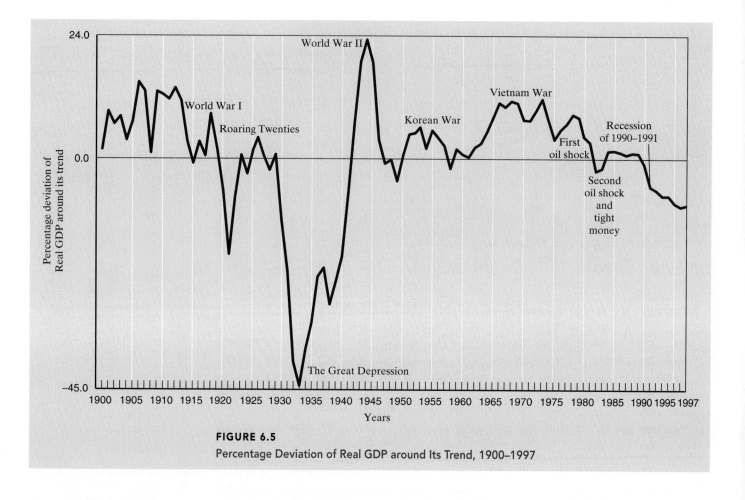

FIGURE 6.5
Percentage Deviation of Real GDP around Its Trend, 1900–1997

THE U.S. ECONOMY SINCE 1970

Since 1970, the U.S. economy has seen three recessions and large fluctuations in the rate of inflation. By analyzing how the various parts of the economy behaved during these hectic times, we can learn a lot about macroeconomic behavior. The following chapters concentrate on these years.

Figures 6.6, 6.7, and 6.8 show the behavior of three key variables during the period since 1970: GDP, the unemployment rate, and the rate of inflation. These graphs are based on quarterly data (data compiled for each quarter of the year) rather than on annual data. The first quarter of a year consists of January, February, and March; the second quarter consists of April, May, and June; and so on. The Roman numerals I, II, III, and IV denote the four quarters. (For example, "1972 III" refers to the third quarter, or summer, of 1972.)

Figure 6.6 plots GDP for the period 1970 I to 1997 IV. In the following chapters we will look at three recessionary periods within this period: 1974 I to 1975 IV, 1980 II to 1983 I, and 1990 III to 1991 I. These periods make useful reference points when we examine how other variables behave during the three periods.[5]

One concern of macroeconomics is unemployment. Unemployment generally rises during recessions and falls during expansions. This can be seen in Figure 6.7, which plots the unemployment rate for the period 1970 I to 1997 IV. Note that unemployment rose

---

[5]As Figure 6.6 shows, GDP rose in the middle of 1981 before falling again in the last quarter of 1981. Given this fact, one possibility would be to treat the 1980 II to 1983 I period as if it included two separate recessionary periods: 1980 II to 1981 I and 1981 IV to 1983 I. Because the expansion in 1981 was so short-lived, however, we have chosen not to separate the period into two parts.

PART TWO
*Concepts and Problems
in Macroeconomics*

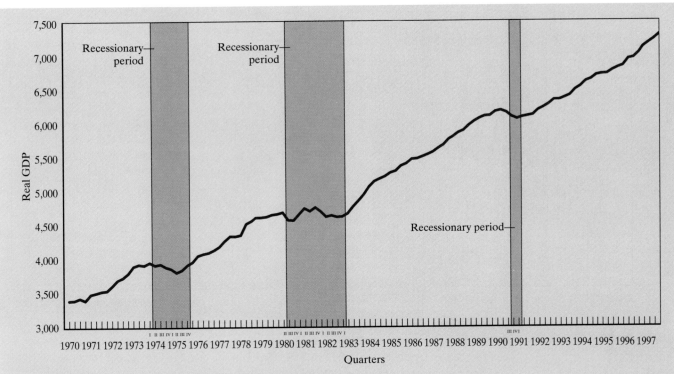

FIGURE 6.6

Real GDP, 1970 I to 1997 IV

Real GDP in the United States since 1970 has risen overall, but there have been three recessionary periods: 1974 I to 1975 IV, 1980 II to 1983 I, and 1990 III to 1991 I.

FIGURE 6.7

Unemployment Rate, 1970 I to 1997 IV

The U.S. unemployment rate since 1970 shows wide variations. The three recessionary reference periods show increases in the unemployment rate.

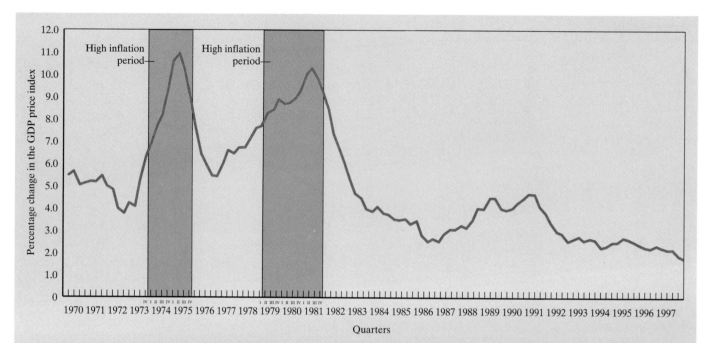

FIGURE 6.8

Percentage Change in the GDP Price Index (four-quarter average), 1970 I to 1997 IV

The percentage change in the GDP price index measures the overall rate of inflation. Since 1970, inflation has been high in two periods: 1973 IV to 1975 IV and 1979 I to 1981 IV. Inflation between 1983 and 1992 was moderate. Since 1992, it has been fairly low.

in all three recessions. In the 1974 to 1975 recession, the unemployment rate reached a maximum of 8.8 percent in the second quarter of 1975. During the 1980 to 1982 recession, it reached a maximum of 10.7 percent in the fourth quarter of 1982. The unemployment rate continued to rise after the 1990 to 1991 recession and reached a peak of 7.6 percent in 1992 III. By the end of 1994 the unemployment rate had fallen to 5.6 percent, and by the end of 1997 it had fallen further to 4.7 percent.

Macroeconomics is also concerned with the inflation rate. A measure of the overall price level is the GDP price index, an economy-wide price index. (The construction of the GDP price index is discussed in the next chapter. It is an index of prices of all domestically produced goods in the economy.) The percentage change in the GDP price index provides one measure of the overall rate of inflation. Figure 6.8 plots the percentage change in the GDP price index for the 1970 I to 1997 IV period.[6] For reference purposes, we have picked two periods within this time as showing particularly high inflation: 1973 IV to 1975 IV and 1979 I to 1981 IV. In the first period, the inflation rate peaked at 10.9 percent in the first quarter of 1975. In the second period, it peaked at 10.3 percent in the first quarter of 1981. Since 1983, the rate of inflation has been quite low by the standards of the 1970s. In the fourth quarter of 1997 it was only 1.8 percent.

Macroeconomics tries to explain the behavior of and the connections among variables such as GDP, the unemployment rate, and the GDP price index. When you can understand the movements shown in Figures 6.6, 6.7, and 6.8, you will have come a long way in understanding how the economy works.

---

[6] The percentage change in Figure 6.8 is the percentage change over four quarters. For example, the value for 1970 I is the percentage change from 1969 I, the value for 1970 II is the percentage change from 1969 II, and so on.

SUMMARY

1. *Microeconomics* examines the functioning of individual industries and the behavior of individual decision-making units. *Macroeconomics* is concerned with the sum, or aggregate, of these individual decisions—the consumption of *all* households in the economy, the amount of labor supplied and demanded by *all* individuals and firms, the total amount of *all* goods and services produced.

THE ROOTS OF MACROECONOMICS

2. Macroeconomics was born out of the effort to explain the *Great Depression* of the 1930s. Since that time, the discipline has evolved, concerning itself with new issues as the problems facing the economy have changed. Through the late 1960s, it was believed that the government could "fine tune" the economy to keep it running on an even keel at all times. The poor economic performance of the 1970s, however, showed that *fine tuning* does not always work.

MACROECONOMIC CONCERNS

3. The three topics of primary concern to macroeconomists are increases in the overall price level, or *inflation*; the growth rate of aggregate output; and the level of unemployment.

GOVERNMENT IN THE MACROECONOMY

4. Among the tools that governments have available to them for influencing the macroeconomy are *fiscal policy* (decisions on taxes and government spending); *monetary policy* (control of the money supply); and *growth or supply-side policies* (policies that focus on increasing the long-run growth rate).

THE COMPONENTS OF THE MACROECONOMY

5. The *circular flow* diagram shows the flow of income received and payments made by the three sectors of the economy—private, public, and international. Everybody's expenditure is someone else's receipt—every transaction must have two sides.

6. Another way of looking at how households, firms, the government, and the international sector relate is to consider the markets in which they interact: the goods-and-services market, labor market, and money (financial) market.

THE METHODOLOGY OF MACROECONOMICS

7. Because macroeconomic behavior is the sum of all the microeconomic decisions made by individual households and firms, we cannot possibly understand the former without some knowledge of the factors that influence the latter. The movements of macroeconomic aggregates reflect decisions made by individual firms and households.

8. A major theme in macroeconomics is the behavior of *aggregate demand* and *aggregate supply*. The logic underlying the aggregate demand and supply curves is more complex than the logic underlying individual market demand and supply curves.

THE U.S. ECONOMY IN THE TWENTIETH CENTURY: TRENDS AND CYCLES

9. Macroeconomics is concerned with both long-run trends and the short-run fluctuations that are part of the *business cycle*. Since 1970, the U.S. economy has seen three *recessions* and large fluctuations in the rate of *inflation*.

REVIEW TERMS AND CONCEPTS

PROBLEM SET

1. Define inflation. Assume that you live in a simple economy in which only three goods are produced and traded: fish, fruit, and meat. Suppose that on January 1, 1998, fish sold for $2.50 per pound, meat was $3.00 per pound, and fruit was $1.50 per pound. At the end of the year, you discover that the catch was low and that fish prices had increased to $5.00 per pound, but fruit prices stayed at $1.50 and meat prices had actually fallen to $2.00. Can you say what happened to the overall "price level"? How might you construct a measure of the "change in the price level"? What additional information might you need to construct your measure?

2. Define unemployment. Should everyone who does not hold a job be considered "unemployed?" To help with your answer, draw a supply and demand diagram depicting the labor market. What is measured along the demand curve? What factors determine the quantity of labor demanded during a given period? What is measured along the labor supply curve? What factors determine the quantity of labor supplied by households during a given period? What is the opportunity cost of holding a job?

3. During 1997, the chairman of the Board of Governors of the Federal Reserve System voiced his concern that the unemployment rate, which was below 5 percent, was getting too low. Because employment is certainly a major concern of macroeconomic policy, and because job *creation* is considered a major goal, what is Mr. Greenspan's concern? What other goal(s) of macro policy might be affected by very low rates of unemployment?

4. The economy was the number one issue during the 1992 presidential campaign. Most people believed that the economy was in recession. However, a careful look at the data shows that GDP stopped falling and began growing in the spring of 1991. In other words, the recession ended a full year and a half before the election. What was it about the economy that led the public to perceive things as so bad?

5. During 1995, the U.S. economy continued to recover from the recession of the early 1990s. However, different regions of the economy were growing at very different rates. The recession hit hardest in California and the Northeast, and the recovery was late in coming in those regions. California and Connecticut had very slow job growth right through 1994.

   Describe the economy of your state. What is the most recently reported unemployment rate? How has the number of payroll jobs changed over the last three months? The last year? How does your state's performance compare to the U.S. economy's performance over the last year? What explanations have been offered in the press? How accurate are these?

6. Explain briefly how macroeconomics is different from microeconomics. How can macroeconomists use microeconomic theory to guide them in their work, and why might they wish to do so?

7. During 1993, when the economy was growing very slowly, President Clinton recommended a series of spending cuts and tax increases designed to reduce the deficit. These were passed by Congress in the Omnibus Budget Reconciliation Act of 1993. Some who opposed the bill argue that the United States was pursuing a "contractionary fiscal policy" at precisely the wrong time. Explain their logic.

8. Many of the expansionary periods during the twentieth century have occurred during wars. Why do you think this is true?

9. In the 1940s, you could buy a soda for 5¢, eat dinner at a restaurant for less than a dollar, and purchase a house for $10,000. From this statement, it follows that consumers today are worse off than consumers in the 1940s. Comment.

*10. During 1994 and 1995, the Federal Reserve became increasingly concerned with inflation. As the economy grew at a more and more rapid rate, the Fed acted to raise interest rates sharply. For example, the interest rate that home buyers had to pay on 30-year fixed-rate mortgages jumped from 7 percent to over 9 percent. This policy was designed to slow the rate of spending growth in the economy. How might higher interest rates be expected to slow the rate of spending growth? Give some examples.

TAKE IT TO THE NET

We invite you to visit the Case and Fair page on the Prentice Hall Web site:
http://www.prenhall.com/casefair
for this chapter's World Wide Web exercise.

Chapter 7

MEASURING NATIONAL OUTPUT AND NATIONAL INCOME

MACROECONOMICS RELIES ON DATA, much of it collected by the government. To study the economy, we need data on total output, total income, total consumption, and the like. One source of these data are the **national income and product accounts**, which describe the components of national income in the economy.

The national income and product accounts do more than convey data about the performance of the economy. They also provide a conceptual framework that macroeconomists use to think about how the pieces of the economy fit together. When an economist thinks about the macroeconomy, the categories and vocabulary he or she uses come from the national income and product accounts.

The national income and product accounts can be compared to the mechanical or wiring diagrams for an automobile engine. The diagrams do not explain how an engine works—they identify the key parts of an engine and show how they are connected. Trying to understand the macroeconomy without understanding national income accounting is like trying to fix an engine without a mechanical diagram and with no names for the engine parts.

GROSS DOMESTIC PRODUCT

The key concept in the national income and product accounts is **gross domestic product**, or **GDP**.

GDP is the total market value of a country's output. It is the market value of all final goods and services produced within a given period of time by factors of production located within a country.

U.S. GDP for 1997—the value of all the output produced by factors of production in the United States in 1997—was $8,079.9 billion.

FINAL GOODS AND SERVICES

final goods and services
Goods and services produced for final use.

intermediate goods *Goods that are produced by one firm for use in further processing by another firm.*

Goods and services produced refers to **final goods and services**. Many goods are **intermediate goods**—they are produced by one firm for use in further processing by another firm. Tires sold to automobile manufacturers are intermediate goods. The value of intermediate goods is not counted in GDP.

Why aren't intermediate goods counted in GDP? Suppose that in producing a car GM pays $100 to Goodyear for tires. GM uses these tires (among other components) to assemble a car, which it sells for $12,000. The value of the car (including its tires) is $12,000, not $12,000 + $100. The final price of the car already reflects the value of all its components. To count in GDP both the value of the tires sold to the automobile manufacturers and the value of the automobiles sold to the consumers would result in double counting.

value added *The difference between the value of goods as they leave a stage of production and the cost of the goods as they entered that stage.*

Double counting can also be avoided by counting only the value added to a product by each firm in its production process. The **value added** during some stage of production is the difference between the value of goods as they leave that stage of production and the cost of the goods as they entered that stage. Value added is illustrated in Table 7.1. The four stages of the production of a gallon of gasoline are (1) oil drilling, (2) refining, (3) shipping, and (4) retail sale. In the first stage, value added is the value of sales. In the second stage, the refiner purchases the oil from the driller, refines it into gasoline, and sells it to the shipper. The refiner pays the driller $0.50 per gallon and charges the shipper $0.65. The value added by the refiner is thus $0.15 per gallon. The shipper then sells the gasoline to retailers for $0.80. The value added in the third stage of production is $0.15. Finally, the retailer sells the gasoline to consumers for $1.00. The value added at the fourth stage is $0.20, and the total value added in the production process is $1.00, the same as the value of sales at the retail level. Adding the total values of sales at each stage of production ($0.50 + $0.65 + $0.80 + $1.00 = $2.95) would significantly overestimate the value of the gallon of gasoline.

> In calculating GDP, we can either sum up the value added at each stage of production or we can take the value of final sales. We do not use the value of total sales in an economy to measure how much output has been produced.

EXCLUSION OF USED GOODS AND PAPER TRANSACTIONS

GDP is concerned only with new, or current, production. Old output is not counted in current GDP because it was already counted back at the time it was produced. It would be double counting to count sales of used goods in current GDP. If someone sells a used

TIRES TAKEN FROM THAT PILE AND MOUNTED ON THE WHEELS OF THE NEW CAR BEFORE IT IS SOLD ARE CONSIDERED INTERMEDIATE GOODS TO THE AUTO PRODUCER. TIRES FROM THAT PILE TO REPLACE TIRES ON YOUR OLD CAR ARE CONSIDERED FINAL GOODS.

TABLE 7.1 VALUE ADDED IN THE PRODUCTION OF A GALLON OF GASOLINE (HYPOTHETICAL NUMBERS)

STAGE OF PRODUCTION	VALUE OF SALES	VALUE ADDED
(1) Oil drilling	$0.50	$0.50
(2) Refining	0.65	0.15
(3) Shipping	0.80	0.15
(4) Retail sale	1.00	0.20
Total value added		$1.00

car to you, the transaction is not counted in GDP, because no new production has taken place. Similarly, a house is counted in GDP only at the time it is built, not each time it is resold. In short:

> GDP ignores all transactions in which money or goods change hands but in which no new goods and services are produced.

Sales of stocks and bonds are not counted in GDP. These sales are exchanges of paper assets and do not correspond to current production. But what if I sell the stock or bond for more than I originally paid for it? Profits from the stock or bond market have nothing to do with current production, so they are not counted in GDP. However, if I pay a fee to a broker for selling a stock of mine to someone else, this fee is counted in GDP, because the broker is performing a service for me. This service is part of current production. Be careful to distinguish between exchanges of stocks and bonds for money (or for other stocks and bonds), which do not involve current production, and fees for performing such exchanges, which do.

EXCLUSION OF OUTPUT PRODUCED ABROAD BY DOMESTICALLY OWNED FACTORS OF PRODUCTION

> GDP is the value of output produced by factors of production *located within a country.*

The three basic factors of production are land, labor, and capital. The labor of U.S. citizens counts as a domestically owned factor of production for the United States. The output produced by U.S. citizens abroad (for example, U.S. citizens working for a foreign company) is *not* counted in U.S. GDP because the output is not produced within the United States. Likewise, profits earned abroad by U.S. companies are not counted in U.S. GDP. However, the output produced by foreigners working in the United States is counted in U.S. GDP because the output is produced within the United States. Also, profits earned in the United States by foreign-owned companies are counted in U.S. GDP.

It is sometimes useful to have a measure of the output produced by factors of production owned by a country's citizens regardless of where the output is produced. This measure is called **gross national product**, or **GNP**. For most countries, including the United States, the difference between GDP and GNP is small.[1] In 1997 GNP for

gross national product (GNP) *The total market value of all final goods and services produced within a given period by factors of production owned by a country's citizens, regardless of where the output is produced.*

---

[1]In a few countries, however, there is a large difference between GDP and GNP. For instance, the tiny country of Lesotho (surrounded entirely by South Africa) has an extremely poor and rudimentary domestic economy. Most residents of Lesotho earn their living by working in the mines and industries of neighboring South Africa. These payments from abroad are not counted in GDP, although they are part of GNP. According to the International Financial Statistics published by the International Monetary Fund, Lesotho's GNP exceeded its GDP by 72 percent in a recent year.

THIS SUBURU PLANT IN LAFAYETTE, INDIANA, IS OWNED BY A JAPANESE FIRM, THOUGH MOST OF THE PLANT'S WORKERS ARE U.S. CITIZENS. ALL OF THE PLANT'S OUTPUT IS INCLUDED IN U.S. GDP, BUT ONLY PART OF IT IS INCLUDED IN U.S. GNP. THE WAGES PAID TO U.S. WORKERS ARE PART OF GNP, WHEREAS THE PLANT'S PROFITS ARE NOT. THE PLANT'S PROFITS ARE PART OF JAPANESE GNP.

the United States was $8,060.1 billion, which is close to the $8,079.9 billion value for U.S. GDP.

The distinction between GDP and GNP can be tricky. Consider the Honda plant in Marysville, Ohio. The plant is owned by the Honda Corporation, a Japanese firm, but most of the workers employed at the plant are U.S. workers. Although all of the output of the plant is included in U.S. GDP, only part of it is included in U.S. GNP. The wages paid to U.S. workers are part of U.S. GNP, while the profits from the plant are not. The profits from the plant are counted in Japanese GNP because this is output produced by Japanese-owned factors of production (Japanese capital in this case). The profits, however, are not counted in Japanese GDP because they were not earned in Japan.

The centrality of GDP as a working concept cannot be overestimated. Just as an individual firm needs to evaluate the success or failure of its operations each year, so the economy as a whole needs to assess itself. GDP, as a measure of the total production of an economy, provides us with a country's economic report card.

CALCULATING GDP

expenditure approach *A method of computing GDP that measures the amount spent on all final goods during a given period.*

income approach *A method of computing GDP that measures the income—wages, rents, interest, and profits—received by all factors of production in producing final goods.*

GDP can be computed in two ways. One is to add up the amount spent on all final goods during a given period. This is the **expenditure approach** to calculating GDP. The other is to add up the income—wages, rents, interest, and profits—received by all factors of production in producing final goods. This is the **income approach** to calculating GDP. These two methods lead to the same value for GDP for the reason we discussed in the previous chapter: *Every payment (expenditure) by a buyer is at the same time a receipt (income) for the seller.* We can measure either income received or expenditures made, and we will end up with the same total output.

Suppose the economy is made up of just one firm and the firm's total output this year sells for $1 million. Because the total amount spent on output this year is $1 million, this year's GDP is $1 million. Remember: The expenditure approach calculates GDP on the basis of total expenditures for final goods and services in the economy.

But *every one* of the million dollars of GDP is either paid to someone or remains with the owners of the firm as profit. Using the income approach, we add up the wages paid to employees of the firm, the interest paid to those who lent money to the firm, and the rents paid to those who leased land, buildings, or equipment to the firm. What is left over is profit, which is, of course, income to the owners of the firm. If we add up the incomes of all the factors of production, including profits to the owners, we get a GDP of $1 million.

THE EXPENDITURE APPROACH

Recall from chapter 6 the four main groups in the economy: households, firms, the government, and the rest of the world. There are also four main categories of expenditure:

Expenditure Categories:

- Consumption (*C*)—household spending on consumer goods.
- Investment (*I*)—spending by firms and households on new capital: plant, equipment, inventory, and new residential structures.
- Government consumption and investment (*G*).
- Net exports (*EX* − *IM*)—net spending by the rest of the world, or exports (*EX*) minus imports (*IM*).

The expenditure approach calculates GDP by adding together these four components of spending. In equation form:

$$GDP = C + I + G + (EX - IM)$$

U.S. GDP was $8,079.9 billion in 1997. The four components of the expenditure approach are shown in Table 7.2, along with their various categories.

▶ **Consumption (C)** A large part of GDP consists of **personal consumption expenditures** (*C*). Table 7.2 shows that in 1997 the amount of personal consumption expenditures accounted for 67.9 percent of GDP. These are expenditures by consumers on goods and services.

There are three main categories of consumer expenditures: durable goods, nondurable goods, and services. **Durable goods,** such as automobiles, furniture, and household appliances, last a relatively long time. **Nondurable goods,** such as food, clothing, gasoline, and cigarettes, are used up fairly quickly. Payments for **services**—those things that we buy that do not involve the production of physical items—include expenditures for doctors, lawyers, and educational institutions. As Table 7.2 shows, in 1997 durable goods expenditures accounted for 8.2 percent of GDP, nondurables for 19.7 percent, and services for 40.0 percent.

personal consumption expenditures (C) *A major component of GDP: expenditures by consumers on goods and services.*

durable goods *Goods that last a relatively long time, such as cars and household appliances.*

nondurable goods *Goods that are used up fairly quickly, such as food and clothing.*

services *The things we buy that do not involve the production of physical things, such as legal and medical services and education.*

TABLE 7.2 COMPONENTS OF GDP, 1997: THE EXPENDITURE APPROACH

	BILLIONS OF DOLLARS	PERCENTAGE OF GDP
Total Gross Domestic Product	8,079.9	100.0
Personal Consumption Expenditures (C)	5,485.8	67.9
Durable goods	659.3	8.2
Nondurable goods	1,592.0	19.7
Services	3,234.5	40.0
Gross Private Domestic Investment (I)	1,242.5	15.4
Nonresidential	846.9	10.5
Residential	327.2	4.0
Change in business inventories	68.4	0.8
Government Consumption and Gross Investment (G)	1,452.7	18.0
Federal	523.8	6.5
State and local	928.9	11.5
Net Exports (EX − IM)	−101.1	−1.3
Exports (EX)	957.1	11.8
Imports (IM)	1,058.1	13.1

Note: Numbers may not add exactly because of rounding.

Source: U.S. Department of Commerce, Bureau of Economic Analysis.

> **Investment (I)** *Investment*, as we use it in economics, refers to the purchase of new capital—housing, plants, equipment, and inventory. The economic use of the term is in contrast to its everyday use, where *investment* often refers to purchases of common stocks, bonds, or mutual funds ("He *invested* in some 8 percent corporate bonds"). Two subjects that have generated much interest lately, foreign investment in the United States and U.S. investment abroad, are discussed in the Global Perspective "Foreign Investment in the United States and U.S. Investment Abroad."

gross private investment (I)
Total investment in capital—that is, the purchase of new housing, plants, equipment, and inventory by the private (or nongovernment) sector.

Total investment in capital by the private sector is called **gross private investment (I)**. Expenditures by firms for machines, tools, plants, and so forth make up **nonresidential investment**.[2] Because these are goods that firms buy for their own final use, they are part of "final sales" and counted in GDP. Expenditures for new houses and apartment buildings constitute **residential investment**. The third component of gross private investment, the **change in business inventories**, is the amount by which firms' inventories change during a period. Business inventories can be looked at as the goods that firms produce now but intend to sell later. In 1997, gross private investment accounted for 15.4 percent of GDP. Of this, 10.5 percent was nonresidential investment, 4.0 percent was residential investment, and 0.8 percent was change in business inventories.

nonresidential investment
Expenditures by firms for machines, tools, plants, and so on.

residential investment
Expenditures by households and firms on new houses and apartment buildings.

change in business inventories
The amount by which firms' inventories change during a period. Inventories are the goods that firms produce now but intend to sell later.

Change in Business Inventories It is sometimes confusing to students that inventories are counted as capital and that changes in inventory are counted as investment. But conceptually it makes some sense. The inventory a firm owns has a value, and it serves a purpose, or provides a service, to the firm. That it has value is obvious. Think of the inventory of a new car dealer or of a clothing store, or stocks of newly produced but unsold computers awaiting shipment. All these have value.

But what *service* does inventory provide? Firms keep stocks of inventory for a number of reasons. One is to meet unforeseen demand. Firms are never sure how much they will sell from period to period. Sales go up and down. To maintain the goodwill of their customers, firms need to be able to respond to unforeseen increases in sales. The only way to do that is with inventory.

Some firms use inventory to provide direct services to customers—the main function of a retail store. A grocery store provides a service—convenience. The store itself doesn't produce any food at all. It simply assembles a wide variety of items and puts them on display so consumers with varying tastes can come and shop in one place for what they want. The same is true for a clothing or hardware store. To provide their services, such stores need light fixtures, counters, cash registers, buildings, and lots of inventory.

Capital stocks are made up of plant, equipment, and inventory; inventory accumulations are part of the change in capital stocks, or investment.

Remember: GDP is not the market value of total final *sales* during a period—it is the market value of total *production*. The relationship between total production and total sales is this: Total production (GDP) equals final sales of domestic goods plus the change in business inventories:

$$\text{GDP} = \text{Final sales} + \text{Change in business inventories.}$$

In 1997, production exceeded sales by $68.4 billion. Inventories at the end of 1997 were $68.4 billion *more* than they were at the beginning of 1997.

Gross Investment versus Net Investment During the process of production, capital (especially machinery and equipment) produced in previous periods gradually wears out. GDP does not give us a true picture of the real production of an economy. GDP

---

[2]The distinction between what is considered investment and what is considered consumption is sometimes fairly arbitrary. A firm's purchase of a car or a truck is counted as investment, but a household's purchase of a car or a truck is counted as consumption of durable goods. In general, expenditures by firms for items that last longer than a year are counted as investment expenditures. Expenditures for items that last less than a year are seen as purchases of intermediate goods.

FOREIGN INVESTMENT IN THE UNITED STATES AND U.S. INVESTMENT ABROAD

In recent years, much concern has been expressed over the fact that many U.S. assets have been sold to foreign investors. For example, Japanese investors have bought hotels, banks, movie companies, and office towers and have invested in factories, colleges, and retail stores in the United States. In 1990, a Japanese firm bought Rockefeller Center in New York City.

Should the United States be worried about profits earned on these investments leaving the country? How much of the United States' capital stock is owned by foreign investors? How much of the capital stock of the rest of the world does the United States own?

As Table 1 shows, total foreign direct investment in the United States did indeed increase dramatically during the 1980s, jumping from $54.5 billion in 1979 to $630.0 billion in 1996. Japan's holdings of U.S. capital assets increased from $3.5 billion at the end of 1979 to $118.1 billion at the end of 1996. That's about $34 in 1996 for every dollar in 1979.

Japan was the second-largest foreign owner of U.S. assets in 1996, behind number one Great Britain. In 1996, Japan owned 18.7 percent of all foreign-owned assets in the United States, while Great Britain owned 22.6 percent. The Dutch came in third at 11.7 percent.

Table 2 presents data on U.S. ownership of capital assets abroad. Currently, about four-fifths of U.S. foreign holdings are in developed countries, with Europe accounting for about 50 percent. The remaining one-fifth of U.S. foreign holdings are located in developing countries, mostly in Latin America. Investment by U.S. multinational firms in developing countries has been very controversial, with some arguing that these companies exert political pressure on host governments. The most famous case of this type involved the alleged

participation of IT&T in a military coup in Chile in the early 1970s.

At the beginning of the 1980s, the United States owned nearly 3.5 times as much capital in foreign countries as foreigners owned in the United States. By 1996, however, foreign direct investment in the United States was about 80 percent of U.S. direct investment abroad. Interestingly, in spite of the dramatic increases during the 1980s, foreign holdings of U.S. capital assets represented only 2.7 percent of total U.S. fixed capital in 1996.

TABLE 1 FOREIGN DIRECT INVESTMENT IN THE UNITED STATES (TOTAL HOLDINGS AT YEAR'S END, 1979 AND 1996)

	1979		1996	
	BILLIONS OF DOLLARS	PERCENT OF TOTAL	BILLIONS OF DOLLARS	PERCENT OF TOTAL
Country				
Canada	7.2	13.2	53.8	8.5
Europe	37.4	68.6	410.4	65.1
U. K.	9.8	18.0	142.6	22.6
Netherlands	NA	NA	73.8	11.7
Japan	3.5	6.4	118.1	18.7
Other	6.4	11.7	47.7	7.7
Total	54.5	100.0	630.0	100.0
Percent of total U.S. fixed capital	0.6	—	2.7	—

Note: NA = not available.

Sources: *Survey of Current Business,* August 1981 and August 1997.

TABLE 2 U.S. DIRECT INVESTMENT IN FOREIGN COUNTRIES (TOTAL HOLDINGS AT YEAR'S END, 1979 AND 1996)

	1979		1996	
	BILLIONS OF DOLLARS	PERCENT OF TOTAL	BILLIONS OF DOLLARS	PERCENT OF TOTAL
Country				
Developed countries	138.6	74.2	631.6	79.3
Europe	82.6	44.2	399.6	50.2
Canada	40.2	21.5	91.6	11.5
Developing countries	44.5	23.8	160.5	20.2
Latin America	35.1	18.8	144.2	18.1
Other	3.6	1.9	4.4	0.6
Total	186.8	100.0	796.5	100.0

Sources: *Survey of Current Business,* August 1981 and August 1997.

includes newly produced capital goods but does not take account of capital goods "consumed" in the production process.

Capital assets decline in value over time. The amount an asset's value falls each period is called its **depreciation**.[3] A personal computer purchased by a business today may be expected to have a useful life of four years before becoming worn out or obsolete. Over that period, the computer steadily depreciates.

What is the relationship between gross private investment (I) and depreciation? **Gross investment** is the total value of all newly produced capital goods (plant, equipment, housing, and inventory) produced in a given period. It takes no account of the fact that some capital wears out and must be replaced. **Net investment** is equal to gross investment minus depreciation. Net investment is a measure of how much the stock of capital *changes* during a period. If net investment is positive, the capital stock has increased; if net investment is negative, the capital stock has decreased. Put another way, the capital stock at the end of a period is equal to the capital stock that existed at the beginning of the period plus net investment:

$$\text{Capital}_{\text{end of period}} = \text{Capital}_{\text{beginning of period}} + \text{Net investment}$$

depreciation *The amount by which an asset's value falls in a given period.*

gross investment *The total value of all newly produced capital goods (plant, equipment, housing, and inventory) produced in a given period.*

net investment *Gross investment minus depreciation.*

▶ **Government Consumption and Investment (G)**   Government consumption and investment (G) include expenditures by federal, state, and local governments for final goods (bombs, pencils, school buildings) and services (military salaries, congressional salaries, school teachers' salaries). Some of these expenditures are counted as government consumption and some are counted as government gross investment. Government transfer payments (social security benefits, veterans' disability stipends, etc.) are not included in G because these transfers are not purchases of anything currently produced. The payments are not made in exchange for any goods or services. Because interest payments on the government debt are also counted as transfers, they are also excluded from GDP on the grounds that they are not payments for current goods or services.

As Table 7.2 shows, government consumption and investment accounted for $1,452.7 billion, or 18.0 percent of U.S. GDP, in 1997. Federal government consumption and investment in 1997 accounted for 6.5 percent of GDP, and state and local government consumption and investment accounted for 11.5 percent.

government consumption and investment (G) *Expenditures by federal, state, and local governments for final goods and services.*

▶ **Net Exports ($EX - IM$)**   The value of **net exports** ($EX - IM$) is the difference between *exports* (sales to foreigners of U.S.-produced goods and services) and *imports* (U.S. purchases of goods and services from abroad). This figure can be positive or negative. In 1997, the United States exported less than it imported, so the level of net exports was negative ($-\$101.1$ billion). Before 1976, the United States had generally been a net exporter—exports exceeded imports, so the net export figure was positive.

The reason for including net exports in the definition of GDP is simple. Consumption, investment, and government spending (C, I, and G) include expenditures on goods produced both domestically and by foreigners. Therefore, $C + I + G$ overstates domestic production because it contains expenditures on foreign-produced goods— that is, imports (IM), which have to be subtracted out of GDP to obtain the correct figure. At the same time, $C + I + G$ understates domestic production because some of what a nation produces is sold abroad and therefore not included in C, I, or G— exports (EX) have to be added in. If a U.S. firm produces computers and sells them in Germany, the computers are part of U.S. production and should be counted as part of U.S. GDP.

net exports ($EX - IM$) *The difference between exports (sales to foreigners of U.S.-produced goods and services) and imports (U.S. purchases of goods and services from abroad). The figure can be positive or negative.*

---

[3]This is the formal definition of economic depreciation. Because depreciation is difficult to measure precisely, accounting rules allow firms to use shortcut methods to approximate the amount of depreciation that they incur each period. To complicate matters even more, the U.S. tax laws allow firms to deduct depreciation for tax purposes under a different set of rules.

TABLE 7.3 COMPONENTS OF GDP, 1997: THE INCOME APPROACH

	BILLIONS OF DOLLARS	PERCENTAGE OF GDP
Gross Domestic Product	8,079.9	100.0
National Income	6,649.7	82.3
Compensation of employees	4,703.6	58.2
Proprietors' income	544.5	6.7
Corporate profits	805.0	10.0
Net interest	448.7	5.6
Rental income	147.9	1.8
Depreciation	867.9	10.7
Indirect Taxes Minus Subsidies	542.5	6.7
Net Factor Payments to the Rest of the World	19.8	0.2

Source: See Table 7.2.

THE INCOME APPROACH

Table 7.3 presents the income approach to calculating GDP, which looks at GDP in terms of who receives it as income, not who purchases it.

The income approach to GDP breaks down GDP into four components: national income, depreciation, indirect taxes minus subsidies, and net factor payments to the rest of the world:

> GDP = National income + Depreciation + (Indirect taxes − Subsidies) + Net factor payments to the rest of the world.

As we examine each, keep in mind that total expenditures always equal total income.

▶ **National Income** National income is the total income earned by factors of production owned by a country's citizens. Table 7.3 shows that national income is the sum of five items: (1) compensation of employees, (2) proprietors' income, (3) corporate profits, (4) net interest, and (5) rental income. **Compensation of employees**, the largest of the five items by far, includes wages and salaries paid to households by firms and by the government, as well as various supplements to wages and salaries such as contributions that employers make to social insurance and private pension funds. **Proprietors' income** is the income of unincorporated businesses, and **corporate profits** are the income of corporate businesses. **Net interest** is the interest paid by business. (Interest paid by households and by the government is not counted in GDP because it is not assumed to flow from the production of goods and services.) **Rental income**, a minor item, is the income received by property owners in the form of rent.

▶ **Depreciation** Recall from our discussion of net versus gross investment that when capital assets wear out or become obsolete, they decline in value. The measure of that decrease in value is called depreciation. This depreciation is a part of GDP in the income approach.

It may seem odd that we must *add* depreciation to national income when we calculate GDP by the income approach. But remember that we want a measure of *all* income, including income that results from the replacement of existing plant and equipment. Because national income does not include depreciation,[4] to get to total

national income *The total income earned by the factors of production owned by a country's citizens.*

compensation of employees *Includes wages, salaries, and various supplements—employer contributions to social insurance and pension funds, for example—paid to households by firms and by the government.*

proprietors' income *The income of unincorporated businesses.*

corporate profits *The income of corporate businesses.*

net interest *The interest paid by business.*

rental income *The income received by property owners in the form of rent.*

---

[4]National income does not include depreciation because depreciation has been subtracted from corporations' total revenue in computing the value of corporate profits, and the value of corporate profits is what is used in computing national income.

income (gross domestic product) we need to add depreciation. In 1997, depreciation accounted for $867.9 billion, or 10.7 percent of U.S. GDP.

> **Indirect Taxes Minus Subsidies**   In calculating final sales on the expenditures side, **indirect taxes**—sales taxes, customs duties, and license fees, for example—are included. These taxes must be accounted for on the income side.

To clarify this, suppose the sales tax is 7 percent and a firm sells 100,000 jelly beans for $100 plus tax. The total sales price is $107—the value of output recorded in the expenditure approach to calculating GDP. Of this $107, $7 goes to pay the tax to the government, some goes to pay wages to the workers in the jelly bean factory, and some goes to pay interest. The rest is the firm's profits plus depreciation.

To have the income and expenditure sides match, the sales tax must be recorded on the income side. If it were not included as part of income, then the basic rule that everyone's expenditure is someone else's income would be violated. Indirect taxes are an expenditure of the households or firms who buy things, but they are not income of firms that sell the products. (Thinking along these lines, indirect taxes can be considered income of the government.) We must add indirect taxes on the income side to make things balance.

Subsidies are payments made by the government for which it receives no goods or services in return. These subsidies are subtracted from national income to get GDP. (Remember: GDP is indirect taxes *minus* subsidies.) For example, farmers receive substantial subsidies from the government. Subsidy payments to farmers are income to farm proprietors and are thus part of national income, but they do not come from the sale of agricultural products, so are not part of GDP. To balance the expenditure side with the income side, these subsidies must be subtracted on the income side.[5]

> **Net Factor Payments to the Rest of the World**   **Net factor payments to the rest of the world** equal the payments of factor income (income to the factors of production) to the rest of the world *minus* the receipts of factor income from the rest of the world. This item is added for the following reason. National income is defined as the income of factors of production *owned* by the country. GDP, however, is output produced by factors of production located *within* the country. In other words, national income includes some income that should not be counted in GDP—namely, the income a country's citizens earn abroad—and this income must be subtracted. In addition, national income does not include some income that is counted in GDP—namely, the foreigners' income in the country whose GDP we are calculating—and this income must be added. Table 7.3 shows that the value of net factor payments to the rest of the world was positive in 1997 ($19.8 billion). This means that U.S. payments of factor income to the rest of the world exceeded U.S. receipts of factor income from the rest of the world in 1997.

As you can see in Table 7.3, U.S. GDP as calculated by the income approach was $8,079.9 billion in 1997—the same amount that we calculated using the expenditure approach.

FROM GDP TO DISPOSABLE PERSONAL INCOME

Although GDP is the most important item in national income accounting, other concepts are also useful to know. Some are presented in Table 7.4. The top of the table shows how GNP is calculated from GDP. Remember that a country's GDP is total

indirect taxes *Taxes like sales taxes, customs duties, and license fees.*

subsidies *Payments made by the government for which it receives no goods or services in return.*

net factor payments to the rest of the world *Payments of factor income to the rest of the world minus the receipt of factor income from the rest of the world.*

---

[5]In Table 7.3, two other items are included in the value for indirect taxes minus subsidies: business transfer payments and the statistical discrepancy. Business transfer payments are deducted from corporate profits, and so they need to be added to income. The statistical discrepancy adjusts for errors in the data collection.

TABLE 7.4 GDP, GNP, NNP, NATIONAL INCOME, PERSONAL INCOME, AND DISPOSABLE PERSONAL INCOME, 1997

	DOLLARS (BILLIONS)
GDP	8,079.9
Plus: Receipts of factor income from the rest of the world	+262.2
Less: Payments of factor income to the rest of the world	−282.0
Equals: **GNP**	8,060.1
Less: Depreciation	−867.9
Equals: **Net national product (NNP)**	7,192.2
Less: Indirect taxes minus subsidies	−542.5
Equals: **National income**	6,649.7
Less: Corporate profits minus dividends	−484.7
Less: Social insurance payments	−732.1
Plus: Personal interest income received from the government and consumers	+319.9
Plus: Transfer payments to persons	+1,121.2
Equals: **Personal income**	6,873.9
Less: Personal taxes	−988.7
Equals: **Disposable personal income**	5,885.2

Source: See Table 7.2.

production by factors of production located within that country, while its GNP is total production by factors of production owned by that country. If we take U.S. GDP, add to it factor income earned by U.S. citizens from the rest of the world (receipts of factor income from the rest of the world), and subtract from it factor income earned in the United States by foreigners (payments of factor income to the rest of the world), we get GNP.

From GNP, we can calculate net national product (NNP). Recall that the expenditure approach to GDP includes gross investment as one of the components of GDP (and of GNP). Gross domestic product does not account for the fact that some of the nation's capital stock is used up in the process of producing the nation's product. **Net national product (NNP)** is gross national product minus depreciation. In a sense, it is a nation's total product minus (or "net of") what is required to maintain the value of its capital stock. Because GDP does not take into account any depreciation of the capital stock that may have occurred, NNP is sometimes a better measure of how the economy is doing than is GDP.

To calculate national income, we subtract indirect taxes minus subsidies from NNP (subtract indirect business taxes and add subsidies). We subtract indirect taxes because they are included in NNP but do not represent payments to factors of production and are not part of national income. We add subsidies because they are payments to factors of production but are not included in NNP.

Personal income is the total income of households. To calculate personal income from national income, two items are subtracted: (1) corporate profits minus dividends, and (2) social insurance payments. Both need explanation. First, some corporate profits are paid to households in the form of dividends, and dividends are part of personal income. The profits that remain after dividends are paid—corporate profits minus dividends—are not paid to households as income. Therefore, corporate profits minus dividends must be subtracted from national income when computing personal income. Second, social insurance payments are payments made to the government, some by firms and some by employees. Because these payments are not received by households, they must be subtracted from national income when computing personal income.

net national product (NNP) *Gross national product minus depreciation; a nation's total product minus what is required to maintain the value of its capital stock.*

personal income *The total income of households. Equals (national income) minus (corporate profits minus dividends) minus (social insurance payments) plus (interest income received from the government and households) plus (transfer payments to households). The income received by households after paying social insurance taxes but before paying personal income taxes.*

TABLE 7.5 DISPOSABLE PERSONAL INCOME AND PERSONAL SAVING, 1997

	DOLLARS (BILLIONS)
Disposable personal income	5,885.2
Less:	
Personal consumption expenditures	−5,485.8
Interest paid by consumers to business	−154.8
Personal transfer payments to foreigners	−17.9
Equals: Personal saving	226.7
Personal saving as a percentage of disposable personal income:	3.9%

Source: See Table 7.2

Two items must be added to national income to calculate personal income: (1) personal interest income received from the government and consumers, and (2) transfer payments to persons. As we have pointed out, interest payments made by the government and consumers (households) are not counted in GDP and not reflected in national income figures.[6] But these payments are income received by households, so they must be added to national income when computing personal income.[7] Similarly, transfer payments to persons are not counted in GDP because they do not represent the production of any goods or services. But social security checks and other cash benefits are income received by households and must also be added to national income when computing personal income.

Personal income is the income received by households before paying personal income taxes but after paying social insurance contributions. The amount of income that households have to spend or save is called **disposable personal income**, or **after-tax income**. It is equal to personal income minus personal taxes.

Because disposable personal income is the amount of income that households can spend or save, it is an important income concept. Table 7.5 shows there are three categories of spending: (1) personal consumption expenditures, (2) interest paid by consumers to business, and (3) personal transfer payments to foreigners. The amount of disposable personal income left after total personal spending is **personal saving**. If your monthly disposable income is $500 and you spend $450, you have $50 left at the end of the month. Your personal saving is $50 for the month. Your personal saving level can be negative: If you earn $500 and spend $600 during the month, you have *dissaved* $100. To spend $100 more than you earn, you will either have to borrow the $100 from someone, take the $100 from your savings account, or sell an asset you own.

The **personal saving rate** is the percentage of disposable personal income saved, an important indicator of household behavior. A low saving rate means households are spending a large amount of their income. A high saving rate means households are

disposable personal income or **after-tax income** *Personal income minus personal income taxes. The amount that households have to spend or save.*

personal saving *The amount of disposable income that is left after total personal spending in a given period.*

personal saving rate *The percentage of disposable personal income that is saved. If the personal saving rate is low, households are spending a large amount relative to their incomes; if it is high, households are spending cautiously.*

---

[6]Interest payments on government bonds are not included in national income, while interest payments on bonds of private firms are, because government debt is assumed to be the result of activities, such as past wars, that do not add to current production. In contrast, it is presumed that firms sell bonds to finance investment that does add to current production. Interest payments by households are not included in national income because they are not considered to add to current production.

[7]Households can pay and receive interest. As a group, households receive more interest than they pay.

cautious in their spending. As Table 7.5 shows, the U.S. personal saving rate in 1997 was 3.9 percent. Saving rates tend to rise during recessionary periods, when consumers become anxious about their future, and fall during boom times, as pent-up spending demand gets released.

NOMINAL VERSUS REAL GDP

So far, we have looked at GDP measured in **current dollars**, or the current prices we pay for things. When a variable is measured in current dollars, it is described in *nominal terms*. **Nominal GDP** is GDP measured in current dollars—all components of GDP valued at their current prices.

In many applications of macroeconomics, nominal GDP is not a very desirable measure of production. Why? Assume there is only one good—say, pizza. In each year 1 and 2, 100 units (slices) of pizza were produced. Production thus remained the same for year 1 and year 2. But suppose the price of pizza increased from $1.00 per slice in year 1 to $1.10 per slice in year 2. Nominal GDP in year 1 is $100 (100 units × $1.00 per unit), and nominal GDP in year 2 is $110 (100 units × $1.10 per unit). Nominal GDP has increased by $10, even though no more slices of pizza were produced. If we use nominal GDP to measure growth, we can be misled into thinking production has grown when all that has really happened is a rise in the price level.

If there were only one good in the economy—like pizza—it would be easy to measure production and compare one year's value to another's. We would add up all the pizza slices produced each year. In the example, production is 100 in both years. If the number of slices had increased to 105 in year 2, we would say production increased by five slices between year 1 and year 2, which is a 5 percent increase. But, alas, there is more than one good in the economy.

At the end of 1995, the Bureau of Economic Analysis (BEA) of the U.S. Department of Commerce—which produces the national income and product accounts—changed the procedure to adjust nominal GDP for price changes. The new procedure has some advantages over the older one, as we will see. To the extent that this change leads to improved measures of GDP, it can have significant and positive effects on policy decisions. The decisions of both monetary policy makers and fiscal policy makers are influenced by GDP growth, and improved measures of growth should lead to better decisions.

As you read the following, keep in mind that the job of adjusting nominal GDP to account for price changes is not easy. Even in an economy of just apples and oranges, it would not be obvious how to add up apples and oranges to get an overall measure of output. The BEA's task is to add up thousands of goods, each of whose price is changing over time.

In the following, we will use the concept of a **weight**, either price weights or quantity weights. What is a weight? It is easiest to define the term by an example. Suppose in your economics course there is a final exam and two other tests. If the final exam counts for one half of the grade and the other two tests for one fourth each, the "weights" are one half, one fourth, and one fourth. If instead the final exam counts for 80 percent of the grade and the other two tests for 10 percent each, the weights are .8, .1, and .1. The more important an item is in a group, the larger its weight.

CALCULATING REAL GDP

Nominal GDP adjusted for price changes is called *real GDP*. All of the main issues involved in computing real GDP can be discussed using a simple three-good economy and two years. Table 7.6 presents all the data that we will need. The table presents

current dollars *The current prices that one pays for goods and services.*

nominal GDP *Gross domestic product measured in current dollars.*

weight *The importance attached to an item within a group of items.*

TABLE 7.6 A THREE-GOOD ECONOMY

	(1)	(2)	(3)	(4)	(5) GDP IN YEAR 1 IN YEAR 1 PRICES $P_1 \times Q_1$	(6) GDP IN YEAR 2 IN YEAR 1 PRICES $P_1 \times Q_2$	(7) GDP IN YEAR 1 IN YEAR 2 PRICES $P_2 \times Q_1$	(8) GDP IN YEAR 2 IN YEAR 2 PRICES $P_2 \times Q_2$
	PRODUCTION		PRICE PER UNIT					
	YEAR 1 Q_1	YEAR 2 Q_2	YEAR 1 P_1	YEAR 2 P_2				
Good A	6	11	$.50	$.40	$3.00	$5.50	$2.40	$4.40
Good B	7	4	$.30	$1.00	$2.10	$1.20	$7.00	$4.00
Good C	10	12	$.70	$.90	$7.00	$8.40	$9.00	$10.80
Total					$12.10 Nominal GDP in year 1	$15.10	$18.40	$19.20 Nominal GDP in year 2

Rates of growth in real GDP vary from country to country. In 1997, U.S. GDP was growing at a rate of 3.6% annually; the figure was −0.3% in Japan, 3.5% in Great Britain, 3.2% in Australia, −0.6% in Russia, 9.6% in China, 8.8% in Mexico, 7.6% in Poland, 7.8% in Argentina, and 8.4% in Malaysia.

Source: The Economist, October 11–17, 1997.

base-year *The year chosen for the weights in a fixed-weight procedure.*

fixed-weight procedure *A procedure that uses weights from a given base year.*

price and quantity data for two years and three goods. The goods are labeled A, B, and C, and the years are labeled 1 and 2. P denotes price, and Q denotes quantity.

The first thing to note from Table 7.6 is that *nominal output*—in current dollars—in year 1 for good A is the price of good A in year 1 ($.50) times the number of units of good A produced in year 1 (6), which is $3.00. Similarly, nominal output in year 1 is $7 \times \$.30 = \$2.10$ for good B and $10 \times \$.70 = \$7.00$ for good C. The sum of these three amounts, $12.10 in column 5, is nominal GDP in year 1 in this simple economy. Nominal GDP in year 2—calculated by using year 2's quantities and year 2's prices—is $19.20 (column 8). Nominal GDP has risen from $12.10 in year 1 to $19.20 in year 2, an increase of 58.7 percent.[8]

You can see that the price of each good changed between year 1 and year 2—the price of good A fell (from $.50 to $.40) and the prices of goods B and C rose (B from $.30 to $1.00; C from $.70 to $.90). Some of the change in nominal GDP between years 1 and 2 is due to price changes and not production changes. How much can we attribute to price changes and how much to production changes? Here, things get tricky. The BEA's old procedure was to pick a **base year** and use the prices in that base year as weights to calculate real GDP. This is a **fixed-weight procedure** because the weights used, which are the prices, are the same for all years—namely, the prices that prevailed in the base year.

Let us use the fixed-weight procedure and year 1 as the base year, which means using year 1 prices as the weights. Then in Table 7.6, real GDP in year 1 is $12.10 (column 5), and real GDP in year 2 is $15.10 (column 6). Note that both columns use year 1 prices, and that nominal and real GDP are the same in year 1 because year 1 is the base year. Real GDP has increased from $12.10 to $15.10, an increase of 24.8 percent.

Let's now use the fixed-weight procedure and year 2 as the base year, which means using year 2 prices as the weights. In Table 7.6, real GDP in year 1 is $18.40 (column 7), and real GDP in year 2 is $19.20 (column 8). Note, both columns use year 2 prices, and nominal and real GDP are the same in year 2 because year 2 is the base year. Real GDP has increased from $18.40 to $19.20, an increase of 4.3 percent.

This example shows that growth rates can be sensitive to the choice of the base year—24.8 percent using year 1 prices as weights and 4.3 percent using year 2 prices as weights. The old BEA procedure simply picked one year as the base year and did all the

[8]The percentage change is calculated as $[(19.20 - 12.10)/12.10] \times 100 = .587 \times 100 = 58.7$ percent.

calculations using the prices in that year as weights. The new procedure made two important changes. The first (using the current example) was to "split the difference" between 24.8 percent and 4.3 percent. What does "splitting the difference" mean? One way would be to take the average of the two numbers, which is 14.55 percent. What the BEA did was to take the *geometric* average, which for the current example is 14.09 percent.[9] These two averages (14.55 percent and 14.09 percent) are quite close, and the use of either would give similar results. The point here is not that the geometric average was used, but that the first change was to split the difference using some average. Note that this new procedure requires two "base" years, because 24.8 percent was computed using year 1 prices as weights and 4.3 percent was computed using year 2 prices as weights.

The second BEA change was to use years 1 and 2 as the base years when computing the percentage change between years 1 and 2, then use years 2 and 3 as the base years when computing the percentage change between years 2 and 3, and so on. The two base years change as the calculations move through time. The series of percentage changes computed in this way is taken to be the series of growth rates of real GDP, and so in this way nominal GDP is adjusted for price changes. To make sure you understand this, review the calculations in Table 7.6; all the data you need to see what is going on are in this table.

CALCULATING THE GDP PRICE INDEX

We now switch gears from real GDP, a quantity measure, to the GDP price index, a price measure. One of economic policy makers' goals is to keep changes in the overall price level small. For this reason policy makers need not only good measures of how real output is changing but also good measures of how the overall price level is changing. The GDP price index is one measure of the overall price level. We can use the data in Table 7.6 to show how the GDP price index is computed by the BEA.

In Table 7.6, the price of good *A* fell from $.50 in year 1 to $.40 in year 2; the price of good *B* rose from $.30 to $1.00; and the price of good *C* rose from $.70 to $.90. If we were interested only in how individual prices change, this is all the information we would need. But if we are interested in how the overall price *level* changes, we need to weight the individual prices in some way. The obvious weights to use are the quantities produced, but which quantities—year 1's or year 2's? The same issues arise here for the quantity weights as for the price weights in computing real GDP.

Let's first use the fixed-weight procedure and year 1 as the base year, which means using year 1 quantities as the weights. Then in Table 7.6, the "bundle" price in year 1 is $12.10 (column 5), and the bundle price in year 2 is $18.40 (column 7). Both columns use year 1 quantities. The bundle price has increased from $12.10 to $18.40, an increase of 52.1 percent.

Next use the fixed-weight procedure and year 2 as the base year, which means using year 2 quantities as the weights. Then the bundle price in year 1 is $15.10 (column 6), and the bundle price in year 2 is $19.20 (column 8). Both columns use year 2 quantities. The bundle price has increased from $15.10 to $19.20, an increase of 27.2 percent.

This example shows that overall price increases can be sensitive to the choice of the base year—52.1 percent using year 1 quantities as weights and 27.2 percent using year 2 quantities as weights. Again, the old BEA procedure simply picked one year as the base year and did all the calculations using the quantities in the base year as weights. The new procedure first splits the difference between 52.1 percent and 27.2 percent by taking the geometric average, which is 39.1 percent. Second, it uses years 1 and 2 as the base years when computing the percentage change between years 1 and 2, years 2 and 3

Between 1970 and 1996, *GDP* increased at an average annual rate of 7.7% for a total increase of over 600%. *Real GDP* increased at a rate of 2.7% during the same period for a total increase of 104%. *Per capita real GDP* increased by only 1.7% for a total increase of 58%.

Source: *1997 Economic Report of the President.*

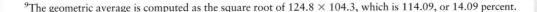

[9]The geometric average is computed as the square root of 124.8 × 104.3, which is 114.09, or 14.09 percent.

as the base years when computing the percentage change between years 2 and 3, and so on. The series of percentage changes computed in this way is taken to be the series of percentage changes in the GDP price index, that is, a series of inflation rates of the overall price level.

THE PROBLEMS OF FIXED WEIGHTS

To see why the BEA switched to the new procedure, let's consider a number of problems with using fixed price weights to compute real GDP. First, 1987 price weights, the last price weights the BEA used before it changed procedures, are not likely to be very accurate for, say, the 1950s. Many structural changes have taken place in the U.S. economy in the last 30 to 40 years, and it seems unlikely that 1987 prices are good weights to use for the 1950s.

Another problem is that the use of fixed price weights does not account for the responses in the economy to supply shifts. Say bad weather leads to a lower production of oranges in year 2. In a simple supply and demand diagram for oranges, this corresponds to a shift of the supply curve to the left, which leads to an increase in the price of oranges and a decrease in the quantity demanded. As consumers move up the demand curve, they are substituting away from oranges. If technical advances in year 2 result in cheaper ways of producing computers, the result is a shift of the computer supply curve to the right, which leads to a decrease in the price of computers and an increase in the quantity demanded. Consumers are substituting toward computers. (You should be able to draw supply-and-demand diagrams for both these cases.) Table 7.6 shows this tendency. The quantity of good A rose between years 1 and 2 and the price decreased (the computer case), whereas the quantity of good B fell and the price increased (the orange case). The computer supply curve has been shifting to the right over time, due primarily to technical advances. The result has been large decreases in the price of computers and large increases in the quantity demanded.

To see why these responses pose a problem for the use of fixed price weights, consider the data in Table 7.6. Because the price of good A was higher in year 1, the increase in production of good A is weighted more if we use year 1 as the base year than if we used year 2 as the base year. Also, because the price of good B was lower in year 1, the decrease in production of good B is weighted less if we use year 1 as the base year. These effects make the overall change in real GDP larger if we use year 1 price weights than if we use year 2 price weights. Using year 1 price weights ignores the kinds of substitution responses discussed in the previous paragraph and leads to what many feel are too-large estimates of real GDP changes. In the past, the BEA tended to move the base year forward about every five years, resulting in the past estimates of real GDP growth being revised downward. It is undesirable to have past growth estimates change simply because of the change to a new base year. (The last change in the base year was from 1982 to 1987.) The new BEA procedure avoids many of these fixed-weight problems.

Similar problems arise when using fixed-quantity weights to compute price indexes. For example, the fixed-weight procedure ignores the substitution away from goods whose prices are increasing and toward goods whose prices are decreasing or increasing less rapidly. The procedure tends to overestimate the increase in the overall price level. As discussed in the next chapter, there are still many price indexes that are computed using fixed weights. The GDP price index differs because it does not use fixed weights. It is also a price index for all the goods and services produced in the economy. Other price indexes cover fewer goods and services.

It should finally be stressed that there is no "right" way of computing real GDP. The economy consists of many goods, each with its own price, and there is no exact way of adding together the production of the different goods. We can say that the BEA's new procedure for computing real GDP avoids the problems associated with the use of fixed weights, and it seems to be an improvement over the old procedure.

LIMITATIONS OF THE GDP CONCEPT

We generally think of increases in GDP as good. Increasing GDP (or preventing its decrease) is usually considered one of the chief goals of the government's macroeconomic policy. Because some serious problems arise when we try to use GDP as a measure of happiness or well-being, we now point out some of the limitations of the GDP concept as a measure of welfare.

GDP AND SOCIAL WELFARE

If crime levels went down, society would be better off, but a decrease in crime is not an increase in output and is not reflected in GDP. Neither is an increase in leisure time. Yet, to the extent that households desire extra leisure time (rather than having it forced on them by a lack of jobs in the economy), an increase in leisure is also an increase in social welfare. Furthermore, some increases in social welfare are associated with a *decrease* in GDP. An increase in leisure during a time of full employment, for example, leads to a decrease in GDP because less time is spent on producing output.

Most nonmarket and domestic activities, such as housework and child care, are not counted in GDP even though they amount to real production. However, if I decide to send my children to day care or hire someone to clean my house or to drive my car for me, GDP increases. The salaries of day-care staff, cleaning people, and chauffeurs are counted in GDP, but the time I spend doing the same things is not counted. A mere change of institutional arrangements, even though no more output is being produced, can show up as a change in GDP.

Furthermore, GDP seldom reflects losses or social ills. GDP accounting rules do not adjust for production that pollutes the environment. The more production there is, the larger is GDP, regardless of how much pollution results in the process.

GDP also has nothing to say about the distribution of output among individuals in a society. It does not distinguish, for example, between the case in which most output goes to a few people and the case in which output is evenly divided among all people. We cannot use GDP to measure the effects of redistributive policies (which take income from some people and give income to others). Such policies have no direct impact on GDP. GDP is also neutral about the kinds of goods an economy produces. Symphony performances, handguns, cigarettes, professional football games, Bibles, soda pop, milk, economics textbooks, and comic books all get counted.

In spite of these limitations, GDP is a highly useful measure of economic activity and well-being. If you doubt this, answer this simple question: Would you rather live in the United States of 200 years ago, when rivers were less polluted and crime rates were probably lower, or in the United States of today? Most people say they prefer the present. Even with all the "negatives," GDP per person and the average standard of living are much higher today than 200 years ago.

THE UNDERGROUND ECONOMY

Many transactions are missed in the calculation of GDP, even though in principle they should be counted. Most illegal transactions are missed unless they are "laundered" into legitimate business. Income that is earned but not reported as income for tax

TABLE 7.7

PER CAPITA GNP
FOR SELECTED
COUNTRIES, 1995

COUNTRY	U.S. DOLLARS
Switzerland	40,630
Japan	39,640
Norway	31,250
Denmark	29,890
Germany	27,510
United States	26,980
Austria	26,890
France	24,990
Sweden	23,750
Finland	20,580
Canada	19,380
Australia	18,720
United Kingdom	18,700
Israel	15,920
Spain	13,580
Portugal	9,740
Greece	8,210
Chile	4,160
Mexico	3,320
Botswana	3,020
Turkey	2,780
Jamaica	1,510
Jordan	1,510
Philippines	1,050
Indonesia	980
Bolivia	800
Egypt	790
Mali	250
Mozambique	80

Source: The World Bank Atlas, 1997.

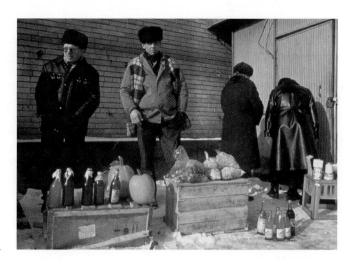

IN SOME COUNTRIES, THE ONLY WAY TO PURCHASE CONSUMER GOODS MAY BE THROUGH THE UNDERGROUND MARKET.

underground economy *The part of the economy in which transactions take place and in which income is generated that is unreported and therefore not counted in GDP.*

per capita GDP or **GNP** *A country's GDP or GNP divided by its population.*

purposes is usually missed, although some adjustments are made in the GDP calculations to take misreported income into account. The part of the economy that should be counted in GDP but is not is sometimes called the **underground economy.**

Tax evasion is usually thought to be the major incentive for people to participate in the underground economy. Studies estimate the size of the U.S. underground economy ranging from 5 percent to 30 percent of GDP,[10] comparable to the size of the underground economy in most European countries and probably much smaller than the size of the underground economy in the Eastern European countries. Estimates of Italy's underground economy range from 10 percent to 35 percent of Italian GDP. At the lower end of the scale, estimates for Switzerland range from 3 percent to 5 percent.

Why should we care about the underground economy? To the extent that GDP reflects only a part of economic activity rather than a complete measure of what the economy produces, it is misleading. Unemployment rates, for example, may be lower than officially measured if people work in the underground economy without reporting this fact to the government. Also, if the size of the underground economy varies between countries—as it does—we can be misled when we compare GDP between countries. For example, Italy's GDP would be much higher if we considered its underground sector as part of the economy, while Switzerland's GDP would change very little.

PER CAPITA GDP/GNP

GDP and GNP are sometimes measured in per capita terms. **Per capita GDP or GNP** is a country's GDP or GNP divided by its population. It is a better measure of well-being for the average person than is total GDP or GNP. Table 7.7 lists the per capita GNP of various countries for 1995. Switzerland has the highest per capita GNP, followed by Japan and Norway. U.S. per capita GNP was $26,980. Mozambique was estimated to have a per capita GNP of only $80 in 1995.

[10]See, for example, Edgar L. Feige, "Defining and Estimating Underground and Informal Economies: The New Industrial Economic Approach," *World Development* 19(7) (1990); and "The Underground Economy in the United States," Occasional Paper No. 2, U.S. Department of Labor, September 1992.

Looking Ahead

This chapter has introduced many key variables that macroeconomists are interested in, including GDP and its components. There is much more to be learned about the data that macroeconomists use. In the next chapter, we will discuss the data on employment, unemployment, and the labor force, and in chapters 11 and 12, we will discuss the data on money and interest rates. Finally, in chapter 21, we will discuss in more detail the data on the relationship between the United States and the rest of the world.

SUMMARY

1. One source of data on the key variables in the macroeconomy are the national income and product accounts. These accounts provide a conceptual framework that macroeconomists use to think about how the pieces of the economy fit together.

GROSS DOMESTIC PRODUCT

2. *Gross domestic product* (*GDP*) is the key concept in national income accounting. GDP is the total market value of all final goods and services produced within a given period by factors of production located within a country. GDP excludes intermediate goods. To include goods both when they are purchased as inputs and when they are sold as final products would be double counting and an overstatement of the value of production.

3. GDP excludes all transactions in which money or goods change hands but in which no new goods and services are produced. GDP includes the income of foreigners working in the United States and the profits that foreign companies earn in the United States. GDP excludes the income of U.S. citizens working abroad and profits earned by U.S. companies in foreign countries.

4. *Gross national product* (*GNP*) is the market value of all final goods and services produced during a given period by factors of production owned by a country's citizens.

CALCULATING GDP

5. The *expenditure approach* to GDP adds up the amount spent on all final goods and services during a given period. The four main categories of expenditures are *personal consumption expenditures* (*C*), *gross private domestic investment* (*I*), *government consumption and investment* (*G*), and *net exports* (*EX* − *IM*). The sum of these equals GDP.

6. The three main components of personal consumption expenditures (*C*) are *durable goods*, *nondurable goods*, and *services*.

7. *Gross private domestic investment* (*I*) is the total investment made by the private sector in a given period. There are three kinds of investment: *nonresidential investment*, *residential investment*, and *changes in business inventories*. Gross investment does not take *depreciation*—the decrease in the value of assets—into account. *Net investment* is equal to gross investment minus depreciation.

8. Government consumption and investment (*G*) include expenditures by state, federal, and local governments for final goods and services. The value of *net exports* (*EX* − *IM*) equals the differences between exports (sales to foreigners of U.S.-produced goods and services) and imports (U.S. purchases of goods and services from abroad).

9. Because every payment (expenditure) by a buyer is a receipt (income) for the seller, GDP can be computed in terms of who receives it as income—the *income approach* to calculating gross domestic product. The GDP equation using the income approach is GDP = National income + Depreciation + (Indirect taxes − Subsidies) + Net factor payments to the rest of the world.

FROM GDP TO DISPOSABLE PERSONAL INCOME

10. GNP minus depreciation is *net national product* (*NNP*). *National income* is the total amount earned by the factors of production in the economy; it is equal to NNP less indirect taxes minus subsidies. *Personal income* is the total income of households. *Disposable personal income* is what households have to spend or save after paying their taxes. The *personal saving rate* is the percentage of disposable personal income saved rather than spent.

NOMINAL VERSUS REAL GDP

11. GDP measured in current dollars (the current prices that one pays for goods) is *nominal GDP*. If we use nominal GDP to measure growth, we can be misled into thinking that production has grown when all that has happened is a

rise in the price level, or inflation. A better measure of production is *real GDP*, which is nominal GDP adjusted for prices changes.

12. The GDP price index is a measure of the overall price level.

LIMITATIONS OF THE GDP CONCEPT

13. We generally think of increases in GDP as good, but some problems arise when we try to use GDP as a measure of happiness or well-being. The peculiarities of GDP accounting mean that institutional changes can change the value of GDP even if real production has not changed. GDP ignores most social ills, such as pollution. Furthermore, GDP tells us nothing about what kinds of goods are being produced or how income is distributed across the population. GDP also ignores many transactions of the underground economy.

14. *Per capita GDP or GNP* is a country's GDP or GNP divided by its population. Per capita GDP or GNP is a better measure of well-being for the average person than is total GDP or GNP.

REVIEW TERMS AND CONCEPTS

base year, 146

change in business inventories, 138

compensation of employees, 141

corporate profits, 141

current dollars, 145

depreciation, 140

disposable personal income, or after-tax, income, 144

durable goods, 137

expenditure approach, 136

final goods and services, 134

fixed-weight procedure, 146

government consumption and investment (G), 140

gross domestic product (GDP), 133

gross investment, 140

gross national product (GNP), 135

gross private investment (I), 138

income approach, 136

indirect taxes, 142

intermediate goods, 134

national income, 141

national income and product accounts, 133

net exports (EX − IM), 140

net factor payments to the rest of the world, 142

net interest, 141

net investment, 140

net national product (NNP), 143

nominal GDP, 145

nondurable goods, 137

nonresidential investment, 138

per capita GDP or GNP, 150

personal consumption expenditures (C), 137

personal income, 143

personal saving, 144

personal saving rate, 144

proprietors' income, 141

rental income, 141

residential investment, 138

services, 137

subsidies, 142

underground economy, 150

value added, 134

weight, 145

Expenditure approach to GDP: GDP = C + I + G + (EX − IM)

GDP = Final sales + GDP − Change in business inventories

Net investment = Capital end of period − Capital beginning of period

Income approach to GDP: GDP = National income + Depreciation + (Indirect taxes − Subsidies) + Net factor payments to the rest of the world

PROBLEM SET

1. From the table for this problem, calculate the following:
   a. Gross private investment
   b. Net exports
   c. Gross domestic product
   d. Gross national product
   e. Net national product
   f. National income
   g. Personal income
   h. Disposable income

Transfer payments	15
Subsidies	5
Social insurance payments	35
Depreciation	50
Receipts of factor income from the rest of the world	4
Government consumption and investment	75
Imports	50
Payments of factor income to the rest of the world	5
Personal interest income from government and households	35
Indirect taxes	20
Exports	60
Net private domestic investment	100
Personal taxes	60
Corporate profits	45
Personal consumption expenditures	250
Dividends	4

2. How do we know that calculating GDP by the expenditure approach yields the same answer as calculating GDP by the income approach?

3. Why do we bother to construct real GDP if we already know nominal GDP?

4. What are some of the problems using fixed weights to compute real GDP and the GDP price index? How does the BEA's approach attempt to solve these problems?

5. Explain what double counting is and discuss why GDP is not equal to total sales.

6. The following table gives some figures from a forecast of real GDP and population done by a well-known consulting firm in 1997. According to the forecast, approximately how much price inflation will there be between 1998 and 1999? What is per capita GDP projected to be in 1998? 1999? Compute the forecast rate of change in real GDP and per capita real GDP between 1998 and 1999.

Real GDP 1998 (billions)	$7,282.7
Real GDP 1999 (billions)	$7,457.1
Population 1998 (millions)	270.3
Population 1999 (millions)	272.6

7. In 1997, in Swaziland and Lesotho, countries in Africa, GNP was substantially bigger than GDP. Locate the two countries on a map of Africa. Given their location, can you explain why this might be the case?

8. During 1997, real GDP in Germany rose about 2.9 percent. During the same period, retail sales in Germany rose only about 1.1 percent in real terms. What are some possible explanations for retail sales to consumers growing more slowly than GDP? (*Hint:* Think of the composition of GDP using the expenditure approach.)

9. Which of the following transactions would not be counted in GDP? Explain your answers.
   a. General Motors issues new shares of stock to finance the construction of a plant.
   b. General Motors builds a new plant.
   c. Company A successfully launches a hostile takeover of Company B, in which it purchases all the assets of Company B.
   d. Your grandmother wins $10 million in the lottery.
   e. You buy a new copy of this textbook.
   f. You buy a used copy of this textbook.
   g. The government pays out social security benefits.
   h. A public utility installs new antipollution equipment in its smokestacks.
   i. Luigi's Pizza buys 30 pounds of mozzarella cheese, holds it in inventory for one month, and then uses it to make pizza, which it sells.
   j. You spend the weekend cleaning your apartment.
   k. A drug dealer sells $500 worth of illegal drugs.

10. If you buy a new car, the entire purchase is counted as consumption in the year in which you make the transaction. Explain briefly why this is in one sense an "error" in national income accounting. (*Hint:* How is the purchase of a car different from the purchase of a pizza?) How might you correct this error?

11. Explain why imports are subtracted in the expenditure approach to calculating GDP.

12. GDP calculations do not directly include the economic costs of environmental damage (for example, global warming, acid rain). Do you think these costs should be included in GDP? Why or why not? How could GDP be amended to include environmental damage costs?

TAKE IT TO THE NET

We invite you to visit the Case and Fair page on the Prentice Hall Web site:

http://www.prenhall.com/casefair

for this chapter's World Wide Web exercise.

Chapter 8

MACROECONOMIC CONCERNS: UNEMPLOYMENT, INFLATION, AND GROWTH

SOMETIME DURING 1990, total employment in the United States stopped growing and began to decline. In May, total employment hit 119.9 million. By October, more than 500,000 people had lost their jobs, and by March 1991, more than 1.5 million people had lost their jobs. At the same time, after nearly eight years of steady growth, real output declined in the third and fourth quarters of 1990 and the first quarter of 1991. For many, this recession was a curiosity, something in the news. After all, 118.5 million out of 120 million workers still had jobs. But for the workers who lost their jobs, the pain was real:

> Standing in the unemployment line today, a cross section of Americans from a beautician to a film editor to a sales manager to a corporate vice president, voiced a shared sense of insecurity about the future as jobs disappear and companies close. They said their hunt for work had taken on new urgency as they watched the economy worsen and opportunities dry up. Gathered at an unemployment office in west Los Angeles, they listened with a very personal concern to the news that the unemployment rate in California had climbed today to its highest point in four years.
>
> "The hardest thing is to see how panicked people are," said Bill Williams, a part owner of a small marketing company in Huntington Beach that recently went out of business. "Right now I don't have a dime. I'm worried about buying things like sugar. I'm close to losing my home."[1]

---

[1]Seth Mydans, "For Jobless, Era of Plenty Fades to Fear," *The New York Times*, December 8, 1990, p. 1.

Twelve years earlier, the United States had wrestled with high inflation. Prices *increased* an average of 11.3 percent in 1979 and 13.5 percent in 1980. As President Jimmy Carter noted in a report to Congress in January 1980:

> It is my strong conviction that inflation remains the nation's number one economic problem. Energy and housing prices are still moving up rapidly, adding directly to inflation and continuing to threaten a new price-wage spiral in the rest of the economy. Our immediate objective must be to prevent the spread of double-digit price increases from oil to the rest of the economy. . . . Halting the spread of inflation is not enough, however. We must take steps to reduce it.[2]

These "twin evils" of unemployment and inflation are concerns of macroeconomists. In this chapter we explore these concerns, describing the periodic ups and downs in the economy that we call the business cycle. Later chapters focus on the likely causes of business cycles and some of the things that government may do to prevent or minimize the damage they create. First, we need to know more about what the business cycle is. What are recessions and depressions? Who is hurt by them? What are the consequences of inflation? Who benefits and who loses when the price level rises rapidly? Why should policy makers in Washington be concerned about the business cycle?

Also, as mentioned in chapter 6, macroeconomists are concerned about the size of the long-run growth rate of output. What factors influence the long-run growth rate? Why do some countries grow faster than others? Can policy makers influence the growth rate? We briefly consider long-run growth issues in this chapter and then return to them in chapter 19.

RECESSIONS, DEPRESSIONS, UNEMPLOYMENT

recession *Roughly, a period in which real GDP declines for at least two consecutive quarters. Marked by falling output and rising unemployment.*

Recall that a **recession** is roughly a period in which real GDP declines for at least two consecutive quarters. Also recall that real GDP is a measure of the actual output of goods and services in the economy during a given period. When real GDP falls, less is being produced. When less output is produced, fewer inputs are used, employment declines, the unemployment rate rises, and a smaller percentage of the capital stock at our disposal is utilized (more plants and equipment are running at less than full capacity). When real output falls, real income declines.

depression *A prolonged and deep recession. The precise definitions of prolonged and deep are debatable.*

A **depression** is a prolonged and deep recession, although there is disagreement over how severe and how prolonged a recession must be to be called a depression. Nearly everyone agrees the U.S. economy experienced a depression between 1929 and the late 1930s. The most severe recession since the 1930s took place between 1980 and 1982.

In Figure 6.6, we divided the period since 1970 into three "recessionary" periods, 1974 to 1975, 1980 to 1982, and 1990 to 1991. Table 8.1 summarizes some of the differences between the recession of 1980 to 1982 and the early part of the Great Depression. Between 1929 and 1933, real GDP declined by 27 percent. In other words, in 1933 the United States produced 27 percent less than in 1929. While only 3.2 percent of the labor force was unemployed in 1929, 25.2 percent was unemployed in 1933. By contrast, between 1980 and 1982 real GDP declined by just 0.2 percent. The unemployment rate rose from 5.8 percent in 1979 to 9.7 percent in 1982. *Capacity utilization rates*, which show the percentage of factory capacity being used in production, are not available for the 1930s, so we have no point of comparison. However, Table 8.1 shows capacity utilization fell from 85.2 percent in 1979 to 72.1 percent in 1982. Although the recession in the early 1980s was severe, it did not come close to the severity of the Great Depression.

[2]Jimmy Carter, *Economic Report of the President*, transmitted to Congress, January 1980.

TABLE 8.1 REAL GDP AND UNEMPLOYMENT RATES, 1929–1933 AND 1980–1982

THE EARLY PART OF THE GREAT DEPRESSION, 1929–1933

	PERCENTAGE CHANGE IN REAL GDP	UNEMPLOYMENT RATE	NUMBER OF UNEMPLOYED (MILLIONS)
1929		3.2	1.5
1930	−9.0	8.9	4.3
1931	−6.3	16.3	8.0
1932	−13.3	24.1	12.1
1933	−1.2	25.2	12.8

Note: Percentage fall in real GDP between 1929 and 1933 was 27.0 percent.

THE RECESSION OF 1980–1982

	PERCENTAGE CHANGE IN REAL GDP	UNEMPLOYMENT RATE	NUMBER OF UNEMPLOYED (MILLIONS)	CAPACITY UTILIZATION (PERCENTAGE)
1979		5.8	6.1	85.2
1980	−0.3	7.1	7.6	80.9
1981	2.3	7.6	8.3	79.9
1982	−2.1	9.7	10.7	72.1

Note: Percentage fall in real GDP between 1979 and 1982 was 0.2 percent.

Sources: Historical Statistics of the United States and U.S. Department of Commerce, Bureau of Economic Analysis.

DEFINING AND MEASURING UNEMPLOYMENT

The most frequently discussed symptom of a recession is unemployment. In September of 1982, the United States' unemployment rate was over 10 percent for the first time since the 1930s. But although unemployment is widely discussed, most people are unaware of what unemployment statistics mean or how they are derived.

The unemployment statistics released to the press on the first Friday of each month are based on a survey of households conducted by the Bureau of Labor Statistics (BLS), a branch of the Department of Labor. Each month the BLS draws a sample of 65,000 households and completes interviews with all but about 2,500 of them. Each interviewed household answers questions regarding the work activity of household members 16 years of age or older during the calendar week that contains the twelfth of the month. (The survey is conducted in the week that follows the week that contains the twelfth of the month.)

If a household member 16 years of age or older worked one hour or more as a paid employee, either for someone else or in his own business or farm, he is classified as **employed**. A household member is also considered employed if he worked 15 hours or more without pay in a family enterprise. Finally, a household member is counted as employed if she held a job from which she was temporarily absent due to illness, bad weather, vacation, labor-management disputes, or personal reasons, whether she was paid or not.

Those who are not employed fall into one of two categories: (1) unemployed or (2) not in the labor force. To be considered **unemployed**, a person must be available for work and have made specific efforts to find work during the previous four weeks.

employed *Any person 16 years old or older (1) who works for pay, either for someone else or in his or her own business for one or more hours per week, (2) who works without pay for 15 or more hours per week in a family enterprise, or (3) who has a job but has been temporarily absent, with or without pay.*

unemployed *A person 16 years old or older who is not working, is available for work, and has made specific efforts to find work during the previous four weeks.*

not in the labor force *People who are not looking for work, either because they do not want a job or because they have given up looking.*

labor force *The number of people employed plus the number of unemployed.*

Persons not looking for work, either because they do not want a job or have given up looking, are classified as **not in the labor force.** People not in the labor force include full-time students, retirees, individuals in institutions, and those staying home to take care of children or elderly parents.

The total **labor force** in the economy is the number of people employed plus the number of unemployed:

$$\text{Labor force} = \text{Employed} + \text{Unemployed}$$

The total population 16 years of age or older is equal to the number of people in the labor force plus the number not in the labor force:

$$\text{Population} = \text{Labor force} + \text{Not in labor force}$$

With these numbers, several ratios can be calculated. The **unemployment rate** is the ratio of the number of people unemployed to the total number of people in the labor force:

$$\text{Unemployment rate} = \frac{\text{Unemployed}}{\text{Employed} + \text{Unemployed}}$$

In January 1998, the labor force contained 137.5 million people, 131.1 million of whom were employed and 6.4 million of whom were unemployed and looking for work. The unemployment rate was 4.7 percent:

$$\frac{6.4}{131.1 + 6.4} = 4.7\%$$

The ratio of the labor force to the population 16 years old or over is called the **labor-force participation rate:**

$$\text{Labor-force participation rate} = \frac{\text{Labor force}}{\text{Population}}$$

Table 8.2 shows the relationship among these numbers for selected years since 1953. The year 1982 shows the effects of the recession. Although the unemployment rate has gone up and down, the labor-force participation rate has grown steadily since 1953. Most of this increase is due to the growth in the participation rate of women between the ages of 25 and 54.

Column 3 in Table 8.2 shows how many new workers the U.S. economy has absorbed in recent years. The number of employed workers increased by about 38 million between 1953 and 1982 and by about 30 million between 1982 and 1997.

COMPONENTS OF THE UNEMPLOYMENT RATE

The unemployment rate by itself conveys a limited amount of information. To understand the level of unemployment better, we must look at unemployment rates across groups of people, regions, and industries.

➤ **Unemployment Rates for Different Demographic Groups** There are big differences in rates of unemployment across demographic groups. Table 8.3 shows the unemployment rate for November 1982—the worst month of the recession in 1982—and for January 1998, broken down by race, sex, and age. In November 1982, when the overall unemployment rate hit 10.8 percent, the rate for whites was 9.6 percent while the rate for African Americans was more than twice that—20.2 percent.

We are paying no rent at all. That, of course, is a very difficult problem because we are continually having evictions, and social workers . . . are hard put to find places for people whose furniture has been put out on the street.[4]

From Birmingham, Alabama, in 1932:

> . . . we have about 108,000 wage and salary workers in my district. Of that number, it is my belief that not exceeding 8000 have their normal incomes. At least 25,000 men are altogether without work. Some of them have not had a stroke of work for more than 12 months. Perhaps 60,000 or 70,000 are working from one to five days a week, and practically all have had serious cuts in wages and many of them do not average over $1.50 per day.[5]

Economic hardship accompanied the recent recessions as well. Between 1979 and 1983, the number of people officially classified as living in poverty in the United States rose from 26.1 million (11.7 percent of the population) to 35.5 million (15.3 percent). In addition to economic hardship, prolonged unemployment may also bring with it social and personal ills: anxiety, depression, a deterioration of physical and psychological health, drug abuse (including alcoholism), and suicide. There is also some evidence that the number of welfare recipients rises and falls with unemployment. See the Issues and Debates box "Unemployment and Welfare: 1991 to 1997."

THE BENEFITS OF RECESSIONS

Do recessions have any benefits? Yes: Recessions are likely to slow the rate of inflation. We saw in Figure 6.8 two serious inflationary periods since 1970: 1974 to 1975 and 1979 to 1981. Each was followed by a recession during which the rate of inflation decreased. As Table 8.7 shows, inflation fell from a 1974 rate of 11.0 percent to 5.8 percent in 1976. In 1983, the inflation rate also fell, to 3.2 percent, from a 1980 rate of 13.5 percent.

It appears recessions do help to counteract inflation, but more analysis is needed before we can understand why (see chapter 14). The point here is:

> Recessions may help to reduce inflation.

Some argue recessions may increase efficiency by driving the least efficient firms in the economy out of business and forcing surviving firms to trim waste and manage their resources better. As we will discuss in chapter 21, a recession leads to a decrease in the demand for imports, which improves a nation's balance of payments—that is, its record of trade with other countries.

INFLATION

Ups in the business cycle often, but not always, seem to encourage inflation. Table 8.8 shows the rate of inflation during the three most recent periods of expansion. The inflation rate rose from 3.2 percent to 11.0 percent from 1972 to 1974. The trend in inflation was also upward from 1976 to 1980. The sustained growth that began in 1983, however, did not seem to bring rapid inflation.

Why is inflation a problem? If you understand that wages and salaries, as well as other forms of income, increase along with prices during periods of inflation, you will see this question is more subtle than you might think. If my income doubles and the prices of the things I buy double, am I any worse off? I can buy exactly the same things

---

TABLE 8.7

INFLATION RATES, 1974–1976 AND 1980–1983

RECESSION BEGINS	INFLATION RATE
→ 1974	11.0
1975	9.1
1976	5.8
→ 1980	13.5
1981	10.3
1982	6.2
1983	3.2

Source: See Table 8.9.

TABLE 8.8

INFLATION DURING THREE EXPANSIONS

	INFLATION RATE
1972	3.2
1973	6.2
1974	11.0
1976	5.8
1977	6.5
1978	7.6
1979	11.3
1980	13.5
1984	4.3
1985	3.6
1986	1.9
1987	3.6
1988	4.1
1989	4.8

Source: See Table 8.9.

---

[4]U.S. Senate Hearings before a subcommittee of the Committee of Manufacturers, 72nd Congress, first session (1931), p. 239. Cited in Lester Chandler, *America's Greatest Depression, 1929–1941* (New York: Harper and Row, 1970), p. 43.

[5]Senate Hearings, in Lester Chandler, *America's Greatest Depression*, p. 43.

UNEMPLOYMENT AND WELFARE: 1991 TO 1997

In the spring of 1991 the U.S. economy began to grow following a brief recession. In 1992, civilian employment totaled 118.5 million, and the unemployment rate stood at 7.5 percent, with 9.6 million looking for work. During the next six years, the economy expanded and unemployment declined.

By August of 1997, the economy had added 18 million jobs, real GDP had expanded over 17 percent, and the number of unemployed was down to 6.7 million, or 4.9 percent of the labor force.

At the same time, there was a steady decline in the number of persons receiving welfare benefits. Although there is much debate about the causes of the decline in welfare, no one doubts that it is partly the result of the strong economy. A 1997 paper written by economists Phillip Levine and Diane Whitmore at the Council of Economic Advisers tries to sort out the link.

The pattern of association between the number of welfare recipients and the number of unemployed is not new and it can be seen in Figure 1.

The authors conclude:

From January 1993 to January 1997, the number of individuals receiving welfare fell by 20 percent, or 2.75 million recipients—the largest decline in over 50 years. Three explanations for this decline are (1) economic growth, which created 12 million new jobs over the period, (2) Federal waivers, which allowed 43 states to experiment with

innovative ideas to help reduce welfare dependency, and (3) other policies affecting work-related incentives, including the 1990 and 1993 expansions of the Earned Income Tax Credit (EITC) and the recent rise in federal and state spending on child care. Over 40 percent of the decline resulted from a falling unemployment rate associated with the economic expansion and almost one-third from statewide welfare reform waivers (Figure 2).[b]

---

*Sources: [a]*Phillip Levine and Diane Whitmore, "Explaining the Decline in Welfare Receipt," Council of Economic Advisers, May 9, 1997; [b]Ibid; [c]Ibid.

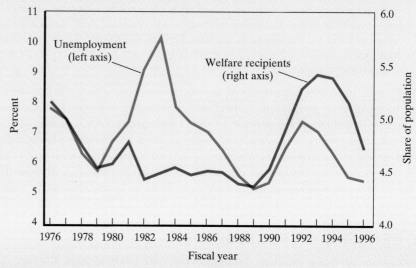

FIGURE 1

Unemployment Rate and Rate of Welfare Receipt[a]

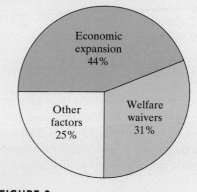

FIGURE 2

Reasons for the Decline in Welfare Caseloads, 1993 to 1996[c]

For more on unemployment and welfare, see the Case and Fair Web page at
http://www.prenhall.com/casefair.

---

that I bought yesterday, so to the extent that my well-being depends on what I am able to buy, the answer is no.

However, incomes and prices do not all increase at the same rate during inflations. For some people, income increases faster than prices; for others, prices increase faster. Some people benefit from inflations, others are hurt.

The remainder of this chapter focuses on the problem of inflation: its measurement, its costs, and the gains and losses experienced during inflationary periods.

DEFINING INFLATION

What is inflation? Not all price increases constitute inflation. Prices of individual goods and services are determined in many ways. In competitive markets, the interaction of many buyers and many sellers—the operation of supply and demand—determines prices. In imperfectly competitive markets, prices are determined by producers' decisions. (This is the core of microeconomic theory.)

In any economy, prices are continuously changing as markets adjust to changing conditions. Lack of rain may dry up corn and wheat fields, reducing supply and pushing up the price of agricultural products. At the same time, high levels of production by oil producers may be driving down the price of oil and petroleum products. Simultaneously, the United Auto Workers may be negotiating a contract with the Ford Motor Company that raises (or lowers) wage rates.

When the price of one good rises, that price increase may or may not be part of a larger inflation. Remember: **inflation** is an increase in the overall price level. It happens when many prices increase simultaneously. We measure inflation by looking at a large number of goods and services and calculating the average increase in their prices during some period of time. **Deflation** is a decrease in the overall price level. It occurs when many prices decrease simultaneously.

It is useful to distinguish between a *one-time* increase in the overall price level and an increase in the overall price level that continues over time. For example, the overall price level could rise 10 percent in a single month and stop rising, or it could increase steadily over some years. Economists often use *inflation* to refer only to increases in the price level that continue over some significant period. We will refer to such periods as periods of **sustained inflation**.

inflation *An increase in the overall price level.*

deflation *A decrease in the overall price level.*

sustained inflation *An increase in the overall price level that continues over a significant period.*

PRICE INDEXES

Price indexes are used to measure overall price levels. We discussed how these indexes are constructed in the previous chapter. The price index that pertains to all goods and services in the economy is the *GDP price index*. As we saw in chapter 7, the BEA does not use fixed weights to construct the GDP price index. Most other price indexes are constructed using fixed weights.

The most popular fixed-weight price index is the **consumer price index (CPI)**. The CPI was first constructed during World War I as a basis for adjusting shipbuilders' wages, which the government controlled during the war. Currently, the CPI is computed by the Bureau of Labor Statistics each month, using a bundle of goods meant to represent the "market basket" purchased monthly by the typical urban consumer. The quantities of each good in the bundle that are used for the weights are based on extensive surveys of consumers.

Table 8.9 shows values of the CPI since 1950. The percentage changes in the table are calculated using the index. (The base period for this index is three years, 1982 to 1984, rather than the more usual one year.) For example, from 1970 to 1971 the CPI increased from 38.8 to 40.5. The percentage change is simply $[(40.5 - 38.8)/38.8] \times 100$, which is 4.4 percent.

Remember from the previous chapter that a fixed-weight price index like the CPI does not account for consumers' substitution away from high-priced goods.

consumer price index (CPI) *A price index computed each month by the Bureau of Labor Statistics using a bundle that is meant to represent the "market basket" purchased monthly by the typical urban consumer.*

Changes in the CPI somewhat overstate changes in the cost of living.

For further discussion of the CPI, see the Issues and Debates box "Controversy Over the CPI—1997."

Other popular price indexes are **producer price indexes (PPIs)**, once called *wholesale price indexes*. These are indexes of prices that producers receive for products at all stages in the production process, not just the final stage. The indexes are calculated

producer price indexes (PPIs) *Measures of prices that producers receive for products at all stages in the production process.*

TABLE 8.9 THE CPI, 1950–1997

YEAR	% Δ IN THE CPI	CPI	YEAR	% Δ IN THE CPI	CPI
1950	1.3	24.1	1974	11.0	49.3
1951	7.9	26.0	1975	9.1	53.8
1952	1.9	26.5	1976	5.8	56.9
1953	0.8	26.7	1977	6.5	60.6
1954	0.7	26.9	1978	7.6	65.2
1955	−0.4	26.8	1979	11.3	72.6
1956	1.5	27.2	1980	13.5	82.4
1957	3.3	28.1	1981	10.3	90.9
1958	2.8	28.9	1982	6.2	96.5
1959	0.7	29.1	1983	3.2	99.6
1960	1.7	29.6	1984	4.3	103.9
1961	1.0	29.9	1985	3.6	107.6
1962	1.0	30.2	1986	1.9	109.6
1963	1.3	30.6	1987	3.6	113.6
1964	1.3	31.0	1988	4.1	118.3
1965	1.6	31.5	1989	4.8	124.0
1966	2.9	32.4	1990	5.4	130.7
1967	3.1	33.4	1991	4.2	136.2
1968	4.2	34.8	1992	3.0	140.3
1969	5.5	36.7	1993	3.0	144.5
1970	5.7	38.8	1994	2.6	148.2
1971	4.4	40.5	1995	2.8	152.4
1972	3.2	41.8	1996	3.0	156.9
1973	6.2	44.4	1997	2.3	160.5

Sources: U.S. Department of Labor, Bureau of Labor Statistics.

separately for various stages in the production process. The three main categories are *finished goods, intermediate materials,* and *crude materials,* although there are subcategories within each of these categories.

One advantage of some of the producer price indexes is that they detect price increases early in the production process. Because their movements sometimes foreshadow future changes in consumer prices, they are considered to be leading indicators of future consumer prices.

THE COSTS OF INFLATION

If you asked most people why inflation is "bad," they would tell you that it lowers the overall standard of living by making goods and services more expensive. That is, it cuts into people's purchasing power. People are fond of recalling the days when a bottle of Coca-Cola cost a dime and a hamburger cost a quarter. Just think what we could buy today if prices had not changed!

What people usually do not think about is what their incomes were in the "good old days." The fact that the cost of a Coke has increased from 10¢ to 50¢ does not mean anything in real terms if people who once earned $5,000 now earn $25,000. Why? The reason is simple:

People's income from wages and salaries, profits, interest and rent increases during inflations. The wage rate is the price of labor, rent is the price of land, and so on. During inflations, most prices—including input prices—tend to rise together, and input prices determine both the incomes of workers and the incomes of owners of capital and land.

CONTROVERSY OVER THE CPI—1997

One function of the Consumer Price Index (CPI) is to adjust programs like social security for changes in the cost of living. For years, the accuracy and appropriateness of the CPI as a measure of the cost of living has been debated. The following excerpt from the 1997 *Economic Report of the President* describes the controversy:

Many researchers have argued that the CPI overstates increases in the cost of living. Much of this research comes from the Bureau of Labor Statistics (BLS), which produces the CPI. This research has identified several possible sources of bias; the degree of consensus on the importance of each varies.

SUBSTITUTION BIAS

The CPI prices a fixed market basket of commodities. Shares of these commodities in the basket are based on spending patterns observed in a base period. But consumers do not buy the same basket of goods from year to year. When the prices of some goods rise more quickly than those of other goods, consumers often substitute away from those that have become relatively expensive and toward others that have become relatively cheap. Increases in the CPI measure how much additional income a typical consumer would need to buy the base-period market basket at the new prices. In contrast, a true cost-of-living index would measure how much more income a consumer needs to maintain the same level of economic well-being, taking into account the ability to substitute among goods. By ignoring substitution, the CPI overstates increases in the cost of living.

QUALITY ADJUSTMENT

Measuring inflation properly requires distinguishing between changes in the underlying price and changes in quality. The BLS measures quality changes when it can. Some are easy to measure, for example when bakers double the size of their chocolate chip cookies. Others are more difficult but straightforward: for example, optional automobile equipment that later becomes standard, such as air bags or antilock brakes, can be quality-adjusted by its price when it was sold as an option. Quality adjustments generally have a significant effect on price increases as measured by the CPI.

NEW PRODUCTS

New products, such as air conditioners in the 1950s or videocassette recorders in the 1980s, usually decline sharply in price during the first years they are available for sale. But these products are not usually included in the CPI basket until years after their introduction, and so the CPI never records their initial price declines.

OUTLET SUBSTITUTION

Over time, consumers may change their shopping patterns, shifting from high-priced to low-priced outlets, where the quality of service is often lower. Current methods assume that all of the difference in price between high- and low-priced outlets reflects differences in the quality of service. To the extent this assumption is not appropriate, current methods overlook one source of price decline.

An advisory commission appointed by the Senate Finance Committee has estimated that the current CPI overstates inflation by 1.1 percentage points per year. Their estimate of bias is the sum of the following parts:

SOURCE OF BIAS	ESTIMATE OF BIAS (PERCENTAGE POINTS)
Substitution	
Upper level (between-category)	0.15
Lower level (within-category)	.25
New products and quality change	.60
Switching to new outlets	.10
Total	1.1
Plausible range	.8–1.6

Others, including Bureau of Labor Statistics commissioner Katherine Abraham, strongly dispute the results of the commission's study. They claim that the bias is significant but much smaller, closer to 0.4 percent in total.

Source: *Economic Report of the President,* 1997, pp. 67–71.

For more on the consumer price index, see the Case and Fair Web page at
http://www.prenhall.com/casefair.

➤ **Inflation Changes the Distribution of Income** Whether you gain or lose during a period of inflation depends on whether your income rises faster or slower than the prices of the things you buy. The group most often mentioned when the impact of inflation is discussed is people living on fixed incomes. If your income is fixed and prices rise, your ability to purchase goods and services falls proportionally. But who are the fixed-income earners?

Most people think of the elderly. Many retired workers living on private pensions receive monthly checks that will never increase. Many pension plans, however, pay benefits that are *indexed* to inflation. The benefits these plans provide automatically increase when the general price level rises. If prices rise 10 percent, benefits also rise 10 percent. The biggest source of income for the elderly is social security. These benefits are fully indexed; when prices rise (that is, when the CPI rises) by 5 percent, social security benefits also increase by 5 percent.

The poor have not fared so well. Welfare benefits, which are not indexed, have not kept pace with the price level over the last two decades. Benefits to families with dependent children under the AFDC program declined 33 percent in real terms between 1970 and 1988. In five states—Idaho, Illinois, Kentucky, New Jersey, and Texas—the average benefits fell by more than 50 percent in real terms.[6]

▶ **Effects on Debtors and Creditors**   It is also commonly believed that debtors benefit at the expense of creditors during an inflation. Certainly, if I loan you $100 to be paid back in a year, and prices increase 10 percent in the meantime, I get back 10 percent less in real terms than what I loaned you.

But suppose we had both anticipated prices would rise 10 percent. I would have taken this into consideration in the deal that I made with you. I would charge you an interest rate high enough to cover the decrease in value due to the anticipated inflation. If we agree on a 15 percent interest rate, then you must pay me $115 at the end of a year. The difference between the interest rate on a loan and the inflation rate is referred to as the **real interest rate**. In our deal, I will earn a real interest rate of 5 percent. By charging a 15 percent interest rate, I have taken into account the anticipated 10 percent inflation rate. In this sense, I am not hurt by the inflation—I keep pace with inflation and earn a profit on my money, too—despite the fact that I am a creditor.

On the other hand, an unanticipated inflation—an inflation that takes people by surprise—can hurt creditors. If the actual inflation rate during the period of my loan to you turns out to be 20 percent, then I as a creditor will be hurt. I charged you 15 percent interest, expecting to get a 5 percent real rate of return, when I needed to charge you 25 percent to get the same 5 percent real rate of return. Because inflation turned out to be higher than expected, I got a negative real return of 5 percent.

> Inflation that is higher than expected benefits debtors; inflation that is lower than expected benefits creditors.

▶ **Administrative Costs and Inefficiencies**   There are costs associated even with anticipated inflation. One is the administrative cost associated with simply keeping up. During the rapid inflation in Israel in the early 1980s, a telephone hotline was set up to give the hourly price index! Store owners have to recalculate and re-post prices frequently, and this takes time that could be used more efficiently.

More frequent banking transactions may be required. For example, interest rates tend to rise with anticipated inflation. When interest rates are high, the opportunity costs of holding cash outside of banks is high. People therefore hold less cash and need to stop at the bank more often. (We discuss this in more detail in the next part of this book.) In addition, if people are not fully informed, or if they do not understand what is happening to prices in general, they may make mistakes in their business dealings. These mistakes can lead to a misallocation of resources.

▶ **Increased Risk and Slower Economic Growth**   When unanticipated inflation occurs regularly, the degree of risk associated with investments in the economy increases.

real interest rate *The difference between the interest rate on a loan and the inflation rate.*

[6]Alicia H. Munnell, "The Current Status of Our Social Welfare System," Federal Reserve Bank of Boston, monograph (1987).

Increases in uncertainty may make investors reluctant to invest in capital and to make long-term commitments. Because the level of investment falls, the prospects for long-term economic growth are lessened.

INFLATION: PUBLIC ENEMY NUMBER ONE?

Economists have debated the seriousness of the costs of inflation for decades. Some, like Alan Blinder, say "inflation, like every teenager, is grossly misunderstood, and this gross misunderstanding blows the political importance of inflation out of all proportion to its economic importance."[7] Others, like Phillip Cagan and Robert Lipsey, argue "it was once thought that the economy would in time make all the necessary adjustments [to inflation], but many of them are proving to be very difficult. . . . for financial institutions and markets, the effects of inflation have been extremely unsettling."[8]

No matter what the real economic cost of inflation, people don't like it. It makes us uneasy and unhappy. In 1974, President Ford verbalized some of this discomfort when he said "our inflation, our public enemy number one, will unless whipped destroy our country, our homes, our liberties, our property, and finally our national pride, as surely as any well-armed wartime enemy."[9] In this belief, our elected leaders have vigorously pursued policies designed to stop inflation. This brings us to where we started. If, as we suggested earlier, the recessions of 1974 to 1975 and 1980 to 1982 were the price we had to pay to stop inflation, stopping inflation is costly.

GLOBAL UNEMPLOYMENT AND INFLATION

Unemployment and inflation are not just concerns of the United States. Other countries at times experience high unemployment or high inflation (or both). The Great Depression of the 1930s was a worldwide phenomenon, and most countries experienced high rates of inflation in the 1970s after the OPEC oil price increases.

The highest rates of inflation in 1997 among countries where we have data were in Bulgaria, Congo, and Rumania. Very high rates of inflation are seen in the other transition economies of Eastern Europe and in developing countries, particularly in Latin America. At the same time, Europe was struggling with high unemployment. Unemployment figures for developing countries are difficult to obtain and hard to interpret. (See Table 8.10.)

OUTPUT GROWTH

It was pointed out in chapter 6 that the average growth rate of output in the U.S. economy since 1900 has been about 3.4 percent per year. Some years are better than others, but on average the rate is 3.4 percent. The key question in the area of economics called "growth theory" is: What determines this rate? Why 3.4 percent and not 2 percent or 4 percent? This question is the subject of chapter 19, but a few points can be made now.

First, machines (capital) and workers (labor) are needed to produce output. Other things being equal, the more capital and labor there is in a country the more output can be produced. Second, machines differ in their efficiency and workers differ in their skills. Other things being equal, the more efficient the capital is, the more output can be produced per unit of capital, and the more skilled labor is, the more output can be produced per worker.

A country's growth rate of output thus depends on (1) how fast its capital stock is growing, (2) how fast the average efficiency of the capital stock is growing, (3) how

TABLE 8.10

INFLATION AND UNEMPLOYMENT IN 1997

COUNTRY	RATE OF INFLATION
Bulgaria	1,268%
Congo	544%
Rumania	175%
Turkey	90%
Venezuela	39%
Mexico	19%
Colombia	18%
Hungary	18%

COUNTRY	RATE OF UNEMPLOYMENT
Spain	20.8%
Belgium	14.1%
France	12.5%
Italy	12.4%
Germany	11.7%
Canada	9.0%

Source: The Economist, October 11, 1997.

---

[7]Alan Blinder, *Hard Heads, Soft Hearts: Tough-Minded Economics for a Just Society* (Reading, Mass.: Addison-Wesley, 1987).

[8]Phillip Cagan and Robert Lipsey, "The Financial Effects of Inflation," National Bureau of Economic Research (Cambridge, Mass.: General Series #103, 1978), pp. 67–68.

[9]U.S. President, Weekly Compilation of Presidential Documents, vol. 10, no. 41, p 1247. Cited in Blinder, *Hard Heads*.

fast the number of workers (labor force) is growing, and (4) how fast the average skill level of the labor force is growing. Let's take each of these four in turn.

We saw in chapter 7 that the capital stock increases when net investment is positive, that is, when the number of new machines produced (gross investment) exceeds the number of machines that wear out (depreciation). Positive net investment values are thus good for output growth because this means that the capital stock is increasing, which allows more output to be produced.

If machines are getting more efficient over time, there is "technical progress." An example of technical progress: Each year personal computers get faster and more efficient. Because the more efficient capital is, the more output can be produced per unit of capital, technical progress increases the growth rate of output.

The labor force of a country can increase either because the population is growing or because there is an increase in labor force participation (the number of workers as a fraction of the total population). Ignoring possible unemployment problems, the faster the growth rate of the labor force, the greater will be the growth rate of output.

Finally, if workers are becoming more skilled over time, this will increase output growth, because on average workers are becoming more efficient. Workers can acquire skills through education and on-the-job training. A worker's skills are sometimes called "human capital." As with physical capital, the more human capital there is, the more output will be produced. Output growth depends in part on the growth of human capital.

Three of the main focuses of growth theory are investment, technical progress, and human capital. A related concern is "productivity," defined as output per worker. If output is growing at 3 percent and the labor force is growing at 1 percent (due, say, to population growth), then productivity is growing at 2 percent. Positive net investment, positive technical progress, and an increase in human capital per worker all contribute to an increase in productivity, because all three lead to an increase in output per worker. We will have more to say about this in chapter 19.

LOOKING AHEAD

This ends our introduction to the basic concepts and problems of macroeconomics. The first chapter of this part introduced the field, the second discussed the measurement of national product and national income, and this chapter discussed three of the macroeconomy's major concerns—unemployment, inflation, and growth.

Thus far, we have said nothing about what *determines* the level of national output, the number of employed and unemployed workers, and the rate of inflation in an economy. The following chapters provide the background in macroeconomic theory you need to understand *how* the macroeconomy functions. With this knowledge, you will be able to understand how the government can influence the economy through its taxing, spending, and monetary policies.

SUMMARY

RECESSIONS, DEPRESSIONS, AND UNEMPLOYMENT

1. A *recession* is a period in which real GDP declines for at least two consecutive quarters. When less output is produced, employment declines, the unemployment rate rises, and a smaller percentage of the capital stock is used. When real output falls, real income declines.

2. A *depression* is a prolonged and deep recession, although there is disagreement over how severe and how prolonged a recession must be to be called a depression.

3. The *unemployment rate* is the ratio of the number of unemployed people to the number of people in the labor force. To be considered unemployed and in the labor force, a person must be looking for work.

4. Big differences in rates of unemployment exist across demographic groups, regions, and industries. African Americans, for example, experience much higher unemployment rates than whites.

5. A person who decides to stop looking for work is considered to have dropped out of the labor force and is no longer classified as unemployed. People who stop looking because they are discouraged about finding a job are sometimes called *discouraged workers*.

6. Some unemployment is inevitable. Because new workers are continually entering the labor force, because industries and firms are continuously expanding and contracting, and because people switch jobs, there is a constant process of job search as workers and firms try to match the best people to the available jobs. This unemployment is both natural and beneficial for the economy.

7. The unemployment that occurs because of short-run job/skill matching problems is called *frictional unemployment*. The unemployment that occurs because of longer-run structural changes in the economy is called *structural unemployment*. The *natural rate of unemployment* is the sum of the frictional rate and the structural rate. The increase in unemployment that occurs during recessions and depressions is called *cyclical unemployment*.

8. The major costs associated with recessions and unemployment are decreased real output, the damage done to the people who are unemployed, and lost output in the future. Benefits of recessions are that they may help to reduce inflation, increase efficiency, and improve a nation's balance of payments.

INFLATION

9. An *inflation* is an increase in the overall price level. It happens when many prices increase simultaneously. Inflation is measured by calculating the average increase in the prices of a large number of goods during some period of time. A *deflation* is a decrease in the overall price level. A *sustained inflation* is an increase in the overall price level that continues over a significant period of time.

10. A number of different indexes are used to measure the overall price level. Among them are the *GDP price index, consumer price index (CPI),* and *producer price indexes (PPIs).*

11. Whether a person gains or loses during a period of inflation depends on whether his or her income rises faster or slower than the prices of the things he or she buys. The elderly are more insulated from inflation than most people think, because social security benefits and many pensions are indexed to inflation. Welfare benefits, which are not indexed to inflation, have not kept pace with inflation since 1970.

12. Inflation that is higher than expected benefits debtors, and inflation that is lower than expected benefits creditors.

GLOBAL UNEMPLOYMENT RATES AND INFLATION

13. Unemployment rates and rates of inflation differ markedly across time and countries and can reach quite high levels at times.

OUTPUT GROWTH

14. Output growth depends on (1) the growth rate of the capital stock, (2) technical progress, (3) the growth rate of the labor force, and (4) the growth rate of human capital per worker.

REVIEW TERMS AND CONCEPTS

1. Labor force = Employed + Unemployed

2. Population = Labor force + Not in labor force

3. Unemployment rate = $\dfrac{\text{Unemployed}}{\text{Employed} + \text{Unemployed}}$

4. Labor-force participation rate = $\dfrac{\text{Labor force}}{\text{Population}}$

1. Between July and August of 1997, total employment in the U.S. economy grew from 129,708,000 to 129,804,000, an increase of 96,000. At the same time, the unemployment rate rose from 4.8 percent to 4.9 percent.
   a. How can unemployment rise when the number employed is also rising?
   b. If 6,677,000 were unemployed, calculate approximately how large the labor force was in August.

2. In August 1997, economists were saying that the U.S. economy was close to full employment even though the unemployment rate was 4.9 percent. How can they make this assertion?

3. Using Table 8.2, calculate the changes in the unemployment rate and the labor-force participation rate that would occur if one million unemployed persons dropped out of the labor force in 1997.

4. "When an inefficient firm or a firm producing a product that people no longer want goes out of business, people are unemployed, but that's part of the normal process of economic growth and development; the unemployment is part of the natural rate and need not concern policy makers." Discuss this and its relevance to the economy today.

5. What is the unemployment rate in your state today? What was it in 1970, 1975, and 1982? How has your state done relative to the national average? Do you know, or can you determine, why?

6. Suppose that all wages, salaries, welfare benefits, and other sources of income were indexed to inflation. Would inflation still be considered a problem? Why or why not?

7. a. What do the CPI and the PPI measure? Why do we need all these price indexes? (Think about what purpose you would use each one for.)
   b. Consider an economy with two goods, gum and lemon drops. Suppose that, between year 1 and year 2, there is a downward shift in the supply schedule for gum and an upward shift in the supply schedule for lemon drops. Explain why the CPI for this two-good economy would overstate the increase in the cost of living.

8. Consider the following statements:
   a. "More people are employed in Tappania now than at any time in the past 50 years."
   b. "The unemployment rate in Tappania is higher now than it has been in 50 years."
   Can both of these statements be true at the same time? Explain.

9. Policy makers talk about the "capacity" of the economy to grow. What specifically is meant by the "capacity" of the economy? How might capacity be measured? In what ways is capacity limited by labor constraints? Capital constraints? What are the consequences if demand in the economy exceeds capacity? What signs would you look for?

10. What was the rate of growth in real GDP during the most recent quarter? You can find the answer in publications such as the *Survey of Current Business*, *The Economist*, or *Businessweek*. Has growth been increasing or decreasing? What policies might you suggest for increasing the economy's potential long-run rate of growth?

11. Suppose the stock of capital and the workforce are both increasing at 3 percent annually in the country of Wholand. At the same time, real output is growing at 6 percent. How is that possible in the short run? In the long run?

TAKE IT TO THE NET

We invite you to visit the Case and Fair page on the Prentice Hall Web site:
http://www.prenhall.com/casefair
for this chapter's World Wide Web exercise.

CRIMINAL BUSINESS CYCLES

Macroeconomic historians will look back on the decade of the 1990s as one of the most remarkable in the post–World War II era. By the end of 1997 the U.S. economy experienced 81 months of uninterrupted growth—nearly twice the post–World War II average for peacetime expansions. If the current expansion persists through the end of 1998, as most economists expect it will, this business cycle boom will be the longest peacetime expansion on record.[1] During the final quarter of 1997 the unemployment rate in the United States had fallen to its lowest level in 24 years and inflation was at its lowest level in 30 years. And it appeared likely that Bill Clinton would be the first president since Lyndon Johnson to witness a budget surplus during his term in office. Coincidentally, as President Clinton noted in his 1998 State of the Union Address, serious crime in the United States has declined for a record five consecutive years.

Economic expansions of this sort have many political and social benefits. Economists and political scientists have shown that the chances of an incumbent president being re-elected increase significantly if the economy is doing well. In fact, economists and political scientists refer to the *political business cycle* to express politicians' attempts to use fiscal or monetary policy to affect the outcome of an election.

To an economist, President Kennedy's "rising tide lifts all boats" means an expanding economy translates into higher living standards, improvements in the distribution of income across classes, and lower poverty rates. All of these factors contribute to the stylized fact that

crime rates tend to fall when the economy is booming, or what might be casually referred to as a *criminal business cycle!*

The idea that crime and economic conditions might be related is not new. In the sixteenth century, Sir Thomas More asked, "What can they then else do but steal. . . ?" when he expressed concern for tenant farmers who were being moved off the land by English landlords and thereby deprived of their livelihood.

More recently, academic studies have established a positive link between employment and crime, especially among young males. A 1994 study sampled a cohort of young men living in Philadelphia between their tenth and eighteenth birthdays and found that working and attending school significantly decreased the probability of committing criminal acts.

However, other studies have found that the link between labor market conditions and crime rates is not so simple and in fact breaks down completely during some periods and for certain types of crime.

Because many factors contribute to crime, it's difficult to measure the precise impact of employment, income, and education on different types of criminal behavior. However, it makes sense that for some segments of the population desperate economic conditions can lead to desperate acts.

For some cities the recent economic boom has coincided with some considerable reductions in crime. For example, employment growth in Boston has averaged about 1 percent from 1991 to 1996, while crime has fallen by 28 percent. In Dallas the story is even more

dramatic. Employment growth has averaged nearly 3 percent since 1991, whereas crime has fallen by over 35 percent. (See Figure 1.)

Researchers in California found that the factor most contributing to a city's gang violence was the unemployment rate. In communities where unemployment ran highest (between 14 percent and 16 percent), the murder rate was almost 15 times greater than in communities where the unemployment rate was between 4 percent and 7 percent.

Questions for Analytical Thinking

1. In New York City, employment has been growing at an annual rate of about 1 percent since 1994, yet the unemployment rate rose 2 full percentage points from the fourth quarter of 1994 to the second quarter of 1997. Why might both the unemployment rate and the number of persons employed increase in an expanding economy?

2. Find data for your state or city on recent employment patterns and crime rates. Visit the FBI Internet site at *http://www.fbi.gov* for crime statistics for your area and the Bureau of Labor Statistics Internet site at *http://www.bls.gov* for employment statistics.

3. What impact might an increase in the minimum wage, like that passed by Congress in 1995, have on crime rates?

4. Some regions of the country, like Detroit, have actually experienced an increase in crime and

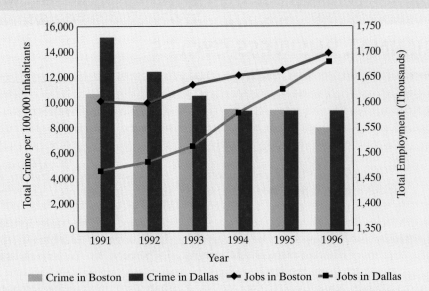

FIGURE 1

More Jobs, Less Crime

Crime in Boston　Crime in Dallas　◆ Jobs in Boston　■ Jobs in Dallas

unemployment during the current expansion. What factors might explain this?

[1] Business cycle troughs and peaks are dated by the National Bureau of Economic Research. The NBER's dating of modern-day business cycles begins with a trough in December 1854. According to the NBER, the longest period of uninterrupted U.S. economic growth coincided with the Vietnam War during the 106 months of February 1961 through December 1969.

Sources: Jason Bram, David Brauer, and Elizabeth Miranda, "New York City's Unemployment Picture," *Current Issues in Economics and Finance,* December 1997, Vol. 3, No. 14, Federal Reserve Bank of New York; Chester Britt, "Crime and Unemployment in the United States, 1958–1990: A Time Series Analysis," *American Journal of Economics and Sociology,* January 1994, Vol. 53, No. 1, pp. 99–109; Bill Clinton, President of the United States, *1998 State of the Union Address,* available on-line at: *http://www.white-house.gov/WH/SOTU98/address.html*; David Dickinson, "Criminal Benefits; Unemployment and Crime," *New Statesman & Society* (UK), January 14, 1994, Vol. 7, No. 285, p. 20; Richard B. Freeman, "Why Do So Many Young American Men Commit Crimes and What Might We Do About It?" *Journal of Economic Perspectives*, Winter 1996, Vol. 10, No. 1, pp. 25–42; Ann Dryden Witte and Helen Tauchen, "Work and Crime: An Exploration Using Panel Data," *NBER Working Paper 4794*, July 1994; Tadashi Yamada, Tetsuji Yamada, and Johan M. Kang, "Crime Rates Versus Labor Market Conditions: Theory and Time Series Evidence," *NBER Working Paper 3801*, August 1991.

AGGREGATE EXPENDITURE AND EQUILIBRIUM OUTPUT

WE NOW BEGIN OUR DISCUSSION of macroeconomic theory. We know how to calculate GDP, but what factors *determine* it? We know how to define and measure inflation and unemployment, but what circumstances *cause* inflation and unemployment? And what, if anything, can government do to reduce unemployment and inflation?

Analyzing the various components of the macroeconomy is a complex undertaking. The level of GDP, the overall price level, and the level of employment—three chief concerns of macroeconomists—are influenced by events in three broadly defined "markets": goods-and-services markets, financial (money) markets, and labor markets. We will explore each market, as well as the links between them, in more detail in the chapters that follow.

▶ **Macroeconomic Markets** Figure 9.1 presents the plan of the next seven chapters, which form the core of macroeconomic theory. In chapters 9 and 10, we describe the market for goods and services, often called the *goods market*. In chapter 9, we explain several basic concepts and show how the equilibrium level of national income is determined in a simple economy with no government and no imports or exports. In chapter 10, we provide a more complete picture of the economy by adding government purchases, taxes, and net exports to the analysis.

In chapters 11 and 12, we focus on the *money market*. Chapter 11 introduces the money market and the banking system and discusses the way the U.S. central bank (the Federal Reserve) controls the money supply. Chapter 12 analyzes the demand for money and the way interest rates are determined. Chapter 13 then examines the relationship between the goods market and the money market. Chapter 14 explores the aggregate demand and supply curves first mentioned in chapter 6. Chapter 14 also analyzes how the overall price level is determined, as well as the relationship between output and the price level. Finally, chapter 15 discusses the supply of and demand for labor and the functioning of the *labor market* in

175

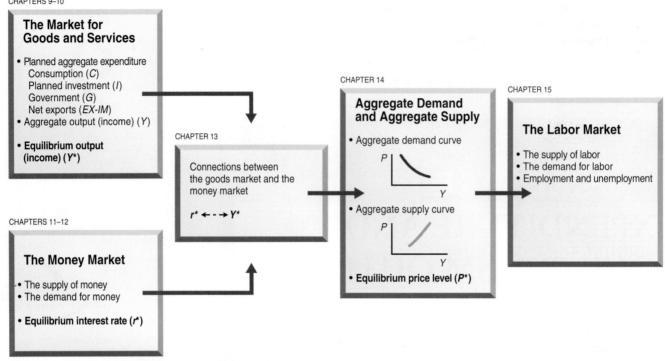

FIGURE 9.1

Understanding Markets in the Macroeconomy

the macroeconomy. This material is essential to an understanding of employment and unemployment.[1]

Before we begin our discussion of aggregate output and aggregate income, we need to stress that production, consumption, and the other activities that we will be discussing in this and the following chapters are ongoing activities. Nonetheless, it is helpful to think about these activities as if they took place in a series of *production periods*. During each period, some output is produced, income is generated, and spending takes place. At the end of each period we can examine the results. Was everything that was produced in the economy sold? What percentage of income was spent? What percentage was saved? Is output (income) likely to rise or fall in the next period? The answers to these questions help us to keep track of the economy's performance.

AGGREGATE OUTPUT AND AGGREGATE INCOME (*Y*)

Each period, firms produce some aggregate quantity of goods and services, which we refer to as *aggregate output* (*Y*). In chapter 7, we introduced real gross domestic product as a measure of the quantity of output produced in the economy, *Y*. Output includes the production of services, consumer goods, and investment goods. It is important to think of these as components of "real" output.

We have already seen that GDP (*Y*) can be calculated in terms of either income or expenditures. Because every dollar of expenditure is received by someone as income, we

[1]Throughout chapters 9 to 15, we provide examples and policy applications relevant to our discussion in each chapter. In chapter 16, we use everything we know about the three broadly defined markets to analyze such macroeconomic topics as stabilization policy and the federal budget deficit.

can compute total GDP (Y) either by adding up the total spent on all final goods during a period *or* by adding up all the income—wages, rents, interest, and profits—received by all the factors of production.

We will use the variable Y to refer to both **aggregate output** and **aggregate income** because they are the same seen from two different points of view. When output increases, additional income is generated. More workers may be hired and paid; workers may put in, and be paid for, more hours; and owners may earn more profits. When output is cut, income falls, workers may be laid off or work fewer hours (and be paid less), and profits may fall.

> In any given period, there is an exact equality between aggregate output (production) and aggregate income. You should be reminded of this fact whenever you encounter the combined term **aggregate output (income)**.

Aggregate output can also be looked on as the aggregate quantity supplied, because it is the amount that firms are supplying (producing) during the period. In the discussions that follow, we use the phrase *aggregate output (income)*, rather than *aggregate quantity supplied*, but keep in mind that the two are equivalent. Also remember that "aggregate output" means "real GDP."

➤ **Think in Real Terms** From the outset you must think in "real terms." For example, when we talk about output (Y), we mean real output, not nominal output. Although we discussed in chapter 7 that the calculation of real GDP is complicated, you can ignore these complications in the following analysis. To help make things easier to read, we will frequently use dollar values for Y, but do not confuse Y with nominal output. The main point is to think of Y as being in real terms—the quantities of goods and services produced, not the dollars circulating in the economy.

INCOME, CONSUMPTION, AND SAVING (Y, C, AND S)

Each period (weeks, months, years, etc.), households receive some aggregate amount of income (Y). We begin our analysis in a simple world with no government and a "closed" economy, that is, no imports and no exports. In such a world, a household can do two, and only two, things with its income: It can buy goods and services—that is, it can *consume*—or it can save. The part of its income that a household does not consume in a given period is called **saving** (Figure 9.2). Total household saving in the economy (S) is by definition equal to income minus consumption (C):

$$\text{Saving} \equiv \text{Income} - \text{Consumption}$$
$$S \equiv Y - C$$

aggregate output *The total quantity of goods and services produced (or supplied) in an economy in a given period.*

aggregate income *The total income received by all factors of production in a given period.*

aggregate output (income) (Y) *A combined term used to remind you of the exact equality between aggregate output and aggregate income.*

saving (S) *The part of its income that a household does not consume in a given period. Distinguished from* savings, *which is the current stock of accumulated saving.*

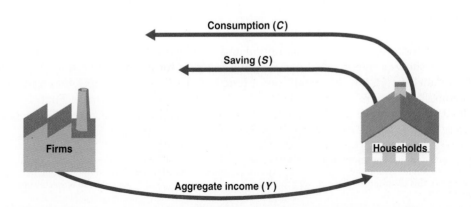

FIGURE 9.2

Saving $\equiv$ Aggregate Income $-$ Consumption

All income is either spent on consumption or saved in an economy in which there are no taxes. Thus, $S \equiv Y - C$.

identity *Something that is always true.*

The triple equal sign means this is an **identity,** or something that is always true. You will encounter several identities in this chapter; be sure to commit them to memory.

Remember: Saving does *not* refer to the total savings accumulated over time. Saving (without the final *s*) refers to the portion of a *single period's* income that is not spent in that period. Saving (*S*) is the amount added to *accumulated savings* in any given period. *Saving* is a flow variable; *savings* is a stock variable. (Review chapter 4 if you are unsure of the difference between stock and flow variables.)

EXPLAINING SPENDING BEHAVIOR

So far, we have said nothing about behavior. We have not described the consumption and saving behavior of households, nor have we speculated about how much aggregate output firms will decide to produce in a given period. Rather, we have only a framework and a set of definitions to work with.

But macroeconomics, you will recall, is the study of behavior. To understand the functioning of the macroeconomy, we must understand the behavior of households and firms. In our simple economy in which there is no government, there are two types of spending behavior: spending by households, or *consumption*, and spending by firms, or *investment*.

➤ **Household Consumption and Saving** How do households decide how much to consume? In any given period, the amount of aggregate consumption in the economy depends on a number of factors, including:

Some Determinants of Aggregate Consumption:	1. Household income
	2. Household wealth
	3. Interest rates
	4. Households' expectations about the future

These factors work together to determine the spending and saving behavior of households, both individually and in the aggregate. No surprise! Households with higher income and higher wealth are likely to spend more than households with less income and less wealth. Lower interest rates reduce the cost of borrowing, so lower interest rates are likely to stimulate spending. (Higher interest rates increase the cost of borrowing and are likely to decrease spending.) Finally, positive expectations about the future are likely to increase current spending, while uncertainty about the future is likely to decrease current spending. In 1990, for example, households began consuming less partly because of their uncertainty about the outcome of the Persian Gulf conflict.

While all these factors are important, we will concentrate for now on the relationship between income and consumption.[2] In *The General Theory*, Keynes argued that the amount of consumption undertaken by a household is directly related to its income:

The higher your income is, the higher your consumption is likely to be. People with more income tend to consume more than people with less income.

consumption function *The relationship between consumption and income.*

The relationship between consumption and income is called a **consumption function.** Figure 9.3 shows a hypothetical consumption function for an individual household. The curve is labeled $c(y)$, which is read "*c* as a function of *y*," or "consumption as a function of income." There are several things you should notice about the curve. First, it has a positive slope. In other words, as *y* increases, so does *c*. Second, the curve intersects the

---

[2]The assumption that consumption is dependent solely on income is, of course, overly simplistic. Nonetheless, many important insights about how the economy works can be obtained through this simplification. In chapter 17, we relax this assumption and consider the behavior of households and firms in the macroeconomy in more detail.

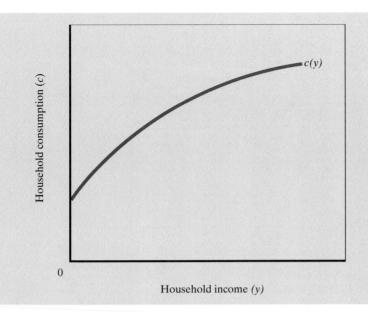

FIGURE 9.3

A Consumption Function for a Household

A consumption function for an individual household shows the level of consumption at each level of household income.

c axis above zero. This means that even at an income of zero, consumption is positive. Even if a household found itself with a zero income, it still must consume to survive. It would borrow or live off its savings, but its consumption could not be zero.

Keep in mind that Figure 9.3 shows the relationship between consumption and income for an individual household. But also remember that macroeconomics is concerned with aggregate consumption. Specifically, macroeconomists want to know how *aggregate* consumption (the total consumption of all households) is likely to respond to changes in *aggregate* income. If all individual households increase their consumption as income increases, and we assume that they do, it is reasonable to assume that a positive relationship exists between aggregate consumption (*C*) and aggregate income (*Y*).

For simplicity, assume that points of aggregate consumption, when plotted against aggregate income, lie along a straight line, as in Figure 9.4. Because the aggregate consumption function is a straight line, we can write the following equation to describe it:

$$C = a + bY$$

Y is aggregate output (income), *C* is aggregate consumption, and *a* is the point at which the consumption function intersects the *C* axis—a constant. The letter *b* is the slope of the line, in this case $\Delta C/\Delta Y$ (because consumption [*C*] is measured on the

UNCERTAINTY ABOUT THE FUTURE TENDS TO DECREASE CURRENT SPENDING, AS IT DID DURING THE PERSIAN GULF WAR IN 1990.

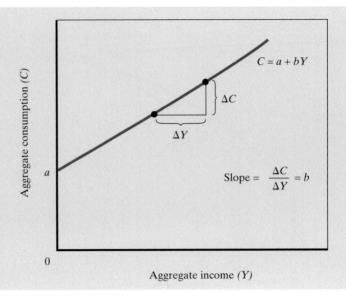

FIGURE 9.4

An Aggregate Consumption Function

The consumption function shows the level of consumption at every level of income. The upward slope indicates that higher levels of income lead to higher levels of consumption spending.

vertical axis, and income [Y] is measured on the horizontal axis).[3] Every time income increases (say by ΔY), consumption increases by b times ΔY. Thus, $\Delta C = b \times \Delta Y$ and $\Delta C/\Delta Y = b$.

Suppose the slope of the line in Figure 9.4 were .75 (that is, $b = .75$). An increase in income (ΔY) of $100 would increase consumption by $b\Delta Y = .75 \times \$100$, or $75.

The **marginal propensity to consume** (**MPC**) is the fraction of a change in income that is consumed. In the consumption function here, b is the *MPC*. An *MPC* of .75 means consumption changes by .75 of the change in income. The slope of the consumption function is the *MPC*.

marginal propensity to consume (MPC) *That fraction of a change in income that is consumed, or spent.*

marginal propensity to save (MPS) *That fraction of a change in income that is saved.*

$$\text{Marginal propensity to consume} \equiv \text{Slope of consumption function} \equiv \frac{\Delta C}{\Delta Y}$$

There are only two places income can go: consumption or saving. If $0.75 of a $1.00 increase in income goes to consumption, $0.25 must go to saving. If income decreases by $1.00, consumption will decrease by $0.75 and saving will decrease by $0.25. The **marginal propensity to save** (**MPS**) is the fraction of a change in income that is saved: $\Delta S/\Delta Y$, where ΔS is the change in saving. Because everything not consumed is saved, the *MPC* and the *MPS* must add up to one.

$$MPC + MPS \equiv 1$$

Because the *MPC* and the *MPS* are important concepts, it may help to review their definitions.

The marginal propensity to consume (*MPC*) is the fraction of an increase in income that is consumed (or the fraction of a decrease in income that comes out of consumption). The marginal propensity to save (*MPS*) is the fraction of an increase in income that is saved (or the fraction of a decrease in income that comes out of saving).

In recent years the average propensity to save (*APS*) seems to be falling in the United States. The following are Department of Commerce figures for personal saving as a percentage of per capita real (1992 dollars) disposable (after-tax) income in the United States:

Year	Real Disposable Income per Capita	Savings Rate
1970	$12,022	8.4%
1980	14,813	8.2
1990	17,941	5.0
1996	19,242	5.3

---

[3]The Greek letter Δ (delta) means "change in." For example, ΔY (read "delta Y") means the "change in income." If income (Y) in 1995 is $100 and income in 1996 is $110, then ΔY for this period is $110 − $100 = $10. For a review of the concept of slope, see the appendix to chapter 1.

TABLE 9.1	CONSUMPTION SCHEDULE DERIVED FROM THE EQUATION $C = 100 + .75Y$	
	AGGREGATE INCOME, Y (BILLIONS OF DOLLARS)	AGGREGATE CONSUMPTION, C (BILLIONS OF DOLLARS)
	0	100
	80	160
	100	175
	200	250
	400	400
	600	550
	800	700
	1,000	850

Because C is aggregate consumption and Y is aggregate income, it follows that the *MPC* is *society's* marginal propensity to consume out of national income and that the *MPS* is *society's* marginal propensity to save out of national income.

➤ **Numerical Example**   The numerical examples used in the rest of this chapter are based on the following consumption function:

$$C = \underbrace{100}_{a} + \underbrace{.75Y}_{b}$$

This equation is simply an extension of the generic $C = a + bY$ consumption function we have been discussing. At a national income of zero, consumption is $100 billion ($a$). As income rises, so does consumption. We will assume that for every $100 billion increase in income (ΔY), consumption rises by $75 billion ($\Delta C$). This means that the slope of the consumption function (b) is equal to $\Delta C/\Delta Y$, or $75 billion/$100 billion = .75. The marginal propensity to consume out of national income is therefore .75; the marginal propensity to save is .25. Some numbers derived from this consumption function appear in Table 9.1 and are graphed in Figure 9.5.

Now consider saving. We already know $Y \equiv C + S$, income equals consumption plus saving. Once we know how much consumption will result from a given level of income, we know how much saving there will be. Recall that saving is everything that is not consumed.

$$S \equiv Y - C$$

From the numbers in Table 9.1, we can easily derive the saving schedule in Table 9.2. At an income of $200 billion, consumption is $250 billion; saving is thus a negative $50 billion ($S \equiv Y - C = 200 billion $-$ 250 billion $= -$50$ billion). At an aggregate income of $400 billion, consumption is exactly $400 billion, and saving is zero. At $800 billion in income, saving is a positive $100 billion.

These numbers are graphed as a saving function in Figure 9.6. The 45° line—the solid black line in the top graph—provides a convenient way of comparing C and Y. (All the points along a 45° line are points at which the value on the horizontal axis equals the value on the vertical axis. Thus, the 45° line in Figure 9.6 represents all the points at which aggregate income equals aggregate consumption.) Where the consumption function is *above* the 45° line, consumption exceeds income, and saving is negative. Where the consumption function *crosses* the 45° line, consumption is equal to income, and saving is zero. Where the consumption function is *below* the 45° line, consumption is less than income, and saving is positive. Note that the slope of the saving function is $\Delta S/\Delta Y$, which is equal to the marginal propensity to save (*MPS*).

FIGURE 9.5

An Aggregate Consumption Function Derived from the Equation $C = 100 + .75Y$

In this simple consumption function, consumption is $100 billion at an income of zero. As income rises, so does consumption. For every $100 billion increase in income, consumption rises by $75 billion. The slope of the line is .75.

The consumption function and the saving function are mirror images of one another. No information appears in one that does not also appear in the other. These functions tell us how households in the aggregate will divide income between consumption spending and saving at every possible income level. In other words, they embody aggregate household behavior.

PLANNED INVESTMENT (*I*)

Consumption, as we've seen, is the spending by households on goods and services. But what kind of spending do firms engage in? The answer is *investment*.

▶ **What Is Investment?** Let's begin with a brief review of terms and concepts. In everyday language, we use *investment* to refer to what we do with our savings: "I invested in

TABLE 9.2 DERIVING A SAVING SCHEDULE FROM A CONSUMPTION SCHEDULE

Y AGGREGATE INCOME (BILLIONS OF DOLLARS)	−	C AGGREGATE CONSUMPTION (BILLIONS OF DOLLARS)	=	S AGGREGATE SAVING (BILLIONS OF DOLLARS)
0		100		−100
80		160		−80
100		175		−75
200		250		−50
400		400		0
600		550		50
800		700		100
1,000		850		150

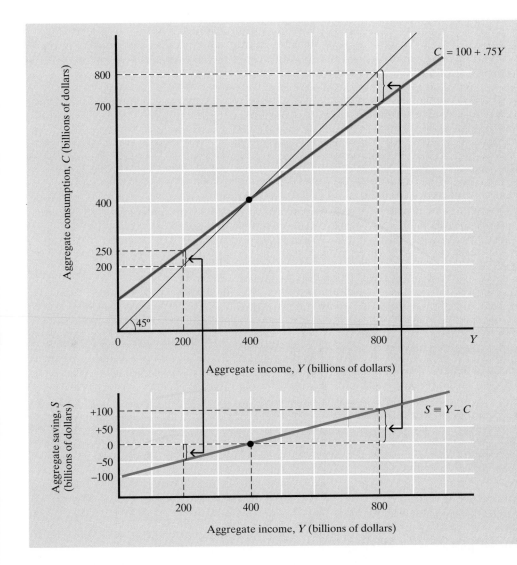

FIGURE 9.6

Deriving a Saving Function from a Consumption Function

Because $S \equiv Y - C$, it is easy to derive a saving function from a consumption function. A 45° line drawn from the origin can be used as a convenient tool to compare consumption and income graphically. At $Y = 200$, consumption is 250. The 45° line shows us that consumption is larger than income by 50. Thus $S \equiv Y - C = -50$. At $Y = 800$, consumption is less than income by 100. Thus, $S = 100$ when $Y = 800$.

a mutual fund and some IBM stock." In the language of economics, however, *investment* always refers to the creation of capital stock. To an economist, an investment is something that is used to create value in the future.

You must not confuse the two uses of the term. When a firm builds a new plant or adds new machinery to its current stock, it is investing. A restaurant owner who buys tables, chairs, cooking equipment, and silverware is investing. When a college builds a new sports center, it is investing. From now on, we use **investment** only to refer to purchases by firms of new buildings and equipment and inventories, all of which add to firms' capital stocks.

Recall that inventories are part of the capital stock. When firms add to their inventories, they are investing—they are buying something that creates value in the future. Most of the capital stock of a clothing store consists of its inventories of unsold clothes in its warehouses and on its racks and display shelves. The service provided by a grocery or department store is the convenience of having a large variety of commodities in inventory available for purchase at a single location.

Manufacturing firms generally have two kinds of inventories: *inputs* and *final products*. General Motors has stocks of tires, rolled steel, engine blocks, valve covers, and thousands of other things in inventory, all waiting to be used in producing new cars. In addition, GM has an inventory of finished automobiles awaiting shipment.

investment *Purchases by firms of new buildings and equipment and additions to inventories, all of which add to firms' capital stock.*

Investment is a flow variable—it represents additions to capital stock in a specific period. A firm's decision on how much to invest each period is determined by many factors. For now, we will focus simply on the effects that given investment levels have on the rest of the economy.

➤ **Actual versus Planned Investment**   One of the most important insights of macroeconomics is deceptively simple: A firm may not always end up investing the exact amount that it planned to. The reason is that a firm does not have complete control over its investment decision; some parts of that decision are made by other actors in the economy. (This is not true of consumption, however. Because we assume households have complete control over their consumption, planned consumption is always equal to actual consumption.)

Generally, firms can choose how much new plant and equipment they wish to purchase in any given period. If GM wants to buy a new robot to stamp fenders or McDonald's decides to buy an extra french-fry machine, it can usually do so without difficulty. There is, however, another component of investment over which firms have less control—inventory investment.

Suppose GM expects to sell one million cars this quarter and has inventories at a level it considers proper. If the company produces and sells one million cars, it will keep its inventories just where they are now (at the desired level). Now suppose GM produces one million cars, but due to a sudden shift of consumer interest it sells only 900,000 cars. By definition, GM's inventories of cars must go up by 100,000 cars. The firm's **change in inventory** is equal to production minus sales. The point here is:

> One component of investment—inventory change—is partly determined by how much households decide to buy, which is not under the complete control of firms. If households do not buy as much as firms expect them to, inventories will be higher than expected, and firms will have made an inventory investment that they did not plan to make.

Because involuntary inventory adjustments are neither desired nor planned, we need to distinguish between actual investment and **desired**, or **planned, investment**. We will use I to refer to desired or planned investment only. In other words, I will refer to planned purchases of plant and equipment and planned inventory changes. **Actual investment**, in contrast, is the *actual* amount of investment that takes place. If actual inventory investment turns out to be higher than firms planned, then actual investment is greater than I, planned investment.

For the purposes of this chapter, we will take the amount of investment that firms plan to make each period (I) as fixed at some given level. We assume this level does not vary with income. In the example that follows, we will assume that $I = \$25$ billion, regardless of income. As Figure 9.7 shows, this means the planned investment function is a horizontal line.

PLANNED AGGREGATE EXPENDITURE (*AE*)

We define total **planned aggregate expenditure** (*AE*) in the economy to be consumption (*C*) plus planned investment (*I*):[4]

> Planned aggregate expenditure ≡ Consumption + Planned investment
> $$AE \equiv C + I$$

change in inventory *Production minus sales.*

desired, or **planned, investment** *Those additions to capital stock and inventory that are planned by firms.*

actual investment *The actual amount of investment that takes place; it includes items such as unplanned changes in inventories.*

planned aggregate expenditure (AE) *The total amount the economy plans to spend in a given period. Equal to consumption plus planned investment: AE ≡ C + I.*

---

[4]In practice, planned aggregate expenditure also includes government spending (G) and net exports ($EX - IM$): $AE \equiv C + I + G + (EX - IM)$. In this chapter we are assuming that G and ($EX - IM$) are zero. This assumption is relaxed in the next chapter.

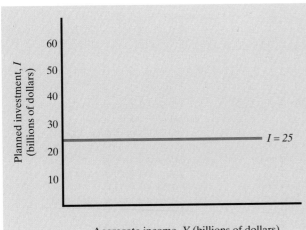

FIGURE 9.7

The Planned Investment Function

For the time being, we will assume that planned investment is fixed. It does not change when income changes, so its graph is just a horizontal line.

AE is the total amount that the economy plans to spend in a given period. We will now use the concept of planned aggregate expenditure to discuss the economy's equilibrium level of output.

EQUILIBRIUM AGGREGATE OUTPUT (INCOME)

Thus far, we have described the behavior of firms and households. We now discuss the nature of equilibrium and explain how the economy achieves equilibrium.

A number of definitions of *equilibrium* are used in economics. They all refer to the idea that at equilibrium, there is no tendency for change. In microeconomics, equilibrium is said to exist in a particular market (say, the market for bananas) at the price for which the quantity demanded is equal to the quantity supplied. At this point, both suppliers and demanders are satisfied. The equilibrium price of a good is the price at which suppliers want to furnish the amount that demanders want to buy.

In macroeconomics, we define **equilibrium** in the goods market as that point at which planned aggregate expenditure is equal to aggregate output.

equilibrium *Occurs when there is no tendency for change. In the macroeconomic goods market, equilibrium occurs when planned aggregate expenditure is equal to aggregate output.*

$$\text{Aggregate output} \equiv Y$$
$$\text{Planned aggregate expenditure} \equiv AE \equiv C + I$$
$$\text{Equilibrium: } Y = AE, \text{ or } Y = C + I$$

This definition of equilibrium can hold if, and only if, planned investment and actual investment are equal. (Remember: we are assuming there is no unplanned consumption.) To understand why, consider Y not equal to AE. First, suppose aggregate output is greater than planned aggregate expenditure:

$$Y > C + I$$
Aggregate output > Planned aggregate expenditure

When output is greater than planned spending, there is unplanned inventory investment. Firms planned to sell more of their goods than they sold, and the difference shows up as an unplanned increase in inventories.

Next, suppose planned aggregate expenditure is greater than aggregate output:

$$C + I > Y$$
Planned aggregate expenditure > Aggregate output

When planned spending exceeds output, firms have sold more than they planned to. Inventory investment is smaller than planned. Planned and actual investment are not

INVENTORIES ACCUMULATING IN 1997: WORRIES ABOUT DECLINING OUTPUT

When GDP data for the second quarter of 1997 were released by the Department of Commerce in August of that year, inventories of unsold goods were up substantially. The following article from the *New York Times* describes the worry:

> Largely ignored in the latest blizzard of economic figures was one indicator that is notoriously hard to interpret but that by autumn could be on every investor's lips. Inventories.
>
> After rising a hefty $64 billion in the January-to-March quarter, the Commerce Department initially estimated that inventories jumped another $67 billion during the spring.
>
> The sum "will be upped to about $95 billion, which would be a record rate of inventory accumulation" for a quarter, said Bruce Steinberg, chief economist at Merrill Lynch. And this, he contended, has "crucial negative implications" for the economy for the rest of 1997.
>
> The theory is straightforward. When goods pile up excessively on store shelves—and in warehouses and factory yards—this costly situation must be redressed sooner or later. This, by ripple effect, means production is cut back and economic growth sags—or even disappears.
>
> Often, a huge stockpile "eventually sows the seeds of a slowdown," said Richard D. Rippe, senior economist at Prudential Securities.
>
> In practice, though, it is often difficult to tell to what extent mounting inventories reflect a retrenchment by consumers or justified confidence by companies that they will be able to sell larger volumes of goods.[a]

Source: [a]Robert D. Hershey Jr., "As Inventories Rise Will There Be a Ripple Effect?" *The New York Times*, August 17, 1997, p. F4. Copyright © 1997 by The New York Times Co. Reprinted by permission.

 For more on aggregate output and aggregate expenditures, see the Case and Fair Web page at http://www.prenhall.com/casefair.

---

equal. Only when output is exactly matched by planned spending will there be no unplanned inventory investment.

> Equilibrium in the goods market is achieved only when aggregate output (Y) and planned aggregate expenditure ($C + I$) are equal, or when actual and planned investment are equal.

Table 9.3 derives a planned aggregate expenditure schedule and shows the point of equilibrium for our numerical example. (Remember, all our calculations are based on $C = 100 + .75Y$.) To determine planned aggregate expenditure, we add consumption spending (C) to planned investment spending (I) at every level of income. Glancing down columns 1 and 4, we see one, and only one, level at which aggregate output and planned aggregate expenditure are equal: $Y = 500$.

Figure 9.8 illustrates the same equilibrium graphically. Figure 9.8a adds planned investment, constant at $25 billion, to consumption at every level of income. Because planned investment is a constant, the planned aggregate expenditure function is simply the consumption function displaced vertically by that constant amount. Figure 9.8b plots the planned aggregate expenditure function with the 45° line. The 45° line, which represents all points on the graph where the variables on the horizontal and vertical axes are equal, allows us to compare measurements along the two axes. The planned aggregate expenditure function crosses the 45° line at a single point, where $Y = \$500$ billion.[5] At that point, $Y = C + I$.

Now let's look at some other levels of aggregate output (income). First, consider $Y = \$800$ billion. Is this an equilibrium output? Clearly not. At $Y = \$800$ billion, planned aggregate expenditure is $725 billion. (See Table 9.3.) This amount is less than

[5]The point at which the two lines cross is sometimes called the *Keynesian cross*.

			(4)	(5)	(6)
			PLANNED	**UNPLANNED**	
			AGGREGATE	**INVENTORY**	
(1)	(2)	(3)	**EXPENDITURE (AE)**	**CHANGE**	**EQUILIBRIUM?**
AGGREGATE OUTPUT (INCOME) (Y)	**AGGREGATE CONSUMPTION (C)**	**PLANNED INVESTMENT (I)**	**C + I**	**Y − (C + I)**	**(Y = AE?)**
100	175	25	200	−100	No
200	250	25	275	−75	No
400	400	25	425	−25	No
500	475	25	500	0	Yes
600	550	25	575	+25	No
800	700	25	725	+75	No
1,000	850	25	875	+125	No

TABLE 9.3 DERIVING THE PLANNED AGGREGATE EXPENDITURE SCHEDULE AND FINDING EQUILIBRIUM (ALL FIGURES IN BILLIONS OF DOLLARS) THE FIGURES IN COLUMN 2 ARE BASED ON THE EQUATION $C = 100 + .75Y$.

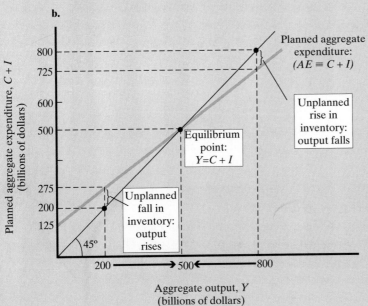

FIGURE 9.8

Equilibrium Aggregate Output

Equilibrium occurs when planned aggregate expenditure and aggregate output are equal. Planned aggregate expenditure is the sum of consumption spending and planned investment spending.

aggregate output, which is $800 billion. Because output is greater than planned spending, the difference ends up in inventory as unplanned inventory investment. In this case, unplanned inventory investment is $75 billion.

Next, consider $Y = \$200$ billion. Is this an equilibrium output? No. At $Y = \$200$ billion, planned aggregate expenditure is $275 billion. Planned spending (AE) is greater than output (Y), and there is unplanned inventory disinvestment of $75 billion.

At $Y = \$200$ billion and $Y = 800$ billion, planned investment and actual investment are unequal. There is unplanned investment, and the system is out of balance. Only at $Y = \$500$ billion, where planned aggregate expenditure and aggregate output are equal, will planned investment equal actual investment.

Finally, let us find the equilibrium level of output (income) algebraically. Recall that we know the following:

(1) $Y = C + I$ (equilibrium)
(2) $C = 100 + .75Y$ (consumption function)
(3) $I = 25$ (planned investment)

Substituting (2) and (3) into (1) we get

$$Y = \underbrace{100 + .75Y}_{C} + \underbrace{25.}_{+\ I}$$

There is only one value of Y for which this statement is true, and we can find it by rearranging terms:

$$Y - .75Y = 100 + 25$$
$$Y - .75Y = 125$$
$$.25Y = 125$$
$$Y = \frac{125}{.25} = 500$$

The equilibrium level of output is 500, as seen in Table 9.3 and Figure 9.8.

THE SAVING/INVESTMENT APPROACH TO EQUILIBRIUM

Because aggregate income must either be saved or spent, by definition, $Y \equiv C + S$—which is an identity. The equilibrium condition is $Y = C + I$—but this is not an identity because it does not hold when we are out of equilibrium.[6] Substituting $C + S$ for Y in the equilibrium condition, we can write:

> Saving/investment approach to equilibrium: $C + S = C + I$
> Because we can subtract C from both sides of this equation, we are left with $S = I$. Thus, only when planned investment equals saving will there be equilibrium.

This saving/investment approach to equilibrium stands to reason intuitively if we recall two things: (1) Output and income are equal, and (2) saving is income that is not spent. Because it is not spent, saving is like a leakage out of the spending stream. Only if that leakage is counterbalanced by some other component of planned spending can the resulting planned aggregate expenditure equal aggregate output. This other component is planned investment (I).

This counterbalancing effect can be seen in Figure 9.9. Aggregate income flows into households, and consumption and saving flow out. The diagram shows saving flowing from households into the financial market. Firms use this saving to finance investment

[6]It would be an identity if I included unplanned inventory accumulations—in other words, if I were actual investment rather than planned investment.

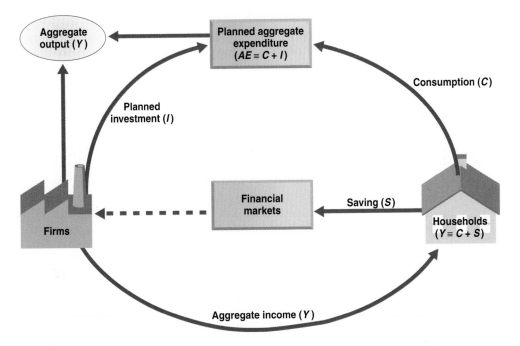

FIGURE 9.9

Planned Aggregate
Expenditure and Aggregate
Output (Income)

Saving is a leakage out of the
spending stream. If planned
investment is exactly equal to
saving, then planned aggregate
expenditure is exactly equal
to aggregate output, and there
is equilibrium.

projects. If the planned investment of firms equals the saving of households, then
planned aggregate expenditure ($AE \equiv C + I$) equals aggregate output (income) (Y), and
there is equilibrium: The *leakage* out of the spending stream—saving—is matched by an
equal *injection* of planned investment spending into the spending stream. For this reason,
the saving/investment approach to equilibrium is also called the *leakages/injections
approach* to equilibrium.

Figure 9.10 reproduces the saving schedule derived in Figure 9.6 and the horizontal investment function from Figure 9.7. Notice that $S = I$ at one, and only one,
level of aggregate output, $Y = 500$. At $Y = 500$, $C = 475$ and $I = 25$. In other words,
$Y = C + I$, and therefore equilibrium exists.

ADJUSTMENT TO EQUILIBRIUM

We have defined equilibrium and learned how to find it, but we have said nothing
about how firms might react to *disequilibrium*. Let's consider the actions firms might
take when planned aggregate expenditure exceeds aggregate output (income).

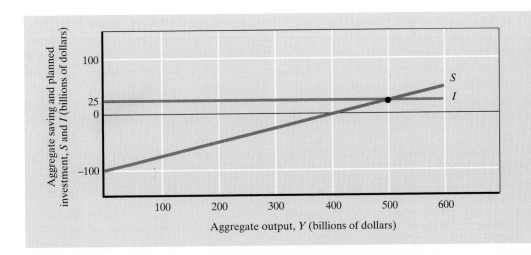

FIGURE 9.10

The $S = I$ Approach to
Equilibrium

Aggregate output will be equal
to planned aggregate expenditure only when saving equals
planned investment ($S = I$).
Saving and planned investment are equal at $Y = 500$.

189

We already know the only way firms can sell more than they produce is by selling some inventory. This means that when planned aggregate expenditure exceeds aggregate output, unplanned inventory reductions have occurred. It seems reasonable to assume firms will respond to unplanned inventory reductions by increasing output. If firms increase output, income must also increase (output and income are two ways of measuring the same thing). As General Motors builds more cars it hires more workers (or pays its existing workforce for working more hours), buys more steel, uses more electricity, and so on. These purchases by GM represent income for the producers of labor, steel, electricity, and so on. If GM (and all other firms) try to keep their inventories intact by increasing production, they will generate more income in the economy as a whole. This will lead to more consumption. Remember, when income rises, consumption also rises.

> The adjustment process will continue as long as output (income) is below planned aggregate expenditure. If firms react to unplanned inventory reductions by increasing output, an economy with planned spending greater than output will adjust to equilibrium, with Y higher than before. If planned spending is less than output, there will be unplanned increases in inventories. In this case, firms will respond by reducing output. As output falls, income falls, consumption falls, and so forth, until equilibrium is restored, with Y lower than before.

As Figure 9.8 shows, at any level of output above $Y = 500$, such as $Y = 800$, output will fall until it reaches equilibrium at $Y = 500$, and at any level of output below $Y = 500$, such as $Y = 200$, output will rise until it reaches equilibrium at $Y = 500$.[7]

THE MULTIPLIER

Now that we know how the equilibrium value of income is determined, we ask: How does the equilibrium level of output change when planned investment changes? If there is a sudden change in planned investment, how will output respond, if it responds at all? As we will see, the change in equilibrium output is *greater* than the initial change in planned investment. Output changes by a multiple of the change in planned investment. So, this multiple is called the **multiplier**!

multiplier *The ratio of the change in the equilibrium level of output to a change in some autonomous variable.*

autonomous variable *A variable that is assumed not to depend on the state of the economy—that is, it is taken as given.*

The multiplier is defined as the ratio of the change in the equilibrium level of output to a change in some autonomous variable. A variable is **autonomous** when it is assumed not to depend on the state of the economy—that is, it is taken as given. In this chapter, we consider planned investment to be autonomous. This simplifies our analysis and provides a foundation for later discussions.

With planned investment as given, we can ask how much the equilibrium level of output changes when planned investment changes. Remember that we are not trying here to explain *why* planned investment changes; we are simply asking how much the equilibrium level of output changes when (for whatever reason) planned investment changes. (Beginning in chapter 13, we will no longer take planned investment as given and will explain how planned investment is determined.)

Consider a sustained increase in planned investment of $25 billion—that is, suppose I increases from $25 billion to $50 billion and stays at $50 billion. If equilibrium

---

[7]In discussing simple supply and demand equilibrium in chapters 4 and 5, we saw that when quantity supplied exceeds quantity demanded, the price falls and the quantity supplied declines. Similarly, when quantity demanded exceeds quantity supplied, the price rises and the quantity supplied increases. In the analysis here we are ignoring potential changes in prices or in the price level and focusing on changes in the level of real output (income). Later, after we have introduced money and the price level into the analysis, prices will be very important. At this stage, however, only aggregate output (income) (Y) adjusts when aggregate expenditure exceeds aggregate output (with inventory falling) or when aggregate output exceeds aggregate expenditure (with inventory rising).

existed at $I = \$25$ billion, an increase in planned investment of $25 billion will cause a disequilibrium, with planned aggregate expenditure greater than aggregate output by $25 billion. Firms immediately see unplanned reductions in their inventories, and, as a result, they begin to increase output.

Let's say the increase in planned investment comes from an anticipated increase in travel that leads airlines to purchase more airplanes, car rental companies to increase purchases of automobiles, and bus companies to purchase more buses (all capital goods). The firms experiencing unplanned inventory declines will be automobile manufacturers, bus producers, and aircraft producers—General Motors, Ford, McDonnell Douglas, Boeing, and so forth. In response to declining inventories of planes, buses, and cars, these firms will increase output.

Now suppose these firms raise output by the full $25 billion increase in planned investment. Does this restore equilibrium? No, because when output goes up, people earn more income and a part of that income will be spent. This increases planned aggregate expenditure even further. In other words, an increase in I also leads indirectly to an increase in C. To produce more airplanes, Boeing has to hire more workers or ask its existing employees to work more hours. It also must buy more engines from General Electric, more tires from Goodyear, and so forth. Owners of these firms will earn more profits, produce more, hire more workers, and pay out more in wages and salaries.

This added income does not vanish into thin air. It is paid to households that spend some of it and save the rest. The added production leads to added income, which leads to added consumption spending.

If planned investment (I) goes up by $25 billion initially *and is sustained at this higher level*, an increase of output of $25 billion will *not* restore equilibrium, because it generates even more consumption spending (C). People buy more consumer goods. There are unplanned reductions of inventories of basic consumption items—washing machines, food, clothing, and so forth—and this prompts other firms to increase output. The cycle starts all over again.[8]

Clearly, output and income can rise by significantly more than the initial increase in planned investment. But how much? How large is the multiplier? This is answered graphically in Figure 9.11. Assume the economy is in equilibrium at point A, where equilibrium output is 500. The increase in I of 25 shifts the $AE \equiv C + I$ curve up by 25, because I is higher by 25 at every level of income. The new equilibrium occurs at point B, where the equilibrium level of output is 600. Like point A, point B is on the 45° line and is an equilibrium value. Output (Y) has increased by 100 (600 − 500), or four times the initial increase in planned investment of 25, between point A and point B. The multiplier in this example is 4. At point B, aggregate spending is also

---

[8]Figure 9.9 can help you understand the multiplier effect. Note in the figure how an increase in planned investment makes its way through the circular flow. Initially, aggregate output is at equilibrium with $Y = C + I$. That is, every period, aggregate output is produced by firms, and every period, planned aggregate expenditure is just sufficient to take all those goods and services off the market.

Now note what happens when planned investment spending increases and is sustained at a higher level. Firms experience unplanned declines in inventories and they increase output; more real output is produced in subsequent periods. But the added output means more income; thus we see added income flowing to households. This means more spending. Households spend some portion of their added income (equal to the added income times the *MPC*) on consumer goods.

The higher consumption spending means that even if firms responded fully to the increase in investment spending in the first round, the economy is still out of equilibrium. Follow the added spending back over to firms in Figure 9.9 and you can see that with higher consumption, planned aggregate expenditure will be greater. Firms again see an unplanned decline in inventories and they respond by increasing the output of consumer goods. This sets off yet another round of income and expenditure increases: Output rises, and income rises as a result, thus increasing consumption. Higher consumption leads to yet another disequilibrium, inventories fall, and output (income) rises again.

FIGURE 9.11

At point A, the economy is in equilibrium at $Y = 500$. When I increases by 25, planned aggregate expenditure is initially greater than aggregate output. As output rises in response, additional consumption is generated, pushing equilibrium output up by a multiple of the initial increase in I. The new equilibrium is found at point B, where $Y = 600$. Equilibrium output has increased by 100 (600 – 500), or *four times* the amount of the increase in planned investment.

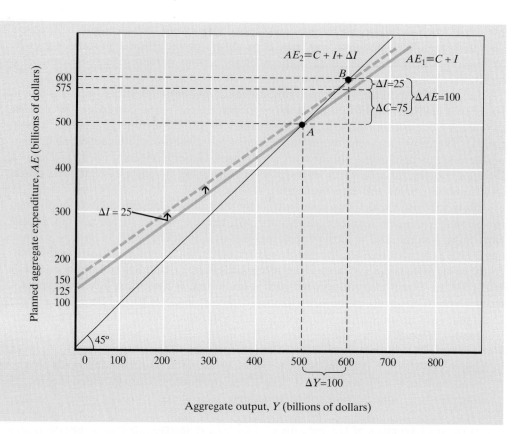

higher by 100. If 25 of this additional 100 is investment (I), as we know it is, the remaining 75 is added consumption (C). From point A to point B then, $\Delta Y = 100$, $\Delta I = 25$, and $\Delta C = 75$.

Why doesn't the multiplier process go on forever? Because only a fraction of the increase in income is consumed in each round. Successive increases in income become smaller and smaller in each round of the multiplier process until equilibrium is restored.

The size of the multiplier depends on the slope of the planned aggregate expenditure line. The steeper the slope of this line, the greater the change in output for a given change in investment. When planned investment is fixed, as in our example, the slope of the $AE \equiv C + I$ line is just the marginal propensity to consume $(\Delta C/\Delta Y)$. The greater the *MPC*, the greater the multiplier. This should not be surprising. A large *MPC* means that consumption increases a lot when income increases. The more consumption changes, the more output has to change to achieve equilibrium.

▶ **The Multiplier Equation** Is there a way to determine the size of the multiplier without using graphic analysis? Yes, there is.

Assume that the market is in equilibrium at an income level of $Y = 500$. Now suppose planned investment (I), and thus planned aggregate expenditure (AE), increases and remains higher by $25 billion. Planned aggregate expenditure is greater than output, there is an unplanned inventory reduction, and firms respond by increasing output (income) (Y). This leads to a second round of increases, and so on.

What will restore equilibrium? Look at Figure 9.10 and recall: planned aggregate expenditure $(AE \equiv C + I)$ is not equal to aggregate output (Y) unless $S = I$; the leakage of saving must exactly match the injection of planned investment spending for the economy to be in equilibrium. Recall also, we assumed that planned investment jumps to a new higher level and stays there; it is a *sustained* increase of $25 billion in planned investment spending. As income rises, consumption rises and so does saving. Our $S = I$ approach to equilibrium leads us to conclude:

> Equilibrium will be restored only when saving has increased by exactly the amount of the initial increase in I.

Otherwise, I will continue to be greater than S, and $C + I$ will continue to be greater than Y. (The $S = I$ approach to equilibrium leads to an interesting paradox in the macroeconomy. See Issues and Debates, "The Paradox of Thrift.")

It is possible to figure how much Y must increase in response to the additional planned investment before equilibrium will be restored. Y will rise, pulling S up with it until the change in saving is exactly equal to the change in planned investment—that is, until S is again equal to I at its new higher level. Because added saving is a *fraction* of added income (the *MPS*), the increase in *income* required to restore equilibrium must be *a multiple* of the increase in planned investment.

Recall that the marginal propensity to save (*MPS*) is the fraction of a change in income that is saved. It is defined as the change in S (ΔS) over the change in income (ΔY):

$$MPS \equiv \frac{\Delta S}{\Delta Y}$$

Because ΔS must be equal to ΔI for equilibrium to be restored, we can substitute ΔI for ΔS and solve:

$$MPS = \frac{\Delta I}{\Delta Y}. \text{ Therefore, } \Delta Y = \Delta I \times \frac{1}{MPS}.$$

As you can see, the change in equilibrium income (ΔY) is equal to the initial change in planned investment (ΔI) times $1/MPS$. The multiplier is $1/MPS$:

$$\text{Multiplier} \equiv \frac{1}{MPS}$$

Because $MPS + MPC \equiv 1$, $MPS \equiv 1 - MPC$. It follows that the multiplier is equal to:

$$\text{Multiplier} \equiv \frac{1}{1 - MPC}$$

In our example, the *MPC* is .75, so the *MPS* must equal $1 - .75$, or .25. Thus, the multiplier is 1 divided by .25, or 4. The change in the equilibrium level of Y is $4 \times \$25$ billion, or \$100 billion.[9] Also note that the same analysis holds when planned investment falls. If planned investment falls by a certain amount and is sustained at this lower level, output will fall by a multiple of the reduction in I. As the initial shock is felt and firms cut output, they lay people off. The result: Income, and subsequently consumption, falls.

▶ **The Size of the Multiplier in the Real World**   In considering the size of the multiplier, it is important to realize that the multiplier we derived in this chapter is based on a *very* simplified picture of the economy. First, we have assumed that planned investment is fixed and does not respond to changes in the economy. Second, we have thus far ignored the role of government, financial markets, and the rest of the world in the macroeconomy. For these reasons, it would be a mistake to move on from this chapter thinking that national income can be increased by \$100 billion simply by increasing planned investment spending by \$25 billion.

---

[9]The multiplier can also be derived algebraically, as the appendix to this chapter demonstrates.

THE PARADOX OF THRIFT

An interesting paradox can arise when households attempt to increase their saving. What happens if households become concerned about the future and want to save more today to be prepared for hard times tomorrow? If households increase their planned saving, the saving schedule in Figure 1 shifts upward, from S to S'. The plan to save more is a plan to consume less, and the resulting drop in spending leads to a drop in income. Income drops by a multiple of the initial shift in the saving schedule. Before the increase in saving, equilibrium exists at point A, where $S = I$ and $Y = \$500$ billion. Increased saving shifts the equilibrium to point B, the point at which $S' = I$. New equilibrium output is $300 billion—a $200 billion decrease ($\Delta Y$) from the initial equilibrium.

By consuming less, households have actually *caused* the hard times about which they were apprehensive. Worse, the new equilibrium finds saving at the same level as it was before consumption dropped ($25 billion). In their attempt to save more, households have caused a contraction in output, and thus in income. They end up consuming less, but they have not saved any more.

It should be clear why saving at the new equilibrium is equal to saving at the old equilibrium. Equilibrium requires that saving equal planned investment, and because planned investment is unchanged, saving must remain unchanged for equilibrium to exist. This paradox shows that the interactions among sectors in the economy can be of crucial importance.

The **paradox of thrift** is "paradoxical" because it contradicts the widely held belief that "a penny saved is a

FIGURE 1

The Paradox of Thrift

An increase in planned saving from S to S' causes equilibrium output to decrease from $500 billion to $300 billion. The decreased consumption that accompanies increased saving leads to a contraction of the economy and to a reduction of income. But at the new equilibrium, saving is the same as it was at the initial equilibrium. Increased efforts to save have caused a drop in income but no overall change in saving.

penny earned." This may be true for an individual, but when society as a whole saves more, the result is a drop in income but no increased saving.

Does the paradox of thrift always hold? Recall our assumption that planned investment is fixed. Let us drop this assumption for a moment. If the extra saving that households want to do to ward off hard times is channeled

into additional investment through financial markets, there is a shift up in the I schedule. The paradox could then be averted. If investment increases, a new equilibrium can be achieved at a higher level of saving and income. This result, however, depends critically on the existence of a channel through which additional household saving finances additional investment.

For more on saving, investment, and the multiplier, see the Case and Fair Web page at http://www.prenhall.com/casefair.

As we relax these assumptions in the following chapters, you will see that most of what we add to make our analysis more realistic has the effect of *reducing* the size of the multiplier. For example:

1. The appendix to chapter 10 shows that when tax payments depend on income (as they do in the real world), the size of the multiplier is reduced. As the economy expands, tax payments increase and act as a drag on the economy. The multiplier effect is smaller.
2. As you will see in chapter 13, planned investment (I) is not fixed; rather, it depends on the interest rate in the economy. This too has the effect of reducing the size of the multiplier.
3. Thus far we have not discussed how the overall price level is determined in the economy. When we do in chapter 14, we will see that part of an expansion of the economy is likely to take the form of an increase in the price level rather than an increase in output. When this happens, the size of the multiplier is reduced.
4. We introduce the role of imports and exports in chapter 10 and treat them in chapter 21. In these chapters, you will see that the multiplier effect on domestic production will be reduced if some domestic spending leaks into foreign markets.

These juicy tidbits give you something to look forward to as you proceed through the rest of this book. For now, however, it is enough to point out that:

> In reality, the size of the multiplier is about 1.4. That is, a sustained increase in autonomous spending of $10 billion into the U.S. economy can be expected to raise real GDP over time by about $14 billion.

This is a far cry from the value of 4.0 that we used in this chapter.

▶ The Multiplier in Action: Recovering From the Great Depression

The Great Depression began in 1930 and lasted nearly a decade. Real output in 1938 was lower than real output in 1929, and the unemployment rate never fell below 14 percent of the labor force between 1930 and 1940. How did the economy get "stuck" at such a low level of income and a high level of unemployment? The Keynesian model that we analyzed in this chapter can help us answer this question.

If firms do not wish to undertake much investment (I is low) or if consumers decide to increase their saving and cut back on consumption, then planned spending will be low. Firms do not want to produce more because, with many workers unemployed, households do not have the income to buy the extra output that firms might produce. And households, who would purchase more if they had more income, cannot find jobs that would enable them to earn additional income. The economy is caught in a vicious circle.

How might such a cycle be broken? One way is for planned aggregate expenditure to increase, increasing aggregate output via the multiplier effect. This increase in *AE* may occur naturally, or it may be caused by a change in government policy.

In the late 1930s, for example, the economy experienced a surge of both residential and nonresidential investment. Between 1935 and 1940, total investment spending (in real terms) increased 64 percent and residential investment more than doubled. There can be no doubt that this increased investment had a multiplier effect. In just five years, employment in the construction industry increased by more than 400,000, employment in manufacturing industries jumped by more than 1 million, and total employment grew by more than 5 million. As more workers were employed, more income was generated, and some of this added income was spent on consumption goods. Inventories declined and firms began to expand output. Between 1935 and 1940, real output (income) increased by more than one third and the unemployment rate dropped from 20.3 percent to 14.6 percent.

But 14.6 percent is a very high rate of unemployment; the Depression was not yet over. Between 1940 and 1943 the Depression ended, with the unemployment rate dropping to 1.9 percent in 1943. This recovery was triggered by the mobilization for World War II and the significant increase in government purchases of goods and services, which rose from $14 billion in 1940 to $88.6 billion in 1943. In the next chapter, we will explore this *government spending multiplier*, and you'll see how the government can help stimulate the economy by increasing its spending.

LOOKING AHEAD: THE GOVERNMENT AND INTERNATIONAL SECTORS

In this chapter, we took the first step in understanding how the economy works. We described the behavior of two sectors (household and firm) and discussed how equilibrium is achieved in the market for goods and services. In the next chapter, we will relax some of the assumptions we have made and take into account the roles of government spending and net exports in the economy. This will give us a more realistic picture of how our economy works.

SUMMARY

AGGREGATE OUTPUT AND AGGREGATE INCOME (Y)

1. Each period, firms produce an aggregate quantity of goods and services called *aggregate output* (Y). Because every dollar of expenditure is received by someone as income, aggregate output and aggregate income are the same thing.

2. The total amount of aggregate consumption that takes place in any given period of time depends on factors such as household income, household wealth, interest rates, and households' expectations about the future.

3. If taxes are zero, households do only two things with their income: They can either spend on consumption or save. C refers to aggregate consumption by households. S refers to aggregate saving by households. By definition, saving equals income minus consumption: $S \equiv Y - C$.

4. The higher someone's income is, the higher his or her consumption is likely to be. This is also true for the economy as a whole: There is a positive relationship between aggregate consumption (C) and aggregate income (Y).

5. The *marginal propensity to consume* (MPC) is the fraction of a change in income that is consumed, or spent. The *marginal propensity to save* (MPS) is the fraction of a change in income that is saved. Because all income must be either saved or spent, $MPS + MPC \equiv 1$.

6. The primary form of spending that firms engage in is investment. Strictly speaking, *investment* refers to the purchase by firms of new buildings and equipment and additions to inventories, all of which add to firms' capital stock.

7. *Actual investment* can differ from planned investment because changes in firms' inventories are part of actual investment and inventory changes are not under the complete control of firms. Inventory changes are partly determined by how much households decide to buy. I refers to planned investment only.

EQUILIBRIUM AGGREGATE OUTPUT (INCOME)

8. In an economy in which government spending and net exports are zero, *planned aggregate expenditure* (AE) equals consumption plus planned investment: $AE \equiv C + I$. *Equilibrium* in the goods market is achieved when planned aggregate expenditure equals aggregate output: $C + I = Y$. This holds if, and only if, planned investment and actual investment are equal.

9. Because aggregate income must be saved or spent, the equilibrium condition $Y = C + I$ can be rewritten as $C + S = C + I$, or $S = I$. Only when planned investment equals saving will there be equilibrium. This approach to equilibrium is the *saving/investment approach* to equilibrium or the *leakages/injections approach* to equilibrium.

10. When planned aggregate expenditure exceeds aggregate output (*income*), there is an unplanned fall in inventories. Firms will increase output. This increased output leads to increased income and even more consumption. This process will continue as long as output (income) is below planned aggregate expenditure. If firms react to unplanned inventory reductions by increasing output, an economy with planned spending greater than output will adjust to equilibrium, with Y higher than before.

11. Equilibrium output changes by a multiple of the change in planned investment or any other autonomous variable. The multiplier is $1/MPS$.

12. When households increase their planned saving, income decreases and saving does not change. Saving does not increase because in equilibrium saving must equal planned investment and planned investment is fixed. If planned investment also increased, this *paradox of thrift* could be averted and a new equilibrium could be achieved at a higher level of saving and income. This result depends on the existence of a channel through which additional household saving finances additional investment.

REVIEW TERMS AND CONCEPTS

actual investment, 184
aggregate income, 177
aggregate output, 177
aggregate output (income) (*Y*), 177
autonomous variable, 190
change in inventory, 184

consumption function, 178
desired, or planned, investment (*I*), 184
equilibrium, 185
identity, 178
investment, 183
marginal propensity to consume (*MPC*), 180

marginal propensity to save (*MPS*), 180
multiplier, 190
paradox of thrift, 194
planned aggregate expenditure (*AE*), 184
saving (*S*), 177

1. $S \equiv Y - C$
2. $MPC \equiv$ slope of consumption function $\equiv \dfrac{\Delta C}{\Delta Y}$
3. $MPC + MPS \equiv 1$
4. $AE \equiv C + I$
5. Equilibrium condition: $Y = AE$ or $Y = C + I$
6. Saving/investment approach to equilibrium: $S = I$
7. Multiplier $\equiv \dfrac{1}{MPS} \equiv \dfrac{1}{1 - MPC}$

PROBLEM SET

1. Briefly define the following terms and explain the relationship between them:

   MPC . . . . Multiplier
   Actual investment . . . . Planned investment
   Aggregate expenditure . . . . Real GDP
   Aggregate output . . . . Aggregate income

2. Crack econometricians in the Republic of Yuck estimate the following:

   Real GNP (*Y*) . . . . 200 billion Yuck dollars
   Planned investment
   spending . . . . 75 billion Yuck dollars

   Yuck is a simple economy with no government, no taxes, and no imports or exports. Yuckers (citizens of Yuck) are creatures of habit. They have a rule that everyone saves exactly 25 percent of income. Assume that planned investment is fixed and remains at 75 billion Yuck dollars.

   You are asked by the business editor of the *Weird Harold*, the local newspaper, to predict the economic events of the next few months. Using the data given, can you make a forecast? What is likely to happen to inventories? What is likely to happen to the level of real GDP? Is the economy at an equilibrium? When will things stop changing?

3. The following questions refer to this table:

AGGREGATE OUTPUT/INCOME	CONSUMPTION	PLANNED INVESTMENT
2,000	2,100	300
2,500	2,500	300
3,000	2,900	300
3,500	3,300	300
4,000	3,700	300
4,500	4,100	300
5,000	4,500	300
5,500	4,900	300

   a. At each level of output, calculate saving. At each level of output, calculate unplanned investment (inventory change). What is likely to happen to aggregate output if the economy were producing at each of the levels indicated? What is the equilibrium level of output?

   b. Over each range of income (2,000 to 2,500, 2,500 to 3,000, and so on), calculate the marginal propensity to consume. Calculate the marginal propensity to save. What is the multiplier?

c. Assuming there is no change in the level of the *MPC* and the *MPS*, and planned investment jumps by 200 and is sustained at that higher level, recompute the table. What is the new equilibrium level of *Y*? Is this consistent with what you compute using the multiplier?

4. Explain the multiplier intuitively. Why is it that an increase in planned investment of $100 raises equilibrium output by more than $100? Why is the effect on equilibrium output finite? How do we know that the multiplier is 1/*MPS*?

5. Explain how planned investment can differ from actual investment.

6. You are given the following data regarding Freedonia, a legendary country:

    (1) Consumption function: $C = 200 + 0.8Y$
    (2) Investment function: $I = 100$
    (3) $AE \equiv C + I$
    (4) $AE = Y$

  a. What is the marginal propensity to consume in Freedonia? The marginal propensity to save?

b. Graph equations (3) and (4) and solve for equilibrium income.

c. Suppose equation (2) were changed to

$$(2') \; I = 110.$$

What is the new equilibrium level of income? By how much does the $10 increase in planned investment change equilibrium income? What is the value of the multiplier?

d. Calculate the saving function for Freedonia. Plot this saving function on a graph with equation (2). Explain why the equilibrium income in this graph must be the same as in part b.

7. If I decide to save an extra dollar, my saving goes up by that amount. But if everyone decides to save an extra dollar, income falls and saving does not rise. Explain.

8. You learned earlier that expenditures and income should always be equal. In this chapter, you've learned that *AE* and aggregate output (income) can be different. Is there an inconsistency here?

TAKE IT TO THE NET

We invite you to visit the Case and Fair page on the Prentice Hall Web site:

http://www.prenhall.com/casefair

for this chapter's World Wide Web exercise.

APPENDIX TO CHAPTER 9

DERIVING THE MULTIPLIER ALGEBRAICALLY

In addition to deriving the multiplier using the simple substitution we used in the chapter, we can also derive the formula for the multiplier by using simple algebra.

Recall that our consumption function is

$$C = a + bY$$

where *b* is the marginal propensity to consume. In equilibrium,

$$Y = C + I$$

Now we solve these two equations for *Y* in terms of *I*. Substituting the first equation into the second, we get

$$Y = \underbrace{a + bY}_{C} + I$$

This equation can be rearranged to yield

$$Y - bY = a + I$$
$$Y(1 - b) = a + I$$

We can then solve for *Y* in terms of *I* by dividing through by $(1 - b)$:

$$Y = (a + I)\left(\frac{1}{1 - b}\right)$$

Now look carefully at this expression and think about increasing *I* by some amount, ΔI, with *a* held constant. If *I* increases by ΔI, income will increase by

$$\Delta Y = \Delta I \times \frac{1}{1 - b}$$

Because $b \equiv MPC$, the expression becomes

$$\Delta Y = \Delta I \times \frac{1}{1 - MPC}$$

The multiplier is

$$\frac{1}{1 - MPC}$$

Finally, because $MPS + MPC \equiv 1$, *MPS* is equal to $1 - MPC$, making the alternative expression for the multiplier 1/*MPS*, just as we saw in this chapter.

Chapter 10

THE GOVERNMENT AND FISCAL POLICY

NOTHING IN MACROECONOMICS or microeconomics arouses as much controversy as the role of government in the economy.

In microeconomics, the active presence of government in regulating competition, providing roads and education, and redistributing income is applauded by those who believe a free market simply does not work well if left to its own devices. Opponents of government intervention say it is the government, not the market, that performs badly. They say bureaucracy and inefficiency could be eliminated or reduced if the government played a smaller role in the economy.

In macroeconomics, the debate over what the government can and should do has a similar flavor, although the issues are somewhat different. At one end of the spectrum are the Keynesians and their intellectual descendants, who believe that the macroeconomy is likely to fluctuate too much if left on its own and that the government should smoothe out fluctuations in the business cycle. These ideas can be traced to Keynes's analysis in *The General Theory*, which suggests that governments can use their taxing and spending powers to increase aggregate expenditure (and thereby stimulate aggregate output) in recessions or depressions. At the other end are those who claim that government spending is incapable of stabilizing the economy, or worse, destabilizing and harmful.

Perhaps the one thing most people can agree on is that, like it or not, governments are important actors in the economies of virtually all countries. For this alone, it is worth our while to analyze the way government influences the functioning of the macroeconomy.

While the government has a variety of powers—including regulating firms' entry into and exit from an industry, setting standards for product quality, setting minimum wage levels, and regulating the disclosure of information—in macroeconomics we study a government with general, but limited, powers. Specifically, government can affect the macroeconomy through two policy channels: fiscal policy and monetary policy. **Fiscal policy,** the focus of this chapter, refers to the government's spending and taxing behavior—in other words, its budget policy.[1] Fiscal policy is generally divided into three categories: (1) policies regarding government purchases of goods

fiscal policy *The government's spending and taxing policies.*

---
[1]The word *fiscal* comes from the root *fisc*, which refers to the "treasury" of a government.

199

monetary policy *The behavior of the Federal Reserve regarding the nation's money supply.*

and services, (2) policies regarding taxes, and (3) policies regarding transfer payments (such as unemployment compensation, social security benefits, welfare payments, and veterans' benefits) to households. **Monetary policy**, in the next two chapters, refers to the behavior of the nation's central bank, the Federal Reserve, regarding the nation's money supply.

GOVERNMENT IN THE ECONOMY

Given the scope and power of local, state, and federal governments, there are some matters over which they exert great control and some matters beyond their control. We need to distinguish between variables that a government controls directly and variables that are a consequence of government decisions *combined with the state of the economy*.

For example, tax rates are controlled by the government. By law, Congress has the authority to decide who and what should be taxed and at what rate. Tax *revenue*, on the other hand, is not subject to complete control by the government. Revenue from the personal income tax system depends both on personal tax rates (which Congress sets) *and* on the income of the household sector (which depends on many factors not under direct government control, such as how much households decide to work). Revenue from the corporate profits tax depends both on corporate profits tax rates and on the size of corporate profits. The government controls corporate tax rates but not the size of corporate profits.

Government expenditures also depends both on government decisions and on the state of the economy. For example, in the United States the unemployment insurance program pays benefits to unemployed people. When the economy goes into a recession, the number of unemployed workers increases and so does the level of government unemployment insurance payments.

Because taxes and expenditures often go up or down in response to changes in the economy rather than as the result of deliberate decisions by policy makers, we will occasionally use **discretionary fiscal policy** to refer to changes in taxes or spending that are the result of deliberate changes in government policy.

discretionary fiscal policy *Changes in taxes or spending that are the result of deliberate changes in government policy.*

GOVERNMENT PURCHASES (G), NET TAXES (T), AND DISPOSABLE INCOME (Y_d)

In the previous chapter, we explored the equilibrium level of national output for a simple economy—no taxes, no government spending, and no exports—to provide a general idea of how the macroeconomy operates.

To get more realistic, we need to consider an economy in which government is an active participant. There are no countries in the world without a government. We begin by adding the government sector into the simple economy in chapter 9.

To keep things simple, we will combine two government activities—the collection of taxes and the payment of transfer payments—into a category we call **net taxes** (T). Specifically, net taxes are equal to the tax payments made to the government by firms and households minus transfer payments made to households by the government. The other variable we will consider is government purchases of goods and services (G).

net taxes (T) *Taxes paid by firms and households to the government minus transfer payments made to households by the government.*

Our earlier discussions of household consumption did not take taxes into account. We assumed that all the income generated in the economy was spent or saved by households. When we take into account the role of government, as Figure 10.1 does, we see that as income (Y) flows toward households, the government takes income from households in the form of net taxes (T). The income that ultimately gets to households is called **disposable, or after-tax, income** (Y_d):

disposable, or **after-tax, income (Y_d)** *Total income minus net taxes:* Y − T.

$$\text{Disposable income} \equiv \text{Total income} - \text{Net taxes}$$
$$Y_d \equiv Y - T$$

200 PART THREE
Macroeconomic Principles and Policy

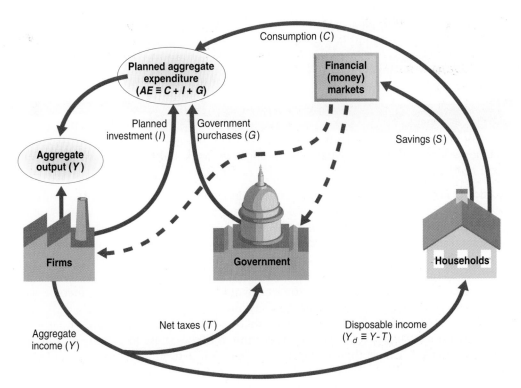

Y_d excludes taxes paid by households and includes transfer payments made to households by the government. For now we are assuming that T does not depend on Y—that is, net taxes do not depend on income. This assumption is relaxed in appendix B to this chapter. Taxes that do not depend on income are sometimes called *lump-sum taxes*.

As Figure 10.1 shows, the disposable income (Y_d) of households must end up either as consumption (C) or saving (S). Thus,

$$Y_d \equiv C + S$$

This equation is an identity—something that is always true.

Because disposable income is aggregate income (Y) minus net taxes (T), we can write another identity:

$$Y - T \equiv C + S$$

Adding T to both sides:

$$Y \equiv C + S + T$$

This identity says aggregate income gets cut into three pieces. Government takes a slice (net taxes, T), and then households divide the rest between consumption (C) and saving (S).

Because governments spend money on goods and services, we need to expand our definition of planned aggregate expenditure. Planned aggregate expenditure (AE) is the sum of consumption spending by households (C), planned investment by business firms (I), *and* government purchases of goods and services (G):[2]

$$AE \equiv C + I + G$$

---

[2]We are still assuming that net exports $(EX - IM)$ are zero. In practice, $AE \equiv C + I + G + (EX - IM)$. We bring net export into the analysis at the end of this chapter.

budget deficit *The difference between what a government spends and what it collects in taxes in a given period:* G − T.

In May 1997 the president and Congress agreed to a budget plan that would reduce the U.S. budget deficit to zero by 2002. The plan involved tax cuts and spending reductions. Little did they know that by the fall of 1997, the budget would be very nearly balanced (G = T) because of the strong economy. A strong economy means higher incomes and higher corporate profits and, thus, higher tax revenues.

A government's **budget deficit** is the difference between what it spends (G) and what it collects in taxes (T) in a given period:

$$\text{Budget deficit} \equiv G - T$$

If G exceeds T, the government must borrow from the public to finance the deficit. It does so by selling Treasury bonds and bills (more on this later). In this case, a part of household saving (S) goes to the government. The dashed lines in Figure 10.1 mean that some S goes to firms to finance investment projects and some goes to the government to finance its deficit.[3]

▶ **Adding Taxes to the Consumption Function** In chapter 9, we examined the consumption behavior of households and noted that aggregate consumption (C) depends on aggregate income (Y): In general, the higher aggregate income is, the higher is aggregate consumption. For the sake of illustration, we used a specific linear consumption function:

$$C = a + bY$$

where a is the amount of consumption that would take place if national income were zero and b is the marginal propensity to consume.

We need to modify this consumption function because we have added government to the economy. With taxes a part of the picture, it makes sense to assume that disposable income (Y_d), rather than before-tax income (Y), determines consumption behavior. If you earn a million dollars, but have to pay $950,000 in taxes, you have no more disposable income than someone who earns only $50,000 but pays no taxes. What you have available for spending on current consumption is your disposable income, not your before-tax income.

To modify our aggregate consumption function to incorporate disposable income rather than before-tax income, instead of $C = a + bY$, we write

$$C = a + bY_d$$

or

$$C = a + b(Y - T)$$

Our consumption function now has consumption depending on disposable income rather than on before-tax income.

▶ **Investment** What about investment? The government can affect investment behavior through its tax treatment of depreciation and other tax policies. Investment may also vary with economic conditions and interest rates, as we will see later. For our present purposes, we continue to assume that planned investment (I) is fixed.

EQUILIBRIUM OUTPUT: $Y = C + I + G$

We know from chapter 9 that equilibrium occurs where Y = AE—that is, where aggregate output equals planned aggregate expenditure. Remember: Planned aggregate expenditure in an economy with a government is $AE \equiv C + I + G$, so the equilibrium condition is:

$$\text{Equilibrium condition: } Y = C + I + G$$

The equilibrium analysis in chapter 9 holds here also. If output (Y) exceeds planned aggregate expenditure (C + I + G), there will be an unplanned increase in

[3]Although it is almost unheard of these days, governments do sometimes run budget surpluses. A *surplus* occurs when net taxes are greater than government purchases of goods and services. A surplus is simply a negative deficit.

TABLE 10.1 FINDING EQUILIBRIUM FOR $I = 100$, $G = 100$, AND $T = 100$
(ALL FIGURES IN BILLIONS OF DOLLARS)

(1) OUTPUT (INCOME) Y	(2) NET TAXES T	(3) DISPOSABLE INCOME $Y_d \equiv Y - T$	(4) CONSUMPTION SPENDING $(C = 100 + .75\,Y_d)$	(5) SAVING S $(Y_d - C)$	(6) PLANNED INVESTMENT SPENDING I	(7) GOVERNMENT PURCHASES G	(8) PLANNED AGGREGATE EXPENDITURE $C + I + G$	(9) UNPLANNED INVENTORY CHANGE $Y - (C + I + G)$	(10) ADJUST-MENT TO DISEQUILI-BRIUM
300	100	200	250	−50	100	100	450	−150	Output↑
500	100	400	400	0	100	100	600	−100	Output↑
700	100	600	550	50	100	100	750	−50	Output↑
900	100	800	700	100	100	100	900	0	Equilibrium
1,100	100	1,000	850	150	100	100	1,050	+50	Output↓
1,300	100	1,200	1,000	200	100	100	1,200	+100	Output↓
1,500	100	1,400	1,150	250	100	100	1,350	+150	Output↓

inventories—actual investment will exceed planned investment. Conversely, if $C + I + G$ exceeds Y, there will be an unplanned decrease in inventories.

An example will illustrate the government's effect on the macroeconomy and the equilibrium condition. First, our consumption function, $C = 100 + .75Y$ before we introduced the government sector, now becomes

$$C = 100 + .75Y_d$$

or

$$C = 100 + .75\,(Y - T)$$

Second, we assume that the government is currently purchasing $100 billion of goods and services and collecting net taxes (T) of $100 billion.[4] In other words, the government is running a balanced budget, financing all of its spending with taxes. Third, we assume that planned investment (I) is $100 billion.

Table 10.1 calculates planned aggregate expenditure at several levels of disposable income. For example, at $Y = 500$, disposable income is $Y - T$, or 400.[5] Therefore, $C = 100 + .75(400) = 400$. Assuming that I is fixed at 100, and assuming that G is fixed at 100, planned aggregate expenditure is 600 ($C + I + G = 400 + 100 + 100$). Because output (Y) is only 500, planned spending is greater than output by 100. As a result, there is an unplanned inventory decrease of 100, giving firms an incentive to raise output. Thus, output of 500 is below equilibrium.

If $Y = 1,300$, then $Y_d = 1,200$, $C = 1,000$, and planned aggregate expenditure is 1,200. Here, planned spending is *less* than output, there will be an unplanned inventory increase of 100, and firms have an incentive to cut back output. Thus, output of 1,300 is above equilibrium. Only when output is 900 are output and planned aggregate expenditure equal, and only at $Y = 900$ does equilibrium exist.

In Figure 10.2, we derive the same equilibrium level of output graphically. First, the consumption function is drawn, taking into account net taxes of 100. The old function was $C = 100 + .75Y$. The new function is $C = 100 + .75(Y - T)$ or $C = 100 + .75(Y - 100)$, rewritten as $C = 100 + .75Y - 75$, or $C = 25 + .75Y$. For example, consumption at an income of zero is 25 ($C = 25 + .75Y = 25 + .75(0) = 25$). The marginal propensity to consume has not changed—we assume it remains .75. Note that the consumption function in Figure 10.2 plots the points in columns 1 and 4 of Table 10.1.

---

[4]As we pointed out earlier, the government does not have complete control over tax revenues and transfer payments. We ignore this problem here, however, and set tax revenues minus transfers at a fixed amount. Things will become more realistic later in this chapter and in appendix B.

[5]For the rest of this discussion, we will understand but not state that figures are in billions of dollars.

FIGURE 10.2

Finding Equilibrium Output/Income Graphically

Because G and I are both fixed at 100, the aggregate expenditure function is the new consumption function displaced upward by $I + G = 200$. Equilibrium occurs at $Y = C + I + G = 900$.

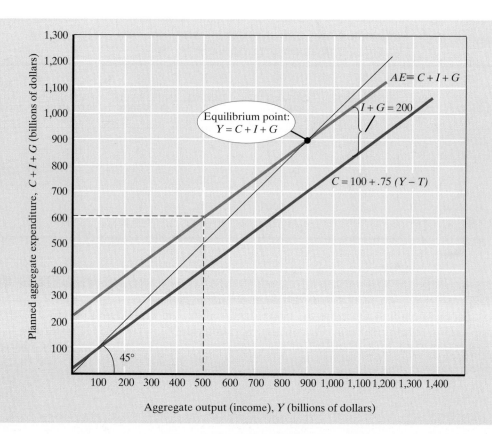

Planned aggregate expenditure, recall, adds planned investment to consumption. But now, in addition to 100 in investment, we have government purchases of 100. Because I and G are constant at 100 each at all levels of income, we add $I + G = 200$ to consumption at every level of income. The result is the new AE curve. This curve is just a plot of the points in columns 1 and 8 of Table 10.1. The 45° line helps us find the equilibrium level of real output, which, we already know, is 900. If you examine any level of output above or below 900, you will find disequilibrium. Look, for example, at $Y = 500$ on the graph. At this level, planned aggregate expenditure is 600, but output is only 500. Inventories will fall below what was planned, and firms will have an incentive to increase output.

▶ **The Leakages/Injections Approach to Equilibrium** As in the last chapter, we can also examine equilibrium using the leakages/injections approach. Look at the circular flow of income in Figure 10.1. The government takes out net taxes (T) from the flow of income—a leakage—and households save (S) some of their income—also a leakage from the flow of income. The planned spending injections are government purchases (G) and planned investment (I). If leakages ($S + T$) equal planned injections ($I + G$), there is equilibrium:

Leakages/injections approach to equilibrium: $S + T = I + G$

To derive this, we know that in equilibrium, aggregate output (income) (Y) equals planned aggregate expenditure (AE). By definition, AE equals $C + I + G$, and by definition Y equals $C + S + T$. Therefore, at equilibrium

$$C + S + T = C + I + G$$

Subtracting C from both sides leaves

$$S + T = I + G$$

Note that equilibrium does *not* require that $G = T$ (a balanced government budget) or that $S = I$. It is only necessary that the sum of S and T equals the sum of I and G.

Column 5 of Table 10.1 calculates aggregate saving by subtracting consumption from disposal income at every level of disposable income ($S \equiv Y_d - C$). Because I and G are fixed, $I + G$ equals 200 at every level of income. The table shows that $S + T$ equals 200 only at $Y = 900$. Thus, the equilibrium level of output (income) is 900, the same answer we arrived at through numerical and graphical analysis.

FISCAL POLICY AT WORK: MULTIPLIER EFFECTS

You can see from Figure 10.2 that if the government were able to change the levels of either G or T, it would be able to change the equilibrium level of output (income). At this point, we are assuming that the government controls G and T.

THE GOVERNMENT SPENDING MULTIPLIER

Suppose you are the chief economic adviser to the president and the economy is sitting at the equilibrium output pictured in Figure 10.2. Output and income are being produced at a rate of $900 billion per year, and the government is currently buying $100 billion worth of goods and services each year and is financing them with $100 billion in taxes. The budget is balanced. In addition, the private sector is investing (producing capital goods) at a rate of $100 billion per year.

The president calls you into the Oval Office and says, "Unemployment is too high. We need to lower unemployment by increasing output and income." After some research, you determine that an acceptable unemployment rate could be achieved only if aggregate output increases to $1,100 billion.

You now need to determine: How can the government use taxing and spending policy—fiscal policy—to increase the equilibrium level of national output? Suppose that the president has let it be known that taxes must remain at present levels—the Congress just passed a major tax reform package—so adjusting T is out of the question for several years. That leaves you with G. Your only option is to increase government spending while holding taxes constant.

To increase spending without raising taxes (which provides the government with revenue to spend), the government must borrow. When G is bigger than T, the government runs a deficit, and the difference between G and T must be borrowed. For the moment we will ignore the possible effect of the deficit and focus only on the effect of a higher G with T constant.

Meanwhile, the president is awaiting your answer. How much of an increase in spending would be required to generate a $200 billion increase in the equilibrium level of output, pushing it from $900 billion up to $1,100 billion and reducing unemployment to the president's acceptable level?

You might be tempted to say that because we need to increase income by 200 (1,100 − 900), we should increase government spending by the same amount—but what would happen? The increased government spending will throw the economy out of equilibrium. Because G is a component of aggregate spending, planned aggregate expenditure will increase by 200. Planned spending will be greater than output, inventories will be lower than planned, and firms will have an incentive to increase output. Suppose output rises by the desired 200. You might think, "We increased spending by 200 and output by 200, so equilibrium is restored."

There is more to the story than this. The moment output rises, the economy is generating more income. This was the desired effect: the creation of more employment. The newly employed workers are also consumers and some of their income gets spent. With higher consumption spending, planned spending will be greater than output,

FAST FACTS

The Taxpayer Relief Act of 1997 was passed by the Congress and signed by the president in August 1997. The act reduced taxes effective in 1997. While the act scaled back government spending in the long run, many cuts do not take effect until after the year 2000. In 1998 and 1999, government spending is expected to rise and tax revenues are expected to fall, increasing the deficit.

Source: Congressional Budget Office, 1997.

inventories will be lower than planned, and firms will raise output, and thus raise income, again. This time firms are responding to the new consumption spending. Already, total income is over 1,100.

This story should sound familiar. It is the multiplier in action. Although this time it is government spending (G) that is changed rather than planned investment (I), the effect is the same as the multiplier effect we described in chapter 9. An increase in government spending has the same impact on the equilibrium level of output and income as an increase in planned investment. A dollar of extra spending from either G or I is identical with respect to its impact on equilibrium output. The equation for the government spending multiplier is the same as the equation for the multiplier for a change in planned investment.[6]

$$\text{Government spending multiplier} \equiv \frac{1}{MPS}$$

government spending multiplier *The ratio of the change in the equilibrium level of output to a change in government spending.*

Formally, the **government spending multiplier** is defined as the ratio of the change in the equilibrium level of output to a change in government spending. This is the same definition we used in the previous chapter, but now the autonomous variable is government spending rather than planned investment.

Remember that we were thinking of increasing government spending (G) by 200. We can use the multiplier analysis to see what the new equilibrium level of Y would be for an increase in G of 200. The multiplier in our example is 4. (Because b—the MPC—is .75, the MPS must be $1 - .75 = .25$. And $1/.25 = 4$). Thus, Y will increase by 800 (4×200). Because the initial level of Y was 900, the new equilibrium level of Y is $900 + 800 = 1,700$ when G is increased by 200.

The level of 1,700 is much larger than the level of 1,100 that we calculated as necessary to lower unemployment to the desired level. Let's back up, then. If we want Y to increase by 200 and if the multiplier is 4, we need G to increase by only $200/4 = 50$. If G changes by 50, the equilibrium level of Y will change by 200, and the new value of Y will be 1,100 ($900 + 200$), as desired.

Looking at Table 10.2, we can check our answer to be sure that it is an equilibrium. Look first at the old equilibrium of 900. When government purchases (G) were 100, aggregate output (income) was equal to planned aggregate expenditure ($AE \equiv C + I + G$) at $Y = 900$. But now G has increased to 150. At $Y = 900$, ($C + I + G$) is greater than Y, there's an unplanned fall in inventories, and output will rise. But by how much? The multiplier told us that equilibrium income would rise by four times the 50 change in G. Y should rise by $4 \times 50 = 200$, from 900 to 1,100 before equilibrium is restored. Let's check. If $Y = 1,100$, then consumption is $C = 100 + .75\ Y_d = 100 + .75(1,000) = 850$. Because I equals 100 and G now equals 100 (the original level of G) + 50 (the additional G brought about by the fiscal policy change) = 150, then $C + I + G = 850 + 100 + 150 = 1,100$. $Y = AE$, and the economy is in equilibrium.

The graphic solution to the president's problem is presented in Figure 10.3. A 50 increase in G shifts the planned aggregate expenditure function up by 50. The new equilibrium income occurs where the new AE line (AE_2) crosses the 45° line, at $Y = 1,100$.

THE TAX MULTIPLIER

Remember that fiscal policy comprises policies regarding government spending *and* policies regarding taxation. To see what effect a change in tax policy has on the economy, imagine the following. You are still chief economic adviser to the president, but now you are instructed to devise a plan to reduce unemployment to an acceptable level *without* increasing the level of government spending. In your plan, instead of increasing

[6]We derive the government spending multiplier algebraically in appendix A to this chapter.

TABLE 10.2 FINDING EQUILIBRIUM AFTER A $50 BILLION GOVERNMENT SPENDING INCREASE
(ALL FIGURES IN BILLIONS OF DOLLARS; G HAS INCREASED FROM 100 IN TABLE 10.1 TO 150 HERE)

(1) OUTPUT (INCOME) Y	(2) NET TAXES T	(3) DISPOSABLE INCOME $Y_d \equiv Y - T$	(4) CONSUMPTION SPENDING $(C = 100 + .75\, Y_d)$	(5) SAVING S $(Y_d - C)$	(6) PLANNED INVESTMENT SPENDING I	(7) GOVERNMENT PURCHASES G	(8) PLANNED AGGREGATE EXPENDITURE $C + I + G$	(9) UNPLANNED INVENTORY CHANGE $Y - (C + I + G)$	(10) ADJUST-MENT TO DISEQUILI-BRIUM
300	100	200	250	−50	100	150	500	−200	Output↑
500	100	400	400	0	100	150	650	−150	Output↑
700	100	600	550	50	100	150	800	−100	Output↑
900	100	800	700	100	100	150	950	−50	Output↑
1,100	100	1,000	850	150	100	150	1,100	0	Equilibrium
1,300	100	1,200	1,000	200	100	150	1,250	+50	Output↓

government spending (G), you decide to cut taxes and maintain the current level of spending. A tax cut increases disposable income, which is likely to lead to added consumption spending. (Remember our general rule that increased income leads to increased consumption.) Would the decrease in taxes affect aggregate output (income) the same as an increase in G?

Clearly, a decrease in taxes would increase income. The government spends no less than it did before the tax cut, and households find they have a larger after-tax, or disposable, income than they had before. This leads to an increase in consumption. Planned aggregate expenditure will increase, which will lead to inventories being lower than planned, which will lead to a rise in output. When output rises, more workers will be employed and more income will be generated, causing a second-round increase in consumption, and so on. Thus, income will increase by a multiple of the decrease in taxes. But there is a wrinkle!

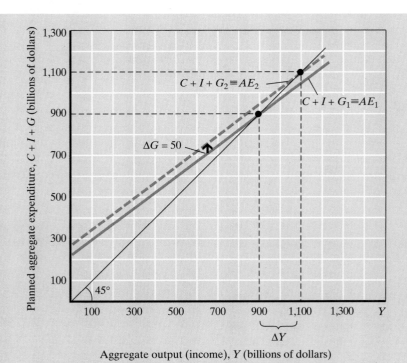

FIGURE 10.3

The Government Spending Multiplier

Increasing government spending by 50 shifts the AE function up by 50. As Y rises in response, additional consumption is generated. Overall, the equilibrium level of Y increases by 200, from 900 to 1,100.

tax multiplier *The ratio of change in the equilibrium level of output to a change in taxes.*

The multiplier for a change in taxes is *not the same* as the multiplier for a change in government spending.

Why does the **tax multiplier**—the ratio of change in the equilibrium level of output to a change in taxes—differ from the spending multiplier? To answer this, we need to compare the ways in which a tax cut and a spending increase work their way through the economy.

Look at Figure 10.1. When the government increases spending, there is an immediate and direct impact on the economy's *total* spending. Because G is a component of planned aggregate expenditure, an increase in G leads to a dollar-for-dollar increase in planned aggregate expenditure. When taxes are cut, there is no direct impact on spending. Taxes enter the picture only because they have an effect on the household's disposable income, which influences household's consumption (which is part of total spending). As Figure 10.1 shows, the tax cut flows through households before affecting aggregate expenditure.

Let's assume the government decides to cut taxes by $1. By how much would spending increase? We already know the answer. The marginal propensity to consume tells us how much consumption spending changes when disposable income changes. In the example running through this chapter, the marginal propensity to consume out of disposable income is .75. This means that if households' after-tax incomes rise by $1, they will increase their consumption not by the full $1, but by only $0.75.[7]

To summarize: When government spending increases by $1, planned aggregate expenditure increases initially by the full amount of the rise in G, or $1. When taxes are cut, however, the initial increase in planned aggregate expenditure is only the MPC times the change in taxes. Because the initial increase in planned aggregate expenditure is smaller for a tax cut than for a government spending increase, the final effect on the equilibrium level of income will be smaller.

We figure the size of the tax multiplier in the same way we derived the multiplier for an increase in investment and an increase in government purchases. The final change in the equilibrium level of output (income) (Y) is:

$$\Delta Y = (\text{initial increase in aggregate expenditure}) \times \left(\frac{1}{MPS}\right)$$

Because the initial change in aggregate expenditure caused by a tax change of ΔT is $(-\Delta T \times MPC)$, we can solve for the tax multiplier by substitution:

$$\Delta Y = (-\Delta T \times MPC) \times \left(\frac{1}{MPS}\right) = -\Delta T \times \left(\frac{MPC}{MPS}\right)$$

Because a tax cut will cause an *increase* in consumption expenditures and output and a tax increase will cause a *reduction* in consumption expenditures and output, the tax multiplier is a negative multiplier:

$$\text{Tax multiplier} \equiv -\left(\frac{MPC}{MPS}\right)$$

We derive the tax multiplier algebraically in appendix A to this chapter.

If the MPC is .75, as in our example, the multiplier is $-.75/.25 = -3$. A tax cut of 100 will increase the equilibrium level of output by $-100 \times -3 = 300$. This is very different than the effect of our government spending multiplier of 4. Under these same conditions, a 100 increase in G will increase the equilibrium level of output by 400 (100×4).

[7]What happens to the other $.25? Remember that whatever households do not consume is, by definition, saved. The other $.25 thus gets allocated to saving.

THE BALANCED-BUDGET MULTIPLIER

We have now discussed (1) changing government spending with no change in taxes, and (2) changing taxes with no change in government spending. But what if government spending and taxes are increased by the same amount? That is, what if the government decides to pay for its extra spending by increasing taxes by the same amount? The government's budget deficit would not change, because the increase in expenditures would be matched by an increase in tax income.

You might think in this case that equal increases in government spending and taxes have no effect on equilibrium income. After all, the extra government spending equals the extra amount of tax revenues collected by the government. But this is not so. Take, for example, a government spending increase of $40 billion. We know from the preceding analysis that an increase in G of 40, with taxes (T) held constant, should increase the equilibrium level of income by 40 × the government spending multiplier. The multiplier is $1/MPS$ or $1/.25 = 4$. The equilibrium level of income should rise by 160 (40 × 4).

Now suppose that instead of keeping tax revenues constant, we finance the 40 increase in government spending with an equal increase in taxes, so as to maintain a balanced budget. What happens to aggregate spending as a result of both the rise in G and the rise in T? There are two initial effects. First, government spending rises by 40. This effect is direct, immediate, and positive. But now the government also collects 40 more in taxes. The tax increase has a *negative* impact on overall spending in the economy, but it does not fully offset the increase in government spending.

The final impact of a tax increase on aggregate expenditure depends on how households respond to it. The only thing we know about household behavior so far is that households spend 75 percent of their added income and save 25 percent. We know that when disposable income falls, both consumption and saving are reduced. A tax *increase* of 40 reduces disposable income by 40, and that means consumption falls by $40 \times MPC$. Because $MPC = .75$, consumption falls by 30 (40 × .75).

The net result in the beginning is that government spending rises by 40 and consumption spending falls by 30. Aggregate expenditure increases by 10 right after the simultaneous balanced-budget increases in G and T.

So, a balanced-budget increase in G and T will raise output. But by how much? How large is this **balanced-budget multiplier**? The answer may surprise you:

> Balanced-budget multiplier $\equiv 1$

Let's combine what we know about the tax multiplier and the government spending multiplier to explain this. To find the final effect of a simultaneous increase in government spending and increase in net taxes, we need to add the multiplier effects of the two. The government spending multiplier is $1/MPS$. The tax multiplier is $-MPC/MPS$. Their sum is $(1/MPS) + (-MPC/MPS) \equiv (1 - MPC)/MPS$. Because $MPC + MPS \equiv 1$, then $1 - MPC \equiv MPS$. This means $(1 - MPC)/MPS \equiv MPS/MPS \equiv 1$.[8]

Back to our example. Using the government spending multiplier, we saw that a 40 increase in G would *raise* output at equilibrium by 160 (40 × the government spending multiplier of 4). Using the tax multiplier, we know that a 40 tax hike will *reduce* the equilibrium level of output by 120 (40 × the tax multiplier, -3). The net effect is 160 minus 120, or 40. It should be clear, then, that the effect on equilibrium Y is equal to the balanced increase in G and T. In other words, the net increase in the equilibrium level of Y resulting from the change in G and the change in T is exactly the size of the initial change in G or T itself.

If the president wanted to raise Y by 200 without increasing the deficit, a simultaneous increase in G and T of 200 would do it. To see why, look at the numbers in

balanced-budget multiplier
The ratio of change in the equilibrium level of output to a change in government spending where the change in government spending is balanced by a change in taxes so as not to create any deficit. The balanced-budget multiplier is equal to one: The change in Y resulting from the change in G and the equal change in T is exactly the same size as the initial change in G or T itself.

---

[8]We also derive the balanced-budget multiplier in appendix A to this chapter.

TABLE 10.3 FINDING EQUILIBRIUM AFTER A $200-BILLION BALANCED-BUDGET INCREASE IN G AND T (ALL FIGURES IN BILLIONS OF DOLLARS; BOTH G AND T HAVE INCREASED FROM 100 IN TABLE 10.1 TO 300 HERE.)

(1) OUTPUT (INCOME) Y	(2) NET TAXES T	(3) DISPOSABLE INCOME $Y_d \equiv Y - T$	(4) CONSUMPTION SPENDING $(C = 100 + .75 Y_d)$	(5) PLANNED INVESTMENT SPENDING I	(6) GOVERNMENT PURCHASES G	(7) PLANNED AGGREGATE EXPENDITURE $C + I + G$	(8) UNPLANNED INVENTORY CHANGE $Y - (C + I + G)$	(9) ADJUSTMENT TO DISEQUILIBRIUM
500	300	200	250	100	300	650	−150	Output↑
700	300	400	400	100	300	800	−100	Output↑
900	300	600	550	100	300	950	−50	Output↑
1,100	300	800	700	100	300	1,100	0	Equilibrium
1,300	300	1,000	850	100	300	1,250	+50	Output↓
1,500	300	1,200	1,000	100	300	1,400	+100	Output↓

Table 10.3. In Table 10.1, we saw an equilibrium level of output at 900. With both G and T up by 200, the new equilibrium is 1,100—higher by 200. At no other level of Y do we find $(C + I + G) = Y$.

> An increase in government spending has a direct initial effect on planned aggregate expenditure; a tax increase does not. The initial effect of the tax increase is that households cut consumption by the MPC times the change in taxes. This change in consumption is less than the change in taxes, because the MPC is less than 1. The positive stimulus from the government spending increase is thus greater than the negative stimulus from the tax increase. The net effect is that the balanced-budget multiplier is 1.

Table 10.4 summarizes everything we have said about fiscal policy multipliers. If anything is still unclear, review the relevant discussions in this chapter.

> **A Warning** Although we have added government, the story we have told about the multiplier is still incomplete and oversimplified. For example, we have been treating net taxes (T) as a lump-sum, fixed amount, whereas in practice, taxes depend on income. Appendix B to this chapter shows that the size of the multiplier is reduced when we make the more realistic assumption that taxes depend on income.

TABLE 10.4 SUMMARY OF FISCAL POLICY MULTIPLIERS

	POLICY STIMULUS	MULTIPLIER	FINAL IMPACT ON EQUILIBRIUM Y
Government-spending multiplier	Increase or decrease in the level of government purchases: ΔG	$\dfrac{1}{MPS}$	$\Delta G \cdot \dfrac{1}{MPS}$
Tax multiplier	Increase or decrease in the level of net taxes: ΔT	$\dfrac{-MPC}{MPS}$	$\Delta T \cdot \dfrac{-MPC}{MPS}$
Balanced-budget multiplier	Simultaneous balanced-budget increase or decrease in the level of government purchases and net taxes: $\Delta G = \Delta T$	1	ΔG

We continue to add more realism to our analysis in the next section and in the chapters that follow. (See the Application box "Fiscal Policy during the Recessions of 1974–1975, 1980–1982, and 1990–1991" for a discussion of the government's use of fiscal policy during the last three recessions.)

ADDING THE INTERNATIONAL SECTOR

In chapter 6, we noted that the U.S. economy does not operate in a vacuum. Rather, it influences and is influenced by the rest of the world. But we have not yet taken into account the role of imports and exports in the macroeconomy.

Opening the economy to foreign trade adds a fourth component to planned aggregate expenditure—exports of goods and services, or EX. Exports are foreign purchases of goods and services produced in the United States. Opening the economy to the rest of the world also means that U.S. consumers and businesses have greater choice because they can buy foreign-produced goods and services (imports, or IM) in addition to domestically produced goods and services.

We can think of imports (IM) as a leakage from the circular flow and exports (EX) as an injection into the circular flow. (Review Figure 6.1.) With imports and exports, the equilibrium condition for the economy is:

Open-economy equilibrium: $Y = C + I + G + (EX - IM)$

The quantity ($EX - IM$) is referred to as **net exports**.

Increases or decreases in net exports can throw the economy out of equilibrium and cause national income to change. For example, a large decrease in exports, *ceteris paribus*, would mean a drop in spending on domestically produced goods and services. The result would be an unplanned rise in inventories and a fall in output. Furthermore, if some domestic spending leaks into foreign markets (imports), the multiplier effect on domestic production will be reduced.

We discuss the international sector and its effects on the macroeconomy in detail in chapter 21. For now, we continue to use $Y = C + I + G$ as the basis of our analysis to keep our discussions clear and concise. Keep in mind that the international sector is an important player in the macroeconomy.

net exports *An economy's total exports* (EX) *minus its total imports* (IM).

THE FEDERAL BUDGET, DEFICIT, AND DEBT

Because fiscal policy is the manipulation of items in the federal budget, we need to consider those aspects of the budget relevant to our study of macroeconomics. The **federal budget** is an enormously complicated document, up to thousands of pages each year. It lists in detail all the things the government plans to spend money on and all the sources of government revenues for the coming year. It is the product of a complex interplay of social, political, and economic forces.

"The budget" is really three different budgets. First, it is a *political document* that dispenses favors to certain groups or regions (the elderly benefit from social security, farmers from agricultural price supports, students from federal loan programs, and so on) and places burdens (taxes) on others. Second, it is a *reflection of goals* the government wants to achieve. For example, in addition to assisting farmers, agricultural price supports are meant to preserve the "family farm." Tax breaks for corporations engaging in research and development of new products are meant to encourage research. Finally, the budget may be an *embodiment of some beliefs about how (if at all) the government should manage the macroeconomy.* The macroeconomic aspects of the budget are only a part of a more complicated story, a story that may be of more concern to political scientists than to economists.

federal budget *The budget of the federal government.*

FISCAL POLICY DURING THE RECESSIONS OF 1974–1975, 1980–1982, AND 1990–1991

As we've seen, the government can stimulate a sluggish economy by increasing government expenditures (G) and cutting taxes (T). Such policies have the effect of increasing aggregate expenditure (demand) and increasing equilibrium output (income). You might expect the government to increase G and/or cut T whenever the economy is in a recession.

Yet, the government has taken very different actions to deal with the three recessions that the U.S. economy has experienced since 1970. The last time the president and Congress consciously used fiscal policy to fight a recession was in 1975, during the administration of President Gerald Ford. The following from the *Economic Report of the President, 1976* suggests the policy succeeded in accomplishing its goals:

AS THE ECONOMY ENTERS A RECESSION, NATIONAL OUTPUT DECREASES AND HOUSEHOLDS HAVE LESS INCOME. WITH LOWER INCOMES, PEOPLE SPEND LESS AND SOME FIRMS MAY GO OUT OF BUSINESS.

> *During the first part of 1975 the economy moved rapidly through the final stages of the most severe recession of the postwar period. Real gross national product (GNP) fell at an annual rate of 9.2 percent in the first quarter and then began to increase. . . .*
>
> *Economic policy shifted early in the year to counter the decline in output. The President proposed a $16-billion tax reduction in the State of the Union message in January and the Congress enacted a $21-billion net reduction in March. Because of these tax cuts, and associated one-time social security payments, real disposable personal income rose sharply in the second quarter. . . .*
>
> *GNP rose sharply in the second half of the year; and by the end of the year the initial phase of a recovery was clearly evident. . . .*

The idea of using fiscal policy to stimulate aggregate expenditure and increase output during a recession was explicitly rejected by President Reagan in the 1980s. Instead, the Reagan administration favored policies designed to stimulate the supply side (rather than the demand side) of the market. These *supply-side policies* (discussed in chapter 19) focused on cutting taxes (a fiscal policy tool) to increase incentives to work, save, and invest. Reagan believed the added labor supply and investment brought about by lower taxes would lead to an expansion of the supply of goods and services, which would reduce inflation and unemployment.

President Reagan's policy worked, partially for reasons he did not intend. There is no question that

the major supply-side tax cuts enacted in 1981 with President Reagan's blessing had the effect of stimulating aggregate *demand* (spending). This outcome makes perfect sense if you remember the theory we've developed so far: Lower taxes mean higher disposable income, and higher disposable income means more consumption and ultimately greater output.

This trend against using fiscal policy to stimulate the economy continued into the 1990s. As the recession of 1990 to 1991 was beginning, Congress and President Bush passed the Omnibus Budget Reconciliation Act, which *cut* federal expenditures and *increased* taxes in an effort to reduce the federal deficit. This policy did not stimulate the economy, which remained sluggish until the end of 1992.

For more on the effects of fiscal policy, see the Case and Fair web page at
http://www.prenhall.com/casefair.

TABLE 10.5 FEDERAL GOVERNMENT RECEIPTS AND EXPENDITURES, 1997 (BILLIONS OF DOLLARS)

	AMOUNT	PERCENTAGE OF TOTAL
Receipts		
Personal taxes	774.4	44.9
Corporate taxes	211.9	12.3
Indirect business taxes	91.3	5.3
Contributions for social insurance	645.9	37.5
Total	1,723.4	100.0
Current Expenditures		
Consumption	463.8	26.5
Transfer payments	795.5	45.4
Grants-in-aid to state and local governments	224.2	12.8
Net interest payments	230.3	13.1
Net subsidies of government enterprises	38.4	2.2
Total	1,752.2	100.0
Current Surplus (+) or deficit (−) (Receipts − Current Expenditures)	−28.8	

Source: U.S. Department of Commerce, Bureau of Economic Analysis.

THE BUDGET

A highly condensed version of the federal budget is shown in Table 10.5. (Some of this reviews material from chapter 3, but here we highlight the budget components of particular importance to macroeconomics.) In 1997, the government had total receipts of $1,723.4 billion, largely from personal income taxes ($774.4 billion) and contributions for social insurance ($645.9 billion).[9] Receipts from corporate taxes accounted for $211.9 billion, or only 12.3 percent of total receipts. Not everyone is aware of the fact that corporate taxes as a percentage of government receipts are quite small relative to personal taxes and social security taxes.

The federal government also made $1,752.2 billion in expenditures in 1997. Of this, $795.5 billion represented transfer payments (social security, military retirement benefits, and unemployment compensation).[10] Consumption ($463.8 billion) was the next largest component, followed by interest on the federal debt ($230.3 billion) and grants-in-aid to state and local governments ($224.2 billion).

THE DEFICIT

The difference between the federal government's expenditures and its receipts is the **federal deficit**. Table 10.5 shows that the federal government spent slightly more than it took in during 1997, resulting in a deficit of $28.8 billion.

The federal deficit was high from the early 1980s until 1997. You can see this in Figure 10.4, where the federal deficit as a percentage of GDP is plotted for the 1970 I to 1997 IV period. As the figure shows, the deficit has been positive throughout the entire

federal deficit *Federal government expenditures minus receipts.*

---

[9]Contributions for social insurance are employer and employee social security taxes.

[10]Remember that there is an important difference between transfer payments and government purchases of goods and services. Much of the government budget goes for things that an economist would classify as transfers (payments that are grants or gifts) rather than purchases of goods and services. It is only the latter that are included in our variable G. Transfers are counted as part of net taxes.

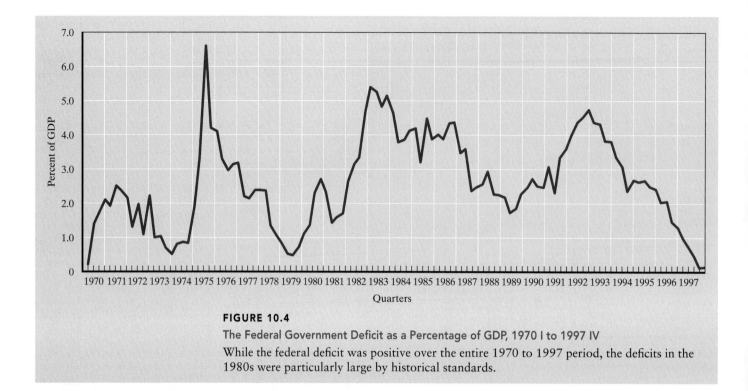

FIGURE 10.4

The Federal Government Deficit as a Percentage of GDP, 1970 I to 1997 IV

While the federal deficit was positive over the entire 1970 to 1997 period, the deficits in the 1980s were particularly large by historical standards.

period. Except for a period in the mid 1970s, the deficit was fairly low until the early 1980s, where it reached 5.4 percent of GDP in 1982 IV. It has fallen rapidly since 1992, and in 1997 IV it was only 0.1 percent of GDP.

How did such large deficits in the 1980s come about? There are several reasons. First, government purchases as a percentage of GDP rose in the early 1980s and then remained high. This increase primarily reflected the defense buildup of the Reagan years. Second, interest payments as a percentage of GDP rose substantially. Third, personal income tax rates fell as a result of the Economic Recovery Tax Act of 1981. With defense spending and interest payments rising rapidly and personal tax rates falling, it is not surprising that the deficit rose substantially during the 1980s. The government simply spent a lot more than it collected in taxes.

THE DEBT

When the government runs a deficit, it must borrow to finance it. To borrow, the federal government sells government securities to the public. It issues pieces of paper promising to pay a certain amount, with interest, in the future. In return, it receives funds from the buyers of the paper and uses these funds to pay its bills. This borrowing increases the **federal debt**, the total amount owed by the federal government. The federal debt is the total of all accumulated deficits minus surpluses over time.

Some of the securities that the government issues end up being held by the federal government itself at the Federal Reserve or in government trust funds. The term **privately held federal debt** refers only to the *privately held* debt of the U.S. government. At the end of October 1997, the federal debt was $5.4 trillion, of which $3.3 trillion was privately held.

Given the large deficits that the federal government has run up since the early 1980s, it should not be surprising that the federal debt has risen sharply from the early

federal debt *The total amount owed by the federal government.*

privately held federal debt *The privately held (non-government-owned) debt of the U.S. government.*

PART THREE
Macroeconomic
Principles and Policy

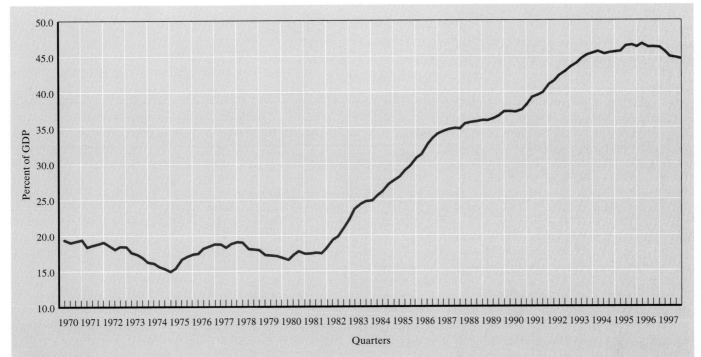

FIGURE 10.5

The Federal Government Debt as a Percentage of GDP, 1970 I to 1997 IV

The federal government debt increased dramatically in the 1980s as a result of the large deficits. The percentage has stabilized during the Clinton administrations.

1980s on. You can see this in Figure 10.5, where the privately held federal debt as a percentage of GDP is plotted for the 1970 I to 1997 IV period. The debt rose rapidly between 1982 and 1992—from 19.4 percent of GDP in 1982 I to 43.5 percent in 1992 IV. With the smaller deficits under the Clinton administration, the debt as a percentage of GDP has remained roughly constant since 1992.

One consequence of the large federal debt is that interest payments by the federal government are large. Table 10.5 shows that interest payments in 1997 were $230.3 billion, or 2.9 percent of GDP. In 1980, before the large increase in the debt, interest payments as a percentage of GDP were only 1.8 percent. Most of the federal debt is owned by U.S. citizens, and so most interest payments are simply a transfer from one group within the country (taxpayers) to another (bondholders). (See Application box, "Who Owns the Public Debt?")

THE ECONOMY'S INFLUENCE ON THE DEFICIT

➤ **Tax Revenues Depend on the State of the Economy**   Some parts of the government's budget depend on the state of the economy, over which the government has no direct control. Consider the revenue side of the budget. The government passes laws that set tax rates and tax brackets, variables the government does control. Tax revenue, on the other hand, depends on taxable income, and income depends on the state of the economy, which the government does *not* control. The government can set a personal income tax rate of 20 percent, but the revenue that the tax brings in will depend on the average income earned by households. The government will collect more revenue when average income is $40,000 than when average income is $20,000.

WHO OWNS THE PUBLIC DEBT?

At the end of October 1997, the total U.S. government debt was $5,369.7 billion, of which $3,346.6 billion was privately held. The difference between the total debt and the privately held debt—$2,023.1 billion—is the amount of the debt held by the government itself, including that held by the Federal Reserve. The Federal Reserve held $424.5 billion, and various government trust funds (such as the trust funds administered by the Social Security Administration) held the rest. Other federal trust funds that own U.S. Treasury obligations include federal employees' retirement funds, highway trust funds, the military retirement fund, and the airport and airway trust fund.

Why does the Federal Reserve hold so much of the debt? The Fed is responsible for controlling the U.S. money supply. As the economy grows, the money supply must be expanded to accommodate that growth. In December 1988, the money supply (M1) was $787.0 billion; by December 1997 it had grown to $1,076.0 billion.

The Fed expands the money supply primarily through open market operations—that is, by buying U.S. government securities in the open market. The Fed pays for these securities by writing a check or by expanding a bank's reserve account at the Fed. In either case, reserves are injected into the system. These additional reserves allow banks to lend more money, which ultimately expands the money supply. In essence, the Fed is creating money when it buys securities.

As a result, the Fed has come to own more than $424.5 billion worth of Treasury securities. The Fed uses the interest it receives on these obligations to finance its operations. It turns the excess interest back to the Treasury each year.

TABLE 1	ESTIMATED PRIVATE OWNERSHIP OF PUBLIC DEBT SECURITIES, DECEMBER 1996	
	BILLIONS OF $	% OF TOTAL
Commercial banks	261.7	7.7
Individuals	356.6	10.5
Insurance companies	214.1	6.3
Money market funds	91.6	2.7
Corporations	258.5	7.6
State and local governments	363.7	10.7
Foreigners	1,131.8	33.2
Other*	733.2	21.5
Total	3,411.2	100.0

*Note: Includes savings and loans, credit unions, mutual savings banks, and pension funds.

Source: Economic Report of the President, 1998, Table B-89.

What happens to the funds held by the various government trust funds? They are used to buy Treasury securities! This makes deficit accounting a very tricky business. Table 10.5 shows that the federal government deficit as reported in the National Income and Product Accounts was $28.8 billion in 1997. However, the social security system ran a surplus of $63.7 billion that year. If we remove this surplus from the official numbers, the 1997 deficit was $92.5 billion.

Most privately held government debt is held in "public debt securities." Table 1 presents the breakdown of the private ownership of these securities in December 1996. "Private ownership" includes state and local governments. Most of the $363.7 billion owned by states and localities is held in pension funds administered by those governments for their employees. For example, many states have a teachers'

retirement fund, and many of the dollars in those funds are invested in Treasury securities. These funds are not really owned by the government because each dollar in them represents an obligation of the state or local government to a retiree.

You can see from Table 1 that the private ownership of Treasury obligations is widespread. Individuals directly own $356.6 billion, or 10.5 percent of the total. Commercial banks account for 7.7 percent, insurance companies for 6.3 percent, and money market funds for 2.7 percent.

In recent years there has been some concern that the United States is relying too much on foreign countries (particularly Japan) to finance its deficits. The table shows that foreigners accounted for 33.2 percent of the total private ownership of public debt securities. This figure is up from 17.3 percent in December 1987.

For more on the public debt, see the Case and Fair web page at http://www.prenhall.com/casefair.

> **Some Government Expenditures Depend on the State of the Economy**   Some items on the expenditure side of the government budget also depend on the state of the economy. As the economy expands, unemployment falls, and the result is a decrease in unemployment benefits. Welfare payments and food stamp allotments also decrease somewhat. Some of the people who receive these benefits during bad times are able to find jobs when the state of the economy improves, and they begin earning enough income that they no longer qualify. Transfer payments tend to go down automatically during an expansion. (During a slump, transfer payments tend to increase because there are more people without jobs and more poor people generally.)

Another reason government spending is not completely controllable is that inflation often picks up when the economy is expanding. This can lead the government to spend more than it had planned to spend. Suppose the government has ordered 20 planes at $2 million each and inflation causes the actual price to be higher than expected. If the government decides to go ahead and buy the planes anyway, it will be forced to increase its spending. Finally, any change in the interest rate changes government interest payments. An increase in interest rates means that the government spends more in interest payments.

> **Automatic Stabilizers**   As the economy expands, the government's tax receipts increase. Also, transfer payments fall as the economy expands, which leads to a decrease in government expenditures. The revenue and expenditure items that change in response to changes in economic activity in such a way as to moderate changes in GDP are known as **automatic stabilizers**. As the economy expands or contracts, "automatic" changes in government revenues and expenditures take place that tend to reduce the change in, or stabilize, GDP.

The fact that some revenues *automatically* tend to rise and some expenditures *automatically* tend to fall in an expansion means that the government surplus is larger, or the deficit is smaller, in an expansion than it otherwise would be. Suppose we wanted to assess whether a government is practicing a policy designed to increase spending and income. If we looked only at the size of the government budget deficit, we might be fooled into thinking that the government is trying to stimulate the economy when, in fact, the real source of the deficit is a slump in the economy that caused revenues to fall and transfer payments to increase.

> **Fiscal Drag**   If the economy is doing well, income will be high and so will tax revenue. Tax revenue rises with increases in income for two reasons. First, there is more income to be taxed when people are earning more. Second, as people earn more income, they move into higher tax brackets and the average tax rate that they pay increases. This

automatic stabilizers *Revenue and expenditure items in the federal budget that automatically change with the state of the economy in such a way as to stabilize GDP.*

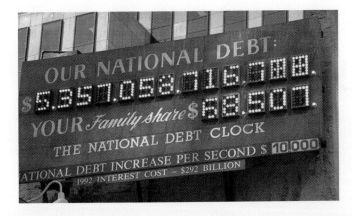

THE NATIONAL DEBT CLOCK IN NEW YORK CITY SHOWS HOW MUCH U.S. DEBT INCREASES EACH SECOND.

fiscal drag *The negative effect on the economy that occurs when average tax rates increase because taxpayers have moved into higher income brackets during an expansion.*

type of increase in tax rates is a **fiscal drag**, because the increase in average tax rates that results when people move into higher brackets acts as a "drag" on the economy. As the economy expands and income increases, the automatic tax increase mechanism built into the system goes to work. Tax rates go up, reducing the after-tax wage, and this slows down the expansion.

Before 1982, people found themselves pushed into higher tax brackets by inflation alone. Suppose my income rose 10 percent in 1981, but the price level also rose by 10 percent in that year. My income did not increase at all in real terms, but because the tax brackets were not legislated in real terms, I ended up paying more taxes. Since 1982, however, tax brackets have been indexed—that is, adjusted for inflation—and this has substantially reduced the automatic fiscal drag built into the system.

> **Full-Employment Budget**   Because the condition of the economy affects the budget deficit so strongly, we cannot accurately judge either the intent or the success of fiscal policies just by looking at the deficit. Instead of looking simply at the size of the deficit, economists have developed an alternative way to measure how effective fiscal policy actually is. By examining what the budget would be like if the economy were producing at the full-employment level of output—the so-called **full-employment budget**—we can establish a benchmark for evaluating fiscal policy.

full-employment budget *What the federal budget would be if the economy were producing at a full-employment level of output.*

The distinction between the actual and full-employment deficits is important. Suppose the economy is in a slump and the deficit is $250 billion. Also suppose that if there were full employment, the deficit would fall to $75 billion. The $75 billion deficit that would remain even with full employment would be due to the structure of tax and spending programs rather than to the state of the economy. This deficit—the deficit that remains at full employment—is sometimes called the **structural deficit**. The $175 billion ($250 billion − $75 billion) part of the deficit caused by the fact the economy is in a slump is known as the **cyclical deficit**. The existence of the cyclical deficit depends on where the economy is in the business cycle, and it ceases to exist when full employment is reached. By definition, the cyclical deficit of the full-employment budget is zero.

structural deficit *The deficit that remains at full employment.*

cyclical deficit *The deficit that occurs because of a downturn in the business cycle.*

DEBT AND DEFICITS: THE REST OF THE WORLD

The United States is not the only country in the world that has had problems with budget deficits. Table 10.6 shows the deficit and debt in 1997 as a percentage of GDP for six countries plus the United States. The table shows that Italy's government ran a deficit equal to 3.2 percent of its GDP in 1997 and had an outstanding debt equal to 116.3 percent of its GDP that year. Canada had the lowest deficit as a percentage of GDP in 1997, followed by the United States and the United Kingdom. Japan's government debt was only 18.2 percent of its GDP, but the values for the other countries were much higher. Canada was the next highest after Italy, with a debt equal to 66.5 percent of GDP in 1997.

TABLE 10.6

GOVERNMENT DEFICITS AND DEBT AS A PERCENTAGE OF NOMINAL GDP, 1997, FOR SELECTED COUNTRIES

	DEFICIT	DEBT
Canada	0.2	66.5
France	3.2	48.6
Germany	3.1	53.4
Italy	3.2	116.3
Japan	2.7	18.2
United Kingdom	2.0	47.9
United States	0.3	51.7

Source: International Monetary Fund, *World Economic Outlook,* October 1997.

THE MONEY MARKET AND MONETARY POLICY: A PREVIEW

We have now seen how households, firms, and the government interact in the goods market, how equilibrium output (income) is determined, and how the government uses fiscal policy to influence the economy. (We've also provided a brief introduction to the international sector's influence on aggregate expenditure and equilibrium output.) In the following two chapters we analyze the money market and monetary policy—the government's other major tool for influencing the economy.

SUMMARY

1. The government can affect the macroeconomy through two specific policy channels. *Fiscal policy* refers to the government's taxing and spending behavior. *Discretionary fiscal policy* refers to changes in taxes or spending that are the result of deliberate changes in government policy. *Monetary policy* refers to the behavior of the Federal Reserve regarding the nation's money supply.

GOVERNMENT IN THE ECONOMY

2. The government does not have complete control over tax revenues and certain expenditures, which are partially dictated by the state of the economy.

3. As a participant in the economy, the government makes purchases of goods and services (G), collects taxes, and makes transfer payments to households. *Net taxes* (T) is equal to the tax payments made to the government by firms and households minus transfer payments made to households by the government.

4. *Disposable*, or *after-tax, income* (Y_d) is equal to the amount of income received by households after taxes: $Y_d \equiv Y - T$. After-tax income determines households' consumption behavior.

5. The *budget deficit* is equal to the difference between what the government spends and what it collects in taxes: $G - T$. When G exceeds T, the government must borrow from the public to finance its deficit.

6. In an economy in which government is a participant, planned aggregate expenditure equals consumption spending by households (C) plus planned investment spending by firms (I) plus government spending on goods and services (G): $AE \equiv C + I + G$. Because the condition $Y = AE$ is necessary for the economy to be in equilibrium, it follows that $Y = C + I + G$ is the macroeconomic equilibrium condition. The economy is also in equilibrium when leakages out of the system equal injections into the system. This occurs when savings and net taxes (the leakages) equal planned investment and government purchases (the injections): $S + T = I + G$.

FISCAL POLICY AT WORK: MULTIPLIER EFFECTS

7. Fiscal policy has a multiplier effect on the economy. A change in government spending gives rise to a multiplier equal to $1/MPS$. A change in taxation brings about a multiplier equal to $-MPC/MPS$. A simultaneous equal increase or decrease in government spending and taxes has a multiplier effect of 1.

ADDING THE INTERNATIONAL SECTOR

8. Opening the economy to foreign trade adds two components to the equilibrium condition: exports (EX) and imports (IM). Exports are an injection into the circular flow; imports are a leakage from the circular flow. The equilibrium condition for the economy becomes $Y = C + I + G + (EX - IM)$ when the international sector is taken into account. The expression ($EX - IM$) is referred to as *net exports*.

THE FEDERAL BUDGET, DEFICIT, AND DEBT

9. The federal deficit was quite large in the 1980s. Reasons for the deficit include the defense buildup of the Reagan years, the high amount of interest paid on already-existing debt, and cuts in personal tax rates. With defense spending and interest payments rising rapidly and personal income tax rates falling, the government has simply been spending more than it has been collecting in taxes.

10. *Automatic stabilizers* are revenue and expenditure items in the federal budget that automatically change with the state of the economy and tend to stabilize GDP. For example, during expansions the government automatically takes in more revenue, because people are making more money that is taxed. Higher income and tax brackets also mean fewer transfer payments.

11. *Fiscal drag* is the negative effect on the economy that occurs when average tax rates increase because taxpayers have moved into higher income brackets during an expansion. These higher taxes reduce disposable income and slow down the expansion. Since 1982, tax brackets have been indexed to inflation, and this has reduced the fiscal drag built into the tax system.

12. The *full-employment budget* is an economist's construction of what the federal budget would be if the economy were producing at a full-employment level of output. The *structural deficit* is the federal deficit that remains even at full employment. *Cyclical deficits* occur when there is a downturn in the business cycle.

REVIEW TERMS AND CONCEPTS

1. Disposable income $Y_d \equiv Y - T$

2. $AE \equiv C + I + G$

3. Government budget deficit $\equiv G - T$

4. Equilibrium in an economy with government: $Y = C + I + G$

5. Leakages/injections approach to equilibrium in an economy with government:
$$S + T = I + G$$

6. Government spending multiplier $\equiv \dfrac{1}{MPS}$

7. Tax multiplier $\equiv -\dfrac{MPC}{MPS}$

8. Balanced-budget multiplier $\equiv 1$

9. Open-economy equilibrium position: $Y = C + I + G + (EX - IM)$

PROBLEM SET

1. Define *saving* and *investment*. Data for the simple closed economy of Newt show that in 1998 saving exceeded investment and the government is running a balanced budget. What is likely to happen? What would happen if the government were instead running a deficit and saving were equal to investment?

2. Crack economists in the economy of Yuk estimate the following:

Real output/income	1,000 billion Yuks
Government purchases	200 billion Yuks
Total net taxes	200 billion Yuks
Investment spending (planned)	100 billion Yuks

   Assume that Yukkers consume 75 percent of their disposable incomes and save 25 percent.
   a. You are asked by the business editor of the *Yuk Gazette* to predict the events of the next few months. Using the data given, can you make a forecast? (Assume that investment is constant.)
   b. If no changes were made, at what level of GDP (Y) would the economy of Yuk settle?
   c. Some local conservatives blame Yuk's problems on the size of the government sector. They suggest cutting government purchases by 25 billion Yuks. What effect would such cuts have on the economy? (Be specific.)

3. On July 3, 1997, the new government of Prime Minister Tony Blair in Great Britain passed its first budget in the Parliament. The top budget priority was a tax cut for business that gave British businesses the lowest tax rates of any Western industrialized country. To offset the business tax cut were a number of tax increases including higher consumption taxes and a windfall tax on profits from privatized utilities. Overall, the result was slightly higher government spending and an increase in tax revenues that exactly matched the spending increase. Would you expect such a package to increase or decrease British GDP? Explain.

4. "A $1 increase in government spending will raise equilibrium income by more than a $1 tax cut, yet both have the same impact on the budget deficit. So if we care about the budget deficit, the best way to stimulate the economy is through increases in spending, not cuts in taxes." Comment.

5. Assume that in 1998, the following prevails in the Republic of Nurd:

$Y = \$200$	$G = \$0$
$C = \$160$	$T = \$0$
$S = \$40$	
I (planned) = $30	

   Assume that households consume 80 percent of their income, they save 20 percent of their income, $MPC = .8$, and $MPS = .2$. That is, $C = .8Y_d$ and $S = .2Y_d$.
   a. Is the economy of Nurd in equilibrium? What is Nurd's equilibrium level of income? What is likely to happen in the coming months if the government takes no action?
   b. If $200 is the "full employment" level of Y, what fiscal policy might the government follow if its goal is full employment?
   c. If the full-employment level of Y is $250, what fiscal policy might the government follow?
   d. Suppose $Y = \$200$, $C = \$160$, $S = \$40$, and $I = \$40$. Is Nurd's economy in equilibrium?
   e. Starting with the situation in d., suppose the government starts spending $30 each year with no taxation and continues to spend $30 every period. If I remains constant, what will happen to the equilibrium level of Nurd's domestic product (Y)? What will the new levels of C and S be?
   f. Starting with the situation in d., suppose the government starts taxing the population $30 each year without spending anything and continues to tax at that rate every period. If I remains constant, what will happen to the equilibrium level of Nurd's domestic product (Y)?

What will be the new levels of C and S? How does your answer to f. differ from your answer to e? Why?

6. Some economists claim World War II ended the Great Depression of the 1930s. The war effort was financed by borrowing massive sums of money from the public. Explain how a war could end a recession. Look at recent and back issues of the *Economic Report of the President* or the *Statistical Abstract of the United States*. How large was the federal government's debt as a percentage of GDP in 1946? How large is it today?

7. Suppose all tax collections are fixed (rather than dependent on income), and all spending and transfer programs are also fixed (in the sense that they do not depend on the state of the economy, as, for example, unemployment benefits now do). If this were the case, would there be any automatic stabilizers in the government budget? Would there be any distinction between the full-employment deficit and the actual budget deficit? Explain.

8. Answer the following:
   a. *MPS* = .4. What is the government spending multiplier?
   b. *MPC* = .9. What is the government spending multiplier?
   c. *MPS* = .5. What is the government spending multiplier?
   d. *MPC* = .75. What is the tax multiplier?
   e. *MPS* = .1. What is the tax multiplier?
   f. If the government spending multiplier is 6, what is the tax multiplier?
   g. If the tax multiplier is −2, what is the government spending multiplier?
   h. If government purchases and taxes are both increased by $100 billion simultaneously, what will the effect be on equilibrium output (income)?

9. What is the relationship between the government budget deficit and the government debt? Suppose that the United States managed to balance its budget in fiscal year 1998. Would there be any effect on the size of the debt?

TAKE IT TO THE NET

We invite you to visit the Case and Fair page on the Prentice Hall Web site:

http://www.prenhall.com/casefair

for this chapter's World Wide Web exercise.

APPENDIX A TO CHAPTER 10

DERIVING THE FISCAL POLICY MULTIPLIERS

THE GOVERNMENT SPENDING AND TAX MULTIPLIERS
In the chapter, we noted that the government spending multiplier is 1/*MPS*. (This is the same as the investment multiplier.) We can also derive the multiplier algebraically using our hypothetical consumption function:

$$C = a + b(Y - T)$$

where b is the marginal propensity to consume. As you know, the equilibrium condition is

$$Y = C + I + G$$

Substituting for C, we get

$$Y = a + b(Y - T) + I + G$$
$$Y = a + bY - bT + I + G$$

This equation can be rearranged to yield

$$Y - bY = a + I + G - bT$$
$$Y(1 - b) = a + I + G - bT$$

Now solve for Y by dividing through by $(1 - b)$:

$$Y = \frac{1}{(1 - b)}(a + I + G - bT)$$

We see from this last equation that if G increases by 1 with the other determinants of Y (a, I, and T) remaining constant, Y increases by $1/(1 - b)$. The multiplier is, as before, simply $1/(1 - b)$, where b is the marginal propensity to consume. And, of course, $1 - b$ equals the marginal propensity to save, so the government spending multiplier is 1/*MPS*.

We can also derive the tax multiplier. The last equation says that when T increases by $1, holding a, I, and G constant, income decreases by $b/(1 - b)$ dollars. The tax multiplier is $-b/(1 - b)$, or $-MPC/(1 - MPC) = -MPC/MPS$. (Remember that we add the negative sign to the tax multiplier because the tax multiplier is a *negative* multiplier.)

THE BALANCED-BUDGET MULTIPLIER
It is easy to show formally that the balanced-budget multiplier = 1. When taxes and government spending are simultaneously increased by the same amount, there are two effects on planned aggregate expenditure: one positive and

one negative. The initial impact of a balanced-budget increase in government spending and taxes on aggregate expenditure would be the *increase* in government purchases (ΔG) minus the *decrease* in consumption (ΔC) caused by the tax increase. The decrease in consumption brought about by the tax increase is equal to $\Delta C = \Delta T(MPC)$.

Increase in spending:	ΔG
−Decrease in spending:	$\Delta C = \Delta T(MPC)$
= Net increase in spending	$\Delta G - \Delta T(MPC)$

In a balanced-budget increase, $\Delta G = \Delta T$, so we can substitute:

Net initial increase in spending:
$$\Delta G - \Delta G(MPC) = \Delta G(1 - MPC).$$

Because $MPS = (1 - MPC)$, the initial increase in spending is

$$\Delta G(MPS).$$

We can now apply the expenditure multiplier $\left(\dfrac{1}{MPS}\right)$ to this net initial increase in spending:

$$\Delta Y = \Delta G\left(\frac{1}{MPS}\right) = \Delta G$$

Thus, the final total increase in the equilibrium level of Y is just equal to the initial balanced increase in G and T. That means the balanced-budget multiplier = 1.

APPENDIX B TO CHAPTER 10

THE CASE IN WHICH TAX REVENUES DEPEND ON INCOME

In this chapter, we used the simplifying assumption that the government collects taxes in a lump sum. This made our discussion of the multiplier effects somewhat easier to follow. But now suppose that the government collects taxes not solely as a lump sum that is paid regardless of income, but also partly in the form of a proportional levy against income. This is a more realistic assumption. Typically, tax collections are either based on income (as with the personal income tax) or they follow the ups and downs in the economy (as with sales taxes). Instead of setting taxes equal to some fixed amount, let's say that tax revenues depend on income. If we call the amount of net taxes collected T, we can write: $T = T_0 + tY$.

This equation contains two parts. First, we note that net taxes (T) will be equal to an amount T_0 if income (Y) is zero. Second, the tax rate (t) indicates how much net taxes change as income changes. Suppose that T_0 is equal to -200 and t is 1/3. The resulting tax function is $T = -200 + 1/3Y$, which is graphed in Figure 10A.1. Note that when income is zero, the government collects "negative net taxes," which simply means that it makes transfer payments of 200. As income rises, tax collections increase because every extra dollar of income generates \$.33 in extra revenues for the government.

How do we incorporate this new tax function into our discussion? All we do is replace the old value of T (in the example in the chapter, T was set equal to 100) with the new value, $-200 + 1/3Y$. Look first at the consumption equation. Consumption (C) still depends on disposable income, as it did before. Also, disposable income is still $Y - T$, or income minus taxes. Instead of disposable

FIGURE 10A.1

The Tax Function

This graph shows net taxes (taxes minus transfer payments) as a function of aggregate income.

Tax function
$T = T_0 + tY = -200 + 1/3Y$

income equaling $Y - 100$, however, the new equation for disposable income is

$$Y_d \equiv Y - T$$

$$Y_d \equiv Y - (-200 + 1/3Y)$$

$$Y_d \equiv Y + 200 - 1/3Y$$

Because consumption still depends on after-tax income, exactly as it did before, we have

$$C = 100 + .75Y_d$$

$$C = 100 + .75\ (Y + 200 - 1/3Y)$$

Nothing else needs to be changed. We solve for equilibrium income exactly as before, by setting planned aggregate expenditure equal to aggregate output. Recall that planned aggregate expenditure is $C + I + G$, and aggregate output is Y. If we assume, as before, that $I = 100$ and $G = 100$, the equilibrium is

$$Y = C + I + G$$

$$Y = \underbrace{100 + .75\ (Y + 200 - 1/3Y)}_{C} + \underbrace{100}_{I} + \underbrace{100.}_{G}$$

This equation may look difficult to solve, but it is not. It simplifies to

$$Y = 100 + .75Y + 150 - .25Y + 100 + 100$$

$$Y = 450 + .5Y$$

$$.5Y = 450$$

This means that $Y = 450/.5 = 900$, the new equilibrium level of income.

Consider the graphic analysis of this equation as shown in Figure 10A.2, where you should note that when we make taxes a function of income (instead of a lump-sum amount), the AE function becomes *flatter* than it was before. Why? When tax collections do not depend on income, an increase in income of $1 means disposable income also increases by a dollar. Because taxes are a constant amount, adding more income does not raise the amount of taxes paid. Disposable income therefore changes dollar-for-dollar with any change in income.

When taxes depend on income, a $1 increase in income does not increase disposable income by a full dollar, because some of the additional dollar goes to pay extra taxes. Under the modified tax function of Figure 10A.2, an extra dollar of income will increase disposable income by only $.67, because $.33 of the extra dollar goes to the government in the form of taxes.

No matter how taxes are calculated, the marginal propensity to consume out of disposable (or after-tax) income is the same—each extra dollar of disposable income will increase consumption spending by $.75. But a $1 change in before-tax income does not have the same effect on disposable income in each case. Suppose we were to increase income by $1. With the lump-sum tax function, disposable income would rise by $1, and consumption would increase by the MPC times the change in Y_d, or $.75. When taxes depend on income, disposable income would rise by only $.67 from the $1 increase in income,

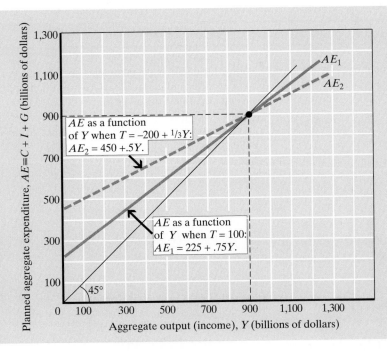

FIGURE 10A.2

Different Tax Systems

When taxes are strictly lump sum ($T = 100$) and do not depend on income, the aggregate expenditure function is steeper than when taxes depend on income.

AE as a function of Y when $T = -200 + 1/3Y$:
$AE_2 = 450 + .5Y$.

AE as a function of Y when $T = 100$:
$AE_1 = 225 + .75Y$.

Planned aggregate expenditure, $AE \equiv C + I + G$ (billions of dollars)

Aggregate output (income), Y (billions of dollars)

and consumption would rise by only the *MPC* times the change in disposable income, or $.75 × .67 = $.50.

If a $1 increase in income raises expenditure by $.75 in one case, and by only $.50 in the other, the second aggregate expenditure function must be flatter than the first.

THE GOVERNMENT SPENDING AND TAX MULTIPLIERS ALGEBRAICALLY

All this means that if taxes are a function of income, the three multipliers (investment, government spending, and tax) are less than they would be if taxes were a lump-sum amount. Using the same linear consumption function we used in chapters 8 and 9, we can derive the multiplier:

$$C = a + b (Y - T)$$

$$C = a + b (Y - T_0 - tY)$$

$$C = a + bY - bT_0 - btY$$

We know that $Y = C + I + G$. Through substitution we get:

$$Y = \underbrace{a + bY - bT_0 - btY}_{C} + I + G$$

Solving for Y:

$$Y = \frac{1}{1 - b + bt} (a + I + G - bT_0)$$

This means that a $1 increase in G or I (holding a and T_0 constant) will increase the equilibrium level of Y by:

$$\frac{1}{1 - b + bt}$$

If $b = MPC = .75$ and $t = .20$, the spending multiplier is 2.5. (Compare this to 4, which would be the value of the spending multiplier if taxes were a lump sum—that is, if $t = 0$.)

Holding a, I, and G constant, a fixed or lump-sum tax cut (a cut in T_0) will increase the equilibrium level of income by:

$$\frac{b}{1 - b + bt}$$

Thus, if $b = MPC = .75$ and $t = .20$, the tax multiplier is -1.875. (Compare this to -3, which would be the value of the tax multiplier if taxes were a lump sum.)

SUMMARY

1. When taxes depend on income, a $1 increase in income does not increase disposable income by a full dollar, because some of the additional dollar must go to pay extra taxes.

This means that if taxes are a function of income, the three multipliers (investment, government spending, and tax) are less than they would be if taxes were a lump-sum amount.

PROBLEM SET

1. Given the following for the economy of a country:
   (1) Consumption function: $C = 85 + 0.5Y_d$
   (2) Investment function: $I = 85$
   (3) Government spending: $G = 60$
   (4) Net taxes: $T = -40 + 0.25Y$
   (5) Disposable income: $Y_d \equiv Y - T$
   (6) Equilibrium: $Y = C + I + G$.

   Solve for equilibrium income. (*Hint:* Be very careful in doing the calculations. They are not difficult, but it is easy to make careless mistakes that produce very wrong results.) How much does the government collect in net taxes when the economy is in equilibrium? What is the government's budget deficit or surplus?

Chapter 11

THE MONEY SUPPLY AND THE FEDERAL RESERVE SYSTEM

IN THE LAST TWO CHAPTERS, we explored how consumers, firms, and the government interact in the goods market. In this chapter and the next we show how money markets work in the macroeconomy. We begin with what money is and the role it plays in the U.S. economy. We then discuss the forces that determine the supply of money and show how banks create money. Finally, we discuss the workings of the nation's central bank, the Federal Reserve, and the tools at its disposal to control the money supply.

Microeconomics has little to say about money. Microeconomic theories and models are concerned primarily with *real* quantities (apples, oranges, hours of labor) and *relative* prices (the price of apples relative to the price of oranges, the price of labor relative to the prices of other goods). Most of the key ideas in microeconomics do not require that we know anything about money. As we shall see, this is not the case in macroeconomics.

AN OVERVIEW OF MONEY

You often hear people say things like "He makes a lot of money" (in other words, "He has a high income") or "She's worth a lot of money" (meaning "She is very wealthy"). It is true that your employer uses money to pay you your income, and your wealth may be accumulated in the form of money. But *money is not income, and money is not wealth*.

To see that money and income are not the same, think of a $20 bill. That bill may pass through a thousand hands in a year, yet never be used to pay anyone a salary. Suppose I get a $20 bill from an automatic teller machine, and I spend it on dinner. The restaurant puts that $20 bill in a bank in the next day's deposit. The bank gives it to a woman cashing a check the following day; she spends it at a baseball game that night. The bill has been through many hands but not as part of anyone's income.

WHAT IS MONEY?

We will soon get to a formal definition of money, but let's start out with the basic idea of what money is.

> Money is anything that is generally accepted as a medium of exchange.

Most people take the ability to obtain and use money for granted. When the whole monetary system works well, as it generally does in the United States, the basic mechanics of the system are virtually invisible. People take for granted that they can walk into any store, restaurant, boutique, or gas station and buy whatever they want, as long as they have enough green pieces of paper.

The idea that you can buy things with money is so natural and obvious that it seems absurd to mention it. But stop and ask yourself: "How is it that a shop owner is willing to part with a steak and a loaf of bread that I can eat in exchange for some pieces of paper that are intrinsically worthless?" And why, on the other hand, are there times and places where it takes a shopping cart full of money to purchase a dozen eggs? The answers to these questions lie in what money is: a means of payment, a store of value, and a unit of account.

> **A Means of Payment, or Medium of Exchange** Money is vital to the working of a market economy. Imagine what life would be like without it. The alternative to a monetary economy is **barter**, people exchanging goods and services for other goods and services directly instead of exchanging via the medium of money.

How does a barter system work? Suppose you want bacon, eggs, and orange juice for breakfast. Instead of going to the store and buying these things with money, you would have to find someone who has these items and is willing to trade them. You would also have to have something the bacon seller, the orange juice purveyor, and the egg vendor want. Having pencils to trade will do you no good if the bacon, orange juice, and egg sellers do not want pencils.

A barter system requires a *double coincidence of wants* for trade to take place. That is, to effect a trade, I not only have to find someone who has what I want, but that person must also want what I have. Where the range of goods traded is small, as it is in relatively unsophisticated economies, it is not difficult to find someone to trade with, and barter is often used. In a complex society with many goods, barter exchanges involve an intolerable amount of effort. Imagine trying to find people who offer for sale all the things you buy in a typical trip to the grocery store, and who are willing to accept goods that you have to offer in exchange for their goods.

Some agreed-upon **medium of exchange** (or, **means of payment**) neatly eliminates the double-coincidence-of-wants problem. Under a monetary system, money is exchanged for goods or services when people buy things; goods or services are exchanged for money when people sell things. No one ever has to trade goods for other goods directly. Money is a lubricant in the functioning of a market economy.

> **A Store of Value** Economists have identified other roles for money aside from its primary function as a medium of exchange. Money also serves as a **store of value**—an asset that can be used to transport purchasing power from one time period to another. If you raise chickens and at the end of the month sell them for more than you want to spend and consume immediately, you may keep some of your earnings in the form of money until the time you want to spend it.

There are many other stores of value besides money. You could have decided to hold your "surplus" earnings by buying such things as antique paintings, baseball cards, or diamonds, which you could sell later when you want to spend your earnings. Money has several advantages over these other stores of value. First, it comes in convenient denominations and is easily portable. You don't have to worry about making change for a

barter *The direct exchange of goods and services for other goods and services.*

medium of exchange, or **means of payment** *What sellers generally accept and buyers generally use to pay for goods and services.*

store of value *An asset that can be used to transport purchasing power from one time period to another.*

Renoir to buy a gallon of gasoline. Second, because money is also a means of payment, it is easily exchanged for goods at all times. (A Renoir is not easily exchanged for other goods.) These two factors compose the **liquidity property of money**. Money is easily spent, flowing out of your hands like liquid. Renoirs and ancient Aztec statues are neither convenient nor portable and are not readily accepted as a means of payment.

The main disadvantage of money as a store of value is that the value of money falls when the prices of goods and services rise. If the price of potato chips rises from $1 per bag to $2 per bag, the value of a dollar bill, in terms of potato chips, falls from one bag to half a bag. When this happens, it may be better to use potato chips (or antiques or real estate) as a store of value.

▶ **A Unit of Account** Money also serves as a **unit of account**—a consistent way of quoting prices. All prices are quoted in monetary units. A textbook is quoted as costing $45, not 140 bananas or 4 videotapes, and a banana is quoted as costing 25¢, not 1.4 apples or 16 pages of a textbook.

Obviously, a standard unit of account is extremely useful when quoting prices. This function of money may have escaped your notice—what else would people quote prices in except money?

COMMODITY AND FIAT MONIES

Introductory economics textbooks are full of stories about the various items that have been used as money by various cultures—candy bars, cigarettes (in World War II prisoner-of-war camps), huge wheels of carved stone (on the island of Yap in the South Pacific), cowrie shells (in West Africa), beads (among North American Indians), cattle (in southern Africa), small green scraps of paper (in contemporary North America). The list goes on. These various kinds of money are generally divided into two groups, commodity monies and fiat money.

Commodity monies are those items used as money that also have an intrinsic value in some other use. For example, prisoners of war made purchases with cigarettes, quoted prices in terms of cigarettes, and held their wealth in the form of accumulated cigarettes. Of course, cigarettes could also be smoked—they had an alternative use apart from serving as money. Gold represents another form of commodity money. For hundreds of years gold could be used directly to buy things, but it also had other uses, ranging from jewelry to dental fillings.

By contrast, money in the United States today is mostly fiat money. **Fiat money**, sometimes called **token money**, is money that is intrinsically worthless. The actual value of a one-, ten-, or fifty-dollar bill is basically zero; what other uses are there for a small piece of paper with some green ink on it?

Why would anyone accept worthless scraps of paper as money instead of something that has some value, such as gold, cigarettes, or cattle? If your answer is "Because the paper money is backed by gold or silver," you are wrong! There was a time when dollar bills were convertible directly into gold. The government backed each dollar bill in circulation by holding a certain amount of gold in its vaults. If the price of gold were $35 per ounce, for example, the government agreed to sell one ounce of gold for 35 dollar bills. But dollar bills are no longer backed by any commodity—gold, silver, or anything else. They are exchangeable only for dimes, nickels, pennies, other dollars, and so on.

The public accepts paper money as a means of payment and a store of value because the government has taken steps to ensure that its money is accepted. The government declares its paper money to be **legal tender**. That is, the government declares that its money must be accepted in settlement of debts. It does this by fiat (hence *fiat money*). It passes laws defining certain pieces of paper printed in certain inks on certain plates to be legal tender, and that is that. Printed on every Federal Reserve note in the United States is "This note is legal tender for all debts, public and private." Often, the government can get a start on gaining acceptance for its paper money by requiring that

liquidity property of money *The property of money that makes it a good medium of exchange as well as a store of value: It is portable and readily accepted and thus easily exchanged for goods.*

unit of account *A standard unit that provides a consistent way of quoting prices.*

SOME OF YAP'S STONE MONEY WHEELS ARE SO LARGE THAT THEY ARE NEVER MOVED.

commodity monies *Items used as money that also have intrinsic value in some other use.*

fiat, or **token**, **money** *Items designated as money that are intrinsically worthless.*

legal tender *Money that a government has required to be accepted in settlement of debts.*

it be used to pay taxes. (Note that you cannot use chickens, baseball cards, or Renoir paintings to pay your taxes, only checks or currency.)

Aside from declaring its currency legal tender, the government usually does one other thing to ensure that paper money will be accepted: It promises the public that it will not print paper money so fast that it loses its value. Expanding the supply of currency so rapidly that it loses much of its value has been a problem throughout history and is known as **currency debasement**. Debasement of the currency has been a special problem of governments that lack the strength to take the politically unpopular step of raising taxes. Printing money to be used on government expenditures of goods and services can serve as a substitute for tax increases, and weak governments have often relied on the printing press to finance their expenditures. A recent example is Bulgaria, where the inflation rate hit a record of 1,268 percent in 1997. We will discuss money and inflation at great length in later chapters.

MEASURING THE SUPPLY OF MONEY IN THE UNITED STATES

We now turn to the various kinds of money in the United States. Recall that money is used: to buy things (a means of payment); to hold wealth (a store of value); and to quote prices (a unit of account). Unfortunately, these characteristics apply to a broad range of assets in the U.S. economy. As we will see, it is not at all clear where we should draw the line and say, "Up to this is money, beyond this is something else."

To solve the problem of multiple monies, economists have given different names to different measures of money. The two most common measures of money are transactions money, also called *M1*, and broad money, also called *M2*.

▶ **M1: Transactions Money** What should be counted as money? Clearly, coins and dollar bills, as well as higher denominations of currency, must be counted as money—they fit all the requirements. But what about checking accounts? Checks too can be used to buy things and can serve as a store of value. In fact, bankers call checking accounts *demand deposits*, because depositors have the right to go to the bank and cash in (demand) their entire checking account balances at any time. That makes your checking account balance virtually equivalent to bills in your wallet, and it should be included as part of the amount of money you hold.

If we take the value of all currency (including coins) held outside of bank vaults and add to it the value of all demand deposits, traveler's checks, and other checkable deposits, we have defined **M1**, or **transactions money**. As its name suggests, this is the money that can be directly used for transactions—to buy things.

> M1 ≡ Currency held outside banks + Demand deposits + Traveler's checks + Other checkable deposits

A *checkable deposit* is any deposit account with a bank or other financial institution on which a check can be written. Checkable deposits include: demand deposits; *negotiable order of withdrawal (NOW) accounts*, which are like checking accounts that pay interest; and *automatic-transfer savings (ATS) accounts*, which automatically transfer funds from savings to checking (or vice versa) when the balance on one of those accounts reaches a predetermined level.

M1 on March 2, 1998, was $1,085.1 billion. M1 is a stock measure—it is measured at a point in time. It is the total amount of coins and currency outside of banks and the total dollar amount in checking accounts *on a specific day*. Until now, we have considered supply as a flow—a variable with a time dimension: the quantity of wheat supplied *per year*, the quantity of automobiles supplied to the market *per year*, and so forth. But M1 is a stock variable.

Cash remains an important part of the U.S. economy, but some people believe it is becoming a thing of the past.

currency debasement *The decrease in the value of money that occurs when its supply is increased rapidly.*

M1, or transactions money *Money that can be directly used for transactions.*

On January 1, 1999, many countries in Europe are scheduled to become part of the new European Monetary Union. The deutsche mark, franc, and lira will be exchanged for the "euro," a common European currency. Europe will become more like the United States, where 50 states share a common monetary unit. The currency will be issued by and controlled by the new European Central Bank.

► **M2: Broad Money** Although $M1$ is the most widely used measure of the money supply, there are others. Should savings accounts be considered money? Many of these accounts cannot be used for transactions directly, but it is easy to convert them into cash or to transfer funds from a savings account into a checking account. And what about money market accounts (which allow only a few checks per month but pay market-determined interest rates) and money market mutual funds (which sell shares and use the proceeds to purchase short-term securities)? These can be used to write checks and make purchases, although only over a certain amount.

If we add **near monies**, close substitutes for transactions money, to $M1$, we get **M2**, called **broad money** because it includes not-quite-money monies such as savings accounts, money market accounts, and other near monies.

> $M2 \equiv M1$ + Savings accounts + Money market accounts + Other near monies

On March 2, 1998, $M2$ was \$4,114.8 billion, considerably larger than the total $M1$ of \$1,085.1 billion. The main advantage of looking at $M2$ instead of $M1$ is that $M2$ is sometimes more stable. For instance, when banks introduced new forms of interest-bearing checking accounts in the early 1980s, $M1$ shot up as people switched their funds from savings accounts to checking accounts. But $M2$ remained fairly constant because the fall in savings account deposits and the rise in checking account balances were both part of $M2$, canceling each other out.

► **Beyond M2** Because a wide variety of financial instruments bear some resemblance to money, some economists have advocated including almost all of them as part of the money supply. In recent years, for example, credit cards have come to be used extensively in exchange. Everyone who has a credit card has a credit limit—you can charge only a certain amount on your card before you have to pay it off. Usually we pay our credit card bills with a check. One of the very broad definitions of money includes the amount of available credit on credit cards (your charge limit minus what you have charged but not paid) as part of the money supply.

There are no rules for deciding what is money and what is not. This poses problems for economists and those in charge of economic policy. However, *for our purposes here, "money" will always refer to transactions money, or M1.* For simplicity, we will say that $M1$ is the sum of two *general* categories: currency in circulation and deposits. Keep in mind, however, that $M1$ has *four* specific components: currency held outside banks, demand deposits, travelers checks, and other checkable deposits.

THE PRIVATE BANKING SYSTEM

Most of the money in the United States today is "bank money" of one sort or another. $M1$ is made up largely of checking account balances rather than currency, and currency makes up an even smaller part of $M2$ and other broader definitions of money. Any understanding of money requires some knowledge of the structure of the private banking system.

Banks and other financial intermediaries borrow from individuals or firms with excess funds and lend to those who need funds. For example, commercial banks receive funds in various forms, including deposits in checking and savings accounts. They take these funds and loan them out in the form of car loans, mortgages, commercial loans, and so forth. Banks and banklike institutions are called **financial intermediaries** because they "mediate," or act as a link between people who have funds to lend and those who need to borrow.

The main types of financial intermediaries are commercial banks, followed by savings and loan associations, life insurance companies, and pension funds. Since about 1970, the legal distinctions between the different types of financial intermediaries have narrowed considerably. It used to be, for example, that checking accounts could be

near monies *Close substitutes for transactions money, such as savings accounts and money market accounts.*

M2, or **broad money** $M1$ *plus savings accounts, money market accounts, and other near monies.*

financial intermediaries *Banks and other institutions that act as a link between those who have money to lend and those who want to borrow money.*

A CASHLESS SOCIETY: DIFFERENT MEANINGS IN THE UNITED STATES AND RUSSIA IN 1997

When Americans talk of the "cashless" society it conjures up images of credit cards, debit cards, internet transactions, electronic bill paying, and so forth. Although about 80 percent of the 360 billion transactions in the United States each year are paid for with cash, the majority of which are under $20, the trend is toward on-line transfers via the computer and toward plastic cards.

But when the Russians talk of the cashless society, they mean there is no money. Because the majority of people still work for the government in Russia, and the government is broke, millions of workers across the country have been going without cash wages for some time. How do they survive? The firms pay people in kind and they engage in barter.

The Russian-European Center for Economic Policy, a monitoring organization sponsored by the European Union, estimated that the proportion of industrial sales in Russia settled with barter rose from about 10 percent in 1993 to 40 percent in 1996. One car company is said to pay nine-tenths of its bills with finished automobiles.

Stories about individual household transactions abound. Siberian

IN SOME PARTS OF WHAT WAS RUSSIA, "CASHLESS SOCIETY" IS LITERALLY WHAT IT SAYS—NO MONEY. WITHOUT CURRENCY, WORKERS MAY BE PAID IN WHAT THEY PRODUCE, SUCH AS THE COFFINS "PAID" TO WORKERS IN SIBERIA IN 1997.

workers in 1997 were paid in coffins; workers at a factory in Volgograd were paid in bras. In Altai, Siberia, a local theater charged two eggs for admission, and when eggs ran out, tickets became denominated in empty bottles.

Source: "The Cashless Society," *The Economist*, March 15, 1997.

For more on cashless economies, see the Case and Fair Web page at http://www.prenhall.com/casefair.

held only in commercial banks and that commercial banks could not pay interest on checking accounts. Savings and loan associations were prohibited from offering certain kinds of deposits and were restricted primarily to making loans for mortgages.

The Depository Institutions Deregulation and Monetary Control Act, enacted by Congress in 1980, eliminated many of the previous restrictions on the behavior of financial institutions. Many types of institutions now offer checking accounts, and interest is paid on many types of checking accounts. Savings and loan associations now make loans for many things besides home mortgages. The Sears Financial Network is one of a number of financial service firms offering, under one roof, a wide variety of services that used to be offered by separate providers such as banks, brokerage houses, insurance companies, and financial planners.

HOW BANKS CREATE MONEY

So far we have described the general way that money works and the way the supply of money is measured in the United States. But how much money is there available at a given time? Who supplies it, and how does it get supplied? We are now ready to analyze these questions in detail. In particular, we want to explore a process that many find mysterious: the way banks *create money*.

A HISTORICAL PERSPECTIVE: GOLDSMITHS

To begin to see how banks create money, consider the origins of the modern banking system. In the fifteenth and sixteenth centuries, citizens of many lands used gold as money, particularly for large transactions. Because gold is both inconvenient to carry around and susceptible to theft, people began to place their gold with goldsmiths for safekeeping. Upon receiving the gold, a goldsmith would issue a receipt to the depositor, charging him a small fee for looking after his gold. After a time, these receipts themselves, rather than the gold that they represented, began to be traded for goods. The receipts became a form of paper money, making it unnecessary to go to the goldsmith to withdraw gold for a transaction.

At this point, all the receipts issued by goldsmiths were backed 100 percent by gold. If a goldsmith had 100 ounces of gold in his safe, he would issue receipts for 100 ounces of gold, and no more. Goldsmiths functioned as warehouses where people stored gold for safekeeping. The goldsmiths found, however, that people did not come often to withdraw gold. Why should they, when paper receipts that could easily be converted to gold were "as good as gold"? (In fact, receipts were better than gold—more portable, safer from theft, and so on.) As a result, goldsmiths had a large stock of gold continuously on hand.

Because they had what amounted to "extra" gold sitting around, goldsmiths gradually realized that they could lend out some of this gold without any fear of running out of gold. Why would they do this? Because instead of just keeping their gold idly in their vaults, they earned interest on loans. Something subtle, but dramatic, happened at this point. The goldsmiths changed from mere depositories for gold into banklike institutions that had the power to create money. This transformation occurred as soon as goldsmiths began making loans. Without adding any more real gold to the system, the goldsmiths increased the amount of money in circulation by creating additional claims to gold (that is, receipts, which entitled the bearer to receive a certain number of ounces of gold on demand).[1] There were thus more claims than there were ounces of gold.

A detailed example may help to clarify this. Suppose you go to a goldsmith who is functioning only as a depository, or warehouse, and ask for a loan to buy a plot of land that costs 20 ounces of gold. Also suppose that the goldsmith has 100 ounces of gold on deposit in his safe and receipts for exactly 100 ounces of gold out to the various people who deposited the gold. If the goldsmith decides he is tired of being a mere goldsmith and wants to become a real bank, he will loan you some gold. You don't want the gold itself, of course; rather, you want a slip of paper that represents 20 ounces of gold. The goldsmith in essence "creates" money for you by giving you a receipt for 20 ounces of gold (even though his entire supply of gold already belongs to various other people).[2] When he does, there will be receipts for 120 ounces of gold in circulation instead of the 100 ounces worth of receipts before your loan, and the supply of money will have increased.

---

[1] Remember, these receipts circulated as money, and people used them to make transactions without feeling the need to cash them in—that is, to exchange them for gold itself.

[2] In return for lending you the receipt for 20 ounces of gold, the goldsmith expects to get an IOU promising to repay the amount (in gold itself or with a receipt from another goldsmith) with interest after a certain period of time.

People think the creation of money is mysterious. Far from it! The creation of money is simply an accounting procedure, among the most mundane of human endeavors. You may suspect the whole process is fundamentally unsound, or somehow dubious. After all, the banking system began when someone issued claims for gold that already belonged to someone else. Here you may be on slightly firmer ground.

Goldsmiths-turned-bankers did face certain problems. Once they started making loans, their receipts outstanding (claims on gold) were greater than the amount of gold they had in their vaults at any given moment. If the owners of the 120 ounces worth of gold receipts all presented their receipts and demanded their gold at the same time, the goldsmith would be in trouble. With only 100 ounces of gold on hand, everyone could not get his or her gold at once.

In normal times, people would be happy to hold receipts instead of real gold, and this problem would never arise. If, however, people began to worry about the goldsmith's financial safety, they might begin to have doubts about whether their receipts really were as good as gold. Knowing there were more receipts outstanding than there were ounces of gold in the goldsmith's vault, people might start to demand gold for receipts.

This situation leads to a paradox. It makes perfect sense to hold paper receipts (instead of gold) if you know you can always get gold for your paper. In normal times, goldsmiths could feel perfectly safe in loaning out more gold than they actually had in their possession. But once you (and everyone else) start to doubt the safety of the goldsmith, then you (and everyone else) would be foolish not to demand your gold back from the vault.

run on a bank *Occurs when many of those who have claims on a bank (deposits) present them at the same time.*

A **run** on a goldsmith (or in our day, a **run on a bank**) occurs when many people present their claims at the same time. These runs tend to feed on themselves. If I see you going to the goldsmith to withdraw your gold, I may become nervous and decide to withdraw my gold as well. It is the *fear* of a run that usually causes the run. Runs on a bank can be triggered by a variety of causes: rumors that an institution may have made loans to borrowers who cannot repay, wars, failures of other institutions that have borrowed money from the bank, and so on. As you will see later in this chapter, today's bankers differ from goldsmiths—today's banks are subject to a "required reserve ratio." Goldsmiths had no legal reserve requirements, although the amount that they loaned out was subject to the restriction imposed on them by their fear of running out of gold.

THE MODERN BANKING SYSTEM

To understand how the modern banking system works, you need to be familiar with some basic principles of accounting. Once you are comfortable with the way banks keep their books, the whole process of money creation will seem logical.

▶ **A Brief Review of Accounting** Central to accounting practices is the statement that "the books always balance." In practice, this means that if we take a snapshot of a firm—any firm, including a bank—at a particular moment in time, then by definition:

$$\text{Assets} - \text{Liabilities} \equiv \text{Net Worth, or}$$
$$\text{Assets} \equiv \text{Liabilities} + \text{Net Worth.}$$

Assets are things a firm owns that are worth something. For a bank, these assets include the bank building, its furniture, its holdings of government securities, cash in its vaults, bonds, stocks, and so forth. Most important among a bank's assets, for our purposes at least, are its *loans*. A borrower gives the bank an *IOU*, a promise to repay a certain sum of money on or by a certain date. This promise is an asset of the bank because it is worth something. The bank could (and sometimes does) sell the IOU to another bank for cash.

Federal Reserve System (the Fed) *The central bank of the United States.*

Other bank assets include cash on hand (sometimes called *vault cash*) and deposits with the United States' central bank—the **Federal Reserve Bank (the Fed)**. As we will

Assets		Liabilities	
Reserves	20	100	Deposits
Loans	90	10	Net worth
Total	110	110	Total

FIGURE 11.1

T Account for a Typical Bank (millions of dollars)

The balance sheet of a bank must always balance, so that the sum of assets (reserves and loans) equals the sum of liabilities (deposits and net worth).

see later in this chapter, federal banking regulations require that banks keep a certain portion of their deposits on hand as vault cash or on deposit with the Fed.

A firm's *liabilities* are its debts—what it owes. A bank's liabilities are the promises to pay, or IOUs, that it has issued. A bank's most important liabilities are its deposits. *Deposits* are debts owed to the depositors, because when you deposit money in your account, you are in essence making a loan to the bank.

The basic rule of accounting says that if we add up a firm's assets and then subtract the total amount it owes to all those who have lent it funds, the difference is the firm's net worth. *Net worth* represents the value of the firm to its stockholders or owners. How much would you pay for a firm that owns $200,000 of diamonds and had borrowed $150,000 from a bank to pay for them? Clearly, the firm is worth $50,000—the difference between what it owns and what it owes. If the price of diamonds were to fall, bringing their value down to only $150,000, the firm would be worth nothing.

We can keep track of a bank's financial position using a simplified balance sheet called a T account. By convention, the bank's assets are listed on the left side of the T account, its liabilities and net worth on the right side. By definition, the balance sheet always balances, so that the sum of the item(s) on the left side of the T account is exactly equal to the sum of the item(s) on the right side.

The T account in Figure 11.1 shows a bank having $110 million in *assets*, of which $20 million are **reserves**, the deposits that the bank has made at the Fed, and its cash on hand (coins and currency). Reserves are an asset to the bank because it can go to the Fed and get cash for them, just the way you can go to the bank and get cash for the amount in your savings account. Our bank's other asset is its loans, worth $90 million.

reserves *The deposits that a bank has at the Federal Reserve bank plus its cash on hand.*

Why do banks hold reserves/deposits at the Fed? There are many reasons, but perhaps the most important is the legal requirement that they hold a certain percentage of their deposit liabilities as reserves. The percentage of its deposits that a bank must keep as reserves is known as the **required reserve ratio**. If the reserve ratio is 20 percent, then a bank with deposits of $100 million must hold $20 million as reserves, either as cash or as deposits at the Fed. To simplify, we will assume that banks hold all of their reserves in the form of deposits at the Fed.

required reserve ratio *The percentage of its total deposits that a bank must keep as reserves at the Federal Reserve.*

On the liabilities side of the T account, the bank has taken deposits of $100 million, so it owes this amount to its depositors. This means that the bank has a net worth of $10 million to its owners ($110 million in assets − $100 million in liabilities = $10 million net worth). The net worth of the bank is what "balances" the balance sheet. Remember:

When some item on a bank's balance sheet changes, there must be at least one other change somewhere else to maintain balance.

If a bank's reserves increase by $1, then one of the following must also be true: (1) its other assets (say, loans) decrease by $1; (2) its liabilities (deposits) increase by $1; or (3) its net worth increases by $1. Various fractional combinations of these are also possible.

► **The Creation of Money** Like the goldsmiths, today's bankers seek to earn income by lending money out at a higher interest rate than they pay depositors for use of their money.

In modern times, the chances of a run on a bank are fairly small; and, even if there is a run, the central bank protects the private banks in various ways. Therefore:

> Banks usually make loans up to the point where they can no longer do so because of the reserve requirement restriction.

A bank's required amount of reserves is equal to the required reserve ratio times the total deposits in the bank. If a bank has deposits of $100 and the required ratio is 20 percent, the required amount of reserves is $20. The difference between a bank's actual reserves and its required reserves is its **excess reserves**:

> Excess reserves ≡ Actual reserves − Required reserves

If banks make loans up to the point where they can no longer do so because of the reserve requirement restriction, this means that banks make loans up to the point where their excess reserves are zero.

To see why, note that when a bank has excess reserves, it has credit available, and it can make loans. Actually, a bank can make loans *only* if it has excess reserves. When a bank makes a loan, it creates a demand deposit for the borrower. This creation of a demand deposit causes the bank's excess reserves to fall because the extra deposits created by the loan use up some of the excess reserves the bank has on hand. An example will help.

Assume there is only one private bank in the country, the required reserve ratio is 20 percent, and the bank starts off with nothing, as shown in Panel 1 of Figure 11.2. Now suppose dollar bills are in circulation and someone deposits 100 of them in the bank. The bank deposits the $100 with the central bank, so it now has $100 in reserves, as shown in Panel 2. The bank now has assets (reserves) of $100 and liabilities (deposits) of $100. If the required reserve ratio is 20 percent, the bank has excess reserves of $80.

How much can the bank lend and still meet the reserve requirement? For the moment, let's suppose anyone who gets a loan keeps the entire proceeds in the bank or pays them to someone else who does. Nothing is withdrawn as cash. In this case, the bank can lend $400 and still meet the reserve requirement, as you can see in Panel 3. With $80 of excess reserves, the bank can have up to $400 of additional deposits. The $100 in reserves plus $400 in loans (which are made as deposits) equal $500 in deposits. With $500 in deposits and a required reserve ratio of 20 percent, the bank must have reserves of $100 (20 percent of $500)—and it does. The bank can lend no more than $400 because its reserve requirement must not exceed $100. When a bank has no excess reserves and thus can make no more loans, it is said to be *loaned up*.

Remember, the money supply (M1) equals cash in circulation plus deposits. Before the initial deposit, the money supply was $100 ($100 cash and no deposits). After the deposit and the loans, the money supply is $500 (no cash outside of bank vaults and $500 in deposits). It is clear, then, that when cash is converted into deposits, the supply of money can change.

The bank whose T accounts are presented in Figure 11.2 is allowed to make loans of $400 based on the assumption that loans that are made *stay in the bank* in the form of deposits. Now suppose I borrow from the bank to buy a personal computer, and I write a check to the computer store. If the store also deposits its money in the bank, my check merely results in a reduction in my account balance and an increase to the store's account balance within the bank. No cash has left the bank. As long as the system is closed in this way—remember that we have so far assumed that there is only one

excess reserves *The difference between a bank's actual reserves and its required reserves.*

FIGURE 11.2

Balance Sheets of a Bank in a Single-Bank Economy

Panel 1

Assets	Liabilities
Reserves 0	0 Deposits

Panel 2

Assets	Liabilities
Reserves 100	100 Deposits

Panel 3

Assets	Liabilities
Reserves 100 Loans 400	500 Deposits

	Panel 1		Panel 2		Panel 3	
	Assets	Liabilities	Assets	Liabilities	Assets	Liabilities
Bank 1	Reserves 100	100 Deposits	Reserves 100 Loans 80	180 Deposits	Reserves 20 Loans 80	100 Deposits
Bank 2	Reserves 80	80 Deposits	Reserves 80 Loans 64	144 Deposits	Reserves 16 Loans 64	80 Deposits
Bank 3	Reserves 64	64 Deposits	Reserves 64 Loans 51.20	115.20 Deposits	Reserves 12.80 Loans 51.20	64 Deposits

Summary:	Deposits
Bank 1	100
Bank 2	80
Bank 3	64
Bank 4	51.20
⋮	⋮
Total	500.00

FIGURE 11.3

The Creation of Money: Balance Sheets of Three Banks

bank—the bank knows that it will never be called upon to release any of its $100 in reserves. It can expand its loans up to the point where its total deposits are $500.

Of course, there are many banks in the country, a situation that is depicted in Figure 11.3. As long as the banking system as a whole is closed, it is still possible for an initial deposit of $100 to result in an expansion of the money supply to $500, but more steps are involved when there is more than one bank.

To see why, assume Mary makes an initial deposit of $100 in Bank 1, and the bank deposits the entire $100 with the Fed (Panel 1 of Figure 11.3). All loans that a bank makes are withdrawn from the bank as the individual borrowers write checks to pay for merchandise. After Mary's deposit, Bank 1 can make a loan of up to $80 to Bill, because it needs to keep only $20 of its $100 deposit as reserves. (We are assuming a 20 percent required reserve ratio.) In other words, Bank 1 has $80 in excess reserves.

Bank 1's balance sheet at the moment of the loan to Bill appears in Panel 2 of Figure 11.3. Bank 1 now has loans of $80. It has credited Bill's account with the $80, so its total deposits are $180 ($80 in loans plus $100 in reserves). Bill then writes a check for $80 for a set of shock absorbers for his car. Bill wrote his check to Sam's Car Shop, and Sam deposits Bill's check in Bank 2. When the check clears, Bank 1 transfers $80 in reserves to Bank 2. Bank 1's balance sheet now looks like the top of Panel 3. Its assets include reserves of $20 and loans of $80; its liabilities are $100 in deposits. Both sides of the T account balance: The bank's reserves are 20 percent of its deposits, as required by law, and it is fully loaned up.

Now look at Bank 2. Because Bank 1 has transferred $80 in reserves to Bank 2, it now has $80 in deposits and $80 in reserves (Panel 1, Bank 2). Its reserve requirement is also 20 percent, so it has excess reserves of $64 on which it can make loans.

Now assume Bank 2 loans the $64 to Kate to pay for a textbook and Kate writes a check for $64 payable to the Manhattan College Bookstore. The final position of Bank 2, after it honors Kate's $64 check by transferring $64 in reserves to the bookstore's bank, is reserves of $16, loans of $64, and deposits of $80 (Panel 3, Bank 2).

The Manhattan College Bookstore deposits Kate's check in its account with Bank 3. Bank 3 now has excess reserves, because it has added $64 to its reserves. With a reserve ratio of 20 percent, Bank 3 can loan out $51.20 (80 percent of $64, leaving 20 percent in required reserves to back the $64 deposit).

As the process is repeated over and over, the total amount of deposits created is $500, the sum of the deposits in each of the banks. Because the banking system can be looked upon as one big bank, the outcome here for many banks is the same as the outcome in Figure 11.2 for one bank.[3]

▶ **The Money Multiplier** In practice, the banking system is not completely closed—there is some leakage out of the system. Still, the point here is:

> An increase in bank reserves leads to a greater than one-for-one increase in the money supply. Economists call the relationship between the final change in deposits and the change in reserves that caused this change the **money multiplier**. Stated somewhat differently, the money multiplier is the multiple by which deposits can increase for every dollar increase in reserves.

money multiplier *The multiple by which deposits can increase for every dollar increase in reserves; equal to one divided by the required reserve ratio.*

Do not confuse the money multiplier with the spending multipliers we discussed in the last two chapters. They are not the same thing.

In the example we just examined, reserves increased by $100 when the $100 in cash was deposited in a bank, and the amount of deposits increased by $500 ($100 from the initial deposit, $400 from the loans made by the various banks from their excess reserves). The money multiplier in this case is $500/$100 = 5. Mathematically, the money multiplier can be defined as:

$$\text{Money multiplier} \equiv \frac{1}{\text{Required reserve ratio}}$$

In the United States, the required reserve ratio varies, depending on the size of the bank and the type of deposit. For large banks and for checking deposits, the ratio is currently 10 percent, which makes the potential money multiplier 1/.10 = 10.0. This means that an increase in reserves of $1 could cause an increase in deposits of $10 if there were no leakage out of the system.

▶ **The Fed and the Money Supply** We have now seen how the private banking system creates money by making loans. However, private banks are not free to create money at will. Their ability to create money is controlled by the volume of reserves in the system, which is controlled by the Federal Reserve. The Federal Reserve, therefore, has the ultimate control over the money supply. Let's examine the structure and function of the Federal Reserve.

THE FEDERAL RESERVE SYSTEM

Founded in 1913 by an act of Congress (to which major reforms were added in the 1930s), the Federal Reserve is the central bank of the United States. The Fed is a complicated institution with many responsibilities, including the regulation and supervision of over 8,000 commercial banks. The organization of the Federal Reserve System is presented in Figure 11.4.

The *Board of Governors* is the most important group within the Federal Reserve System. The board consists of seven members, each appointed for 14 years by the president of the United States. The *chair* of the Federal Reserve, who is appointed by the

[3]If banks create money when they make loans, does repaying a loan "destroy" money? The answer is yes.

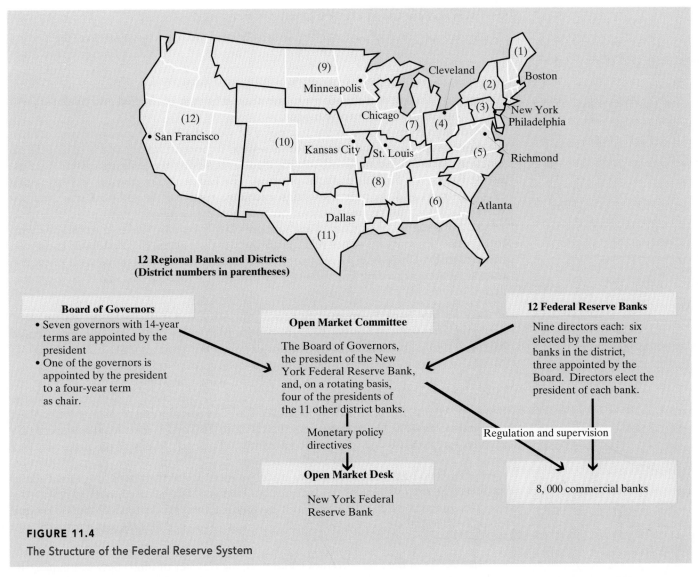

FIGURE 11.4

The Structure of the Federal Reserve System

The following text appears within the figure:

Board of Governors
- Seven governors with 14-year terms are appointed by the president
- One of the governors is appointed by the president to a four-year term as chair.

Open Market Committee

The Board of Governors, the president of the New York Federal Reserve Bank, and, on a rotating basis, four of the presidents of the 11 other district banks.

Monetary policy directives

Open Market Desk

New York Federal Reserve Bank

12 Federal Reserve Banks

Nine directors each: six elected by the member banks in the district, three appointed by the Board. Directors elect the president of each bank.

Regulation and supervision

8,000 commercial banks

12 Regional Banks and Districts (District numbers in parentheses)

president and whose term runs for four years, usually dominates the entire Federal Reserve System and is sometimes said to be the second most powerful person in the United States. The Fed is an independent agency in that it does not take orders from the president or from Congress.

The United States is divided into 12 Federal Reserve districts, each with its own Federal Reserve bank. These districts are indicated on the map in Figure 11.4. The district banks are like branch offices of the Federal Reserve in that they carry out the rules, regulations, and functions of the central system in their districts and report to the Board of Governors on local economic conditions.

U.S. monetary policy—the behavior of the Federal Reserve regarding the money supply—is formally set by the **Federal Open Market Committee (FOMC)**. The FOMC consists of the seven members of the Federal Reserve System's Board of Governors, the president of the New York Federal Reserve Bank, and, on a rotating basis, four of the presidents of the 11 other district banks. The FOMC sets goals regarding the money supply and interest rates, and it directs the **Open Market Desk** in the New York Federal Reserve Bank to buy and/or sell government securities. (We discuss the specifics of open market operations later in this chapter.)

Federal Open Market Committee (FOMC) *A group composed of the seven members of the Fed's Board of Governors, the president of the New York Federal Reserve Bank, and four of the other eleven district bank presidents on a rotating basis; it sets goals regarding the money supply and interest rates and directs the operation of the Open Market Desk in New York.*

Open Market Desk *The office in the New York Federal Reserve Bank from which government securities are bought and sold by the Fed.*

FUNCTIONS OF THE FED

The Fed is the central bank of the United States. (A brief discussion of the central banks of other countries, and the challenges they faced in 1998, is found in this chapter's Global Perspective.) Central banks are sometimes known as "bankers' banks" because only banks (and occasionally foreign governments) can have accounts in them. As a private citizen, you cannot go to the nearest branch of the Fed and open a checking account or apply to borrow money.

Although from a macroeconomic point of view the Fed's crucial role is to control the money supply, the Fed also performs several important functions for banks. These functions include clearing interbank payments, regulating the banking system, and assisting banks in a difficult financial position. The Fed is also responsible for managing exchange rates and the nation's foreign exchange reserves.[4] In addition, it is often involved in intercountry negotiations on international economic issues. In the early 1980s, for example, then Chair Paul Volcker played a major role in negotiations with foreign governments on issues relating to the debt problems of developing countries. More recently, Chair Alan Greenspan has been involved in discussions with European central bankers regarding the monetary problems of reuniting East and West Germany and "opening up" Eastern Europe.

➤ **Clearing Interbank Payments**   Suppose you write a $100 check, drawn on your bank, the First Bank of Fresno (FBF), to pay for tulip bulbs from Crockett Importers of Miami, Florida. Because Crockett Importers does not bank at FBF, but at Banco de Miami, how does your money get from your bank to the bank in Florida?

The answer: The Fed does it. Both FBF and Banco de Miami have accounts at the Federal Reserve. When Crockett Importers receives your check and deposits it at the Banco de Miami, the bank submits the check to the Federal Reserve, asking it to collect the funds from FBF. The Fed presents the check to FBF and is instructed to debit FBF's account for the $100 and to credit the account of Banco de Miami. Accounts at the Fed count as reserves, so FBF loses $100 in reserves and Banco de Miami gains $100 in reserves. The two banks effectively have traded ownerships of their deposits at the Federal Reserve. The *total* volume of reserves has not changed, nor has the money supply.

This function of clearing interbank payments allows banks to shift money around virtually instantaneously. All they need to do is wire the Fed and request a transfer, and the funds move at the speed of electricity from one computer account to another.

➤ **Other Duties of the Fed**   Besides facilitating the transfer of funds between banks, the Fed performs several other important duties. It is responsible for many of the regulations governing banking practices and standards. For example, the Federal Reserve has the authority to control mergers between banks, and it is responsible for examining banks to ensure they are financially sound and they conform to a host of government accounting regulations. And, as we saw earlier, the Fed also sets reserve requirements for all financial institutions.

One of the most important responsibilities of the Fed is to act as the **lender of last resort** for the banking system. As our discussion of goldsmiths suggested, banks are subject to the possibility of runs on their deposits. In the United States, most deposits of less than $100,000 are insured by the Federal Deposit Insurance Corporation (FDIC). Deposit insurance makes panics less likely. Because depositors know they can always get their money, even if the bank fails, they are less likely to withdraw their deposits. Not all deposits are insured, so the possibility of bank panics remains. But the Federal Reserve stands ready to provide funds to a troubled bank that cannot find any other sources of funds.

lender of last resort *One of the functions of the Fed: It provides funds to troubled banks that cannot find any other sources of funds.*

---

[4]*Foreign exchange reserves* are holdings of the currencies of other countries (for example, French francs) by the U.S. government. We discuss exchange rates and foreign exchange markets at length in chapter 21.

FOUR CENTRAL BANKS IN 1998

Virtually every country has a central bank run by the government. Banking systems and financial institutions differ from country to country, but the essential function of the central bank is the same in all countries: to control the supply of money and to regulate the banking system. As you will see in subsequent chapters, central banks can influence behavior and thus have an impact on the functioning of the economy. Four of the most important central banks in the world are described briefly here with a discussion of the major problem each faced in 1998.

THE UNITED STATES: THE FEDERAL RESERVE SYSTEM (NICKNAME: "THE FED")

The Fed chair in 1998 was Alan Greenspan. Greenspan was known for his strong anti-inflation views. As you will see in later chapters, excess monetary expansion can lead to inflation. Although no inflation was on the radar screens during 1997, labor markets were very tight and wage inflation was a big worry as the economy continued to expand at a healthy clip. But in October, stock markets around the world came crashing down and that took some of the wind out of the economy. Greenspan called the stock market crash a "salutatory" event.

GERMANY: THE DEUTSCHE BUNDESBANK (NICKNAME: "THE BUBA")

The biggest problem facing Germany in recent years has been the economic effects of reunification. The monetary problem was enormous. The East German currency had to be exchanged for new West German deutsche marks without creating wild inflationary swings. This was accomplished in an amazingly orderly way, and inflation remained in check. In early 1998, Bundesbank president Tietmeyer's major concern was similar to Alan Greenspan's. The economy was beginning to recover from recession and the Bundesbank's position was to hold down money supply growth to prevent inflation. In October 1997, the Bundesbank raised its key money market interest rate from 3.0 percent to 3.3 percent; it was the first move toward tightening in five years.

JAPAN: THE BANK OF JAPAN (NICKNAME: "BOJ")

The Bank of Japan faced one major problem in 1998: recession. During the second quarter of 1997, real GDP in Japan fell at an 11.2 percent annual rate! The banking system had been feeling great pressure from defaulted loans based on real estate and land values that had fallen sharply between 1992 and 1995. This is similar to the savings and loan crisis in the United States a few years earlier. Second, the recession had been hanging around for a long time. On December 16, 1994, Mr. Yasuro Matsushita took over as governor of the Bank of Japan and has continued a policy of modest monetary expansion to help bring Japan out of its recession.

RUSSIA: THE CENTRAL BANK OF RUSSIA

The Central Bank of Russia has problems dwarfing those of Germany, the United States, and Japan. Though the list of economic woes in the New Russia was long, near the top was hyperinflation. In 1992, prices rose about 2,000 percent. By the beginning of 1995, inflation was *down* to about 15 percent per month and by the beginning of 1998 it was 15 percent per year. As the economy moved from central planning to the market, the government found it very difficult to maintain salaries and to finance a collapsing industrial structure. Ultimately it resorted to printing money to make up for the shortfall. In addition to breaking the addiction to printing money, the Central Bank has a new private banking system of over 2,000 banks that will need supervision and regulation.

For more on central banks, see the Case and Fair Web page at
http://ww.prenhall.com/casefair.

The Fed is the ideal lender of last resort for two reasons. First, providing funds to a bank that is in dire straits is risky and not likely to be very profitable, and it is hard to find private banks or other private institutions willing to do this. The Fed is a nonprofit institution whose function is to serve the overall welfare of the public. Thus, the Fed would certainly be interested in preventing catastrophic banking panics such as those that occurred in the late 1920s and the 1930s.

Second, the Fed has an essentially unlimited supply of funds with which to bail out banks facing the possibility of runs. The reason, as we shall see, is that the Fed can create reserves at will. A promise by the Fed that it will support a bank is very

TABLE 11.1 ASSETS AND LIABILITIES OF THE FEDERAL
RESERVE SYSTEM, DECEMBER 31, 1997
(millions of dollars)

ASSETS			LIABILITIES
Gold	$ 11,047	$457,469	Federal Reserve notes (outstanding)
Loans to banks	2,035		Deposits:
U.S. government securities	451,924	30,838	Bank reserves (from depository institutions)
		5,444	U.S. Treasury
All other assets	52,841	24,096	All other liabilities and net worth
Total	$517,847	$517,847	Total

Source: Federal Reserve Bulletin, March 1998.

convincing. Unlike any other lender, the Fed can never run out of money. Therefore, the explicit or implicit support of the Fed should be enough to assure depositors they are in no danger of losing their funds.

THE FED'S BALANCE SHEET

Although it is a special bank, the Federal Reserve is in some ways similar to an ordinary commercial bank. Like an ordinary bank, the Fed has a balance sheet that records its asset and liability position at any moment in time. The balance sheet for the Federal Reserve is presented in Table 11.1.

As the asset side of the balance sheet shows, the Fed owns about $11 billion of gold. *Do not think that this gold has anything to do with the supply of money.* Most of the gold was acquired during the 1930s, when it was purchased from the U.S. Treasury Department. Since 1934, the dollar has not been backed by (not convertible into) gold. You cannot take a dollar bill to the Fed to receive gold for it; all you can get for your old dollar bill is a new dollar bill.[5] Although it is unrelated to the money supply, the Fed's gold counts as an asset on its balance sheet, because it is something of value the Fed owns.

The balance sheet mentions an asset called "loans to banks." These loans are an asset of the Federal Reserve in the same way a private commercial bank's loans are among its assets. The Fed sometimes makes loans to commercial banks that are short of reserves.[6] The $2,035 billion in Table 11.1 represents these kinds of loans.

The largest of the Fed's assets by far consists of government securities: about $452 billion worth at the end of December 1997. Government securities are obligations of the federal government, such as Treasury bills and government bonds, which the Fed has purchased over the years. The way in which these bonds are acquired has important implications for the Fed's control of the money supply. (We return to this topic after our survey of the Fed's balance sheet.)

The bulk of the Fed's liabilities are Federal Reserve notes. The dollar bill you use to buy a quart of milk is clearly an asset from your point of view—it is something you own that has value. But because every financial asset is by definition a liability of some other agent in the economy, whose liability is that dollar bill? That dollar bill, and bills of all other denominations in the economy, are a liability—an IOU—of the Federal Reserve.

---

[5]The fact that the Fed is not obliged to provide gold for currency means it can never go bankrupt. When the currency was backed by gold, it would have been possible for the Fed to run out of gold if too many of its depositors came to it at the same time and asked to exchange their deposits for gold. But if depositors come to the Fed to withdraw their deposits today, all they can get are dollar bills. The dollar was convertible into gold internationally until August 15, 1971.

[6]Recall that commercial banks are required to keep a set percentage of their deposit liabilities on deposit at the Fed. If a bank suddenly finds itself short of reserves, one of its alternatives is to borrow the reserves it needs from the Fed.

They are rather strange IOUs, because all they can be redeemed for are other IOUs of exactly the same type. They are, nonetheless, classified as liabilities of the Fed.

The balance sheet shows that, like an ordinary commercial bank, the Fed has accepted deposits. These deposits are liabilities. The bulk of the Fed's deposits come from commercial banks. Remember: commercial banks are required to keep a certain share of their own deposits as deposits at the Fed. A bank's deposits at the Fed (its reserves) are an asset from the bank's point of view, and those same reserves must be a liability from the Fed's point of view.

Table 11.1 shows the Fed has accepted a small volume of deposits from the U.S. Treasury. In effect, the Fed acts as the bank for the U.S. government. When the government needs to pay for something like a new aircraft carrier, it may write out a check to the supplier of the ship drawn on its "checking account" at the Fed. Similarly, when the government receives revenues from tax collections, fines, or sales of government assets, it may deposit these funds in its account at the Fed.

HOW THE FED CONTROLS THE MONEY SUPPLY

To see how the Fed controls the supply of money in the U.S. economy we need to understand the role of reserves. As we have said, the required reserve ratio establishes a link between the reserves of the commercial banks and the deposits (money) that commercial banks are allowed to create.

The reserve requirement effectively determines how much a bank has available to lend. If the required reserve ratio is 20 percent, each $1 of reserves can support $5 in deposits. A bank that has reserves of $100,000 cannot have more than $500,000 in deposits. If it did, it would fail to meet the required reserve ratio.

If you recall that the *money supply* is equal to the sum of deposits inside banks and the currency in circulation outside of banks, you can see that reserves provide the leverage that the Fed needs to control the money supply.

> If the Fed wants to increase the supply of money, it creates more reserves, thereby freeing banks to create additional deposits by making more loans. If it wants to decrease the money supply, it reduces reserves.

Three tools are available to the Fed for changing the money supply: (1) changing the required reserve ratio; (2) changing the discount rate; and (3) open market operations.

THE REQUIRED RESERVE RATIO

The simplest way for the Fed to alter the supply of money is to change the required reserve ratio. This process is shown in Table 11.2. Let's assume the initial required reserve ratio is 20 percent.

In Panel 1, a simplified version of the Fed's balance sheet (in billions of dollars) shows that reserves are $100 billion and currency outstanding is $100 billion. The total value of the Fed's assets is $200 billion, which we assume to be all in government securities. Assuming there are no excess reserves—banks stay fully loaded up—the $100 billion in reserves supports $500 billion in deposits at the commercial banks. (Remember: The money multiplier equals 1/required reserve ratio = 1/.20 = 5. Thus, $100 billion in reserves can support $500 billion [$100 billion × 5] in deposits when the required reserve ratio is 20 percent.) The supply of money (M1, or transactions money) is therefore $600 billion: $100 billion in currency and $500 billion in (checking account) deposits at the commercial banks.

Now suppose the Fed wants to increase the supply of money to $900 billion. If it lowers the required reserve ratio from 20 percent to 12.5 percent (as in Panel 2 of Table 11.2), then the same $100 billion of reserves could support $800 billion in

FAST FACTS

The Federal Open Market Committee meets eight times a year to determine the monetary policy of the Federal Reserve. Prior to meeting, the board publishes a regional outlook report, the "Beige Book," based on data compiled by the 12 district Federal Reserve Banks. During the week prior to publication, Fed economists are busy talking on the phone to businesses about recent trends.

PANEL 1: REQUIRED RESERVE RATIO = 20%

Federal Reserve				Commercial Banks			
Assets		Liabilities		Assets			Liabilities
Government securities	$200	$100	Reserves	Reserves	$100	$500	Deposits
		$100	Currency	Loans	$400		

Note: Money supply (M1) = Currency + Deposits = $600.

PANEL 2: REQUIRED RESERVE RATIO = 12.5%

Federal Reserve				Commercial Banks			
Assets		Liabilities		Assets			Liabilities
Government securities	$200	$100	Reserves	Reserves	$100	$800	Deposits (+$300)
		$100	Currency	Loans (+$300)	$700		

Note: Money supply (M1) = Currency + Deposits = $900.

deposits instead of only $500 billion. In this case, the money multiplier is 1/.125, or 8. At a required reserve ratio of 12.5 percent, $100 billion in reserves can support $800 billion in deposits. The total money supply would be $800 billion in deposits plus the $100 billion in currency, for a total of $900 billion.[7]

Put another way, with the new lower reserve ratio, banks have excess reserves of $37.5 billion. At a required reserve ratio of 20 percent, they needed $100 billion in reserves to back their $500 billion in deposits. At the lower required reserve ratio of 12.5 percent, they need only $62.5 billion of reserves to back their $500 billion of deposits, so the remaining $37.5 billion of the existing $100 billion in reserves are "extra." With that $37.5 billion of excess reserves, banks can lend out more money. If we assume the system loans money and creates deposits to the *maximum* extent possible, the $37.5 billion of reserves will support an additional $300 billion of deposits ($37.5 billion × the money multiplier of 8 = $300 billion). The change in the required reserve ratio has injected an additional $300 billion into the banking system, at which point the banks will be fully loaned up and unable to increase their deposits further.

> Decreases in the required reserve ratio allow banks to have more deposits with the existing volume of reserves. As banks create more deposits by making loans, the supply of money (currency + deposits) increases. The reverse is also true: If the Fed wants to restrict the supply of money, it can raise the required reserve ratio, in which case banks will find that they have insufficient reserves and must therefore reduce their deposits by "calling in" some of their loans.[8] The result is a decrease in the money supply.

---

[7]To find the maximum volume of deposits (D) that can be supported by an amount of reserves (R), divide R by the required reserve ratio. If the required reserve ratio is g, because $R = gD$, then $D = R/g$.

[8]Banks never really have to "call in" loans before they are due, to reduce the money supply. First, the Fed is almost always expanding the money supply slowly because the real economy grows steadily and, as we shall see, growth brings with it the need for more circulating money. So when we speak of "contractionary monetary policy," we mean the Fed is slowing down the rate of money growth, not reducing the money supply. Second, even if the Fed were actually to cut reserves (rather than curb their expansion), banks would no doubt be able to comply by reducing the volume of new loans they make while old ones are coming due.

For many reasons, the Fed has tended not to use changes in the reserve requirement to control the money supply. In part, this reluctance stems from the era when only some banks were members of the Federal Reserve System and, therefore, subject to reserve requirements. The Fed reasoned that if it raised the reserve requirement to contract the money supply, banks might choose to stop being members. (Because reserves pay no interest, the higher the reserve requirement, the more the penalty imposed on those banks holding reserves.) This argument no longer applies. Since the passage of the Depository Institutions Deregulation and Monetary Control Act in 1980, all depository institutions are subject to Federal Reserve requirements.

It is also true that changing the reserve requirement ratio is a crude tool. Because of lags in banks' reporting to the Fed on their reserve and deposit positions, a change in the requirement today does not affect banks for about two weeks. (However, the fact that changing the reserve requirement expands or reduces credit in every bank in the country makes it a very powerful tool when the Fed does use it.) A much better tool for controlling week-to-week changes in the money supply, as we shall see shortly, is open market operations.

THE DISCOUNT RATE

Banks may borrow from the Fed. The interest rate they pay the Fed is the **discount rate**. When banks increase their borrowing, the money supply increases.

To simplify, let's assume there is only one bank in the country and the required reserve ratio is 20 percent. The initial position of the bank and the Fed appear in Panel 1 of Table 11.3, where the money supply (currency + deposits) is $480. In Panel 2, the bank has borrowed $20 from the Fed. By using this $20 as a reserve, the bank can increase its loans by $100, from $320 to $420. (Remember: A required reserve ratio of 20 percent gives a money multiplier of 5; excess reserves of $20 allows the bank to create an additional $20 × 5, or $100, in deposits.)

discount rate *Interest rate that banks pay to the Fed to borrow from it.*

> Bank borrowing from the Fed leads to an increase in the money supply.

TABLE 11.3   THE EFFECT ON THE MONEY SUPPLY OF COMMERCIAL BANK BORROWING FROM THE FED
(ALL FIGURES IN BILLIONS OF DOLLARS)

PANEL 1: NO COMMERCIAL BANK BORROWING FROM THE FED

Federal Reserve				Commercial Banks			
Assets			Liabilities	Assets			Liabilities
Securities	$160	$80	Reserves	Reserves	$80	$400	Deposits
		$80	Currency	Loans	$320		

Note: Money supply (M1) = Currency + Deposits = $480.

PANEL 2: COMMERCIAL BANK BORROWING $20 FROM THE FED

Federal Reserve				Commercial Banks			
Assets			Liabilities	Assets			Liabilities
Securities	$160	$100	Reserves (+$20)	Reserves (+$20)	$100	$500	Deposits (+$100)
Loans	$20	$80	Currency	Loans (+$100)	$420	$20	Amount owed to Fed (+$20)

Note: Money supply (M1) = Currency + Deposits = $580.

Banks that borrow from the Fed must eventually repay, and when they do, the money supply goes back down by exactly the amount by which it initially increased.

The Fed can influence bank borrowing through the discount rate:

> The higher the discount rate, the higher the cost of borrowing, and the less borrowing banks will want to do.

If the Fed wants to curtail the growth of the money supply, for example, it raises the discount rate and discourages banks from borrowing from it, restricting the growth of reserves (and ultimately deposits).

In practice, the Fed does not often use the discount rate to control the money supply. It does change the discount rate from time to time to keep it in line with other interest rates, but most often the discount rate follows the other rates rather than leads them.

Changing the discount rate to control the supply of money has several problems associated with it. First, although raising the discount rate does discourage borrowing by banks (and therefore reduces their ability to expand the money supply), it is never clear in advance exactly how much of an effect a change in the discount rate will have. If banks are very short of reserves, they may decide to borrow from the Fed even though the discount rate is quite high.

> The discount rate cannot be used to control the money supply with great precision, because its effects on banks' demand for reserves are uncertain.

Second, changes in the discount rate can be largely offset by movements in other interest rates. If the discount rate is set at 10 percent and the rate paid by Treasury bills is 9 percent, banks will not borrow from the Fed to purchase Treasury bills. Because they would be paying more in borrowing costs than they would be making in interest revenue, they would lose by borrowing from the Fed. If the Treasury bill rate were to rise to 11 percent, banks could profitably borrow from the Fed to purchase Treasury bills. So, a discount rate that is high enough to discourage borrowing in some circumstances may not be high enough in others.

You may wonder whether the discount rate can ever be below the rate banks charge for loans or below the rate offered on Treasury bills. If this were the case, wouldn't banks borrow enormous quantities from the Fed at the lower rate and lend at the higher rate? In practice, the discount rate is at times lower than the rate that banks charge for their loans, and yet this kind of behavior is not common. This is because the Fed places other constraints on the borrowing behavior of banks. The Fed practices **moral suasion** to discourage heavy borrowing. Because member banks know that the Fed would look disapprovingly at heavy borrowing, they do not borrow heavily, and the amount that they do borrow responds only slightly to changes in the discount rate.

OPEN MARKET OPERATIONS

By far the most significant of the Fed's tools for controlling the supply of money is **open market operations**. Congress has authorized the Federal Reserve to buy and sell U.S. government securities in the open market. When the Fed purchases a security, it pays for it by writing a check that, when cleared, *expands* the quantity of reserves in the system, increasing the money supply. When the Fed sells a bond, private citizens or institutions pay for it with a check that, when cleared, *reduces* the quantity of reserves in the system.

To see how open market transactions and reserve controls work, we need to review several key ideas.

moral suasion *The pressure exerted by the Fed on member banks to discourage them from borrowing heavily from the Fed.*

open market operations *The purchase and sale by the Fed of government securities in the open market; a tool used to expand or contract the amount of reserves in the system and thus the money supply.*

▶ **Two Branches of Government Deal in Government Securities**   The fact that the Fed is able to buy and sell government securities—bills and bonds—may confuse students. In fact, *two* branches of government deal in financial markets for different reasons, and you must keep the two separate in your mind.

First, keep in mind that the Treasury Department is responsible for collecting taxes and paying the federal government's bills. Salary checks paid to government workers, payments to General Dynamics for a new Navy ship, social security checks to retirees, and so forth are all written on accounts maintained by the Treasury. Tax receipts collected by the Internal Revenue Service, a Treasury branch, are deposited to these accounts.

If total government spending exceeds tax receipts, the law requires the Treasury to borrow the difference. Recall that the government deficit is $(G - T)$, or government purchases minus net taxes. $(G - T)$ is the amount the Treasury must borrow each year to finance the deficit. This means:

> The Treasury *cannot* print money to finance the deficit.

The Treasury borrows by issuing bills, bonds, and notes that pay interest. These government securities, or IOUs, are sold to individuals and institutions. Often foreign countries, as well as U.S. citizens, buy them. As discussed in chapter 10, the total amount of privately held government securities is the *privately held federal debt.*

The Fed is not the Treasury. Rather, it is a quasi-independent agency authorized by Congress to buy and sell *outstanding* (preexisting) U.S. government securities on the open market. The bonds and bills initially sold by the Treasury to finance the deficit are continuously resold and traded among ordinary citizens, firms, banks, pension funds, and so forth. The Fed's participation in that trading affects the quantity of reserves in the system, as we will see.

Because the Fed owns some government securities, some of what the government owes, it owes to itself. Recall that the Federal Reserve System's largest single asset is government securities. These securities are nothing more than bills and bonds initially issued by the Treasury to finance the deficit. They were acquired by the Fed over time through direct open market purchases that the Fed made to expand the money supply as the economy expanded.

▶ **The Mechanics of Open Market Operations**   How do open market operations affect the money supply? Look again at Table 11.1. As you can see, most of the Fed's assets consist of the government securities we have just been talking about.

Suppose the Fed wants to decrease the supply of money. If it can reduce the volume of bank reserves on the liabilities side of its balance sheet, it will force banks in turn to reduce their own deposits (to meet the required reserve ratio). Since these deposits are part of the supply of money, the supply of money will contract.

What will happen if the Fed sells some of its holdings of government securities to the general public? The Fed's holdings of government securities must decrease, because the securities it sold will now be owned by someone else. How do the purchasers of securities pay for what they have bought? By writing checks drawn on their banks and payable to the Fed.

Let's look more carefully at how this works, with the help of Table 11.4. In Panel 1, the Fed initially has $100 billion of government securities. Its liabilities consist of $20 billion of deposits (which are the reserves of commercial banks) and $80 billion of currency. With the required reserve ratio at 20 percent, the $20 billion of reserves can support $100 billion of deposits in the commercial banks. The commercial banking system is fully loaned up. Panel 1 also shows the financial position of a private citizen, Jane Q. Public. Jane has assets of $5 billion (a large checking account deposit in the bank) and no debts, so her net worth is $5 billion.

TABLE 11.4 OPEN MARKET OPERATIONS (THE NUMBERS IN PARENTHESES IN PANELS 2 AND 3 SHOW THE DIFFERENCES BETWEEN THOSE PANELS AND PANEL 1. ALL FIGURES IN BILLIONS OF DOLLARS)

PANEL 1

Federal Reserve				Commercial Banks				Jane Q. Public			
Assets		Liabilities		Assets		Liabilities		Assets		Liabilities	
Securities	$100	$20	Reserves	Reserves	$20	$100	Deposits	Deposits	$5	$0	Debts
		$80	Currency	Loans	$80					$5	Net Worth

Note: Money supply (M1) = Currency + Deposits = $180.

PANEL 2

Federal Reserve				Commercial Banks				Jane Q. Public			
Assets		Liabilities		Assets		Liabilities		Assets		Liabilities	
Securities (−$5)	$95	$15 (−$5)	Reserves	Reserves (−$5)	$15	$95 (−$5)	Deposits	Deposits (−$5)	$0	$0	Debts
		$80	Currency	Loans	$80			Securities (+$5)	$5	$5	Net Worth

Note: Money supply (M1) = Currency + Deposits = $175.

PANEL 3

Federal Reserve				Commercial Banks				Jane Q. PuBlic			
Assets		Liabilities		Assets		Liabilities		Assets		Liabilities	
Securities (−$5)	$95	$15 (−$5)	Reserves	Reserves (−$5)	$15	$75 (−$25)	Deposits	Deposits (−$5)	$0	$0	Debts
		$80	Currency	Loans (−$20)	$60			Securities (+$5)	$5	$5	Net Worth

Note: Money supply (M1) = Currency + Deposits = $155.

Now imagine that the Fed sells $5 billion in government securities to Jane. Jane pays for the securities by writing a check to the Fed, drawn on her bank. The Fed then reduces the reserve account of her bank by $5 billion. The balance sheets of all the participants after this transaction are shown in Panel 2. Note that the supply of money (currency plus deposits) has fallen from $180 billion to $175 billion.

This is not the end of the story. As a result of the Fed's sale of securities, the amount of reserves has fallen from $20 billion to $15 billion, while deposits have fallen from $100 billion to $95 billion. With a required reserve ratio of 20 percent, banks must have .20 × $95 billion, or $19 billion in reserves. Banks are under their required reserve ratio by $4 billion ($19 billion [the amount they should have] minus $15 billion [the amount they do have]). To comply with the federal regulations, banks must decrease their loans and their deposits.[9]

The final equilibrium position is shown in Panel 3, where commercial banks have reduced their loans by $20 billion. Notice that the change in deposits from Panel 1 to Panel 3 is $25 billion, which is five times the size of the change in reserves that the Fed brought about through its $5 billion open market sale of securities. This corresponds exactly to our earlier analysis of the money multiplier. The change

---

[9]Once again, banks never really have to call in loans. Loans and deposits would probably be reduced by slowing the rate of new lending as old loans come due and are paid off.

in money (−$25 billion) is equal to the money multiplier (5) times the change in reserves (−$5 billion).

Now consider what happens when the Fed *purchases* a government security. Suppose I hold $100 in Treasury bills, which the Fed buys from me. The Fed writes me a check for $100, and I turn in my Treasury bills. I then take the $100 check and deposit it in my local bank. This increases the reserves of my bank by $100 and begins a new episode in the money expansion story. With a reserve requirement of 20 percent, my bank can now lend out $80. If that $80 is spent and ends up back in a bank, that bank can lend $64, and so forth. (Review Figure 11.3.) The Fed can expand the money supply by buying government securities from people who own them, just the way it reduces the money supply by selling these securities.

Each business day, the Open Market Desk in the New York Federal Reserve Bank buys or sells millions of dollars' worth of securities, usually to large security dealers who act as intermediaries between the Fed and the private markets. We can sum up the effect of these open market operations this way:

- An open market *purchase* of securities by the Fed results in an increase in reserves and an *increase* in the supply of money by an amount equal to the money multiplier times the change in reserves.
- An open market *sale* of securities by the Fed results in a *decrease* in reserves and a *decrease* in the supply of money by an amount equal to the money multiplier times the change in reserves.

Open market operations are the Fed's preferred means of controlling the money supply for several reasons. First, open market operations can be used with some precision. If the Fed needs to change the money supply by just a small amount, it can buy or sell a small volume of government securities. If it wants a larger change in the money supply, it can buy or sell a larger amount. Second, open market operations are extremely flexible. If the Fed decides to reverse course, it can easily switch from buying securities to selling them. Finally, open market operations have a fairly predictable effect on the supply of money. Because banks are obliged to meet their reserve requirements, an open market sale of $100 in government securities will reduce reserves by $100, which will reduce the supply of money by $100 times the money multiplier.

Where does the Fed get the money to buy government securities when it wants to expand the money supply? The Fed creates it. In effect, it tells the bank from which it has bought a $100 security that its reserve account (deposit) at the Fed now contains $100 more than it did previously. This is where the power of the Fed, or any central bank, lies. The Fed has the ability to create money at will. In the United States, the Fed exercises this power when it creates money to buy government securities.

THE SUPPLY CURVE FOR MONEY

Thus far we know how the Fed can control the money supply by controlling the amount of reserves in the economy. If the Fed wants the quantity of money to be $1,200 billion on a given date, it can aim for this target by changing the discount rate, by changing the required reserve ratio, or by engaging in open market operations. In this sense, the supply of money is completely determined by the Fed, and the money supply curve in Figure 11.5 is a vertical line.

A vertical money supply curve says the Fed sets the money supply independent of the interest rate. A vertical money supply curve means the interest rate does not affect the Fed's decision on how much money to supply. We will see in chapter 16 that the Fed's money supply behavior is influenced by the state of the economy, but perhaps

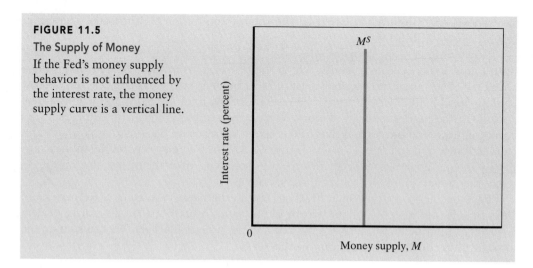

FIGURE 11.5

The Supply of Money
If the Fed's money supply behavior is not influenced by the interest rate, the money supply curve is a vertical line.

also by the interest rate. In practice, the money supply curve is not likely to be vertical. It would complicate matters at this stage of our analysis to consider Fed behavior in more detail, so we will assume for now that the money supply curve is vertical. This assumption is relaxed in chapter 16.[10]

LOOKING AHEAD

This chapter has discussed only the supply side of the money market. We have seen what money is, how banks create money by making loans, and how the Fed controls the money supply. In the next chapter we turn to the demand side of the money market. We will examine the demand for money and how the supply of and demand for money determine the equilibrium interest rate.

SUMMARY

AN OVERVIEW OF MONEY

1. Money has three distinguishing characteristics: (1) a means of payment, or medium of exchange; (2) a store of value; and (3) a unit of account. The alternative to using money is *barter*, in which goods are exchanged directly for other goods. Barter is costly and inefficient in an economy with many different kinds of goods.

2. *Commodity monies* are items used as money and also have an intrinsic value in some other use (for example, gold and cigarettes). *Fiat monies* are intrinsically worthless apart from their use as money. To ensure the acceptance of fiat monies, governments use their power to declare money *legal tender* and promise the public they will not debase the currency by expanding its supply rapidly.

3. There are various definitions of money. Currency plus demand deposits plus traveler's checks plus other checkable deposits compose M1, or *transactions money*—money that can be used directly to buy things. The addition of savings accounts and money market accounts (*near monies*) to M1 gives M2, or *broad money*.

---

[10]There is another reason the money supply curve may not be vertical. If bank borrowing from the Fed responds positively to the difference between the market interest rate and the discount rate, then as the market interest rate rises (with the discount rate fixed), banks will borrow more. We have seen that an increase in bank borrowing leads to an increase in the money supply. Therefore, the supply of money responds positively to the market interest rate, so the money supply schedule should have a positive slope. In practice this effect is fairly small, and for simplicity we will ignore it. The Fed could offset this effect completely if it raised the discount rate in line with the market interest rate.

HOW BANKS CREATE MONEY

4. The *required reserve ratio* is the percentage of a bank's deposits that must be kept as reserves at the nation's central bank, the Federal Reserve.

5. Banks create money by making loans. When a bank makes a loan to a customer, it creates a deposit in that customer's account. This deposit becomes part of the money supply. Banks can create money only when they have *excess reserves*—reserves in excess of the amount set by the required reserve ratio.

6. The *money multiplier* is the multiple by which the total supply of money can increase for every dollar increase in reserves. The money multiplier is equal to 1/required reserve ratio.

THE FEDERAL RESERVE SYSTEM

7. The Fed's most important function is controlling the nation's money supply. The Fed also performs several other functions: It clears interbank payments, is responsible for many of the regulations governing banking practices and standards, and acts as a *lender of last resort* for troubled banks that cannot find any other sources of funds. The Fed also acts as the bank for the U.S. government.

HOW THE FED CONTROLS THE MONEY SUPPLY

8. The key to understanding how the Fed controls the money supply is the role of reserves. If the Fed wants to increase the supply of money, it creates more reserves, freeing banks to create additional deposits. If it wants to decrease the money supply, it reduces reserves.

9. The Fed has three tools to control the money supply: (1) change the required reserve ratio; (2) change the *discount rate* (the interest rate member banks pay when they borrow from the Fed); or (3) engage in *open market operations* (the buying and selling of already-existing government securities). To increase the money supply, the Fed can create additional reserves by lowering the discount rate or by buying government securities, or the Fed can increase the number of deposits that can be created from a given quantity of reserves by lowering the required reserve ratio. To decrease the money supply, the Fed can reduce reserves by raising the discount rate or by selling government securities, or it can raise the required reserve ratio.

10. If the Fed's money supply behavior is not influenced by the interest rate, the supply curve for money is a vertical line.

REVIEW TERMS AND CONCEPTS

1. $M1 \equiv$ Currency held outside banks + Demand deposits + Traveler's checks + Other checkable deposits

2. $M2 \equiv M1$ + Savings accounts + Money market accounts + Other near monies

3. Assets $\equiv$ Liabilities + Capital (or Net Worth)

4. Excess reserves $\equiv$ Actual reserves − Required reserves

5. Money multiplier $\equiv \dfrac{1}{\text{Required reserve ratio}}$

PROBLEM SET

1. Define money. What is meant by the "store of value" function of money? What is meant by the "medium of exchange" function of money? Think of your current cash holdings and checking account balances. How much do you think you have on hand for purposes of engaging in transactions (buying stuff) on a daily basis? How much is serving as a store of value? Would the amount you hold onto as cash and in your checking account change if your local bank started paying 15 percent interest on three-month certificates of deposit? Why or why not?

2. For each of the following say whether it is an asset on the accounting books of a bank or a liability. Explain why in each case.

>Cash in the vault
>Demand deposits
>Savings deposits
>Reserves
>Loans
>Deposits at the Federal Reserve

3. If the head of the Central Bank of Japan wanted to expand the supply of money in Japan in 1999, which of the following would do it? Explain your answer.

>Increase the required reserve ratio
>Decrease the required reserve ratio
>Increase the discount rate
>Decrease the discount rate
>Buy government securities in the open market
>Sell government securities in the open market

4. In 1997, the U.S. money supply (M1) was $1,077 billion, broken down as follows: $396 billion in currency, $86 billion in traveler's checks, and $672 billion in checking deposits. Suppose the Fed has decided to reduce the money supply by increasing the reserve requirement from 10 percent to 11 percent. Assuming all banks were initially loaned up (had no excess reserves) and currency held outside of banks did not change, how large a change in the money supply would have resulted from the change in the reserve requirement?

5. As King of Medivalia, you are constantly strapped for funds to pay your army. Your chief economic wizard suggests the following plan: "When you collect your tax payments from your subjects, insist on being paid in gold coins. Take these gold coins, melt them down, and then remint them with an extra 10 percent of brass thrown in. You will then have 10 percent more money than you started with." What do you think of the plan? Will it work?

6. Why is M2 sometimes a more stable measure of money than M1? Explain in your own words, using the definitions of M1 and M2.

7. Do you agree or disagree with each of the following statements? Explain your answers.
   a. "When the Treasury of the United States issues bonds and sells them to the public to finance the deficit, the money supply remains unchanged because every dollar of money taken in by the Treasury goes right back into circulation through government spending. This is not true when the Fed sells bonds to the public."
   b. "The money multiplier depends on the marginal propensity to save."

*8. When the Fed adds new reserves to the system, some of these new reserves find their way out of the country into foreign banks or foreign investment funds. In addition, some portion of new reserves ends up in people's pockets and mattresses rather than in bank vaults. These "leakages" reduce the money multiplier and sometimes make it very difficult for the Fed to control the money supply precisely. Explain why this is true.

9. You are given this T account for a bank:

ASSETS		LIABILITIES	
Reserves	$500	$3,500	Deposits
Loans	3,000		

The required reserve ratio is 10 percent.
   a. How much is the bank required to hold as reserves, given its deposits of $3,500?
   b. How much are its excess reserves?
   c. By how much can the bank increase its loans?
   d. Suppose a depositor comes to the bank and withdraws $200 in cash. Show the bank's new balance sheet, assuming the bank obtains the cash by drawing down its reserves. Does the bank now hold excess reserves? Is it meeting the required reserve ratio? If not, what can it do?

10. What are the major functions of the Federal Reserve? Could any of these functions be performed by private banks, or is the central bank the only agent capable of filling these roles? Explain.

TAKE IT TO THE NET

We invite you to visit the Case and Fair page on the Prentice Hall Web site:

http://www.prenhall.com/casefair

for this chapter's World Wide Web exercise.

Chapter 12

MONEY DEMAND, THE EQUILIBRIUM INTEREST RATE, AND MONETARY POLICY

HAVING DISCUSSED THE *SUPPLY* of money in the last chapter, we now turn to the *demand* for money. One goal of this and the previous chapter is to provide a theory of how the interest rate is determined in the macroeconomy. Once we have seen how the interest rate is determined, we can turn to how the Fed affects the interest rate through **monetary policy**.

It is important that you understand exactly what the interest rate is. **Interest** is the fee a borrower pays to a lender for the use of his or her funds. Firms and the government borrow funds by issuing bonds, and they pay interest to the firms and households (the lenders) that purchase those bonds. Households and firms that have borrowed from a bank must pay interest on those loans to the bank.

The **interest rate** is the annual interest payment on a loan expressed as a percentage of the loan. A $1,000 bond (representing a $1,000 loan from a household to a firm) that pays $100 in interest per year has an interest rate of 10 percent. The interest rate is expressed as an *annual* rate. It is the amount of interest received *per year* divided by the amount of the loan.

While there are many different interest rates, we will assume that there is only one. This simplifies our analysis yet provides a valuable tool for us to understand how the parts of the macroeconomy relate to one another. Appendix A to this chapter provides more detail on the various types of interest rates.

THE DEMAND FOR MONEY

What factors and what forces determine the demand for money are central issues in macroeconomics. As we shall see, the interest rate and the level of national income (Y) influence how much money households and firms wish to hold.

Before we proceed, we must stress one point students find troublesome. When we speak of the demand for money, we are not asking "How much

monetary policy *The behavior of the Federal Reserve regarding the money supply.*

interest *The fee that a borrower pays to a lender for the use of his or her funds.*

interest rate *The annual interest payment on a loan expressed as a percentage of the loan. Equal to the amount of interest received per year divided by the amount of the loan.*

cash do you wish you could have?" or "How much income would you like to earn?" or "How much wealth would you like?" (The answer to these questions is presumably "as much as possible.") Rather, we are concerned with how much of your financial assets you want to hold *in the form of money*, which does not earn interest, versus how much you want to hold in interest-bearing securities, such as bonds. We take as given the *total* amount of financial assets; our concern here is with how these assets are divided between money and interest-bearing securities.

THE TRANSACTION MOTIVE

How much money to hold involves a trade-off between the liquidity of money and the interest income offered by other kinds of assets. The main reason for holding money instead of interest-bearing assets is that money is useful for buying things. Economists call this the **transaction motive**. This rationale for holding money is at the heart of the discussion that follows.[1]

transaction motive *The main reason that people hold money— to buy things.*

➤ **Assumptions**   To keep our analysis of the demand for money clear, we need a few simplifying assumptions. First, we assume there are only two kinds of assets available to households: bonds and money. By "bonds" we mean interest-bearing securities of all kinds. By "money" we mean currency in circulation and deposits, neither of which is assumed to pay interest.[2]

Second, we assume that income for the typical household is "bunched up." It arrives once a month, at the beginning of the month. Spending, by contrast, is spread out over time; we assume that spending occurs at a completely uniform rate throughout the month—that is, that the same amount is spent each day (see Figure 12.1). The mismatch between the timing of money inflow and the timing of money outflow is sometimes called the **nonsynchronization of income and spending**.

nonsynchronization of income and spending *The mismatch between the timing of money inflow to the household and the timing of money outflow for household expenses.*

Finally, we assume that spending for the month is exactly equal to income for the month. Because we are focusing on the transactions demand for money and not on its use as a store of value, this assumption is perfectly reasonable.

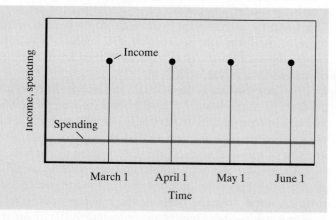

FIGURE 12.1
The Nonsynchronization of Income and Spending

Income arrives only once a month, but spending takes place continuously.

---

[1]The model that we discuss here is known in the economics profession as the Baumol/Tobin model, after the two economists who independently derived it, William Baumol of Princeton University and James Tobin of Yale University.

[2]Remember that the category "deposits" includes checking accounts. Many checking accounts pay interest. This turns out not to matter for the purposes of our discussion, however. Suppose bonds pay 10 percent interest and checking accounts pay 5 percent. (Checking accounts must pay less than bonds. Otherwise, everyone would hold all their wealth in checking accounts and none in bonds, because checking accounts are more convenient.) When it comes to choosing whether to hold bonds or money, it is the difference in the interest rates on the two that matters. People are concerned about how much extra interest they will get from holding bonds rather than money. In the example above, we could say that bonds pay 5 percent and money pays 0 percent, which makes our discussion simpler.

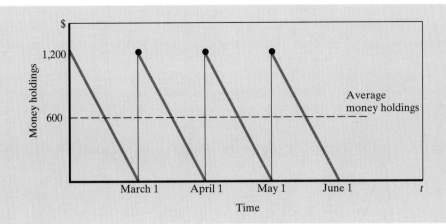

FIGURE 12.2

Jim's Monthly Checking Account Balances: Strategy 1

Jim could decide to deposit his entire paycheck ($1,200) into his checking account at the start of the month and run his balance down to zero by the end of the month. In this case, his average balance would be $600.

MONEY MANAGEMENT AND THE OPTIMAL BALANCE

Given these assumptions, how would a rational person (household) decide how much of monthly income to hold as money and how much to hold as interest-bearing bonds? Suppose Jim decides to deposit his entire paycheck in his checking account. Let's say Jim earns $1,200 per month. The pattern of Jim's bank account balance is illustrated in Figure 12.2. At the beginning of the month, Jim's balance is $1,200. As the month rolls by, Jim draws down his balance, writing checks or withdrawing cash to pay for the things he buys. At the end of the month, Jim's bank account balance is down to zero. Just in time, he receives his next month's paycheck, deposits it, and the process begins again.

One useful statistic we will need to calculate is the *average balance* in Jim's account. Jim spends his money at a constant $40 per day ($40 per day times 30 days per month = $1,200). His average balance is just his starting balance ($1,200) plus his ending balance (0) divided by 2, or ($1,200 + 0)/2 = $600. For the first half of the month Jim has more than his average of $600 on deposit, and for the second half of the month he has less than his average.

Anything wrong with Jim's strategy? Yes. If he follows the plan described, Jim is giving up interest on his funds, interest he could be earning if he held some of his funds in interest-bearing bonds instead of in his checking account. How could he manage his funds to give himself more interest?

Instead of depositing his entire paycheck in his checking account at the beginning of the month, Jim could put half his paycheck into his checking account and buy a bond with the other half. Doing this, he would run out of money in his checking account halfway through the month. At a spending rate of $40 per day, his initial deposit of $600 would last only 15 days. Jim would have to sell his bond halfway through the month and deposit the $600 from the sale of the bond in his checking account to pay his bills during the second half of the month.

Jim's money holdings (checking account balances) if he follows this strategy are shown in Figure 12.3. When he follows the buy-a-$600-bond strategy, Jim reduces the average amount of money in his checking account. Comparing the dashed green lines (old strategy) with the solid green lines (buy-$600-bond strategy), his average bank balance is exactly half of what it was with the first strategy.[3]

The buy-a-$600-bond strategy seems sensible. The object of this strategy was to keep some funds in bonds, where they could earn interest, instead of as "idle"

---

[3]Jim's average balance for the first half of the month is (starting balance + ending balance)/2, or ($600 + 0)/2 = $300. His average for the second half of the month is also $300. His average for the month as a whole is $300.

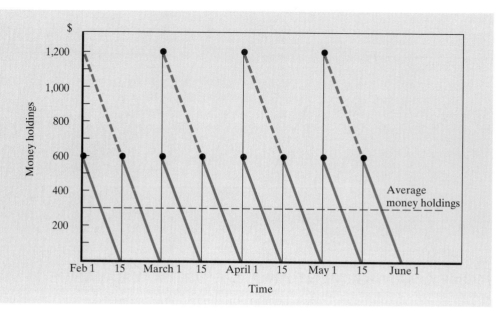

FIGURE 12.3

Jim's Monthly Checking
Account Balances: Strategy 2

Jim could also choose to put
one half of his paycheck into
his checking account and buy
a bond with the other half of
his income. At mid-month,
Jim would sell the bond and
deposit the $600 into his
checking account to pay the
second half of the month's
bills. Following this strategy,
Jim's average money holdings
would be $300.

money. But why stop there? Another possibility would be for Jim to put only $400
into his checking account on the first of the month and buy two $400 bonds. The
$400 in his account will last only 10 days if he spends $40 per day, so after 10 days
he must sell one of the bonds and deposit the $400 from the sale in his checking ac-
count. This will last through the 20th of the month, at which point he must sell the
second bond and deposit the other $400. This strategy lowers Jim's average money
holding (checking account balance) even further, reducing his money holdings to an
average of only $200 per month, with correspondingly higher average holdings of
interest-earning bonds.

You can imagine Jim going even further. Why not hold all wealth in the form of
bonds (where it earns interest) and make transfers from bonds to money every time he
makes a purchase? If selling bonds, transferring funds to checking accounts, and making trips to the bank were without cost, Jim would never hold money for more than an
instant. Each time he needed to pay cash for something or write a check, he would go
to the bank or call the bank, transfer the exact amount of the transaction to his checking account, and either withdraw the cash or write the check to complete the transaction. If he did this constantly, he would squeeze the most interest possible out of his
funds because he would never hold assets that did not earn interest.

In practice, money management of this kind is costly. There are brokerage fees and
other costs to buy or sell bonds, and time must be spent waiting in line at the bank. At
the same time, it is costly to hold assets in non-interest-bearing form, because they lose
potential interest revenue.

We have a trade-off problem of the type that pervades economics. Switching more
often from bonds to money raises the interest revenue Jim earns (because the more
times he switches, the less, on average, he has to hold in his checking account and the
more he can keep in bonds), but this increases his money management costs. Less
switching means more interest revenue lost (because average money holdings are
higher) but lower money management costs (fewer purchases and sales of bonds, less
time spent waiting in bank lines, fewer trips to the bank, and so on).

▶ **The Optimal Balance** There is a level of average money balances that earns Jim the
most profit, taking into account both the interest earned on bonds and the costs paid
for switching from bonds to money. This level is his *optimal balance*.

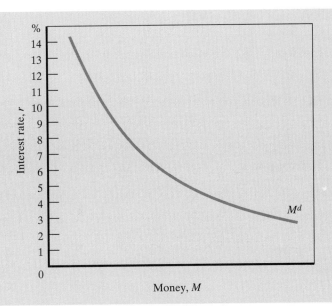

FIGURE 12.4

The Demand Curve for Money Balances

The quantity of money demanded (the amount of money households and firms wish to hold) is a function of the interest rate. Because the interest rate is the opportunity cost of holding money balances, increases in the interest rate will reduce the quantity of money that firms and households want to hold, and decreases in the interest rate will increase the quantity of money that firms and households want to hold.

How does the interest rate affect the number of switches that Jim makes and thus the average money balance he chooses to hold? It is easy to see why an increase in the interest rate lowers the optimal money balance. If the interest rate were only 2 percent, it would not be worthwhile to give up much liquidity by holding bonds instead of cash or checking balances. But if the interest rate were 30 percent, the opportunity cost of holding money instead of bonds would be quite high, and we would expect people to keep most of their funds in bonds and to spend considerable time in managing their money balances. The interest rate represents the opportunity cost of holding money (and therefore not holding bonds, which pay interest). The higher the interest rate, the higher the opportunity cost of holding money, and the less money people will want to hold. This leads us to conclude:

> When interest rates are high, people want to take advantage of the high return on bonds, so they choose to hold very little money.

Appendix B to this chapter provides a detailed example of this principle.

A demand curve for money, with the interest rate representing the "price" of money, would look like the curve labeled M^d in Figure 12.4. At higher interest rates, bonds are much more attractive than money, so people hold less money because they must make a larger sacrifice in interest for each dollar of money they hold. The curve in Figure 12.4 slopes downward, just like an ordinary demand curve for oranges or shoes. There is an inverse relationship between the interest rate and the quantity of money demanded.[4]

---

[4]The theory of money demand presented here assumes that a person knows the exact timing of her or his income and spending. In practice, both have some uncertainty attached to them. For example, some income payments may be unexpectedly delayed a few days or weeks, and some expenditures may arise unexpectedly (such as a plumbing problem). Because people know that this uncertainty exists, they may choose to hold more money than the strict transactions motive would suggest, as a precaution against unanticipated delays in income receipts or unanticipated expenses. This reason for holding money is sometimes called the *precautionary motive.*

THE SPECULATION MOTIVE

A number of theories have been offered to explain why the quantity of money households desire to hold may rise when interest rates fall, and fall when interest rates rise. One involves household expectations and the relationship of interest rates to bond values.

To understand this theory, you need to realize that the market value of most interest-bearing bonds is inversely related to the interest rate. Suppose I bought an 8 percent bond a year ago for $1,000. Now suppose the market interest rate rises to 10 percent. If I offered to sell my bond for $1,000, no one would buy it because anyone can buy a new bond and earn 10 percent in the market rather than 8 percent of my bond. But at some lower selling price, my bond becomes attractive to buyers. This is because a lower price increases the actual yield to the buyer of my bond. Suppose I sell you my bond for $500. Because the bond is paying 8 percent annually on the original $1,000 (that is, $80 per year), it is actually paying you an annual amount that comes to 16 percent of your investment in the bond ($500 × .16 = $80). If you bought that same bond from me for about $800, it would effectively pay you 10 percent interest ($800 × .10 = $80). The point here is simple:

> When market interest rates fall, bond values rise; when market interest rates rise, bond values fall.

Now consider my desire to hold money balances rather than bonds. If market interest rates are higher than normal, I may expect them to come down in the future. If and when interest rates fall, the bonds that I bought when they were high will increase in value. When interest rates are high, the opportunity cost of holding cash balances is high and there is a **speculation motive** for holding bonds in lieu of cash. I am "speculating" that interest rates will fall in the future.

Similarly, when market interest rates are lower than normal, I may expect them to rise in the future. Rising interest rates will bring about a decline in the value of bonds. Thus, when interest rates are low, it is a good time to be holding money and not bonds. When interest rates are low, not only is the opportunity cost of holding cash balances low, but there is also a speculative motive for holding a larger amount of money. Why should I put money into bonds now when I expect interest rates to rise in the future? (For more on the interaction between the bond market and the money market, see Application Box "The Bond Market, the Money Market, and the Speculation Motive.")

speculation motive *One reason for holding bonds instead of money: Because the market value of interest-bearing bonds is inversely related to the interest rate, investors may wish to hold bonds when interest rates are high with the hope of selling them when interest rates fall.*

THE PRIMARY MOTIVE FOR HOLDING CASH IS TO ENGAGE IN TRANSACTIONS. MOST PEOPLE WALK AROUND WITH SOME MONEY IN THEIR POCKETS AND KEEP SOME MONEY IN THEIR CHECKING ACCOUNTS, BUT USUALLY NOT THOUSANDS OF DOLLARS. THE COST OF HOLDING MONEY IS FORGONE INTEREST.

THE BOND MARKET, THE MONEY MARKET, AND THE SPECULATION MOTIVE

People are often confused when business-page headlines read "Bonds Fall, Pushing up Interest Rates" or "Bonds Rise, Driving Yields Down." Nonetheless, it is true that the current market price or value of all fixed-rate bonds, whether U.S. Treasury Bonds or German corporate bonds, fall in value when interest rates rise, and rise in value when interest rates fall.

To see why, consider Heidi, a German house painter who bought for $1,000 a 10-year German government bond with a fixed rate of 10 percent. By buying that bond, Heidi has agreed to accept a return on her money of 10 percent for 10 years. This means a check for $100 every year with a promise that her $1,000 will be returned at the end of 10 years.

Though the German government has no obligation to pay the $1,000 back before the bond matures in 10 years, Heidi may need the money before 10 years is up. To get her money back earlier, she can call a broker and sell the bond. In fact, there is a huge market for existing bonds, and existing bond prices are posted in the newspapers every day. To sell the bond, the broker has to find a buyer, and the amount that a buyer would be willing to pay depends on the current rate of interest.

Suppose Heidi wants to sell her bond two years after she purchased it. The bond still has eight years left to maturity. Assume that the Bundesbank (the German central bank) has pushed

rates for eight-year bonds to 12 percent. Someone who paid $1,000 for Heidi's bond today would be getting only $100 (10 percent) interest per year. The same person could be getting interest of $120 per year, or 12 percent, by buying a newly issued $1,000 bond. The result: Heidi's broker will not be able to sell her bond for $1,000. Instead, Heidi will have to take a loss because her bond's value has fallen.

Do bond values really fall in the real world? Absolutely. When the Federal Reserve raised U.S. interest rates in 1994, the value of outstanding bonds traded in the market fell substantially. Similarly, during Mexico's peso crises in 1995, Mexican interest rates shot up sharply, and Mexican government bonds lost a lot of their value. (U.S. holders of Mexican securities got hit even harder because the value of the peso fell too—but that's covered later in the chapter on open-market macroeconomics.)

Another way to see the same connection between the bond market and the money market is to think of a case in which the demand for bonds increases. Suppose that because of excess demand for bonds in Germany, the value of Heidi's bond goes up to $1,100. Someone who is willing to pay $1,100 for Heidi's bond *must reveal that he is willing to accept an annual yield of less than 10 percent*. After all, $100 is only 9.1 percent of $1,100. In addition, the buyer who pays $1,100 will get back only $1,000 when the bond matures.

Higher bond prices mean the interest rate bond buyers are willing to accept is lower than before! If buyers are willing to accept 9 percent on old bonds, they will accept 9 percent on new bonds.

Bond prices and interest rates are two sides of the same coin. A "rally" in the bond market means bond prices have gone up and interest rates, or bond "yields," have gone down. Similarly, when the bond market "drops," interest rates, or yields, have gone up.

These effects have important implications for money demand. Assume households choose only between holding their assets as money (which does not earn interest) or as bonds (which do earn interest). If households and firms believe interest rates are historically high and they are likely to fall, it is a *good* time to hold bonds. Why? Because a drop in rates means bond values will rise, in a sense earning bondholders a bonus. When interest rates are high and expected to fall, demand for bonds is likely to be high and money demand is likely to be low. Similarly, if people see interest rates as low and expect them to rise, it is *not* a good time to be holding bonds. Why? Because if interest rates rise, bond holders suffer losses. When interest rates are low, money demand is likely to be high and the demand for bonds is likely to be low. Thus, we have another reason for the negative relationship between interest rates and money demand. As we mentioned in the text, this is the *speculation motive* for holding money.

For more on the bond market, the money market, and the relationships between them, see the Case and Fair Web page at **http://www.prenhall.com/casefair.**

THE TOTAL DEMAND FOR MONEY

So far we have talked only about household demand for checking account balances. But the total quantity of money demanded in the economy is the sum of the demand for checking account balances *and cash* by both households *and firms*.

The trade-off for firms is the same as it was for Jim. Like households, firms must manage their money. They have payrolls to meet and purchases to make; they receive cash and checks from sales; and many firms that deal with the public must make change—they need cash in the cash register. Thus, just like Jim, firms need money to engage in ordinary transactions.

But firms as well as households can hold their assets in interest-earning form. Firms manage their assets just as households do, keeping some in cash, some in their checking accounts, and some in bonds. A higher interest rate raises the opportunity cost of money for firms as well as for households and thus reduces the demand for money.

The same trade-off holds for cash. We all walk around with some money in our pockets, but not thousands of dollars, for routine transactions. We carry, on average, about what we think we will need. Why not more? Because there are costs—risks of being robbed and forgone interest.

> At any given moment, there is a demand for money—for cash and checking account balances. Although households and firms need to hold balances for everyday transactions, their demand has a limit. For both households and firms, the quantity of money demanded at any moment depends on the opportunity cost of holding money, a cost determined by the interest rate.

TRANSACTIONS VOLUME AND THE PRICE LEVEL

The money demand curve in Figure 12.4 is a function of the interest rate. There are other factors besides the interest rate that influence total desired money holdings. One is the dollar value of transactions made during a given period of time.

Suppose Jim's income were to double. Instead of making $1,200 in purchases each month, he makes $2,400 in purchases. He needs to hold more money. Why? Simple: To buy more things, he needs more money.

What is true for Jim is true for the economy as a whole. The total demand for money in the economy depends on the total dollar volume of transactions made. The total dollar volume of transactions in the economy, in turn, depends on two things: the total *number* of transactions and the average transaction *amount*. Although there are no data on the actual number of transactions in the economy, a reasonable indicator is likely to be aggregate output (income) (Y). A rise in aggregate output—real GDP—means there is more economic activity. Firms are producing and selling more output, more people are on payrolls, and household incomes are higher. In short, there are more transactions, and firms and households together will hold more money when they are engaging in more transactions. Thus, an increase in aggregate output (income) will increase the demand for money.

Figure 12.5 shows a shift of the money demand curve resulting from an increase in Y:

> For a given interest rate, a higher level of output means an increase in the *number* of transactions and more demand for money. The money demand curve shifts to the right when Y rises. Similarly, a decrease in Y means a decrease in the number of transactions and a lower demand for money. The money demand curve shifts to the left when Y falls.

The amount of money needed by firms and households to facilitate their day-to-day transactions also depends on the average *dollar amount* of each transaction. In turn, the average amount of each transaction depends on prices, or rather, on the *price level*. If all prices, including the price of labor (the wage rate) were to double, firms and households would need more money balances to carry out their day-to-day transactions—each transaction would require twice as much money. If the price of your lunch increases from $3.50 to $7.00, you will begin carrying more cash. If your

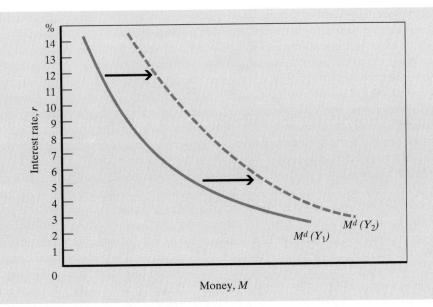

An increase in Y means there is more economic activity. Firms are producing and selling more, and households are earning more income and buying more. There are more transactions, for which money is needed. As a result, both firms and households are likely to increase their holdings of money balances at a given interest rate.

end-of-the-month bills are twice as high as they used to be, you will keep more money in your checking account.

> Increases in the price level shift the money demand curve to the right, and decreases in the price level shift the money demand curve to the left. Even though the number of transactions may not have changed, the quantity of money needed to engage in them has.

THE DETERMINANTS OF MONEY DEMAND: REVIEW

Table 12.1 summarizes everything we have said about the demand for money. First, because the interest rate (r) is the opportunity cost of holding money balances for both firms and households: increases in the interest rate are likely to decrease the quantity of money demanded; decreases in the interest rate will increase the quantity of money demanded. Thus, the quantity of money demanded is a negative function of the interest rate.

The demand for money also depends on the dollar volume of transactions in a given period. The dollar volume of transactions depends on both aggregate output (income), Y, and the price level, P. The relationship of money demand to Y and the relationship of money demand to P are both positive. Increases in Y or in P will shift the money demand curve to the right; decreases in Y or P will shift the money demand curve to the left.

➤ **Some Common Pitfalls** We need to consider several pitfalls in thinking about money demand. First, when we spoke in earlier chapters about the demand for goods and

TABLE 12.1 DETERMINANTS OF MONEY DEMAND

1. The interest rate: r (negative effect)
2. The dollar volume of transactions (positive effect)
   a. Aggregate output (income): Y (positive effect)
   b. The price level: P (positive effect)

services, we were speaking of demand as a *flow variable*—something measured over a period of time. If you say your demand for coffee is three cups, you need to specify whether you are talking about three cups per hour, three cups per day, or three cups per week. In macroeconomics, consumption and saving are flow variables. We consume and save continuously, but we express consumption and saving in time-period terms, such as $600 *per month*.

Money demand is *not* a flow measure. Rather it is a *stock variable*, measured at a given point in time. It answers the question: How much money do firms and households desire to hold at a specific point in time, given the current interest rate, volume of economic activity, and price level?

Second, many people think of money demand and saving as roughly the same—they are not. Say that in a given year a household had income of $50,000 and expenses of $47,000. It saved $3,000 during the year. At the beginning of the year the household had no debt and $100,000 in assets. Because the household saved $3,000 during the year, it has $103,000 in assets at the end of the year. Some of the $103,000 is held in stocks, some in bonds, some in other forms of securities, and some in money. How much the household chooses to hold in the form of money is its demand for money. Depending on the interest rate and the household's transactions, the amount of the $103,000 that it chooses to hold in the form of money could be anywhere from a few hundred dollars to many thousands. How much of its assets a household holds in the form of money is different from how much of its income it spends during the year.

Finally, recall the difference between a shift in a demand curve and a movement along the curve. The money demand curve in Figure 12.4 shows optimal money balances as a function of the interest rate *ceteris paribus*, all else equal. Changes in the interest rate cause movements *along* the curve—*changes in the quantity of money demanded*. Changes in real GDP (Y) or in the price level (P) cause shifts of the curve as shown in Figure 12.5—*changes in demand*.

THE EQUILIBRIUM INTEREST RATE

We are now in a position to consider one of the key questions in macroeconomics: How is the interest rate determined in the economy?

Financial markets (what we call the money market) work very well in the United States. Almost all financial markets clear—that is, almost all reach an equilibrium where quantity demanded equals quantity supplied. In the money market,

> The point at which the quantity of money demanded equals the quantity of money supplied determines the equilibrium interest rate in the economy.

Sounds simple, but it requires elaboration.

SUPPLY AND DEMAND IN THE MONEY MARKET

We saw in chapter 11 that the Fed controls the money supply through its manipulation of the amount of reserves in the economy. Because we are assuming that the Fed's money supply behavior does not depend on the interest rate, the money supply curve is a vertical line. (Review Figure 11.5.) In other words, we are assuming that the Fed uses its three tools (the required reserve ratio, the discount rate, and open market operations) to achieve its fixed target for the money supply.

Figure 12.6 superimposes the vertical money supply curve on the downward-sloping money demand curve. Only at interest rate r^* is the quantity of money in circulation (the money supply) equal to the quantity of money demanded. To understand why r^* is an equilibrium, we need to ask what adjustments would take place if the interest rate were not r^*.

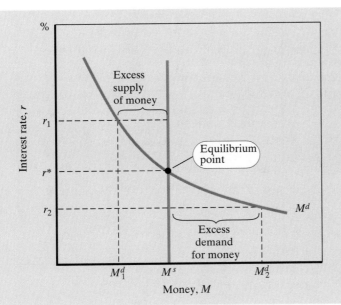

FIGURE 12.6

Adjustments in the
Money Market

Equilibrium exists in the money
market when the supply of
money is equal to the demand
for money: $M^d = M^s$. At r_1, the
quantity of money supplied
exceeds the quantity of money
demanded, and the interest rate
will fall. At r_2, the quantity
demanded exceeds the quantity
supplied, and the interest rate
will rise. Only at r^* is
equilibrium achieved.

To understand the adjustment mechanism, keep in mind that borrowing and lending is a continuous process. The Treasury sells U.S. government securities (bonds) more or less continuously to finance the deficit. When it does, it is borrowing, and must pay interest to attract bond buyers. Buyers of government bonds are, in essence, lending money to the government, just as buyers of corporate bonds are lending money to corporations that wish to finance investment projects.

Consider first r_1 in Figure 12.6. At r_1, the quantity of money demanded is M_1^d, and the quantity of money supplied exceeds the quantity of money demanded. This means there is more money in circulation than households and firms want to hold. At r_1, firms and households will attempt to reduce their money holdings by buying bonds. When there is money in circulation looking for a way to earn interest—when demand for bonds is high—those looking to borrow money by selling bonds will find that they can do so at a lower interest rate.

If the interest rate is initially high enough to create an excess supply of money, the interest rate will immediately fall, discouraging people from moving out of money and into bonds.

Now consider r_2, where the quantity of money demanded (M_2^d) exceeds the supply of money currently in circulation—households and firms do not have enough money on hand to facilitate ordinary transactions. They will try to adjust their holdings by shifting assets out of bonds and into their checking accounts. At the same time, the continuous flow of new bonds being issued must also be absorbed. The Treasury and corporations can sell bonds in an environment where people are adjusting their asset holdings to shift *out* of bonds only by offering a higher interest rate to the people who buy them.

If the interest rate is initially low enough to create an excess demand for money, the interest rate will immediately rise, discouraging people from moving out of bonds and into money.

FIGURE 12.7

The Effect of an Increase in the Supply of Money on the Interest Rate

An increase in the supply of money from M_0^s to M_1^s lowers the rate of interest from 14 percent to 7 percent.

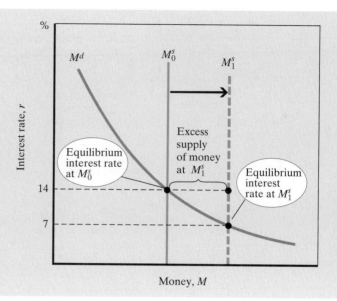

CHANGING THE MONEY SUPPLY TO AFFECT THE INTEREST RATE

With an understanding of equilibrium in the money market, we can now see how the Federal Reserve can affect the interest rate. Suppose the current interest rate is 14 percent and the Fed wants to reduce the interest rate. To do so, it would expand the money supply. Figure 12.7 shows how such an expansion would work. To expand M^s, the Fed can reduce the reserve requirement, cut the discount rate, or buy U.S. government securities on the open market. All of these practices expand the quantity of reserves in the system. Banks can make more loans, and the money supply expands. (Review chapter 11 if you are unsure why.) In Figure 12.7, the initial money supply curve, M_0^s, shifts to the right, to M_1^s.

At the 14 percent interest rate there is an excess supply of money. This immediately puts downward pressure on the interest rate as households and firms try to buy bonds with their money to earn that high interest rate. As this happens, the interest rate falls, and it will continue to fall until it reaches the new equilibrium interest rate of 7 percent. At this point, $M_1^s = M^d$, and the market is in equilibrium.

If the Fed wanted to drive the interest rate *up*, it would contract the money supply. It could do so by increasing the reserve requirement, by raising the discount rate, or by selling U.S. government securities in the open market. Whichever tool the Fed chooses, the result would be lower reserves and a lower supply of money. M_0^s in Figure 12.7 would shift to the left, and the equilibrium interest rate would rise. (As an exercise, draw a graph of this situation.)

INCREASES IN Y AND SHIFTS IN THE MONEY DEMAND CURVE

Changes in the supply of money are not the only factors that influence the equilibrium interest rate. Shifts in money demand can do the same thing.

Recall that the demand for money depends on both the interest rate and the volume of transactions. As a rough measure of the volume of transactions, we use Y, the level of aggregate output (income). Remember that the relationship between money demand and Y is positive—increases in Y mean a higher level of real economic activity. More is being produced, income is higher, and there are more transactions in the economy.

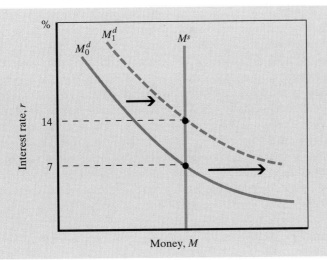

FIGURE 12.8

The Effect of an Increase in Income on the Interest Rate

An increase in aggregate output (income) shifts the money demand curve from M_0^d to M_1^d, which raises the equilibrium interest rate from 7 percent to 14 percent.

Consequently, the demand for money on the part of firms and households in aggregate is higher.

> An increase in Y shifts the money demand curve to the right.

Figure 12.8 illustrates such a shift. Y increases, causing money demand to shift from M_0^d to M_1^d. The result is an increase in the equilibrium level of the interest rate from 7 percent to 14 percent. A decrease in Y would shift M^d to the left, and the equilibrium interest rate would fall.

The money demand curve also shifts when the price level changes. If the price level rises, the money demand curve shifts to the right, because people need more money to engage in their day-to-day transactions. With the quantity of money supplied unchanged, however, the interest rate must rise to reduce the quantity of money demanded to the unchanged quantity of money supplied—a movement *along* the money demand curve.

> An increase in the price level is like an increase in Y in that both events increase the demand for money. The result is an increase in the equilibrium interest rate.

If the price level *falls*, the money demand curve shifts to the left, because people need less money for their transactions. But with the quantity of money supplied unchanged, the interest rate must fall to increase the quantity of money demanded to the unchanged quantity of money supplied.

> A decrease in the price level leads to a decrease in the equilibrium interest rate.

We explore this relationship in more detail in chapter 14.

LOOKING AHEAD: THE FED AND MONETARY POLICY

We now know that the Fed can change the interest rate by changing the quantity of money supplied. If the Fed increases the quantity of money, the interest rate falls; if it decreases the quantity of money, the interest rate rises.

But we have not yet said *why* the Fed might want to change the interest rate or what happens to the economy when the interest rate changes. We have hinted at why:

A low interest rate stimulates spending, particularly investment; a high interest rate reduces spending. By changing the interest rate the Fed can change aggregate output (income). In the next chapter, we will combine our discussions of the goods and money markets and discuss how the interest rate affects the equilibrium level of aggregate output (income) (Y) in the goods market.

The Fed's use of its power to influence events in the goods market, as well as in the money market, is the center of the government's monetary policy. When the Fed moves to contract the money supply in an effort to restrain the economy, economists call it a **tight monetary policy**. Conversely, when the Fed stimulates the economy by expanding the money supply, it has an **easy monetary policy**. The Fed moved aggressively to expand the money supply and lower interest rates in 1975, in 1982, and early in 1991. These easy money policies contributed to economic recovery from the recessions of those years. Tight money policies caused aggregate spending to decline in 1974 and 1981, contributing to the recessions of those years. During the summer of 1981, tight money helped to push some key interest rates above 20 percent!

From the end of the recession in 1991 through 1997, the U.S. economy experienced steady growth with no signs of inflation. During the spring of 1994, the Fed raised rates to slow an accelerating economy because of inflation worries. During 1995, the economy slowed down but growth resumed in 1996 and 1997. By 1997, the economy had grown so much that the Fed was worried about a labor shortage. A labor shortage could trigger inflation if wages rise. But by the end of 1997, the Fed had not acted to raise rates.

We will discuss the way in which the economy affects the Fed's behavior in chapter 16. In that chapter, we'll also discuss some of the Fed's recent policies in more detail and examine the effects of these policies on the economy.

tight monetary policy *Fed policies that contract the money supply in an effort to restrain the economy.*

easy monetary policy *Fed policies that expand the money supply in an effort to stimulate the economy.*

SUMMARY

1. *Interest* is the fee a borrower pays to a lender for the use of his or her funds. The *interest rate* is the annual interest payment on a loan expressed as a percentage of the loan; it is equal to the amount of interest received per year divided by the amount of the loan. Although there are many different interest rates in the United States, we assume there is only one interest rate in the economy. This simplifies our analysis but still provides a tool for understanding how the various parts of the macroeconomy relate to each other.

THE DEMAND FOR MONEY

2. The demand for money depends negatively on the interest rate. The higher the interest rate, the higher the opportunity cost (more interest forgone) from holding money, and the less money people will want to hold. An increase in the interest rate reduces the demand for money, and the money demand curve slopes downward.

3. The volume of transactions in the economy affects money demand. The total dollar volume of transactions depends on both the total number of transactions and the average transaction amount.

4. A reasonable measure of the number of transactions in the economy is aggregate output (income) (Y). When Y rises, there is more economic activity, more is being produced and sold, and more people are on payrolls—there are more transactions in the economy. An increase in Y causes the money demand curve to shift to the right. This follows because households and firms need more money when they are engaging in more transactions. A decrease in Y causes the money demand curve to shift left.

5. Changes in the price level affect the average dollar amount of each transaction. *Increases* in the price level will increase the demand for money (shift the money demand curve to the right) because households and firms will need more money for their expenditures. *Decreases* in the price level will decrease the demand for money (shift the money demand curve to the left).

THE EQUILIBRIUM INTEREST RATE

6. The point at which the quantity of money supplied equals the quantity of money demanded determines the equilibrium interest rate in the economy. An excess supply of

money will cause households and firms to buy more bonds, driving the interest rate down. An excess demand for money will cause households and firms to move out of bonds, driving the interest rate up.

7. The Fed can affect the equilibrium interest rate by changing the supply of money using one of its three tools—the required reserve ratio, the discount rate, or open market operations.

8. An increase in the price level is like an increase in Y in that both events cause an increase in money demand. The result

is an increase in the equilibrium interest rate. A decrease in the price level leads to reduced money demand and a decrease in the equilibrium interest rate.

9. *Tight monetary policy* refers to Fed policies that contract the money supply in an effort to restrain the economy. *Easy monetary policy* refers to Fed policies that expand the money supply in an effort to stimulate the economy. The Fed chooses between these two types of policies for different reasons at different times.

REVIEW TERMS AND CONCEPTS

easy monetary policy, 264
interest, 251
interest rate, 251

monetary policy, 251
nonsynchronization of income and
    spending, 252

speculation motive, 256
tight monetary policy, 264
transaction motive, 252

PROBLEM SET

1. During the fall of 1997, a debate was going on among the members of the Board of Governors of the Federal Reserve. One view: The economy was growing too rapidly and labor was in such short supply that wages were bound to rise, pushing up prices with them. This view argued for the Fed to make a "preemptive strike" against inflation by raising interest rates. The alternative view: The economic turmoil taking place in Asia and a downturn in the stock market in late 1997 would slow the economy enough and a preemptive strike was not needed. How explicitly does the Fed go about raising and lowering rates? In what ways would raising rates slow the economy?

2. At the beginning of 1998, interest rates in Japan were very low. However, households believed interest rates were likely to rise eventually. This implies that the quantity of money demanded in Japan at the beginning of 1998 was quite high. Using the concepts of speculative motive and transaction motive for money, explain why.

3. During the fourth quarter of 1993, real GDP in the United States grew at an annual rate of over 7 percent. During 1994, the economy continued to expand with modest inflation (Y rose at a rate of 4 percent and P increased about 3 percent). At the beginning of 1994, the prime interest rate (the interest rate that banks offer their best, least risky customers) stood at 6 percent, where it remained for over a year. By the beginning of 1995, the prime rate had increased to over 8.5 percent.
   a. Using money supply and money demand curves, show the effects of the increase in Y and P on interest rates assuming *no change* in the money supply.

   b. On a separate graph, show that the interest rate can rise even if the Federal Reserve expands the money supply as long as it does so more slowly than money demand is increasing.

4. Illustrate the following situations using supply and demand curves for money:
   a. The Fed buys bonds in the open market during a recession.
   b. During a period of rapid inflation, the Federal Reserve increases the reserve requirement.
   c. The Fed acts to hold interest rates constant during a period of high inflation.
   d. During a period of no growth in GDP and zero inflation, the Fed lowers the discount rate.
   e. During a period of rapid real growth of GDP, the Fed acts to increase the reserve requirement.

5. During a recession, interest rates may fall even if the Fed takes no action to expand the money supply. Why? Use a graph to explain.

6. During the summer of 1997, the Congress and the president agreed on a budget package to balance the federal budget. The "deal," signed into law by President Clinton in August as the Taxpayer Relief Act of 1997, contained substantial tax cuts and expenditure reductions. The tax reductions were scheduled to take effect immediately, however, while the expenditure cuts mostly come in the years 1999 to 2002. Thus, in 1998, the package was seen by economists to be mildly expansionary. If the result is an increase in the growth of real output/income, what would you expect to happen to interest rates if the Fed holds the money supply (or the rate of growth of the money supply)

constant? What would the Fed do if it wanted to raise interest rates? What if it wanted to lower interest rates? Illustrate with graphs.

7. The demand for money in a country is given by

$$M^d = 10,000 - 10,000r + Y,$$

where M^d is money demand in dollars, r is the interest rate (a 10 percent interest rate means $r = 0.1$), and Y is national income. Assume Y is initially 5,000.

a. Graph the amount of money demanded (on the horizontal axis) against the interest rate (on the vertical axis).

b. Suppose the money supply (M^s) is set by the Central Bank at $10,000. On the same graph you drew for part a., add the money supply curve. What is the equilibrium rate of interest? Explain how you arrived at your answer.

c. Suppose income rises from $Y = 5,000$ to $Y = 7,500$. What happens to the money demand curve you drew in part a? Draw the new curve, if there is one. What happens to the equilibrium interest rate if the Central Bank doesn't change the supply of money?

d. If the Central Bank wants to keep the equilibrium interest rate at the same value as it was in part b., by how much should it increase or decrease the supply of money, given the new level of national income?

e. Suppose the shift in part b. has occurred, and the money supply remains at $10,000, but there is no observed change in the interest rate. What might have happened that could explain this?

TAKE IT TO THE NET

We invite you to visit the Case and Fair page on the Prentice Hall Web site:

http://www.prenhall.com/casefair

for this chapter's World Wide Web exercise.

APPENDIX A TO CHAPTER 12

THE VARIOUS INTEREST RATES IN THE U.S. ECONOMY

Although there are many different interest rates in the economy, they tend to move up or down with one another. Here, we discuss some of their differences. We will first discuss the relationship between interest rates on securities with different *maturities*, or terms. We then discuss briefly some of the main interest rates in the U.S. economy.

THE TERM STRUCTURE OF INTEREST RATES

The *term structure of interest rates* is the relationship between the interest rates offered on securities of different maturities. The key here is understanding things like: How are these different rates related? Does a two-year security (an IOU that promises to repay principal, plus interest, after two years) pay a lower annual rate than a one-year security (an IOU to be repaid, with interest, after one year)? What happens to the rate of interest offered on one-year securities if the rate of interest on two-year securities increases?

Assume you want to invest some money for two years and at the end of the two years you want it back. Assume you want to buy government securities. For this analysis, we restrict your choices to two: (1) You can buy a two-year security today and hold it for two years, at which time you cash it in (we will assume that the interest rate on the two-year security is 9 percent per year), or (2) you can buy a one-year security today. At the end of one year, you must cash this security in; you can then buy another one-year security. At the end of the second year, you will cash in the second security. Assume the interest rate on the first one-year security is 8 percent.

Which would you prefer? Currently, you don't have enough data to answer this question. To consider choice 2 sensibly, you need to know the interest rate on the one-year security that you intend to buy in the second year. This rate will not be known until the second year. All you know now is the rate on the two-year security and the rate on the current one-year security. To decide what to do, you must form an *expectation* of the rate on the one-year security a year from now. If you expect the one-year rate (8 percent) to remain the same in the second year, you should buy the two-year security. You would earn 9 percent per year on the two-year security but only 8 percent per year on the two one-year securities. If you expect the one-year rate to rise to 12 percent a year from now, you should make the second choice. You would earn 8 percent in the first year, and you expect to earn 12 percent in the second year. The expected rate of return over the two years is about 10 percent, which is better than the 9 percent you can get on the two-year security. If you expected the one-year rate a year from now to be 10 percent, it would not matter very much which of the two choices you made. The rate of return over the two-year period would be roughly 9 percent for both choices.

We now alter the focus of our discussion to get to the topic we are really interested in—how the two-year rate is determined. Assume the one-year rate has been set by the Fed and it is 8 percent. Also assume that people expect the one-year rate a year from now to be 10 percent. What is the two-year rate? According to a theory called the *expectations theory of the term structure of interest rates*, the two-year rate is equal to the average of the current one-year rate and the one-year rate expected a year from now. In this example, the two-year rate would be 9 percent (the average of 8 percent and 10 percent).

If the two-year rate were lower than the average of the two one-year rates, people would not be indifferent as to which security they held. They would want to hold only the short-term, one-year securities. To find a buyer for a two-year security, the seller would be forced to increase the interest rate it offers on the two-year security until it is equal to the average of the current one-year rate and the expected one-year rate for next year. The interest rate on the two-year security will continue to rise until people are once again indifferent between one two-year security and two one-year securities.[1]

Let's now return to Fed behavior. We know the Fed can affect the short-term interest rate by changing the money supply. But does it also affect long-term interest rates? The answer is "somewhat." Because the two-year rate is an average of the current one-year rate and the expected one-year rate a year from now, the Fed influences the two-year rate to the extent that it influences the current one-year rate. The same holds for three-year rates and beyond. The current short-term rate is a means by which the Fed can influence longer-term rates.

In addition, Fed behavior may directly affect people's expectations of the future short-term rates, which will then affect long-term rates. If the chair of the Federal Reserve testifies before Congress that he or she is thinking about raising short-term interest rates, people's expectations of

---

[1]For longer terms, additional future rates must be averaged in. For a three-year security, for example, the expected one-year rate a year from now and the expected one-year rate two years from now are added to the current one-year rate and averaged.

higher future short-term interest rates are likely to increase. These expectations will then be reflected in current long-term interest rates.

TYPES OF INTEREST RATES

The following are some widely followed interest rates in the United States.

Three-Month Treasury Bill Rate

Government securities that mature in less than a year are called *Treasury bills*, or sometimes *T bills*. The interest rate on three-month Treasury bills is probably the most widely followed short-term interest rate.

Government Bond Rate

Government securities with terms of one year or more are called *government bonds*. There are 1-year bonds, 2-year bonds, and so on up to 30-year bonds. Bonds of different terms have different interest rates. The relationship among the interest rates on the various maturities is the term structure of interest rates that we discussed in the first part of this appendix.

Federal Funds Rate

Banks borrow not only from the Fed but also from each other. If one bank has excess reserves, it can lend some of those reserves to other banks through the federal funds market. The interest rate in this market is called the *federal funds rate*—the rate banks are charged to borrow reserves from other banks.

The federal funds market is really a desk in New York City. From all over the country, banks with excess reserves to lend and banks in need of reserves call the desk and negotiate a rate of interest. Account balances with the Fed are changed for the period of the loan without any physical movement of money.

This borrowing and lending, which takes place near the close of each working day, is generally for one day ("overnight"), so the federal funds rate is a one-day rate. It is the rate that the Fed controls most closely through its open market operations.

Commercial Paper Rate

Firms have several alternatives for raising funds. They can sell stocks, issue bonds, or borrow from a bank. Large firms can also borrow directly from the public by issuing "commercial paper," which are essentially short-term corporate IOUs that offer a designated rate of interest. The interest rate offered on commercial paper depends on the financial condition of the firm and the maturity date of the IOU.

Prime Rate

Banks charge different interest rates to different customers. You would expect to pay a higher interest rate for a car loan than General Motors would pay for a $1 million loan to finance investment. Also, you would pay more interest for an unsecured loan, a "personal" loan, than for one that was secured by some asset, such as a house or car, to be used as collateral.

The *prime rate* is a benchmark that banks often use in quoting interest rates to their customers. A very low risk corporation might be able to borrow at (or even below) the prime rate. A less well known firm might be quoted a rate of "prime plus three-fourths," which means that if the prime rate is say, 10 percent, the firm would have to pay interest of 10.75 percent. The prime rate depends on the cost of funds to the bank, it moves up and down with changes in the economy.

AAA Corporate Bond Rate

Corporations finance much of their investment by selling bonds to the public. Corporate bonds are classified by various bond dealers according to their risk. Bonds issued by General Motors are in less risk of default than bonds issued by a new, risky biotech research firm. Bonds differ from commercial paper in one important way: Bonds have a longer maturity.

Bonds are graded in much the same way students are. The highest grade is AAA, the next highest AA, and so on. The interest rate on bonds rated AAA is the *triple A corporate bond rate*, the rate that the least risky firms pay on the bonds that they issue.

PROBLEM SET

1. The following table gives three key U.S. interest rates in 1980 and again in April 1993:

	1980	1993
Three-month U.S. government bills	11.39%	2.92%
Long-term U.S. government bonds	10.81%	6.85%
Prime rate	15.26%	6.00%

Can you give an explanation for the extreme differences that you see? Specifically, comment on: (1) the fact that rates in 1980 were much higher than in 1993, and (2) the long-term rate was higher than the short-term rate in 1993 but lower in 1980.

APPENDIX B TO CHAPTER 12

THE DEMAND FOR MONEY: A NUMERICAL EXAMPLE

This appendix presents a numerical example showing how optimal money management behavior can be derived.

We have seen that the interest rate represents the opportunity cost of holding funds in non-interest-bearing checking accounts (as opposed to bonds, which yield interest). We have also seen that there are costs involved in switching from bonds to money. Given these costs, our objective is to determine the optimum amount of money for an individual to hold. The optimal average level of money holdings is the amount that maximizes the profits from money management. Interest is earned on average bond holdings, but the cost per switch multiplied by the number of switches must be subtracted from interest revenue to obtain the net profit from money management.

Suppose the interest rate is .05 (5 percent), it costs $2 each time a bond is sold,[1] and the proceeds from the sale are deposited in one's checking account. Suppose also that the individual's income is $1,200 and that this income is spent evenly throughout the period. This situation is depicted in the top half of Table 12B.1. The optimum value for average money holdings is the value that achieves the largest possible profit in column 6 of the table. When the interest rate is 5 percent, the optimum average money holdings are $150 (which means the individual makes three switches from bonds to money).

In the bottom half of Table 12B.1, the same calculations are performed for an interest rate of 3 percent rather than 5 percent. In this case, the optimum average money holding is $200 (which means the person/household makes two switches from bonds to money rather than three). The lower interest rate has led to an increase in the optimum average money holdings. Under the assumption that people behave optimally, the demand for money is a negative function of the interest rate: The lower the rate, the more money on average is held, and the higher the rate, the less money on average is held.

---

[1]In this example we will assume that the $2 cost does not apply to the original purchase of bonds.

TABLE 12B.1   OPTIMUM MONEY HOLDINGS

1 NUMBER OF SWITCHES[1]	2 AVERAGE MONEY HOLDINGS[2]	3 AVERAGE BOND HOLDINGS[3]	4 INTEREST EARNED[4]	5 COST OF SWITCHING[5]	6 NET PROFIT[6]
		r = 5 percent			
0	$600.00	$ 0.00	$ 0.00	$0.00	$ 0.00
1	300.00	300.00	15.00	2.00	13.00
2	200.00	400.00	20.00	4.00	16.00
3	150.00*	450.00	22.50	6.00	16.50
4	120.00	480.00	24.00	8.00	16.00

Assumptions: Interest rate $r = 0.05$. Cost of switching from bonds into money equals $2 per transaction.

		r = 3 percent			
0	$600.00	$ 0.00	$ 0.00	$0.00	$ 0.00
1	300.00	300.00	9.00	2.00	7.00
2	200.00*	400.00	12.00	4.00	8.00
3	150.00	450.00	13.50	6.00	7.50
4	120.00	480.00	14.40	8.00	6.40

Assumptions: Interest rate $r = 0.03$. Cost of switching from bonds into money equals $2 per transaction.

---

*Optimum money holdings.   [1]That is, the number of times you sell a bond.   [2]Calculated as 600/(col. 1 + 1).   [3]Calculated as 600 – col. 2.
[4]Calculated as r × col. 3, where r is the interest rate.   [5]Calculated as t × col. 1, where t is the cost per switch ($2).   [6]Calculated as col. 4 – col. 5.

PROBLEM SET

1. Sherman Peabody earns a monthly salary of $1,500, which he receives at the beginning of each month. He spends the entire amount each month, at the rate of $50 per day. (Assume 30 days in a month.) The interest rate paid on bonds is 10 percent per month. It costs $4 every time Peabody sells a bond.
   a. Describe briefly how Mr. Peabody should decide how much money to hold.
   b. Calculate Peabody's optimal money holdings. (*Hint:* It may help to formulate a table such as the one in this appendix. You can round to the nearest $.50, and you need to consider only average money holdings of more than $100.)
   c. Suppose the interest rate rises to 15 percent. Find Peabody's optimal money holdings at this new interest rate. What would happen if the interest rate increases to 20 percent?
   d. Graph your answers to b. and c. with the interest rate on the vertical axis and the amount of money demanded on the horizontal axis. Explain why your graph slopes downward.

LOCAL CURRENCIES: A DO-IT-YOURSELF GUIDE TO MAKING MONEY

When governments finance spending by printing money, economists call it *seigniorage*. If you were to do the same thing it would be called counterfeiting, right? Not necessarily. It depends on how you do it.

In Unity, Maine, Gary Robb has been printing currency for the residents of Waldo County since 1995 using a system pioneered in Ithaca, New York, in 1991. In fact, dozens of communities around the country are experimenting with alternative currency schemes designed as a means of payment for goods and services. And it's perfectly legal! IRS and Federal

Reserve officials say that there is nothing illegal about local currency, provided that it does not look like a Federal Reserve note, comes in denominations of at least $1.00, and is treated as taxable income.

There's really nothing new about local currencies. Before the Civil War, different currencies were issued by local banks. The National Bank Act of 1863 established a single currency via the charter of "national banks," which were privately owned commercial banks with the authority to create a limited amount of national bank notes. In 1914 the U.S. banking

system as we now know it was established and Federal Reserve notes were introduced to end the currency confusion and facilitate transactions throughout the country.

Today, local currencies, like the Ithaca HOURS currency, function as an extension of a barter economy designed to support local businesses and nonprofit organizations and help foster a sense of community (see Figure 1).

Here's how the Ithaca HOURS system works. One Ithaca HOUR is worth $10—roughly equal to the average hourly wage in Tompkins

FIGURE 1

Ithaca HOURS Currency

Source: Courtesy Paul Glover, Ithaca HOURS.

County, New York. The currency comes in five different denominations, ranging from one-eighth of an HOUR to two HOURS, and is printed using multicolored ink on a variety of different papers, including paper made from cattail and hemp. It is protected by law from counterfeiting.

Ithaca HOURS are used to buy just about every sort of good or service, including bicycles, attorney services, groceries, movie theater tickets, eyeglasses, and chiropractic and nursing care. Over $62,000 worth of Ithaca HOURS are in circulation today. Hundreds of local merchants and service providers accept HOURS as a means of payment. There's even a local, federally charted credit union that provides interest-free HOUR loans, provides HOUR grants for new businesses, and accepts HOURS for mortgage and loan fees.

However, Ithaca HOURS have no value outside Ithaca, and businesses often take HOURS as only partial payment for a purchase, the other part in U.S. dollars, to be able to pay out-of-town suppliers. Banks and national brand chain stores generally don't accept them at all.

The supply of HOURS is overseen by an advisory board that meets regularly. Worn out HOURS are replaced and new HOURS are issued in exchange for $10 in Federal Reserve notes. A writer named Paul Glover started the system by getting 90 merchants and service providers to agree to accept Ithaca HOURS in exchange for a listing in a barter directory entitled *HOUR Town* and two Ithaca HOURS, worth $20. Every eight months, merchants and individuals listed in *HOUR Town* may apply for an additional HOUR as compensation for continued participation in the system. In this way the advisory board controls the growth in the supply of HOURS. Today over 1,500 listings make *HOUR Town* a rough equivalent of the Yellow Pages of the local phone directory.

Questions for Analytical Thinking

1. Why do you think Paul Glover set the value of an Ithaca HOUR equal to the average hourly wage in Tompkins County?

2. Does an Ithaca HOUR possess all three properties of money: unit of account; store of value; and medium of exchange? What if the Ithaca HOUR is owned by a student at Ithaca College and she takes it with her to Orlando, Florida, for spring break?

3. Why must the currency advisory board in Ithaca control the growth of the supply of Ithaca HOURS?

4. What difficulties might you confront if you tried to establish an Ithaca HOURS monetary system in your town or on your college campus?

Sources: Ellen Grahm, "Community Groups Print Local (and Legal) Currencies," *The Wall Street Journal*, June 27, 1996; Adam Corrigan, "Dealing for Hours," *Bangor Daily News*, Bangor, Maine, November 19, 1996; Lewis Solomon, *Rethinking Our Centralized Monetary System: The Case for Local Currency*, (New York: Praeger, 1996); Internet Web site: *http://www.lightlink.com/hours/ithacahours/index.html*.

MACROECONOMIC ANALYSIS AND ISSUES

MONEY, THE INTEREST RATE, AND OUTPUT: ANALYSIS AND POLICY

IN CHAPTERS 9 and 10, we discussed the market for goods and services—the **goods market**—without mentioning money, the money market, or the interest rate. We described how the equilibrium level of aggregate output (income) (Y) is determined in the goods market. At given levels of planned investment spending (I), government spending (G), and net taxes (T), we were able to determine the equilibrium level of output in the economy.

In chapters 11 and 12, we discussed the financial market, or **money market**, barely referring to the goods market, as we explained how the equilibrium level of the interest rate is determined in the money market.

The goods market and the money market do not operate independently, however. Events in the money market affect what goes on in the goods market, and events in the goods market affect what goes on in the money market. Only by analyzing the two markets together can we determine the values of aggregate output (income) (Y) and the interest rate (r) that are consistent with the existence of equilibrium in *both* markets.

Looking at both markets simultaneously also reveals how fiscal policy affects the money market and how monetary policy affects the goods market. This is what we'll do in this chapter. By establishing how the two markets affect each other, we will show how open market purchases of government securities (which expand the money supply) affect the equilibrium level of national output and income. Similarly, we will show how fiscal policy measures (such as tax cuts) affect interest rates and investment spending.

goods market *The market in which goods and services are exchanged and in which the equilibrium level of aggregate output is determined.*

money market *The market in which financial instruments are exchanged and in which the equilibrium level of the interest rate is determined.*

THE LINKS BETWEEN THE GOODS MARKET AND THE MONEY MARKET

There are two key *links* between the goods market and the money market.

▶ **Link 1: Income and the Demand for Money** The first link between the goods market and the money market exists because the demand for money depends on income. As aggregate output (income) (Y) increases, the number of transactions requiring the use of money increases. (You just saw this in chapter 12.) An increase in output, with the interest rate held constant, leads to an increase in money demand.

> Income, which is determined in the goods market, has considerable influence on the demand for money in the money market.

▶ **Link 2: Planned Investment Spending and the Interest Rate**   The second link between the goods market and the money market exists because planned investment spending (I) depends on the interest rate (r). In chapters 9 and 10 we assumed that planned investment spending is fixed at a certain level, but we did so only to simplify that discussion. In practice, investment is not fixed. Rather, it depends on a number of key economic variables. One is the interest rate. The higher the interest rate, the lower the level of planned investment spending.

> The interest rate, which is determined in the money market, has significant effects on planned investment in the goods market.

INVESTMENT, THE INTEREST RATE, AND THE GOODS MARKET

It should come as no surprise that the relationship between the level of planned investment and the interest rate is negative.

> When the interest rate falls, planned investment rises.
> When the interest rate rises, planned investment falls.

To see why, recall that *investment* refers to the purchase of new capital—new machines and plants. Whether a firm decides to invest in a project depends on whether the expected profits from the project justify its costs. Usually, a big cost of an investment project is the interest cost.

Consider a firm opening a new plant, or the investment required to open a new ice-cream store. When a manufacturing firm builds a new plant, the contractor must be paid at the time the plant is built. When an entrepreneur decides to open a new ice-cream parlor, she needs freezers, tables, chairs, light fixtures, and signs. These too must be paid for when they are installed.

The money needed to carry out such projects is generally borrowed and paid back over an extended period. The real cost of an investment project depends in part on the interest rate—the cost of borrowing. When the interest rate rises, it becomes more expensive to borrow, and fewer projects are likely to be undertaken; increasing the interest rate, *ceteris paribus*, is likely to reduce the level of planned investment spending. When the interest rate falls, it becomes less costly to borrow, and more investment projects are likely to be undertaken; reducing the interest rate, *ceteris paribus*, is likely to increase the level of planned investment spending.

The relationship between the interest rate and planned investment is illustrated by the downward-sloping demand curve in Figure 13.1. The higher the interest rate, the lower the level of planned investment. At an interest rate of 3 percent, planned investment is I_0. When the interest rate rises from 3 percent to 6 percent, planned investment falls from I_0 to I_1. As the interest rate falls, however, more projects become profitable, so more investment is undertaken.

We can now use the fact that planned investment depends on the interest rate to consider how this relationship affects planned aggregate expenditure (AE). Recall that

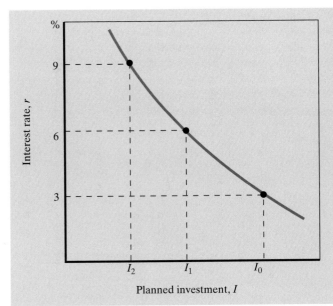

FIGURE 13.1

Planned Investment Schedule

Planned investment spending is a negative function of the interest rate.

planned aggregate expenditure is the sum of consumption, planned investment, and government purchases.[1] That is,

$$AE \equiv C + I + G$$

We now know that there are actually many possible levels of I, each corresponding to a different interest rate (as illustrated in Figure 13.1). When the interest rate changes, planned investment changes. Therefore, a change in the interest rate (r) will lead to a change in total planned spending ($C + I + G$) as well.[2]

Figure 13.2 shows what happens to planned aggregate expenditure when the interest rate rises from 3 percent to 6 percent. At the higher interest rate, planned investment is lower; planned aggregate expenditure thus shifts *downward*. Recall from chapters 9 and 10: A fall in any component of aggregate spending has an even larger (or "multiplier") effect on equilibrium income (Y). When the interest rate rises, planned investment (and planned aggregate expenditure) falls, and equilibrium output (income) falls by even more than the fall in planned investment. In Figure 13.2, equilibrium Y falls from Y_0 to Y_1 when the interest rate rises from 3 percent to 6 percent.

We can summarize the effects of a change in the interest rate on the equilibrium level of output:

The Effects of a Change in the Interest Rate:	■ A high interest rate (r) discourages planned investment (I).
	■ Planned investment is a part of planned aggregate expenditure (AE).
	■ Thus, when the interest rate rises, planned aggregate expenditure (AE) at every level of income falls.
	■ Finally, a decrease in planned aggregate expenditure lowers equilibrium output (income) (Y) by a multiple of the initial decrease in planned investment.

---

[1]As we saw in chapter 10, planned aggregate expenditure also includes net exports ($EX - IM$). The impact of adding exports and imports to our analysis is complex and will be discussed in chapter 21. For now, we are assuming that net exports are zero.

[2]When we look at the behavior of households in the macroeconomy in detail in chapter 17, you will see that consumption spending (C) is also stimulated by lower interest rates and discouraged by higher interest rates.

FIGURE 13.2

The Effect of an Interest
Rate Increase on Planned
Aggregate Expenditure

An increase in the interest
rate from 3 percent to 6
percent lowers planned
aggregate expenditure and
thus reduces equilibrium
income from Y_0 to Y_1.

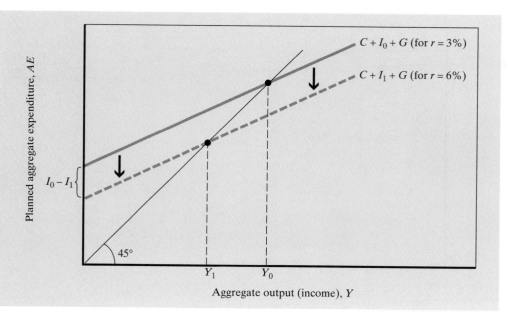

Using a convenient shorthand:

$$r\uparrow \rightarrow I\downarrow \rightarrow AE\downarrow \rightarrow Y\downarrow$$

$$r\downarrow \rightarrow I\uparrow \rightarrow AE\uparrow \rightarrow Y\uparrow$$

As you see, the equilibrium level of output (Y) is not determined solely by events in the goods market, as we assumed in our earlier simplified discussions. The reason is that the money market affects the level of the interest rate, which then affects planned investment in the goods market. There is a different equilibrium level of Y for every possible level of the interest rate (r). The final level of equilibrium Y depends on what the interest rate turns out to be, which depends on events in the money market.

MONEY DEMAND, AGGREGATE OUTPUT (INCOME), AND THE MONEY MARKET

We have just seen how the interest rate—which is determined in the money market—influences the level of planned investment spending and thus the goods market. Now let's look at the other half of the story: the ways in which the goods market affects the money market.

In chapter 12, we explored the demand for money by households and firms and explained why the demand for money depends negatively on the interest rate. An increase in the interest rate raises the opportunity cost of holding non-interest-bearing money (as compared to interest-bearing bonds), encouraging people to keep more of their funds in bonds and less in checking account balances. The downward-sloping money demand curve (M^d) is shown in Figure 13.3.

We also saw in chapter 12 that the demand for money depends on the level of income in the economy. More income means more transactions, and an increased volume of transactions implies a greater demand for money. With more people earning higher incomes and buying more goods and services, more money will be demanded to meet the increased volume of transactions. An increase in income therefore shifts the money demand curve to the right. (Review Figure 12.5.)

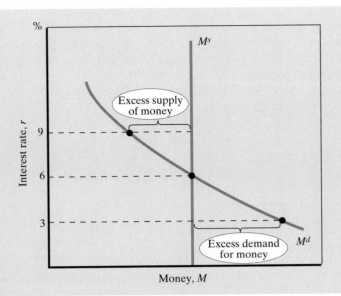

FIGURE 13.3

Equilibrium in the Money Market

If the interest rate were 9 percent, the quantity of money in circulation would exceed the amount households and firms want to hold. The excess money balances would cause the interest rate to drop as people try to shift their funds into interest-bearing bonds. At 3 percent the opposite is true. Excess demand for money balances would push interest rates up. Only at 6 percent would the actual quantity of money in circulation be equal to what the economy wants to hold in money balances.

If, as we are assuming, the Fed's choice of the amount of money to supply does not depend on the interest rate, then the money supply curve is simply a vertical line. The equilibrium interest rate is the point at which the quantity of money demanded equals the quantity of money supplied. This equilibrium is shown at a 6 percent interest rate in Figure 13.3. If the amount of money demanded by households and firms is less than the amount in circulation as determined by the Fed, as it is at an interest rate of 9 percent in Figure 13.3, the interest rate will fall. If the amount of money demanded is greater than the amount in circulation, as it is at an interest rate of 3 percent in Figure 13.3, the interest rate will rise.

Now consider what will happen to the interest rate when there is an increase in aggregate output (income) (Y). This increase in Y will cause the money demand curve to shift to the right. This is illustrated in Figure 13.4, where an increase in income from Y_0 to Y_1 has shifted the money demand curve from M_0^d to M_1^d. At the initial interest rate of 6 percent, there is now excess demand for money, and the interest rate rises from 6 percent to 9 percent.

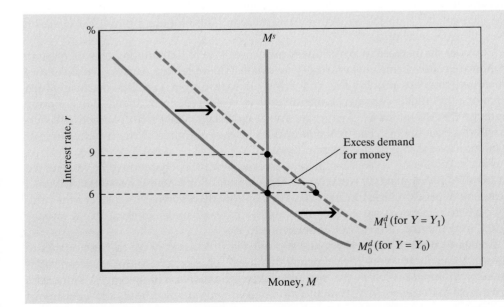

FIGURE 13.4

The Effect of an Increase in Income (Y) on the Interest Rate (r)

An increase in income from Y_0 to Y_1 shifts the M^d curve to the right. With a fixed supply of money, there is now an excess demand for money ($M^d > M^s$) at the initial interest rate of 6 percent. This causes the interest rate to rise. At an interest rate of 9 percent the money market is again in equilibrium with $M^s = M^d$, but at a higher interest rate than before the increase in income.

The equilibrium level of the interest rate is not determined exclusively in the money market. Changes in aggregate output (income) (Y), which take place in the goods market, shift the money demand curve and cause changes in the interest rate. With a given quantity of money supplied, higher levels of Y will lead to higher equilibrium levels of r. Lower levels of Y will lead to lower equilibrium levels of r. Represented in symbols:

$$Y\uparrow \rightarrow M^d\uparrow \rightarrow r\uparrow$$

$$Y\downarrow \rightarrow M^d\downarrow \rightarrow r\downarrow$$

COMBINING THE GOODS MARKET AND THE MONEY MARKET

Now that we are aware of the links between the goods market and the money market, we can examine the two markets simultaneously. To see how the two markets interact, it will be convenient to consider the effects of changes in fiscal and monetary policy on the economy. We want to examine what happens to the equilibrium levels of aggregate output (income) (Y) and the interest rate (r) when certain key variables—notably government spending (G), net taxes (T), and the money supply (M^s)—increase or decrease.

EXPANSIONARY POLICY EFFECTS

Any government policy aimed at stimulating aggregate output (income) (Y) is said to be expansionary. An **expansionary fiscal policy** is an increase in government spending (G) or a reduction in net taxes (T) aimed at increasing aggregate output (income) (Y). An **expansionary monetary policy** is an increase in the money supply aimed at increasing aggregate output (income) (Y).

▶ **Expansionary Fiscal Policy: An Increase in Government Purchases (G) or Decrease in Net Taxes (T)** As you know from chapter 10, government purchases (G) and net taxes (T) are the two tools of government fiscal policy. The government can stimulate the economy—that is, it can increase aggregate output (income) (Y)—either by *increasing* government purchases or by *reducing* net taxes. Though the impact of a tax cut is somewhat smaller than the impact of an increase in G, both have a multiplier effect on the equilibrium level of Y.

Consider an increase in government purchases (G) of $10 billion. This increase in expenditure causes firms' inventories to be smaller than planned. Unplanned inventory reductions stimulate production, and firms increase output (Y). But because added output means added income, some of which is subsequently spent, consumption spending (C) also increases. Again, inventories will be smaller than planned and output will rise even further. The final equilibrium level of output is higher by a multiple of the initial increase in government purchases.

This multiplier story is incomplete, however. Until this chapter, we have assumed that planned investment (I) is fixed at a certain level. But we now know that planned investment depends on the interest rate. We can now discuss what happens to the multiplier when investment varies because we now have an understanding of the money market, in which the interest rate is determined.

Return to our multiplier story at the point that firms first begin to raise output in response to an increase in government purchases. As aggregate output (income) (Y) increases, an impact is felt in the money market—the increase in income (Y) increases the demand for money (M^d). (For the moment, assume the Fed holds the quantity of

expansionary fiscal policy *An increase in government spending or a reduction in net taxes aimed at increasing aggregate output (income)* (Y).

expansionary monetary policy *An increase in the money supply aimed at increasing aggregate output (income)* (Y).

FAST FACTS

The countries with the most expansionary fiscal policy (biggest annual government deficit [$G - T$] as a percentage of GDP) in 1995 were Finland (9%), Greece (14.4%) and Brazil (13.3%). In 1995, Singapore ran a surplus ($G < T$) equal to 15% of its GDP.

Source: World Bank, *World Development Report, 1997.*

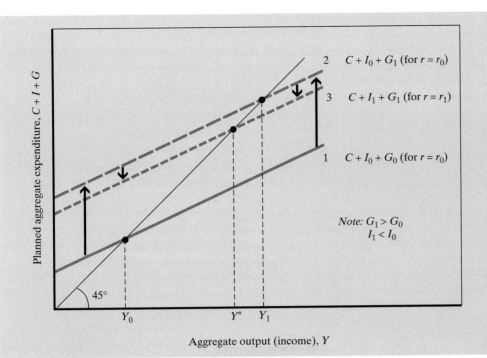

FIGURE 13.5
The Crowding-Out Effect

An increase in government spending G from G_0 to G_1 shifts the planned aggregate expenditure schedule from 1 to 2. The crowding-out effect of the decrease in planned investment (brought about by the increased interest rate) then shifts the planned aggregate expenditure schedule from 2 to 3.

money supplied [M^s] constant.) The resulting disequilibrium, with the quantity of money demanded greater than the quantity of money supplied, causes the interest rate to rise. The increase in G increases both Y and r.

The increase in r has a side effect—a higher interest rate causes planned investment spending (I) to decline. Because planned investment spending is a component of planned aggregate expenditure ($C + I + G$), the decrease in I works against the increase in G. An increase in government spending (G) increases planned aggregate expenditure and increases aggregate output, but a decrease in planned investment reduces planned aggregate expenditure and *decreases* aggregate output.

This tendency for increases in government spending to cause reductions in private investment spending is called the **crowding-out effect**. Without any expansion in the money supply to accommodate the rise in income and increased money demand, planned investment spending is partially crowded out by the higher interest rate. The extra spending created by the rise in government purchases is somewhat offset by the fall in planned investment spending. Income still rises, but the multiplier effect of the rise in G is lessened because of the higher interest rate's negative effect on planned investment.

This crowding-out effect is illustrated graphically in Figure 13.5. An increase in government purchases from G_0 to G_1 shifts the planned aggregate expenditure curve ($C + I_0 + G_0$) upward. The increase in (Y) from Y_0 to Y_1 causes the demand for money to rise, which results in a disequilibrium in the money market. The excess demand for money raises the interest rate (r) from r_0 to r_1, causing I to decrease from I_0 to I_1. The fall in I pulls the planned aggregate expenditure curve back down, which lowers the equilibrium level of income to Y^*. (Remember that equilibrium is achieved when $Y = AE$.)

Note that the size of the crowding-out effect, and the ultimate size of the government spending multiplier, depend on several things. First, we assumed the Fed did not change the quantity of money supplied. If we were to assume instead that the Fed expanded the quantity of money to accommodate the increase in G, the multiplier would be larger. In this case, the higher demand for money would be satisfied with a higher quantity of money supplied, and the interest rate would not rise. Without a higher interest rate, there would be no crowding out.

crowding-out effect *The tendency for increases in government spending to cause reductions in private investment spending.*

interest sensitivity or **insensitivity of planned investment** *The responsiveness of planned investment spending to changes in the interest rate. Interest sensitivity means that planned investment spending changes a great deal in response to changes in the interest rate; interest insensitivity means little or no change in planned investment as a result of changes in the interest rate.*

Second, the crowding-out effect depends on the **sensitivity** or **insensitivity of planned investment** spending to changes in the interest rate. Crowding out occurs because a higher interest rate reduces planned investment spending. Investment depends on factors other than the interest rate, however, and investment may at times be quite insensitive to changes in the interest rate. If planned investment does not fall when the interest rate rises, there is no crowding-out effect. For more details on one type of investment sensitive to interest-rate changes, see the Application box "Lower Interest Rates Stimulate Investment: Mortgages and Housing in 1998."

To summarize the effects of an expansionary fiscal policy:

Effects of an Expansionary Fiscal Policy:

$$G\uparrow \rightarrow Y\uparrow \rightarrow M^d\uparrow \rightarrow r\uparrow \rightarrow I\downarrow$$

Y increases less than if r did not increase.

Exactly the same reasoning holds for changes in net taxes. The ultimate effect of a tax cut on the equilibrium level of output depends on how the money market reacts. The expansion of Y that a tax cut brings about will lead to an increase in the interest rate and thus a decrease in planned investment spending. The ultimate increase in Y will therefore be less than it would be if the interest rate did not rise.

▶ **Expansionary Monetary Policy: An Increase in the Money Supply** Now let's consider what will happen when the Fed decides to increase the supply of money through open market operations. At first, open market operations inject new reserves into the system and expand the quantity of money supplied (the money supply curve shifts to the right). Because the quantity of money supplied is now greater than the amount households want to hold, the equilibrium rate of interest falls. Planned investment spending (which is a component of planned aggregate expenditure) increases when the interest rate falls.

Increased planned investment spending means planned aggregate expenditure is now greater than aggregate output. Firms experience unplanned decreases in inventories, and they raise output (Y). An increase in the money supply decreases the interest rate and increases Y. However, the higher level of Y increases the demand for money (the demand for money curve shifts to the right), and this keeps the interest rate from falling as far as it otherwise would.

If you review the sequence of events that follows the monetary expansion, you can see the links between the injection of reserves by the Fed into the economy and the increase in output. First, the increase in the quantity of money supplied pushes down the interest rate. Second, the lower interest rate causes planned investment spending to rise. Third, the increased planned investment spending means higher planned aggregate expenditure, which means increased output as firms react to unplanned decreases in inventories. Fourth, the increase in output (income) leads to an increase in the demand for money (the demand for money curve shifts to the right), which means the interest rate decreases less than it would have if the demand for money had not increased.

Effects of an Expansionary Monetary Policy:

$$M^s\uparrow \rightarrow r\downarrow \rightarrow I\uparrow \rightarrow Y\uparrow \rightarrow M^d\uparrow$$

r decreases less than if M^d did not increase.

The power of monetary policy to affect the goods market depends on how much of a reaction occurs at each link in this chain. Perhaps the most critical link is the link between r and I. Monetary policy can be effective *only* if I reacts to changes in r. If firms sharply increase the number of investment projects undertaken when the interest rate falls, expansionary monetary policy works well at stimulating the economy. If, however, firms are reluctant to invest even at a low interest rate, expansionary monetary policy will have limited success. In other words, the effectiveness of monetary policy depends

LOWER INTEREST RATES STIMULATE INVESTMENT: MORTGAGES AND HOUSING IN 1998

One component of planned investment spending that is quite sensitive to interest rate changes is investment in housing. Home purchases are generally financed with a mortgage. A mortgage is a long-term loan. Higher mortgage rates increase the cost of buying and owning a home. Between January and December of 1994, the interest rate on 30-year fixed-rate mortgages jumped from 6.75 percent to 9.25 percent, largely as the result of an expanding economy (which was shifting the money demand curve to the right) and an increasingly resistant Fed holding the line on money supply growth. Between 1994 and 1998, rates fell with a few bumps along the way back to 6.75 percent.

Consider the effect of such a reduction in rates on the real monthly cost of a home. A potential buyer considering purchase of a $100,000 home with a 20 percent down payment faces a $658 monthly payment when mortgage rates are 9.25 percent. If interest rates fell to 6.75 percent, the same buyer would face a monthly payment of only $519. The cut in rates has the same effect as a 21 percent decrease in the price of the house!

In addition, falling mortgage rates can stimulate spending by homeowners even if they do not use the opportunity to buy a new house. How? If Sally borrowed money in 1994 to pay for a $100,000 home at 9.25 percent, she could pay off the mortgage in 1998, and "refinance" the loan and reduce her monthly payment to $494. She would

AS MORTGAGE INTEREST RATES GO DOWN, NEW HOME BUILDING PICKS UP.

benefit from the fact that some of the loan had been paid off and that the mortgage rate was down to 6.75 percent.

The effects of falling rates are discussed in the following article from the *New York Times*:

Housing starts rose 4.8 percent in June, reversing a decline in the previous month and signaling that demand for homes could rebound as the economy enters the third quarter.

Real estate markets have been bolstered by the highest levels of consumer confidence in the economy in decades, the lowest unemployment rate in a quarter-century and historic gains in the stock market. Home builders, like economists, are optimistic about the housing industry, a survey by the National Association of Home Builders showed.

Mortgage rates have declined steadily since mid-April. The average rate on a 30-year fixed mortgage fell to 7.69 percent in June from 7.93 percent in May.

"With the fall in mortgage rates over the last few weeks, the housing sector will modestly contribute to overall economic growth" in the third quarter, said Stan Shipley, an economist at Merrill Lynch & Company in New York. Mortgage refinancings should also rise, putting more money in consumers' pockets to spend, analysts said.[a]

[a]"Builders Start New Homes at Faster Pace," *The New York Times*, July 18, 1997, p. C6. Copyright © 1997 by The New York Times Co. Reprinted by permission.

For more on interest rates and homebuilding, see the Case and Fair Web page at
http://www.prenhall.com/casefair.

on the shape of the investment function. If it is nearly vertical, indicating very little responsiveness of investment to the interest rate, the middle link in this chain is weak, rendering monetary policy ineffective.

▶ **Expansionary Policy in Action: The Recessions of 1974 to 1975, 1980 to 1982, and 1990 to 1991** The United States has experienced three recessions since 1970. In two, 1974 to

FIGURE 13.6

Fed Accommodation of an Expansionary Fiscal Policy

An expansionary fiscal policy, like the 1975 tax cut, will increase aggregate output (income) and shift the money demand curve to the right, from M_0^d to M_1^d. If the money supply were unchanged, the interest rate would rise from r_0 to r_1 and planned investment would be negatively affected. But if the Fed were to "accommodate" the fiscal expansion by increasing the money supply from M_0^s to M_1^s, the interest rate would not rise.

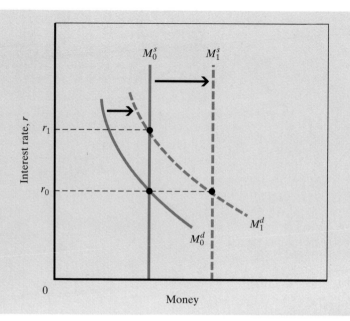

1975 and 1980 to 1982, the government engaged in tax cuts that had the effect of stimulating consumer spending (C). Because C is a component of planned aggregate expenditure, these tax cuts had the effect of increasing aggregate output (income) (Y).

Consider the recession of 1974 to 1975. The Tax Reduction Act of 1975 resulted in a 1974 tax rebate of $8 billion that was paid to consumers in the second quarter of 1975. This rebate and other tax reductions led to increased consumer spending, which contributed to the economic recovery that began soon after the new tax laws went into effect.

But what about the crowding-out effect? Did the 1975 expansionary fiscal policy drive up interest rates and crowd out private spending? In this case, no. At the same time that Congress was cutting taxes to stimulate spending, the Fed was trying to stimulate the economy by expanding the money supply. Even though the increased output during the expansion caused the *demand* for money to rise, the Fed was simultaneously expanding the *supply* of money, and interest rates did not change very much. This situation is illustrated in Figure 13.6.

A similar sequence of events took place during the recession of 1980 to 1982. On the recommendation of President Reagan, Congress passed a huge tax cut during the summer of 1981. Like the 1975 tax cut, the 1981 tax cut led to an increase in consumer spending, which helped lift the economy out of the recession.

Recovery from the 1980 to 1982 recession was also helped along by the Fed, which began to increase the supply of money sharply in the spring of 1982. So, even though output and income were expanding by late 1982, thereby increasing the demand for money, interest rates actually *declined* because the supply of money was expanding at the same time. There was no crowding-out effect.

The recession of 1990 to 1991 began soon after Iraq's invasion of Kuwait in the late summer of 1990. The recession was short-lived and shallow compared with the two previous recessions. Real GDP began to rise in the second quarter of 1991. But this recovery became known as the "jobless recovery." Because productivity increased and large firms continued to trim payrolls even as output was expanding, the unemployment rate stayed high right into the presidential election of 1992.

President Bush debated calling for a tax cut to stimulate the economy, but concern with the already large government deficit and pressure from the Fed convinced him to wait. The Fed did push interest rates lower in an effort to get the economy moving. Even so, little response was evident by election time.

President Clinton called for some modest fiscal stimulus when he took office, but the Congress balked. Then, in the summer of 1993, Congress passed the Clinton deficit reduction package, which *increased* taxes and *reduced* government spending. In the meantime, monetary policy continued to be expansionary. Eventually, interest rates hit 30-year lows! For much of 1993, the three-month T-bill rate was under 3 percent for the first time since 1962, and the 30-year bond rate fell below 6 percent for the first time since the government began selling 30-year-bonds.

In late 1994, the slow-growth recovery ended and a real expansion began. To the extent that policy was responsible for the expansion, it was monetary (rather than fiscal) policy that finally got things moving.

CONTRACTIONARY POLICY EFFECTS

Any government policy that is aimed at reducing aggregate output (income) (Y) is said to be *contractionary*. Where expansionary policy is used to boost the economy, contractionary policy is used to slow the economy.

Considering that one of the four major economic goals is economic growth (chapter 1), why would the government adopt policies designed to reduce aggregate spending? As we will see in the next two chapters, one way to fight inflation is to reduce aggregate spending. When the inflation rate is high, the government may feel compelled to use its powers to contract the economy. Before we discuss the contractionary policies that the government has undertaken in recent years, we need to discuss how contractionary fiscal and monetary policy work.

> **Contractionary Fiscal Policy: A Decrease in Government Spending (G) or an Increase in Net Taxes (T)** A **contractionary fiscal policy** is a decrease in government spending (G) or an increase in net taxes (T) aimed at decreasing aggregate output (income) (Y). The effects of this policy are the opposite of the effects of an expansionary fiscal policy.

contractionary fiscal policy *A decrease in government spending or an increase in net taxes aimed at decreasing aggregate output (income)* (Y).

A decrease in government purchases or an increase in net taxes leads to a decrease in aggregate output (income) (Y), a decrease in the demand for money (M^d), and a decrease in the interest rate (r). The decrease in Y that accompanies a contractionary fiscal policy is less than it would be if we did not take the money market into account because the decrease in r also causes planned investment (I) to *increase*. This increase in I offsets some of the decrease in planned aggregate expenditure brought about by the decrease in G. (This also means the multiplier effect is smaller than it would be if we did not take the money market into account.) The effects of a decrease in G, or an increase in T, can be represented as:

Effects of a Contractionary Fiscal Policy:	$G\downarrow$ or $T\uparrow \rightarrow Y\downarrow \rightarrow M^d\downarrow \rightarrow r\downarrow \rightarrow I\uparrow$ ⌐
	└→ Y decreases less than if r did not decrease.

> **Contractionary Monetary Policy: A Decrease in the Money Supply** A **contractionary monetary policy** is a decrease in the money supply aimed at decreasing aggregate output (income) (Y). As you recall, the level of planned investment spending is a negative function of the interest rate: The higher the interest rate, the less planned investment there will be. The less planned investment there is, the lower planned aggregate expenditure will be, and the lower the equilibrium level of output (income) (Y) will be. The lower equilibrium income results in a decrease in the demand for money, which means that the increase in the interest rate will be less than it would be if we did not take the goods market into account.

contractionary monetary policy *A decrease in the money supply aimed at decreasing aggregate output (income)* (Y).

Effects of a Contractionary Monetary Policy:	$M^s \downarrow \rightarrow r \uparrow \rightarrow I \downarrow \rightarrow Y \downarrow \rightarrow M^d \downarrow$ ——— $\longrightarrow$ r increases less than if M^d did not decrease.

➤ **Contractionary Policy in Action: 1973 to 1974, 1979 to 1980, and 1994** The Fed has pursued strong contractionary policies twice in the last two decades: first in 1973 to 1974 and again in 1979 to 1980. In both cases, the tight monetary policies led to very high interest rates. In 1974, short-term rates exceeded 12 percent, and in 1981, some short-term rates exceeded 20 percent! These high interest rates had a negative effect on planned aggregate expenditure and contributed to the recessions that followed. The Fed's purpose in following a tight monetary policy was to slow the inflation rate. (We will see in the next chapter why a contractionary policy may bring the inflation rate down.)

In 1994, worries about inflation surfaced again as the economy began to push toward full employment. Once again, the Fed began to pull on the reins. In February, it announced the first of several increases in the discount rate and the target federal funds rate. By the end of the year, the prime rate had jumped from 6 percent to 8.5 percent. Between 1994 and 1997 the Fed made only modest changes in the discount rate.

THE MACROECONOMIC POLICY MIX

Although we've been treating fiscal and monetary policy separately, it should be clear that fiscal and monetary policy can be used simultaneously. For example, both government purchases (G) and the money supply (M^s) can be increased at the same time. We have seen that an increase in G by itself raises both Y and r, while an increase in M^s by itself raises Y but lowers r. Therefore, if the government wanted to increase Y without changing r, it could do so by increasing both G and M^s by the appropriate amounts.

policy mix *The combination of monetary and fiscal policies in use at a given time.*

Policy mix refers to the combination of monetary and fiscal policies in use at a given time. A policy mix that consists of a decrease in government spending and an increase in the money supply would favor investment spending over government spending. This is because both the increased money supply and the fall in government purchases would cause the interest rate to fall, which would lead to an increase in planned investment. The opposite is true for a mix that consists of an expansionary fiscal policy and a contractionary monetary policy. This mix favors government spending over investment spending. Such a policy will have the effect of increasing government spending and reducing the money supply. Tight money and expanded government spending would drive the interest rate up and planned investment down.

There is no rule about what constitutes the "best" policy mix or the "best" composition of output. On this, as on many other issues, economists (and others) disagree. In part, someone's preference for a certain composition of output—say, one weighted heavily toward private spending with relatively little government spending—depends on how that person stands on such issues as the proper role of government in the economy.

Table 13.1 summarizes the effects of various combinations of policies on several important macroeconomic variables. If you can explain the reasoning underlying each of the effects shown in the figure, you can be satisfied that you have a good understanding of the links between the goods market and the money market.

OTHER DETERMINANTS OF PLANNED INVESTMENT

We have assumed in this chapter that planned investment depends only on the interest rate. In reality, planned investment depends on other factors. We will discuss these factors more in chapter 17, but provide a brief description here.

TABLE 13.1 THE EFFECTS OF THE MACROECONOMIC POLICY MIX

		FISCAL	
		Expansionary ($\uparrow G$ or $\downarrow T$)	Contractionary ($\downarrow G$ or $\uparrow T$)
MONETARY	Expansionary ($\uparrow M^s$)	$Y\uparrow$, r?, I?, $C\uparrow$	Y?, $r\downarrow$, $I\uparrow$, C?
	Contractionary ($\downarrow M^s$)	Y?, $r\uparrow$, $I\downarrow$, C?	$Y\downarrow$, r?, I?, $C\downarrow$

Key:
$\uparrow$: variable increases.
$\downarrow$: variable decreases.
?: Forces push the variable in different directions. Without additional information, we cannot specify which way the variable moves.

> **Expectations and Animal Spirits**   Firms' expectations about their future sales play an important role in their investment decisions. When a firm invests, it adds to its capital stock, and capital is used in the production process. If a firm expects that its sales will increase in the future, it may begin to build up its capital stock (that is, to invest) now so that it will be able to produce more in the future to meet the increased level of sales. The optimism or pessimism of entrepreneurs about the future course of the economy can have an important effect on current planned investment. Keynes used the phrase *animal spirits* to describe the feelings of entrepreneurs, and he argued that these feelings affect investment decisions.

> **Capital Utilization Rates**   The degree of utilization of a firm's capital stock is also likely to affect planned investment. If the demand for a firm's output has been decreasing and the firm has been lowering output in response to this decline, the firm may have a low rate of capital utilization. It can be costly to get rid of capital quickly once it is in place, and firms sometimes respond to a fall in output by keeping the capital in place but utilizing it less (for example, by running machines fewer hours per day or at slower speeds). Firms tend to invest less in new capital when their capital utilization rates are low than when they are high.

> **Relative Labor and Capital Costs**   The cost of capital (of which the interest rate is the main component) *relative* to the cost of labor can affect planned investment. If labor is expensive relative to capital (high wage rates), firms tend to substitute away from labor toward capital. They aim to hold more capital relative to labor when wage rates are high than when they are low.

The Determinants of Planned Investment:
- The interest rate
- Expectations of future sales
- Capital utilization rates
- Relative capital and labor costs

LOOKING AHEAD: THE PRICE LEVEL

Our discussion of aggregate output (income) and the interest rate in the goods market and the money market is now complete. You should now have a good understanding of how the two markets work together. However, we have not yet discussed the price level in any detail.

We cannot begin to understand the economic events of the last three decades without an understanding of the aggregate price level. The two periods of rapid increases in the price level, 1974 to 1975 and 1979 to 1981, had dramatic effects on the economy. What causes the price level to change? Are there policies that might prevent large changes in the price level or stop them once they have started? Is inflation in 1998 so low that we don't have to worry about it? Before we can answer such questions, we must understand the factors that affect the overall price level. This is the task of the next chapter. Up to this point we have taken the price level as fixed. Now it is time to relax this assumption.

SUMMARY

1. The *goods market* and the *money market* do not operate independently. Events in the money market have considerable effects on the goods market, and events in the goods market have considerable effects on the money market.

THE LINKS BETWEEN THE GOODS MARKET AND THE MONEY MARKET

2. There are two important links between the goods market and the money market: The level of real output (income) (Y), which is determined in the goods market, determines the volume of transactions each period and thus affects the demand for money in the money market; And, the interest rate (r), which is determined in the money market, affects the level of planned investment spending in the goods market.

3. There is a negative relationship between planned investment and the interest rate because the interest rate determines the cost of investment projects. When the interest rate rises, planned investment will decrease; when the interest rate falls, planned investment will increase.

4. For every value of the interest rate, there is a different level of planned investment spending and a different equilibrium level of output. The final level of equilibrium output depends on what the interest rate turns out to be, which depends on events in the money market.

5. For a given quantity of money supplied the interest rate depends on the demand for money. Money demand depends on the level of output (income). With a given money supply, then, increases and decreases in Y will affect money demand, which will affect the equilibrium interest rate.

COMBINING THE GOODS MARKET AND THE MONEY MARKET

6. An *expansionary fiscal policy* is an increase in government spending (G) or a reduction in net taxes (T) aimed at increasing aggregate output (income) (Y). An expansionary fiscal policy based on increases in government spending tends to lead to a *crowding-out effect*: Because increased government expenditures mean more transactions in the economy and thus an increased demand for money, the interest rate will rise. The decrease in planned investment spending that accompanies the higher interest rate will then partially offset the increase in aggregate expenditures brought about by the increase in G.

7. The size of the crowding-out effect, affecting the size of the government-spending multiplier, depends on two things: the assumption that the Fed does not change the quantity of money supplied and the *sensitivity* or *insensitivity of planned investment* to changes in the interest rate.

8. An *expansionary monetary policy* is an increase in the money supply aimed at increasing aggregate output (income) (Y). An increase in the money supply leads to a lower interest rate, increased planned investment, increased planned aggregate expenditure, and ultimately a higher equilibrium level of aggregate output (income) (Y). Expansionary policies have been used to lift the economy out of recessions.

9. A *contractionary fiscal policy* is a decrease in government spending or an increase in net taxes aimed at decreasing aggregate output (income) (Y). A decrease in government spending or an increase in net taxes leads to a decrease in aggregate output (income) (Y), a decrease in the demand for money, and a decrease in the interest rate. However, the decrease in Y is somewhat offset by the additional planned investment resulting from the lower interest rate.

10. A *contractionary monetary policy* is a decrease in the money supply aimed at decreasing aggregate output (income) (Y). The higher interest rate brought about by the reduced money supply causes a decrease in planned investment spending and a lower level of equilibrium output. However, the lower equilibrium level of output brings about a decrease in the demand for money, which means the increase in the interest rate will be less than it would be if we did not take the goods market into account. Contractionary policies have been used to fight inflation.

11. The *policy mix* is the combination of monetary and fiscal policies in use at a given time. There is no rule about what constitutes the best policy mix or the best composition of output. In part, one's preference for a certain composition of output depends on one's stance regarding such issues as the proper role of government in the economy.

OTHER DETERMINANTS OF PLANNED INVESTMENT

12. In addition to the interest rate, the level of planned investment in the economy also depends on expectations and animal spirits, capital utilization rates, and relative capital and labor costs.

REVIEW TERMS AND CONCEPTS

contractionary fiscal policy, 283
contractionary monetary policy, 283
crowding-out effect, 279
expansionary fiscal policy, 278

expansionary monetary policy, 278
goods market, 273
interest sensitivity or insensitivity of
   planned investment, 280

money market, 273
policy mix, 284

PROBLEM SET

1. On October 9, 1997, the German central bank, the Bundesbank, surprised the world by announcing it would take action to raise interest rates. This set off a protest in Germany because unemployment is above 12 percent. What impact is an interest rate increase likely to have on the level of output?

2. During the third quarter of 1997, Japanese GDP was falling at an annual rate of over 11 percent. Many blame the big increase in Japan's taxes in the spring of 1997 designed to balance the budget. Explain how an increase in taxes with the economy growing slowly could precipitate a recession; do not skip steps in your answer. If you were head of the Japanese central bank, how would you respond? What impact would your policy have on the level of investment?

3. Some economists argue that the "animal spirits" of investors are so important in determining the level of investment in the economy that interest rates don't matter at all. Suppose that this were true—that investment in no way depends on interest rates.
   a. How would Figure 13.1 be different?
   b. What would happen to the level of planned aggregate expenditures if the interest rate changed?
   c. What would be different about the relative effectiveness of monetary and fiscal policy?

4. For each of the following, tell a story and predict the effects on the equilibrium levels of aggregate output (Y) and the interest rate (r):
   a. During the summer of 1997, the Congress passed and the president signed the *Taxpayer Relief Act of 1997*. The act contained a number of tax cuts and expenditure reductions designed to ultimately balance the budget. Many of the tax cuts took effect immediately and in 1998. The expenditure cuts were scheduled to take effect in 1999 to 2002. Assume the Fed holds M^s fixed. You may give a different answer for 1998 and for 1999 to 2002.
   b. In 1993, the Congress and the president raised taxes. At the same time, the Federal Reserve was pursuing an expansionary monetary policy.
   c. In 1990, the Perisan Gulf War led to a sharp drop in consumer confidence and a drop in consumption. Assume the Fed holds the money supply constant.

   d. The Fed attempts to increase the money supply to stimulate the economy, but plants are operating at 65 percent of their capacities and businesses are pessimistic about the future.

5. Occasionally, the Federal Reserve Open Market Committee sets a policy designed to "track" the interest rate. This means that the OMC is pursuing policies designed to keep the interest rate constant. If, in fact, the Fed were acting to counter any increases or decreases in the interest rate to keep it constant, what specific actions would you expect to see the Fed take if the following were to occur? (In answering, indicate the effects of each set of events on Y, C, S, I, M^s, M^d, and r.)
   a. There is an unexpected increase in investor confidence, leading to a sharp increase in orders for new plant and equipment.
   b. A major New York bank fails, causing a number of neurotic people (not trusting even the FDIC) to withdraw a substantial amount of cash from other banks and put it in their cookie jars.

6. Paranoia, the largest country in Central Antarctica, receives word of an imminent penguin attack. The news causes expectations about the future to be shaken. As a consequence, there is a sharp decline in investment spending plans.
   a. Explain in detail the effects of such an event on the economy of Paranoia, assuming no response on the part of the Central Bank or the Treasury (M^s, T, and G all remain constant). Be sure to discuss the adjustments in the goods market and the money market.
   b. To counter the fall in investment, the king of Paranoia calls for a proposal to increase government spending. To finance the program, the Chancellor of the Exchequer has proposed three alternative options:
      (1) Finance the expenditures with an equal increase in taxes.
      (2) Keep tax revenues constant and borrow the money from the public by issuing new government bonds.
      (3) Keep taxes constant and finance the expenditures by printing new money.
   Consider the three financing options and rank them from most expansionary to least expansionary. Explain your ranking.

7. Why might investment not respond positively to low interest rates during a recession? Why might investment not respond negatively to high interest rates during a boom?

8. In the early 1980s, the Federal Reserve was tightening the money supply to fight inflation at the same time that President Reagan was increasing defense spending and reducing taxes. What would you expect the effects of this policy mix to be?

TAKE IT TO THE NET

We invite you to visit the Case and Fair page on the Prentice Hall Web site:

http://www.prenhall.com/casefair

for this chapter's World Wide Web exercise.

APPENDIX TO CHAPTER 13

THE *IS-LM* DIAGRAM

There is a useful way of depicting graphically the determination of aggregate output (income) and the interest rate in the goods and money markets. Two curves are involved in this diagram, the *IS* curve and the *LM* curve. In this appendix, we will derive these two curves and use them to see how changes in government purchases (G) and the money supply (M^s) affect the equilibrium values of aggregate output (income) and the interest rate. The effects we describe here are the same as the effects we described in the main text; here we illustrate the effects graphically.

THE *IS* CURVE

We know that in the goods market, there is an equilibrium level of aggregate output (income) (Y) for each value of the interest rate (r). For a given value of r, we can determine the equilibrium value of Y. We also know from Figure 13.5 that the equilibrium value of Y falls when r rises and rises when r falls. There is thus a *negative* relationship between the equilibrium value of Y and r. The reason for this negative relationship is the negative relationship between planned investment and the interest rate. When the interest rate rises, planned investment (I) falls, and this decrease in I leads to a decrease in the equilibrium value of Y. The negative relationship between the equilibrium value of Y and r is shown in Figure 13A.1. This curve is called the **IS curve**.[1] Each point on the *IS* curve represents the equilibrium point in the goods market for the given interest rate.

We also know from our earlier analysis of the goods market that when government purchases (G) increase with a constant interest rate, the equilibrium value of Y increases. This means the *IS* curve shifts to the right when G increases. With the same value of r and a higher value of G, the equilibrium value of Y is larger; when G decreases, the *IS* curve shifts to the left.

THE *LM* CURVE

In the money market, there is an equilibrium value of the interest rate (r) for every value of aggregate output (income) (Y). The equilibrium value of r is determined at the point at which the quantity of money demanded equals the quantity

FIGURE 13A.1

The *IS* Curve

Each point on the *IS* curve corresponds to the equilibrium point in the goods market for the given interest rate. When government spending (G) increases, the *IS* curve shifts to the right, from IS_0 to IS_1.

Interest rate, r

Aggregate output (income), Y

---

[1] The letter *I* stands for investment, and the letter *S* stands for saving. *IS* refers to the fact that in equilibrium in the goods market, planned investment equals saving.

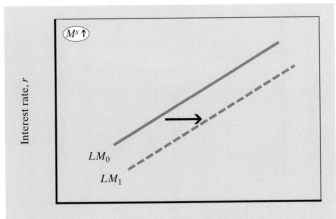

FIGURE 13A.2

The *LM* Curve

Each point on the *LM* curve corresponds to the equilibrium point in the money market for the given value of aggregate output (income). Money supply (M^s) increases shift the *LM* curve to the right, from LM_0 to LM_1.

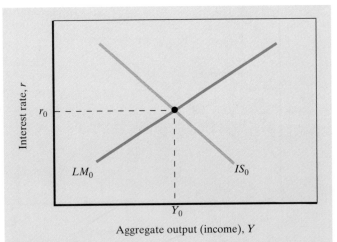

FIGURE 13A.3

The *IS-LM* Diagram

The point at which the *IS* and *LM* curves intersect corresponds to the point at which both the goods market and the money market are in equilibrium. The equilibrium values of aggregate output and the interest rate are Y_0 and r_0.

of money supplied. For a given value of Y, we can determine the equilibrium value of r in the money market. We also know from Figure 13.4 that the equilibrium value of r rises when Y rises and falls when Y falls—a *positive* relationship between the equilibrium value of r and Y. The reason for this positive relationship is the positive relationship between the demand for money and Y. When Y increases, the demand for money increases because more money is demanded for the increased volume of transactions in the economy. An increase in the demand for money increases the equilibrium value of r—thus the positive relationship between the equilibrium value of r and Y.

The positive relationship between the equilibrium value of r and Y is shown in Figure 13A.2. This curve is called the **LM curve**.[2] Each point on the **LM** curve represents equilibrium in the money market for the given value of aggregate output (income).

We also know from our analysis of the money market that when the money supply (M^s) increases with a constant level of Y, the equilibrium value of r decreases. As Figure 13A.2 shows, this means the *LM* curve shifts to the right when M^s increases. With the same value of Y and a higher value of M^s, the equilibrium value of r is lower. When M^s decreases, the *LM* curve shifts to the left.

THE *IS-LM* DIAGRAM

Figure 13A.3 shows the *IS* and *LM* curves together on one graph. The point at which the two curves intersect is the point at which equilibrium exists in *both* the goods market and the money market. There is equilibrium in the goods market because the point is on the *IS* curve, and there is equilibrium in the money market because the point is on the *LM* curve.

We now have only two tasks left. The first is to see how the equilibrium values of Y and r are affected by changes in G—fiscal policy. This is easy. We have just seen that an increase in G shifts the *IS* curve to the right. Thus, an increase in G leads to higher equilibrium values of Y and r. This situation is illustrated in Figure 13A.4. Conversely, a decrease in G leads to lower equilibrium values of Y and r because the lower level of G causes the *IS* curve to shift to the left. (The effects are similar for changes in net taxes, T.)

Our second task is to see how the equilibrium values of Y and r are affected by changes in M^s—monetary policy. This is also easy. We have just seen that an increase in M^s shifts the *LM* curve to the right. Thus, an increase in M^s leads to a higher equilibrium value of Y and a lower equilibrium value of r. This is illustrated in Figure 13A.5. Conversely, a decrease in M^s leads to a lower equilibrium value of Y and a higher equilibrium value of r because a decreased money supply causes the *LM* curve to shift to the left.

The *IS-LM* diagram is a useful way of seeing the effects of changes in monetary and fiscal policies on equilibrium

---

[2]The letter L stands for liquidity, a characteristic of money, and the letter M stands for money.

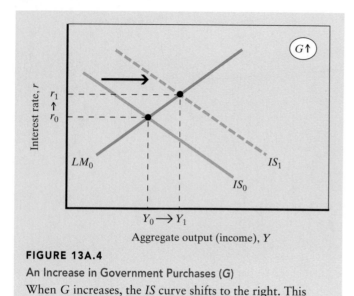

FIGURE 13A.4

An Increase in Government Purchases (G)

When G increases, the IS curve shifts to the right. This increases the equilibrium value of both Y and r.

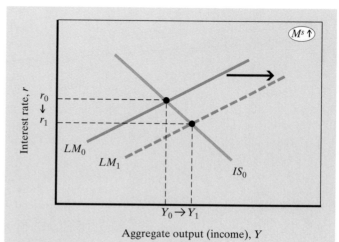

FIGURE 13A.5

An Increase in the Money Supply (M^S)

When M^s increases, the LM curve shifts to the right. This increases the equilibrium value of Y and decreases the equilibrium value of r.

aggregate output (income) and the interest rate through shifts in the two curves. Always keep in mind the economic theory that lies *behind* the two curves. Do not memorize what curve shifts when; be able to understand and explain *why* the curves shift. This means always going back to the behavior of households and firms in the goods and money markets.

It is easy to use the *IS-LM* diagram to see how there can be a monetary and fiscal policy mix that leads to, say, an increase in aggregate output (income) but no increase in the interest rate. If both G and M^s increase, both curves shift to the right, and the shifts can be controlled in such a way as to bring about no change in the equilibrium value of the interest rate.

SUMMARY

1. An *IS curve* illustrates the negative relationship between the equilibrium value of aggregate output (income) (Y) and the interest rate in the goods market. An *LM curve* illustrates the positive relationship between the equilibrium value of the interest rate and aggregate output (income) (Y) in the money market. The point at which the *IS* and *LM* curves intersect is the point at which equilibrium exists in both the goods market and the money market.

REVIEW TERMS AND CONCEPTS

IS curve A curve illustrating the negative relationship between the equilibrium value of aggregate output (income) (Y) and the interest rate in the goods market. 288

LM curve A curve illustrating the positive relationship between the equilibrium value of the interest rate and aggregate output (income) (Y) in the money market. 289

PROBLEM SET

1. Illustrate each of the following situations with *IS/LM* curves:
   a. An increase in G with the money supply held constant by the Fed.
   b. An increase in G with the Fed changing M^s by enough to keep interest rates constant.
   c. The president cuts G and increases T while the chair of the Fed expands M^s.
   d. The president increases G and holds T constant while the chair of the Fed holds M^s constant during a period of inflation.

Chapter 14

AGGREGATE DEMAND, AGGREGATE SUPPLY, AND INFLATION

ONE OF THE MOST IMPORTANT ISSUES in macroeconomics is the determination of the overall price level. Recall that inflation—an increase in the overall price level—is one of the key concerns of macroeconomists and government policy makers. Understanding the factors that affect the price level is essential to understanding macroeconomics.

In chapter 8, we discussed how inflation is measured and the costs of inflation, but made no mention of the *causes* of inflation. For simplicity, our analysis in chapters 9 through 13 took the price level as fixed. This allowed us to discuss the links between the goods market and the money market without the complication of a changing price level. Having considered how the two markets work, we are ready to take up flexible prices.

We begin by discussing the *aggregate demand curve* and the *aggregate supply curve*, introduced briefly in chapter 6. We then put the two curves together and discuss how the equilibrium price level is determined in the economy. This analysis allows us to see how the price level affects the economy and how the economy affects the price level. Finally, we consider monetary and fiscal policy effects and the causes of inflation.

THE AGGREGATE DEMAND CURVE

The place to begin our exploration of the price level is the money market. (If you have forgotten the details of how the overall price level is calculated or what it means, review chapters 7 and 8.) As we saw in Chapter 12, people's demand for money depends on income (Y), the interest rate (r), and the price level (P).

It is not hard to understand why the price level affects the demand for money. Suppose you plan to purchase one pound of chocolate, one bag of potato chips, and a Hostess Twinkie. If these items cost $2.00, $1.00, and $.50 respectively, you would need $3.50 in cash or in your checking account to make your purchases. Suppose that the price of these goods doubles. To make the same purchases, you will need $7.00.

In general, the amount of money required to make a given number of transactions depends directly and proportionately on the average price of those transactions. Doubling the price level will double the demand for money. As prices and wages rise, households will want to keep more money in their wallets and in their checking accounts, firms will need more in their cash drawers, and so forth. If prices and wages are rising at 6 percent per year, we can expect the demand for money to increase at about 6 percent per year, *ceteris paribus.*

> Money demand is a function of three variables: the interest rate (r), the level of real income (Y), and the price level (P). (Remember: Y is *real* output, or income. It measures the actual volume of output, without regard to changes in the price level.) Money demand will increase if the real level of output (income) increases, the price level increases, or the interest rate declines.

DERIVING THE AGGREGATE DEMAND CURVE

aggregate demand *The total demand for goods and services in the economy.*

Recall that **aggregate demand** is the total demand for goods and services in the economy. To derive the aggregate demand curve, we examine what happens to aggregate output (income) (Y) when the price level (P) changes. Does it increase, decrease, or remain constant when the price level increases? Our discussions of the goods market and the money market provide the tools to answer this.

The aggregate demand curve is derived assuming the fiscal policy variables [government purchases (G) and net taxes (T)] and the monetary policy variable (M^s) remain unchanged. In other words, assuming the government does not take any action to affect the economy in response to changes in the price level.

As you know, an increase in the price level increases the demand for money and shifts the money demand curve to the right, as illustrated in Figure 14.1a. At the initial interest rate of 6 percent, an increase in the price level leads to an excess demand for money. Because of the higher price level, households and firms need to hold larger

FIGURE 14.1

The Impact of an Increase in the Price Level on the Economy—Assuming No Changes in G, T, and M^s

a. An increase in the price level increases the demand for money from M_0^d to M_1^d. With the supply of money unchanged, the interest rate increases from 6% to 9%.

b. The higher interest rate decreases planned investment from I_0 to I_1.

c. Decreased planned investment reduces planned aggregate expenditure and causes equilibrium output (income) to fall from Y_0 to Y_1.

292

money balances than before. However, the quantity of money supplied remains the same. (Remember, we are assuming that the Fed takes no action to change the money supply.) The money market is now out of equilibrium. Equilibrium is reestablished at a higher interest rate, 9 percent.

As indicated in Figure 14.1b, with the interest rate now higher, fewer investment projects are desirable, and planned investment spending (I) falls from I_0 to I_1. Lower I means planned aggregate expenditure (AE) is lower, shown in Figure 14.1c as a downward shift of the AE curve. Lower AE means inventories are greater than planned, firms cut back on output, and Y falls from Y_0 to Y_1.

> An increase in the price level causes the level of aggregate output (income) to fall.

The situation is reversed when the price level declines. A lower price level causes money demand to fall, which leads to a lower interest rate. A lower interest rate stimulates planned investment spending, increasing planned aggregate expenditure, which leads to an increase in Y.

> A decrease in the price level causes the level of aggregate output (income) to rise.

This negative relationship between aggregate output (income) and the price level is called the **aggregate demand (AD) curve**, shown in Figure 14.2.

Each point on the aggregate demand curve represents equilibrium in both the goods market *and* the money market. We have derived the AD curve by using the analysis we did in chapter 13, in which the goods market and the money market were linked together. Therefore,

> Each pair of values of P and Y on the aggregate demand curve corresponds to a point at which both the goods market and the money market are in equilibrium.

aggregate demand (AD) curve *A curve that shows the negative relationship between aggregate output (income) and the price level. Each point on the* AD *curve is a point at which both the goods market and the money market are in equilibrium.*

THE AGGREGATE DEMAND CURVE: A WARNING

It is very important that you realize what the aggregate demand curve represents. As we pointed out in chapter 6, the aggregate demand curve is much more complex than a simple individual or market demand curve. The AD curve is *not* a market demand curve, and it is *not* the sum of all market demand curves in the economy.

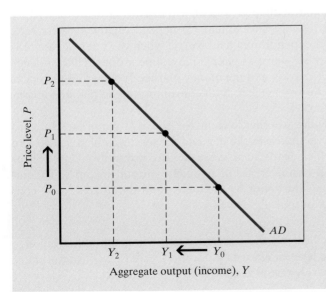

FIGURE 14.2

The Aggregate Demand (AD) Curve

At all points along the AD curve, both the goods market and the money market are in equilibrium.

To understand why, recall the logic behind a simple downward-sloping household demand curve. A demand curve shows the quantity of output demanded (by an individual household or in a single market) at every possible price, *ceteris paribus*. In drawing a simple demand curve, we are assuming that *other prices* and *income* are fixed. From these assumptions, it follows that one reason the quantity demanded of a particular good falls when its price rises is that other prices do *not* rise. The good in question therefore becomes more expensive relative to other goods, which leads households to substitute other goods for the good whose price increased. In addition, if income does not rise when the price of a good does, real income falls. This may also lead to a lower quantity demanded of the good whose price has risen.

Things are different when the *overall price level* rises. When the overall price level rises, many prices—including many wage rates (many people's income)—rise together. For this reason, we cannot use the *ceteris paribus* assumption to draw the *AD* curve. The logic that explains why a simple demand curve slopes downward fails to explain why the *AD* curve also has a negative slope.

> Aggregate demand falls when the price level increases because the higher price level causes the demand for money (M^d) to rise. With the money supply constant, the interest rate will rise to reestablish equilibrium in the money market. *It is the higher interest rate that causes aggregate output to fall.*

You do not need to understand anything about the money market to understand a simple individual or market demand curve. However, to understand what the *aggregate* demand curve represents, you must understand the interaction between the goods market and the money market. The *AD* curve in Figure 14.2 embodies everything we have learned about the goods market and the money market up to now.

> The *AD* curve is *not* the sum of all the market demand curves in the economy. It is *not* a market demand curve.

OTHER REASONS FOR A DOWNWARD-SLOPING AGGREGATE DEMAND CURVE

In addition to the effects of money supply and money demand on the interest rate, two other factors lie behind the downward slope of the *AD* curve. These are the consumption link and the real wealth effect.

▶ **The Consumption Link**   We noted in chapter 9 (and will discuss in detail in chapter 17) that consumption (C) and planned investment (I) depend on the interest rate. Other things equal, consumption expenditures tend to rise when the interest rate falls and to fall when the interest rate rises—just as planned investment does. This tendency is another link between the goods market and the money market. If something happens to change the interest rate in the money market, both consumption and planned investment are affected in the goods market.

The *consumption* link provides another reason for the *AD* curve's downward slope. An increase in the price level increases the demand for money, which leads to an increase in the interest rate, which leads to a decrease in consumption (as well as planned investment), which leads to a decrease in aggregate output (income). The initial decrease in consumption (brought about by the increase in the interest rate) contributes to the overall decrease in output.

> Planned investment does not bear all the burden of providing the link from a higher interest rate to a lower level of aggregate output. Decreased consumption brought about by a higher interest rate also contributes to this effect.

> **The Real Wealth Effect** We also noted in chapter 9 (and will discuss in detail in chapter 17) that consumption depends on wealth. Other things equal, the more wealth households have, the more they consume. Wealth includes holdings of money, shares of stock, bonds, and housing, among other things. If household wealth decreases, the result will be less consumption now and in the future.

The price level has an effect on some kinds of wealth. Suppose you are holding $1,000 in a checking account or in a money market fund and the price level rises by 10 percent. Your holding is now worth 10 percent less because the prices of the goods that you could buy with your $1,000 have all increased by 10 percent. The purchasing power (or "real value") of your holding has decreased by 10 percent.

An increase in the price level may also lower the real value of stocks and housing, although whether it does depends on what happens to stock prices and housing prices when the overall price level rises. If stock prices and housing prices rise by the same percentage as the overall price level, the real value of stocks and housing will remain unchanged. The point is:

> An increase in the price level lowers the real value of *some* types of wealth.

The fact that the price level lowers the real value of wealth provides another reason for the downward slope of the *AD* curve. An increase in the price level lowers the real value of wealth. This leads to a decrease in consumption, which leads to a decrease in aggregate output (income). So, there is a negative relationship between the price level and output through this **real wealth effect** or **real balance effect**.

AGGREGATE EXPENDITURE AND AGGREGATE DEMAND

Throughout our discussion of macroeconomics so far, we have referred to the total planned spending by households (C), firms (I), and the government (G) as planned aggregate expenditure. At equilibrium, planned aggregate expenditure ($AE \equiv C + I + G$) and aggregate output (Y) are equal:[1]

$$\text{Equilibrium condition: } C + I + G = Y$$

How does planned aggregate expenditure relate to aggregate demand?

> At every point along the aggregate demand curve, the aggregate quantity demanded is exactly equal to planned aggregate expenditure, $C + I + G$.

You can see this in Figures 14.1 and 14.2. When the price level rises, it is planned aggregate expenditure that decreases, moving us up the aggregate demand curve.

But the aggregate demand curve represents more than just planned aggregate expenditure. Each point on the *AD* curve represents the *particular* level of planned aggregate expenditure that is consistent with equilibrium in the goods market and money market at the given price. Notice that the variable on the horizontal axis of the aggregate demand curve in Figure 14.2 is *Y*. At every point along the *AD* curve, $Y = C + I + G$.

SHIFTS OF THE AGGREGATE DEMAND CURVE

The aggregate demand curve in Figure 14.2 is based on the assumption that the government policy variables G, T, and M^s are fixed. If any of these variables change, the aggregate demand curve will shift.

Consider an increase in the quantity of money supplied. If the quantity of money is expanded at any given price level, the interest rate will fall, causing planned investment

real wealth, or **real balance, effect** *The change in consumption brought about by a change in real wealth that results from a change in the price level.*

FAST FACTS

During 1997, the Japanese economy was in a severe recession. In an attempt to shift the aggregate demand curve to the right, the Bank of Japan increased the money supply and pushed down interest rates to near zero. During the year ending in November 1997, the Japanese money supply increased by 8%. The prime interest rate on November 12 was 1.63% and the three-month money market interest rate was 0.43%!

Source: The Economist, November 15, 1997, p. 109.

[1]If we include the rest of the world, the equilibrium condition is $C + I + G + (EX - IM) = Y$.

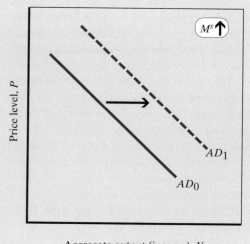

FIGURE 14.3

The Effect of an Increase in Money Supply on the *AD* Curve

An increase in the money supply (M^s) causes the aggregate demand curve to shift to the right, from AD_0 to AD_1. This shift occurs because the increase in M^s lowers the interest rate, which increases planned investment (and thus planned aggregate expenditure). The final result is an increase in output at each possible price level.

spending (and planned aggregate expenditure) to rise. The result is an increase in output at the given price level. As Figure 14.3 shows:

> An increase in the quantity of money supplied at a given price level shifts the aggregate demand curve to the right.

An increase in government purchases or a decrease in net taxes also increases aggregate output (income) at each possible price level, even though some of the increase will be crowded out if the money supply is held constant. (If you are unsure of what crowding-out is, review chapter 12.) An increase in government purchases directly increases planned aggregate expenditure, which leads to an increase in output. A decrease in net taxes results in a rise in consumption, which increases planned aggregate expenditure, which also leads to an increase in output. As Figure 14.4 shows:

> An increase in government purchases or a decrease in net taxes shifts the aggregate demand curve to the right.

FIGURE 14.4

The Effect of an Increase in Government Purchases or a Decrease in Net Taxes on the *AD* Curve

An increase in government purchases (G) or a decrease in net taxes (T) causes the aggregate demand curve to shift to the right, from AD_0 to AD_1. The increase in G increases planned aggregate expenditure, which leads to an increase in output at each possible price level. A decrease in T causes consumption to rise. The higher consumption then increases planned aggregate expenditure, which leads to an increase in output at each possible price level.

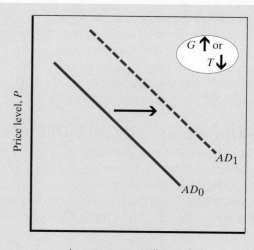

FIGURE 14.5

Shifts in the Aggregate
Demand Curve: A Summary

Expansionary monetary policy	**Contractionary monetary policy**
$M^s\uparrow \rightarrow AD$ curve shifts to the right.	$M^s\downarrow \rightarrow AD$ curve shifts to the left.
Expansionary fiscal policy	**Contractionary fiscal policy**
$G\uparrow \rightarrow AD$ curve shifts to the right.	$G\downarrow \rightarrow AD$ curve shifts to the left.
$T\downarrow \rightarrow AD$ curve shifts to the right.	$T\uparrow \rightarrow AD$ curve shifts to the left.

The same kind of reasoning applies to decreases in the quantity of money supplied, decreases in government purchases, and increases in net taxes. All of these shift the aggregate demand curve to the left.

Figure 14.5 summarizes the ways the aggregate demand curve shifts in response to changes in M^s, G, and T. To test your understanding of the AD curve, go through the figure piece by piece and explain each of its components.

THE AGGREGATE SUPPLY CURVE

Aggregate supply is the total supply of goods and services in an economy. Although there is little disagreement among economists about the logic behind the aggregate demand curve, there is a great deal of disagreement about the logic behind the aggregate supply curve. There is also disagreement about its shape.

aggregate supply *The total supply of all goods and services in an economy.*

THE AGGREGATE SUPPLY CURVE: A WARNING

The **aggregate supply (AS) curve** shows the relationship between the aggregate quantity of output supplied by all the firms in an economy and the overall price level. To understand the aggregate supply curve, we need to understand something about the behavior of the individual firms that make up the economy.

aggregate supply (AS) curve *A graph that shows the relationship between the aggregate quantity of output supplied by all firms in an economy and the overall price level.*

It may seem logical to derive the aggregate supply curve by adding together the supply curves of all the individual firms in the economy. However, the logic behind the relationship between the overall price level in the economy and the level of aggregate output (income)—that is, the AS curve—is very different from the logic behind an individual firm's supply curve. The aggregate supply curve is *not* a market supply curve, and it is *not* the simple sum of all the individual supply curves in the economy. (Recall a similar warning for the aggregate demand curve.)

To understand why, recall the logic behind a simple supply curve, first introduced in chapter 4. A supply curve shows the quantity of output an individual firm would supply at each possible price *ceteris paribus*. When we draw a firm's supply curve, we assume that input prices, including wage rates, are constant. An individual firm's supply curve shows what would happen to the firm's output if the price of its output changes with *no* corresponding increase in costs. Such an assumption for an individual firm is reasonable because an individual firm is small relative to the economy as a whole. (It is unlikely that one firm raising the price of its output will lead to significant increases in input prices in the economy.) If the price of a profit-maximizing firm's output rises with *no* increase in the costs of any inputs, the firm is likely to increase output.

But what would happen if there were an increase in the overall price level? It is unrealistic to believe that costs are constant for individual firms if the overall price level is increasing, for two reasons. First, the outputs of some firms are the inputs of other firms. Therefore, if output prices rise, there will be an increase in at least some input prices. Second, it is unrealistic to assume that wage rates (an important input cost) do not rise at all when the overall price level rises. Because all input prices (including wage rates) are not constant as the overall price level changes, individual firms' supply curves *shift* as the overall price level changes, so we cannot sum them to get an aggregate supply curve.

Another reason the aggregate supply curve cannot be the sum of the supply curves of all the individual firms in the economy is that many firms (some would argue most firms) do not simply respond to prices determined in the market. Rather, they actually *set prices*. Only in perfectly competitive markets do firms simply react to prices determined by market forces. Firms in other kinds of industries (imperfectly competitive industries, to be exact) make both output *and* price decisions based on their perceptions of demand and costs. Price-setting firms do not have individual supply curves because these firms are choosing both output and price at the same time. To derive an individual supply curve, we need to imagine calling out a price to a firm and having the firm tell us how much output it will supply at that price. We cannot do this if firms are also setting prices. If supply curves do not exist for imperfectly competitive firms, we certainly cannot add them together to get an aggregate supply curve!

What, then, can we say about the relationship between aggregate output and the overall price level? Because input prices change when the overall price level changes and because many firms in the economy set prices as well as output, it is clear that an "aggregate supply curve" in the traditional sense of the word *supply* does not exist. What does exist is what we might call a "price/output response" curve—a curve that traces out the price decisions and output decisions of all the markets and firms in the economy under a given set of circumstances.

What might such a curve look like?

AGGREGATE SUPPLY IN THE SHORT RUN

Many argue that the aggregate supply curve (or the "price/output response" curve) has a positive slope, at least in the short run. (We will discuss the short-run/long-run distinction in more detail later in this chapter.) In addition, many argue that at very low levels of aggregate output (for example, when the economy is in a recession), the aggregate supply curve is fairly flat, and at high levels of output (for example, when the economy is experiencing a boom), it is vertical or nearly vertical. Such a curve is shown in Figure 14.6.

To understand the shape of the *AS* curve in Figure 14.6, consider the output and price response of markets and firms to a steady increase in aggregate demand brought about by an increasingly expansionary fiscal or monetary policy. The reaction of firms to such an expansion is likely to depend on two factors: (1) how close the economy is to capacity at the time of the expansion, and (2) how rapidly input prices (such as wage rates) respond to increases in the overall price level.

▶ **Capacity Constraints** In microeconomics, "short run" describes the time in which firms' decisions are constrained by some *fixed factor of production*. A farmer is constrained in the short run by the number of acres of land on his or her farm—the amount of land owned is the fixed factor of production. Manufacturing firms' short-run production decisions are constrained by the size of their physical production facilities. In the longer run, individual firms can overcome these types of constraints by investing in greater capacity—for example, by purchasing more acreage or building a new factory.

The idea of a fixed capacity in the short run also plays a role in macroeconomics. Macroeconomists tend to focus on whether or not *individual firms* are producing at or

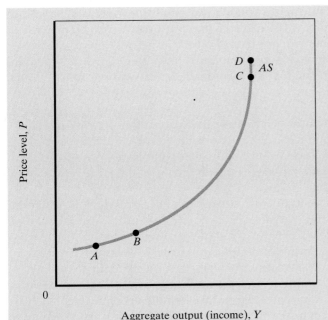

FIGURE 14.6

The Short-Run Aggregate Supply Curve

In the short run, the aggregate supply curve (the price/output response curve) has a positive slope. At low levels of aggregate output, the curve is fairly flat. As the economy approaches capacity, the curve becomes nearly vertical. At capacity, the curve is vertical.

close to full capacity. A firm is producing at full capacity if it is fully utilizing the capital and labor it has on hand. As we will discuss in detail in chapter 17, firms may at times have *excess capital* and *excess labor* on hand—amounts of capital and labor not needed to produce the current level of output. If, for example, there are costs of getting rid of capital once it is in place, a firm may choose to hold on to some of this capital, even if the economy is in a downturn and the firm has decreased its output. In this case, the firm will not be fully utilizing its capital stock. Firms may be especially likely to behave this way if they expect that the downturn will be short and that they will need the capital in the future to produce a higher level of output. Firms may have similar reasons for holding excess labor. It may be costly, both in worker morale and administrative costs, to lay off a large number of workers.

The Federal Reserve reports on the nation's "capacity utilization rate" monthly. In December of 1990, for example, during the recession of 1990 to 1991, the capacity utilization rate for manufacturing firms was 79.3 percent. This suggests about 20 percent of the nation's factory capacity was idle. During the recessions of 1974 to 1975 and 1980 to 1982, capacity utilization fell below 75 percent. At the beginning of 1998, with real output growing at a healthy pace, U.S. capacity utilization stood at 83.3 percent.

Macroeconomists also focus on whether or not the *economy as a whole* is operating at full capacity. If there is cyclical unemployment (unemployment above the frictional and structural amounts), the economy is not fully utilizing its labor force. There are people who want to work at the current wage rates who cannot find jobs.

> Even if firms are not holding excess labor and capital, the economy may be operating below its capacity if there is cyclical unemployment.

Output Levels and Price/Output Responses   At low levels of output in the economy, there is likely to be excess capacity both in individual firms and in the economy as a whole. Firms are likely to be producing at levels of output below their existing capacity constraints. That is, they are likely to be holding excess capital and labor. It is also likely that there will be cyclical unemployment in the economy as a whole in periods of low output. When this is the case, it is likely that firms will respond to an increase in demand by increasing output much more than they increase prices. Firms are below capacity, so the extra cost of producing more output is likely to be small. In addition, firms can get more labor (from the ranks of the unemployed) without much, if any, increase in wage rates.

> An increase in aggregate demand when the economy is operating at low levels of output is likely to result in an increase in output with little or no increase in the overall price level. That is, the aggregate supply (price/output response) curve is likely to be fairly flat at low levels of aggregate output.

Refer to Figure 14.6. Aggregate output is considerably higher at *B* than at *A*, but the price level at *B* is only slightly higher than it is at *A*.

If aggregate output continues to expand, things will change. As firms and the economy as a whole begin to move closer and closer to capacity, firms' response to an increase in demand is likely to change from mainly increasing output to mainly increasing prices. Why? As firms continue to increase their output, they will begin to bump into their short-run capacity constraints. In addition, unemployment will be falling as firms hire more workers to produce the increased output, so the economy as a whole will be approaching its capacity. As aggregate output rises, the prices of labor and capital (input costs) will begin to rise more rapidly, leading firms to increase their output prices.

At some level of output, it is virtually impossible for firms to expand any further. At this level, all sectors are fully utilizing their existing factories and equipment. Plants are running double shifts, and many workers are on overtime. In addition, there is little or no cyclical unemployment in the economy. At this point, firms will respond to any further increases in demand only by raising prices.

> When the economy is producing at its maximum level of output—that is, at capacity—the aggregate supply curve becomes vertical.

Between *C* and *D* in Figure 14.6, the *AS* curve is vertical. Moving from *C* to *D* results in no increase in aggregate output but a large increase in the price level.

> **The Response of Input Prices to Changes in the Overall Price Level** Whether or not the economy is producing a level of output close to capacity, there must be some time lag between changes in input prices and changes in output prices for the aggregate supply (price/output response) curve to slope upward. If input prices changed at exactly the same rate as output prices, the *AS* curve would be vertical.

It is easy to see why. It is generally assumed that firms make decisions with the objective of maximizing profits. If all output and input prices increase 10 percent, no firm would find it advantageous to change its level of output. Why? Because the output level that maximized profits before the 10 percent increase will be the same as the level that maximizes profits after the 10 percent increase.[2] So, if input prices adjusted immediately to output prices, the aggregate supply (price/output response) curve would be vertical.

Wage rates may increase at exactly the same rate as the overall price level if the price-level increase is *fully anticipated*. If inflation were expected to be 5 percent this

---

[2]All prices going up by the same percentage is analogous to changing the monetary unit of account from, say, green dollars to red dollars, where 1.1 red dollars equals one green dollar. A change in the monetary unit of account has no effect on the firms' profit-maximizing decisions. If the nominal value of all output and input prices increases by 10 percent, then nothing *real* happens. When all nominal values go up by 10 percent, firms' decisions regarding *real* output will not change.

year, this expected increase might be built into wage and salary contracts. Most employees, however, do not receive automatic pay raises as the overall price level increases, and sometimes increases in the price level are unanticipated. Input prices—particularly wage rates—tend to lag increases in output prices for a variety of reasons. (We discuss these in chapter 15.) At least in the short run, wage rates tend to be slow to adjust to overall macroeconomic changes. It is precisely this point that has led to an important distinction between the AS curve in the long run and the AS curve in the short run.[3] We will return to this distinction shortly, but for now we will assume that the AS curve is shaped like the one in Figure 14.6.

SHIFTS OF THE SHORT-RUN AGGREGATE SUPPLY CURVE

Just as the aggregate demand curve can shift, so too can the aggregate supply (price/output response) curve. Recall the individual firm behavior we just considered in describing the shape of the short-run AS curve. Firms with the power to set prices choose the price/output combinations that maximize their profits. Firms in perfectly competitive industries choose the quantities of output to supply at given price levels. The AS curve traces out these price/output responses to economic conditions.

Anything that affects these individual firm decisions can shift the AS curve. Some of these factors include cost shocks, economic growth, stagnation, public policy, and natural disasters.

▶ **Cost Shocks** Firms' decisions are heavily influenced by costs. Some costs change at the same time the overall price level changes, some costs lag behind changes in the price level, and some may not change at all. Changes in costs that occur at the same time that the price level changes are built into the shape of the short-run AS curve. For example, when the price level rises, wage rates might rise by half as much in the short run. (This could happen if half of all wage contracts in the economy had cost-of-living increase clauses and half did not.) The shape of the short-run AS curve would reflect this response.

But sometimes cost changes occur that are *not* the result of changes in the overall price level. Example: the cost of energy. During the fall of 1990, world crude oil prices doubled from about $20 to $40 a barrel. Once it became clear the Persian Gulf War would not lead to the destruction of the Saudi Arabian oil fields, the price of crude oil on world markets fell back to below $20 per barrel. In contrast, in 1973 to 1974 and again in 1979, the price of oil increased substantially and remained at a higher level. Oil is an important input in many firms and industries, and when the price of firms' inputs rises, firms respond by raising prices and lowering output. At the aggregate level, this means an increase in the price of oil (or a similar cost increase) *shifts* the AS curve to the left, as in Figure 14.7a. A leftward shift of the AS curve means a higher price level for a given level of output.

A decrease in costs shifts the AS curve to the right, as in Figure 14.7b. A rightward shift of the AS curve means a lower price level for a given level of output.

Shifts in the AS curve brought about by a change in costs are referred to as **cost shocks** or **supply shocks**.

cost shock, or **supply shock**
A change in costs that shifts the aggregate supply (AS) curve.

▶ **Economic Growth** Economic growth shifts the AS curve to the right. Recall that the vertical part of the short-run AS curve represents the economy's maximum (capacity) output. This maximum output is determined by the economy's existing resources and

---

[3]Some textbooks derive the short-run aggregate supply curve by assuming *all* input prices are fixed. "Fixed input prices" means input prices do not change as the overall price level changes. This assumption is not realistic because the outputs of some firms (such as intermediate goods and capital goods) are the inputs of other firms. It is also unrealistic to assume that wage rates do not respond at all to changes in the overall price level. It is more realistic to assume that wage rates do not *fully* respond in the short run than it is to assume no response at all.

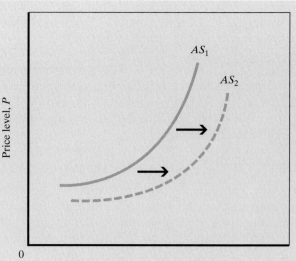

a. A decrease in aggregate supply

A leftward shift of the AS curve from AS_1 to AS_2 could be caused by an increase in costs (for example, an increase in wage rates or energy prices), natural disasters, economic stagnation, and the like.

b. An increase in aggregate supply

A rightward shift of the AS curve from AS_1 to AS_2 could be caused by a decrease in costs, economic growth, public policy that stimulates supply, and the like.

FIGURE 14.7
Shifts of the Aggregate Supply Curve

the current state of technology. If the supply of labor increases or the stock of capital grows, the AS curve will shift to the right. The labor force grows naturally with the population, but it can also increase for other reasons. Since the 1960s, for example, the percentage of women in the labor force has grown sharply. This increase in the supply of women workers has shifted the AS curve to the right.

Immigration can also shift the AS curve. During the 1970s, Germany, faced with a serious labor shortage, opened its borders to large numbers of "guest workers," largely from Turkey. The United States has recently experienced significant immigration, legal and illegal, from Mexico, from Central and South American countries, and from Asia. Increases in the stock of capital over time and technological advances can also shift the AS curve to the right. We will discuss economic growth in more detail in chapter 20.

▶ **Stagnation and Lack of Investment** The opposite of economic growth is stagnation and decline. Over time, capital deteriorates and eventually wears out completely if it is not properly maintained. If an economy fails to invest in both public capital (sometimes called *infrastructure*) and private capital (plant and equipment) at a sufficient rate, the stock of capital will decline. If the stock of capital declines, the AS curve will shift to the left.

▶ **Public Policy** Public policy can shift the AS curve. In the 1980s, for example, the Reagan administration put into effect a form of public policy based on supply-side economics. The idea behind these supply-side policies was to deregulate the economy and reduce taxes to increase the incentives to work, engage in entrepreneurial activity, and invest. The main purpose of these policies was to shift the AS curve to the right. (We discuss supply-side economics in chapter 19.)

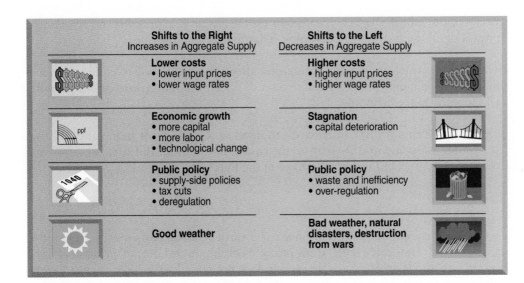

FIGURE 14.8

Factors That Shift the Aggregate Supply Curve

Shifts to the Right Increases in Aggregate Supply	Shifts to the Left Decreases in Aggregate Supply
Lower costs • lower input prices • lower wage rates	**Higher costs** • higher input prices • higher wage rates
Economic growth • more capital • more labor • technological change	**Stagnation** • capital deterioration
Public policy • supply-side policies • tax cuts • deregulation	**Public policy** • waste and inefficiency • over-regulation
Good weather	**Bad weather, natural disasters, destruction from wars**

➤ **Weather, Wars, and Natural Disasters** Changes in weather can shift the *AS* curve. A severe drought will reduce the supply of agricultural goods; the perfect mix of sun and rain will produce a bountiful harvest. If an economy is damaged by war or natural disaster, the *AS* curve will shift to the left. Whenever part of the resource base of an economy is reduced or destroyed, the *AS* curve shifts to the left.

Figure 14.8 shows some factors that might cause the *AS* curve to shift.

THE EQUILIBRIUM PRICE LEVEL

The **equilibrium price level** in the economy occurs at the point at which the *AD* curve and the *AS* curve intersect, shown in Figure 14.9, where the equilibrium price level is P_0 and the equilibrium level of aggregate output (income) is Y_0.

Figure 14.9 looks simple, but it is a powerful device for analyzing a number of macroeconomic questions. Consider first what is true at the intersection of the *AS* and *AD* curves. Each point on the *AD* curve corresponds to equilibrium in both the goods

equilibrium price level *The point at which the aggregate demand and aggregate supply curves intersect.*

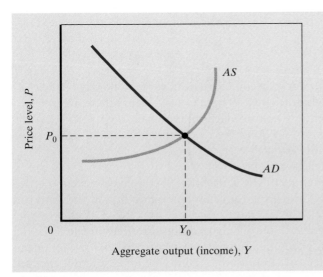

FIGURE 14.9

The Equilibrium Price Level

At each point along the *AD* curve, both the money market and the goods market are in equilibrium. Each point on the *AS* curve represents the price/output decisions of all the firms in the economy. P_0 and Y_0 correspond to equilibrium in the goods market and the money market and to a set of price/output decisions on the part of all the firms in the economy.

market and the money market. Each point on the *AS* curve represents the price/output responses of all the firms in the economy. That means:

> The point at which the *AS* and *AD* curves intersect corresponds to equilibrium in the goods and money markets and to a set of price/output decisions on the part of all the firms in the economy.

We will use this *AS/AD* framework to analyze the effects of monetary and fiscal policy on the economy and to analyze the causes of inflation. But first we need to return to the *AS* curve and discuss its shape in the long run.

THE LONG-RUN AGGREGATE SUPPLY CURVE

As we noted earlier, for the *AS* curve not to be vertical, some costs must lag behind increases in the overall price level. If all prices (both input and output prices) change at the same rate, the level of aggregate output does not change. We have assumed that in the short run at least some cost changes lag behind price level changes. But what happens in the long run?

Many economists believe costs lag behind price-level changes in the short run but ultimately move with the overall price level. For example, wage rates tend to move very closely with the price level *over time*. If the price level increases at a steady rate, inflation may come to be fully anticipated and built into most labor contracts.

If costs and the price level move in tandem in the long run, the *AS* curve is vertical. We can see why in Figure 14.10. Initially, the economy is in equilibrium at a price level of P_0 and aggregate output of Y_0 (the point at which AD_0 and AS_0 intersect). Now imagine a shift of the *AD* curve from AD_0 to AD_1. In response to this shift, both the price level and aggregate output rise in the short run, to P_1 and Y_1 respectively. But recall: the movement along the upward-sloping *AS* curve as *Y* increases from Y_0 to Y_1 assumes some costs lag behind the increase in the overall price level.

Now suppose costs fully adjust to prices in the long run. Suppose labor unions renegotiate wage contracts to catch up with the increase in prices. These kinds of cost increases, which come in later periods, cause the *AS* curve to shift to the left, from AS_0 to AS_1. If, in the final analysis, costs and prices have risen by exactly the same percentage, aggregate output will be back at Y_0 (the point at which AD_1 and AS_1 intersect).

> If wage rates and other costs fully adjust to changes in prices in the long run, then the long-run *AS* curve is vertical.

POTENTIAL GDP

Recall that even the short-run *AS* curve becomes vertical at some particular level of output. The vertical portion of the short-run *AS* curve exists because there are physical limits to the amount that an economy can produce in any given time period. At the physical limit, all plants are operating around the clock, many workers are on overtime, and there is no cyclical unemployment.

Note that the vertical portions of the short-run *AS* curves in Figure 14.10 are to the right of Y_0. If the vertical portions of the short-run *AS* curves represent "capacity," then what is the nature of Y_0, the level of output corresponding to the long-run *AS* curve?

Y_0 represents the level of aggregate output that can be *sustained* in the long run without inflation. It is sometimes called **potential output** or **potential GDP**. Output can be pushed above Y_0 under a variety of circumstances, but when it is, there is upward

potential output, or **potential GDP** *The level of aggregate output that can be sustained in the long run without inflation.*

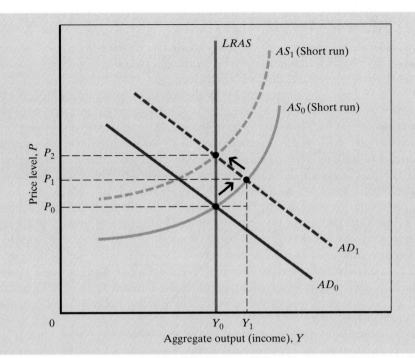

FIGURE 14.10

The Long-Run Aggregate Supply Curve

When the *AD* curve shifts from AD_0 to AD_1, the equilibrium price level initially rises from P_0 to P_1 and output rises from Y_0 to Y_1. Costs respond in the longer run, shifting the *AS* curve from AS_0 to AS_1. If costs ultimately increase by the same percentage as the price level, the quantity supplied will end up back at Y_0. Y_0 is sometimes called "potential GDP."

pressure on costs. As the economy approaches short-run capacity, wage rates tend to rise as firms try to attract more people into the labor force and to induce more workers to work overtime. Rising costs shift the short-run *AS* curve to the left (in Figure 14.10, from AS_0 to AS_1) and drive output back to Y_0.

The underlying idea here is simple. It is possible to try to squeeze too much from an existing resource base. Labor can be overemployed. In recent years, some states experienced unemployment rates below 3 percent. When the unemployment rate is this low, there is an upward pressure on wages that ultimately constrains growth.

➤ **Short-Run Equilibrium below Potential GDP**   Thus far we have argued that if the short-run aggregate supply and aggregate demand curves intersect to the right of Y_0 in Figure 14.10, wages and other input prices will rise, causing the short-run *AS* curve to shift left and pushing GDP back down to Y_0. Although different economists have different opinions on how to determine whether an economy is operating at or above potential GDP, there is general agreement that there is a maximum level of output (below the vertical portion of the short-run aggregate supply curve) that can be sustained without inflation.

But what about short-run equilibria that occur to the *left* of Y_0? If the short-run aggregate supply and aggregate demand curves intersect at a level of output below potential GDP, what will happen? Here again economists disagree. Those who believe the aggregate supply curve is vertical in the long run believe that when short-run equilibria exist below Y_0, GDP will tend to rise—just as GDP tends to fall when short-run equilibrium exists above Y_0. The argument is that when the economy is operating below full employment with excess capacity and high unemployment, input prices (including wages) are likely to *fall*. A decline in input prices shifts the aggregate supply curve to the *right,* causing the price level to fall and the level of real GDP to rise back to Y_0. This automatic adjustment works only if input prices fall when excess capacity and unemployment exist. We will discuss wage adjustment during periods of unemployment in detail in chapter 15.

AD, AS, AND MONETARY AND FISCAL POLICY

We are now ready to use the AS/AD framework to consider the effects of monetary and fiscal policy. We will first consider the short-run effects.

Recall that the two fiscal policy variables are government purchases (G) and net taxes (T). The monetary policy variable is the quantity of money supplied (M^s). An *expansionary* policy aims at stimulating the economy through an increase in G or M^s or a decrease in T. A *contractionary* policy aims at slowing down the economy through a decrease in G or M^s or an increase in T. We saw earlier in this chapter that an expansionary policy shifts the AD curve to the right and that a contractionary policy shifts the AD curve to the left. But how do these policies affect the equilibrium values of the price level (P) and the level of aggregate output (income)?

When considering the effects of a policy change, we must be careful to note where along the (short-run) AS curve the economy is at the time of the change. If the economy is initially on the flat portion of the AS curve, as shown by point A in Figure 14.11, then an expansionary policy, which shifts the AD curve to the right, results in a small price increase relative to the output increase: The increase in equilibrium Y (from Y_0 to Y_1) is much greater than the increase in equilibrium P (from P_0 to P_1). This is the case in which an expansionary policy works well. There is an increase in output with little increase in the price level.

If the economy is initially on the steep portion of the AS curve, as shown by point B in Figure 14.12, then an expansionary policy results in a small increase in equilibrium output (from Y_0 to Y_1) and a large increase in the equilibrium price level (from P_0 to P_1). In this case, an expansionary policy does not work well. It results in a much higher price level with little increase in output. The multiplier is therefore close to zero: Output is initially close to capacity, and attempts to increase it further lead mostly to a higher price level.

Figures 14.11 and 14.12 show it is important to know where the economy is *before* a policy change is put into effect. The economy is producing on the nearly flat part of the AS curve if most firms are producing well below capacity. When this is the case, firms will respond to an increase in demand by increasing output much more than they increase prices. If the economy is producing on the steep part of the AS curve, firms are close to capacity and will respond to an increase in demand by increasing prices much more than they increase output.

FIGURE 14.11

A Shift of the Aggregate Demand Curve When the Economy Is on the Nearly Flat Part of the AS Curve

Aggregate demand can shift to the right for a number of reasons, including an increase in the money supply, a tax cut, or an increase in government spending. If the shift occurs when the economy is on the nearly flat portion of the AS curve, the result will be an increase in output with little increase in the price level.

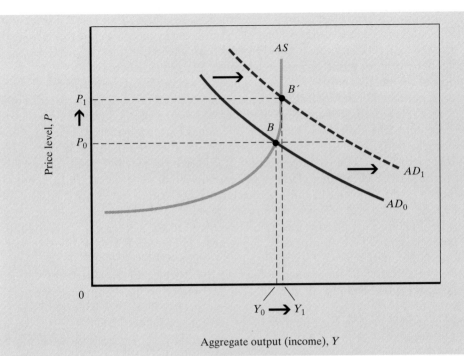

If a shift of aggregate demand occurs while the economy is operating near full capacity, the result will be an increase in the price level with little increase in output.

To see what happens when the economy is on the steep part of the *AS* curve, consider the effects of an increase in *G* with no change in the money supply. Why, when *G* is increased, will there be virtually no increase in *Y*? In other words, why will the expansionary fiscal policy fail to stimulate the economy? To answer this we need to go back to chapter 13 and consider what is behind the *AD* curve.

The first thing that happens when *G* increases is an unanticipated decline in firms' inventories. Because firms are very close to capacity output when the economy is on the steep part of the *AS* curve, they cannot increase their output very much. The result, as Figure 14.12 shows, is a substantial increase in the price level. The increase in the price level increases the demand for money, which (with a fixed money supply) leads to an increase in the interest rate, decreasing planned investment. *There is nearly complete crowding out of investment*. If firms are producing at capacity, prices and interest rates will continue to rise until the increase in *G* is completely matched by a decrease in planned investment and there is complete crowding out.

LONG-RUN AGGREGATE SUPPLY AND POLICY EFFECTS

We have so far been considering monetary and fiscal policy effects in the short run. Regarding the long run, it is important to realize:

> If the *AS* curve is vertical in the long run, neither monetary policy nor fiscal policy has any effect on aggregate output in the long run.

Look back at Figure 14.10. Monetary and fiscal policy shift the *AD* curve. If the long-run *AS* curve is vertical, output always comes back to Y_0. In this case, policy affects *only* the price level in the long run, and the multiplier effect of a change in government spending on aggregate output in the long run is zero. Under the same circumstances, the tax multiplier is also zero.

The conclusion that policy has no effect on aggregate output in the long run is perhaps startling. Do most economists agree that the aggregate supply curve is vertical in the long run?

Most economists agree that input prices tend to lag output prices in the short run, giving the *AS* curve some positive slope. Most also agree the *AS* curve is likely to be steeper in the long run. But how long is the long run? The longer the lag time, the greater the potential impact of monetary and fiscal policy on aggregate output. If the long run is only three to six months, policy has little chance to affect output; if the long run is three or four years, policy can have significant effects. A good deal of research in macroeconomics focuses on the length of time lags between input and output prices. In a sense, the length of the long run is one of the most important open questions in macroeconomics.

Another source of disagreement centers on whether equilibria below potential GDP, Y_0 in Figure 14.10, are self-correcting. Recall that those who believe in a vertical long-run *AS* curve believe that slack in the economy will put downward pressure on input prices (including wages), causing the short-run *AS* curve to shift to the right and pushing GDP back toward Y_0. However, some argue that wages and other input prices do *not* fall during slack periods and that the economy can get "stuck" at an equilibrium below potential GDP. In this case, monetary and fiscal policy would be necessary to restore full employment. We will return to this debate in chapter 15.

The "new classical" economics, which we discuss in chapter 19, assumes prices and wages are fully flexible and adjust very quickly to changing conditions. New classical economists believe, for example, that wage rate changes do not lag price changes. The new classical view is consistent with the existence of a vertical *AS* curve, even in the short run. At the other end of the spectrum is what is sometimes called the simple "Keynesian" view of aggregate supply. Those who hold this view believe there is a kink in the *AS* curve at capacity output, as we discuss in the Issues and Debates box "The Simple 'Keynesian' Aggregate Supply Curve."

CAUSES OF INFLATION

We now turn to inflation and use the *AS/AD* framework to consider the causes of inflation.

> **Inflation versus Sustained Inflation: A Reminder**   Before we discuss the specific causes of inflation, recall the distinction we made in chapter 8. **Inflation**, as you know, is an increase in the overall price level. Anything that shifts the *AD* curve to the right or the *AS* curve to the left causes inflation. But it is often useful to distinguish between a *one-time increase* in the price level (a one-time inflation) and an inflation that is sustained. A **sustained inflation** occurs when the overall price level continues to rise over some fairly long period of time. When we speak of a sustained inflation rate of 7 percent, for example, we generally mean that the price level has been rising at a rate of 7 percent per year over a number of years.

It is generally accepted that there are many possible causes of a one-time increase in the price level. (We discuss the main causes next.) But for the price level to continue to increase period after period, most economists believe it must be "accommodated" by an expanded money supply. This leads to the assertion that a sustained inflation, whatever the initial cause of the increase in the price level, is essentially a monetary phenomenon.

DEMAND-PULL INFLATION

Inflation initiated by an increase in aggregate demand is called **demand-pull inflation**. You can see how demand-pull inflation works by looking at Figures 14.11 and 14.12. In both, the inflation begins with a shift of the aggregate demand schedule from AD_0 to AD_1, which causes the price level to increase from P_0 to P_1. (Output also increases, from Y_0 to Y_1.) If the economy is operating on the steep portion of the *AS* curve at the time of the increase in aggregate demand, as in Figure 14.12, most of the effect will be

inflation *An increase in the overall price level.*

sustained inflation *Occurs when the overall price level continues to rise over some fairly long period of time.*

demand-pull inflation *Inflation that is initiated by an increase in aggregate demand.*

THE SIMPLE "KEYNESIAN" AGGREGATE SUPPLY CURVE

There is a great deal of disagreement regarding the shape of the *AS* curve. One view of the aggregate supply curve, the simple "Keynesian" view, holds that at any given moment, the economy has a clearly defined capacity, or maximum, output. This maximum output, denoted by Y_F, is defined by the existing labor force, the current capital stock, and the existing state of technology. If planned aggregate expenditure increases when the economy is producing *below* this maximum capacity, this view holds, inventories will be lower than planned and firms will increase output, but the price level will not change. Firms are operating with underutilized plants (excess capacity) and there is unemployment. Expansion does not exert any upward pressure on prices. However, if planned aggregate expenditure increases when the economy is producing near or at its maximum (Y_F), inventories will be lower than planned, but firms cannot increase their output. The result will be an increase in the price level, or inflation.

This view is illustrated in Figure 1. In the top half of the diagram, aggregate output (income) (Y) and planned aggregate expenditure ($C + I + G \equiv AE$) are initially in equilibrium at AE_1, Y_1, and price level P_1. Now suppose a tax cut or an increase in government spending increases planned aggregate expenditure. If such an increase shifts the *AE* curve from AE_1 to AE_2 and the corresponding aggregate demand curve from AD_1 to AD_2, the equilibrium level of output will rise from Y_1 to Y_F. (Remember, an expansionary policy shifts the *AD* curve to the right.) Because we were initially producing below

capacity output (Y_1 is lower than Y_F), the price level will be unaffected, remaining at P_1.

But now consider what would happen if *AE* were to increase even further. Suppose planned aggregate expenditure were to shift from AE_2 to AE_3, with a corresponding shift of AD_2 to AD_3. If the economy were producing below capacity output, the equilibrium level of output would rise to Y_3. But the output of the economy cannot exceed the maximum output of Y_F. As inventories fall below what was planned, firms encounter a fully employed labor market and fully utilized plants. Therefore, they cannot increase their output. The result is that the aggregate supply curve becomes vertical at Y_F, and the price level is driven up to P_3.

FIGURE 1

With planned aggregate expenditure of AE_1 and aggregate demand of AD_1, equilibrium output is Y_1. A shift of planned aggregate expenditure to AE_2, corresponding to a shift of the *AD* curve to AD_2, causes output to rise but the price level to remain at P_1. If planned aggregate expenditure and aggregate demand exceed Y_F, however, there is an inflationary gap and the price level rises to P_3.

The difference between planned aggregate expenditure and aggregate output at full capacity is sometimes referred to as an **inflationary gap**. You can see the inflationary gap in the top half of Figure 1. At Y_F (capacity output), planned aggregate expenditure (shown by AE_3) is greater than Y_F. The price level rises to P_3 until the aggregate quantity supplied and the aggregate quantity demanded are equal.

Despite the fact that the kinked aggregate supply curve provides some insights, most economists find it unrealistic. It does not seem likely that the whole economy suddenly runs into a capacity "wall" at a specific level of output. As output expands, some firms and industries will hit capacity before others.

For more on the aggregate supply curve, see the Case and Fair Web page at
http://www.prenhall.com/casefair.

FIGURE 14.13

Cost-Push, or Supply-Side
Inflation

An increase in costs shifts the
AS curve to the left. Assuming
the government does not react
to this shift, the *AD* curve
does not shift, the price level
rises, and output falls.

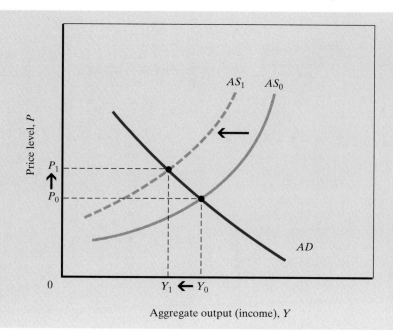

an increase in the price level rather than an increase in output. If the economy is operating on the flat portion of the *AS* curve, as in Figure 14.11, most of the effect will be
an increase in output rather than an increase in the price level.

Remember: In the long run the initial increase in the price level will cause the *AS*
curve to shift to the left as input prices (costs) respond to the increase in output prices.
If the long-run *AS* curve is vertical, as depicted in Figure 14.10, the increase in costs
will shift the short-run *AS* curve (AS_0) to the left to AS_1, pushing the price level even
higher, to P_2. If the long-run *AS* curve is vertical, a shift in aggregate demand from
AD_0 to AD_1 will result, in the long run, in *no* increase in output and a price-level increase from P_0 to P_2.

COST-PUSH, OR SUPPLY-SIDE, INFLATION

cost-push, or **supply-side,**
inflation *Inflation caused by an*
increase in costs.

Inflation can also be caused by an increase in costs, referred to as **cost-push,** or **supply-**
side, inflation. Several times in the last two decades oil prices on world markets increased
sharply. Because oil is used in virtually every line of business, costs increased.

An increase in costs (a cost shock) shifts the *AS* curve to the left, as Figure 14.13
shows. If we assume the government does not react to this shift in *AS* by changing fiscal
or monetary policy, the *AD* curve will not shift. The supply shift will cause the equilibrium price level to rise (from P_0 to P_1) and the level of aggregate output to decline (from
Y_0 to Y_1). Recall from chapter 6 that **stagflation** occurs when output is falling at the

stagflation *Occurs when output*
is falling at the same time that
prices are rising.

same time prices are rising—in other words, when the economy is experiencing both a
contraction and inflation simultaneously. Figure 14.13 shows that one possible cause of
stagflation is an increase in costs.

To return to monetary and fiscal policy for a moment, note from Figure 14.13
that the government could counteract the increase in costs (the cost shock) by engaging in an expansionary policy (an increase in *G* or M^s or a decrease in *T*). This would
shift the *AD* curve to the right, and the new *AD* curve would intersect the new *AS*
curve at a higher level of output. The problem with this policy, however, is that the
intersection of the new *AS* and *AD* curves would take place at a price even higher
than P_1 in Figure 14.13.

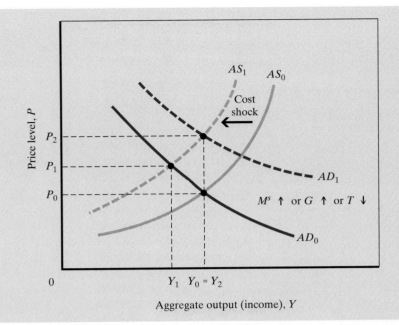

FIGURE 14.14

Cost Shocks Are Bad News for Policy Makers

A cost shock with no change in monetary or fiscal policy would shift the aggregate supply curve from AS_0 to AS_1, lower output from Y_0 to Y_1, and raise the price level from P_0 to P_1. Monetary or fiscal policy could be changed enough to have the AD curve shift from AD_0 to AD_1. This would prevent output from falling, but it would raise the price level further, to P_2.

> Cost shocks are bad news for policy makers. The only way they can counter the output loss brought about by a cost shock is by having the price level increase even more than it would without the policy action.

This situation is illustrated in Figure 14.14.

EXPECTATIONS AND INFLATION

When firms are making their price/output decisions, their *expectations* of future prices may affect their current decisions. If a firm expects that its competitors will raise their prices, in anticipation it may raise its own price.

Consider a firm that manufactures toasters. The toaster maker must decide what price to charge retail stores for its toaster. If it overestimates price and charges much more than other toaster manufacturers are charging, it will lose many customers. If it underestimates price and charges much less than other toaster makers are charging, it will gain customers but at a considerable loss in revenue per sale. The firm's *optimum price*—the price that maximizes the firm's profits—is presumably not too far from the average of its competitors' prices. If it does not know its competitors' projected prices before it sets its own price, as is often the case, it must base its price on what it expects its competitors' prices to be.

Suppose inflation has been running at about 10 percent per year. Our firm probably expects its competitors will raise their prices about 10 percent this year, so it is likely to raise the price of its own toaster by about 10 percent. This is how expectations can get "built into the system." If every firm expects every other firm to raise prices by 10 percent, every firm will raise prices by about 10 percent. Every firm ends up with the price increase it expected.

The fact that expectations can affect the price level is vexing. Expectations can lead to an inertia that makes it difficult to stop an inflationary spiral. If prices have been rising, and if people's expectations are *adaptive*—that is, if they form their expectations on the basis of past pricing behavior—then firms may continue raising prices even if demand is slowing or contracting.

In terms of the *AS/AD* diagram, an increase in inflationary expectations that causes firms to increase their prices shifts the *AS* curve to the left. Remember that the *AS* curve represents the price/output responses of firms. If firms increase their prices because of a change in inflationary expectations, the result is a leftward shift of the *AS* curve.

MONEY AND INFLATION

It is easy to see that an increase in the money supply can lead to an increase in the aggregate price level. As Figures 14.11 and 14.12 show, an increase in the money supply (M^s) shifts the *AD* curve to the right and results in a higher price level. This is simply a demand-pull inflation.

But the supply of money may also play a role in creating a sustained inflation. Consider an initial increase in government spending (G) with the money supply (M^s) unchanged. Because the money supply is unchanged, this is an increase in G that is not "accommodated" by the Fed. The increase in G shifts the *AD* curve to the right and results in a higher price level. This is shown in Figure 14.15 as a shift from AD_0 to AD_1. (In Figure 14.15, the economy is assumed to be operating on the vertical portion of the *AS* curve.)

Remember what happens when the price level increases. The higher price level causes the demand for money to increase. With an unchanged money supply and an increase in the quantity of money demanded, the interest rate will rise, and the result will be a decrease in planned investment (I) spending. The new equilibrium corresponds to higher G, lower I, a higher interest rate, and a higher price level.

Now let's take our example one step further. Suppose that the Fed is sympathetic to the expansionary fiscal policy (the increase in G we just discussed) and decides to expand the supply of money to keep the interest rate constant. As the higher price level pushes up the demand for money, the Fed expands the supply of money with the goal of keeping the interest rate unchanged, eliminating the crowding-out effect of a higher interest rate.

When the supply of money is expanded, the *AD* curve shifts to the right again, from AD_1 to AD_2. This shift of the *AD* curve, brought about by the increased money supply, pushes prices up even further. Higher prices in turn increase the demand for money further, which requires a further increase in the money supply, and so on.

What would happen if the Fed tried to keep the interest rate constant when the economy is operating on the steep part of the *AS* curve? The situation could lead to a **hyperinflation**, a period of very rapid increases in the price level. If no more output can be coaxed out of the economy and if planned investment is not allowed to fall (because the interest rate is kept unchanged), then it is not possible to increase G. As the Fed keeps pumping more and more money into the economy to keep the interest rate unchanged, the price level will keep rising.

SUSTAINED INFLATION AS A PURELY MONETARY PHENOMENON

Virtually all economists agree that an increase in the price level can be caused by anything that causes the *AD* curve to shift to the right or the *AS* curve to shift to the left. These include expansionary fiscal policy actions, monetary expansion, cost shocks, changes in expectations, and so forth. It is also generally agreed that for a *sustained* inflation to occur, the Federal Reserve must accommodate it. In this sense, a sustained inflation can be thought of as a purely monetary phenomenon.

This argument, first put forth by monetarists (coming in chapter 19), has gained wide acceptance. It is easy to show, as we just did, how expanding the money supply can continuously shift the *AD* curve. It is not as easy to come up with other reasons for continued shifts of the *AD* curve if the money supply is constant. One possibility is for the government to increase spending continuously without increasing taxes. But this process cannot continue forever. To finance spending without taxes, the government

hyperinflation *A period of very rapid increases in the price level.*

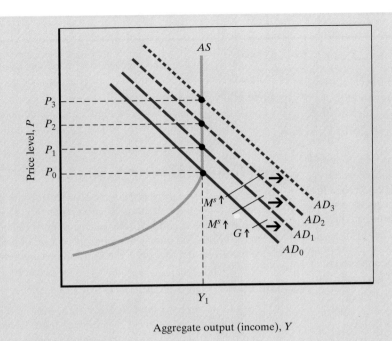

FIGURE 14.15

Sustained Inflation from an Initial Increase in *G* and Fed Accommodation

An increase in *G* with the money supply constant shifts the *AD* curve from AD_0 to AD_1. Although not shown in the figure, this leads to an increase in the interest rate and crowding out of planned investment. If the Fed tries to keep the interest rate unchanged by increasing the money supply, the *AD* curve will shift farther and farther to the right. The result is a sustained inflation, perhaps a hyperinflation.

must borrow. Without any expansion of the money supply, the interest rate will rise dramatically, making the cost of borrowing very high. But more importantly, the public must be willing to buy the government bonds that are being issued to finance the spending increases. At some point, the public may be unwilling to buy any more bonds even though the interest rate is very high.[4] At this point, the government is no longer able to increase non-tax-financed spending without the Fed's cooperation. If this is true, then a sustained inflation cannot exist without the Fed's cooperation.

In recent years, the governments of several struggling eastern European and Latin American nations have expanded their money supplies significantly. The result has been very high inflation in those countries.

LOOKING AHEAD

In chapters 9 and 10, we discussed the concept of an equilibrium level of aggregate output and income, the idea of the multiplier, and the basics of fiscal policy. Those two chapters centered on the workings of the goods market alone.

In chapters 11 and 12, we analyzed the money market by discussing the supply of money, the demand for money, the equilibrium interest rate, and the basics of monetary policy. Chapter 13 brought our analysis of the goods market together with our analysis of the money market.

In this chapter, we used everything learned so far to discuss the aggregate supply and aggregate demand curves, first mentioned in chapter 6. Using aggregate supply and aggregate demand curves, we can determine the equilibrium price level in the economy and understand some causes of inflation.

We have said little about employment, unemployment, and the functioning of the labor market in the macroeconomy. The next chapter will link everything we have done so far to this third major market arena—the labor market—and to the problem of unemployment.

---

[4]This means that the public's demand for money no longer depends on the interest rate. Even though the interest rate is very high, the public cannot be induced to have its real money balances fall any further. There is a limit regarding how much the public can be induced to have its real money balances fall.

SUMMARY

THE AGGREGATE DEMAND CURVE

1. Money demand is a function of three variables: (1) the interest rate (r); (2) the level of real income (Y); and (3) the price level (P). Money demand will increase if the real level of output (income) increases, the price level increases, or the interest rate declines.

2. At a higher price level, households and firms need to hold larger money balances. If the money supply remains the same, this increased demand for money will cause the interest rate to increase and planned investment spending to fall. As a result, planned aggregate expenditure will be lower, inventories will be greater than planned, firms will cut back on output, and Y will fall. An increase in the price level causes the level of aggregate output (income) to fall: a decrease in the price level causes the level of aggregate output (income) to rise.

3. *Aggregate demand* is the total demand for goods and services in the economy. The *aggregate demand* (*AD*) *curve* illustrates the negative relationship between aggregate output (income) and the price level. Each point on the *AD* curve is a point at which both the goods market and the money market are in equilibrium. The *AD* curve is *not* the sum of all the market demand curves in the economy.

4. At every point along the aggregate demand curve, the aggregate quantity demanded in the economy is exactly equal to planned aggregate expenditure.

5. An increase in the quantity of money supplied, an increase in government purchases, or a decrease in net taxes at a given price level shifts the aggregate demand curve to the right. A decrease in the quantity of money supplied, a decrease in government purchases, or an increase in net taxes shifts the aggregate demand curve to the left.

THE AGGREGATE SUPPLY CURVE

6. *Aggregate supply* is the total supply of goods and services in an economy. The *aggregate supply* (*AS*) *curve* shows the relationship between the aggregate quantity of output supplied by all the firms in an economy and the overall price level. The *AS* curve is *not* a market supply curve, and it is *not* the simple sum of all the individual supply curves in the economy. For this reason, it is helpful to think of the *AS* curve as a "price/output response" curve—that is, a curve that traces out the price decisions and output decisions of all the markets and firms in the economy under a given set of circumstances.

7. The shape of the short-run *AS* curve is a source of much controversy in macroeconomics. Many economists believe that at very low levels of aggregate output the *AS* curve is fairly flat, and at high levels of aggregate output the *AS* curve is vertical or nearly vertical. Thus, the *AS* curve slopes upward and becomes vertical when the economy reaches its capacity, or maximum, output.

8. Anything that affects individual firms' decisions can shift the *AS* curve. Some of these factors include cost shocks, economic growth, stagnation, public policy, and natural disasters.

THE EQUILIBRIUM PRICE LEVEL

9. The *equilibrium price level* in the economy occurs at the point at which the *AS* and *AD* curves intersect. The intersection of the *AS* and *AD* curves corresponds to equilibrium in the goods and money markets *and* to a set of price/output decisions on the part of all the firms in the economy.

THE LONG-RUN AGGREGATE SUPPLY CURVE

10. For the *AS* curve to slope upward, some input prices must lag behind increases in the overall price level. If wage rates and other costs fully adjust to changes in prices in the long run, then the long-run *AS* curve is vertical.

11. The level of aggregate output that can be sustained in the long run without inflation is called *potential output* or *potential GDP*.

AD, AS, AND MONETARY AND FISCAL POLICY

12. If the economy is initially producing on the flat portion of the *AS* curve, an expansionary policy—which shifts the *AD* curve to the right—will result in a small increase in the equilibrium price level relative to the increase in equilibrium output. If the economy is initially producing on the steep portion of the *AS* curve, an expansionary policy results in a small increase in equilibrium output and a large increase in the equilibrium price level.

13. If the *AS* curve is vertical in the long run, neither monetary nor fiscal policy has any effect on aggregate output in the long run. For this reason, the exact length of the long run is one of the most pressing questions in macroeconomics.

CAUSES OF INFLATION

14. *Inflation* is an increase in the overall price level. A *sustained inflation* occurs when the overall price level continues to rise over some fairly long period of time. Most economists believe that sustained inflations can occur only if the Fed continuously increases the money supply.

15. *Demand-pull inflation* is inflation initiated by an increase in aggregate demand. *Cost-push*, or *supply-side*, *inflation* is inflation initiated by an increase in costs. An increase in costs may also lead to *stagflation*—the situation in which the economy is experiencing both a contraction and inflation simultaneously.

16. Inflation can become "built into the system" as a result of expectations. If prices have been rising and people form their expectations on the basis of past pricing behavior, firms may continue raising prices even if demand is slowing or contracting.

17. When the price level increases, so too does the demand for money. If the economy is operating on the steep part of the *AS* curve and the Fed tries to keep the interest rate constant by increasing the supply of money, the result could be a hyperinflation—a period of very rapid increases in the price level.

REVIEW TERMS AND CONCEPTS

aggregate demand, 292
aggregate demand (*AD*) curve, 293
aggregate supply, 297
aggregate supply (*AS*) curve, 297
cost-push, or supply-side, inflation, 310

cost shock, or supply shock, 301
demand-pull inflation, 308
equilibrium price level, 303
hyperinflation, 312
inflation, 308

inflationary gap, 309
potential output, or potential GDP, 304
real wealth, or real balance, effect, 295
stagflation, 310
sustained inflation, 308

PROBLEM SET

1. "The aggregate demand curve slopes downward, because when the price level is lower, people can afford to buy more, and aggregate demand rises. When prices rise, people can afford to buy less, and aggregate demand falls." Is this a good explanation of the shape of the *AD* curve? Why or why not?

2. Using aggregate supply and demand curves to illustrate your points, discuss the impacts of the following events on the price level and on equilibrium GDP (*Y*) in the *short run:*
   a. A tax cut holding government purchases constant with the economy operating at near full capacity.
   b. An increase in the money supply during a period of high unemployment and excess industrial capacity.
   c. An increase in the price of oil caused by a war in the Middle East, assuming that the Fed attempts to keep interest rates constant by accommodating inflation.
   d. The Clinton plan from early 1993: an increase in taxes and a cut in government spending, supported by a cooperative Fed acting to keep output from falling.

3. During 1997 and 1998, a debate raged over whether the United States was at or above potential GDP (see the Application box in this chapter). Some economists feared the economy was operating at a level of output above potential GDP and inflationary pressures were building. They urged the Fed to tighten monetary policy and increase interest rates to slow the economy. Others argued that a worldwide glut of cheap products was causing input prices to be lower, keeping prices from rising.

Using aggregate supply and demand curves and other useful graphs, illustrate the following:
   a. Those pushing the Fed to act were right and prices start to rise more rapidly in 1998 and 1999. The Fed acts belatedly to slow money growth (contract the money supply), driving up interest rates and pushing the economy back to potential GDP.
   b. The worldwide glut gets worse and the result is a *falling* price level (deflation) in the United States despite expanding aggregate demand.

4. Show the effects of the following stories on the position of the aggregate demand curve. Use graphs of the money demand curve, the investment function, and aggregate expenditure function if useful. What is likely to happen to *Y, C, I,* and *r* as a result?
   a. In 1997 the Congress enacted a substantial tax cut (the Taxpayer Relief Act of 1997) that lowered taxes for many immediately. While the act contained some expenditure reductions, they did not kick in until 1999. Assume that the Fed expands the money supply to keep interest rates constant.
   b. The Federal Reserve sharply decreases the money supply to fight inflation.

5. Using aggregate supply and aggregate demand curves to illustrate, describe the effects of the following events on the price level and on equilibrium GDP in the *long run,* assuming that input prices fully adjust to output prices after some lag:
   a. An increase in the money supply above potential GDP.
   b. A decrease in government spending and in the money supply with GDP above potential GDP.
   c. Starting with the economy at potential GDP, a war in the Middle East pushes up energy prices temporarily. The Fed expands the money supply to accommodate the inflation.

6. Two separate capacity constraints are discussed in this chapter: (1) the actual physical capacity of existing plants and equipment, shown as the vertical portion of the short-run *AS* curve, and (2) potential GDP, leading to a vertical *LRAS* curve. Explain the difference between the two. Which is greater, full-capacity GDP or potential GDP? Why?

7. In country A, all wage contracts are indexed to inflation. That is, each month wages are adjusted to reflect increases in the cost of living as reflected in changes in the price level. In country B, there are no cost-of-living adjustments to wages, but the workforce is completely unionized. Unions negotiate three-year contracts. In which country is an expansionary monetary policy likely to have a larger effect on aggregate output? Explain your answer using aggregate supply and aggregate demand curves.

8. In an effort to fight inflation in 1974 and 1975, the U.S. government acted with contractionary monetary policy. Using aggregate supply and aggregate demand curves, illustrate the effects that the government expected this policy to have on aggregate output and on the price level.

The contractionary monetary policy had the effect of reducing aggregate output; the United States experienced a recession from 1974 to 1975. But although output was reduced, prices continued to increase throughout the recession. Give two alternative explanations for why prices might continue to rise even though output is falling.

TAKE IT TO THE NET

We invite you to visit the Case and Fair page on the Prentice Hall Web site:

http://www.prenhall.com/casefair

for this chapter's World Wide Web exercise.

Chapter 15

THE LABOR MARKET, UNEMPLOYMENT, AND INFLATION

IN CHAPTER 6, we stressed the three broadly defined markets in which households, firms, the government, and the rest of the world interact: (1) the *goods market*, discussed in chapters 9 and 10, (2) the *money market*, discussed in chapters 11 and 12, and (3) the *labor market*. In chapter 8 we described some features of the U.S. labor market and explained how the unemployment rate is measured. Then, in chapter 14, we considered the labor market briefly in our discussion of the aggregate supply curve. Because labor is an input, what goes on in the labor market affects the shape of the *AS* curve. If wages and other input costs lag price increases, the *AS* curve will be upward sloping; if wages and other input costs are completely flexible and rise every time prices rise by the same percentage, the *AS* curve will be vertical.

In this chapter we look further at the labor market's role in the macroeconomy. First, we consider the classical view, which holds that wages always adjust to clear the labor market. We then consider why the labor market may not always clear and why unemployment may exist. Finally, we discuss the relationship between inflation and unemployment.

➤ **The Labor Market: Basic Concepts** Let's review briefly what the unemployment rate measures. The **unemployment rate** is the number of people unemployed as a percentage of the labor force. To be unemployed, a person must be out of a job and actively looking for work. When a person stops looking for work, he or she is considered *out of the labor force* and is no longer counted as unemployed.

It is important to realize that even if the economy is running at or near full capacity, the unemployment rate will never be zero. The economy is dynamic. Students graduate from schools and training programs; some businesses make profits and grow, while others suffer losses and go out of business; people move in and out of the labor force and change careers. It takes time for people to find the right job and for employers to match the right worker with the jobs they have. This **frictional** and **structural unemployment** is inevitable and in many ways desirable. (Review chapter 8 if these terms are hazy to you.)

unemployment rate *The ratio of the number of people unemployed to the total number of people in the labor force.*

frictional unemployment *The portion of unemployment that is due to the normal working of the labor market; used to denote short-run job/skill matching problems.*

structural unemployment *The portion of unemployment that is due to changes in the structure of the economy that result in a significant loss of jobs in certain industries.*

In this chapter, we are concerned with **cyclical unemployment**, the increase in unemployment that occurs during recessions and depressions. When the economy contracts, the number of people unemployed and the unemployment rate rise. The United States has experienced several periods of high unemployment. During the Great Depression, the unemployment rate remained over 17 percent for nearly a decade. In December of 1982, more than 12 million people were unemployed, putting the unemployment rate at 10.8 percent.

In one sense, the reason employment falls when the economy experiences a downturn is obvious. When firms cut back on production, they need fewer workers, so people get laid off.

> Employment tends to fall when aggregate output falls and rise when aggregate output rises.

But a decline in the demand for labor does not necessarily mean that unemployment will rise. If markets work as we described in chapters 4 and 5, a decline in the demand for labor will initially create an excess supply of labor. As a result, the wage rate will fall until the quantity of labor supplied again equals the quantity of labor demanded, restoring equilibrium in the labor market. At the new lower wage rate, everyone who wants a job will have one.

If the quantity of labor demanded and the quantity of labor supplied are brought into equilibrium by rising and falling wage rates, there should be no persistent unemployment above the frictional and structural amount. This was the view held by the classical economists who preceded Keynes, and it is still the view of a number of economists today.

THE CLASSICAL VIEW OF THE LABOR MARKET

The classical view of the labor market is illustrated in Figure 15.1. Classical economists assumed the wage rate adjusts to equate the quantity of labor demanded with the quantity of labor supplied, thereby implying that unemployment does not exist. To see how this adjustment takes place, assume there is a decrease in the demand for labor that shifts the demand curve in Figure 15.1 from D_0 to D_1. This decreased demand will cause the wage rate to fall from W_0 to W^* and the amount of labor demanded to fall from L_0 to L^*. The decrease in the quantity of labor supplied is a movement along the labor supply curve.

labor supply curve *A graph that illustrates the amount of labor that households want to supply at the particular wage rate.*

Each point on the **labor supply curve** in Figure 15.1 represents the amount of labor households want to supply at the particular wage rate. Each household's decision regarding how much labor to supply is part of the overall consumer choice problem of a household.[1] Each household member looks at the market wage rate, the prices of outputs, and the value of leisure time (including the value of staying at home and working in the yard or raising children) and chooses the amount of labor to supply (if any). A household member not in the labor force has decided his or her time is more valuable in nonmarket activities.

It is easy to see why. If you choose to stay out of the labor force, it is because you (a member of society) place a higher value on the use of your time than society is currently placing on the product that you would produce if you were employed. Consider households in less-developed countries. In many, the alternative to working for a wage is subsistence farming. If the wage rate in the labor market is very low, many will choose to farm for themselves. In this case, the value of what these people produce in farming must be greater than the value that society currently places on what they would produce if they worked for a wage. If this were not true, wages would rise and more people would join the labor force.

---

[1] The household choice problem is discussed in detail in chapter 6.

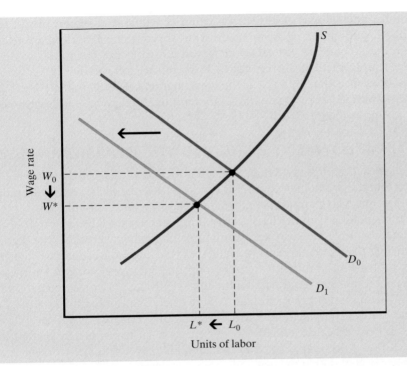

FIGURE 15.1

The Classical Labor Market

Classical economists believe that the labor market always clears. If the demand for labor shifts from D_0 to D_1, the equilibrium wage will fall from W_0 to W^*. Everyone who wants a job at W^* will have one.

Each point on the **labor demand curve** in Figure 15.1 represents the amount of labor firms want to employ at the particular wage rate. Each firm's decision about how much labor to demand is part of its overall profit-maximizing decision.[2] A firm makes a profit by selling output to households. It will hire workers if the value of its output is sufficient to justify the wage that is being paid. Thus, the amount of labor that a firm hires depends on the value of the output that workers produce.

The classical economists saw the workings of the labor market—the behavior of labor supply and labor demand—as optimal from the standpoint of both individual households and firms and from the standpoint of society. If households want more output than is currently being produced, output demand will increase, output prices will rise, the demand for labor will increase, the wage rate will rise, and more workers will be drawn into the labor force. (Some of those who preferred not to be a part of the labor force at the lower wage rate will be lured into the labor force at the higher wage rate.) At equilibrium, prices and wages reflect a trade-off between the value households place on outputs and the value of time spent in leisure and nonmarket work. At equilibrium, the people who are not working have *chosen* not to work at that market wage. There is always *full employment* in this sense. The classical economists believed the market will achieve the optimal result if left to its own devices, and there is nothing the government can do to make things better.

labor demand curve *A graph that illustrates the amount of labor that firms want to employ at the particular wage rate.*

THE CLASSICAL LABOR MARKET AND THE AS CURVE

We can now relate the classical view of the labor market to the theory of the vertical *AS* curve in chapter 14. The classical idea that wages adjust to clear the labor market is consistent with the view that wages respond quickly to price changes. Recall that the argument that the *AS* curve is vertical in the long run involves input-price adjustments. If the short-run *AS* and *AD* curves intersected above potential GDP (Y_0 in Figure 14.10), then input prices, *including wages*, would rise, shifting the *AS* curve to the left and pushing Y back down to Y_0. Similarly, if the short-run *AS* and *AD* curves intersected to

[2]The demand for inputs by firms, including the demand for labor, is discussed in chapter 10.

the left of Y_0, unemployment and excess capacity would cause input prices, *including wages*, to fall, shifting the *AS* curve to the right and pushing *Y* back up to Y_0. Also remember: if the *AS* curve is vertical, monetary and fiscal policy cannot affect the level of output and employment in the economy. It, therefore, follows that those who believe the wage rate adjusts quickly to clear the labor market are likely to believe the *AS* curve is vertical (or almost vertical) and monetary and fiscal policy have little or no effect on output and employment.

THE UNEMPLOYMENT RATE AND THE CLASSICAL VIEW

If, as the classical economists assumed, the labor market works well, how can we account for the fact that the unemployment rate at times seems high? There seem to be times when millions of people who want jobs at prevailing wage rates cannot find them. How can we reconcile this situation with the classical assumption about the labor market?

Some economists answer by arguing that the unemployment rate is not a good measure of whether the labor market is working well. We know the economy is dynamic and at any given time some industries are expanding and some are contracting. In California the construction industry contracted in the mid-1990s. Consider a carpenter who is laid off because of the industry's contraction. This person had probably developed specific skills related to the construction industry—skills not necessarily useful for jobs in other industries. If he were earning $30,000 per year as a carpenter, it may be that he could earn only $20,000 per year in another industry. He may eventually work his way back up to a salary of $30,000 in the new industry as he develops new skills, but this will take time. Will the carpenter take a job at $20,000? There are at least two reasons he may not. First, he may believe the slump in the construction industry is temporary and he will soon get his job back. Second, he may believe he can earn more than $20,000 in another industry and will continue to look for a better job.

If our carpenter decides to continue looking for a job paying more than $20,000 per year, he will be considered unemployed because he is actively looking for work. This does not necessarily mean the labor market is not working properly. The carpenter has *chosen* not to work for a wage of $20,000 per year, but if his value to any firm outside the construction industry is no more than $20,000 per year, we would not expect him to find a job paying more than $20,000. The unemployment rate as measured by the government is not necessarily an accurate indicator of whether the labor market is working properly.

If the degree to which industries are changing in the economy fluctuates over time, there will be more people like our carpenter at some times than at others. This will cause the measured unemployment rate to fluctuate. Some economists argue the measured

SOME ECONOMISTS BELIEVE UNEMPLOYMENT IS NOT A MAJOR PROBLEM. HOWEVER, THE IMAGES OF THE 1930S ARE STILL WITH US, AND MORE THAN 12 MILLION PEOPLE WERE LOOKING FOR WORK DURING THE RECESSION OF 1982.

unemployment rate may sometimes *seem* high even though the labor market is working well. The quantity of labor supplied at the current wage is equal to the quantity demanded at the current wage. The fact that there are people willing to work at a wage higher than the current wage does not mean the labor market is not working. Whenever there is an upward-sloping supply curve in a market (as is usually the case in the labor market), the quantity supplied at a price higher than the equilibrium price is always greater than the quantity supplied at the equilibrium price.

Economists who view unemployment in this way do not see it as a major problem. Yet the images of the bread lines in the 1930s are still with us, and many find it difficult to believe everything was optimal when over 12 million people were looking for work at the end of 1982. There are other views of unemployment, as we now will see.

EXPLAINING THE EXISTENCE OF UNEMPLOYMENT

If unemployment is a major macroeconomic problem—and many economists believe it is—then we need to explore some of the reasons that have been suggested for its existence. Among these are sticky wages, efficiency wage theory, imperfect information, and minimum wage laws.

STICKY WAGES

One explanation for unemployment (above and beyond normal frictional and structural unemployment) is that wages are **"sticky"** on the downward side. That is, the equilibrium wage gets stuck at a particular level and does not fall when the demand for labor falls. This is illustrated in Figure 15.2, where the equilibrium wage gets stuck at W_0 (the original wage) and does not fall to W^* when demand decreases from D_0 to D_1. The result is unemployment of the amount $L_0 - L_1$, where L_0 is the quantity of labor that households want to supply at wage rate W_0 and L_1 is the amount of labor that firms want to hire at wage rate W_0. $L_0 - L_1$ is the number of workers who would like to work at W_0 but cannot find jobs.

The sticky wage explanation of unemployment begs the question. *Why* are wages sticky, if they are, and why do wages not fall to clear the labor market during periods of

sticky wages *The downward rigidity of wages as an explanation for the existence of unemployment.*

FAST FACTS

With unemployment at a 24-year low (4.7%) late in 1997, it was not considered a big problem in the United States. If anything, there were worries about a shortage of skilled workers. In Europe, unemployment has been a chronic problem. In November 1997, unemployment was 13.4% in Belgium, 12.5% in France, 11.8% in Germany, 12.8% in Italy, and 20.8% in Spain.

Source: The Economist, November 15, 1997, p. 108.

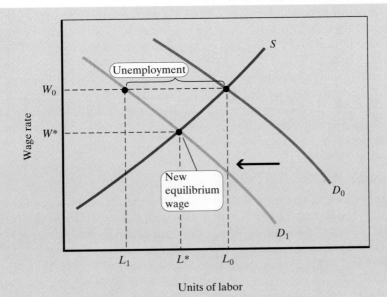

FIGURE 15.2

Sticky Wages

If wages "stick" at W_0 rather than fall to the new equilibrium wage of W^* following a shift of demand from D_0 to D_1, the result will be unemployment equal to $L_0 - L_1$.

high unemployment? Many answers have been proposed, but as yet no one answer has been agreed upon. This is one reason macroeconomics has been in a state of flux for so long. The existence of unemployment continues to be a puzzle. Although we will discuss the major theories that have been proposed to explain why wages may not clear the labor market, we can offer no conclusions. The question is still open.

> **Social, or Implicit, Contracts**   One explanation for downwardly sticky wages is that firms enter into **social**, or **implicit**, **contracts** with workers not to cut wages. It seems that extreme events—a deep recession, deregulation, or threat of bankruptcy—are necessary for firms to cut wages. Wage cuts did occur during the Great Depression, in the airline industry following deregulation of the industry in the 1980s, and recently when some U.S. manufacturing firms found themselves in danger of bankruptcy from stiff foreign competition. These are exceptions to the general rule. For reasons that may be more sociological than economic, cutting wages seems close to being a taboo.

A related argument, the **relative-wage explanation of unemployment**, holds that workers are concerned about their wages *relative* to the wages of other workers in other firms and industries and may be unwilling to accept wage cuts unless they know other workers are receiving similar cuts. Because it is difficult to reassure any one group of workers that all other workers are in the same situation, workers may resist any cut in their wages. There may be an implicit understanding between firms and workers that firms will not do anything that would make their workers worse off relative to workers in other firms.

> **Explicit Contracts**   Many workers—in particular, unionized workers—sign one- to three-year employment contracts with firms. These contracts stipulate the workers' wages for each year of the contract. Wages set in this way do not fluctuate with economic conditions, either upward or downward. If the economy slows down and firms demand fewer workers, the wage will not fall. Rather, some workers will be laid off.

Although **explicit contracts** can explain why some wages are sticky, a deeper question must also be considered. Workers and firms surely know at the time a contract is signed that unforeseen events may cause the wages set by the contract to be too high or too low. Why do firms and workers bind themselves in this way? One explanation is that negotiating wages is costly. Negotiations between unions and firms can take a considerable amount of time—time that could be spent producing output—and it would be very costly to negotiate wages weekly or monthly. Contracts are a way of bearing these costs at no more than one-, two-, or three-year intervals. There is a trade-off between the costs of locking workers and firms into contracts for long periods of time and the costs of wage negotiations. The length of contracts that minimizes negotiation costs seems to be (from what we observe in practice) between one and three years.

Some multiyear contracts adjust for unforeseen events by **cost-of-living adjustments (COLAs)** written into the contract. COLAs tie wages to changes in the cost of living: The greater the rate of inflation, the more wages are raised. COLAs thus protect workers from unexpected inflation, although many COLAs adjust wages by a smaller percentage than the percentage increase in prices.

EFFICIENCY WAGE THEORY

Another explanation for unemployment centers on the **efficiency wage theory**, which holds that the productivity of workers increases with the wage rate. If this is true, firms may have an incentive to pay wages *above* the wage at which the quantity of labor supplied is equal to the quantity of labor demanded.

An individual firm has an incentive to hire workers as long as the value of what they produce is equal to or greater than the wage rate. With no efficiency effects, the market in Figure 15.1 would produce an equilibrium wage of W^*. But suppose the

---

social, or implicit, contracts *Unspoken agreements between workers and firms that firms will not cut wages.*

relative-wage explanation of unemployment *An explanation for sticky wages (and therefore unemployment): If workers are concerned about their wages relative to other workers in other firms and industries, they may be unwilling to accept a wage cut unless they know that all other workers are receiving similar cuts.*

explicit contracts *Employment contracts that stipulate workers' wages, usually for a period of one to three years.*

cost-of-living adjustments (COLAs) *Contract provisions that tie wages to changes in the cost of living. The greater the inflation rate, the more wages are raised.*

efficiency wage theory *An explanation for unemployment that holds that the productivity of workers increases with the wage rate. If this is so, firms may have an incentive to pay wages above the market-clearing rate.*

firm could increase the productivity of all its workers by raising the wage rate above W^*. The firm's demand for labor would be no lower, but the higher wage rate would cause the quantity of labor supplied to increase. The quantity of labor supplied would exceed the quantity of labor demanded at the new higher wage—the *efficiency wage*—and the result is unemployment.

Empirical studies of labor markets have identified several potential benefits that firms receive from paying workers more than the market-clearing wage. Among them are lower turnover, improved morale, and reduced "shirking" of work.[3] But even though the efficiency wage theory predicts some unemployment, it is unlikely that the behavior it is describing accounts for much of the observed large cyclical fluctuations in unemployment over time.

IMPERFECT INFORMATION

Thus far we have been assuming that firms know exactly what wage rates they need to set to clear the labor market. They may not choose to set their wages at this level, but at least they know what the market-clearing wage is. In practice, firms may not have enough information at their disposal to know what the market-clearing wage is. In this case, firms are said to have *imperfect information*. If firms have imperfect or incomplete information, they may simply set wages wrong—wages that do not clear the labor market.

If a firm sets its wages too high, more workers will want to work for that firm than the firm wants to employ, and some potential workers will be turned away. The result is, of course, unemployment. One objection to this explanation is that it explains the existence of unemployment only in the very short run. As soon as a firm sees that it has made a mistake, why wouldn't it immediately correct its mistake and adjust its wage to the correct, market-clearing level? Why would unemployment *persist*?

If the economy were simple, it should take no more than a few months for firms to correct their mistakes. But the economy is complex. Although firms may be aware of their past mistakes and may try to correct them, new events are happening all the time. Because constant change—including a constantly changing equilibrium wage level—is characteristic of the economy, firms may find it hard to adjust wages to the market-clearing level. The labor market is not like the stock market or the market for wheat, where prices are determined in organized exchanges every day. Rather, thousands of firms are setting wages and millions of workers are responding to these wages. It may take considerable time for the market-clearing wages to be determined after they have been disturbed from an equilibrium position.

MINIMUM WAGE LAWS

Minimum wage laws explain at least a small fraction of unemployment. These laws set a floor for wage rates—a minimum hourly rate for any kind of labor. In 1998, the federal minimum wage was \$5.15 per hour. If the market-clearing wage for some groups of workers is below this amount, this group will be unemployed. In Figure 15.2, if the minimum wage is W_0 and the market-clearing wage is W^*, then the number of unemployed will be $L_0 - L_1$.

Teenagers, who have relatively little job experience, are most likely to be hurt by minimum wage laws. If some teenagers can produce only \$4.50 worth of output per hour, no firm would be willing to hire them at a wage of \$5.15. To do so would incur a loss of \$0.65 per hour. In an unregulated market, these teenagers would be able to find work at the market-clearing wage of \$4.50 per hour. If the minimum wage laws prevent the wage from falling below \$5.15, these workers will not be able to find jobs, and they will be unemployed.

A recent paper argues that unemployment rates in Europe are consistently higher than in the United States because European labor markets are less flexible than in the United States. Proposals to reduce unemployment go beyond increasing GDP. They include cutting jobless benefits, reducing minimum wages, and relaxing job protection laws.

See David Coe and Dennis Snower, "Policy Complementarities: The Case for Fundamental Labor Market Reform," IMF Staff Papers, Volume 44, No. 1, 1997.

minimum wage laws *Laws that set a floor for wage rates—that is, a minimum hourly rate for any kind of labor.*

---

[3]For a good summary, see George Akerlof and Janet Yellen, *Efficiency Wage Models of the Labor Market* (Cambridge: Cambridge University Press, 1986).

In response to this argument against the minimum wage, Congress established a subminimum wage for teenagers. The new law allows employers to hire teenagers at an "Opportunity Wage" of $4.25 for up to 90 days.

AN OPEN QUESTION

As we've seen, there are many explanations for why the labor market may not clear. The theories we have just set forth are not necessarily mutually exclusive, and there may be elements of truth in all of them. The aggregate labor market is very complicated, and there are no simple answers to why there is unemployment. Much current work in macroeconomics is concerned directly or indirectly with this question, and it is an exciting area of study. Which argument or arguments will win out in the end is an open question.

THE SHORT-RUN RELATIONSHIP BETWEEN THE UNEMPLOYMENT RATE AND INFLATION

The relationship between the unemployment rate and inflation—two of the most important variables in macroeconomics—has been the subject of much debate. We now have enough knowledge of the macroeconomy to explore this relationship.

We must begin by considering the relationship between aggregate output (income) (Y) and the unemployment rate (U). An increase in Y means firms are producing more output. To produce more output, more labor is needed in the production process. Therefore, an increase in Y leads to an increase in employment. An increase in employment means more people working (fewer people unemployed) and a lower unemployment rate. An increase in Y corresponds to a *decrease* in U. Thus U and Y are *negatively* related:[4]

> When Y rises, the unemployment rate falls, and when Y falls, the unemployment rate rises.

Next consider an upward-sloping aggregate supply (AS) curve, as shown in Figure 15.3. This curve represents the relationship between Y and the overall price level (P). The relationship is a positive one: When Y increases, P increases, and when Y decreases, P decreases.

As you will recall from the last chapter, the shape of the AS curve is determined by the behavior of firms and how they react to an increase in demand. If aggregate demand shifts to the right and the economy is operating on the nearly flat part of the AS curve—far from capacity—output will increase but the price level will not change much. However, if the economy is operating on the steep part of the AS curve—close to capacity—an increase in demand will drive up the price level, but output will be constrained by capacity and will not increase much.

Think about what will happen following an event that leads to an increase in aggregate demand. First, firms experience an unanticipated decline in inventories. They respond by increasing output (Y) and hiring workers—the unemployment rate falls. If the economy is not close to capacity, there will be little increase in the price level. But if aggregate demand continues to grow, the ability of the economy to increase output will eventually reach its limit. As aggregate demand shifts further and further to the right along the AS curve, the price level increases more and more, and output begins to reach its limit. At the point at which the AS curve becomes vertical, output cannot rise any further. If output cannot grow, the unemployment rate cannot be pushed any lower.

[4]We will see in chapter 17 that this relationship is not simple; all we need to know for now is that the two variables are negatively related.

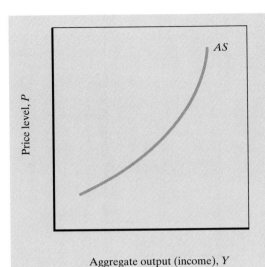

FIGURE 15.3

The Aggregate Supply Curve

The *AS* curve shows a positive relationship between the price level (*P*) and aggregate output (income) (*Y*).

There is a negative relationship between the unemployment rate and the price level. As the unemployment rate declines in response to the economy moving closer and closer to capacity output, the overall price level rises more and more, as shown in Figure 15.4.

The curve in Figure 15.4 has *not* been a major focus of attention in macroeconomics. Rather, the curve that has been extensively studied is shown in Figure 15.5, which plots the inflation rate on the vertical axis and the unemployment rate on the horizontal axis. The **inflation rate** is the percentage change in the price level, not the price level itself.

Figures 15.4 and 15.5 imply different things. Figure 15.4 says the *price level* remains the same if the unemployment rate remains unchanged. Figure 15.5 says that the *inflation rate* remains the same if the unemployment rate remains unchanged. The curve in Figure 15.5 is called the **Phillips Curve**, after A. W. Phillips, who first examined it using data for the United Kingdom. In simplest terms, the Phillips Curve is a graph showing the relationship between the inflation rate and the unemployment rate.

The rest of this chapter focuses on the Phillips Curve in Figure 15.5 because it is the macroeconomic relationship that has been studied the most. Keep in mind, however, that it is not easy to go from the *AS* curve to the Phillips Curve. We have

inflation rate *The percentage change in the price level.*

Phillips Curve *A graph showing the relationship between the inflation rate and the unemployment rate.*

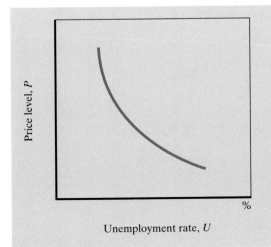

FIGURE 15.4

The Relationship between the Price Level and the Unemployment Rate

There is a negative relationship between the price level (*P*) and the unemployment rate (*U*). As the unemployment rate declines in response to the economy's moving closer and closer to capacity output, the price level rises more and more.

FIGURE 15.5

The Phillips Curve

The Phillips Curve shows the relationship between the inflation rate and the unemployment rate.

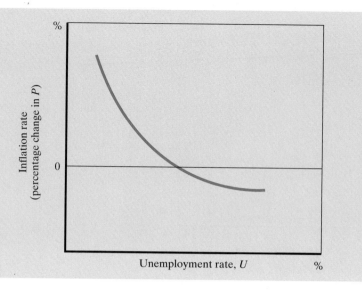

moved from graphs in which the price level is on the vertical axis (Figures 15.3 and 15.4) to a graph in which the *percentage change* in the price level is on the vertical axis (Figure 15.5). Put another way, the theory behind the Phillips Curve is somewhat different from the theory behind the *AS* curve. Fortunately, most of the insights gained from the *AS/AD* analysis regarding the behavior of the price level also apply to the behavior of the inflation rate.

THE PHILLIPS CURVE: A HISTORICAL PERSPECTIVE

In the 1950s and 1960s, there was a remarkably smooth relationship between the unemployment rate and the rate of inflation, as Figure 15.6 shows for the 1960s. As you can see, the data points fit fairly closely around a downward-sloping curve; in general,

FIGURE 15.6

Unemployment and Inflation, 1960 to 1969

During the 1960s there seemed to be an obvious trade-off between inflation and unemployment. Policy debates during the period revolved around this apparent trade-off.

Source: Table 8.9; *Economic Report of the President*, 1998, Table B-42.

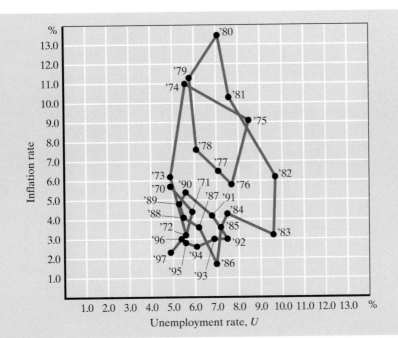

FIGURE 15.7

Unemployment and Inflation, 1970 to 1997

During the 1970s and 1980s, it became clear that the relationship between unemployment and inflation was anything but simple.

Source: Table 8.9; *Economic Report of the President*, 1998, Table B-42.

the higher the unemployment rate, the lower the rate of inflation. The Phillips Curve in Figure 15.6 shows a trade-off between inflation and unemployment. To lower the inflation rate, we must accept a higher unemployment rate, and to lower the unemployment rate, we must accept a higher rate of inflation.

Textbooks written in the 1960s and early 1970s relied on the Phillips Curve as the main explanation of inflation. Things seemed simple—inflation appeared to respond in a fairly predictable way to changes in the unemployment rate. For this reason, policy discussions in the 1960s revolved around the Phillips Curve. The role of the policy maker, it was thought, was to choose a point on the curve. Conservatives usually argued for choosing a point with a low rate of inflation and were willing to accept a higher unemployment rate in exchange for this. Liberals usually argued for accepting more inflation to keep unemployment at a low level.

Life did not turn out to be quite so simple. The Phillips Curve broke down in the 1970s and 1980s. This can be seen in Figure 15.7, which graphs the unemployment rate and inflation rate for the period from 1970 to 1997. The points in Figure 15.7 show no particular relationship between inflation and unemployment.

AS/AD ANALYSIS AND THE PHILLIPS CURVE

How can we explain the stability of the Phillips Curve in the 1950s and 1960s and the lack of stability after that? To answer, we need to return to *AS/AD* analysis.

If the *AD* curve shifts from year to year but the *AS* curve does not, the values of *P* and *Y* each year will lie along the *AS* curve (Figure 15.8a). The plot of the relationship between *P* and *Y* will be upward sloping. Correspondingly, the plot of the relationship between the unemployment rate (which decreases with increased output) and the rate of inflation will be a curve that slopes downward. In other words, we would expect to see a negative relationship between the unemployment rate and the inflation rate.

But the relationship between the unemployment rate and the inflation rate will look different if the *AS* curve shifts from year to year but the *AD* curve does not. A leftward shift of the *AS* curve will cause an *increase* in the price level (*P*) and a

a.
AD shifts with no *AS* shifts trace out the *AS* curve (a positive relationship between *P* and *Y*).

b.
AS shifts with no *AD* shifts trace out the *AD* curve (a negative relationship between *P* and *Y*).

c.
If both *AD* and *AS* are shifting, there is no systematic relationship between *P* and *Y*.

FIGURE 15.8

Changes in the Price Level and Aggregate Output Depend on Both Shifts in Aggregate Demand and Shifts in Aggregate Supply

decrease in aggregate output (*Y*) (Figure 15.8b). When the *AS* curve shifts to the left, the economy experiences both inflation *and* an increase in the unemployment rate (because decreased output means increased unemployment). In other words, if the *AS* curve is shifting from year to year, we would expect to see a positive relationship between the unemployment rate and the inflation rate.

If both the *AS* and the *AD* curves are shifting simultaneously, however, there is no systematic relationship between *P* and *Y* (Figure 15.8c) and thus no systematic relationship between the unemployment rate and the inflation rate.

➤ **The Role of Import Prices**   One of the main factors that causes the *AS* curve to shift is the price of imports. (Remember: The *AS* curve shifts when input prices change, and input prices are affected by the price of imports, particularly the price of imported oil.) The price of imports is plotted in Figure 15.9 for the 1960 I to 1997 IV period. As you can see, the price of imports changed very little between 1960 and 1970. There were no large shifts in the *AS* curve in the 1960s due to changes in the price of imports. There were also no other large changes in input prices in the 1960s, so overall the *AS* curve shifted very little during the decade. The main variation in the 1960s was in aggregate demand, so the shifting *AD* curve traced out points along the *AS* curve.

Figure 15.9 also shows that the price of imports increased considerably in the 1970s. This led to large shifts in the *AS* curve during the decade. But the *AD* curve was also shifting throughout the 1970s. With both curves shifting, the data points for *P* and *Y* were scattered all over the graph, and the observed relationship between *P* and *Y* was not at all systematic.

This story about import prices and the *AS* and *AD* curves in the 1960s and 1970s carries over to the Phillips Curve. The Phillips Curve was stable in the 1960s because the primary source of variation in the economy was demand, not costs. In the 1970s both demand *and* costs were varying, so no obvious relationship between the unemployment rate and the inflation rate was apparent.

To some extent, what is remarkable about the Phillips Curve is not that it was not smooth after the 1960s but that it ever was smooth.

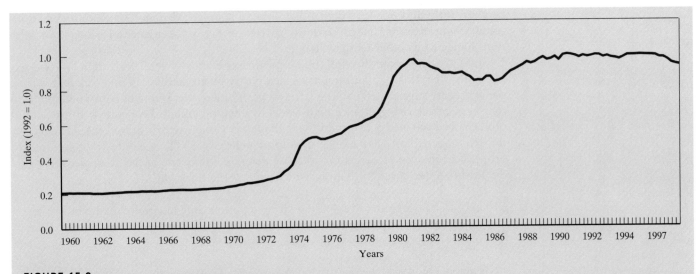

FIGURE 15.9

The Price of Imports, 1960 I to 1997 IV

The price of imports changed very little in the 1960s and early 1970s. It increased substantially in 1974 and again in 1979 to 1980. Since 1981, the price of imports has changed very little.

EXPECTATIONS AND THE PHILLIPS CURVE

Another reason the Phillips Curve is not stable concerns expectations. We saw in chapter 14 that if a firm expects other firms to raise their prices, the firm may raise the price of its own product. If all firms are behaving in this way, then prices will rise because they are expected to rise. In this sense, expectations are self-fulfilling. Similarly, if inflation is expected to be high in the future, negotiated wages are likely to be higher than if inflation is expected to be low. Wage inflation is thus affected by expectations of future price inflation. Because wages are input costs, prices rise as firms respond to the higher wage costs. Price expectations that affect wage contracts eventually affect prices themselves.

If the rate of inflation depends on expectations, then the Phillips Curve will shift as expectations change. For example, if inflationary expectations increase, the result will be an increase in the rate of inflation even though the unemployment rate may not have changed. In this case, the Phillips Curve will shift to the right. If inflationary expectations decrease, the Phillips curve will shift to the left—there will be less inflation at any given level of the unemployment rate.

It so happened that inflationary expectations were quite stable in the 1950s and 1960s. The inflation rate was moderate during most of this period, and people expected it to remain moderate. With inflationary expectations not changing very much, there were no major shifts of the Phillips Curve, which helps explain its stability during the period.

Near the end of the 1960s, inflationary expectations began to increase, primarily in response to the actual increase in inflation that was occurring because of the tight economy caused by the Vietnam War. Inflationary expectations increased even further in the 1970s as a result of large oil price increases. These changing expectations led to shifts of the Phillips Curve, which is another reason the curve was not stable during the 1970s.

IS THERE A SHORT-RUN TRADE-OFF BETWEEN INFLATION AND UNEMPLOYMENT?

Does the fact that the Phillips Curve broke down during the 1970s mean there is no trade-off between inflation and unemployment in the short run? Not at all. It simply means other things affect inflation aside from unemployment. Just as the relationship between price and quantity demanded along a standard demand curve shifts when income or other factors change, so does the relationship between unemployment and inflation change when other factors change.

In 1975, for example, inflation and unemployment were both high. As we explained earlier, this stagflation was caused partly by an increase in oil costs that shifted the aggregate supply curve to the left and partly by expectations of continued inflation that kept prices rising despite high levels of unemployment. In response to this situation, the Fed pursued a contractionary monetary policy, which shifted the AD curve to the left and led to even higher unemployment. By 1977, the rate of inflation had dropped from over 11 percent to about 6 percent. So the rise in the unemployment rate did lead to a decrease in inflation, which reflects the trade-off.

> There *is* a short-run trade-off between inflation and unemployment, but other factors besides unemployment affect inflation. Policy involves much more than simply choosing a point along a nice, smooth curve.

Back in chapter 8, we mentioned that recessions may be the price that the economy pays to eliminate inflation. We can now understand this statement better. When unemployment rises, *other things being equal*, inflation falls. We explore the trade-off between inflation and unemployment in other nations—and caution against generalizing too much—in the Global Perspective box "Inflation and Unemployment around the World, 1990 to 1992."

THE LONG-RUN *AS* CURVE, POTENTIAL GDP, AND THE NATURAL RATE OF UNEMPLOYMENT

Recall from chapter 14 that many economists believe the AS curve is vertical in the long run. In the short run, we know that some input prices (which are costs to firms) lag increases in the overall price level. If the price level rises without a full adjustment of costs, firms' profits will be higher and output will increase. In the long run, however, input prices may catch up to output price increases. If input prices rise in subsequent periods, driving up costs, the short-run aggregate supply curve will shift to the left, and aggregate output will fall.

This situation is illustrated in Figure 15.10. Assume the initial equilibrium is at the intersection of AD_0 and the long-run aggregate supply curve. Now consider a shift of the aggregate demand curve from AD_0 to AD_1. If input prices lag changes in the overall price level, aggregate output will rise from Y_0 to Y_1. (This is a movement along the short-run AS curve AS_0.) But in the longer run, input prices may catch up. For example, next year's labor contracts may make up for the fact that wage increases did not keep up with the cost of living this year. If input prices catch up in the longer run, the AS curve will shift from AS_0 to AS_1 and drive aggregate output back to Y_0. If input prices ultimately rise by exactly the same percentage as output prices, firms will produce the same level of output as they did before the increase in aggregate demand.

In chapter 14 we said Y_0 is sometimes called *potential GDP*. Aggregate output can be pushed above Y_0 in the short run. When aggregate output exceeds Y_0, however, there is upward pressure on input prices and costs. The unemployment rate is already quite low, firms are beginning to encounter the limits of their plant capacities, and so forth. At levels of aggregate output above Y_0, costs will rise, the AS curve will shift to the left, and the price level will rise. Thus potential GDP is the level of aggregate output that can be sustained in the long run without inflation.

This story is directly related to the Phillips Curve. Those who believe the AS curve is vertical in the long run at potential GDP also believe the Phillips Curve is vertical in the long run at some natural rate of unemployment. The **natural rate of unemployment** is the rate of unemployment that is consistent with the notion of a fixed long-run output

natural rate of unemployment
A concept consistent with the notion of a fixed long-run output at potential GDP. Generally considered the sum of the frictional and structural unemployment rates.

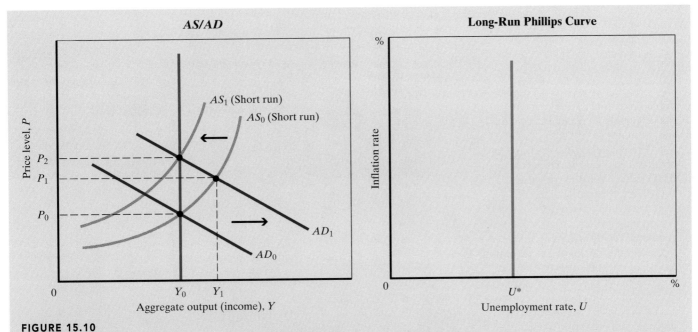

FIGURE 15.10

The Long-Run Phillips Curve: The Natural Rate of Unemployment

If the *AS* curve is vertical in the long run, so is the Phillips Curve. In the long run, the Phillips Curve corresponds to the natural rate of unemployment—that is, the unemployment rate that is consistent with the notion of a fixed long-run output at potential GDP. *U** is the natural rate of unemployment.

at potential GDP. The logic behind the vertical Phillips Curve is that whenever the unemployment rate is pushed below the natural rate, wages begin to rise, thus pushing up costs. This leads to a *lower* level of output, which pushes the unemployment rate back up to the natural rate. At the natural rate, the economy can be considered to be at full employment.

THE NAIRU—THE NONACCELERATING INFLATION RATE OF UNEMPLOYMENT

In Figure 15.10 the long-run vertical Phillips Curve is a graph with the inflation rate on the vertical axis and the unemployment rate on the horizontal axis. The natural rate of unemployment is U^*. In the long run, according to advocates of the long-run vertical Phillips Curve, the actual unemployment rate moves to U^* because of the natural workings of the economy.

Another graph of interest is Figure 15.11, a graph with the *change in* the inflation rate on the vertical axis and the unemployment rate on the horizontal axis. Many economists believe the relationship between the change in the inflation rate and the unemployment rate is as depicted by the *PP* curve in the figure. The value of the unemployment rate where the *PP* curve crosses zero is called the **NAIRU**, the "nonaccelerating inflation rate of unemployment." If the actual unemployment rate is to the left of the NAIRU, the change in the inflation rate will be positive. As depicted in the figure, at U_1 the change in the inflation rate is 1. Conversely, if the actual unemployment rate is to the right of the NAIRU, the change in the inflation rate is negative: At U_2 the change is -1.

Consider what happens if the unemployment rate decreases from the NAIRU to U_1 and stays at U_1 for many periods. Assume also that the inflation rate at the NAIRU was 2 percent. Then in the first period the inflation rate will increase from 2 percent to

NAIRU *The non-accelerating inflation rate of unemployment.*

INFLATION AND UNEMPLOYMENT AROUND THE WORLD, 1990 TO 1992

Table 1 presents unemployment and inflation figures for a number of industrial economies.

These numbers make clear that economic generalizations across countries can be hazardous, for two reasons. First, the economic events experienced by one country in a given period may be very different from the economic events experienced by another country during the same period. (For example, one country may encounter a supply shock that shifts its aggregate supply curve at the same time that another is experiencing demand-pull inflation.) Second, the trade-off between inflation and unemployment, to the extent that one exists, is determined by the institutions within the country. For example, Japan had a tradition of "lifetime" employment for male workers in the country's largest industries. Although 1992 and 1993 saw the rules beginning to change,

UNEMPLOYMENT HAS EMERGED AS A SERIOUS PROBLEM IN EUROPE IN THE 1990S. HERE, THESE WORKERS AT AN EMPLOYMENT CENTER IN GERMANY ARE HOPING TO FIND WORK.

FIGURE 15.11

The NAIRU Diagram

To the left of the NAIRU the price level is accelerating (positive changes in the inflation rate), and to the right of the NAIRU the price level is decelerating (negative changes in the inflation rate). Only when the unemployment rate is equal to the NAIRU is the price level changing at a constant rate (no change in the inflation rate).

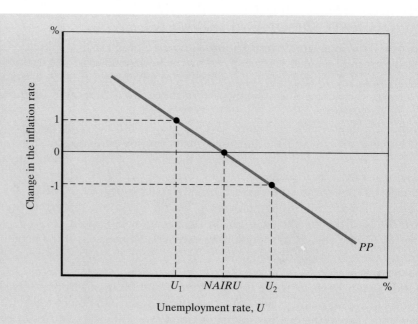

Japanese firms are still more reluctant than their U.S. counterparts to lay off workers during economic hard times. This means Japanese workers do much less "job searching" and Japan probably has a lower natural rate of unemployment than the United States. The opposite is true in the Netherlands, which has a very liberal unemployment insurance program that pays virtually 100% of lost wages to the unemployed for an extended time. Such a system is likely to lead to a higher natural rate because it makes the cost of being unemployed quite low.

A number of patterns emerge from the numbers. Seven of the 10 countries in the group experienced an increase in unemployment between 1990 and 1992. Those same seven countries experienced a simultaneous decline in inflation. Only Germany and the Netherlands saw unemployment decline, and both experienced an increase in inflation. Japan had no change in the unemployment rate. All nine countries in which the unemployment rate changed seemed to exhibit a trade-off between inflation and unemployment.

TABLE 1	UNEMPLOYMENT AND INFLATION RATES IN SELECTED COUNTRIES, 1990 TO 1992			
	UNEMPLOYMENT RATE		INFLATION RATE	
	1990	1992	1990	1992
Canada	8.1	11.3 ↑	5.0	2.0 ↓
Australia	6.9	10.8 ↑	7.0	1.0 ↓
France	9.2	10.1 ↑	3.1	2.3 ↓
United Kingdom	6.8	9.6 ↑	6.4	4.3 ↓
Italy	11.4	11.6 ↑	7.6	4.5 ↓
United States	5.5	6.8 ↑	5.0	3.0 ↓
Netherlands	8.0	6.6 ↓	3.0	4.0 ↑
Sweden	1.5	4.7 ↑	11.0	2.0 ↓
Germany	6.2	5.8 ↓	3.1	4.4 ↑
Japan	2.2	2.2 -	2.2	1.6 ↓

Sources: OECD, IMF, and *Statistical Abstract of the United States*, 1994, Tables 1379, 1381.

The similarity of patterns across the seven countries experiencing higher unemployment and lower inflation demonstrates that linkages across economies do exist. All countries experienced falling commodity prices (including oil) on world markets during 1991 and 1992. In addition, countries are linked through imports and exports and through capital flows. For example, one of the reasons that the U.S. economy did not grow more quickly following the 1990 to 1991 recession was that its major trading partners (Europe and Japan) were experiencing recessions of their own and were buying less from the United States.

For more on inflation and unemployment in other countries, see the Case and Fair Web page at http://www.prenhall.com/casefair.

3 percent. The inflation rate does not, however, just stay at the higher 3 percent value. In the next period the inflation rate will increase from 3 percent to 4 percent, and so on. The price level will be accelerating (that is, the change in the inflation rate will be positive) when the actual unemployment rate is below the NAIRU. Conversely, the price level will be decelerating (that is, the change in the inflation rate will be negative) when the actual unemployment rate is above the NAIRU.[5]

The *PP* curve in Figure 15.11 is like the *AS* curve in Figure 15.3—the same factors that shift the *AS* curve, such as cost shocks, can also shift the *PP* curve. Figure 14.8 summarizes the various factors that can cause the *AS* curve to shift, and these are also relevant for the *PP* curve. A favorable shift for the *PP* curve is to the left, because the *PP* curve crosses zero at a lower unemployment rate, which means that the NAIRU is lower. Some have argued that one possible recent source of favorable shifts is increased foreign competition, which may have kept both wage costs and other input costs down.

---

[5] The NAIRU is actually misnamed. It is the *price level* that is accelerating or decelerating, not the inflation rate, when the actual unemployment rate differs from the NAIRU. The inflation rate is not accelerating or decelerating, but simply changing by the same amount each period. The namers of the NAIRU forgot their physics.

Before about 1995, proponents of the NAIRU theory argued that the value of the NAIRU in the United States was around 6 percent. By the end of 1995 the unemployment rate declined to about 5.5 percent, and by 1997 the unemployment rate was under 5 percent. If the NAIRU were 6 percent, one should have seen a continuing increase in the inflation rate beginning about 1995. In fact, the 1995 to 1997 period saw slightly declining inflation. Not only did inflation not continually increase, it did not even increase once to a new higher value and then stay there. As the unemployment rate declined during this period, proponents of the NAIRU lowered their estimates of it, more or less in line with the actual fall in the unemployment rate. This can be justified by arguing that there have been continuing favorable shifts of the *PP* curve, such as possible increased foreign competition. Critics have argued that this procedure is close to making the NAIRU theory vacuous. Can the theory really be tested if the estimate of the NAIRU is changed whenever it is not consistent with the data? How trustworthy is the appeal to favorable shifts?

Macroeconomists are currently debating whether equations estimated under the NAIRU theory are good approximations. More time is needed before any definitive answers can be given.

LOOKING AHEAD

This chapter concludes our basic analysis of how the macroeconomy works. In the preceding seven chapters, we have examined how households and firms behave in the three market arenas—the goods market, the money market, and the labor market. We have seen how aggregate output (income), the interest rate, and the price level are determined in the economy, and we have examined the relationship between two of the most important macroeconomic variables, the inflation rate and the unemployment rate. In chapter 16, we use everything we have learned up to this point to examine a number of important policy issues.

SUMMARY

1. Because the economy is dynamic, *frictional* and *structural unemployment* are inevitable and in some ways desirable. Times of *cyclical unemployment* are of concern to macroeconomic policy makers.
2. In general, employment tends to fall when aggregate output falls and rise when aggregate output rises.

THE CLASSICAL VIEW OF THE LABOR MARKET

3. Classical economists believe the interaction of supply and demand in the labor market brings about equilibrium and that unemployment (beyond the frictional and structural amounts) does not exist.
4. The classical view of the labor market is consistent with the theory of a vertical aggregate supply curve.

EXPLAINING THE EXISTENCE OF UNEMPLOYMENT

5. Some economists argue that the unemployment rate is not an accurate indicator of whether the labor market is working properly. Unemployed people who are considered part

of the labor force may be offered jobs but may be unwilling to take those jobs at the offered salaries. Some of the unemployed may have chosen not to work, but this does not mean that the labor market has malfunctioned.

6. Those who do not subscribe to the classical view of the labor market suggest several reasons why unemployment exists. Downwardly *sticky wages* may be brought about by *implicit* or *explicit contracts* not to cut wages. If the equilibrium wage rate falls but wages are prevented from falling also, the result will be unemployment.

7. *Efficiency wage theory* holds that the productivity of workers increases with the wage rate. If this is true, firms may have an incentive to pay wages above the wage at which the quantity of labor supplied is equal to the quantity of labor demanded. At all wages above the equilibrium, there will be an excess supply of labor and therefore unemployment.

8. If firms are operating with incomplete or imperfect information, they may not know what the market-clearing wage is. As a result, they may set their wages incorrectly and bring about unemployment. Because the economy is so

complex, it may take considerable time for firms to correct these mistakes.

9. *Minimum wage laws,* which set a floor for wage rates, are one factor contributing to teenagers' unemployment. If the market-clearing wage for some groups of workers is below the minimum wage, some members of this group will be unemployed.

THE SHORT-RUN RELATIONSHIP BETWEEN THE UNEMPLOYMENT RATE AND INFLATION

10. There is a negative relationship between the unemployment rate (U) and aggregate output (income) (Y): When Y rises, U falls. When Y falls, U rises.

11. The relationship between the unemployment rate and the price level is negative: As the unemployment rate declines and the economy moves closer to capacity, the price level rises more and more.

12. The *Phillips Curve* represents the relationship between the *inflation rate* and the *unemployment rate*. During the 1950s and 1960s, this relationship was stable, and there seemed to be a predictable trade-off between inflation and

unemployment. As a result of import price increases (which led to shifts in aggregate supply) and shifts in aggregate demand brought about partially by inflationary expectations, the relationship between the inflation rate and the unemployment rate was erratic in the 1970s. There *is* a short-run trade-off between inflation and unemployment, but other things besides unemployment affect inflation.

THE LONG-RUN *AS* CURVE, POTENTIAL GDP, AND THE NATURAL RATE OF UNEMPLOYMENT

13. Those who believe the *AS* curve is vertical in the long run also believe the Phillips Curve is vertical in the long run at the *natural rate of unemployment.* The natural rate is generally the sum of the frictional and structural rates. If the Phillips Curve is vertical in the long run, then there is a limit to how low government policy can push the unemployment rate without setting off inflation.

14. The NAIRU theory says that the price level will accelerate when the unemployment rate is below the NAIRU and decelerate when the unemployment rate is above the NAIRU.

REVIEW TERMS AND CONCEPTS

cost-of-living adjustments (COLAs), 322
cyclical unemployment, 318
efficiency wage theory, 322
explicit contracts, 322
frictional unemployment, 317
inflation rate, 325

labor demand curve, 319
labor supply curve, 318
minimum wage laws, 323
NAIRU, 331
natural rate of unemployment, 330
Phillips Curve, 325

relative-wage explanation of unemployment, 322
social, or implicit, contracts, 322
sticky wages, 321
structural unemployment, 317
unemployment rate, 317

PROBLEM SET

1. Obtain monthly data on the unemployment rate and the inflation rate for the last two years. (These data can be found in a recent issue of the *Survey of Current Business* or in the *Monthly Labor Review* or *Employment and Earnings*, all published by the government and available in many college libraries.)
   a. What trends do you observe? Can you explain what you see using aggregate supply and aggregate demand curves?
   b. Plot the 24 monthly rates on a graph with the unemployment rate measured on the X axis and the inflation rate on the Y axis. Is there evidence of a trade-off between these two variables? Can you offer an explanation?

2. In 1998, the country of Ruba was suffering a period of high unemployment. The new president Clang appointed as his chief economist Laurel Tiedye. Ms. Tiedye and her staff

estimated these supply and demand curves for labor from data obtained from the secretary of labor, Robert Small:

$$Q_D = 100 - 5W$$
$$Q_S = 10W - 20,$$

where Q is the quantity of labor supplied/demanded in millions of workers and W is the wage rate in slugs, the currency of Ruba.
   a. Currently, the law in Ruba says no worker shall be paid less than nine slugs per hour. Estimate the quantity of labor supplied, the number of unemployed, and the unemployment rate.
   b. President Clang, over the objection of Secretary Small, has recommended to the Congress that the law be

changed to allow the wage rate to be determined in the market. If such a law were passed, and the market adjusted quickly, what would happen to total employment, the size of the labor force, and the unemployment rate? Show the results graphically.

   c. Will the Rubanese labor market adjust quickly to such a change in the law? Why or why not?

3. The following policies have at times been advocated for coping with unemployment. Briefly explain how each might work, and explain which type or types of unemployment (frictional, structural, or cyclical) each policy is designed to alter.

   a. A computer list of job openings and a service that matches employees with job vacancies (sometimes called an "economic dating service").

   b. Lower minimum wage for teenagers.

   c. Retraining programs for workers who need to learn new skills in order to find employment.

   d. Public employment for people without jobs.

   e. Improved information about available jobs and current wage rates.

   f. The president goes on nationwide TV and attempts to convince firms and workers that the inflation rate next year will be low.

4. Your boss offers you a wage increase of 10 percent. Is it possible that you are worse off, even with the wage increase, than you were before?

5. How will the following affect labor force participation rates? Labor supply? Unemployment?

   a. Because the retired elderly are a larger and larger fraction of the U.S. population, Congress and the president decide to raise the social security tax on individuals in order to continue paying benefits to the elderly.

   b. A national child care program is enacted, requiring employers to provide free child care services.

   c. The U.S. government reduces restrictions on immigration into the United States.

   d. The welfare system is eliminated.

   e. The government subsidizes the purchase of new capital by firms (an investment tax credit).

6. Draw a graph to illustrate the following:

   a. A Phillips Curve based on the assumption of a vertical long-run aggregate supply curve.

   b. The effect of a change in inflationary expectations on a recently stable Phillips Curve.

   c. Unemployment caused by a recently enacted minimum wage law.

7. Obtain data on "average hourly earnings of production workers" and the unemployment rate for your state or area over a recent two-year period. Has unemployment increased or decreased? What has happened to wages? Does the pattern of unemployment help explain the movement of wages? Can you offer an explanation?

8. Suppose the inflation-unemployment relationship depicted by the Phillips Curve was stable. Do you think the U.S. trade-off and the Japanese trade-off would be identical? If not, what kinds of factors might make the trade-offs dissimilar?

TAKE IT TO THE NET

We invite you to visit the Case and Fair page on the Prentice Hall Web site:
http://www.prenhall.com/casefair
for this chapter's World Wide Web exercise.

Chapter 16

DEFICIT REDUCTION, FED BEHAVIOR, STABILIZATION, STOCK MARKET EFFECTS, AND MACRO ISSUES ABROAD

NEWSPAPERS CARRY ARTICLES dealing with macro-economic problems daily, and macroeconomic issues are a heavy part of many political campaigns. Using what we've learned about how the macro-economy works, we now examine in greater depth some current issues and problems.

In this chapter, we take up five issues: (1) legislation concerned with setting targets for the federal deficit; (2) the way the Fed reacts to the state of the economy; (3) the lags in the economy's response to monetary and fiscal policy changes; (4) the effects of the stock market on the economy; and (5) the cyclical behavior since 1980 of the economies of Japan and five European countries.

DEFICIT REDUCTION AND MACROPOLICY

The federal government's deficit was a concern to policy makers for many years. As discussed in chapter 10, the deficit problem began in the early 1980s, when huge increases in the deficit occurred, and it continued until the late 1990s. When the deficit reached 4.7 percent of GDP in 1986, the U.S. Congress passed and President Reagan signed the **Gramm-Rudman-Hollings Bill** (named for its three congressional sponsors), referred to as GRH.

GRH set a target for reducing the federal deficit by a set amount each year. As Figure 16.1 shows, the deficit was to decline by $36 billion per year between 1987 and 1991, with a deficit of zero slated for fiscal year 1991. What was interesting about the GRH legislation was that the targets were not merely guidelines. If Congress, through its decisions about taxes and

Gramm-Rudman-Hollings Bill
Passed by the U.S. Congress and signed by President Reagan in 1986, this law set out to reduce the federal deficit by $36 billion per year, with a deficit of zero slated for 1991.

FIGURE 16.1

Deficit Reduction Targets under Gramm-Rudman-Hollings

The GRH legislation, passed in 1986, set out to lower the federal deficit by $36 billion per year. If the plan had worked, a zero deficit would have been achieved by 1991.

spending programs, produced a budget with a deficit larger than the targeted amount, GRH called for automatic spending cuts. The cuts were divided proportionately among most federal spending programs, so that a program that made up 5 percent of total spending was to endure a cut equal to 5 percent of the total spending cut.[1]

In 1986, the U.S. Supreme Court declared part of the GRH bill unconstitutional. In effect, the court said the Congress would have to approve the "automatic" spending cuts before they could take place. The law was changed in 1986 to meet the Supreme Court ruling and again in 1987, when new targets were established. The new targets had the deficit reaching zero in 1993 rather than 1991. The targets were changed again in 1991, when the year to achieve a zero deficit was changed from 1993 to 1996.

In practice, these targets never came close to being achieved. As time wore on, even the revised targets became completely unrealistic, and by the end of the 1980s the GRH legislation was not taken seriously.

The deficit problem continued in the 1990s, and one of President Clinton's goals when he took office in 1993 was to reduce the deficit. The first step was the Omnibus Budget Reconciliation Act of 1993. The act, which barely made it through Congress, was projected to reduce the deficit in the five fiscal years 1994 to 1998 by $504.8 billion—$254.7 billion would come from cuts in federal spending, and $250.1 billion would come from tax increases. Most of the tax increases were levied on high-income taxpayers.

There was also some sentiment in the mid 1990s for the passage of a "balanced-budget amendment," intended to prevent Congress from doing what it did in the 1980s. The balanced-budget amendment passed the House in early 1995, but it failed by one vote in the Senate. It turned out that the passage of the Omnibus Budget Reconciliation Act of 1993 and a robust economy from 1994 to 1997 was enough to lead to a roughly balanced budget by 1998. As of 1998, there was no longer a federal government deficit problem, although there was no assurance that the problem would not resurface in the future, especially as the baby boomers begin to retire and start drawing social security.

Although the government deficit is not currently a problem, it is instructive to see what the macroeconomic consequences are of legislation or amendments that target the deficit. Many economists who favored deficit reduction were opposed to the GRH legislation and the balanced-budget amendment, and we will now see why.

THE EFFECTS OF SPENDING CUTS ON THE DEFICIT

Suppose the terms of the balanced-budget amendment or some other deficit-reduction measure dictate that the deficit must be cut by $20 billion. By how much must government spending be cut to achieve this goal? You might be tempted to think the spending cuts should add up to the amount the deficit is to be cut—$20 billion. (This is what GRH dictated: If the deficit needed to be cut by a certain amount, automatic spending cuts were to be equal to this amount.) Seems reasonable! If you decrease your personal spending by $100 over a year, your personal deficit will fall by the full $100 of your spending cut.

But the government is not an individual household. A cut in government spending shifts the *AD* curve to the left and results in a decrease in aggregate output (income) (*Y*) and a contraction in the economy. When the economy contracts, both the taxable income of households and the profits of firms fall. This means revenue from the personal income tax and the corporate profits tax will fall.

How do these events affect the size of the deficit? To estimate the response of the deficit to changes in government spending, we need to go through two steps. First, we must decide how much a $1 change in government spending will change GDP. That means we need to know the size of the government spending multiplier. (Recall that the government spending multiplier measures the increase [or decrease] in GDP [*Y*]

---

[1]Programs like social security were exempt from cuts or were treated differently. Interest payments on the federal debt were also immune from cuts.

brought about by a $1 increase [or decrease] in government spending.) Based on empirical evidence, a reasonable value for the government spending multiplier seems to be around 1.4 after one year, and this is the value we will use. A $1 billion decrease in government spending lowers GDP by about $1.4 billion after one year.

Next, we must see what happens to the deficit when GDP changes. We have just noted that when GDP falls—the economy contracts—taxable income and corporate profits fall, so tax revenues fall. In addition, some categories of government expenditures tend to rise when the economy contracts. For example, unemployment insurance benefits (a transfer payment) rise as the economy contracts because more people become unemployed and eligible for benefits. Both the decrease in tax revenues and the rise in government expenditures cause the deficit to increase.

> The deficit tends to rise when GDP falls, and tends to fall when GDP rises.

Assume the **deficit response index (DRI)** is −.22. That is, for every $1 billion decrease in GDP, the deficit rises by $0.22 billion. This number seems close to what is true in practice.

We can now use the multiplier and the DRI to answer the question that began this section. Suppose government spending is reduced by $20 billion, the exact amount of the necessary deficit reduction. This will lower GDP by 1.4 × $20 billion, or $28 billion, if the value of the multiplier is 1.4. A $28 billion fall in GDP will increase the deficit by .22 × $28 billion, or $6.2 billion, if the value of the DRI is −.22. Because we initially cut government spending (and therefore lowered the deficit from this source) by $20 billion, the net effect of the spending cut is to lower the deficit by $20 billion − $6.2 billion = $13.8 billion.

A $20 billion government spending cut does not lower the deficit by $20 billion. To lower the deficit by $20 billion, we need to cut government spending by about $30 billion. Using 1.4 as the value of the government spending multiplier and −.22 as the value of the DRI, we see that a spending cut of $30 billion lowers GDP by 1.4 × $30 billion, or $42 billion. This raises the deficit by .22 × $42 billion, or $9.2 billion. The net effect on the deficit is −$30 billion (from the government spending cut) + $9.2 billion, which is −$20.8 billion (slightly larger than the necessary $20 billion reduction). This means the spending cut must be nearly 50 percent larger than the deficit reduction we wish to achieve! Clearly, Congress would have had trouble achieving the deficit targets under the GRH legislation even if it had allowed GRH's automatic spending cuts to take place.

> **Monetary Policy to the Rescue?** Was Congress so poorly informed about macroeconomics that it would pass legislation that could not possibly work? In other words, are there any conditions under which it would be reasonable to assume that a spending cut needs to be only as large as the desired reduction in the deficit? If the government spending multiplier is zero, government spending cuts will not contract the economy, and the cut in the deficit will be equal to the cut in government spending.

Could the government spending multiplier ever be zero? Before the GRH bill was passed, some argued it could. The argument went as follows: If households and firms are worried about the large government deficits and hold back on consumption and investment because of these worries, the passage of GRH might make them more optimistic and induce them to consume and invest more. This increased consumption and investment would offset the effects of the decreased government spending, and the net result would be a multiplier effect of zero.

Another argument in favor of the GRH bill centered on the Fed and monetary policy. We know from chapter 14 that an increase in the money supply shifts the AD curve to the right. Because a cut in government spending shifts the AD curve to the left, the Fed could respond to the spending cut by increasing the money supply enough to shift the AD curve

deficit response index (DRI)
The amount by which the deficit changes with a one-dollar change in GDP.

back (to the right) to its original position, preventing any change in aggregate output (income). Some argued the Fed would behave in this way after the passage of the GRH bill because it would see that Congress finally "got its house in order."

From chapter 13 we know an increase in the money supply leads to a decrease in the equilibrium interest rate. If the Fed were to offset the effects of a decrease in government spending by increasing the money supply, the interest rate would fall, stimulating planned investment and offsetting the effects of the decrease in G. This would be a multiplier of zero. However, studies at the time of the original GRH bill showed the decrease in the interest rate that would be necessary to have the multiplier be zero (that is, for a government spending cut to have no effect on aggregate output [income]) is quite large. The Fed would have had to engage in extreme behavior with respect to interest rate changes for the multiplier to be zero.

A zero multiplier can come about through renewed optimism on the part of households and firms or through very aggressive behavior on the part of the Fed. But because neither of these situations is very plausible, the multiplier is likely to be greater than zero. Thus, it is likely that to lower the deficit by a certain amount, the cut in government spending must be larger than that amount.

ECONOMIC STABILITY AND DEFICIT REDUCTION

So, lowering the deficit by a given amount is likely to require a government spending decrease larger than this amount. However, this is not the only point to learn from our analysis of deficit targeting. We will now show how deficit targeting can adversely affect the way the economy responds to a variety of stimuli.

In a world with no GRH, no balanced-budget amendment, no similar deficit-targeting measure, the Congress and the president make decisions each year about how much to spend and how much to tax. The federal government deficit is a result of these decisions and the state of the economy. But, with GRH or the balanced-budget amendment, the size of the deficit is set in advance. Taxes and government spending must be adjusted to produce the required deficit. In this situation, the deficit is no longer a consequence of the tax and spending decisions. Rather, taxes and spending become a consequence of the deficit decision.

What difference does it make whether Congress chooses a target deficit and adjusts government spending and taxes to achieve this target or decides how much to spend and tax and lets the deficit adjust itself? The difference may be substantial! Consider a leftward shift of the AD curve caused by some negative demand shock. A **negative demand shock** is something that causes a negative shift in consumption or investment schedules or that leads to a decrease in U.S. exports.

We know that a leftward shift of the AD curve lowers aggregate output (income), which causes the government deficit to increase. In a world without deficit targeting, the increase in the deficit during contractions provides an **automatic stabilizer** for the economy. (Review chapter 10 if this is hazy.) The contraction-induced decrease in tax revenues and increase in transfer payments tends to boost consumer incomes and stimulate consumer spending at a time when spending would otherwise be weak. Thus, the decrease in aggregate output (income) caused by the negative demand shock is lessened somewhat by the growth of the deficit (Figure 16.2a).

In a world with deficit targeting, the deficit is not allowed to rise. Some combination of tax increases and government spending cuts would be needed to offset what would have otherwise been an increase in the deficit. We know that increases in taxes or cuts in spending are contractionary in themselves. The contraction in the economy will therefore be larger than it would have been without deficit targeting, because the initial effect of the negative demand shock is worsened by the rise in taxes or the cut in government spending required to keep the deficit from rising. As Figure 16.2b shows,

negative demand shock *Something that causes a negative shift in consumption or investment schedules or that leads to a decrease in U.S. exports.*

automatic stabilizers *Revenue and expenditure items in the federal budget that automatically change with the economy in such a way as to stabilize GDP.*

PART FOUR
*Macroeconomic
Analysis and Issues*

a. Without Deficit Targeting

Positive boost to demand reduces the shock

(automatic stabilizers)

Negative demand shock → Income falls → Tax revenues drop; transfers increase → Deficit increases

b. With Deficit Targeting

Negative demand shock → Income falls → Tax revenues drop; transfers increase → Deficit increases

Second negative demand shock reinforces first shock and worsens the contraction ← Tax rates raised or spending cut to reach deficit target

(automatic destabilizer)

FIGURE 16.2

Deficit Targeting as an Automatic Destabilizer

Deficit targeting changes the way the economy responds to negative demand shocks because it does not allow the deficit to increase. The result is a smaller deficit, but a larger decline in income than would have otherwise occurred.

deficit targeting acts as an **automatic destabilizer**. It requires taxes to be raised and government spending to be cut during a contraction. This reinforces, rather than counteracts, the shock that started the contraction.

▶ **Summary** It's clear the GRH legislation, the balanced-budget amendment, and similar deficit-targeting measures have some undesirable macroeconomic consequences. Deficit targeting requires cuts in spending or increases in taxes at times when the economy is already experiencing problems. This does not mean Congress should ignore the deficit. Rather, it means that locking the economy into spending cuts during periods of negative demand shocks, as deficit-targeting measures do, is not a good way to manage the economy.

automatic destabilizers
Revenue and expenditure items in the federal budget that automatically change with the economy in such a way as to destabilize GDP.

THE FED'S RESPONSE TO THE STATE OF THE ECONOMY

We know from chapter 11 that the Fed can control the money supply through open market operations, and from chapters 13 and 14 that changes in the money supply can affect aggregate output (income) (Y), the interest rate, and the price level. The Fed has the power to affect the economy through open market operations. But what factors affect its decisions? Why does the Fed sometimes increase the money supply and sometimes decrease the money supply?

Two of the Fed's main goals are high levels of output and employment and a low rate of inflation. From the Fed's point of view, the best situation is a fully employed economy with a low inflation rate. The worst situation is *stagflation*—high unemployment and high inflation.

FIGURE 16.3

The Fed's Response to Low Output/Low Inflation

During periods of low output/low inflation, the economy is on the relatively flat portion of the AS curve. In this case, the Fed is likely to expand the money supply. This will shift the AD curve to the right, from AD_0 to AD_1, and lead to an increase in output with very little increase in the price level.

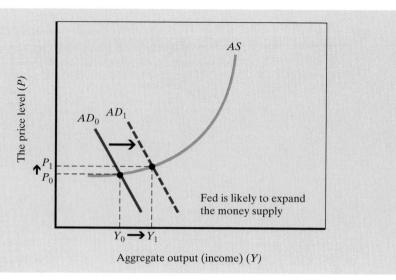

If the economy is in a low output/low inflation situation, it will be producing on the relatively flat portion of the AS curve (Figure 16.3). In this case, the Fed can increase output by increasing the money supply with little effect on the price level. The increase in the money supply will shift the AD curve to the right, leading to an increase in output with little change in the price level.

> The Fed is likely to increase the money supply during times of low output and low inflation.

The opposite is true in times of high output and high inflation. In this situation, the economy is producing on the relatively steep portion of the AS curve (Figure 16.4), and the Fed can decrease the money supply with little effect on output. The decrease in the money supply will shift the AD curve to the left, which will lead to a fall in the price level and little effect on output.[2]

> The Fed is likely to decrease the money supply during times of high output and high inflation.

Stagflation is a more difficult problem to solve. If the Fed expands the money supply, output will rise, but so will the inflation rate (which is already too high). If the Fed contracts the money supply, the inflation rate will fall, but so will output (which is already too low). (You should be able to draw AS/AD diagrams to see why this is true.) The Fed is faced with a trade-off. In this case, the Fed's decisions depend on how it weighs output relative to inflation. If it dislikes high inflation more than low output, it will contract the money supply; if it dislikes low output more than high inflation, it will expand the money supply. In practice, the Fed probably dislikes high inflation more than low output, but how the Fed behaves depends in part on the beliefs of the chair of the Fed.

The Fed sometimes "leans against the wind," meaning as the economy expands, the Fed uses open market operations to raise interest rates gradually to try to prevent the economy from expanding too quickly. Conversely, as the economy contracts, the

---

[2]In practice, the price level rarely falls. What the Fed actually achieves in this case is a decrease in the *rate of inflation* (that is, in the percentage change in the price level), not a decrease in the price level itself. The discussion here is sliding over the distinction between the price level and the rate of inflation. Recall our discussion of this distinction in chapter 15.

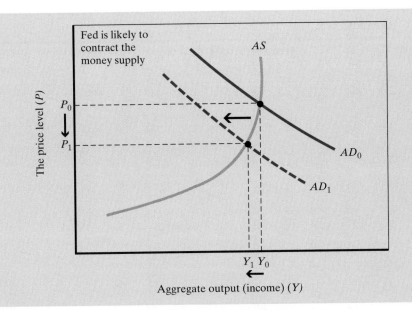

FIGURE 16.4

The Fed's Response to High Output/High Inflation

During periods of high output/high inflation, the economy is on the relatively steep portion of the AS curve. In this case, the Fed is likely to contract the money supply. This will shift the AD curve to the left, from AD_0 to AD_1, and lead to a decrease in the price level with very little decrease in output.

Fed lowers interest rates gradually to lessen (and eventually stop) the contraction. This type of stabilization is not easily achieved, as we will see later in this chapter.

▶ **The Behavior of the Fed During the 1990 to 1991 Recessions**   Table 16.1 presents data on selected variables for the 1989 I to 1997 IV period. We can use this table to see how the Fed behaved both before and after the 1990 to 1991 recession. In the first quarter of 1990 the growth rate was 3.9 percent, the unemployment rate 5.3 percent, the inflation rate 5.0 percent, and the three-month Treasury bill rate 7.8 percent. You can see that the Fed kept the bill rate fairly high in 1989. The economy was at or close to full employment, and the Fed wanted to keep the inflation rate in check.

In the second half of 1990, the economy went into a recession. Because inflation seemed to be under control at that time, experts expected the Fed would begin following an expansionary monetary policy to lessen the contraction of the economy. At the end of 1990, the Fed began to follow exactly this policy. Table 16.1 shows the three-month T-bill rate fell from 7.0 percent in the fourth quarter of 1990 to 6.1 percent in the first quarter of 1991. By the fourth quarter of 1991, the bill rate was down to 4.6 percent. This lowering of interest rates was designed to stimulate private spending and bring the economy out of the recession.

The Fed's behavior during the 1990 to 1991 recession is an example of its tendency to lean against the wind. After the Fed became convinced a recession was at hand, it responded by engaging in open market operations to lower interest rates. Inflation was not a problem, so the Fed could expand the economy in this way without worrying much about the inflationary consequences of its actions. Some argue that the Fed should have acted sooner, but with the Persian Gulf situation uncertain until February 1991, the Fed did not want to expand too much in the face of a possibly lengthy war that could have led to inflationary pressures. Once the outcome of the Persian Gulf War was known, the Fed responded rapidly.

▶ **The Behavior of the Fed in 1993 and 1994**   The economy was slow to recover from the 1990 to 1991 recession, and the growth rate did not pick up much until the beginning of 1992. Even at the end of 1992, the unemployment rate was still high at 7.4 percent (Table 16.1). The Fed kept the bill rate relatively low in 1992 and 1993 in an attempt to stimulate the economy. This was simply an extension of its expansionary policy in 1991. Again, inflation was not a problem in 1992 and 1993, so the Fed had room to stimulate.

TABLE 16.1 DATA FOR SELECTED VARIABLES FOR THE 1989–1997 PERIOD

QUARTER	REAL GDP GROWTH RATE (%)	UNEMPLOYMENT RATE (%)	INFLATION RATE (%)	THREE-MONTH T-BILL RATE	AAA BOND RATE	FEDERAL GOVERNMENT DEFICIT	DEFICIT/GDP
1989 I	4.0	5.2	4.7	8.5	9.7	92.1	0.017
II	3.0	5.2	4.3	8.4	9.5	100.3	0.019
III	2.2	5.3	3.3	7.8	9.0	124.8	0.023
IV	0.4	5.4	3.4	7.6	8.9	136.4	0.025
1990 I	3.9	5.3	5.0	7.8	9.2	154.1	0.027
II	1.2	5.3	5.2	7.8	9.4	144.2	0.025
III	−1.9	5.7	4.2	7.5	9.4	142.7	0.025
IV	−4.0	6.1	4.2	7.0	9.3	177.7	0.031
1991 I	−2.1	6.6	5.0	6.1	8.9	134.6	0.023
II	1.8	6.8	3.1	5.6	8.9	196.8	0.033
III	1.0	6.9	2.9	5.4	8.8	213.9	0.036
IV	1.0	7.1	2.5	4.6	8.4	238.9	0.040
1992 I	4.7	7.4	3.4	3.9	8.3	267.5	0.044
II	2.5	7.6	2.7	3.7	8.3	279.5	0.045
III	3.0	7.6	1.6	3.1	8.0	297.5	0.047
IV	4.3	7.4	2.9	3.1	8.0	278.9	0.044
1993 I	0.1	7.2	3.8	3.0	7.7	278.2	0.043
II	2.0	7.1	2.0	3.0	7.4	249.2	0.038
III	2.1	6.8	1.9	3.0	6.9	250.4	0.038
IV	5.3	6.6	2.7	3.1	6.8	224.7	0.034
1994 I	3.0	6.6	2.5	3.3	7.2	209.0	0.031
II	4.7	6.2	2.2	4.0	7.9	163.1	0.024
III	1.8	6.0	2.6	4.5	8.2	187.7	0.027
IV	3.6	5.6	2.7	5.3	8.6	186.9	0.026
1995 I	0.9	5.5	3.3	5.8	8.3	191.6	0.027
II	0.3	5.7	2.0	5.6	7.7	179.5	0.025
III	3.0	5.7	2.1	5.4	7.4	176.4	0.024
IV	2.2	5.6	2.2	5.3	7.0	150.3	0.020
1996 I	1.8	5.6	2.8	5.0	7.0	153.6	0.021
II	6.0	5.4	1.8	5.0	7.6	111.6	0.015
III	1.0	5.3	2.6	5.1	7.6	99.6	0.013
IV	4.3	5.3	1.8	5.0	7.2	77.0	0.010
1997 I	4.9	5.3	2.4	5.1	7.4	55.6	0.007
II	3.3	4.9	1.8	5.1	7.6	36.6	0.005
III	3.1	4.9	1.4	5.1	7.2	10.7	0.001
IV	3.9	4.7	1.4	5.1	6.9	8.3	0.001

Note: The inflation rate is the percentage change in the GDP price index.

By the fourth quarter of 1993 the unemployment rate had fallen to 6.6 percent and the growth rate was 5.3 percent.

At the end of 1993 the Fed decided to begin slowing down the economy. The bill rate rose from 3.1 percent in the fourth quarter of 1993 to 5.8 percent in the first quarter of 1995. Why was the Fed pursuing a contractionary policy? You can see from the table that the inflation rate in 1993 and 1994 was quite low, and there were no signs even at the end of 1994 of any inflationary pressures building in the economy. But the Fed was worried about inflation picking up in the future. The growth rate in 1994 was relatively high (about 3.3 percent) and the unemployment rate was down to 5.6 percent by the fourth quarter, and the Fed felt these trends might spell inflation problems in the future.

The Fed's behavior in 1994 is an example of leaning against the wind quite far in advance, long before any observed sign of increasing inflation. Some people felt that the Fed was acting too hastily and should have waited for direct signs of inflationary pressures before tightening.

> **The Behavior of the Fed in 1995–1997** Inflation in fact did not become a problem after 1994, and by 1997 the inflation rate was below 2 percent. After slow growth in the first half of 1995, the economy picked up the pace, and by the end of 1997, the unemployment rate was down to 4.7 percent. The Fed lowered the T-bill rate from 5.8 percent in the first quarter of 1995 to 5.0 percent in the first quarter of 1996, and then it kept the T-bill rate at roughly 5.0 percent throughout 1996 and 1997. You can see from Table 16.1 that the federal government deficit fell to essentially zero by the end of 1997. What better outcome could the Fed want: good growth, low unemployment, low inflation, and a balanced government budget!

Needless to say, Chairman Greenspan was fairly popular in 1997 (as was President Clinton). The economy was doing well. It was clear from Greenspan's testimony in 1996 and 1997, however, that he was nervous about the possibility of inflation increasing and that the Fed was watching very carefully for signs of this. It seemed very likely that the Fed would lean against wind (i.e., raise interest rates) at the first sign of inflation picking up. At the end of 1997, the Fed was also concerned about possible negative effects on the U.S. economy from the Asian crisis, and if the U.S. economy was adversely affected, the Fed would likely respond by lowering interest rates. Barring either inflation picking up or growth falling, the Fed seemed inclined to just sit and wait, as it had essentially done for all of 1996 and 1997.

LAGS IN THE ECONOMY'S RESPONSE TO MONETARY AND FISCAL POLICY

One of the objectives of monetary and fiscal policy is stabilization of the economy. Consider the two possible time paths for aggregate output (income) (Y) shown in Figure 16.5. In path B (the dashed line), the fluctuations in GDP are smaller than those in path A (the solid line). One aim of **stabilization policy** is to smooth out fluctuations in output, to try to move the economy along a path like B instead of A. Stabilization policy is also concerned with the stability of prices. Here the goal is not to prevent the overall price level from rising at all but rather to achieve an inflation rate that is as low as possible given the government's other goals of high and stable levels of output and employment.

Stabilization goals are not easy to achieve. The existence of various kinds of **time lags**, or delays in the response of the economy to stabilization policies, can make the economy difficult to control. Economists generally recognize three kinds of time lags: recognition lags, implementation lags, and response lags. We will consider each. But we will begin with an analogy.

stabilization policy *Describes both monetary and fiscal policy, the goals of which are to smooth out fluctuations in output and employment and to keep prices as stable as possible.*

time lags *Delays in the economy's response to stabilization policies.*

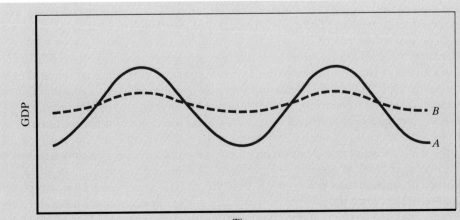

FIGURE 16.5

Two Time Paths for GDP

Path A is less stable—it varies more over time—than path B. Other things being equal, society prefers path B to path A.

THE GOVERNMENT'S ATTEMPTS TO STABILIZE THE ECONOMY ARE LIKE TRYING TO GET THE WATER TEMPERATURE JUST RIGHT IN THE SHOWER, ACCORDING TO MILTON FRIEDMAN.

➤ **"The Fool in the Shower"** Milton Friedman, a leading critic of stabilization policy, likened the government's attempts to stabilize the economy to a "fool in the shower." The shower starts out too cold, because the pipes have not yet warmed up. So the fool turns up the hot water. Nothing happens, so he turns up the hot water further. The hot water comes on and scalds him. He immediately turns up the cold water. Nothing happens right away, so he turns up the cold further. When the cold water finally starts to come up, he finds the shower too cold. And so it goes.

In Friedman's view, the government is constantly behaving like the fool in the shower, stimulating or contracting the economy at the wrong time. How this might happen is shown in Figure 16.6. Suppose the economy reaches a peak and begins to slide into recession at point A (at time t_0). Policy makers do not observe the decline in GDP until it has sunk to point B (at time t_1). By the time they have begun to stimulate the economy (point C, time t_2), the recession is well advanced and the economy has almost bottomed out. When the policies finally begin to take effect (point D, time t_3), the economy is already on its road to recovery. The policies push the economy to point F'—a much greater fluctuation than point F, which is where the economy would have been without the stabilization policy. Sometime after point D, policy makers may begin to realize that the economy is expanding too quickly. But by the time they have implemented contractionary policies and the policies have made their effects felt, the economy is starting to weaken. The contractionary policies therefore end up pushing GDP to point G' instead of point G.

Because of the various time lags, the expansionary policies that should have been instituted at time t_0 do not begin to have an effect until time t_3, when they are no longer needed. The dashed lines in Figure 16.6 show how the economy behaves as a result of the "stabilization" policies; the solid lines show the time path of GDP if the economy had been allowed to run its course and no stabilization policies had been attempted. In this case, stabilization policy makes income more erratic, not less—the policy results in a peak income of F' as opposed to F and a trough income of G' instead of G.

Critics of stabilization policy argue that the situation in Figure 16.6 is typical of the interaction between the government and the rest of the economy. This is not necessarily true. We need to know more about the nature of the various kinds of lags before deciding whether stabilization policy is good or bad.

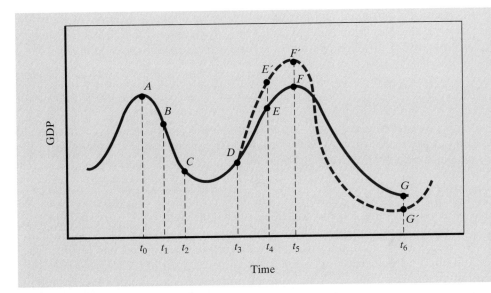

Attempts to stabilize the economy
can prove destabilizing because of
time lags. An expansionary policy
that should have begun to take effect
at point *A* does not actually begin
to have an impact until point *D*,
when the economy is already on an
upswing. Hence the policy pushes the
economy to points *F'* and *G'* (rather
than points *F* and *G*). Income varies
more widely than it would have if no
policy had been implemented.

RECOGNITION LAGS

It takes time for policy makers to recognize a boom or a slump. Many important data—those from the national income and product accounts, for example—are available only quarterly. It usually takes several weeks to compile and prepare even the preliminary estimates for these figures. If the economy goes into a slump on January 1, the recession may not show up until the data for the first quarter are available at the end of April.

Moreover, the early national income and product accounts data are only preliminary, based on an incomplete compilation of the various data sources. These estimates can, and often do, change as better data become available. This makes the interpretation of the initial estimates difficult, and **recognition lags** result.

recognition lag *The time it takes for policy makers to recognize the existence of a boom or a slump.*

IMPLEMENTATION LAGS

The problems that lags pose for stabilization policy do not end once economists and policy makers recognize that the economy is in a slump or a boom. Even if everyone knows that the economy needs to be stimulated or reined in, it takes time to put the desired policy into effect, especially for actions that involve fiscal policy. **Implementation lags** result.

Each year Congress decides on the federal government's budget for the coming year. The tax laws and spending programs embodied in this budget are not subject to change once they are in place. If it becomes clear that the economy is entering a recession and is in need of a fiscal stimulus during the middle of the year, there is little that can be done. Until Congress authorizes more spending or a cut in taxes, changes in fiscal policy are not possible.[3]

Implementation lags vary in length. In May of 1975, for example, the U.S. economy was in a deep recession and needed immediate stimulation. Although many economists had called for government action earlier, general agreement that action was necessary did not come about until late spring. Once the consensus emerged, President Ford asked Congress for an immediate tax cut retroactive to 1974. (See Application box in chapter 10.) Congress responded, and rebate checks were mailed to millions of people within weeks. As those dollars were spent, the economy began to recover.

Monetary policy is less subject to the kinds of restrictions that slow down changes in fiscal policy. As we saw in chapter 11, the Fed's chief tool to control the supply of money

implementation lag *The time it takes to put the desired policy into effect once economists and policy makers recognize that the economy is in a boom or a slump.*

---

[3]Don't forget, however, about the existence of automatic stabilizers. Many programs contain built-in countercyclical features that expand spending or cut tax collections automatically (without the need for congressional or executive action) during a recession.

or the interest rate is open market operations—buying and selling government securities. Transactions in these securities take place in a highly developed market, and if the Fed wishes, it can buy or sell a large volume of securities in a very short period of time.

> The implementation lag for monetary policy is generally much shorter than for fiscal policy.

When the Fed wishes to increase the supply of money, it goes into the open market and purchases government securities. This instantly increases the stock of money (bank reserves held at the Fed), and an expansion of the money supply begins.

RESPONSE LAGS

response lag *The time that it takes for the economy to adjust to the new conditions after a new policy is implemented; the lag that occurs because of the operation of the economy itself.*

Even after a macroeconomic problem has been recognized and the appropriate policies to correct it have been implemented, there are **response lags**—lags that occur because of the operation of the economy itself. Even after the government has formulated a policy and put it into place, the economy takes time to adjust to the new conditions.

Although monetary policy can be adjusted and implemented more quickly than fiscal policy, it may actually take longer to make its effect felt on the economy because of response lags. What is most important is the total lag between the time a problem first occurs and the time the corrective policies are felt.

▶ **Response Lags for Fiscal Policy** One way to think about the response lag in fiscal policy is through the government spending multiplier. This multiplier measures the change in GDP caused by a given change in government spending or net taxes. It takes time for the multiplier to reach its full value. The result is a lag between the time a fiscal policy action is initiated and the time the full change in GDP is realized.

The reason for the response lag in fiscal policy—the delay in the multiplier process—is simple. During the first few months after an increase in government spending or a tax cut, there is not enough time for the firms or individuals who benefit directly from the extra government spending or the tax cut to increase their own spending.

Suppose you are the owner of Transylvania Trucking, a small fleet of trucks. The government decides to increase its spending, and one of the things it spends more on is trucking services, including some extra purchases from your company. In the first months after you receive this extra business from the government, however, you are unlikely to increase your own purchases. Most of the things you buy—trucks, office furniture, stationery—are already contained in your inventories. It will generally take you some time before your own purchases are increased to reflect the extra income that you have received, and the multiplier effect of government spending will not be felt until this occurs.

> Neither individuals nor firms revise their spending plans instantaneously. Until they can make those revisions, extra government spending does not stimulate extra private spending.

Changes in government purchases are a component of aggregate expenditure. When *G* rises, aggregate expenditure increases directly; when *G* falls, aggregate expenditure decreases directly. When personal taxes are changed, however, an additional step intervenes, giving rise to another lag. Suppose a tax cut has lowered personal income taxes across the board. Each household must decide what portion of its tax cut to spend and what portion to save. This decision is the extra step. Before the tax cut gets translated into extra spending, households must take the step of increasing their spending, which usually takes some time.

With a business tax cut, there is a further complication. Firms must decide what to do with their added after-tax profits. If they pay out their added profits to households

348 PART FOUR
*Macroeconomic
Analysis and Issues*

as dividends, the result is the same as with a personal tax cut. Households must decide whether to spend or to save the extra funds. Firms may also retain their added profits and use them for investment, but investment is a component of aggregate expenditure that requires planning and time.

In practice, it takes about a year for a change in taxes or in government spending to have its full effect on the economy. This means that if we increase spending to counteract a recession today, the full effects will not be felt for 12 months. By that time, the state of the economy might be very different.

➤ **Response Lags for Monetary Policy** Monetary policy works by changing interest rates, which then change planned investment. Interest rates can also affect consumption spending, as we discuss further in the next chapter. For now, it is enough to know that lower interest rates usually stimulate consumption spending and higher interest rates decrease consumption spending.

The response of consumption and investment to interest rate changes takes time. Even if interest rates were to drop by five percentage points overnight, firms would not immediately increase their investment purchases. Firms generally make their investment plans several years in advance. If General Motors wants to respond to a decrease in interest rates by investing more, it will take some time—perhaps up to a year—to come up with plans for a new factory or assembly line. While such plans are being drawn, GM may spend little on new investments. The effect of the decrease in interest rates may not make itself felt for quite some time.

It is likely that the response lags for monetary policy will be even longer than response lags for fiscal policy. When government spending changes, there is a direct change in the sales of firms, which sell more as a result of the increased government purchases. When interest rates change, however, the sales of firms do not change until households change their consumption spending and/or firms change their investment spending. It takes time for households and firms to respond to interest rate changes. In this sense, interest rate changes are like tax-rate changes. The resulting change in firm sales must wait for households and firms to change their purchases of goods.

➤ **Summary** Stabilization is not easily achieved. It takes time for policy makers to recognize the existence of a problem, more time for them to implement a solution, and yet more time for firms and households to respond to the stabilization policies taken. Monetary policy can be adjusted more quickly and easily than taxes or government spending, making it a useful instrument in stabilizing the economy. But because the economy's response to monetary changes is probably slower than its response to changes in fiscal policy, tax and spending changes can also play a useful role in macroeconomic management.

THE EFFECTS OF THE STOCK MARKET ON THE ECONOMY

We mentioned in chapter 9 that one of the factors that affects consumption is wealth, something we consider in more detail in chapter 17. If a household has a sudden increase in wealth, its current and future consumption levels will increase. One of the main components of household wealth is the value of stocks held by households. When stock prices rise, household wealth increases, and when stock prices fall, household wealth decreases. Stock prices affect the economy by affecting household wealth, which affects household consumption. (This chapter's Application boxes explain how to follow both the bond market and the stock market by reading the financial pages of the daily newspaper.)

As you should recall from chapter 3, one of the key aspects of the modern corporation is its limited liability. Stockholders are entitled to a share of the firm's profits, but if the firm incurs losses, stockholders' liability is limited to the amount of their initial contribution. This is not true with partnerships or proprietorships.

READING A BOND TABLE

WHAT IS A BOND?

When a business wishes to make a large purchase—to build a new factory, or to buy an expensive piece of machinery—it often cannot pay for the purchase all at once, entirely out of its normal revenues. The obvious solution is to borrow the money, make the purchase, and then repay the lender of the funds over a longer period of time. This is called "financing" an investment, and the "pieces of paper" that are involved in these transactions are called **financial instruments**. *Bonds* are one type of financial instrument that firms issue in exchange for cash. If you buy a bond, you are making a loan to the firm that sold it to you.

Bonds have several properties. First, they are issued with a *face value*, typically in denominations of $1,000, that represent the amount you (the buyer) agree to lend the bond issuer. They also come with a *maturity date* on which the firm promises to pay back the funds you lent it. (However, you can sell the bond to someone else before the maturity date if you want.) Finally, there is a fixed payment of a specified amount (usually made annually), paid by the bond issuer to the bondholder. This payment, known as the *coupon*, is calculated using the prevailing interest rate at the time the bond is issued. Even if interest rates change over the life of the bond, which they almost always do, the amount you receive as interest on your bond remains fixed. (This is why bonds are sometimes referred to as fixed-income securities. The bondholder receives a set amount, known in advance, no matter what happens to interest rates, stock prices, and so on.)

If you bought a $10,000, 10 percent, 15-year bond from Company XYZ on January 1, 1998, this is what would happen. You would give XYZ, or perhaps your broker, a check for $10,000. Every January for the next 14 years, XYZ would send you a check for $1,000 (10 percent of the $10,000 face value). On January 1, 2013, XYZ would send you a check for the face value of the bond—$10,000—plus the interest for that year—$1,000—and that would square all accounts.

Does the fact that the annual interest payment (coupon) on a bond does not change with fluctuations in the interest rate mean that bonds are completely insulated from interest rate movements? Absolutely not!

Instead of the coupon responding to a change in the interest rate, it is the *price of the bond* that changes. To see why, suppose you had a choice of putting $10,000 into the bond described here or into a bank account that pays 10 percent per year interest. In either case, you would earn $1,000 per year in interest payments, so you should be indifferent between the two choices.

But now suppose that the interest rate on the bank account goes up to 20 percent instead of 10 percent. The bond still promises to pay $1,000 per year. If you want to earn $1,000 in interest, you need to put only $5,000 into the bank account (.20 × $5,000 = $1,000). You would obviously prefer to put $5,000 into the bank rather than tie up $10,000 in the bond. The only way anyone would willingly buy the bond is if it cost no more than other investments that yield the same stream of income in the future. The bond would thus be worth much less than $10,000 if the interest rate were 20 percent. It follows, then, that when interest rates rise, bond prices fall, and bondholders suffer a *capital loss*—that is, a reduction in the value of the securities they own.

> **The Crash of October 1987**   To see how events in the stock market affect the economy, let's consider a particular episode in the history of the stock market—the stock market crash of October 1987. The value of stocks in the United States fell by about a trillion dollars between August 1987 and the end of October 1987. In one day—October 19, 1987—the value of stocks fell nearly $700 billion. This corresponded to a large drop in household wealth.

In practice, it seems that a $1.00 decrease in wealth leads roughly to a $0.05 decrease in consumption spending per year. In other words, consumption seems to be lower in each future year by about 5 percent of the decrease in wealth. Using this estimate, we can see that the $1 trillion decrease in wealth in 1987 implies a $50 billion lower level of consumption in 1988. The level of GDP was around $4 trillion in 1987, so a $50 billion decrease in consumption is around 1.25 percent of GDP. A multiplier effect would also be at work here. A decrease in consumption spending leads to a

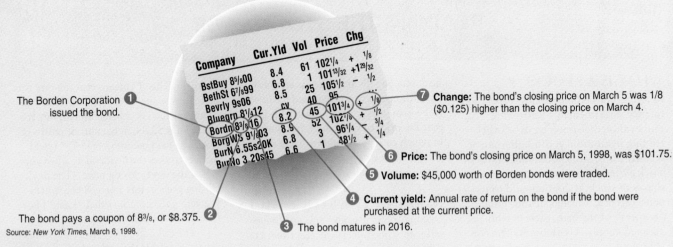

The Borden Corporation issued the bond. **1**

The bond pays a coupon of 8⅜, or $8.375. **2**

Source: *New York Times*, March 6, 1998.

3 The bond matures in 2016.

4 **Current yield:** Annual rate of return on the bond if the bond were purchased at the current price.

5 **Volume:** $45,000 worth of Borden bonds were traded.

6 **Price:** The bond's closing price on March 5, 1998, was $101.75.

7 **Change:** The bond's closing price on March 5 was 1/8 ($0.125) higher than the closing price on March 4.

FIGURE 1

New York Stock Exchange Bonds

READING A BOND TABLE

Figure 1 shows a small section of the *New York Times*'s corporate bond price quotations for March 5, 1998. What do all these signs and symbols mean?

The first column, under "Company," gives the name of the corporation that issued the bond and certain information about the terms under which the bond was originally issued. Let's take the last bond listed in the figure as an example. This bond was issued by the Borden Corporation. The "8⅜" means the bond pays a coupon of 8⅜, or $8.375, per $100 of face value of the bond. The "16" means the bond matures in 2016. The column titled "Cur. Yld" shows the annual rate of return on the bond if the bond were purchased at the current price. If the current price were $100, then the annual rate of return would be 8.375 percent. The bond yields 8.2 percent, however, so the current price of the bond must be higher than its face value of $100. (Remember: A decrease in the interest rate raises the value of a bond.) The column "Vol" tells how many thousands of dollars in bonds were traded during the day.

Here we see $45,000 (at face value) of the Borden bond was traded on March 5, 1998.

"Price" is the closing price of the bond. This is how much you would have to pay for the bond per $100 of face value. The Borden bond's closing price was 101¾, which means the bond was worth $101.75 at the end of the trading day. The last column, "Chg," tells us by how much the closing bond price differs from the closing price on the previous day. In this case, the price of the Borden bond rose by one eighth of a point—$0.125.

For more on bonds, see the Case and Fair Web page at
http://www.prenhall.com/casefair.

decrease in aggregate output (income), which leads to a further decrease in spending, and so on. The total decrease in GDP would be somewhat larger than the initial decrease in consumption of $50 billion. If the multiplier is 1.4, the total decrease in GDP would be about 1.4 × $50 billion = $70 billion, or about 1.75 percent of GDP.

Although 1.75 percent of GDP is a large amount, it is not large enough to imply that a recession would result from the crash. The life-cycle theory, which we discuss in chapter 17, helps explain why. If households are making lifetime decisions and want to have as smooth a consumption path as possible over their lifetimes, they will respond to a decrease in wealth by cutting consumption a little each year. They will *not* decrease their consumption in the current year by the full amount of the decrease in wealth. As we already noted, it has been estimated that households adjust their consumption by about 5 percent of the decrease in wealth each year.

Why were people predicting the economy would go into a recession, worse, a depression, after the crash? The reasons all pertain to expectations. If households and

READING THE STOCK PAGE

WHAT IS A STOCK?

In addition to issuing bonds, firms can finance investments by borrowing money directly from a bank or other lending institution. A third alternative is for firms to issue additional shares of stock. When a corporation issues new shares of stock, it does not add to its debt. Instead, it brings in additional "owners" of the firm, owners who agree to supply it with funds. The contributions of such owners are treated differently from loans made by outsiders, which are considered liabilities.

What is a share of stock? If you buy one share of Company QRS, and the firm has 1 million total shares outstanding, you have purchased a one-millionth ownership of the firm. You have a right—along with the owners of the other 999,999 shares—to select the management of the firm and to share in its profits. (This is not true of bondholders and other creditors of the firm, who have no say in its management.) Unlike bonds or direct borrowing, your stock does not promise a fixed annual payment. Rather, the returns you receive on your investment depend on how well Company QRS performs. If its profits are high, the firm may pay dividends to its shareholders, although it is not required to do so. If the firm does well, you may also find that the price of QRS stock has gone up, in which case you could realize a *capital gain* by selling your stock for more than you originally paid for it.

READING THE STOCK PAGES

Once you buy a stock, you are free to sell it to someone else at any time. Developments in the stock market, where such transactions take place, are constantly followed in the news.

Figure 1 reproduces part of the stock quotations from the *New York Times* for March 5, 1998. Let's take the stock of Chevron and see what information the stock pages provide.

The first two columns, under the heading "52-Week," give the stock's highest and lowest prices over the past year. The price of a share of Chevron stock reached a high of 89 $3/16$ and a low of 61$3/4$ during this period. (Stock prices are quoted in dollars per share, so "61$3/4$" means that the stock sold for $61.75 per share at its low point during the past 52 weeks.) The column "Div" gives the current annual rate of dividend

payment. The "f" means that the rate was increased by the most recent dividend announcement. The current annual rate for Chevron is $2.44. What sort of return is this? The next column, "Yld %" (yield percent), takes the dividend as a percentage of the day's closing price. (The day's closing price in this case is 84$9/16$, which is given in the column titled "Last.") For Chevron the yield is 2.9 percent.

The column "P/E" (price-earnings ratio) calculates the ratio of the price of a share of stock to the company's *total earnings per share* (which includes not only dividends paid to shareholders but also retained earnings). The PE ratio is a measure of how highly a stock is valued. Chevron's PE ratio is 17. The column "Sales 100s" tells how many hundreds of shares changed hands during the day's trading. On March 5, 1998, 1,958,600 shares of Chevron's stock were traded. The last four columns give the stock's highest, lowest, and closing price during the day's trading, as well as the change in the closing price from the closing price of the previous day.

Source: The New York Times, March 6, 1998.

FIGURE 1

New York Stock Exchange Issues

The stock was issued by Chevron. ❶

Over the past year, ❷ Chevron's stock sold at a high of $89.1875 and a low of $61.75.

Dividend: The annual rate ❸ of dividend payment is $2.44.

Source: *New York Times*, March 6, 1998.

❹ **Yield percent:** Dividend as a percentage of the stock's closing price. The stock is yielding 2.9% per year at the day's closing price of $84.5625.

❺ **Price-earnings ratio:** Ratio of the price of a share of stock to the company's total earnings per share.

❻ **Sales:** On March 5, 1998, 1,958,600 shares of Chevron's stock were traded.

❼ On March 5, 1998, Chevron stock sold for a high of $84.875 and a low of $82.6875.

❽ Chevron stock sold for $84.5625 at the end of the trading day. This price was $1.0625 higher than the previous day's closing price.

For more on stocks, see the Case and Fair Web page at
http://www.prenhall.com/casefair.

firms expected the economy would contract sharply after the crash, they probably would have cut back on consumption and investment. (This would be Keynes's animal spirits at work.) These expectations would have become self-fulfilling in the sense that the economy would have gone into a recession because of the cuts in consumption and investment brought about by lowered expectations.

But, the economy did not go into a recession in 1988. Expectations were not changed drastically following the crash. The Fed helped out by easing monetary policy right after the crash to counteract any large negative reaction. The three-month Treasury bill rate fell from 6.4 percent to 5.8 percent between October and November of 1987. In addition, the value of stocks gradually increased over time to their earlier levels. Because the initial decrease in wealth turned out to be temporary, the negative wealth effect was not nearly as large as it otherwise would have been. The crash affected consumption only slightly.

▶ **The Stock Market Boom of 1995 to 1997** Between the end of 1994 and the end of 1997, stock prices, on average, roughly doubled, adding over $3 trillion to household wealth. If this increase is sustained, and if households spend about 5 percent of the increase each year, we should expect to see consumption expenditures in the future about $150 billion higher per year than otherwise. This is a fairly large percentage of GDP. With GDP running around $8.5 trillion in 1998, the increased consumption would be about 1.8 percent of GDP, not counting any multiplier effects. Whether the stock market boom will have this much effect on GDP is hard to say. It may be that the 5 percent figure is a little high, but perhaps more importantly, it may be that not all of the increase in stock prices will be sustained. Even if only half of the increase is sustained, however, this should still have a fairly expansionary effect on the U.S. economy over the next few years.

BUSINESS CYCLES IN OTHER COUNTRIES

The United States is not the only developed nation to have business cycles. We now turn to inflation and unemployment in Japan, the United Kingdom, (West) Germany, France, Italy, and Spain. Figure 16.7 gives data for 1980 to 1996 for each country's (1) growth rate, (2) inflation rate, (3) unemployment rate, and (4) short-term interest rate.

The overall performance of the Japanese economy was quite good until 1992, when the growth rate slowed considerably. The slower growth led the unemployment rate to rise from 2.1 percent in 1991 to 3.4 percent in 1996. The Bank of Japan eased monetary policy during this period in an attempt to stimulate the economy, and by 1996 the short-term interest rate was down to 0.5 percent. This "leaning against the wind" behavior of the Bank of Japan is similar to the Fed's behavior discussed earlier in this chapter. Alas, this monetary-policy stimulus was not enough to prevent the slowdown from lasting a number of years.

The United Kingdom's economy shows distinct cycles. The U.K. growth rate was negative in 1980 to 1981 and then again in 1991 to 1992, whereas growth in the mid-1980s was strong. Note that inflation was very high in 1980 and 1981, even though growth was negative—a clear period of stagflation. By 1990, the unemployment rate had fallen to 7.1 percent, but it then began rising as the growth rate turned negative. The interest rate dropped substantially during the 1991 to 1993 period, which reflects the Bank of England's easing of monetary policy to try to stimulate the economy. The U.K. economy recovered moderately in 1994 to 1996, with the unemployment rate falling to 8.2 percent by 1996.

The general U.K. pattern of low or negative growth in the early 1980s and then again in the early 1990s also holds for the other four European countries in Figure 16.7. Also, the inflation rate has been generally falling over time in the European countries. Another trend is the fairly high level of unemployment across all of Europe for the period 1980 to 1996: Spain experienced the worst problems in this area.

There has been much discussion in Europe as to why the unemployment rates have remained so high for so long. Some say the problem is caused by the generous social welfare benefits in Europe—especially unemployment benefits—which may lead the

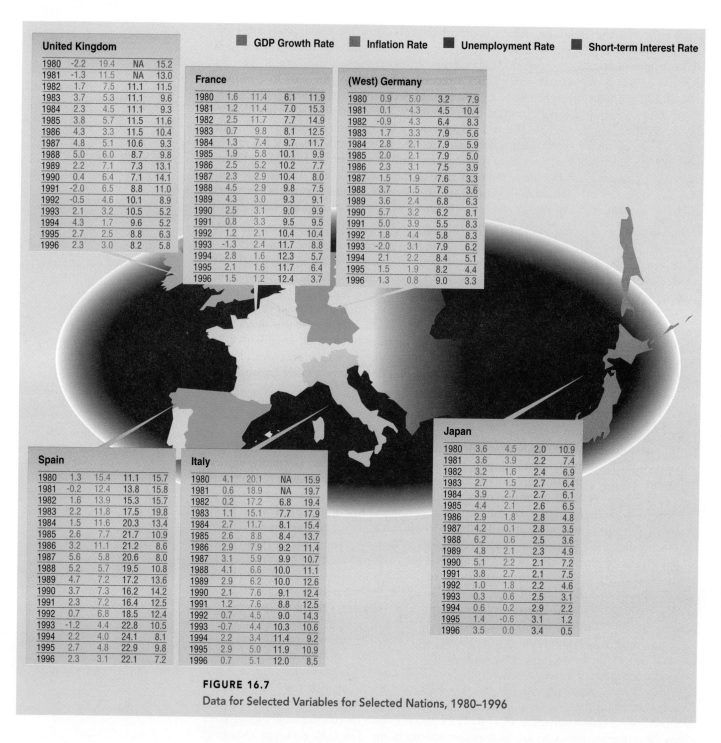

	GDP Growth Rate	Inflation Rate	Unemployment Rate	Short-term Interest Rate

United Kingdom

Year	GDP Growth Rate	Inflation Rate	Unemployment Rate	Short-term Interest Rate
1980	-2.2	19.4	NA	15.2
1981	-1.3	11.5	NA	13.0
1982	1.7	7.5	11.1	11.5
1983	3.7	5.3	11.1	9.6
1984	2.3	4.5	11.1	9.3
1985	3.8	5.7	11.5	11.6
1986	4.3	3.3	11.5	10.4
1987	4.8	5.1	10.6	9.3
1988	5.0	6.0	8.7	9.8
1989	2.2	7.1	7.3	13.1
1990	0.4	6.4	7.1	14.1
1991	-2.0	6.5	8.8	11.0
1992	-0.5	4.6	10.1	8.9
1993	2.1	3.2	10.5	5.2
1994	4.3	1.7	9.6	5.2
1995	2.7	2.5	8.8	6.3
1996	2.3	3.0	8.2	5.8

France

Year	GDP Growth Rate	Inflation Rate	Unemployment Rate	Short-term Interest Rate
1980	1.6	11.4	6.1	11.9
1981	1.2	11.4	7.0	15.3
1982	2.5	11.7	7.7	14.9
1983	0.7	9.8	8.1	12.5
1984	1.3	7.4	9.7	11.7
1985	1.9	5.8	10.1	9.9
1986	2.5	5.2	10.2	7.7
1987	2.3	2.9	10.4	8.0
1988	4.5	2.9	9.8	7.5
1989	4.3	3.0	9.3	9.1
1990	2.5	3.1	9.0	9.9
1991	0.8	3.3	9.5	9.5
1992	1.2	2.1	10.4	10.4
1993	-1.3	2.4	11.7	8.8
1994	2.8	1.6	12.3	5.7
1995	2.1	1.6	11.7	6.4
1996	1.5	1.2	12.4	3.7

(West) Germany

Year	GDP Growth Rate	Inflation Rate	Unemployment Rate	Short-term Interest Rate
1980	0.9	5.0	3.2	7.9
1981	0.1	4.3	4.5	10.4
1982	-0.9	4.3	6.4	8.3
1983	1.7	3.3	7.9	5.6
1984	2.8	2.1	7.9	5.9
1985	2.0	2.1	7.9	5.0
1986	2.3	3.1	7.5	3.9
1987	1.5	1.9	7.6	3.3
1988	3.7	1.5	7.6	3.6
1989	3.6	2.4	6.8	6.3
1990	5.7	3.2	6.2	8.1
1991	5.0	3.9	5.5	8.3
1992	1.8	4.4	5.8	8.3
1993	-2.0	3.1	7.9	6.2
1994	2.1	2.2	8.4	5.1
1995	1.5	1.9	8.2	4.4
1996	1.3	0.8	9.0	3.3

Spain

Year	GDP Growth Rate	Inflation Rate	Unemployment Rate	Short-term Interest Rate
1980	1.3	15.4	11.1	15.7
1981	-0.2	12.4	13.8	15.8
1982	1.6	13.9	15.3	15.7
1983	2.2	11.8	17.5	19.8
1984	1.5	11.6	20.3	13.4
1985	2.6	7.7	21.7	10.9
1986	3.2	11.1	21.2	8.6
1987	5.6	5.8	20.6	8.0
1988	5.2	5.7	19.5	10.8
1989	4.7	7.2	17.2	13.6
1990	3.7	7.3	16.2	14.2
1991	2.3	7.2	16.4	12.5
1992	0.7	6.8	18.5	12.4
1993	-1.2	4.4	22.8	10.5
1994	2.2	4.0	24.1	8.1
1995	2.7	4.8	22.9	9.8
1996	2.3	3.1	22.1	7.2

Italy

Year	GDP Growth Rate	Inflation Rate	Unemployment Rate	Short-term Interest Rate
1980	4.1	20.1	NA	15.9
1981	0.6	18.9	NA	19.7
1982	0.2	17.2	6.8	19.4
1983	1.1	15.1	7.7	17.9
1984	2.7	11.7	8.1	15.4
1985	2.6	8.8	8.4	13.7
1986	2.9	7.9	9.2	11.4
1987	3.1	5.9	9.9	10.7
1988	4.1	6.6	10.0	11.1
1989	2.9	6.2	10.0	12.6
1990	2.1	7.6	9.1	12.4
1991	1.2	7.6	8.8	12.5
1992	0.7	4.5	9.0	14.3
1993	-0.7	4.4	10.3	10.6
1994	2.2	3.4	11.4	9.2
1995	2.9	5.0	11.9	10.9
1996	0.7	5.1	12.0	8.5

Japan

Year	GDP Growth Rate	Inflation Rate	Unemployment Rate	Short-term Interest Rate
1980	3.6	4.5	2.0	10.9
1981	3.6	3.9	2.2	7.4
1982	3.2	1.6	2.4	6.9
1983	2.7	1.5	2.7	6.4
1984	3.9	2.7	2.7	6.1
1985	4.4	2.1	2.6	6.5
1986	2.9	1.8	2.8	4.8
1987	4.2	0.1	2.8	3.5
1988	6.2	0.6	2.5	3.6
1989	4.8	2.1	2.3	4.9
1990	5.1	2.2	2.1	7.2
1991	3.8	2.7	2.1	7.5
1992	1.0	1.8	2.2	4.6
1993	0.3	0.6	2.5	3.1
1994	0.6	0.2	2.9	2.2
1995	1.4	-0.6	3.1	1.2
1996	3.5	0.0	3.4	0.5

FIGURE 16.7

Data for Selected Variables for Selected Nations, 1980–1996

unemployed not to search very hard for a job. Others say the problem has mushroomed as people who are laid off lose more work skills the longer they remain unemployed and over time suffer a lower likelihood of being hired again. Others say because of union power the real wage rate has been kept too high to allow full employment to be achieved. Finally, some say monetary and fiscal policies, especially monetary policies, have not been expansionary enough. They argue, for example, that more expansionary monetary policies could have led to lower unemployment rates without much of an increase in inflation. (Note that short-term interest rates were fairly high in Europe throughout the period, even after the inflation rates fell substantially.)

It is hard to resolve these debates, and it could be that each explanation has some validity. Although customs and institutions differ across countries, the basic tools of macroeconomics can be applied to many countries.

SUMMARY

DEFICIT REDUCTION AND MACROPOLICY: GRAMM-RUDMAN-HOLLINGS

1. In fiscal year 1986, Congress passed and President Reagan signed the *Gramm-Rudman-Hollings Bill*, which set out to reduce the federal deficit by $36 billion per year, with a zero deficit slated for fiscal year 1991. If Congress passed a budget with a deficit larger than the targeted amount, the law called for automatic spending cuts. A Supreme Court ruling later overturned this provision, and the actual figures for each year never came close to the targets. Thanks to the Omnibus Budget Reconciliation Act of 1993, and a robust economy, there was roughly a balanced federal budget in 1998.

2. The deficit tends to rise when GDP falls, and to fall when GDP rises. The *deficit response index (DRI)* is the amount by which the deficit changes with a one-dollar change in GDP.

3. For spending cuts of a certain amount to reduce the deficit by the same amount, the government spending multiplier must be zero. Before GRH was passed, some argued that a government spending multiplier of zero can be achieved through renewed optimism on the part of households or through very aggressive behavior by the Fed to decrease the interest rate. Empirical evidence has shown that neither situation is very plausible, so to lower the deficit by a certain amount, government spending cuts must be larger than that to lower the deficit.

4. Deficit-targeting measures that call for automatic spending cuts to eliminate or reduce the deficit may have the effect of destabilizing the economy because they prevent automatic stabilizers from working.

THE FED'S RESPONSE TO THE STATE OF THE ECONOMY

5. Because the Fed can control the money supply through open market operations, it has the ability to affect aggregate output (income) (Y), the interest rate, and the price level. The Fed is likely to increase the money supply during times of low output and low inflation, and to decrease the money supply during periods of high output and high inflation. The Fed's behavior during stagflation (periods of high unemployment and high inflation) depends on how the Fed weighs output relative to inflation.

6. As the economy expands, the Fed tends to use open market operations to raise interest rates gradually to try to prevent

the economy from expanding too quickly. The Fed lowers interest rates gradually to lessen (and eventually stop) a contraction. This is called "leaning against the wind."

LAGS IN THE ECONOMY'S RESPONSE TO MONETARY AND FISCAL POLICY

7. *Stabilization policy* describes both fiscal and monetary policy, the goals of which are to smooth out fluctuations in output and employment and to keep prices as stable as possible. Stabilization goals are not necessarily easy to achieve because of the existence of certain *time lags*, or delays in the response of the economy to macropolicies.

8. A *recognition lag* is the time it takes for policy makers to recognize the existence of a boom or slump. An *implementation lag* is the time it takes to put the desired policy into effect once economists and policy makers recognize that the economy is in a boom or a slump. A *response lag* is the time that it takes for the economy to adjust to the new conditions after a new policy is implemented—in other words, a lag that occurs because of the operation of the economy itself. In general, monetary policy can be implemented more rapidly than fiscal policy, but fiscal policy generally has a shorter response lag than monetary policy.

THE EFFECTS OF THE STOCK MARKET ON THE ECONOMY

9. When stock prices rise, household wealth increases. When stock prices fall, household wealth decreases. Stock prices affect the economy by affecting household wealth, which affects household consumption.

BUSINESS CYCLES IN OTHER COUNTRIES

10. Since 1980, the nations of Europe have shown considerable fluctuation in growth rates, unemployment rates, and inflation rates. Japan suffered a slowdown in 1992–1995.

11. Explanations offered for the persistence of high unemployment in Europe are: (1) generous social welfare benefits, (2) structural unemployment as workers lose more skills the longer they are laid off, (3) union-imposed above-equilibrium wages, and (4) monetary and fiscal policies that have not been expansionary enough. Each explanation may have some validity.

REVIEW TERMS AND CONCEPTS

automatic destabilizer, 341
automatic stabilizer, 340
deficit response index (DRI), 339

Gramm-Rudman-Hollings Bill, 337
implementation lag, 347

negative demand shock, 340
recognition lag, 347
response lag, 348

stabilization policy, 345
time lag, 345

1. What is meant by an automatic destabilizer?

2. The term *fine tuning* was sometimes used during the 1950s and 1960s to describe federal monetary and fiscal policy. At the time the U.S. economy was on a fairly steady growth path with little inflation. The term went out of fashion during the 1970s and 1980s when the economy experienced severe inflation followed by a deep recession twice within a decade. Between 1991 and 1998, the economy once again returned to steady growth with little inflation and the term came back into use. Explain what is meant by fine tuning. During the fall of 1993, growth accelerated. What moves would you anticipate by the Fed in early 1994? During 1995, growth slowed considerably. What would you expect the Fed to do?

3. During 1997, stock markets in Asia collapsed. Hong Kong's was down nearly 30 percent, Thailand's down 62 percent, Malaysia's down 60 percent. Big drops were also experienced in Japan and Korea. What impacts would these events have on the economies of the countries themselves? Explain your answer. In what ways would you have expected these events to influence the U.S. economy? How might the spending of Asians on American goods be affected? What about Americans who have invested in these countries?

4. Explain carefully why the government deficit rises as the economy contracts.

5. You are given the following information about the economy in 1996 (all in billions of dollars):

(1) Consumption function:	$C = 100 + (0.8 \times Y_d)$
(2) Taxes:	$T = -150 + (0.25 \times Y)$
(3) Investment function:	$I = 60$
(4) Disposable income:	$Y_d = Y - T$
(5) Government spending:	$G = 80$
(6) Equilibrium:	$Y = C + I + G$

   Hint: Deficit is $D = G - T = G - [-150 + (0.25 \times Y)]$

   a. Find equilibrium income. Show that the government budget deficit (the difference between government spending and tax revenues) is $5 billion.

   b. Congress passes the Foghorn-Leghorn amendment, which requires that the deficit be zero this year. If the budget adopted by Congress has a deficit that is larger than zero, the deficit target must be met by cutting spending. Suppose spending is cut by $5 billion (to $75 billion). What is the

   new value for equilibrium GDP? What is the new deficit? Explain carefully why the deficit is not zero.

   c. What is the deficit response index and how is it defined? Explain why the DRI must equal 0.25 in this example. Using this information, by how much must we cut spending to achieve a deficit of zero?

   d. Suppose the Foghorn-Leghorn amendment was not in effect and planned investment falls to $I = 55$. What is the new value of GDP? What is the new government budget deficit? What happens to GDP if the F-L amendment is in effect and spending is cut to reach the deficit target? (*Hint:* Spending must be cut by $21.666 billion to balance the budget.)

6. During the first six months of 1995, the U.S. economy appeared to slow significantly. Many people point to Federal Reserve decisions made during 1994. What specific actions did the Fed take that might have caused economic slowing during 1995? Why were such actions taken? In retrospect, was the Fed right or wrong in doing what it did? Was the Fed a "fool in the shower"?

7. Some states are required to balance their budgets. Is this measure stabilizing or destabilizing? Suppose all states were committed to a balanced-budget philosophy and the economy moved into a recession. What effects would this philosophy have on the size of the federal deficit?

8. Describe the Fed's tendency to "lean against the wind." Do the Fed's policies tend to stabilize or destabilize the economy?

9. Explain why stabilization policy may be difficult to carry out. How is it possible that stabilization policies can actually be destabilizing?

10. It takes about one year for the multiplier to reach its full value. Explain this phenomenon? Does this have any implications for fiscal policy?

11. The unemployment rate in Japan has been much lower than the unemployment rate in the United States, and the unemployment rate in the United States has been much lower than unemployment rates in European countries. Look up the most recent unemployment figures for Europe, Japan, and the United States. Does this pattern still hold? Why might unemployment rates be consistently lower in one country *vis-à-vis* another?

TAKE IT TO THE NET

We invite you to visit the Case and Fair page on the Prentice Hall Web site:
http://www.prenhall.com/casefair
for this chapter's World Wide Web exercise.

Chapter 17

HOUSEHOLD AND FIRM BEHAVIOR IN THE MACROECONOMY

IN CHAPTERS 9 through 15, we considered the interactions of households, firms, the government, and the rest of the world in the goods, money, and labor markets. The macroeconomy is complicated, and there is a lot to learn about these interactions. To keep our discussions as uncomplicated as possible, we have so far assumed simple behavior of households and firms—the two basic decision-making units in the economy. We assumed household consumption (C) depends only on income and firms' planned investment (I) depends only on the interest rate. We did not consider that households make consumption and labor supply decisions simultaneously and that firms make investment and employment decisions simultaneously.

Now that we understand the basic interactions in the economy, we must relax these assumptions. In the first part of this chapter, we present a more realistic picture of the influences on households' consumption and labor supply decisions. In the second part, we present a more detailed and realistic picture of the influences on firms' investment and employment decisions. We then use what we have learned to analyze more macroeconomic issues.

HOUSEHOLDS: CONSUMPTION AND LABOR SUPPLY DECISIONS

Before discussing household behavior, let's review what we have learned so far.

THE KEYNESIAN THEORY OF CONSUMPTION: A REVIEW

The assumption that household consumption (C) depends on income, which we have used as the basis of our analysis so far, is one that Keynes stressed in his *General Theory of Employment, Interest, and Money*. While Keynes believed many factors, including interest rates and wealth, are likely to influence the level of consumption spending, he focused on current income:

357

The amount of aggregate consumption depends mainly on the amount of aggregate income. The fundamental psychological law, upon which we are entitled to depend with great confidence both . . . from our knowledge of human nature and from the detailed facts of experience, is that men [and women, too] are disposed, as a rule and on average, to increase their consumption as their incomes increase, but not by as much as the increase in their income.[1]

Keynes is making two points here. First, he suggests that consumption is a positive function of income. The more income you have, the more consuming you are likely to do. Except for a few rich misers who save scraps of soap and bits of string despite million-dollar incomes, this proposition makes sense. Rich people typically consume more than poor people.

Second, Keynes suggests, high-income households consume a smaller proportion of their income than low-income households. (If rich households consume relatively less of their incomes, then by definition they save a higher proportion of their incomes than poor households.) The proportion of income that households spend on consumption is measured by the **average propensity to consume (APC)**.[2] The APC is defined as consumption divided by income:

$$APC \equiv \frac{C}{Y}$$

If a household earns $30,000 per year and spends $25,000 (saving $5,000), it has an *APC* of $25,000/$30,000, or 0.833. Keynes argues that someone who earns, say, $30,000 is likely to spend a larger portion of his or her income than is someone who earns $100,000.

Although the idea that consumption depends on income is a useful starting point, it is far from a complete description of the consumption decision. We need to consider other theories of consumption.

THE LIFE-CYCLE THEORY OF CONSUMPTION

The **life-cycle theory of consumption** is an extension of Keynes's theory. The idea of the life-cycle theory is that people make lifetime consumption plans. Realizing that they are likely to earn more in their prime working years than they earn earlier or later, they make consumption decisions based on their expectations of lifetime income. People tend to consume less than they earn during their main working years—they *save* during those years—and they tend to consume more than they earn during their early and later years—they *dissave*, or use up savings, during those years. Students in medical school generally have very low current incomes, but few live in the poverty that those incomes might predict. Instead, they borrow now and plan to pay back later when their incomes improve.

The lifetime income and consumption pattern of a representative individual is shown in Figure 17.1. As you can see, this person has a low income during the first part of her life, high income in the middle, and low income again in retirement. Her income in retirement is not zero because she has income from sources other than her own labor—social security payments, interest and dividends, and the like.

The consumption path as drawn in Figure 17.1 is constant over the person's life. This is an extreme assumption, but it illustrates the point that the path of consumption over a lifetime is likely to be much more stable than the path of income. We consume an amount

average propensity to consume (APC) *The proportion of income households spend on consumption. Determined by dividing consumption (C) by income (Y).*

life-cycle theory of consumption *A theory of household consumption: Households make lifetime consumption decisions based on their expectations of lifetime income.*

---

[1]John Maynard Keynes, *The General Theory of Employment, Interest, and Money* (1936), First Harbinger Ed. (New York: Harcourt Brace Jovanovich, 1964), p. 96.

[2]Whereas the *APC* measures the proportion of total income households spend on consumption, the marginal propensity to consume (*MPC*), which we introduced in chapter 9, measures the proportion of a *change* in income that households spend on consumption. We could interpret Keynes's theory as implying that the marginal propensity to consume falls as income rises. If the *MPC* falls as income rises, it follows that the average propensity to consume (*APC*) falls also.

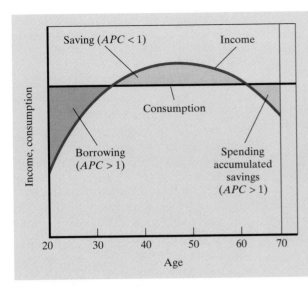

FIGURE 17.1

Life-Cycle Theory of Consumption

In their early working years, people consume more than they earn. This is also true in the retirement years. In between, people save (consume less than they earn) to pay off debts from borrowing and to accumulate savings for retirement.

greater than our incomes during our early working careers. We do this by borrowing against future income, by taking out a car loan, a mortgage to buy a house, or a loan to pay for college. This debt is repaid when our incomes have risen and we can afford to use some of our income to pay off past borrowing without substantially lowering our consumption. The reverse is true for our retirement years. Here, too, our incomes are low. But because we consume less than we earn during our prime working years, we can save up a "nest egg" that allows us to maintain an acceptable standard of living during retirement.

Fluctuations in wealth are also an important component of the life-cycle story. Many young households borrow in anticipation of higher income in the future. Some households actually have *negative wealth*—the value of their assets is less than the debts they owe. A household in its prime working years saves to pay off debts and to build up assets for its later years, when income typically goes down. Households whose assets are greater than the debts they owe have *positive wealth*. With its wage earners retired, a household consumes its accumulated wealth. Generally speaking, wealth starts out negative, turns positive, and then approaches zero near the end of life. Wealth, therefore, is intimately linked to the cumulative saving and dissaving behavior of households.

The key difference between the Keynesian theory of consumption and the life-cycle theory is that the life-cycle theory suggests consumption and saving decisions are likely to be based not just on current income but on expectations of future income as well. The consumption behavior of households immediately following World War II clearly supports the life-cycle story. Just after the war ended, income fell as wage earners moved out of war-related work. However, consumption spending did not fall commensurately, as Keynesian theory would predict. People expected to find jobs in other sectors eventually, and they did not adjust their consumption spending to the temporarily lower incomes they were earning in the meantime.

The phrase **permanent income** is sometimes used to refer to the average level of a person's expected future income stream. If you expect your income will be high in the future (even though it may not be high now), your permanent income is said to be high. With this concept, we can sum up the life-cycle theory by saying that current consumption decisions are likely to be based on permanent income rather than on current income.[3] This means that policy changes like tax-rate changes are likely to have more of an effect on household behavior if they are expected to be permanent rather than temporary.

permanent income *The average level of one's expected future income stream.*

[3] The pioneering work on this topic was done by Milton Friedman, *A Theory of the Consumption Function* (Princeton, N.J.: Princeton University Press, 1957). In the mid-1960s, Franco Modigliani did closely related work that included the formulation of the life-cycle theory.

From October 1996 to October 1997, employment grew by 2,277,000—1.7% over the 1996 labor force. But the unemployment rate only fell from 5.2 to 4.7%. Why such a small decrease? Because during the same time the labor force grew by 2,225,000. Most new workers were new labor force entrants rather than previously in the workforce but unemployed.

Source: Bureau of Labor Statistics release, November 1997.

But although this insight enriches our understanding of the consumption behavior of households, the analysis is still missing something. What's missing is the other main decision of households: the labor supply decision.

THE LABOR SUPPLY DECISION

The size of the labor force in an economy is of obvious importance. A growing labor force is one of the ways in which national income/output can be expanded, and the larger the percentage of people who work, the higher is the potential output per capita.

So far, we have said little about the things that determine the size of the labor force. Of course, demographics are a key; the number of children born in 2000 will go a long way toward determining the potential number of 20-year-old workers in 2020. In addition, immigration, both legal and illegal, plays a role.

But so does behavior. Households make decisions about whether to work and how much to work. These decisions are closely tied to consumption decisions, because for most households the bulk of their spending is financed out of wages and salaries.

> Households make consumption and labor supply decisions simultaneously. Consumption cannot be considered separately from labor supply, because it is precisely by selling your labor that you earn income to pay for your consumption.

As we discussed in chapter 4, the alternative to supplying your labor in exchange for a wage or a salary is leisure or other nonmarket activities. Nonmarket activities include raising a child, going to school, keeping a house, or, in a developing economy, working as a subsistence farmer.

But what determines the quantity of labor supplied by a household? Among the list of factors are the wage rate, prices, wealth, and nonlabor income.

▶ **The Wage Rate** A changing wage rate can affect labor supply, but whether the effect is positive or negative is ambiguous. For example, an increase in the wage rate affects a household in two ways. First, work becomes more attractive relative to leisure and other nonmarket activities. Because every hour spent in leisure now requires giving up a higher wage, the opportunity cost of leisure is higher. As a result, you would expect a higher wage would lead to a larger labor supply—a larger workforce. This is called the *substitution effect of a wage rate increase.*

On the other hand, households who work are clearly better off after a wage rate increase. By working the same number of hours as they did before, they will earn more income. If we assume that leisure is a normal good, people with higher income will spend some of it on leisure by working less. This is the *income effect of a wage rate increase.*

When wage rates rise, the substitution effect suggests that people will work more, while the income effect suggests that they will work less. The ultimate effect depends on which separate effect is more powerful. The data suggest that the substitution effect seems to win in most cases. That is, higher wage rates usually lead to a larger labor supply, while lower wage rates usually lead to a lower labor supply.

▶ **Prices** Prices also play a major role in the consumption/labor supply decision. In our discussions of the possible effects of an increase in the wage rate, we have been assuming that the prices of goods and services do not rise at the same time. If the wage rate and all other prices rise simultaneously, the story is different. To make things clear we need to distinguish between the nominal wage rate and the real wage rate.

The **nominal wage rate** is the wage rate in current dollars. When we adjust the nominal wage rate for changes in the price level, we obtain the **real wage rate**. The real wage rate measures the amount that wages can buy in terms of goods and services. Workers do not care about their nominal wage—they care about the purchasing power of this wage—the real wage.

nominal wage rate *The wage rate in current dollars.*

real wage rate *The amount that the nominal wage rate can buy in terms of goods and services.*

Suppose skilled workers in Indianapolis were paid a wage rate of $15 per hour in 1995. Now suppose that their wage rate rose to $18 in 1996, a 20 percent increase. If the prices of goods and services were exactly the same in 1996 as they were in 1995, the real wage rate would have increased by 20 percent. An hour of work in 1996 ($18) buys 20 percent more than an hour of work in 1995 ($15).

But what if the prices of all goods and services also increased by 20 percent between 1995 and 1996? The purchasing power of an hour's wages has not changed. The real wage rate has not increased at all. Eighteen dollars in 1996 buys the same quantity of goods and services that $15 bought in 1995.

To measure the real wage rate, we adjust the nominal wage rate with a price index. As we saw in chapter 8, there are several such indexes that we might use, including the consumer price index and the GDP price index.[4]

We can now apply what we have learned from the life-cycle theory to our wage/price story. Recall the life-cycle theory says people look ahead in making their decisions. Translated to real wage rates, this idea says:

> Households look at expected future real wage rates as well as the current real wage rate in making their current consumption and labor supply decisions.

Consider the medical student who expects his or her real wage rate will be higher in the future. This expectation obviously has an effect on current decisions about things like how much to buy and whether or not to take a part-time job.

▶ **Wealth and Nonlabor Income** Life-cycle theory says wealth fluctuates over the life cycle. Households accumulate wealth during their working years to pay off debts accumulated when they were young and to support themselves in retirement. This role of wealth is clear, but the existence of wealth poses another question. Consider two households that are at the same stage in their life cycle and have pretty much the same expectations about future wage rates, prices, and so forth. They expect to live the same length of time, and both plan to leave the same amount to their children. They differ only in their wealth. Because of a past inheritance, Household 1 has more wealth than Household 2. Which household is likely to have a higher consumption path for the rest of its life? Household 1, because it has more wealth to spread out over the rest of its life.

> Holding everything else constant (including the stage in the life cycle), the more wealth a household has, the more it will consume, both now and in the future.

Now consider a household that has a sudden unexpected increase in wealth, perhaps an inheritance from a distant relative. How will the household's consumption pattern be affected? The household will increase its consumption, both now and in the future, as it spends the inheritance over the course of the rest of its life.

An increase in wealth can also be looked upon as an increase in nonlabor income. **Nonlabor, or nonwage, income** is income received from sources other than working—inheritances, interest, dividends, and transfer payments such as welfare payments and social security payments. As with wealth:

nonlabor, or nonwage, income *Any income received from sources other than working— inheritances, interest, dividends, transfer payments, and so on.*

> An unexpected increase in nonlabor income will have a positive effect on a household's consumption.

---

[4]To calculate the real wage rate, we divide the nominal wage rate by the price index. Suppose the wage rate rose from $5.00 per hour in 1984 to $9.00 per hour in 1994 and the price level rose 50 percent during the same period. Using 1984 as the base year, the price index would be 1.00 in 1984 and 1.50 in 1994. The real wage rate is W/P, where W is the nominal wage rate and P is the price level. The real wage rate is $5.00 in 1984 ($5.00/$1.00) and $6.00 in 1994 ($9.00/$1.50), using 1984 as the base year.

But what about the effect of an increase in wealth or nonlabor income on labor supply? We already know an increase in income results in an increase in the consumption of normal goods, including leisure. Therefore, an unexpected increase in wealth or nonlabor income results in both an increase in consumption and an increase in leisure. With leisure increasing, labor supply must fall, so:

> An unexpected increase in wealth or nonlabor income leads to a *decrease* in labor supply.

This point should be obvious. If I suddenly win a million dollars in the state lottery or make a killing in the stock market, I will probably work less in the future than I otherwise would have.

INTEREST RATE EFFECTS ON CONSUMPTION

Recall from the last few chapters that the interest rate affects a firm's investment decision. A higher interest rate leads to a lower level of planned investment, and vice versa. This was a key link between the money market and the goods market, and it was the channel through which monetary policy had an impact on planned aggregate expenditure.

We can now expand on this link: The interest rate also affects household behavior. Consider the effect of a fall in the interest rate on consumption. A fall in the interest rate lowers the reward to saving. If the interest rate falls from 10 percent to 5 percent, I earn 5 cents instead of 10 cents per year on every dollar saved. This means that the opportunity cost of spending a dollar today (instead of saving it and consuming it plus the interest income a year from now) has fallen. I will substitute toward current consumption and away from future consumption when the interest rate falls: I consume more today and save less. A rise in the interest rate leads me to consume less today and save more. This effect is called the *substitution effect*.

There is also an *income effect* of an interest rate change on consumption. If a household has positive wealth and is earning interest on that wealth, a fall in the interest rate leads to a fall in interest income. This is a decrease in its nonlabor income, which, as we just saw, will have a negative effect on consumption. For households with positive wealth, the income effect works in the opposite direction from the substitution effect. On the other hand, if a household is a debtor and is paying interest on its debt, a fall in the interest rate leads to a fall in interest payments. The household is better off in this case and will consume more. In this case the income and substitution effects work in the same direction. The total household sector in the United States has positive wealth, and so in the aggregate the income and substitution effects work in the opposite direction.

On balance, the data suggest that the substitution effect dominates the income effect, so that the interest rate has a negative net effect on consumption. There is also some evidence, however, that the income effect is getting larger over time. U.S. households own most of the U.S. government debt, and the size of this debt has increased dramatically in the last 20 years. This means the change in government interest payments, and so the change in household interest income, is now larger for a given change in interest rates than before, which leads to a larger income effect than before for a given change in interest rates. This may help explain why the easing of monetary policy in 1991 and 1992 was not very effective in stimulating the economy: The negative income effect from the falling interest rates nearly offset the positive substitution effect.

GOVERNMENT EFFECTS ON CONSUMPTION AND LABOR SUPPLY: TAXES AND TRANSFERS

The government influences household behavior mainly through income tax rates and transfer payments.

MORTGAGE REFINANCING GETS HOT IN 1997

One of the ways lower interest rates may affect consumption is that home owners may take advantage of lower rates to lower the monthly payments on the loans they used to finance their home purchases.

When most people purchase a home, they finance the purchase by borrowing most of the money through a *mortgage*. A mortgage loan is a long-term loan secured with real estate. The borrower secures the loan with the real estate purchased. In the case of a single family home purchase, if the borrower does not pay back the loan, the lender can "foreclose" (take possession of the house).

Houses are expensive, so most people spread their payments over long periods. Most loans are for 30 years. Because the loan is for a long time, small changes in interest rates can make a big difference. For example, the following table gives the approximate monthly payment required to finance a $100,000, 30-year-fixed-rate mortgage at various interest rates:

RATE	MONTHLY PAYMENT
10%	$878
9%	$805
8%	$734
7%	$665
6%	$600
5%	$537

When interest rates fall, as they did during 1997, some people take advantage of the lower rates by "refinancing." That is, they borrow the same amount of money at a lower rate and pay off the older, higher-rate loan. They end up with a lower monthly payment. The result may well be higher consumption spending on other goods and services.

During 1997, mortgage interest rates dropped steadily from over 8 percent to under 7 percent at the end of the year. At the same time, according to the Mortgage Bankers Association of the United States, the percentage of U.S. mortgage applications that were for refinancing of existing loans grew from 19.4 percent in April to 41.6 percent in November.

The following appeared in the *Boston Globe* on November 23, 1997:

When Maryanne Palladino discovered that interest rates were falling, she decided it was time to refinance the mortgage on her four-bedroom home in North Andover.

It would be Palladino's third time refinancing the $213,000 mortgage in the three-and-a-half years since she purchased the Cape Cod-style house.

With competition for customers growing, lenders are using other methods to attract business. They may waive the application fee, throw in a free appraisal, or hawk a slightly lower interest rate, especially for first-time buyers. Many have launched aggressive advertising campaigns, using radio, television, or direct-mail to catch the attention of consumers. And an increasing number of homeowners are refinancing over the Internet, though experts don't recommend that method for most consumers.[a]

---

[a]Jennifer Babson, "Refinancing Frenzy," *Boston Globe*, November 23, 1997, p. G1.

 For more on refinancing loans, see the Case and Fair Web page at http://www.prenhall.com/casefair.

When the government raises income tax rates, after-tax real wages decrease, lowering consumption. When the government lowers income tax rates, after-tax real wages increase, raising consumption.

A change in income tax rates also affects labor supply. If the substitution effect dominates, as we are generally assuming, then an increase in income tax rates, which lowers after-tax wages, will lower labor supply. A decrease in income tax rates will increase labor supply.

Transfer payments are payments such as social security benefits, veterans benefits, and welfare benefits. An increase in transfer payments is an increase in nonlabor income, which we have seen has a positive effect on consumption and a negative effect on labor supply. Increases in transfer payments thus increase consumption and decrease labor supply, while decreases in transfer payments decrease consumption and increase labor supply. Table 17.1 summarizes these results.

TABLE 17.1 THE EFFECTS OF GOVERNMENT ON HOUSEHOLD CONSUMPTION AND LABOR SUPPLY

| | INCOME TAX RATES | | TRANSFER PAYMENTS | |
	Increase	Decrease	Increase	Decrease
Effect on consumption	Negative	Positive	Positive	Negative
Effect on labor supply	Negative*	Positive*	Negative	Positive

*If the substitution effect dominates.

Note: The effects are larger if they are expected to be permanent rather than temporary.

In 1996, the Congress passed and the president signed a controversial package of reforms to the welfare system. It gave much more freedom to states to design programs to get people off welfare and into the workforce. The new legislation took effect on July 1, 1997. "Aid to Families with Dependent Children" was changed to "Temporary Assistance for Needy Families." States are required to limit most recipients to no more than 5 years of benefits over a lifetime.

A POSSIBLE EMPLOYMENT CONSTRAINT ON HOUSEHOLDS

Our discussion of the labor supply decision has so far proceeded as if households were free to choose how much to work each period. If a member of a household decides to work five additional hours a week at the current wage rate, we have assumed the person *can* work five hours more—that work is available. If someone who has not been working decides to work at the current wage rate, we have assumed that the person *can find a job*.

There are times when these assumptions do not hold. The Great Depression, when unemployment rates reached 25 percent of the labor force, led to the birth of macroeconomics in the 1930s. Since the mid-1970s, the United States has experienced three recessions, with millions of unemployed workers unable to find work.

All households face a budget constraint, regardless of the state of the economy. This budget constraint, which separates those bundles of goods that are available to a household from those that are not, is determined by income, wealth, and prices. When there is unemployment, some households feel an additional constraint on their behavior. Some people may want to work 40 hours per week at the current wage rates but can find only part-time work. Others may not find any work at all.

How does a household respond when it is constrained from working as much as it would like? It consumes less. If your current wage rate is $10 per hour and you normally work 40 hours a week, your normal income from wages is $400 per week. If your average tax rate is 20 percent, your after-tax wage income is $320 per week. You are likely to spend much of this income during the week. If you are prevented from working, this income will not be available to you, and you will have less to spend.

You will spend something, of course. You may receive some form of nonlabor income, and you may have assets, such as savings deposits or stocks and bonds, that can be withdrawn or sold. You may also be able to borrow during your period of unemployment. But even though you will spend something during the week, it is almost certain that you will spend less than you would have if you had your usual income of $320 in after-tax wages.

Households consume less if they are constrained from working.

A household constrained from working as much as it would like at the current wage rate faces a different decision from the decision facing a household that can work as much as it wants. The work decision of the former household is, in effect, forced on it. The household works as much as it can—a certain number of hours per week or perhaps none at all—but this amount is less than the household would choose to work at the current wage rate if it could find more work. The amount that a household would like to work at the current wage rate if it could find the work is called its **unconstrained supply of labor**. The amount that the household actually works in a given period at current wage rates is called its **constrained supply of labor**.

A household's constrained supply of labor is not a variable over which it has any control. The amount of labor the household supplies is imposed on it from the outside by the

unconstrained supply of labor *The amount a household would like to work within a given period at the current wage rate if it could find the work.*

constrained supply of labor *The amount a household actually works in a given period at the current wage rate.*

workings of the economy. However, the household's consumption *is* under its control. We have just seen that the less a household works—that is, the smaller the household's constrained supply of labor—the lower is its consumption. Constraints on the supply of labor are an important determinant of consumption when there is unemployment.

▶ **Keynesian Theory Revisited** Recall the Keynesian theory that current income determines current consumption. We now know the consumption decision is made jointly with the labor supply decision and the two depend on the real wage rate. It is incorrect to think consumption depends only on income, at least when there is full employment. But if there is unemployment, Keynes is closer to being correct because income is not determined by households. When there is unemployment, the level of income (at least workers' income) depends exclusively on the employment decisions made by firms. There are unemployed workers who are willing to work at the current wage rate, and their income is in effect determined by firms' hiring decisions. This income affects current consumption, which is consistent with Keynes's theory. This is one of the reasons Keynesian theory is considered to pertain to periods of unemployment. It was, of course, precisely during such a period that the theory was developed.

A SUMMARY OF HOUSEHOLD BEHAVIOR

This completes our discussion of household behavior in the macroeconomy. Clearly, household consumption depends on more than current income. Households determine consumption and labor supply simultaneously, and they look ahead in making their decisions.

> The following factors affect household consumption and labor supply decisions:
> - current and expected future real wage rates
> - the initial value of wealth
> - current and expected future nonlabor income
> - interest rates
> - current and expected future tax rates and transfer payments

If households are constrained in their labor supply decisions, income is directly determined by firms' hiring decisions. In this case, we can say (in the traditional, Keynesian way) that "income" affects consumption.

THE HOUSEHOLD SECTOR SINCE 1970

To better understand household behavior, let's examine how some of the aggregate household variables have changed over time. We will discuss the period 1970 I to 1997 IV. (Remember, Roman numerals refer to quarters. 1970 I means the first quarter of 1970.) Within this span, there have been three recessionary periods, 1974 I to 1975 IV, 1980 II to 1983 I, and 1990 III to 1991 I. How did the household variables behave during each period?

▶ **Consumption** Data on the total consumption of the household sector are in the national income accounts. As we saw in Table 7.2, personal consumption expenditures accounted for 67.9 percent of GDP in 1997. The three basic categories of consumption expenditures are services, nondurable goods, and durable goods.

Figure 17.2 presents the data for consumption of services and nondurable goods combined and for durable goods. The variables are in real terms. You can see that expenditures on services and nondurable goods are "smoother" over time than expenditures on durable goods. For example, the decrease in expenditures on services and nondurable goods was much smaller during the three recessionary periods than the decrease in expenditures on durable goods.

Why do expenditures on durables fluctuate more than expenditures on services and nondurables? When times are bad, people can postpone the purchase of durable

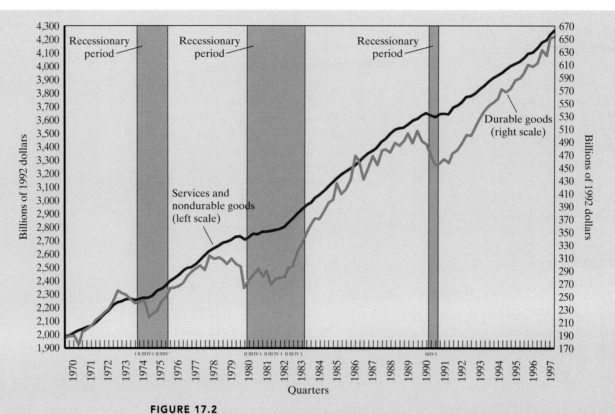

FIGURE 17.2

Consumption Expenditures, 1970 I to 1997 IV

Over time, expenditures for services and nondurable goods are "smoother" than expenditures for durable goods.

goods, and they do. It follows that expenditures on these goods change the most. When times are tough, you do not *have* to have a new car or a new washer-dryer; you can make do with your old Chevy or Maytag until things get better. But when your income falls, it is less easy to postpone the service costs of day care or health care. Non-durables fall into an intermediate category, with some items (like new clothes) easier to postpone than others (like food).

➤ **Housing Investment**   Another important expenditure of the household sector is housing investment (purchases of new housing), plotted in Figure 17.3. This variable fluctuates greatly, for at least two reasons. Housing investment is the most easily postponable of all household expenditures. Also, housing investment is sensitive to the general level of interest rates, and interest rates fluctuate considerably over time. When interest rates are low, housing investment is high, and vice versa.

➤ **Labor Supply**   As we noted in chapters 8 and 15, a person is considered a part of the labor force when he or she either is working or has been actively looking for work in the past few weeks. The ratio of the labor force to the total working-age population—those 16 and over—is the *labor-force participation rate*.

It is informative to divide the labor force into three categories: males 25 to 54, females 25 to 54, and all others 16 and over. Ages 25 to 54 are sometimes called "prime" ages, presuming that a person is in the prime of working life during these ages. The participation rates for these three groups are plotted in Figure 17.4.

As the figure shows, most men of prime age are in the labor force, although the participation rate has fallen slightly since 1970—from .961 in 1970 I to .920 in 1997 IV.

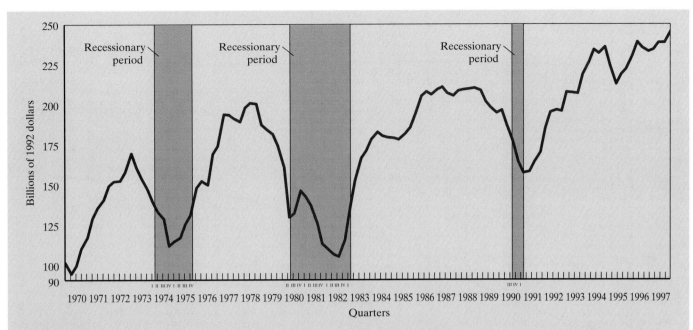

FIGURE 17.3

Housing Investment of the Household Sector, 1970 I to 1997 IV

Housing investment fell sharply during the three recessionary periods since 1970. Like expenditures for durable goods, expenditures for housing investment are postponable.

(A rate of .920 means that 92.0 percent of prime-age men were in the labor force.) The participation rate for prime-age women, on the other hand, has risen dramatically since 1970—from .501 in 1970 I to .766 in 1997 IV. Although economic factors account for some of this increase, a change in social attitudes and preferences probably explains much of the increase. Although the participation rate of prime-age women is still below the rate for prime-age men, this difference will narrow even further in the future if the rate for men keeps falling and the rate for women keeps rising.

Figure 17.4 also shows the participation rate for all individuals 16 and over except prime-age men and women. This rate has some cyclical features—it tends to fall in recessions and to rise or fall less during expansions. These features reveal the operation of the *discouraged-worker effect*, discussed in chapter 8. During recessions, some people get discouraged about ever finding a job. They stop looking and are then not considered a part of the labor force. During expansions, people become encouraged again. Once they begin looking for jobs, they are again considered a part of the labor force. Because prime-age women and men are likely to be fairly attached to the labor force, the discouraged-worker effect for them is quite small.

The participation rate for non-prime-age men and women has fallen since 1970. Part of this decrease reflects an increase in early retirement. When someone retires, he or she is no longer considered a part of the labor force.

FIRMS: INVESTMENT AND EMPLOYMENT DECISIONS

Having taken a closer look at the behavior of households in the macroeconomy, we now look more closely at the behavior of firms—the other major decision-making unit in the economy. In discussing firm behavior earlier, we assumed that planned investment depends only on the interest rate. However, there are several other determinants

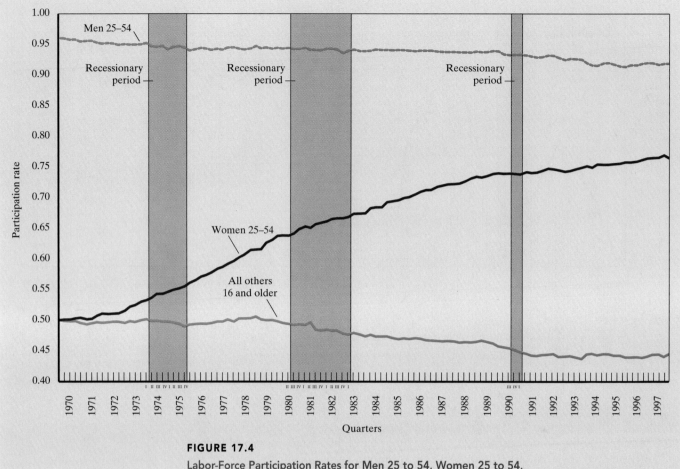

FIGURE 17.4

Labor-Force Participation Rates for Men 25 to 54, Women 25 to 54, and All Others 16 and Over, 1970 I to 1997 IV

Since 1970, the labor-force participation rate for prime-age men has been decreasing slightly. The rate for prime-age women has been increasing dramatically. The rate for all others 16 and over has been declining since 1979 and shows a tendency to fall during recessions (the discouraged-worker effect).

of planned investment. We now discuss them and the factors that affect firms' employment decisions. Once again, microeconomic theory can help us gain some insights into the working of the macroeconomy.

In a market economy, firms determine which goods and services are available to consumers today and which will be available in the future, how many workers are needed for what kinds of jobs, and how much investment will be undertaken. Stated in macroeconomic terms, the decisions of firms, taken together, determine output, labor demand, and investment.

inputs *The goods and services that firms purchase and turn into output.*

In this section, we concentrate on the input choices made by firms. By **inputs**, we mean the goods and services that firms purchase and turn into output. Two important inputs that firms use are capital and labor. (Other inputs are energy, raw materials, and semifinished goods.) Each period, firms must decide how much capital and labor to use in producing output. Let's look first at the decision about how much capital to use.

▶ **Investment Decisions**   At any point in time a firm has a certain stock of capital on hand. *Stock of capital* means the factories and buildings (sometimes called "plants") firms own, the equipment they need to do business, and their inventories of partly or wholly finished goods. There are two basic ways a firm can add to its capital stock.

One is to buy more machinery or build new factories or buildings. This kind of addition to the capital stock is **plant-and-equipment investment**.

The other way a firm adds to its capital stock is to increase its inventories. When a firm produces more than it sells in a given period, the firm's stock of inventories increases.[5] This type of addition to the capital stock is **inventory investment**. Recall from chapter 9 that unplanned inventory investment is different from planned inventory investment. When a firm sells less than it expected to, it experiences an unplanned increase in its inventories and is forced to invest more than it planned to. Unplanned increases in inventories result from factors beyond the firm's control. (We take up inventory investment in detail later in this chapter.)

➤ **Employment Decisions**   In addition to investment decisions, firms make *employment* decisions. At the beginning of each period, a firm has a certain number of workers on its payroll. On the basis of its current situation and its upcoming plans, the firm must decide whether to hire additional workers, keep the same number, or reduce its workforce by laying off some employees.

Until this point, our description of firm behavior has been quite simple. In chapter 9 we argued that firms increase production when they experience unplanned decreases in inventory and reduce production when they experience unplanned increases in inventory. We have also alluded to the fact that the demand for labor increases when output grows. In reality, the set of decisions facing firms is much more complex. A decision to produce additional output is likely to involve additional demand for both labor *and* capital.

The demand for labor is quite important in macroeconomics. If the demand for labor increases at a time of less-than-full employment, the unemployment rate will fall. If the demand for labor increases when there is full employment, wage rates will rise. The demand for capital (which is partly determined by the interest rate) is important as well. Recall, planned investment spending is a component of planned aggregate expenditure. When planned investment spending (I, the demand for new capital) increases, the result is additional output (income). We discussed the investment multiplier effect in chapter 9.

➤ **Decision Making and Profit Maximization**   To understand the complex behavior of firms in input markets, we must assume that firms make decisions to maximize their profits. One of the most important profit-maximizing decisions that a firm must make is how to produce its output. In most cases, a firm must choose among alternative methods of production, or *technologies*. Different technologies generally require different combinations of capital and labor.

Consider a factory that manufactures shirts. Shirts can be made entirely by hand, with workers cutting the pieces of fabric and sewing them together. But shirts exactly like those can be made on huge complex machines that cut and sew and produce shirts with very little human supervision. Between these two extremes are dozens of alternative technologies. Shirts can be partly hand sewn, with the stitching done on electric sewing machines.

Firms' decisions regarding the amount of capital and labor that they will use in production are closely related. If firms maximize profits, they will choose the technology that minimizes the cost of production. That is, it is logical to assume that firms will choose the technology that is most efficient.

The most efficient technology depends on the relative prices of capital and labor. A shirt factory in the Philippines that decides to increase its production faces a large supply of relatively inexpensive labor. Wage rates in the Philippines are quite low. Capital equipment must be imported and is very expensive. A shirt factory in the Philippines is likely to choose a **labor-intensive technology**—a large amount of labor relative to capital.

plant-and-equipment investment *Purchases by firms of additional machines, factories, or buildings within a given period.*

inventory investment *Occurs when a firm produces more output than it sells within a given period.*

labor-intensive technology *A production technique that uses a large amount of labor relative to capital.*

---

[5]The change in inventories is exactly equal to the difference between production and sales. If a firm sells 20 units more than it produces in the course of a month, its inventories fall by 20 units; if it produces 20 units more than it sells, its inventories rise by 20 units.

When labor-intensive technologies are used, expansion is likely to increase the demand for labor substantially while increasing the demand for capital only modestly.

A shirt factory in Germany that decides to expand production is likely to buy a large amount of capital equipment and to hire relatively few new workers. It will probably choose a **capital-intensive technology**—a large amount of capital relative to labor. German wage rates are quite high, higher in many occupations than in the United States. Capital, however, is plentiful.

capital-intensive technology
A production technique that uses a large amount of capital relative to labor.

> Firms' decisions about labor demand and investment are likely to depend on the relative costs of labor and capital. The relative impact of an expansion of output on employment and on investment demand depends on the wage rate and the cost of capital.

EXPECTATIONS AND ANIMAL SPIRITS

In addition to the cost of capital and the cost of labor, firms' expectations about the future play a big role in investment and employment decisions.

Time is a key factor in investment decisions. Capital has a life that typically extends over many years. A developer who decides to build an office tower is making an investment that will be around (barring earthquakes, floods, or tornadoes) for several decades. In deciding where to build a plant, a manufacturing firm is committing a large amount of resources to purchase capital that will presumably yield services over a long time. Furthermore, the decision to build a plant or to purchase large equipment must often be made years before the actual project is completed. While the acquisition of a small business computer may take only a few days, the planning process for downtown developments in large U.S. cities has been known to take decades.

For these reasons, investment decisions require looking into the future and forming expectations about it. In forming their expectations, firms consider numerous factors. At a minimum, they gather information about the demand for their specific products, about what their competitors are planning, and about the macroeconomy's overall health. A firm is not likely to increase its production capacity if it does not expect to sell more of its product in the future. Hilton will not put up a new hotel if it does not expect to fill the rooms at a profitable rate. Ford will not build a new plant if it expects the economy to enter a long recession.

Forecasting the future is fraught with dangers. Many events cannot be foreseen. Investments are therefore always made with imperfect knowledge. Keynes pointed this out in 1936:

> The outstanding fact is the extreme precariousness of the basis of knowledge on which our estimates of prospective yield have to be made. Our knowledge of the factors which will govern the yield of an investment some years hence is usually very slight and often negligible. If we speak frankly, we have to admit that our basis of knowledge for estimating the yield ten years hence of a railway, a copper mine, a textile factory, the goodwill of a patent medicine, an Atlantic liner, a building in the City of London amounts to little and sometimes nothing.

Keynes concludes from this that much investment activity depends on psychology and on what he calls the **animal spirits of entrepreneurs:**

animal spirits of entrepreneurs
A phrase coined by Keynes to describe investors' feelings.

> Our decisions . . . can only be taken as a result of animal spirits. In estimating the prospects of investment, we must have regard, therefore, to nerves and hysteria and even the digestions and reactions to the weather of those upon whose spontaneous activity it largely depends.[6]

[6]John Maynard Keynes, *The General Theory of Employment, Interest, and Money* (1936), First Harbinger Ed. (New York: Harcourt Brace Jovanovich, 1964), pp. 149, 152.

Because expectations about the future are, as Keynes points out, subject to great uncertainty, they may change often. Thus animal spirits help to make investment a volatile component of GDP.

> **The Accelerator Effect** Expectations, at least in part, determine the level of planned investment spending. At any interest rate, the level of investment is likely to be higher if businesses are optimistic. If businesses are pessimistic, the level of planned investment will be lower. But what determines expectations?

One possibility borne out empirically is that expectations are optimistic when aggregate output (Y) is rising and pessimistic when aggregate output is falling.

> At any given level of the interest rate, expectations are likely to be more optimistic and planned investment is likely to be higher when output is growing rapidly than when it is growing slowly or falling.

It is easy to see why. If firms expect future output to grow, they must plan now to add productive capacity. One indicator of future prospects is the current growth rate.

If this is the case in reality, and evidence indicates it is, the ultimate result will be an **accelerator effect**. If aggregate output (income) (Y) is rising, investment will increase even though the level of Y may be low. Higher investment spending leads to an added increase in output, further "accelerating" the growth of aggregate output. If Y is falling, expectations are dampened, and investment spending will be cut even though the level of Y may be high, accelerating the decline.

accelerator effect *The tendency for investment to increase when aggregate output increases and decrease when aggregate output decreases, accelerating the growth or decline of output.*

EXCESS LABOR AND EXCESS CAPITAL EFFECTS

We need to make one more point about firms' investment and employment decisions: Firms may sometimes choose to hold **excess labor** and/or **excess capital**. A firm holds excess labor (or capital) if it could reduce the amount of labor it employs (or capital it holds) and still produce the same amount of output.

Why would a firm want to employ more workers or have more capital on hand than it needs? Both labor and capital are costly—a firm has to pay wages to its workers, and it forgoes interest on funds tied up in machinery or buildings. Why would a firm want to incur costs that do not yield revenue?

To see why, suppose a firm suffers a sudden and large decrease in sales, but it expects the lower sales level to last only a few months, after which it believes sales will pick up again. In this case, the firm is likely to lower production in response to the sales change to avoid too large an increase in its stock of inventories. This decrease in production means the firm could get rid of some workers and some machines, because it now needs less labor and less capital to produce the now-lower level of output.

Alas, things are not this simple. Decreasing its workforce and capital stock quickly can be costly for a firm. Abrupt cuts in the workforce hurt worker morale and may increase personnel administration costs, and abrupt reductions in capital stock may be disadvantageous because of the difficulty of selling used machines. These types of costs are sometimes called **adjustment costs** because they are the costs of adjusting to the new level of output. There are also adjustment costs to increasing output. For example, it is usually costly to recruit and train new workers.

Adjustment costs may be large enough that a firm chooses not to decrease its workforce and capital stock when production falls. The firm may at times choose to have more labor and capital on hand than it needs to produce its current amount of output, simply because it would be more costly to get rid of them than to keep them. In practice, excess labor takes the form of workers not working at their normal level of activity (more coffee breaks and more idle time, for instance). Some of this excess labor may receive new training so that productivity will be higher when production picks up again.

excess labor, excess capital *Labor and capital that are not needed to produce the firm's current level of output.*

adjustment costs *The costs that a firm incurs when it changes its production level—for example, the administration costs of laying off employees or the training costs of hiring new workers.*

The existence of excess labor and capital at any given moment is likely to affect future employment and investment decisions. Suppose a firm already has excess labor and capital due to a fall in its sales and production. When production picks up again, the firm will not need to hire as many new workers or acquire as much new capital as it otherwise would need to.

> The more excess capital a firm already has, the less likely it is to invest in new capital in the future. The more excess labor it has, the less likely it is to hire new workers in the future.

INVENTORY INVESTMENT

We now turn to a brief discussion of the inventory investment decision. This decision is quite different from the plant-and-equipment investment decision.

➤ The Role of Inventories   Recall the distinction between a firm's sales and its output. If a firm can hold goods in inventory, which is usually the case unless the good is perishable or unless the firm produces services, then within a given period it can sell a quantity of goods that differs from the quantity of goods it produces during that period. When a firm sells more than it produces, its stock of inventories decreases; when it sells less than it produces, its stock of inventories increases.

> Stock of inventories (end of period) = Stock of inventories (beginning of period)
> + Production − Sales

If a firm starts a period with 100 umbrellas in inventory, produces 15 umbrellas during the period, and sells 10 umbrellas in this same interval, it will have 105 umbrellas (100 + 15 − 10) in inventory at the end of the period. A change in the stock of inventories is actually investment because inventories are counted as part of a firm's capital stock. In our example, inventory investment during the period is a positive number, 5 umbrellas (105 − 100). When the number of goods produced is less than the number of goods sold, inventory investment is negative.

➤ The Optimal Inventory Policy   We can now consider firms' inventory decisions. Firms are concerned with what they are going to sell and produce in the future, as well as what they are selling and producing currently. At each point in time, a firm has some idea of how much it is going to sell in the current period and in future periods. Given these expectations and its knowledge of how much of its good it already has in stock, a firm must decide how much to produce in the current period.

Inventories are costly to a firm because they take up space and they tie up funds that could be earning interest. However, if a firm's stock of inventories gets too low, the firm may have difficulty meeting the demand for its product, especially if demand increases unexpectedly. The firm may lose sales. The point between too low and too high a stock of inventory is called the **desired**, or **optimal**, **level of inventories**. This is the level at which the extra cost (in lost sales) from decreasing inventories by a small amount is just equal to the extra gain (in interest revenue and decreased storage costs).

A firm that had no costs other than inventory costs would always aim to produce in a period exactly the volume of goods necessary to make its stock of inventories at the end of the period equal to the desired stock. If the stock of inventory fell lower than desired, the firm would produce more than it expected to sell to bring the stock up. If the stock of inventory grew above the desired level, the firm would produce less than it expected to sell to reduce the stock.

desired, or **optimal, level of inventories** *The level of inventory at which the extra cost (in lost sales) from lowering inventories by a small amount is just equal to the extra gain (in interest revenue and decreased storage costs).*

There are other costs to running a firm besides inventory costs. In particular, large and abrupt changes in production can be very costly because it is often disruptive to change a production process geared to a certain rate of output. If production is to be increased, there may be adjustment costs for hiring more labor and increasing the capital stock. If production is to be decreased, there may be adjustment costs in laying off workers and decreasing the capital stock.

Because holding inventories and changing production levels are both costly, firms face a trade-off between them. Because of adjustment costs, a firm is likely to smooth its production path relative to its sales path. This means a firm is likely to have its production fluctuate less than its sales, with changes in inventories to absorb the difference each period. However, because there are incentives not to stray too far from the optimal level of inventories, fluctuations in production are not eliminated completely. Production is still likely to fluctuate, just not as much as sales fluctuate.

Two other points need to be made here. First, if a firm's stock of inventories is unusually or unexpectedly high, the firm is likely to produce less in the future than it would have, to decrease its high stock of inventories. In other words, although the stock of inventories fluctuates over time because production is smoothed relative to sales, at any point in time inventories may be unexpectedly high or low because sales have been unexpectedly low or high. An unexpectedly high stock will have a negative effect on production in the future, and an unexpectedly low stock will have a positive effect on production in the future.

> An unexpected increase in inventories has a negative effect on future production, and an unexpected decrease in inventories has a positive effect on future production.

Second, firms do not know their future sales exactly. They have expectations of future sales, and these expectations may not turn out to be exactly right.

This has important consequences. If sales turn out to be less than expected, inventories will be higher than expected, and there will be less production in the future. Furthermore, *future* sales expectations are likely to have an important effect on *current* production. If a firm expects its sales to be high in the future, it will adjust its planned production path accordingly. Even though a firm smoothes production relative to sales, over a long time it must produce as much as it sells. If it did not, it would eventually run out of inventories.

> The level of a firm's planned production path depends on the level of its expected future sales path. If a firm's expectations of the level of its future sales path decrease, the firm is likely to decrease the level of its planned production path, including its actual production in the current period. Current production depends on expected future sales.

Because production is likely to depend on expectations of the future, animal spirits may play a role. If firms become more optimistic about the future, they are likely to produce more now. Keynes's view that animal spirits affect investment is also likely to pertain to output.

A SUMMARY OF FIRM BEHAVIOR

The following factors affect firms' investment and employment decisions:

- the wage rate and the cost of capital. (An important component of the cost of capital is the interest rate.)
- firms' expectations of future output.
- the amount of excess labor and excess capital on hand.

The most important points to remember about the relationship between production, sales, and inventory investment are:

- inventory investment (that is, the change in the stock of inventories) equals production minus sales.
- an unexpected increase in the stock of inventories has a negative effect on future production.
- current production depends on expected future sales.

THE FIRM SECTOR SINCE 1970

To close our discussion of firm behavior, we now examine some aggregate investment and employment variables for the period 1970 I to 1997 IV.

➤ **Plant and Equipment Investment**   Plant and equipment investment by the firm sector is plotted in Figure 17.5. Investment fared poorly in the three recessionary periods after 1970. This observation is consistent with the observation that investment depends in part on output. An examination of the plot of real GDP in Figure 6.6 and the plot of investment in Figure 17.5 shows investment generally does poorly when GDP does poorly and investment generally does well when GDP does well.

Figure 17.5 also shows that investment fluctuates greatly. Not surprising! The animal spirits of entrepreneurs are likely to be volatile, and if animal spirits affect investment, it follows that investment too will be volatile.

Despite the volatility of plant and equipment investment, however, it is still true that housing investment fluctuates more than plant and equipment investment (as you can see by comparing Figures 17.3 and 17.5). Plant and equipment investment is not the most volatile component of GDP.

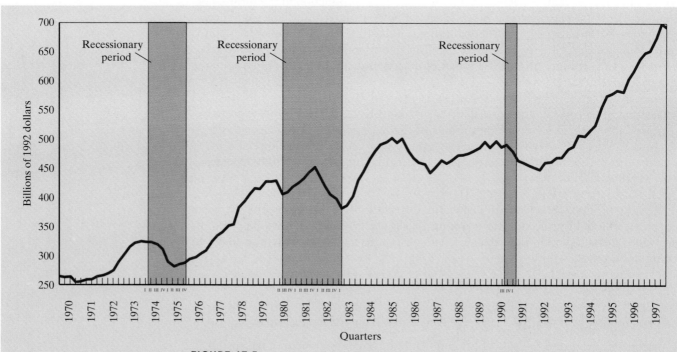

FIGURE 17.5

Plant and Equipment Investment of the Firm Sector, 1970 I to 1997 IV

Overall, plant and equipment investment declined in the three recessionary periods since 1970.

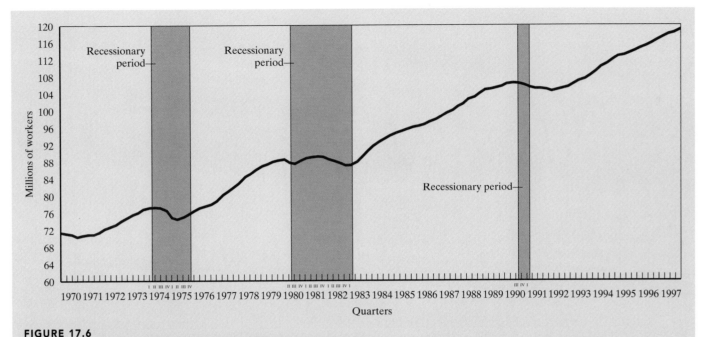

FIGURE 17.6

Employment in the Firm Sector, 1970 I to 1997 IV

Growth in employment was generally negative in the three recessions the U.S. economy has experienced since 1970.

➤ **Employment**   Employment in the firm sector is plotted in Figure 17.6, which shows that employment fell in all three recessionary periods. This is consistent with the theory that employment depends in part on output. Otherwise, employment has grown over time in response to the growing economy. Employment in the firm sector rose from 71.4 million in 1970 I to 118.9 million in 1997 IV.

➤ **Inventory Investment**   Recall that *inventory investment* is the difference between the level of output and the level of sales. Recall also that some inventory investment is usually unplanned. This occurs when the actual level of sales is different from the expected level of sales.

Inventory investment of the firm sector is plotted in Figure 17.7. Also plotted in this figure is the ratio of the stock of inventories to the level of sales—the *inventory/sales ratio*. The figure shows that inventory investment is very volatile—more volatile than housing investment and plant and equipment investment. Some of this volatility is undoubtedly due to the unplanned component of inventory investment, which is likely to fluctuate greatly from one period to the next.

When the inventory/sales ratio is high, the actual stock of inventories is likely to be larger than the desired stock. In such a case, firms have overestimated demand and produced too much relative to sales, and they are likely to want to produce less in the future to draw down their stock. You can find several examples of this in Figure 17.7—the clearest occurred during the 1974 to 1975 period. At the end of 1974, the stock of inventories was very high relative to sales, which means that firms probably had undesired inventories at the end of 1974. In 1975, firms worked off these undesired inventories by producing less than they sold. Thus inventory investment was very low in 1975. The year 1975 is clearly a year in which output would have been higher had the stock of inventories at the beginning of the year not been so high.

On average the inventory/sales ratio has been declining over time, which suggests that firms are becoming more efficient in their management of inventory stocks. They

FIGURE 17.7

Inventory Investment of the Firm Sector and the Inventory/Sales Ratio, 1970 I to 1997 IV

The inventory/sales ratio is the ratio of the firm sector's stock of inventories to the level of sales. Inventory investment is very volatile.

are becoming more efficient in the sense of being able (other things equal) to hold smaller and smaller stocks of inventories relative to sales.

PRODUCTIVITY AND THE BUSINESS CYCLE

productivity, or **labor productivity** *Output per worker hour; the amount of output produced by an average worker in one hour.*

We can now use what we have just learned about firm behavior to analyze movements in productivity. **Productivity,** sometimes called **labor productivity,** is defined as output per worker hour. If output is Y and the number of hours worked in the economy is H, then productivity is Y/H. Simply stated, productivity measures how much output an average worker produces in one hour.

Productivity fluctuates over the business cycle, tending to rise during expansions and fall during contractions. The fact that firms at times hold excess labor explains why productivity fluctuates in the same direction as output.

Figure 17.8 shows the pattern of employment and output for a hypothetical economy over time. Employment does not fluctuate as much as output over the business cycle. It is precisely this pattern that leads to higher productivity during periods of high output and lower productivity during periods of low output. During expansions in the economy, output rises by a larger percentage than employment, and the ratio of output to workers rises. During downswings, output falls faster than employment and the ratio of output to workers falls.

The existence of excess labor when the economy is in a slump means productivity as measured by the ratio Y/H tends to fall at such times. Does this mean labor is in some sense "less productive" during recessions than before? Not really: It means only that firms choose to employ more labor than they need. For this reason, some workers are in effect idle some of the time, even though they are considered employed. They are not

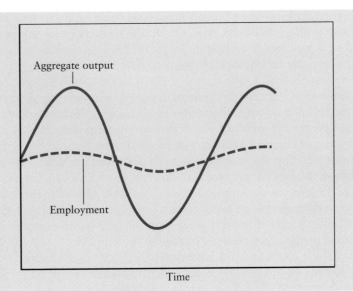

FIGURE 17.8

Employment and Output
over the Business Cycle

In general, employment does
not fluctuate as much as output
over the business cycle. As a
result, measured productivity
(the output-to-labor ratio)
tends to rise during expansionary periods and decline during
contractionary periods.

less productive in the sense of having less potential to produce output; they are merely not working part of the time that they are *counted* as working.

▶ **Productivity in the Long Run**   Theories of long-run economic behavior, which attempt to explain how and why economies grow over time, focus on productivity, usually measured in this case as *output per worker*, or its closely related measure, *GDP per capita*. Productivity defined this way is a key index of an economy's performance over the long run. For example, in comparing how the economies of the United States and Japan have performed over the past 90 years, we would probably begin by noting that although the United States had a substantially higher income per person in 1900, the two countries' incomes per person are now comparable. As we shall see in chapter 19, the growth of output per worker depends on technological progress and on the growth of the capital stock, both of which have been more rapid in Japan than in the United States.

Productivity figures can be misleading when used to diagnose the health of the economy over the short run, because business cycles can distort the meaning of productivity measurements. Output per worker falls in recessions because firms hold excess labor during slumps. Output per worker rises in expansions because firms put the excess labor back to work. Neither of these conditions has anything to do with the economy's long-run potential to produce output.

THE RELATIONSHIP BETWEEN OUTPUT AND UNEMPLOYMENT

We can also use what we have learned about household and firm behavior to analyze the relationship between output and unemployment. When we discussed the connections between the *AS/AD* diagram and the Phillips Curve in chapter 15, we mentioned that output (Y) and the unemployment rate (U) are inversely related. When output rises, the unemployment rate falls, and when output falls, the unemployment rate rises. At one time, it was believed that the relationship between the two variables was fairly stable. **Okun's Law** (after Arthur Okun, who first studied the relationship) stated that the unemployment rate decreased about one percentage point for every 3 percent increase in real GDP. As with the Phillips Curve, Okun's Law has not turned out to be a "law." The economy is far too complex for there to be such a simple and stable relationship between two macroeconomic variables.

Okun's Law *The theory, put forth by Arthur Okun, that the unemployment rate decreases about one percentage point for every 3 percent increase in real GDP. Later research and data have shown that the relationship between output and unemployment is not as stable as Okun's "law" predicts.*

Although the relationship between output and the unemployment rate is not the simple relationship Okun believed, it is true that a 1 percent increase in output tends to correspond to a less than 1 percentage point decrease in the unemployment rate. In other words, there are a number of "slippages" between changes in output and changes in the unemployment rate.

The first slippage is between the change in output and the change in the number of jobs in the economy. When output increases by 1 percent, the number of jobs does not tend to rise by 1 percent in the short run. There are two reasons for this. First, a firm is likely to meet some of the increase in output by increasing the number of hours worked per job. Instead of having the labor force work 40 hours per week, the firm may pay overtime and have the labor force work 42 hours per week. Second, if a firm is holding excess labor at the time of the output increase, at least part of the increase in output can come from putting the excess labor back to work. For both reasons, the number of jobs is likely to rise by a smaller percentage than the increase in output.

The second slippage is between the change in the number of *jobs* and the change in the *number of people employed*. If I have two jobs, I am counted twice in the job data but only once in the persons-employed data. Because some people have two jobs, there are more jobs than there are people employed. When the number of jobs increases, some of the new jobs are filled by people who already have one job (rather than by people who are unemployed). This means the increase in the number of people employed is less than the increase in the number of jobs. This is a slippage between output and the unemployment rate because the unemployment rate is calculated from data on the number of people employed, not the number of jobs.

The third slippage concerns the response of the labor force to an increase in output. Let E denote the number of people employed, let L denote the number of people in the labor force, and let u denote the unemployment rate. In these terms, the unemployment rate is

$$u = 1 - E/L.$$

discouraged-worker effect
The decline in the measured unemployment rate that results when people who want to work but cannot find work grow discouraged and stop looking for jobs, dropping out of the ranks of the unemployed and the labor force.

The unemployment rate is one minus the employment rate, E/L.

When we discussed how the unemployment rate is measured in chapter 8, we introduced the **discouraged-worker effect**. A discouraged worker is one who would like a job but has stopped looking for one because the prospects seem so bleak. When output increases, job prospects begin to look better, and some people who had stopped looking for work begin looking again. When they do, they are once again counted as part of the labor force. The labor force increases when output increases because discouraged workers are moving back into the labor force. This is another reason the unemployment rate does not fall as much as might be expected when output increases.

These three slippages show that the link from changes in output to changes in the unemployment rate is complicated. All three combine to make the change in the unemployment rate less than the percentage change in output in the short run. They also show that the relationship between changes in output and changes in the unemployment rate is not likely to be stable. The size of the first slippage, for example, depends on how much excess labor is being held at the time of the output increase, and the size of the third slippage depends on what else is affecting the labor force (like changes in real wage rates) at the time of the output increase.

> The relationship between output and unemployment depends on the state of the economy at the time of the output change.

THE SIZE OF THE MULTIPLIER

We can finally bring together the material in this chapter and in previous chapters to consider the size of the multiplier. We mentioned in chapter 9 that much of the analysis we would do after deriving the simple multiplier would have the effect of decreasing the size of the multiplier. We can now summarize why.

- First, there are *automatic stabilizers*. We saw in the appendix to chapter 10 that if taxes are not a fixed amount but rather depend on income (which is surely the case in practice), the size of the multiplier is decreased. When the economy expands and income increases, the amount of taxes collected increases. This acts to offset some of the expansion (thus a smaller multiplier). When the economy contracts and income decreases, the amount of taxes collected decreases. This helps to lessen the contraction. Some transfer payments also respond to the state of the economy and act as automatic stabilizers, lowering the value of the multiplier. Unemployment benefits are the best example of transfer payments that increase during contractions and decrease during expansions.
- Second, there is the *interest rate*. We saw in chapter 13 that if government spending increases and the money supply remains unchanged, the interest rate increases, which decreases planned investment and aggregate output (income). This *crowding out* of planned investment decreases the value of the multiplier. And, as we saw in chapter 17, increases in the interest rate also have a negative effect on consumption. Consumption is also crowded out in the same way that planned investment is, and this lowers the value of the multiplier even further.
- Third, there is the response of the *price level*. We saw in chapter 14 that some of the effect of an expansionary policy is to increase the price level. The multiplier is smaller because of this price response. The multiplier is particularly small when the economy is on the steep part of the *AS* curve, where most of the effect of an expansionary policy is to increase prices.
- Fourth, there are *excess capital* and *excess labor*. If firms are holding excess labor and capital, then part of any output increase can come from putting the excess labor and capital back to work rather than from increasing employment and investment. This lowers the value of the multiplier because (1) investment increases less than it would have if there were no excess capital, and (2) consumption increases less that it would have if employment (and thus household income) had increased more.
- Fifth, there are *inventories*. Part of any initial increase in sales can come from drawing down inventories rather than increasing output. To the extent that firms draw down their inventories in the short run, the value of the multiplier is lower because output does not respond as quickly to demand changes.
- Sixth, there are the *life-cycle story* and *expectations*. People look ahead, and they respond less to temporary changes than to permanent changes. The multiplier effects for policy changes perceived to be temporary are smaller than those for policy changes perceived to be permanent.
- Finally, the fact that the United States imports a good deal of what it consumes makes the multiplier smaller than it would be if the U.S. economy were closed. Consider the effects of an increase in government purchases. Initially, most government spending is spending on domestically produced goods and services. But the multiplier effect results from consumption spending by those who earn more income as a result of the additional government spending. Consumers in the United States buy automobiles from Germany and Japan, electronics from Korea, and textiles from the Philippines. When spending "leaks" into imports, the size of the multiplier is reduced. (We discuss this in chapter 21.)

➤ **The Size of the Multiplier in Practice** In practice, the multiplier probably has a value of around 1.4. Its size also depends on how long ago the spending increase began. For example, in the first quarter of an increase in government spending, the multiplier is only about 1.1. If government spending rises by $1 billion, then GDP increases by only about $1.1 billion during the first quarter. In the second quarter, the multiplier rises to about 1.3. The multiplier then rises to its peak of about 1.4 in the third or fourth quarter.

One of the main points to remember here is that if the government is contemplating a monetary or fiscal policy change, the response of the economy to the change is not likely to be large and quick. It takes time for the full effects to be felt, and in the final analysis the effects are much smaller than the simple multiplier we discussed in chapter 9 would lead one to believe.

A good way to review much of the material since chapter 9 is to make sure that you clearly understand how the value of the multiplier is affected by each of the additions to the simple model in chapter 9. We have come a long way since then, and this review may help you to put all the pieces together.

SUMMARY

HOUSEHOLDS: CONSUMPTION AND LABOR SUPPLY DECISIONS

1. The Keynesian theory of consumption holds that household consumption (C) is positively related to current income: The more income you have, the more you are likely to consume. Keynes also believed high-income households consume a smaller proportion of their income than low-income households. The proportion of income households spend on consumption is measured by the *average propensity to consume* (*APC*), which is equal to consumption divided by income (C/Y).

2. The *life-cycle theory of consumption* says households make lifetime consumption decisions based on their expectations of lifetime income. Generally, households consume an amount less than their incomes during their prime working years and an amount greater than their incomes during their early working years and after they have retired.

3. Households make consumption and labor supply decisions simultaneously. Consumption cannot be considered separately from labor supply, because it is precisely by selling your labor that you earn the income that makes consumption possible.

4. There is a trade-off between the goods and services that wage income will buy and leisure or other nonmarket activities. The wage rate is the key variable that determines how a household responds to this trade-off.

5. Changes in the wage rate have both an income effect and a substitution effect. The evidence suggests the substitution effect seems to dominate for most people, which means the aggregate labor supply responds positively to an increase in the wage rate.

6. Consumption increases when the wage rate increases.

7. The *nominal wage rate* is the wage rate in current dollars. The *real wage rate* is the amount the nominal wage can buy in terms of goods and services. Households look at expected future real wage rates as well as the current real wage rate in making their consumption and labor supply decisions.

8. Holding all else constant (including the stage in the life cycle), the more wealth a household has, the more it will consume, both now and in the future.

9. An unexpected increase in *nonlabor income* (any income received from sources other than working, such as inheritances, interest, and dividends) will have a positive effect on a household's consumption and will lead to a decrease in labor supply.

10. The interest rate also affects consumption, although the direction of the total effect depends on the relative sizes of the income and substitution effects. There is some evidence the income effect is larger now than it used to be, making monetary policy less effective than it used to be.

11. The government influences household behavior mainly through income tax rates and transfer payments. If the substitution effect dominates, an increase in tax rates lowers after-tax income, decreases consumption, and decreases the labor supply; a decrease in tax rates raises after-tax income, increases consumption, and increases labor supply. Increases in transfer payments increase consumption and decrease labor supply; decreases in transfer payments decrease consumption and increase labor supply.

12. During times of unemployment, households' labor supply may be constrained. Households may wish to work a certain number of hours at current wage rates but may not be allowed to do so by firms. In this case, the level of income (at least workers' income) depends exclusively on the employment decisions made by firms. Households consume less if constrained from working.

FIRMS: INVESTMENT AND EMPLOYMENT DECISIONS

13. Firms purchase *inputs* and turn them into outputs. Each period, firms must decide how much capital and labor (two major inputs) to use in producing output. Firms can invest in plants and equipment or in inventory.

14. Because output can be produced using many different technologies, firms must make capital and labor decisions simultaneously. A *labor-intensive technique* uses a large amount of labor relative to capital. A *capital-intensive technique* uses a large amount of capital relative to labor. Which technology to use depends on the wage rate and the cost of capital.

15. Expectations affect investment and employment decisions. Keynes used *animal spirits of entrepreneurs* to refer to investors' feelings.

16. At any level of the interest rate, expectations are likely to be more optimistic and planned investment is likely to be higher when output is growing rapidly than when it is growing slowly or falling. The result is an *accelerator effect* that can cause the economy to expand more rapidly during an expansion and contract more quickly during a recession.

17. *Excess labor and capital* are labor and capital not needed to produce a firm's current level of output. Holding excess labor and capital may be more efficient than laying off workers or selling used equipment. The more excess capital a firm has, the less likely it is to invest in new capital in the future. The more excess labor it has, the less likely it is to hire new workers in the future.

18. Holding inventories is costly to a firm because they take up space and they tie up funds that could be earning interest. Not holding inventories can cause a firm to lose sales if demand increases. The *desired*, or *optimal*, *level of inventories* is the level at which the extra cost (in lost sales) from lowering inventories by a small amount is equal to the extra gain (in interest revenue and decreased storage costs).

19. An unexpected increase in inventories has a negative effect on future production, and an unexpected decrease in inventories has a positive effect on future production.

20. The level of a firm's planned production path depends on the level of its expected future sales path. If a firm's expectations of its future sales path decrease, the firm is likely to decrease the level of its planned production path, including its actual production in the current period.

PRODUCTIVITY AND THE BUSINESS CYCLE

21. *Productivity*, or *labor productivity*, is output per worker hour—the amount of output produced by an average worker in one hour. Productivity fluctuates over the business cycle, tending to rise during expansions and fall during contractions. That workers are less productive during contractions does not mean they have less potential to produce output; it means excess labor exists and workers are not working at their capacity.

THE RELATIONSHIP BETWEEN OUTPUT AND UNEMPLOYMENT

22. There is a negative relationship between output and unemployment: When output (Y) rises, the unemployment rate (U) falls, and when output falls, the unemployment rate rises. *Okun's Law* stated that the unemployment rate decreases about one percentage point for every 3 percent increase in GDP. Okun's Law is not a "law"—the economy is too complex for there to be a stable relationship between two macroeconomic variables. In general, the relationship between output and unemployment depends on the state of the economy at the time of the output change.

THE SIZE OF THE MULTIPLIER

23. There are several reasons why the actual value of the multiplier is smaller than the size that would be predicted by a simple model of a closed economy: (1) Automatic stabilizers help to offset contractions or limit expansions. (2) When government spending increases, the increased interest rate crowds out planned investment and consumption spending. (3) Expansionary policies increase the price level. (4) Firms sometimes hold excess capital and excess labor. (5) Firms may meet increased demand by drawing down inventories rather than increasing output. (6) Households and firms change their behavior less when they expect changes to be temporary rather than permanent. (7) A significant portion of spending is spent on foreign-produced goods.

24. In practice, the size of the multiplier at its peak is about 1.4.

REVIEW TERMS AND CONCEPTS

accelerator effect, 371

adjustment costs, 371

animal spirits of entrepreneurs, 370

average propensity to consume (APC), 358

capital-intensive technology, 370

constrained supply of labor, 364

desired, or optimal, level of inventories, 372

discouraged-worker effect, 378

excess capital, 371

excess labor, 371

income effect of a wage rate increase, 360

inputs, 368

inventory investment, 369

labor-intensive technology, 369

life-cycle theory of consumption, 358

nominal wage rate, 360

nonlabor, or nonwage, income, 361

Okun's law, 377

permanent income, 359

plant-and-equipment investment, 369

productivity, or labor productivity, 376

real wage rate, 360

substitution effect of a wage rate increase, 360

unconstrained supply of labor, 364

$$APC \equiv \frac{C}{Y}$$

PROBLEM SET

1. In October 1997, the unemployment rate hit a 24-year low of 4.7 percent. Partly as a result of very tight labor markets, wages rose 4.2 percent and were expected to rise further. What effect would rising wages likely have on the labor supply? Explain your answer using income and substitution effects. If rising wages and welfare reform succeeded in increasing the labor force, how would this affect the unemployment rate relative to what would have happened without the labor force increase? What about the rate of growth in real output/income (Y)?

2. The year 2000 is a presidential election year. What happens to the economy may have a large impact on the outcome. Candidates and the Congress will be taking positions that depend on the state of the economy. Get a copy of the latest employment release from the Bureau of Labor Statistics (their web site is: http://stats.bls.gov). What has happened to employment and wages during the last year? The last month? Is the labor force growing or shrinking? Can you say why? From the newspapers, what has been happening to real GDP? How fast is it growing or shrinking? What position has the Federal Reserve been taking most recently? Are interest rates up or down relative to six months ago? Explain the logic of what the Fed is doing using the concepts explored in this chapter.

3. At the beginning of 1998, the Federal Reserve Bank was poised to raise interest rates in an effort to slow the U.S. economy's rate of growth. Its goal: to prevent inflation.
   a. What direct effects do higher interest rates have on household and firm behavior?
   b. One of the consequences of higher interest rates was that the value of existing bonds (both corporate bonds and government bonds) fell by more than $1.7 trillion. Explain why higher interest rates would reduce the value of existing fixed rate bonds held by the public.
   c. Some economists argue that the wealth effect of higher interest rates on consumption is as important as the direct effect of higher interest rates on consumption. Explain what economists mean by "wealth effects on consumption" and illustrate with AS/AD curves.

4. In 1993, President Clinton proposed and Congress enacted an increase in taxes. One of the increases was in the income tax rate for higher-income wage earners. Republicans claimed that reducing the rewards for working (the net after-tax wage rate), would lead to less work effort and a lower labor supply. Supporters of the tax increase replied that this criticism was baseless because it "ignored the income effect of the tax increase (net wage reduction)." Explain what these supporters meant.

5. Graph the following two consumption functions:
   (1) C = 300 + 0.5 Y
   (2) C = 0.5Y.
   a. For each function, calculate and graph the average propensity to consume (APC) when income is $100, $400, and $800.
   b. For each function, what happens to the APC as income rises?
   c. For each function, what is the relationship between the APC and the marginal propensity to consume?
   d. Under consumption function (1), a family with income of $50,000 consumes a smaller proportion of its income than a family with income of $20,000; yet if we take a dollar of income away from the rich family and give it to the poor family, total consumption by the two families does not change. Explain how this could be.

6. During the late 1990s the price of houses increased steadily around the country.
   What impact would you expect increases and decreases in home value to have on the consumption behavior of home owners? Explain. In what ways might events in the housing market have influenced the rest of the economy through their effects on consumption spending? Be specific.

7. Adam Smith is 45 years old. He has assets (wealth) of $20,000 and has no debts or liabilities. He knows he will work for 20 more years and will live 5 years after that when he will earn nothing. His salary each year for the rest of his working career is $14,000. (There are no taxes.) He wants to distribute his consumption over the rest of his life in such a way that he consumes the same amount each year. He cannot consume in total more than his current wealth plus the sum of his income for the next 20 years. Assume the rate of interest is zero and Smith decides not to leave any inheritance to his children.
   a. How much will Adam consume this year? Next year? How did you arrive at your answer?
   b. Plot on a graph Adam's income, consumption, and wealth from the time he is 45 until he is 70 years old. What is the relationship between the annual increase in his wealth and his annual saving (income minus consumption)? In what year does Adam's wealth start to decline? Why? How much wealth does he have when he dies?
   c. Suppose Adam receives a tax rebate of $100 per year, so his income is $14,100 per year for the rest of his working career. By how much does his consumption increase this year? Next year?
   d. Now suppose Adam receives a one-year-only tax refund of $100—his income this year is $14,100, but in all succeeding years his income is $14,000. What happens to his consumption this year? In succeeding years?

8. Explain why a household's consumption and labor supply decisions are interdependent. What impact does this interdependence have on the way in which consumption and income are related?

9. Why do expectations play such an important role in investment demand? How, if at all, does this explain why investment is so volatile?

10. How can a firm maintain a smooth production schedule even when sales are fluctuating? What are the benefits of a smooth production schedule? What are the costs?

TAKE IT TO THE NET

 We invite you to visit the Case and Fair page on the Prentice Hall Web site:
http://www.prenhall.com/casefair
for this chapter's World Wide Web exercise.

WHAT WOULD YOU DO WITH A BUDGET SURPLUS?

In February 1998 President Clinton submitted the first balanced budget to Congress in 30 years. The proposed $1.7 trillion in federal spending for fiscal year 1999 would result in a surplus of nearly $10 billion—if the Administration's economic projections come true. Many analysts believe that a budget surplus during the next fiscal year is possible, provided Congress and the Administration can avoid the temptation to create new ways to spend the increase in revenue that has resulted from a booming economy. However, this raises an interesting question. If we can't spend it, what should we do with it? After all, it has been so long since the United States has had a federal budget surplus.

Federal budget deficits are not a new phenomenon. The government incurred its first deficit in 1792, and has produced 70 annual deficits since 1900. Historically, deficits were the result of either wars or recessions. Wars required increased amounts of military spending, whereas recessions reduced Federal income tax revenues from households and businesses.

The government ran budget deficits during the War of 1812, the recession of 1837, the Civil War, the depression of the 1890s, and World War I. Each time, after the war was over or the economy recovered, the government used the budget surpluses that followed to pay down the debt it had accumulated.

During the Great Depression, and the increase in spending associated with President Roosevelt's New Deal, the government ran up sizable deficits once again. Then, World War II forced the government to spend more than ever before on defense—and the deficit grew to unprecedented levels. Since the end of World War II, the government has balanced its books only eight times—primarily because spending has grown faster than revenues. The total amount of accumulated deficits at the end of 1997 totaled $5.4 trillion.

During the 1990s, the Bush and Clinton Administrations, together with the Congress, finally began to enact serious deficit reduction measures, and their efforts have begun to pay off. Although the government held the line on spending, an expanding economy began to yield dividends in the form of increased revenues. According to the most recent estimates from the Office of Management and Budget, there was a cyclical surplus of $21 billion in 1997 that, when added to the actual deficit of $22 billion, amounted to an estimated structural deficit of $43 billion.

The rapid return to fiscal prosperity has surprised many, including analysts at the U.S. Treasury who watched their coffers fill with unexpected revenues. According to the 1998 *Economic Report of the President*, the deficit projections for fiscal 1997 were off by more than $100 billion. Roughly three-quarters of the forecast error was due to higher than expected revenues. A complete understanding of this revenue surprise will have to wait until the 1997 tax returns are completely processed, but a large share of it undoubtedly can be attributed to better-than-expected economic growth in 1997.

The prospect of an estimated $1 trillion in total surpluses over the next 10 years has some members of Congress scrambling for creative ways to spend it. It's clear that these days, using the surplus as a payment on past debt does not seem to have the same appeal it did at the turn of the century. We've lived with deficits for so long that the $5.4 trillion accumulated thus far doesn't seem to be an impediment to growth, and $10 billion is so small relative to the debt outstanding that it feels like a waste of resources to many people. Besides, there's some evidence that some predictable level of government securities in circulation are a good thing because they provide risk-free assets with which to balance a portfolio of financial assets.

Many Republicans are proposing a reduction in income taxes—giving back to the tax payers the surplus the government collected. Democrats are proposing increases in social spending as a way to take advantage of the windfall. Economists warn, however, that a reduction in tax rates hurts the government's ability to fund existing programs during times of economic recession, when incomes fall.

A *rainy-day* fund, where money is set aside for use during hard economic times, is popular with many citizens and indeed exists in many state budgets. State revenues have also enjoyed surprisingly strong growth during the past few years and the debates going on in state legislatures today mirror those at the federal level. Some states have decided to increase their rainy-day funds, whereas others are rolling back taxes.

One thing is clear, you can't just leave the money in the bank. Treasury deposits are held by the

Federal Reserve, but generally earn no interest.[1]

Increasingly, the proposal that gets the most favorable reviews is to use the forthcoming surpluses to fix the social security system. The number of baby boomers approaching retirement age threatens to bankrupt the social security system early in the next century unless something is done to make sure the system can afford to finance them. According to the Administration, simply transferring the projected surpluses to the social security trust fund would delay the fund's depletion by 10 years.

There are no easy answers, and the projected surpluses could vanish just as quickly as they came if an unexpected shock should drive the economy into recession. However,

the debate is certain to be full of interesting proposals . . . which is one of the things that makes economics so interesting.

Questions for Analytical Thinking

1. Write a memo to the President describing your proposals for the projected budget surplus.

2. Suppose you had $5,000 worth of credit card debt and you suddenly inherited $500. Would you spend it, save it, or retire some of your debt? Suppose, instead, you received a promotion in your first job and a $500 per month raise. Now what would you do?

3. Although the government is projecting a budget surplus for fiscal year 1999, the structural budget is projected to be in deficit until fiscal year 2001. Explain what these estimates imply about

the government's projections of the gap between actual and potential GDP.

4. Many members of Congress support a balanced budget amendment to the Constitution. What impact would a balanced budget amendment have on fiscal automatic stabilizers and business cycles in this country.

Sources: Jacob Schlesinger and Christopher Georges, "Uses of Surpluses to Save Social Security Gains Fed Chairman's Support," *The Wall Street Journal*, January 30, 1998, p. A2; David Wessel and Christopher Georges, "Federal Overhaul," *The Wall Street Journal*, February 3, 1998, p. A1; Jackie Calmes, "Clinton's Plan to Put 'Social Security First' Took Months of Debate and Changes Budget Politics," *The Wall Street Journal*, January 29, 1998, p. A20; *The Budget of the United States Government, FY 1999, Analytical Perspectives*, Office of Management and Budget, Washington, D.C., 1998; *A Citizen's Guide to the Federal Budget, FY 1999*, Office of Management and Budget, Washington, D.C., 1998; *Economic Report of the President*, President's Council of Economic Advisers, 1998.

---

[1] *In some instances, Treasury deposits are lent out via so-called "Repurchase Agreements" with brokers of government securities, and the yield on these loans are deposited in the Treasury's accounts.*

Chapter

18

DEBATES IN MACROECONOMICS: MONETARISM, NEW CLASSICAL THEORY, AND SUPPLY-SIDE ECONOMICS

THROUGHOUT THIS BOOK, we have noted there are many disagreements and questions in macroeconomics. For example, economists disagree on whether the aggregate supply curve is vertical, either in the short run or the long run. Some even doubt that the aggregate supply curve is a useful macroeconomic concept! There are different views on whether cyclical employment exists and, if it does, what causes it. Economists disagree about whether monetary and fiscal policies are effective at stabilizing the economy, and they support different views on the primary determinants of consumption and investment spending.

We discussed some of these disagreements in previous chapters, but only briefly. In this chapter, we discuss in more detail a number of alternative views of how the macroeconomy works.

KEYNESIAN ECONOMICS

John Maynard Keynes's *General Theory of Employment, Interest and Money*, published in 1936, remains one of the most important works in economics. While a great deal of the material in the previous 10 chapters is drawn from modern research that postdates Keynes, much of it is built around a framework constructed by Keynes.

But what exactly is *Keynesian economics*? In one sense, it is the foundation of all of macroeconomics. Keynes was the first to stress aggregate demand and the links between the money market and the goods market. And it was Keynes who stressed the possible problem of sticky wages. Virtually all the debates in this chapter can be understood in terms of the aggregate output/aggregate expenditure framework suggested by Keynes.

Keynes was an activist! In his words, "The central controls necessary to ensure full employment will, of course, involve a large extension of the traditional functions of government." But he also believed in the efficiency of markets. He felt it was possible to "cure the disease while preserving efficiency and freedom."

Source: J. M. Keynes, *The General Theory,* pp. 379, 381.

In recent years, the term *Keynesian* has been used narrowly. Keynes believed in an activist federal government. He believed the government had a role to play in fighting inflation and unemployment, and he believed monetary and fiscal policy should be used to manage the macroeconomy. This is why *Keynesian* is sometimes used to refer to economists who advocate active government intervention in the macroeconomy.

During the 1970s and 1980s, it became clear that managing the macroeconomy was more easily accomplished on paper than in practice. The inflation problems of the 1970s and early 1980s and the seriousness of the recessions of 1974 to 1975 and 1980 to 1982 led many economists to challenge the idea of active government intervention in the economy. Some were simple attacks on the bureaucracy's ability to act in a timely manner. Others were theoretical assaults that claimed to show that monetary and fiscal policy could have *no effect whatsoever* on the economy, even if it were efficiently managed.

Two major schools decidedly *against* government intervention have developed: monetarism and new classical economics.

MONETARISM

The debate between "monetarist" and "Keynesian" economics is complicated because they mean different things to different people. If we consider the main monetarist message to be that "money matters," then almost all economists would agree. In the *AS/AD* story, for example, an increase in the money supply shifts the *AD* curve to the right, which leads to an increase in both aggregate output (Y) and the price level (P). Monetary policy thus has an effect on output and the price level. **Monetarism**, however, is usually considered to go beyond the notion that money matters.

THE VELOCITY OF MONEY

velocity of money *The number of times a dollar bill changes hands, on average, during a year; the ratio of nominal GDP to the stock of money.*

To understand monetarist reasoning, you must understand the **velocity of money.** Think of velocity as the number of times a dollar bill changes hands, on average, during a year.

Suppose on January 1 you buy a new ballpoint pen with a $5 bill. The owner of the stationery store does not spend your $5 right away. She may hold it until, say, May 1, when she uses it to buy a dozen doughnuts. The doughnut store owner does not spend the $5 he receives until July 1, when he uses it (along with other cash) to buy 100 gallons of oil. The oil distributor uses the bill to buy an engagement ring for his fiancée on September 1, but the $5 bill is not used again in the remaining three months of the year. Because this $5 bill has changed hands four times during the year, its velocity of circulation is four. A velocity of four means the $5 bill stays with each owner for an average of three months, or one quarter of a year.

In practice, we use GDP, rather than the total value of all transactions in the economy, to measure velocity,[1] because GDP data are more available. The income velocity of money (V) is the ratio of nominal GDP to the stock of money (M):

$$V \equiv \frac{GDP}{M}$$

If $6 trillion worth of final goods and services are produced in a year and if the money stock is $1 trillion, then the velocity of money is $6 trillion ÷ $1 trillion, or 6.0.

---

[1]Recall GDP does not include transactions in intermediate goods (e.g., flour sold to a baker to be made into bread) or in existing assets (the sale of a used car). If these transactions are made using money, however, they do influence the number of times money changes hands during the course of a year. GDP is an imperfect measure of transactions to use in calculating the velocity of money.

We can expand this definition slightly by noting that nominal income (GDP) is equal to real output (income) (Y) times the overall price level (P):

$$GDP \equiv P \times Y$$

Through substitution,

$$V \equiv \frac{P \times Y}{M}$$

or

$$M \times V \equiv P \times Y$$

At this point, it is worth pausing to ask if our definition has provided us with any insights into the workings of the economy. The answer is no. Because we defined V as the ratio of GDP to the money supply, the statement $M \times V \equiv P \times Y$ is an identity—it is true by definition. It contains no more useful information than the statement "a bachelor is an unmarried man." The definition does not, for example, say anything about what will happen to $P \times Y$ when M changes. The final value of $P \times Y$ depends on what happens to V. If V falls when M increases, the product $M \times V$ could stay the same, in which case the change in M would have had no effect on nominal income. To give monetarism some economic content, we turn to a simple version of monetarism known as the **quantity theory of money**.

quantity theory of money
The theory based on the identity $M \times V \equiv P \times Y$ *and the assumption that the velocity of money* (V) *is constant (or virtually constant).*

THE QUANTITY THEORY OF MONEY

The key assumption of the quantity theory of money is that the velocity of money is constant (or virtually constant) over time. If we let $\overline{V}$ denote the constant value of V, the equation for the quantity theory can be written:

$$M \times \overline{V} = P \times Y$$

Note the double equal sign has replaced the triple equal sign because the equation is no longer an identity. The equation is true if velocity is constant (and equal to $\overline{V}$), but not otherwise. If the equation is true, it provides an easy way to explain nominal GDP. Given M, which can be considered a policy variable set by the Federal Reserve, nominal GDP is just $M \times \overline{V}$. In this case, the effects of monetary policy are clear. Changes in M cause equal percentage changes in nominal GDP. For example, if the money supply doubles, nominal GDP also doubles. If the money supply remains unchanged, nominal GDP remains unchanged.

The key is whether the velocity of money is really constant. Early economists believed the velocity of money was determined largely by institutional considerations, such as how often people are paid and how the banking system clears transactions between banks. Because these factors change gradually, early economists believed velocity was essentially constant.

If there is equilibrium in the money market, then the quantity of money supplied is equal to the quantity of money demanded. That could mean M in the quantity-theory equation equals both the quantity of money supplied and the quantity of money demanded. If the quantity-theory equation is looked on as a demand-for-money equation, it says that the demand for money depends on nominal income (GDP, or $P \times Y$), but *not* on the interest rate.[2] If the interest rate changes and nominal income does not, the equation says that the quantity of money demanded will not change. This is contrary to the theory of the demand for money in chapter 12, which had the demand for money depending on both income and the interest rate.

---

[2]In terms of the appendix to chapter 13, this means the *LM* curve is vertical.

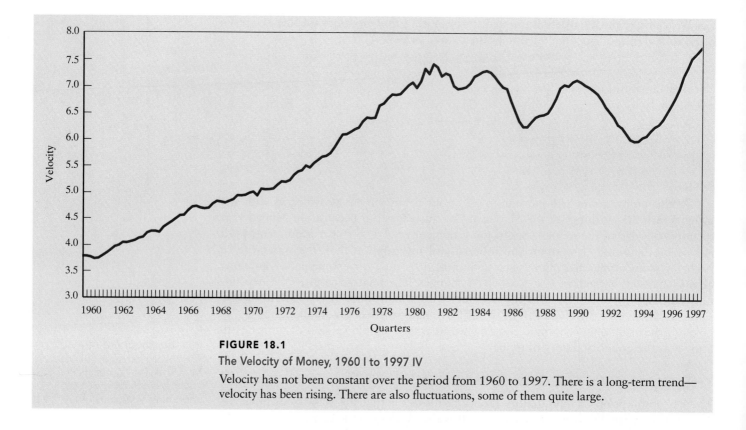

FIGURE 18.1

The Velocity of Money, 1960 I to 1997 IV

Velocity has not been constant over the period from 1960 to 1997. There is a long-term trend—velocity has been rising. There are also fluctuations, some of them quite large.

▶ **Testing the Quantity Theory of Money**   One way to test the validity of the quantity theory of money is to look at the demand for money using recent data on the U.S. economy. The key is: Does money demand depend on the interest rate? Most empirical work says yes. When demand-for-money equations are estimated (or "fit to the data"), the interest rate usually turns out to be a factor. The demand for money does not appear to depend only on nominal income.

Another way of testing the quantity theory is to plot velocity over time and see how it behaves. Figure 18.1 plots the velocity of money for the 1960 I to 1997 IV period. The data show that velocity is far from constant. There is a long-term trend—on average, velocity has been rising during these years—but fluctuations around this trend have also occurred, and some have been quite large. Velocity rose from 6.8 in 1980 III to 7.2 in 1981 III; fell to 6.7 in 1983 I; rose to 7.0 in 1984 III; and fell to 6.1 in 1986 IV. Changes of a few tenths of a point may seem small, but they are actually large. For example, the money supply in 1986 IV was $709 billion. If velocity changes by 0.3 with a money supply of this amount, and if the money supply is unchanged, we have a change in nominal GDP ($P \times Y$) of $213 billion (0.3 × $709 billion), which is about 5 percent of GDP.

The debate over monetarist theories is more subtle than our discussion so far indicates. First, there are many definitions of the money supply. $M1$ is the money supply variable used for the graph in Figure 18.1, but there may be some other measure of the money supply that would lead to a smoother plot. For example, many people shifted their funds from checking account deposits to money market accounts when the latter became available in the late 1970s. Because GDP did not change as a result of this shift while $M1$ decreased, velocity—the ratio of GDP to $M1$—must have gone up. But suppose instead we measured the supply of money by $M2$ (which includes both checking accounts and money market accounts). In this case, the decrease in checking deposits would be exactly offset by the rise in money market account deposits, and $M2$ would not change. With no change in GDP and no change in $M2$, the velocity of money would not change. Whether velocity is constant or not may depend partly on how we measure the money supply.

Second, there may be a time lag between a change in the money supply and its effects on nominal GDP. Suppose we experience a 10 percent increase in the money supply today, but it takes one year for nominal GDP to increase by 10 percent. If we measured the ratio of today's money supply to today's GDP, it would seem that velocity had fallen by 10 percent. But if we measured today's money supply against GDP one year from now, when the increase in the supply of money had its full effect on income, then velocity would have been constant.

The debate over the usefulness of monetarist theory is primarily empirical. It is a debate that can be resolved by looking at facts about the real world and seeing whether they are in accord with the predictions of theory. Is there a measure of the money supply and a choice of the time lag between a change in the money supply and its effects on nominal GDP such that V is in effect constant? If so, then the monetarist theory is a useful approach to understanding how the macroeconomy works. If not, then some other theory is likely to be more appropriate. (We discuss the testing of alternative theories at the end of this chapter.)

INFLATION AS A PURELY MONETARY PHENOMENON

So far we have talked only about nominal output ($P \times Y$). We have said nothing about how a monetarist would break down a change in nominal output (due to a money-supply change) into a change in P and a change in Y. Here again it is not possible to make a general statement about what all monetarists believe. Some may believe that all of the change occurs in P, and others may believe that at least sometimes some of the change occurs in Y. If all of the change occurs in P, then there is a proportional relationship between changes in the money supply and changes in the price level. For example, a 10 percent change in M will lead to a 10 percent change in P if Y remains unchanged. In this case, inflation (an increase in P) is always a purely monetary phenomenon. The price level will not change if the money supply does not change. We will call this view, that changes in M affect only P and not Y, the "strict monetarist" view.

There is considerable disagreement as to whether the strict monetarist view is a good approximation of reality. For example, the strict view is not compatible with a nonvertical AS curve in the AS/AD model in chapter 14. In the case of a nonvertical AS curve, an increase in M, which shifts the AD curve to the right, increases both P and Y. (You may want to review why.)

Almost all economists agree, however, that *sustained* inflation—inflation that continues over many periods—is a purely monetary phenomenon. We pointed out in chapter 14

FAST FACTS

Monetarists say figures like these support their contention that inflation is a monetary phenomenon:

| Country | Annual average percentage change 1985 to 1995 in: | |
	Money Supply	Prices (GDP Deflator)
Brazil	995.5%	875.3%
Peru	388.5	398.5
Sierra Leone	51.4	61.6
Jamaica	32.8	28.3
Israel	22.1	17.1
United States	3.9	3.2

Source: World Bank, *World Development Report*, 1997, Table 2.

in the context of the *AS/AD* framework that inflation cannot continue indefinitely unless the Fed "accommodates" it by increasing the money supply. Let's review this.

Consider a continuously increasing level of government spending (*G*) without any corresponding increase in taxes. The increases in *G* keep shifting the *AD* curve to the right, which leads to an increasing price level (*P*). (You may find it useful to draw a graph here.) With a fixed money supply, the increases in *P* lead to a higher and higher interest rate, but there is a limit to how far this can go. Because taxes are unchanged, the government must finance the increases in *G* by issuing bonds, and there is a limit to how many bonds the public is willing to hold regardless of how high the interest rate goes. At the point at which the public cannot be induced to hold any more bonds, the government will be unable to borrow any more to finance its expenditures. Only if the Fed is willing to increase the money supply (buy some of the government bonds) can the government spending (with its inflationary consequences) continue.

> Inflation cannot continue indefinitely without increases in the money supply.

THE KEYNESIAN/MONETARIST DEBATE

The leading spokesman for monetarism over the last few decades has been Professor Milton Friedman, formerly of the University of Chicago and currently at the Hoover Institute in California. Most monetarists, including Friedman, blame most of the instability in the economy on the federal government, arguing that the inflation the United States encountered over the years could have been avoided if only the Fed had not expanded the money supply so rapidly.

Most monetarists do not advocate an activist monetary stabilization policy—expanding the money supply during bad times and slowing the growth of the money supply during good times. Monetarists tend to be skeptical of the government's ability to "manage" the macroeconomy. The most common argument against such management is the one expressed in chapter 16: Time lags make it likely that conscious attempts to stimulate and contract the economy make the economy more, not less, unstable.

Friedman has for many years advocated a policy of steady and slow money growth—specifically, that the money supply should grow at a rate equal to the average growth of real output (income) (*Y*). That is, the Fed should pursue a constant policy that accommodates real growth but not inflation.

Keynesianism and monetarism are at odds with each other. Many Keynesians advocate the application of coordinated monetary and fiscal policy tools to reduce instability in the economy—to fight inflation and unemployment. But not all Keynesians advocate an activist federal government. Some reject the strict monetarist position that changes in money only affect the price level in favor of the view that both monetary and fiscal policies make a difference and *at the same time* believe the best possible policy for government to pursue is basically noninterventionist.

Most Keynesians agree after the experience of the 1970s that monetary and fiscal tools are not finely calibrated. The notion that monetary and fiscal expansions and contractions can "fine-tune" the economy is gone forever. Still, many feel the experiences of the 1970s also show that stabilization policies can help prevent even bigger economic disasters. Had the government not cut taxes and expanded the money supply in 1975 and in 1982, they argue, the recessions of those years might have been significantly worse. The same people would argue that had the government not resisted the inflations of 1974 to 1975 and 1979 to 1981 with tight monetary policies, they would probably have become much worse.

Thirty years ago, the debate between Keynesians and monetarists was the central controversy in macroeconomics. That controversy, while still alive today, is no longer at the forefront. For the past two decades, the focus of current thinking in macroeconomics has been on the new classical macroeconomics.

NEW CLASSICAL MACROECONOMICS

The challenge to Keynesian and related theories has come from a school sometimes referred to as the **new classical macroeconomics**.[3] Like *monetarism* and *Keynesianism*, this term is vague. No two new classical macroeconomists think exactly alike, and no single model completely represents this school. The following discussion, however, conveys the flavor of the new classical views.

THE DEVELOPMENT OF NEW CLASSICAL MACROECONOMICS

New classical macroeconomics has developed from two different, though related, sources. These sources are the theoretical and the empirical critiques of existing, or traditional, macroeconomics.

On the theoretical level, there has been growing dissatisfaction with the way traditional models treat expectations. Keynes himself recognized that expectations (in the form of "animal spirits") play a big part in economic behavior. The problem is, traditional models have assumed that expectations are formed in naive ways. A common assumption, for example, is that people form their expectations of future inflation by assuming present inflation will continue. If they turn out to be wrong, they adjust their expectations by some fraction of the difference between their original forecast and the actual inflation rate. Suppose I expect 10 percent inflation next year. When next year comes, the inflation rate turns out to be only 5 percent, so I have made an error of 5 percent. I might then predict an inflation rate for the following year of 7.5 percent, halfway between my earlier expectation (10 percent) and actual inflation last year (5 percent).

The problem with this treatment of expectations is that it is not consistent with the assumptions of microeconomics. It implies people systematically overlook information that would allow them to make better forecasts, even though there are costs to being wrong. If, as microeconomic theory assumes, people are out to maximize their satisfaction and firms are out to maximize their profits, they should form their expectations in a smarter way. Instead of naively assuming the future will be like the past, they should actively seek to forecast the future. Any other behavior is not in keeping with the microeconomic view of the forward-looking, rational people who compose households and firms.

On the empirical level, there was stagflation in the U.S. economy during the 1970s. Remember, stagflation is simultaneous high unemployment and rising prices. The Phillips Curve theory of the 1960s predicted that demand pressure pushes up prices, so that when demand is weak—in times of high unemployment, for example—prices should be stable (or perhaps even falling). The new classical theories were an attempt to explain the apparent breakdown in the 1970s of the simple inflation-unemployment trade-off predicted by the Phillips Curve. Just as the Great Depression of the 1930s motivated the development of Keynesian economics, so the stagflation of the 1970s helped motivate the formulation of new classical economics.

RATIONAL EXPECTATIONS

In previous chapters, we stressed households' and firms' expectations about the future. A firm's decision to build a new plant depends on its expectations of future sales. The amount of saving a household undertakes today depends on its expectations about future interest rates, wages, and prices.

How are expectations formed? Do people assume things will continue as they are at present? (Like predicting rain tomorrow because it is raining today.) What information

---

[3]The term *new classical* is used because many of the assumptions and conclusions of this group of economists resemble those of the classical economists—that is, those who wrote before Keynes.

EVEN THOUGH UNCERTAINTY EXISTS, IF YOU KNOW THE "MODEL" GENERATING THE UNCERTAINTY, IT IS POSSIBLE TO HAVE EXPECTATIONS ABOUT THE FUTURE THAT ARE "ON AVERAGE" CORRECT. YOU DON'T KNOW WHETHER A RANDOM COIN TOSS WILL COME UP HEADS OR TAILS. BUT YOU DO KNOW THAT IF YOU TOSS A FAIR COIN 1,000 TIMES, IT WILL COME UP HEADS ABOUT 500 TIMES.

do people use to make their guesses about the future? Questions like these have become central to current macroeconomic thinking and research. One theory, the **rational-expectations hypothesis**, offers a powerful way of thinking about expectations.

Suppose we want to forecast inflation. What does it mean to say that my expectations of inflation are "rational"? The rational-expectations hypothesis assumes people know the "true model" that generates inflation—they know how inflation is determined in the economy—and they use this model to forecast future inflation rates. If there were no random, unpredictable events in the economy, and if people knew the true model generating inflation, their forecasts of future inflation rates would be perfect. Because it is true, the model would not permit mistakes, and thus the people using it would not make mistakes.

However, many events that affect the inflation rate are not predictable—they are random. By "true" model, then, we mean a model that is *on average* correct in forecasting inflation. Sometimes the random events have a positive effect on inflation, which means the model underestimates the inflation rate, and sometimes they have a negative effect, which means the model overestimates the inflation rate. On average, the model is correct. Therefore, rational expectations are correct on average, even though their predictions are not exactly right all the time.

To see this, suppose you have to forecast how many times a fair coin will come up heads out of 100 tosses. The true model in this case is that the coin has a 50–50 chance of coming up heads on any one toss. Because the outcome of the 100 tosses is random, you cannot be sure of guessing correctly. If you know the true model—that the coin is fair—your rational expectation of the outcome of 100 tosses is 50 heads. You are not likely to be exactly right—the actual number of heads is likely to be slightly higher or slightly lower than 50—but *on average* you will be correct.

Sometimes people are said to have rational expectations if they use "all available information" in forming their expectations. This definition is vague, because it is not always clear what "all available information" means. The definition is precise, if by "all available information" we mean that people know and use the true model. We cannot have more or better information than the true model.

If information can be obtained at no cost, then someone is not behaving rationally if he or she fails to use all available information. Because there are almost always costs to making a wrong forecast, it is not rational to overlook information that could help improve the accuracy of a forecast as long as the costs of acquiring that information do not outweigh the benefits of improving its accuracy.

> **Rational Expectations and Market Clearing** If firms have rational expectations and if they set prices and wages on this basis, then, on average, prices and wages will be set at levels that ensure equilibrium in the goods and labor markets. When a firm has rational expectations, it knows the demand curve for its output and the supply curve of labor that it faces, except when random shocks disrupt those curves. Therefore, on average the firm will set the market-clearing prices and wages. The firm knows the true model, and it will not set wages different from those it expects will attract the number of workers it wants. If all firms behave this way, then wages will be set in such a way that the total amount of labor supplied will, on average, be equal to the total amount of labor that firms demand. In other words, on average there will be no unemployment.

In chapter 15, we argued that there might be disequilibrium in the labor market (either in the form of unemployment or in excess demand for workers) because firms may make mistakes in their wage-setting behavior due to expectation errors. If, on average, firms do not make errors, then, on average, there is equilibrium. When expectations are rational, disequilibrium exists only temporarily as a result of random, unpredictable shocks—obviously an important conclusion. If true, it means disequilibrium in any market is only temporary, because firms, on average, set market-clearing wages and prices.

The assumption that expectations are rational radically changes the way we can view the economy. We go from a world in which unemployment can exist for substantial periods and the multiplier can operate to a world in which (on average) all markets clear and there is full employment. In this world there is no need for government stabilization policies. Unemployment is not a problem that governments need to worry about; if it exists at all, it is because of unpredictable shocks that, on average, amount to zero. There is no more reason for the government to try to change the outcome in the labor market than there is for it to change the outcome in the banana market. On average, prices and wages are set at market-clearing levels.

THE LUCAS SUPPLY FUNCTION

The **Lucas supply function**, after Robert E. Lucas of the University of Chicago, is an important part of a number of new classical macroeconomic theories. It yields, as we shall see, a surprising policy conclusion. The function is deceptively simple. It says real output (Y) depends on (is a function of) the difference between the actual price level (P) and the expected price level (P^e):

$$Y = f(P - P^e)$$

The actual price level minus the expected price level ($P - P^e$) is the **price surprise**. Before considering the policy implications of this function, we should look at the theory behind it.

Lucas begins by assuming people and firms are specialists in production but generalists in consumption. If someone you know is a manual laborer, the chances are she sells only one thing—labor. If she is a lawyer, she sells only legal services. In contrast, people buy a large bundle of goods—ranging from gasoline to ice cream and pretzels—on a regular basis. The same is true for firms. Most companies tend to concentrate on producing a small range of products, but they typically buy a larger range of inputs—raw materials, labor, energy, capital. According to Lucas, this divergence between buying and selling creates an asymmetry. People know much more about the prices of the things they sell than they do about the prices of the things they buy.[4]

At the beginning of each period, a firm has some expectation of the average price level for that period. If the actual price level turns out to be different, there is a price surprise. Say the average price level is higher than expected. Because the firm learns about the actual price level slowly, some time goes by before it realizes all prices have gone up. The firm *does* learn *quickly* that the price of its *output* has gone up. The firm perceives—incorrectly, it turns out—that its price has risen relative to other prices, and this leads it to produce more output.

A similar argument holds for workers. When there is a positive price surprise, workers at first believe their "price"—their wage rate—has increased relative to other prices. Workers believe their real wage rate has risen. We know from theory that an increase in the real wage is likely to encourage workers to work more hours.[5] The real wage has not actually risen, but it takes workers a while to figure this out. In the meantime, they supply more hours of work than they would have. This means the economy will produce more output when prices are unexpectedly higher than when prices are at their expected level.

This is the rationale for the Lucas supply function. Unexpected increases in the price level can fool workers and firms into thinking relative prices have changed, causing them to alter the amount of labor or goods they choose to supply.

Lucas supply function *The supply function embodies the idea that output* (Y) *depends on the difference between the actual price level and the expected price level.*

price surprise *Actual price level minus expected price level.*

---

[4]It is not entirely obvious why this should be true, and some critics of the new classical school have argued that this is unrealistic. Some have also criticized the Lucas supply function as too simple, arguing that other things besides price surprises affect aggregate output.

[5]This is true if we assume that the substitution effect dominates the income effect (see chapter 17).

> ► **Policy Implications of the Lucas Supply Function**   The Lucas supply function in combination with the assumption that expectations are rational implies that anticipated policy changes have no effect on real output. Consider a change in monetary policy. In general, the change will have some effect on the average price level. If the policy change is announced to the public, then people know what the effect on the price level will be, because they have rational expectations (and know the way changes in monetary policy affect the price level). This means the change in monetary policy affects both the actual price level and the expected price level in the same way. The new price level minus the new expected price level is zero—no price surprise. In such a case, there will be no change in real output, because the Lucas supply function states that real output can change from its fixed level only if there is a price surprise.

The general conclusion is that *any* announced policy change—in fiscal policy or any other policy—has no effect on real output, because the policy change affects both actual and expected price levels in the same way. If people have rational expectations, known policy changes can produce no price surprises—and no increases in real output. The only way any change in government policy can affect real output is if it is kept in the dark so it is not generally known. Government policy can affect real output only if it surprises people; otherwise, it cannot. Rational-expectations theory combined with the Lucas supply function proposes a very small role for government policy in the economy.

EVALUATING RATIONAL-EXPECTATIONS THEORY

What are we to make of all this? It should be clear that the key question regarding the new classical macroeconomics is how realistic is the assumption of rational expectations. If it approximates the way expectations are actually formed, then it calls into question any theory that relies at least in part on expectation errors for the existence of disequilibrium. The arguments in favor of the rational-expectations assumption sound persuasive from the perspective of microeconomic theory. If expectations are not rational, there are likely to be unexploited profit opportunities—most economists believe such opportunities are rare and short-lived.

The argument *against* rational expectations is that it requires households and firms to know too much. This argument says it is unrealistic to think these basic decision-making units know as much as they need to know to form rational expectations. People must know the true model (or at least a good approximation of the true model) to form rational expectations, and this is a lot to expect. Even if firms and households are capable of learning the true model, it may be costly to take the time and gather the relevant information to learn it. The gain from learning the true model (or a good approximation of it) may not be worth the cost. In this sense, there may not be unexploited profit opportunities around. Gathering information and learning economic models may be too costly to bother with, given the expected gain from improving forecasts.

Although the assumption that expectations are rational seems consistent with the satisfaction-maximizing and profit-maximizing postulates of microeconomics, the rational-expectations assumption is more extreme and demanding because it requires more information on the part of households and firms. Consider a firm engaged in maximizing profits. In some way or other, it forms expectations of the relevant future variables, and given these expectations, it figures out the best thing to do from the point of view of maximizing profits. Given a set of expectations, the problem of maximizing profits may not be too hard. What may be hard is forming accurate expectations in the first place. This requires firms to know much more about the overall economy than they are likely to, so the assumption that their expectations are rational is not necessarily realistic. Firms, like the rest of us—so the argument goes—grope around in a world that is difficult to understand, trying to do their best but not always understanding enough to avoid mistakes.

In the final analysis, the issue is empirical. Does the assumption of rational expectations stand up well against empirical tests? This is difficult to answer. Much work is currently being done to answer it. There are no conclusive results yet, but it is one of the questions that makes macroeconomics an exciting area of research.

REAL BUSINESS CYCLE THEORY

Recent work in new classical macroeconomics has been concerned with whether the existence of business cycles can be explained under the assumptions of complete price and wage flexibility (market clearing) and rational expectations. This work is called **real business cycle theory**. As we discussed in chapter 14, if prices and wages are completely flexible, then the AS curve is vertical, even in the short run. If the AS curve is vertical, then events or phenomena that shift the AD curve (such as changes in the money supply, changes in government spending, and shocks to consumer and investor behavior) have no effect on real output. Real output does fluctuate over time, so the puzzle is how these fluctuations can be explained if they are not due to policy changes or other shocks that shift the AD curve. Solving this puzzle is one of the main missions of real business cycle theory.

real business cycle theory
An attempt to explain business cycle fluctuations under the assumptions of complete price and wage flexibility and rational expectations. It emphasizes shocks to technology and other shocks.

It is clear that if shifts of the AD curve cannot account for real output fluctuations (because the AS curve is vertical), then shifts of the AS curve must be responsible. However, the task is to come up with convincing stories as to what causes these shifts and why they persist over a number of periods. The problem is particularly difficult when it comes to the labor market. If prices and wages are completely flexible, then there is never any unemployment aside from frictional unemployment. For example, because the measured U.S. unemployment rate was 9.7 percent in 1982 and 4.9 percent in 1997, the puzzle is to explain why so many more people choose not to work in 1982 than in 1997.

Early real business cycle theorists emphasized shocks to the production technology. Say there is a negative shock in a given year that causes the marginal product of labor to decline. This leads to a fall in the real wage, which leads to a decrease in labor supply. People have been led to work less because the negative technology shock has led to a lower return from working. The opposite happens when there is a positive shock: The marginal product of labor rises, the real wage rises, and people choose to work more. This early work was not as successful as some had hoped because it required what seemed to be unrealistically large shocks to explain the observed movements in labor supply over time.

Since this initial work, different types of shocks have been introduced, and work is actively continuing in this area. To date, fluctuations of some variables, but not all, have been explained fairly well. Some argue that this work is doomed to failure because it is based on the unrealistic assumption of complete price and wage flexibility, while others hold more hope. Real business cycle theory is another example of the current state of flux in macroeconomics.

SUPPLY-SIDE ECONOMICS

From our discussion of equilibrium in the goods market, beginning with the simple multiplier in chapter 9 and continuing through chapter 14, we have focused primarily on *demand*. Supply increases and decreases in response to changes in aggregate expenditure (which is closely linked to aggregate demand). Fiscal policy works by influencing aggregate expenditure through tax policy and government spending. Monetary policy works by influencing investment and consumption spending through increases and decreases in the interest rate. The theories we have been discussing are "demand oriented."

The 1970s were difficult times for the U.S. economy. The United States found itself in 1974 to 1975 with stagflation—high unemployment and inflation. The late 1970s saw inflation return to the high levels of 1974 to 1975. It seemed as if policy makers were incapable of controlling the business cycle.

As a result of these seeming failures, orthodox economics came under fire. One assault was from a group of economists who expounded **supply-side economics**. The argument of the supply-siders was simple. Basically, they said, all the attention to demand in orthodox macro theory distracted our attention from the real problem with the U.S. economy. The real problem, said supply-siders, was that high rates of taxation and heavy regulation had reduced the incentive to work, to save, and to invest. What was needed was not a demand stimulus but better incentives to stimulate *supply*.

If we cut taxes so people take home more of their paychecks, the argument continued, they will work harder and save more. If businesses get to keep more of their profits and can get away from government regulations, they will invest more. This added labor supply and investment, or capital supply, will lead to an expansion of the supply of goods and services, which will reduce inflation and unemployment at the same time. The ultimate solution to the economy's woes, the supply-siders concluded, was on the *supply side* of the economy.

At their most extreme, supply-siders argued that the incentive effects of supply-side policies were likely to be so great that a major cut in tax rates would actually *increase* tax revenues. Even though tax *rates* would be lower, more people would be working and earning income and firms would earn more profits, so that the increases in the *tax bases* (profits, sales, and income) would outweigh the decreases in rates, resulting in increased government revenues.

▶ **The Laffer Curve** Figure 18.2 presents a key diagram of supply-side economics. The tax rate is measured on the vertical axis, and tax revenue is measured on the horizontal axis. The assumption behind this curve is that there is some tax rate beyond which the supply response is large enough to lead to a decrease in tax revenue for further increases in the tax rate. There is obviously some tax rate between zero and 100 percent at which tax revenue is at a maximum. At a tax rate of zero, work effort is high, but there is no tax revenue. At a tax rate of 100, the labor supply is presumably zero, because no one is allowed to keep any of his or her income. Somewhere in between zero and 100 is the maximum-revenue rate.

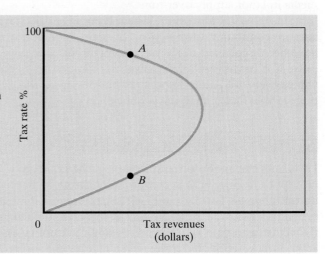

FIGURE 18.2

The Laffer Curve

The Laffer Curve shows the amount of revenue the government collects is a function of the tax rate. It shows that when tax rates are very high, an increase in the tax rate could cause tax revenues to fall. Similarly, under the same circumstances, a cut in the tax rate could generate enough additional economic activity to cause revenues to rise.

The big debate in the 1980s was whether tax rates in the United States put the country on the upper or lower part of the curve in Figure 18.2. The supply-side school claimed the United States was around *A* and taxes should be cut. Others argued that the United States was nearer *B* and tax cuts would lead to lower tax revenue.

The diagram in Figure 18.2 is the **Laffer Curve**, after Arthur Laffer, who, legend has it, first drew it on the back of a napkin at a cocktail party. The Laffer Curve had some influence on the passage of the Economic Recovery Tax Act of 1981, the tax package put forward by the Reagan administration that brought with it substantial cuts in both personal and business taxes. The individual income tax was to be cut 25 percent over three years. Corporate taxes were cut sharply in a way designed to stimulate capital investment. The new law allowed firms to depreciate their capital at a rapid rate for tax purposes, and the bigger deductions led to taxes that were significantly lower than before.

Laffer Curve *With the tax rate measured on the vertical axis and tax revenue measured on the horizontal axis, the Laffer Curve shows there is some tax rate beyond which the supply response is large enough to lead to a decrease in tax revenue for further increases in the tax rate.*

EVALUATING SUPPLY-SIDE ECONOMICS

Among the criticisms of supply-side economics is that it is unlikely a tax cut would substantially increase the supply of labor.

Supporters of supply-side economics claim that Reagan's tax policies were successful in stimulating the economy. They point to the fact that almost immediately after the tax cuts of 1981 were put into place, the economy expanded and the recession of 1980 to 1982 came to an end. In addition, inflation rates fell sharply from the high rates of 1980 and 1981. And, except for one year, federal receipts continued to rise throughout the 1980s despite the cut in tax rates.

Critics of supply-side policies do not dispute these facts but offer an alternative explanation of how the economy recovered. The Reagan tax cuts were enacted just as the U.S. economy was in the middle of its deepest recession since the Great Depression. The unemployment rate stood at 10.8 percent in the fourth quarter of 1982. It was the recession, critics argue, that was responsible for the reduction in inflation—not the supply-side policies. In addition, in theory, a tax cut could even lead to a *reduction* in labor supply. Recall our discussion of income and substitution effects in chapter 4. Although it is true a higher after-tax wage rate provides a higher reward for each hour of work and thus more incentive to work, a tax cut also means households receive a higher income for a given number of hours of work. Because they can earn the same amount of money working fewer hours, households might actually choose to work *less*. They might spend some of their added income on leisure. Research done during the 1980s suggests tax cuts seem to increase the supply of labor somewhat but the increases are very modest.

But what about the recovery from the recession? Why did real output begin to grow rapidly in late 1982, precisely when the supply-side tax cuts were taking effect? Two reasons have been suggested. First, the supply-side tax cuts had large *demand*-side effects that stimulated the economy. Second, the Federal Reserve pumped up the money supply and drove interest rates down at the same time that the tax cuts were being put into effect. The money supply expanded about 20 percent between 1981 and 1983, and interest rates succumbed. In 1981, the average three-month U.S. Treasury bill paid 14 percent interest. In 1983, the figure had dropped to 8.6 percent.

Certainly, traditional theory suggests that a huge tax cut will lead to an increase in disposable income and, in turn, an increase in consumption spending (a component of aggregate expenditure). In addition, although an increase in planned investment (brought about by a lower interest rate) leads to added productive capacity and added supply in the long run, it also increases expenditures on capital goods (new plant and equipment investment) in the short run.

THE SUPPLY-SIDE DEBATE: THEN AND NOW

THEN

In 1979 the Consumer Price Index rose 11.3 percent and in 1980 it rose 13.5 percent. So, in 1980 the Fed began pursuing a policy of slowing the rate of money growth to fight inflation. As the Fed tightened, interest rates rose. In 1978 the 90-day T-Bill interest rate was 7.2 percent. It rose to an average level of 10.0 percent in 1979, to 11.5 percent in 1980, and over 14 percent in 1981.

Ronald Reagan was elected in 1980 on an economic platform based on supply-side principles, promising to get the economy under control. Because Keynesian economics focuses on demand, Keynesian economists believe the appropriate fiscal-policy response to inflation is to increase taxes and reduce government spending. The idea is to reduce aggregate expenditure and shift the aggregate demand curve to the left. But supply-siders believe the policy prescription is exactly the opposite: *Cut* taxes and shift the aggregate supply curve to the right! The clearest statement of this logic is contained in the following excerpt from the *Joint Economic Report* of the 96th Congress:

[The policy of the United States should be to increase] real economic growth through tax reductions designed, not to pump money into the economy, but to restructure the tax code to increase the reward to additional saving, investment and employment. . . . The tax cuts to stimulate saving, investment, and competitiveness will put more goods on the shelves and lower prices, thus reinforcing anti-inflation monetary policy.[a]

NOW

In 1993, the Congress passed and the president signed the Omnibus Budget Reconciliation Act of 1993 that raised taxes substantially as part of a deficit reduction package. There were dire warnings from the supply-siders. But by 1997, the performance of the economy was cited by the administration in its critique of the supply-side position:

In 1993 the President submitted to the Congress a package of measures to reduce the Federal budget deficit that cut Federal spending and raised income tax rates for the roughly 1.2 percent of taxpayers with the highest incomes. At the time, some critics said that these higher tax rates could hurt the economy by blunting incentives to work and to save. Adherents of supply-side theory went further, arguing that a combination of weaker economic performance and increased tax avoidance would result in little or no additional revenue from these higher tax rates. The 1994 Report explored this issue and concluded that the proposed increases in tax rates for high-income taxpayers would increase tax revenue without adversely affecting the economy. Three years later this conclusion has been justified. Between 1993 and 1994, households with adjusted gross incomes of $100,000 or more saw those incomes increase by an average of 9.0 percent while their income tax liability increased by 8.9 percent.[b]

Sources: [a]*Joint Economic Report*, 96th Congress, March 1980. [b]*Economic Report of the President*, 1997, p. 43.

For more on supply-side economics, see the Case and Fair Web page at
http://www.prenhall.com/casefair.

Whether the recovery from the 1981 to 1982 recession was the result of supply-side expansion or supply-side policies that had demand-side effects, one thing is clear: The extreme promises of the supply-siders did not materialize. President Reagan argued that because of the effect depicted in the Laffer Curve, the government could maintain expenditures (and even increase defense expenditures sharply), cut tax rates, *and* balance the budget. This was clearly not the case. Government revenues fell sharply from levels that would have been realized without the tax cuts. After 1982, the federal government ran huge deficits, with nearly $2 trillion added to the national debt between 1983 and 1992.

For more on the supply-side story, see the Issues and Debates box, "The Supply-Side Debate: Then and Now."

TESTING ALTERNATIVE MACRO MODELS

You may wonder why there is so much disagreement in macroeconomics. Why cannot macroeconomists test their models against one another and see which performs best?

One problem is that macroeconomic models differ in ways that are hard to standardize. If one model takes the price level to be given, or not explained within the model, and another one does not, the model with the given price level may do better in, say, predicting output—not because it is a better model but simply because the errors in predicting prices have not been allowed to affect the predictions of output. The model that takes prices as given has a head start, so to speak.

Another problem arises in the testing of the rational-expectations assumption. Remember, if people have rational expectations, they are using the true model to form their expectations. Therefore, to test this assumption we need the true model. But there's no way to be sure that whatever model is taken to be the true model is in fact the true one. Any test of the rational-expectations hypothesis is therefore a *joint* test (1) that expectations are formed rationally, and (2) that the model being used is the true one. If the test rejects the hypothesis, it may be that the model is wrong rather than that expectations are not rational.

Another problem for macroeconomists is the small amount of data available. Most empirical work uses data beginning about 1950, which in 1998 was about 49 years' (196 quarters) worth of data. While this may seem like a lot of data, it is not. Macroeconomic data are fairly "smooth," which means a typical variable does not vary much from quarter to quarter or year to year. For example, the number of business cycles within this 49-year period is small, about seven. Testing various macroeconomic hypotheses on the basis of seven business cycle observations is not easy, and any conclusions must be interpreted with caution.

To give an example of the problem of a small number of observations, consider trying to test the hypothesis that import prices affect domestic prices. Import prices changed very little in the 1950s and 1960s. Therefore, it would have been very difficult at the end of the 1960s to estimate the effect of import prices on domestic prices. The variation in import prices was not great enough to show any effects. We cannot demonstrate that changes in import prices explain changes in domestic prices if import prices do not change! The situation was different by the end of the 1970s, because by then import prices had varied considerably. By the end of the 1970s, there were good estimates of the import price effect, but not before. This kind of problem is encountered again and again in empirical macroeconomics. In many cases there are not enough observations for much to be said, hence considerable room for disagreement.

We said in chapter 1 that it is difficult in economics to perform controlled experiments. Economists are for the most part at the mercy of the historical data. If we were able to perform experiments, we could probably learn more about the economy in a shorter time. Alas, we must wait. In time, the current range of disagreements in macroeconomics should be considerably narrowed.

SUMMARY

KEYNESIAN ECONOMICS

1. In a broad sense, Keynesian economics is the foundation of modern macroeconomics. In a narrower sense, *Keynesian* refers to economists who advocate active government intervention in the economy.

MONETARISM

2. The monetarist analysis of the economy places a great deal of emphasis on the *velocity of money*, which is defined as the number of times a dollar bill changes hands, on average, during the course of a year. The

velocity of money is the ratio of nominal GDP to the stock of money, or $V \equiv GDP/M \equiv P \times Y/M$. Alternately, $M \times V \equiv P \times Y$.

3. The *quantity theory of money* assumes that velocity is constant (or virtually constant). This implies that changes in the supply of money will lead to equal percentage changes in nominal GDP. The quantity theory of money equation is $M \times V = P \times Y$. The equation says demand for money does not depend on the interest rate.

4. Most economists believe sustained inflation is a purely monetary phenomenon. Inflation cannot continue indefinitely unless the Fed "accommodates" it by expanding the money supply.

5. Most monetarists blame most of the instability in the economy on the federal government and are skeptical of the government's ability to manage the macroeconomy. They argue that the money supply should grow at a rate equal to the average growth of real output (income) (Y)—the Fed should expand the money supply to accommodate real growth but not inflation.

NEW CLASSICAL MACROECONOMICS

6. The *new classical macroeconomics* has developed from two different but related sources: the theoretical and the empirical critiques of traditional macroeconomics. On the theoretical level, there has been growing dissatisfaction with the way traditional models treat expectations. On the empirical level, the stagflation in the U.S. economy during the 1970s caused many people to look for alternative theories to explain the breakdown of the Phillips Curve.

7. The *rational-expectations hypothesis* assumes people know the "true model" that generates economic variables. For example, rational expectations assumes that people know how inflation is determined in the economy and use this model to forecast future inflation rates.

8. The *Lucas supply function* assumes that real output (Y) depends on the actual price level minus the expected price level, or the *price surprise*. This function combined with the assumption that expectations are rational implies that anticipated policy changes have no effect on real output.

9. *Real business cycle theory* is an attempt to explain business-cycle fluctuations under the assumptions of complete price and wage flexibility and rational expectations. It emphasizes shocks to technology and other shocks.

SUPPLY-SIDE ECONOMICS

10. *Supply-side economics* focuses on incentives to stimulate supply. Supply-side economists believe that if we lower taxes, workers will work harder and save more and firms will invest more and produce more. At their most extreme, supply-siders argue that incentive effects are likely to be so great that a major cut in taxes will actually increase tax revenues.

11. The *Laffer Curve* shows the relationship between tax rates and tax revenues. Supply-side economists use it to argue that it is possible to generate higher revenues by cutting tax rates, but evidence does not appear to support this. The lower tax rates by the Reagan administration decreased tax revenues significantly and contributed to the massive increase in the federal debt during the 1980s.

TESTING ALTERNATIVE MACRO MODELS

12. Economists disagree about which macroeconomic model is best for several reasons: (1) macroeconomic models differ in ways that are hard to standardize; (2) when testing the rational-expectations assumption, we are never sure that whatever model is taken to be the true model is the true one; (3) the amount of data available is fairly small.

REVIEW TERMS AND CONCEPTS

Laffer Curve, 397	quantity theory of money, 387	$V \equiv \dfrac{GDP}{M}$
Lucas supply function, 393	rational-expectations hypothesis, 392	
monetarism, 386	real business cycle theory, 395	$M \times V \equiv P \times Y$
new classical macroeconomics, 391	supply-side economics, 396	$M \times \overline{V} = P \times Y$
price surprise, 393	velocity of money (V), 386	

PROBLEM SET

1. The table gives estimates of the rate of money supply growth and the rate of real GDP growth for six countries in 1997:

	RATE OF GROWTH IN MONEY SUPPLY (M1)	RATE OF GROWTH OF REAL GDP
Britain	+6.1%	+3.9%
Canada	+13.8	+3.7
Japan	+8.1	−0.3
Netherlands	+9.8	+3.1
Spain	+12.8	+3.1
United States	−2.1	+4.0

   a. If you were a monetarist, what would you predict about the rate of inflation across the six countries?
   b. If you were a Keynesian, and assuming activist central banks, how might you interpret the same data?

2. The three diagrams in Figure 1 represent in a simplified way the predictions of the three theories presented in this chapter about the likely effects of a major tax cut.
   a. Match each of the following theories with a graph: (1) Keynesian economics, (2) supply-side economics, (3) rational expectations/monetarism. Explain the logic behind the three graphs.
   b. Which theory do you find the most convincing? Explain.

3. In 1998, a well-known economist was heard to say, "The problem with supply-side economics is that when you cut taxes, they have both supply and demand side effects and you can't separate them." Explain what he meant. Be specific and use either the 1997 tax cuts or the Reagan tax cuts of 1981 as an example.

4. A cornerstone of new classical economics is the notion that expectations are "rational." What do you think will happen to the prices of single-family homes in your community over the next several years? On what do you base your expectations? Is your thinking consistent with the notion of rational expectations? Explain.

5. You are a monetarist given the following information. The money supply is $1,000. The velocity of money is 5. What is nominal income? Real income? What happens to nominal income if the money supply is doubled? What happens to real income?

6. When Bill Clinton took office in January 1993, he faced two major economic problems: a large federal budget deficit and high unemployment resulting from a very slow recovery from the recession of 1990 to 1991. In his first State of the Union message, the president called for spending cuts and substantial tax increases to reduce the deficit. Most of these proposed spending cuts were in the defense budget. The following day, Alan Greenspan, chair of the Federal Reserve Board of Governors, signaled his support for the president's plan. Many elements of the president's original plan were later incorporated into the deficit reduction bill passed in 1993.
   a. Some said at the time that without the Fed's support, the Clinton plan would be a disaster. Explain this argument.
   b. Supply-side economists and monetarists were very worried about the plan and the support it received from the Fed. What specific problems might a monetarist worry about? A supply-side economist?
   c. Suppose you were hired by the Fed Bank of St. Louis to report on the events of 1995 and 1996. What specific evidence would you look for to see if the Clinton plan was effective or whether the critics were right to be skeptical?

7. "In an economy with reasonably flexible prices and wages, full employment is almost always maintained." Explain why this is true.

FIGURE 1

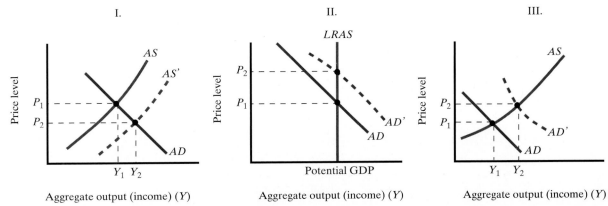

I.

Aggregate output (income) (Y)

II.

Aggregate output (income) (Y)

III.

Aggregate output (income) (Y)

8. During the 1980 presidential campaign, Ronald Reagan promised to cut taxes, increase expenditures on national defense, and balance the budget. During the New Hampshire primary of 1980, George Bush called this policy "voodoo economics." The two men were arguing about the relative merits of supply-side economics. Explain their disagreement.

*9. In a hypothetical economy there is a simple proportional tax on wages imposed at a rate t. There are plenty of jobs around so if people enter the labor force they can find work. We define total government receipts from the tax as

$$T = t \times W \times L$$

where t = the tax rate, W = the gross wage rate, and L = the total supply of labor. The net wage rate is

$$W_n = (1 - t)W.$$

The elasticity of labor supply is defined as

$$\frac{\text{percentage change in } L}{\text{percentage change in } W_n} = \frac{\Delta L/\Delta L}{\Delta W_n/W_n}$$

Suppose t were cut from .25 to .20. For such a cut to *increase* total government receipts from the tax, how elastic must the supply of labor be? (Assume a constant gross wage.) What does your answer imply about the supply-side assertion that a cut in taxes can increase tax revenues?

TAKE IT TO THE NET

We invite you to visit the Case and Fair page on the Prentice Hall Web site:

http://www.prenhall.com/casefair

for this chapter's World Wide Web exercise.

Chapter 19

ECONOMIC GROWTH AND PRODUCTIVITY

RECALL FROM CHAPTER 1 that **economic growth** occurs when an economy experiences an increase in total output. The increase in real output that began in the Western World with the Industrial Revolution and continues today has been so sustained and so rapid that economists refer to this as the period of **modern economic growth**. These three simple words describe the complex phenomenon that is the subject of this chapter.

It is through economic growth that living standards improve. But growth brings change. New things are produced, while others become obsolete. Some believe growth is the fundamental objective of a society, because it lifts people out of poverty and enhances the quality of their lives. Others say economic growth erodes traditional values and leads to exploitation, environmental destruction, and corruption.

The first part of this chapter describes economic growth in some detail and identifies sources of economic growth. After a review of the U.S. economy's growth record since the nineteenth century, we examine the role of public policy in the growth process. We conclude with a review of the debate over the benefits and costs of growth.

THE GROWTH PROCESS: FROM AGRICULTURE TO INDUSTRY

The easiest way to understand the growth process and to identify its causes is to think about a simple economy. Recall from chapter 2 Colleen and Bill, washed up on a deserted island. At first they had only a few simple tools and whatever human capital they brought with them to the island. They gathered nuts and berries and built a small cabin. Their "GDP" consisted of basic food and shelter.

Over time, things improved. The first year, they cleared some land and began to cultivate a few vegetables that they found growing on the island. They made some tools and dug a small reservoir to store rainwater. As their agricultural efforts became more efficient, they shifted their resources—their time—into building a larger, more comfortable home.

Colleen and Bill were accumulating capital in two forms. First, they built *physical capital*, material things used in the production of goods and

economic growth *An increase in the total output of an economy. Defined by some economists as an increase of real GDP per capita.*

modern economic growth
The period of rapid and sustained increase in real output per capita that began in the Western World with the Industrial Revolution.

services—a better house, tools, and a water system. Second, they acquired more *human capital*—knowledge, skills, and talents. Through trial and error, they learned about the island, its soil and its climate, what worked and what didn't. Both kinds of capital made them more efficient and increased their productivity. Because it took less time to produce the food they needed to survive, they could devote more energy to producing other things or to leisure.

At any given time, Colleen and Bill faced limits on what they could produce. These limits were imposed by the existing state of their technical knowledge and the resources at their disposal. Over time, they expanded their possibilities, developed new technologies, accumulated capital, and made their labor more productive. In chapter 2 we defined a society's *production possibilities frontier (ppf)*, which shows all possible combinations of output that can be produced given present technology and if all available resources are fully and efficiently employed. Economic growth expands those limits and shifts society's production possibilities frontier out to the right, as Figure 19.1 shows.

▶ **From Agriculture to Industry: The Industrial Revolution** Before the Industrial Revolution in Great Britain, every society in the world was agrarian. Towns and cities existed here and there, but almost everyone lived in rural areas. People spent most of their time producing food and other basic subsistence goods. Then, beginning in England around 1750, technical change and capital accumulation increased productivity significantly in two important industries: agriculture and textiles. New and more efficient methods of farming were developed. New inventions and new machinery in spinning, weaving, and steel production meant that more could be produced with fewer resources. Just as new technology, capital equipment, and the resulting higher productivity made it possible for Colleen and Bill to spend time working on other projects and new "products," the British turned from agricultural production to industrial production. In both cases, growth meant new products, more output, and wider choice.

There was one big difference. Colleen and Bill were fully in charge of their own lives. Peasants and workers in eighteenth-century England ended up with a very different set of choices. It was no longer possible to make a living as a peasant farmer. The cities offered the only real alternative, and a rural agrarian society was very quickly transformed into an urban industrial society.

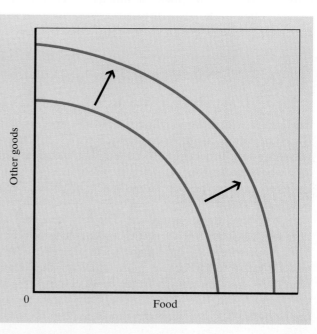

FIGURE 19.1

Economic Growth Shifts Society's Production Possibility Frontier Up and to the Right

The production possibility frontier shows all the combinations of output that can be produced if all of society's scarce resources are fully and efficiently employed. Economic growth expands society's production possibilities, shifting the ppf up and to the right.

Small changes in growth rates can make a big difference over time. Here's what can happen to an income of $10,000 over 10- and 20-year periods at various growth rates:

| | The value of $10,000: | |
Growth rate	after 10 years	after 20 years
1%	$11,046	$12,202
3%	13,439	18,061
5%	16,289	26,533
10%	26,931	67,275

▶ **Growth in an Industrial Society** The process of economic growth in an industrial society such as the United States is more complex but follows the same steps we have just described for growth in an agrarian society.

Consider the development of the electronic calculator. Prior to 1970, calculators that could add, subtract, multiply, and divide weighed fifty pounds, performed calculations slowly, and were expensive (a good calculator cost hundreds of dollars). Today, electronic calculators retail for as low as $3 or come free with a magazine subscription. Some are small enough to fit into a wristwatch.

During the past 15 years, the growth of computing technology has changed the way we live and do business. Access to the World Wide Web is becoming cheaper and easier. Computers with Pentium processors and massive memory and storage capacity are selling for the price of small electronic calculators 25 years ago.

Technological change, innovation, and capital production (calculators, computers, and software) have increased productivity. If a diner spends less on accounting, its sandwiches will cost less. Sandwich buyers thus may go to see another movie or have another soda. The entertainment and soft drink sectors expand, and so on. That is economic growth.

THE SOURCES OF ECONOMIC GROWTH

Economic growth occurs either when (1) society acquires more resources, or (2) society discovers ways of using available resources more efficiently. For economic growth to increase living standards, the rate of growth must exceed the rate of population increase. Economic growth is generally defined as *an increase in real GDP per capita.*

As we discuss the factors that contribute to economic growth, it will be helpful to think of an **aggregate production function.** An individual firm's production function is a mathematical representation of the relationship between the firm's inputs and its output. Output for an aggregate production function is national output, or gross domestic product. Stated simply, gross domestic product (output) (Y), depends upon the amount of labor (L) and the amount of capital (K) available in the economy (assuming the amount of land is fixed).[1]

If you think of GDP as a function of both labor and capital, you can see that:

> An increase in GDP can come about through:
>
> 1. an increase in the labor supply,
> 2. an increase in physical or human capital, or
> 3. an increase in productivity (the amount of product produced by each unit of capital or labor).

aggregate production function
The mathematical representation of the relationship between inputs and national output, or gross domestic product.

---

[1]All the numbers in the tables to follow were derived from the simple production function: $Y = 3 \times K^{1/3}L^{2/3}$.

AN INCREASE IN LABOR SUPPLY

Consider what would happen if another person joined Colleen and Bill on the island. She would join in the work and produce, and so GDP would rise. Or suppose that a person who had not been a part of the labor force were to begin to work and use his time and energy to produce pottery. Real output would rise in this case also. An increasing labor supply can generate more output.

Whether output *per capita* rises when the labor supply increases is another matter. If the capital stock remains fixed while labor increases, the new labor will likely be less productive than the old labor. This is called *diminishing returns*, and it worried Thomas Malthus, David Ricardo, and other early economists.

Malthus and Ricardo, who lived in England during the nineteenth century, were concerned that the fixed supply of land would lead to diminishing returns. With land in strictly limited supply, the ppf could be pushed out only so far as population increased. To increase agricultural output, people would be forced to farm less productive land or to farm land more intensively. In either case, the returns to successive increases in population would diminish. Both Malthus and Ricardo predicted a gloomy future as population outstripped the land's capacity to produce. What both economists left out of their calculations was technological change and capital accumulation. New and better farming techniques have raised agricultural productivity so much that less than 3 percent of the U.S. population now provide enough food for the country's entire population.

Diminishing returns can also occur if a nation's capital stock grows more slowly than its workforce. Capital enhances workers' productivity. A person with a shovel digs a bigger hole than a person without one, and a person with a steam shovel outdoes them both. If a society's stock of plant and equipment does not grow and the technology of production does not change, additional workers will not be as productive, because they do not have machines to work with.

Table 19.1 illustrates how growth in the labor force, without a corresponding increase in the capital stock or technological change, might lead to growth of output but declining productivity and a lower standard of living. As labor increases, output rises from 300 units in Period 1 to 320 in Period 2, to 339 in Period 3, and so forth, but **labor productivity** (output per worker hour) falls. Output per worker hour, Y/L, is a measure of labor's productivity.

The fear that new workers entering the labor force will displace existing workers and generate unemployment has been with us for a long time. New workers can come from many places. They might be immigrants, young people looking for their first jobs, or older people entering the labor force for the first time. Between 1947 and 1997, the number of women in the labor force more than tripled, jumping from

labor productivity *Output per worker hour; the amount of output produced by an average worker in one hour.*

TABLE 19.1 ECONOMIC GROWTH FROM AN INCREASE IN LABOR— MORE OUTPUT BUT DIMINISHING RETURNS AND LOWER LABOR PRODUCTIVITY

PERIOD	QUANTITY OF LABOR L (HOURS)	QUANTITY OF CAPITAL K (UNITS)	TOTAL OUTPUT Y (UNITS)	MEASURED LABOR PRODUCTIVITY Y/L
1	100	100	300	3.0
2	110	100	320	2.9
3	120	100	339	2.8
4	130	100	357	2.7

TABLE 19.2 EMPLOYMENT, LABOR FORCE, AND POPULATION GROWTH, 1947 TO 1997

	CIVILIAN NONINSTITUTIONAL POPULATION OVER 16 YEARS OLD (MILLIONS)	CIVILIAN LABOR FORCE		EMPLOYMENT (MILLIONS)
		NUMBER (MILLIONS)	PERCENTAGE OF POPULATION	
1947	101.8	59.4	58.3	57.0
1960	117.3	69.6	59.3	65.8
1970	137.1	82.8	60.4	78.7
1980	167.7	106.9	63.7	99.3
1990	189.2	125.8	66.5	118.8
1997	203.1	136.3	67.1	129.6
Percentage change, 1947–1997	+99.5	+129.5		+127.4
Annual Rate	+1.4%	+1.7%		+1.7%

Source: *Economic Report of the President, 1998,* Table B-35.

17 million to 63 million. Table 19.2 shows that in the United States since World War II, the civilian noninstitutional population (those not in jails or mental institutions) over 16 years of age roughly doubled, while the labor force grew by 129.5 percent. The U.S. economy, however, has shown a remarkable ability to expand right along with the labor force. The number of persons employed jumped by 72.6 million—127.4 percent—during the same period.

> As long as the economy and the capital stock are expanding rapidly enough, new entrants into the labor force do not displace other workers.

INCREASES IN PHYSICAL CAPITAL

An increase in the stock of capital can also increase output, even if it is not accompanied by an increase in the labor force. Physical capital both enhances the productivity of labor and provides valuable services directly.

It is easy to see how capital provides services directly. Consider what happened on Bill and Colleen's island. In the first few years, they built a house, putting many hours of work into it that could have gone into producing other things for immediate consumption. With the house for shelter, Colleen and Bill can spend time on other things. In the same way, capital equipment produced in one year can add to the value of a product over many years. For example, we still derive use and value from bridges and tunnels built decades ago.

It is also easy to see how capital used in production enhances the productivity of labor. Computers enable us to do almost instantly tasks that once were impossible or might have taken years to complete. An airplane with a small crew can transport hundreds of people thousands of miles in a few hours. A bridge over a river at a critical location may save thousands of labor hours that would be spent transporting materials and people the long way around. It is precisely this yield in the form of future valuable services that provides both private and public investors with the incentive to devote resources to capital production.

Table 19.3 shows how an increase in capital without a corresponding increase in labor might increase output. Observe several things about these numbers. First, additional capital increases measured productivity; output per worker hour (Y/L) increases from 3.0 to 3.1, to 3.2, and finally to 3.3 as the quantity of capital (K)

TABLE 19.3 ECONOMIC GROWTH FROM AN INCREASE IN CAPITAL—MORE OUTPUT, DIMINISHING RETURNS TO ADDED CAPITAL, HIGHER MEASURED LABOR PRODUCTIVITY

PERIOD	QUANTITY OF LABOR L (HOURS)	QUANTITY OF CAPITAL K (UNITS)	TOTAL OUTPUT Y (UNITS)	MEASURED LABOR PRODUCTIVITY Y/L
1	100	100	300	3.0
2	100	110	310	3.1
3	100	120	319	3.2
4	100	130	327	3.3

WORKERS REPAIR THE BROOKLYN BRIDGE, WHICH CONNECTS THE NEW YORK CITY BOROUGHS OF MANHATTAN AND BROOKLYN. MAINTENANCE AND DEVELOPMENT OF INFRASTRUCTURE PLAY AN IMPORTANT ROLE IN ECONOMIC GROWTH.

increases. Second, there are diminishing returns to capital. Increasing capital by 10 units first increases output by 10 units—from 300 in Period 1 to 310 in Period 2. But the second increase of 10 units yields only 9 units of output, and the third increase yields only 8 units.

Table 19.4 shows the values of the private nonresidential capital stock in the United States since 1960. The increase in capital stock is the difference between gross investment and depreciation. (Remember, some capital becomes obsolete and some wears out every year.) Between 1960 and 1995, the stock of equipment has increased at a rate of 4.3 percent per year and the stock of structures has increased at a rate of 2.6 percent per year.

By comparing Tables 19.2 and 19.4, you can see that capital has been increasing faster than labor since 1960. In all economies experiencing modern economic growth, capital expands at a more rapid rate than labor. That is, the ratio of capital to labor (K/L) increases, and this too is a source of increasing productivity. Another source of increased productivity is public capital, the subject of the Application "Infrastructure and Economic Growth."

INCREASES IN HUMAN CAPITAL

Investment in human capital is another source of economic growth. People in good health are more productive than people in poor health; people with skills are more productive than people without them.

TABLE 19.4 FIXED PRIVATE NONRESIDENTIAL NET CAPITAL STOCK, 1960 TO 1995 (BILLIONS OF 1992 DOLLARS)

	EQUIPMENT	STRUCTURES
1960	660.6	1,768.8
1970	1,117.3	2,419.9
1980	1,855.4	3,176.9
1990	2,507.3	4,142.2
1995	2,885.5	4,399.1
Percentage change, 1960–1995	+336.8	+148.7
Annual rate	+4.3%	+2.6%

Source: Survey of Current Business, May 1997, Table 15, p. 92.

TABLE 19.5 YEARS OF SCHOOL COMPLETED BY PEOPLE OVER 25 YEARS OLD, 1940 TO 1996

	PERCENTAGE WITH LESS THAN FIVE YEARS OF SCHOOL	PERCENTAGE WITH FOUR YEARS OF HIGH SCHOOL OR MORE	PERCENTAGE WITH FOUR YEARS OF COLLEGE OR MORE
1940	13.7	24.5	4.6
1950	11.1	34.3	6.2
1960	8.3	41.1	7.7
1970	5.5	52.3	10.7
1980	3.6	66.5	16.2
1990	NA	77.6	21.3
1996	NA	81.7	23.6

Source: Statistical Abstract of the United States, 1990, Table 215; and 1997, Table 243.
NA = not available.

Human capital can be produced in many ways. Individuals can invest in themselves by going to college or vocational training programs. Firms can invest in human capital through on-the-job training. The government invests in human capital with programs to improve health and to provide schooling and job training.

Table 19.5 shows the level of educational attainment has risen significantly since 1940. The percentage of the population with at least four years of college rose from under 5 percent in 1940 to 23.6 percent in 1996. In 1940 fewer than 1 person in 4 had completed high school; in 1996, more than 8 in 10 had.

INCREASES IN PRODUCTIVITY

Growth that cannot be explained by increases in the *quantity* of inputs can be explained only by an increase in the *productivity* of those inputs—each unit of input must be producing more output. The **productivity of an input** can be affected by factors including technological change, other advances in knowledge, and economies of scale.

productivity of an input *The amount of output produced per unit of an input.*

➤ **Technological Change** The Industrial Revolution was in part sparked by new technological developments. New techniques of spinning and weaving—the invention of the "mule" and the "spinning jenny," for example—were critical. The high-tech boom that swept the United States in the early 1980s was driven by the rapid development and dissemination of semiconductor technology.

Technological change affects productivity in two stages. First, there is an advance in knowledge, or an **invention**. But knowledge by itself does nothing unless it is used. When new knowledge is used to produce a new product or to produce an existing product more efficiently, there is **innovation**.

invention *An advance in knowledge.*

innovation *The use of new knowledge to produce a new product or to produce an existing product more efficiently.*

Technological change cannot be measured directly. Some studies have presented data on "indicators" of the rate of technical change—the number of new patents, for example—but none are satisfactory. Still, we know technological changes that have improved productivity are all around us. Computer technology has revolutionized the office, hybrid seeds have increased the productivity of land, and more efficient and powerful aircraft have made air travel routine and inexpensive.

➤ **Other Advances in Knowledge** Over and above invention and innovation, advances in other kinds of knowledge can also improve productivity. One is what we might call "managerial knowledge." For example, because of the very high cost of capital during

INFRASTRUCTURE AND ECONOMIC GROWTH

A major source of economic growth is the accumulation of capital. When we think of capital's role in economic growth, we tend to focus on private capital—the plant, equipment, and inventory of business firms. But what about *public* capital?

Recall from our earlier discussions that *capital goods* are used to produce other goods and services over time. One form of capital is infrastructure. **Infrastructure**, also called **public capital**, refers to the roads, bridges, water treatment plants, fire stations, and so on that collectively contribute to the public good.

Infrastructure has the potential for increasing productivity and growth. Good highways and bridges reduce transportation costs and make it easier to transport goods. Readily available clean water improves health and is often essential for production.

Governments are usually responsible for putting public capital into place. Throughout the 1980s, however, there was strong pressure to reduce government spending and to increase growth in the private sector. One of the consequences of these pressures was a significant slowdown in public infrastructure investment. Some have pointed to this slowdown as a cause of the slower economic growth in the 1980s.

In June 1990, the Federal Reserve Bank of Boston held a conference on the topic of infrastructure and growth. Professor David Aschauer of Bates College opened the conference with the following challenge:

As the decade of the 1990s begins, new challenges present themselves to the citizenry of the United States. Among the most important are concerns about the environment, economic productivity, and international competitiveness, and a rearrangement of standing strategic military relationships. Our future quality of life, economic prosperity, and security depend crucially on how we choose to meet these new challenges. . . .

The first direction, expenditure reduction, certainly has merit to a broad class of individuals. Many would point to the fact that total federal government outlays, expressed relative to gross national product, rose from 14.8 percent in 1950 to 21.6 percent in 1980 and, in 1989, to 21.8 percent. Others would point to the persistence of federal budget deficits. To both groups, expenditure reduction would be of benefit to economic performance, either by reducing the overall scale of government activity in the economy or by allowing a reduction in interest rates and an expansion in domestic investment activity.

But the second direction, expenditure reorientation, may also have merit. It could well be the case that quality of life and economic performance would be best served by retaining the resources within the public sector and expanding expenditure in certain critical areas. One candidate area is infrastructure, the public stock of social and economic overhead capital. Indeed, it has been claimed in the popular press that "it's hard to escape America's crumbling infrastructure" and that "even though the deterioration of U.S. highways, bridges, airports, harbors, sewage systems, and other building blocks of the economy has been exhaustively documented in recent years, there has been scant progress" in addressing the postulated need to renew the public capital stock (Industry Week, May 21, 1990).[a]

Clearly, someone was listening. Prior to taking office, President Bill Clinton held an economic summit to discuss ideas for stimulating economic growth. A major focus of the discussion was infrastructure, and it led to Clinton's call for $16 billion in public works spending in his 1993 State of the Union address.

The president's proposal was defeated by Congress, which argued that the infrastructure's role in economic growth is not significant enough to justify spending such huge sums of money. The debate continues to rage. In his 1995 *Economic Report*, Clinton summarized this situation as follows: "Declining trends in public capital suggest that infrastructure investment has been a net drag on the growth of productivity since 1970, but there is no consensus as to the quantitative importance of this effect."

---

[a]"Is There a Shortfall in Public Capital Investment?" Proceedings of a Conference sponsored by the Federal Reserve Bank of Boston, Alicia Munnell, Editor, June 1990.

For more on economic growth, see the Case and Fair Web page at
http://www.prenhall.com/casefair.

the early 1980s, firms learned to manage their inventories much better. Many were able to keep production lines and distribution lines flowing with a much lower stock of inventories. Inventories are part of a firm's capital stock, and trimming them reduces costs and raises productivity. This is an example of a *capital-saving* innovation; many of the advances that we are used to thinking about, such as the introduction of robotics, are *labor-saving*.

In addition to managerial knowledge, improved personnel management techniques, accounting procedures, data management, and the like can also make production more efficient, reduce costs, and increase measured productivity.

> **Economies of Scale** *External economies of scale* are cost savings that result from increases in the size of industries. The economies that accompany growth in size may arise from a variety of causes. For example, as firms in a growing industry build plants at new locations, they may lower transport costs. There may also be some economies of scale associated with R&D (research and development) spending and job-training programs.

> **Other Influences on Productivity** In addition to technological change, other advances in knowledge, and economies of scale, other forces may affect productivity. During the 1970s and 1980s, the U.S. government required many firms to reduce the air and water pollution they were producing. These requirements diverted capital and labor from the production of measured output, therefore *reducing* measured productivity. Similarly, in recent years requirements imposed by the Occupational Safety and Health Act (OSHA) have required firms to protect workers better from accidental injuries and potential health problems. These laws also divert resources from measured output.

Negative effects such as these are more a problem of *measurement* than of truly declining productivity. The EPA (Environmental Protection Agency) regulates air and water quality because clean air and water presumably have a value to society. The resources diverted to produce that value are not wasted. A perfect measure of output produced that is of value to society would include environmental quality and good health.

The list of factors that can affect productivity is large. Weather can have a big impact on agricultural productivity. The early 1990s saw huge floods and massive crop losses in the Midwest. Floods in California in 1995 had similar effects.

Having presented the major factors that influence productivity, we now turn to the growth record for the United States and how these factors have combined to produce a record of steady growth that has lasted over 100 years.

GROWTH AND PRODUCTIVITY IN THE UNITED STATES

Modern economic growth in the United States began in the middle of the nineteenth century. After the Civil War, the railroads spread across the country and the economy took off. Table 19.6 shows the growth rate of real output in the United States since 1871.

Over the long haul, real output in the United States has been growing at about 3.3 percent annually. Between 1871 and 1909, the growth rate was very healthy, ranging from 4.0 percent to 5.5 percent per year. Because of the dislocations of the Great Depression, growth was slower during the 1930s and 1940s, but the 1950s and 1960s saw renewed growth and vigor in the economy. Although the 1970s contained some good years and some bad, during the decade output rose by an average of 3.1 percent per year, a credible performance. In the 1990 to 1997 period, the rate of growth was only 2.3 percent; it was brought down by the recession from 1990 to 1991.

TABLE 19.6 GROWTH OF REAL GDP IN THE UNITED STATES, 1871 TO 1997

PERIOD	AVERAGE GROWTH RATE PER YEAR	PERIOD	AVERAGE GROWTH RATE PER YEAR
1871–1889	5.5	1960–1970	4.1
1889–1909	4.0	1970–1980	3.1
1909–1929	2.8	1980–1990	2.9
1929–1950	3.4	1990–1997	2.3
1950–1960	3.5	1950–1997	3.2

Sources: Historical Statistics of the United States: Colonial Times to 1970, Tables F47-70, F98-124; U.S. Department of Commerce, Bureau of Economic Analysis.

Figure 19.2 shows growth rates of real GDP since 1961 for the United States and several other countries. Growth has been slowing everywhere. Virtually all the countries in the table experienced less growth during the 1970s than during the 1960s and continued to grow more slowly during the 1980s. The early 1990s saw a recession sweep across the world; in 1991, GDP declined in many countries, including the

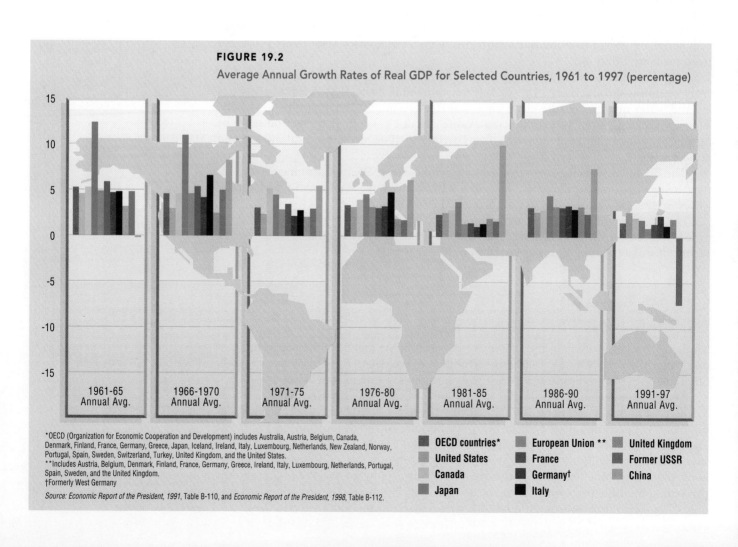

FIGURE 19.2

Average Annual Growth Rates of Real GDP for Selected Countries, 1961 to 1997 (percentage)

*OECD (Organization for Economic Cooperation and Development) includes Australia, Austria, Belgium, Canada, Denmark, Finland, France, Germany, Greece, Japan, Iceland, Ireland, Italy, Luxembourg, Netherlands, New Zealand, Norway, Portugal, Spain, Sweden, Switzerland, Turkey, United Kingdom, and the United States.
**Includes Austria, Belgium, Denmark, Finland, France, Germany, Greece, Ireland, Italy, Luxembourg, Netherlands, Portugal, Spain, Sweden, and the United Kingdom.
†Formerly West Germany

Source: Economic Report of the President, 1991, Table B-110, and Economic Report of the President, 1998, Table B-112.

Legend:
- OECD countries*
- United States
- Canada
- Japan
- European Union **
- France
- Germany†
- Italy
- United Kingdom
- Former USSR
- China

United States. In most of the countries of the European Union, recession lasted through 1993, but by 1994 virtually all of the world's industrial countries were growing again. The economies of the former Soviet Union did very poorly in the 1991 to 1997 period, with real GDP falling at an annual rate of 7.3 percent.

SOURCES OF GROWTH IN THE U.S. ECONOMY SINCE 1929

For many years, Edward Denison of the Brookings Institution in Washington has been studying the growth process in the United States and sorting out the relative importance of the various causal factors. Table 19.7 presents the results of his most recently published major work.

Denison estimates that about half of U.S. growth in output over the entire period from 1929 to 1982 has come from increases in factors of production and the other half from increases in productivity. Growth in the labor force accounted for about 20 percent of overall growth, while growth in capital stock (both human and physical) accounted for 33 percent. Of the capital stock growth figure, human capital (education and training) accounted for 19 percent of the total, and physical capital accounted for 14 percent. Growth of knowledge was the most important factor contributing to increases in the productivity of inputs.

The relative importance of these causes of growth varied considerably over the years. Between 1929 and 1948, for example, physical capital played a much smaller role than it did in other periods. But each period included times that were atypical for one reason or another. The period between 1929 and 1948 included the dislocations and uncertainties of the Great Depression and World War II. From 1948 to 1973, the economy enjoyed a period of unusual stability and expansion.

A 1997 study by Charles Jones comes to the gloomy conclusion that a slowdown of growth in the United States is imminent. Jones's paper finds that much of the post WWII growth in the United States comes from three factors: (1) an increase in educational attainment, (2) a sharp increase in the share of the labor force devoted to

---

TABLE 19.7 SOURCES OF GROWTH IN THE UNITED STATES, 1929 TO 1982

	PERCENT OF GROWTH ATTRIBUTABLE TO EACH SOURCE			
	1929–1982	1929–1948	1948–1973	1973–1979
Increases in inputs	53	49	45	94
Labor	20	26	14	47
Capital	14	3	16	29
Education (human capital)	19	20	15	18
Increases in productivity	47	51	55	6
Advances in knowledge	31	30	39	8
Other factors*	16	21	16	−2
Total	100	100	100	100
Annual growth rate in real national income	2.8	2.4	3.6	2.6

Note: Economies of scale, weather, pollution abatement, worker safety and health, crime, labor disputes, and so forth.

Source: Edward Denison, *Trends in American Economic Growth, 1929–1982* (Washington: Brookings Institution, 1985).

FIGURE 19.3

Labor Productivity Growth: Rate of Change of Real Output per Hour of Labor in the United States, 1960–1997

Source: Economic Report of the President, 1998, Table B-50.

research, and (3) an increase in the openness of the world economy—the expansion of trade. He concludes that these increases must ultimately level off, and when they do, the growth rate in the United States could fall by as much as 75 percent.[2]

THE PRODUCTIVITY "PROBLEM"

The years since 1973 have deserved the attention they received. During the early years of the Reagan administration, the "productivity problem" was much discussed. Some economics textbooks published in the early 1980s had entire chapters discussing the decline in productivity that seemed to be taking place during the late 1970s. In January of 1981, the Congressional Budget Office published a report, "The Productivity Problem: Alternatives for Action."

What exactly is this productivity problem? Figure 19.3 shows that the growth rate of *output per hour of labor* has generally fallen since 1960, and in the 1980s and early 1990s it was only slightly above 1 percent.

Many explanations were offered for the productivity decline of the late 1970s and early 1980s. Some economists pointed to the low rate of saving in the United States compared to other parts of the world. Others blamed increased environmental and government regulation of U.S. businesses. Still others argued that the country was not spending as much on research and development as it should have been. Finally, some suggested, high energy costs in the 1970s led to investment designed to save energy rather than to enhance productivity. (We discuss exactly how each of these factors influence growth later in this chapter.)

During the 1980s many of these factors seemed to turn around. Private investment in plant and equipment increased from long-run levels of under 8 percent of GDP to nearly 10 percent during the decade. Energy prices cascaded. There was some reduction in regulation under the Reagan administration. Research and development spending rose to its highest percentage of GDP since 1970. Productivity, on the other hand, did not respond; the growth rate of productivity remained low in the last half of the 1980s.

The late 1990s have seen a slight upward trend, with the growth rate of productivity averaging 1.5 percent in the 1995 to 1997 period.

To conclude our discussion of productivity, we must point out that the productivity statistics we have been examining are hotly debated. For more details, see Issues and Debates box "Can We Really Measure Productivity Changes?"

ECONOMIC GROWTH AND PUBLIC POLICY

The decline in productivity that has caused so much concern has led to a protracted national discussion about the role of government in stimulating economic growth. This debate was spurred in part by increasing concern in the United States that the United States was not doing as well as Japan. The enormous success of the Japanese in world markets and their extraordinary postwar annual rates of growth have led more and more people to look to the Far East for economic instruction.

Several strategies for increasing the rate of growth in the United States have been suggested, and some have been enacted into law. These strategies include policies aimed toward improving the quality of education, increasing the saving rate, stimulating

---

[2]Charles I. Jones, "The Coming Slowdown in U.S. Economic Growth," mimeo, Stanford University, September 15, 1997.

CAN WE REALLY MEASURE PRODUCTIVITY CHANGES?

When the government publishes numbers like those in Figure 19.3, most people take them as "true." Even though we don't really know much about how they are constructed, we assume they are the best measurements we can get.

Yet such data are often the source of controversy. Some have argued that the mix of products produced in the United States and the increased pace of technological change in recent years have made it increasingly difficult to measure productivity changes accurately. The observed productivity decline in recent decades may be measurement error.

These arguments make a certain amount of sense at an intuitive level. Even in agriculture, where it is relatively easy to measure productivity growth, the possibility of mismeasurement exists. The output of a soybean farm can be measured in bushels, and labor, capital, and land inputs present no serious measurement problems. So, over time, as farming techniques improved and farmers acquired new and better machinery, output per acre and output per worker rose and have continued to rise. But today we have biotechnology. Genetic engineering now makes it possible to make soybeans higher in protein and more disease resistant. Technology has improved and "output" has increased, but these increases do not show up in the data because of crude measures of output.

A similar problem exists with computers. If you simply counted the number of personal computers produced and measured the cost of the inputs used in their production, you would no doubt see some productivity advances. But computers being produced for under $1,000 in 1998 contained processors capable of performing tasks literally thousands of times faster than computers produced a few years earlier. If we were to measure computer outputs not in terms of units produced but in terms of the actual "services" they provide to users, we would find massive productivity advances. Most new PCs now contain CD-ROM slots and can be easily connected to the new and growing "information superhighway," a source of cheap and plentiful information. In short, the problem is that many of the products we now use are qualitatively different from the comparable products we used only a few years ago, and the standard measures of productivity miss much of these quality changes.

The problems are greater in the service sector, where output is extremely difficult to measure. It is easy to understand the problem if you think of what information technology has done for legal services. As recently as 10 years ago, a lawyer doing research to support a legal case might spend hundreds of hours looking through old cases and public documents. Today's lawyers can log on to a computer and in seconds do a key word search on a massive legal database. Such time- and labor-saving productivity advances are not counted in the official data.

One of the leading experts on technology and productivity estimates that we have reasonably good measures of output and productivity in only about 31 percent of the U.S. economy. Does this mean that productivity is not a problem? On this topic economists have agreed to disagree.[a]

_____

[a]This argument was described most clearly by Professor Zvi Grilliches of Harvard in his presidential address to the American Economic Association in January 1994. The full text, entitled "Productivity, R&D, and the Data Constraint," is published in the _American Economic Review_, March 1994. The counterargument is best advanced by Professor Dale Jorgenson in _Productivity_ (Harvard University Press, 1995).

For more on measuring productivity, see the Case and Fair Web page at
http://www.prenhall.com/casefair.

---

investment, increasing research and development, reducing regulation, and pursuing an industrial policy.

▶ **Policies to Improve the Quality of Education** The Denison study shows that the contribution of education and training (human capital production) to growth in the United States has remained relatively constant at about 20 percent since 1929.

During the 1970s, public education was criticized. Teachers' salaries declined sharply in real terms, while property tax limitations and cuts in federal programs forced the curtailment of school budgets. In the last few years, battles have been waged in Congress over the amount of federal dollars set aside for scholarships and loans to college students. Whatever the policies of the moment, however, all federal, state, and local expenditures on education acknowledge the need to build the nation's stock of human capital.

The Taxpayer Relief Act of 1997 contained provisions that focused on education. First, the HOPE Scholarship credit allows taxpayers to claim a credit up to $1,500 for postsecondary education expenses on behalf of any family member. Other provisions include a new Education Individual Retirement Account that allows savings to earn tax free returns as long as the balance is used to pay educational expenses.

> **Policies to Increase the Saving Rate** The amount of capital accumulation in an economy is ultimately constrained by its rate of saving. The more saving in an economy, the more funds are available for investment. The national saving rate in Japan is twice as high as in the United States, and investment is a much higher fraction of GDP in Japan than in the United States. Many people have argued that the tax system and the social security system in the United States are biased against saving. Some public finance economists favor shifting to a system of consumption taxation rather than income taxation to reduce the tax burden on saving.

Others claim the social security system, by providing guaranteed retirement incomes, reduces the incentive for people to save. Private pension plans make deposits to workers' accounts, the balances of which are invested in the stock market and bond market and are made available to firms for capital investment. Social security benefits, in contrast, are paid out of current tax receipts, and no such accumulations are available for investment. Thus, the argument goes, if social security substitutes for private saving, the national saving rate is reduced. Evidence on the extent to which taxes and social security reduce the saving rate has not been clear to date.

A provision of the 1997 Taxpayer Relief Act allowed for new "backloaded" retirement accounts (the so-called Roth IRAs) to stimulate savings. Individuals can deposit up to $2,000 annually to specified retirement accounts that accumulate earnings without paying income tax. Withdrawals made after age 59½ or for the purchase of a first home can be made tax free.

> **Policies to Stimulate Investment** For the growth rate to increase, saving must be used to finance new investment. In an effort to revive a slowly growing economy in 1961, President Kennedy proposed and the Congress passed the *investment tax credit*. The ITC provided a tax reduction for firms that invest in new capital equipment. For most investments, the reduction took the form of a direct credit equal to 10 percent of the investment. A firm investing in a new computer system costing $100,000 would have its tax liability reduced by $10,000. The investment tax credit was changed periodically over the years, and it was on the books until it was repealed in 1986. Many states have adopted investment tax credits against their state corporation taxes.

In 1982, the federal Economic Recovery Tax Act contained a number of provisions designed to encourage investment. Among them was the *Accelerated Cost Recovery System (ACRS)*, which gave firms the opportunity to reduce their taxes by using artificially rapid rates of depreciation for purposes of calculating taxable profits. While these rules were complicated, their effect was similar to the effect of the investment tax credit. The government effectively reduced the cost of capital to firms that undertook investment in plant or equipment.

Another provision of the 1997 Taxpayer Relief Act cut the rate of taxation of income earned in the form of capital gains (taxes on increases in the value of assets such as shares of stock). For asset sales after May 6, 1997, the maximum rate of tax is 20 percent, down from 28 percent. The hope is to stimulate investment, especially in new start-up companies, but the evidence on the likely effects of such changes is mixed.

> **Policies to Increase Research and Development**   As Table 19.7 shows, increases in knowledge accounted for 31 percent of total growth in the United States between 1929 and 1982. Although not shown in the table, during the years of high R&D expenditures, 1953 to 1973, the figure reached 40 percent. Research also shows that the rate of return on investment in R&D is quite high. Estimates place the rate of return at around 30 percent.[3]

It can be argued that new knowledge is like a public good. Although the United States has a patent system to protect the gains of R&D for inventors and innovators, many of the benefits flow to imitators and others, including the public. This logic has been used to justify public subsidization of R&D spending.

> **Reduced Regulations**   The Reagan and Bush administrations, and the Republicans' "Contract with America" in 1995, were committed to reducing government regulation, which many believe stands in the way of U.S. industry.

Critics of these policies say many regulations on the books serve legitimate economic purposes. For example, environmental regulations, if properly administered, improve efficiency. Judicious use of antitrust laws can also improve the allocation of resources and stimulate investment and production.

Denison estimated that regulation of occupational health and safety, and of the environment, reduced the annual growth rate between 1973 and 1979 by 0.13 percentage points, from 2.74 percent to 2.61 percent per year. But has the value of the improved environment and increased safety been worth it?

> **Industrial Policy**   In the last few years, a number of economists have called for increased government involvement in the allocation of capital across manufacturing sectors, a practice known as **industrial policy**. Those who favor industrial policy believe that because governments of other countries are "targeting" industries for special subsidies and rapid investment, the United States should do likewise to avoid losing out in international competition. The Japanese Ministry of Trade and Industry, for example, picked the automobile industry very early on and decided to expand its role in world markets. The strategy succeeded very well; the Japanese auto industry has been remarkably successful.

Critics of industrial policy argue that having the government involved in the allocation of capital would be disastrous. Investment always involves risk, they believe, and the best people to judge the extent and appropriateness of that risk are those making the investments and those actually involved in the industry.

industrial policy *Government involvement in the allocation of capital across manufacturing sectors.*

GROWTH POLICY: A LONG-RUN PROPOSITION

When President Ford and Congress passed the dramatic tax cuts of 1975 to stimulate the economy and end the deep recession, the results were observable within a few months. Fiscal and monetary policies designed to counteract the cyclical up-and-down swings in the economy can produce measurable results in a short time.

However, the effects of policies designed to increase the rate of growth may not have observable effects for many years—they are by definition designed to mold the economy's long-run growth path. For example, a policy that succeeded in raising the rate of growth by one percentage point, say from 2.5 percent to 3.5 percent, would be viewed by all as a tremendous success. Yet it would be almost a decade before such a policy would raise GDP by 10 percent.

---

[3]See M. Nadiri, "Contributions and Determinants of Research and Development Expenditures in the U.S. Manufacturing Industries," in *Capital Efficiency and Growth*, ed. George M. von Furstenberg, (Cambridge, Mass.: Ballinger Press, 1980).

The fact that pro-growth policies can be costly in the short run and do not produce measurable results for a long time often pushes them far down on politicians' lists of priorities. Some economists who opposed the Tax Reform Act of 1986 argued that the elements of the tax code that had been favorable to capital investment and growth were cut for precisely these reasons. Defenders of the Tax Reform Act claim that it is indeed possible to oversubsidize investment and that the pre-1986 tax code had been doing just that.

Not everyone agrees that the top priority in a developed economy should be continued growth. We'll see why as we close the chapter.

THE PROS AND CONS OF GROWTH

There are those who believe growth should be the primary objective of any society and those who believe the costs of growth are too great.

THE PRO-GROWTH ARGUMENT

Advocates of growth believe growth *is* progress. Resources in a market economy are used to produce what people want; if you produce something people do not want, you are out of business. Even in a centrally planned economy, resources are targeted to fulfill needs and wants. If a society is able to produce those things more efficiently and at less cost, how can that be bad?

By applying new technologies and better production methods, resources are freed to produce new and better products. For Colleen and Bill accumulation of capital—a house, a water system, and so forth—and advancing knowledge were necessary to improve life on a formerly uninhabited island. In a modern industrial society, capital accumulation and new technology improve the quality of life.

One way to think about the benefits of growth is to compare two periods, say 1950 and 1995. In 1995, real GDP per capita was more than twice what it was in 1950. This means incomes have grown twice as fast as prices so that we can buy that much more. (Remember, no one is telling anyone what to buy, and most people can spend much more now than they could then.)

Although things available in both periods are not exactly the same, growth has given us *more* choice, not less. Consider transportation. In the 1950s, the interstate highway system (social capital) had not been built. Driving from Chicago to New York took several days. We had automobiles, but the highway system did not compare to what we have today. And greater advances have been made in air travel. Flying between the two cities was possible, but more costly, less comfortable, and slower in 1950 than it is today.

Do these changes improve the quality of life? Yes, because they give us more freedom. We can travel more frequently. I can see my mother more often. I spend less time getting where I want to go so I can spend more time there. People are able to get to more places for less money.

What about consumer durables—dishwashers, microwave ovens, compact disc players, power lawn mowers, and so forth? Do they enhance the quality of life? If not, why do we buy them? In 1950, about 3 percent of all homes had dishwashers; today it's close to 50 percent. In 1950, fewer than 2 percent of all homes had air conditioners; today over 60 percent do.

What makes a dishwasher worthwhile? It saves the most valuable commodity—*time*. Many consumer durables have no intrinsic value—they don't provide satisfaction directly. They free us from tasks and chores that are not fun (no one likes to wash clothes or dishes). If a product allows us to perform these tasks more easily and quickly, it gives us more time for other things.

And think of the improvement in the *quality* of things that yield satisfaction directly. Record players in the 1950s reproduced sound imperfectly; high fidelity was just being developed, and stereo was in the future. Today you can get a compact disc player for your car. Small "boxes" available at discount stores for under $30 reproduce sound far better than the best machines available in the early 1950s. And the range of tapes and compact discs available is extraordinary.

Growth also makes it possible to improve conditions for the less fortunate. The logic is simple: When there is more to go around, the sacrifice required to help the needy is smaller. With higher incomes, we can better afford the sacrifices needed to help the poor. Growth also produces jobs. When population growth is not accompanied by growth in output, unemployment and poverty increase.

Those in advanced societies can be complacent about growth, or critical of it. But leaders of developing countries understand its benefits. When 75 percent of a country's population is poor, redistributing existing incomes does not do much. The only hope for improvement in the long run is economic growth.

THE ANTI-GROWTH ARGUMENT

Those who argue against economic growth generally make four major points:

1. Any measure of output measures only the value of things exchanged in the market. Many things that affect the quality of life are not traded in the market, and those things generally lose value when growth occurs.
2. For growth to occur, industry must cause consumers to develop new tastes and preferences. Therefore, we have no real need for many of the things we now consume. Wants are created, and consumers have become the servants, rather than the masters, of the economy.
3. The world has a finite quantity of resources, and rapid growth is consuming them at a rate that cannot continue. Because the available resources impose limits to growth, we should begin now to plan for the future, when growth will be impossible.
4. Growth requires that income be distributed unfairly.

▶ **Growth Has Negative Effects on the Quality of Life** Perhaps the most significant "unmeasurable" changes that affect the quality of life occur in the early stages of growth when societies become industrialized. More is produced: Agricultural productivity is higher, more manufactured goods are available, and so forth. But most people are crowded into cities, and their lives change drastically.

Before industrialization, most people in the Western World lived in small towns in the country. Most were poor, and they worked long hours to produce enough food to survive. After industrialization and urbanization in eighteenth-century England, men, women, and children worked long hours at routine jobs in hot, crowded factories. They were paid low wages and had very little control over their lives.

Even today, growth continues to change the quality of life in ways that are observable but not taken into account when we calculate growth rates. U.S. agriculture, for example, is becoming more productive every year. As productivity goes up, food prices drop, and fewer resources are needed in the agricultural sector. States in New England that once had thriving farms have found their climates and soils not good enough to compete anymore. In 1959, 56,000 farms covered 9.3 million acres in the six New England states; in 1998, fewer than 30,000 farms covered fewer than 5 million acres. The agricultural sector had been cut in half.

During the early 1970s, small family farmers all over the United States found that making a living was becoming nearly impossible. The villain? Growth and progress. The cost? The decline of a lifestyle that many people want to maintain and that many others think of as an important part of America.

FOLLOWING INDUSTRIAL MERCURY DUMPING INTO THE WATERS OF MINIMATA BAY, JAPAN, THERE WERE CONSIDERABLE NUMBERS OF BIRTH DEFECTS.

There are other consequences of growth that are not counted in the growth calculation. Perhaps the most significant is environmental damage. As the industrial engine is fed, waste is produced. Often both the feeding and the waste cause massive environmental damage. A dramatic example is the surface, or strip, mining of coal that has ravaged many parts of the United States. Another is the uncontrolled harvesting of U.S. forests. Modern growth requires paper and wood products, and large areas of timber in many states have been cleared and never replanted.

The disposal of industrial wastes has not begun to keep pace with industrial growth. It is now clear that growing and prosperous chemical companies have for decades been dumping hazardous, often carcinogenic, waste products into the nation's soil and water. It is costing billions to clean them up. Those costs were never taken into account when the market was allocating resources to the growing chemical industry.

Growth-related problems are everywhere. Japan paid little attention to the environment during the early years of its rapid economic growth. Many of the results were disastrous. The best known of these results were the horrifying birth defects following the dumping of industrial mercury into the waters of Minamata Bay. In addition to birth defects, thousands of cases of "Minamata disease" in adults have been documented, and hundreds have died.

➤ **Growth Encourages the Creation of Artificial Needs**   The nature of preferences has been debated within the economics profession for many years. The orthodox view, which lies at the heart of modern welfare economics, is that preferences exist among consumers and that the economy's purpose is to serve those needs. According to the notion of **consumer sovereignty**, people are free to choose, and things that people do not want will not sell. The consumer rules.

The opposite view is that preferences are formed within the economic system. To continue growing, firms need a continuously expanding set of demands. To ensure that demand grows, firms create it by managing our minds and manipulating our behavior with elaborate advertising, fancy packaging, and other marketing techniques that persuade us to buy things for which we have no intrinsic need.

➤ **Growth Means the Rapid Depletion of a Finite Quantity of Resources**   In 1972, the Club of Rome, a group of "concerned citizens," contracted with a group at MIT to do a study entitled *The Limits to Growth*.[4] The book-length final report presented the

consumer sovereignty
The notion that people are free to choose, and that things that people do not want will not sell. "The customer rules."

[4]Dennis L. Meadows, et al., *The Limits to Growth* (Washington: Potomac Associates, 1972).

results of computer simulations that assumed present growth rates of population, food, industrial output, and resource exhaustion. According to these data, sometime after the year 2000 the limits will be reached, and the entire world economy will come crashing down:

> Collapse occurs because of nonrenewable resource depletion. The industrial capital stock grows to a level that requires an enormous input of resources. In the very process of that growth, it depletes a large fraction of the resource reserves available. As resource prices rise and mines are depleted, more and more capital must be used for obtaining resources, leaving less to be invested for future growth. Finally, investment cannot keep up with depreciation and the industrial base collapses, taking with it the service and agricultural systems, which have become dependent on industrial inputs (such as fertilizers, pesticides, hospital laboratories, computers, and especially energy for mechanization. . . . Population finally decreases when the death rate is driven upward by the lack of food and health services.[5]

This argument is similar to one offered almost 200 years ago by Thomas Malthus, mentioned earlier in this chapter.

In the early 1970s, many thought that the Club of Rome's predictions had come true. It seemed the world was starting to run up against the limits of world energy supplies; the prices of energy products shot up, and there were serious shortages. But in the years since, new reserves have been found, new sources of energy have been discovered and developed, and conservation measures have been tremendously successful (automobile gas mileage has been pushed up to levels that were inconceivable 15 years ago). Energy prices have fallen to levels that in real terms are about the same as they were before the oil price shocks of the 1970s.

A variation of the depletion-of-resources argument stops short of predicting doomsday. It does point out that unchecked growth in the developed world may have undesirable distributional consequences. To fuel our growth, we are buying vast quantities of minerals and other resources from the developing countries, which have become dependent on the proceeds of those sales to buy food and other commodities on world markets. If this continues, by the time these countries have grown to the point that they need mineral resources, their resources may be gone.

▶ **Growth Requires an Unfair Income Distribution and Propagates It** One cause of growth is capital accumulation. Capital investment requires saving, and saving comes mostly from the rich. The rich save more than the poor, and in the developing countries most people are poor and need to use whatever income they have for survival.

Critics also claim that the real beneficiaries of growth are the rich. Choices open to the "haves" in society are greatly enhanced, but the choices open to the "have-nots" remain severely limited. If the benefits of growth trickle down to the poor, why are there more homeless today than there were 20 years ago?

▶ **Summary: No Right Answer** We have presented the arguments for and against economic growth in simple terms. In reality, even those who take extreme positions in this debate acknowledge there is no "right answer." To suggest that all economic growth is bad is wrong; to suggest that economic growth should run unchecked is equally wrong. The question is: How can we derive the benefits of growth and at the same time minimize its undesirable consequences?

Society must make some hard choices, and there are many trade-offs. For example, we can grow faster if we pay less attention to environmental concerns. But how much environmental damage should we accept to get how much economic growth? Many

---

[5]Meadows, *Limits*, pp. 131–132.

argue that we can achieve an acceptable level of economic growth *and* protect the environment at the same time. There is also a trade-off between growth and the distribution of income. More financial inequality would probably lead to more saving and ultimately to more capital and faster growth. Using taxes and income transfers to redistribute some of the benefits of growth to the poor probably does slow the rate of growth. But it is not a question of all or nothing; society must decide how much inequality is desirable.

As long as these trade-offs exist, people will disagree. The debate in contemporary politics is largely about the costs and benefits of shifting more effort toward the goal of economic growth and away from environmental and social welfare goals.

SUMMARY

1. *Modern economic growth* is the period of rapid and sustained increase in real output per capita that began in the Western World with the Industrial Revolution.

THE GROWTH PROCESS: FROM AGRICULTURE TO INDUSTRY

2. All societies face limits imposed by the resources and technologies available to them. Economic growth expands these limits and shifts society's production possibilities frontier up and to the right.

THE SOURCES OF ECONOMIC GROWTH

3. If growth in output outpaces growth in population, and if the economic system is producing what people want, growth will increase the standard of living. Growth occurs when (1) society acquires more resources, or (2) society discovers ways of using available resources more efficiently.

4. An *aggregate production function* embodies the relationship between inputs—the labor force and the stock of capital—and total national output.

5. A number of factors contribute to *economic growth:* (1) an increase in the labor supply; (2) an increase in physical capital—plant and equipment—and/or human capital—education, training, and health; (3) an increase in productivity brought about by technological change; other advances in knowledge (managerial skills and so forth); and/or economies of scale.

GROWTH AND PRODUCTIVITY IN THE UNITED STATES

6. Modern economic growth in the United States dates to the middle of the nineteenth century. For the last 100 years, the nation's growth in real output has averaged about 3.0 percent per year. Between 1929 and 1982, about half of U.S. growth in output came from increases in factors of production and half from increases in productivity.

7. There has been much concern that the rate of growth in the United States is slowing. The growth rate of measured labor productivity decreased from 3.7 percent in the 1960 to 1964 period to 1.1 percent in the 1985 to 1989 period.

ECONOMIC GROWTH AND PUBLIC POLICY

8. A number of public policies have been pursued with the aim of improving the growth of real output. These policies include efforts to improve the quality of education, to encourage saving, to stimulate investment, to increase research and development, and to reduce regulation. Some economists also argue for increased government involvement in the allocation of capital across manufacturing sectors, a practice known as *industrial policy*.

THE PROS AND CONS OF GROWTH

9. Advocates of growth argue that growth is progress. Growth gives us more freedom—meaning more choices. It saves time, improves the standard of living, and is the only way to improve conditions for the poor. Growth creates jobs and increases income simply because there is more to go around.

10. Those who argue against growth make four points. First, many things that affect the quality of life are not traded in the market, and these things generally lose value when there is growth. Second, to have growth, industry must cause consumers to develop new tastes and preferences for many things that they have no real need for. Third, the world has a finite quantity of resources, and rapid growth is eating them up at a rate that cannot continue. Fourth, growth requires that income be distributed inequitably.

REVIEW TERMS AND CONCEPTS

aggregate production function, 407
consumer sovereignty, 422
economic growth, 405
industrial policy, 419

infrastructure, or public capital, 412
innovation, 411
invention, 411

labor productivity, 408
modern economic growth, 405
productivity of an input, 411

PROBLEM SET

1. During 1997, real GDP in the United States was growing at a rate of about 4 percent per year. The Federal Reserve was contemplating an increase in interest rates to slow the growth rate to about 2.5 percent per year. If growth is a good thing for an economy, why would the Fed try to slow it down?

2. Tables 1, 2, and 3 present some data on three hypothetical economies. Complete the tables by figuring the measured productivity of labor and the rate of output growth. What do the data tell you about the causes of economic growth? (*Hint:* How fast are L and K growing?)

TABLE 1

PERIOD	L	K	Y	Y/L	GROWTH RATE OF OUTPUT
1	1,052	3,065	4,506		
2	1,105	3,095	4,674		
3	1,160	3,126	4,842		
4	1,218	3,157	5,019		

TABLE 2

PERIOD	L	K	Y	Y/L	GROWTH RATE OF OUTPUT
1	1,052	3,065	4,506		
2	1,062	3,371	4,683		
3	1,073	3,709	4,866		
4	1,084	4,079	5,055		

TABLE 3

PERIOD	L	K	Y	Y/L	GROWTH RATE OF OUTPUT
1	1,052	3,065	4,506		
2	1,062	3,095	4,731		
3	1,073	3,126	4,967		
4	1,084	3,157	5,216		

3. Between 1995 and 1998, according to the Departments of Commerce and Labor, measured productivity growth (the increase in Y/L) was less than the rate of growth of real output (the increase in Y). Explain this seeming paradox. Be specific. Provide any statistical evidence to support your theory.

4. One of the provisions of the Taxpayer Relief Act of 1997 was a reduction in the rate of income taxation on capital gains to 20 percent from 28 percent. The hope is that lower capital gains taxation will lead to a higher rate of growth. How might a lower rate of tax on capital gains affect household behavior? Firm behavior? In what ways are these changes in behavior likely or not likely to lead to more growth?

5. In earlier chapters, you learned that aggregate expenditure $(C + I + G)$ must equal aggregate output for the economy to be in equilibrium. You also saw that when consumption spending rises, $C + I + G$ increases, inventories fall, and aggregate output rises. Thus, policies that simultaneously increase consumer spending and reduce saving would lead to a higher level of GDP. In this chapter, we have argued that a higher saving rate, even with lower consumption spending, is the key to long-run GDP growth. How can both arguments be correct?

6. Suppose you have just been elected to Congress and you find yourself on the Ways and Means Committee—the committee in the House that decides on tax matters. The committee is debating a bill that would make major changes in tax policy. First, the corporate tax would be lowered substantially in an effort to stimulate investment. The bill contains a 15 percent investment tax credit—firms would be able to reduce their taxes by 15 percent of the value of investment projects that they undertake. To keep revenues constant, the bill would impose a national sales tax that would raise the price of consumer goods and reduce consumption. What trade-offs do you see implied in this bill? What are the pros and cons? How would you vote?

7. If you wanted to measure productivity (output per worker) in the following sectors over time, how would you measure "output"? How easy is it to measure productivity in each of the sectors?

a. Software
b. Vegetable farming
c. Education
d. Airline transportation

8. Economists generally agree high budget deficits today will reduce the growth rate of the economy in the future. Why? Do the reasons for the high budget deficit matter? In other words, does it matter whether the deficit is caused by lower taxes, increased defense spending, more job-training programs, and so on?

9. Why can growth lead to a more unequal distribution of income? Assuming this is true, how is it possible for the poor to benefit from economic growth?

TAKE IT TO THE NET

We invite you to visit the Case and Fair page on the Prentice Hall Web site:
http://www.prenhall.com/casefair
for this chapter's World Wide Web exercise.

NEW IDEAS ABOUT ECONOMIC GROWTH

The data reported for the U.S. economy during the current expansion continues to confound traditional theories about the way mature economies are supposed to behave. In 1997 real GDP grew by nearly 4 percent over the year, the strongest annual rate of growth in nearly a decade. Even more surprising was that, during that same year, the GDP price index rose by less than 2 percent, the smallest annual rate of inflation since 1964, whereas the overall unemployment rate for 1997 was 4.9 percent, its lowest annual average since 1973.

Traditional economic theory about the business cycle says that tight labor markets are supposed to lead to higher prices, which then leads the Federal Reserve to raise interest rates and slow down the expansion, or even bring about a modest recession. But few economists are predicting anything like a traditional boom-bust cycle for the U.S. economy in the near future. In fact, more and more economists are coming to believe that we've entered a new era of economic growth—one in which the traditional theories no longer apply.

One of the key differences underlying this expansion has been the rapid developments in the high technology sectors of the economy, particularly in the area of computer hardware and software. According to traditional theorists, over the course of a business cycle prices rise and productivity slows as businesses bump up against their capacity constraints—that is, diminishing returns represent a speed limit to economic growth. In high-tech industries, however, although investments in microprocessor technology and computer software require large initial outlays, the costs of production and distribution are relatively small and decline over time. Such technological improvements lead to higher productivity and declining prices—a phenomenon that spreads as the new technology is adopted across industries.

Add to this increased global competitiveness and the growing importance of international financial markets and you have the seeds for a new era of economic growth. The changing complexion of the economy has led many economists to rethink their ideas about economic growth and its causes.

One of the leading proponents of what has become known as New Growth Theory is Paul Romer, an economist at Stanford University. Romer believes that the reason per capita GDP is so much higher in the United States than in other developed countries is because the United States has invested proportionately more in knowledge and discovery during the last century, leading to innovations and technological advancements that have paid significant dividends in terms of prospects

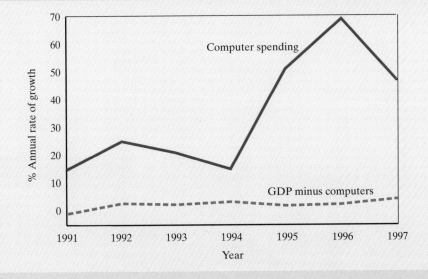

FIGURE 1

Computer Spending's Share of GDP Growth

Source: U.S. Department of Commerce, Bureau of Economic Analysis.

425

for long-term economic growth. Rather than focusing on the stock of capital and the supply of labor as primary determinants of growth, Romer believes that the keys to economic growth are a well-educated workforce and an adequate stock of ideas and innovation. New Growth Theory thus offers the promise of *increasing returns* as knowledge feeds on itself, enabling the rate of economic growth to actually increase over time.

Romer uses companies like Microsoft Corporation as an example of his New Growth Theory. Microsoft produces computer software—literally "bits" of information consisting of the ones and zeros that make up the instructions that make computers work. The company occupies just a handful of buildings and employs a few thousand people, yet it produces billions of dollars worth of output. Although the cost of the design and development of these computer applications was significant, the physical product itself is relatively unimportant, because it is inexpensive to replicate and can be distributed over the Internet at almost no cost. Microsoft is just one of hundreds of high-tech companies in the information processing and telecommunications industries that have accounted for roughly one-third of total GDP growth in recent years.

Questions for Analytical Thinking

1. Just as technological progress improves the prospects for employment in certain industries, it also makes other jobs obsolete. Should university professors be concerned about "technological unemployment"?

2. According to the U.S. Department of Labor, farmers and textile workers are two of the occupations projected to decline by the greatest amount between 1994 and 2005. What factors might be responsible for the decline in these occupations?

3. What sort of government policies could you recommend that might promote the growth of ideas in this country?

4. It's been argued that jobs in high-tech industries like the design of new microprocessors or computer software have a larger multiplier effect on the economy than traditional manufacturing industries like automobile production. Why?

Sources: Michael Mandel, "The New Business Cycle," *Business Week*, March 31, 1997; Thomas I. Palley, "Growth theory in a Keynesian Mode: Some Keynesian Foundations for New Endogenous Growth Theory," *Journal of Post Keynesian Economics*, Fall 1996, Vol. 19, No. 1; Paul M. Romer, "The Origins of Economic Growth," *The Journal of Economic Perspectives*, Winter 1994, Vol. 8, No. 1; Bernard Wysocki, Jr., "For Economist Paul Romer, Prosperity Depends on Ideas," *The Wall Street Journal*, January 21, 1997; U.S. Bureau of Labor Statistics, *Occupational Outlook Handbook*, available on-line at *http://www.bls.gov.*

INTERNATIONAL ECONOMICS

PART SIX

THE GLOBAL ECONOMY

INTERNATIONAL TRADE, COMPARATIVE ADVANTAGE, AND PROTECTIONISM

OVER THE LAST 25 YEARS, international transactions have become increasingly important to the U.S. economy. In 1970, imports represented only about 7 percent of U.S. gross domestic product. It's now around 13 percent. In 1997, the United States imported $1,058 billion worth of goods and services.

The "internationalization" or "globalization" of the U.S. economy has occurred in the private and public sectors, in input and output markets, and in business firms and households. Once uncommon, foreign products are now everywhere, from the utensils we eat with to the cars we drive. In 1970, foreign-produced cars made up only a small percentage of all the cars in the United States. At that time, it was difficult to find mechanics who knew how to repair foreign cars, and replacement parts were hard to obtain. Today the roads are full of Toyotas and Nissans from Japan, Volvos from Sweden, and BMWs from Germany, and any service station that cannot repair foreign-produced automobiles probably won't get much business. Half of all the cars and 80 percent of all the consumer electronics (televisions, CD players, and so forth) that U.S. consumers buy are produced abroad.

At the same time, the United States exports billions of dollars worth of agricultural goods, aircraft, and industrial machinery. Financial capital flows smoothly and swiftly across international boundaries in search of high returns. In 1997, for example, a downturn in some Asian economies, including Korea and Thailand, caused an outflow of international capital and a sharp decline in stock market prices.

The inextricable connection of the U.S. economy to the economies of the rest of the world has had a profound impact on the discipline of economics and is the basis of one of its most important insights:

All economies, regardless of their size, depend to some extent on other economies and are affected by events outside their borders.

427

TABLE 20.1

U.S. BALANCE OF TRADE (EXPORTS MINUS IMPORTS), 1929 TO 1997 (BILLIONS OF DOLLARS)

	EXPORTS MINUS IMPORTS
1929	+0.4
1933	+0.1
1945	−0.9
1955	+0.4
1960	+2.4
1965	+3.9
1970	+1.2
1975	+13.6
1976	−2.3
1977	−23.7
1978	−26.1
1979	−24.0
1980	−14.9
1981	−15.0
1982	−20.5
1983	−51.7
1984	−102.0
1985	−114.2
1986	−131.5
1987	−142.1
1988	−106.1
1989	−80.4
1990	−71.3
1991	−20.5
1992	−29.5
1993	−60.7
1994	−90.9
1995	−86.0
1996	−94.8
1997	−101.1

Source: U.S. Department of Commerce, Bureau of Economic Analysis.

trade surplus *The situation when a country exports more than it imports.*

trade deficit *The situation when a country imports more than it exports.*

Corn Laws *The tariffs, subsidies, and restrictions enacted by the British Parliament in the early nineteenth century to discourage imports and encourage exports of grain.*

To get you more acquainted with the international economy, this chapter discusses the economics of international trade. First, we describe the recent tendency of the United States to import more than it exports. Next, we explore the basic logic of trade. Why should the United States or any other country engage in international trade? Finally, we address the controversial issue of protectionism. Should a country provide certain industries with protection in the form of import quotas, tariffs, or subsidies?

TRADE SURPLUSES AND DEFICITS

Until the 1970s, the United States generally exported more than it imported. When a country exports more than it imports, it runs a **trade surplus**. When a country imports more than it exports, it runs a **trade deficit**. Table 20.1 shows that before 1975 the United States generally ran a trade surplus. This changed in 1976, and since 1976 the United States has run a trade deficit. The deficit reached a peak of $142.1 billion in 1987, fell to $20.5 billion in 1991, and then rose again to $101.1 billion in 1997.

The large trade deficits in the middle and late 1980s touched off political controversy that continues today. Foreign competition hit U.S. markets hard. Less expensive foreign goods—among them steel, textiles, and automobiles—began driving U.S. manufacturers out of business, and thousands of jobs were lost in important industries. Cities such as Pittsburgh, Youngstown, and Detroit had major unemployment problems.

The natural reaction was to call for protection of U.S. industries. Many people wanted the president and Congress to impose taxes and import restrictions that would make foreign goods less available and more expensive, protecting U.S. jobs. This argument was not new. For hundreds of years, industries have petitioned governments for protection, and societies have debated the pros and cons of free and open trade. For the last century and a half, the principal argument against protection has been the theory of comparative advantage, first discussed in chapter 2.

THE ECONOMIC BASIS FOR TRADE: COMPARATIVE ADVANTAGE

Perhaps the best-known debate on the issue of free trade took place in the British Parliament during the early years of the nineteenth century. At that time, the landed gentry—the landowners—controlled Parliament. For a number of years, imports and exports of grain had been subject to a set of tariffs, subsidies, and restrictions collectively called the **Corn Laws**. Designed to discourage imports of grain and encourage exports, the Corn Laws' purpose was to keep the price of food high. The landlords' incomes, of course, depended on the prices they got for what their land produced. The Corn Laws clearly worked to the advantage of those in power.

With the Industrial Revolution, a class of wealthy industrial capitalists began to emerge. The industrial sector had to pay workers at least enough to live on, and a living wage depended greatly on the price of food. Tariffs on grain imports and export subsidies that kept grain and food prices high increased the wages that capitalists had to pay, cutting into their profits. The political battle raged for years. But as time went by, the power of the landowners in the House of Lords was significantly reduced. When the conflict ended in 1848, the Corn Laws were repealed.

On the side of repeal was David Ricardo, a businessman, economist, member of Parliament, and one of the fathers of modern economics. Ricardo's principal work, *Principles of Political Economy and Taxation*, was published in 1817, two years before he entered Parliament. Ricardo's **theory of comparative advantage**, which he used to argue against the Corn Laws, claimed that trade enables countries to specialize in producing the products they produce best. According to the theory:

> Specialization and free trade will benefit all trading partners (real wages will rise), even those that may be absolutely less efficient producers.

theory of comparative advantage *Ricardo's theory that specialization and free trade will benefit all trading partners (real wages will rise), even those that may be absolutely less efficient producers.*

This basic argument remains at the heart of free-trade debates even today. It was invoked numerous times by Presidents Reagan and Bush as they wrestled with Congress over various pieces of protectionist legislation.

▶ **Specialization and Trade: The Two-Person Case** The easiest way to understand the theory of comparative advantage is to examine a simple two-person society. Suppose Bill and Colleen, stranded on a deserted island in chapter 2, have only two tasks to accomplish each week: gathering food to eat and cutting logs that will be used in constructing a house. If Colleen could cut more logs than Bill in a day and Bill could gather more berries and fruits, specialization would clearly benefit both of them.

But suppose Bill is slow and clumsy and Colleen is better at both cutting logs *and* gathering food. Ricardo's point is that it still pays for them to specialize. They can produce more in total by specializing than they can by sharing the work equally. (It may be helpful to review the discussion of comparative advantage in chapter 2 before proceeding.)

ABSOLUTE ADVANTAGE VERSUS COMPARATIVE ADVANTAGE

A country enjoys an **absolute advantage** over another country in the production of a product if it uses fewer resources to produce that product than the other country does. Suppose country A and country B produce wheat, but A's climate is more suited to wheat and its labor is more productive. Country A will produce more wheat per acre than country B and use less labor in growing it and bringing it to market. Country A enjoys an absolute advantage over country B in the production of wheat.

A country enjoys a **comparative advantage** in the production of a good if that good can be produced at lower cost *in terms of other goods*. Suppose countries C and D both produce wheat and corn and C enjoys an absolute advantage in the production of both—that is, C's climate is better than D's, and fewer of C's resources are needed to produce a given quantity of both wheat and corn. Now C and D must each choose between planting land with either wheat or corn. To produce more wheat, either country must transfer land from corn production; to produce more corn, either country must transfer land from wheat production. The cost of wheat in each country can be measured in bushels of corn, and the cost of corn can be measured in bushels of wheat.

Suppose that in country C, a bushel of wheat has an opportunity cost of two bushels of corn. That is, to produce an additional bushel of wheat, C must give up two bushels of corn. At the same time, producing a bushel of wheat in country D requires the sacrifice of only one bushel of corn. Even though C has an *absolute* advantage in the production of both products, D enjoys a *comparative* advantage in the production of wheat because the *opportunity cost* of producing wheat is lower in D. Under these circumstances, Ricardo claims, D can benefit from trade if it specializes in the production of wheat.

absolute advantage *The advantage in the production of a product enjoyed by one country over another when it uses fewer resources to produce that product than the other country does.*

comparative advantage *The advantage in the production of a product enjoyed by one country over another when that product can be produced at lower cost in terms of other goods than it could be in the other country.*

▶ **Gains from Mutual Absolute Advantage** To illustrate Ricardo's logic in more detail, suppose Australia and New Zealand each have a fixed amount of land and do not trade with the rest of the world. There are only two goods—wheat, to produce bread, and cotton, to produce clothing. This kind of two-country/two-good world does not exist, but its operations can be generalized to many countries and many goods.

To proceed, we have to make some assumptions about the preferences of the people living in New Zealand and the people living in Australia. If the citizens of both countries go around naked, there is no need to produce cotton; all the land can be used to produce wheat. However, assume that people in both countries have similar preferences

TABLE 20.2 YIELD PER ACRE OF WHEAT AND COTTON

	NEW ZEALAND	AUSTRALIA
Wheat	6 bushels	2 bushels
Cotton	2 bales	6 bales

Australia and New Zealand are more heavily trade dependent than the United States. In 1995 trade accounted for 40% of GDP in Australia and 62% of GDP in New Zealand.

Source: World Bank, *World Development Report 1997.*

with respect to food and clothing: The populations of both countries use both cotton and wheat. And preferences for food and clothing are such that both countries consume equal amounts of wheat and cotton.

Finally, we assume that each country has only 100 acres of land for planting and land yields are given in Table 20.2. New Zealand can produce three times the wheat that Australia can on one acre of land, and Australia can produce three times the cotton that New Zealand can in the same space. New Zealand has an absolute advantage in the production of wheat, and Australia has an absolute advantage in the production of cotton. In cases like this, we say the two countries have *mutual absolute advantage.*

If there is no trade and each country divides its land to obtain equal units of cotton and wheat production, each country produces 150 bushels of wheat and 150 bales of cotton. New Zealand puts 75 acres into cotton but only 25 acres into wheat, while Australia does the reverse. (See Table 20.3.)

We can organize the same information in graphical form as production possibility frontiers for each country. In Figure 20.1, which presents the positions of the two countries before trade, each country is constrained by its own resources and productivity. If Australia put all its land into cotton, it would produce 600 bales of cotton (100 acres × 6 bales/acre) and no wheat; if it put all its land into wheat, it would produce 200 bushels of wheat (100 acres × 2 bushels/acre) and no cotton. The opposite is true for New Zealand. Recall from chapter 2, a country's production possibility frontier represents all combinations of goods that can be produced, given the country's resources and state of technology. Each country must pick a point along its own production possibility curve.

Because both countries have an absolute advantage in the production of one product, specialization and trade will benefit both. Australia should produce cotton, New Zealand should produce wheat. Transferring all land to wheat production in New Zealand yields 600 bushels; transferring all land to cotton production in Australia yields 600 bales. An agreement to trade 300 bushels of wheat for 300 bales of cotton would double both wheat and cotton consumption in both countries. (Remember, before trade both countries produced 150 bushels of wheat and 150 bales of cotton. After trade, each country will have 300 bushels of wheat and 300 bales of cotton to consume. Final production and trade figures are in Table 20.4 and Figure 20.2.)

> Trade enables both countries to move beyond their previous resource and productivity constraints.

TABLE 20.3 TOTAL PRODUCTION OF WHEAT AND COTTON ASSUMING NO TRADE, MUTUAL ABSOLUTE ADVANTAGE, AND 100 AVAILABLE ACRES

	NEW ZEALAND	AUSTRALIA
Wheat	25 acres × 6 bushels/acre 150 bushels	75 acres × 2 bushels/acre 150 bushels
Cotton	75 acres × 2 bales/acre 150 bales	25 acres × 6 bales/acre 150 bales

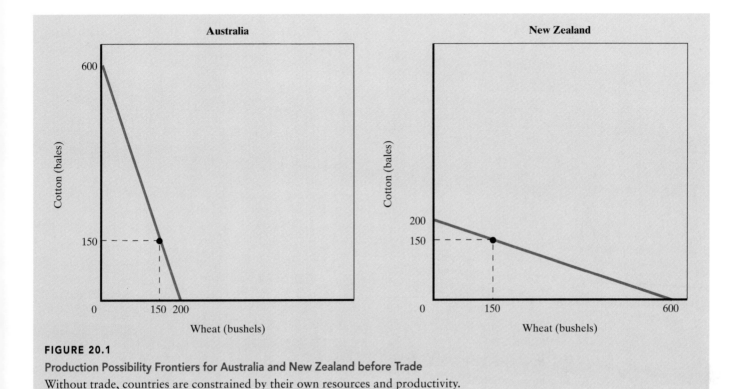

FIGURE 20.1

Production Possibility Frontiers for Australia and New Zealand before Trade

Without trade, countries are constrained by their own resources and productivity.

The advantages of specialization and trade seem obvious when one country is technologically superior at producing one product and another country is technologically superior at producing another product. But, let us turn to the case in which one country has an absolute advantage in the production of *both* goods.

> **Gains from Comparative Advantage** Table 20.5 contains different land yield figures for New Zealand and Australia. Now New Zealand has a considerable absolute advantage in the production of both cotton and wheat, with one acre of land yielding six times as much wheat and twice as much cotton as one acre in Australia. Ricardo would argue that *specialization and trade are still mutually beneficial.*

Again, preferences imply consumption of equal units of cotton and wheat in both countries. With no trade, New Zealand would divide its 100 available acres evenly, or 50/50, between the two crops. The result would be 300 bales of cotton and 300 bushels of wheat. Australia would divide its land 75/25. Table 20.6 shows that final production in Australia would be 75 bales of cotton and 75 bushels of wheat. (Remember, we are assuming that in each country, people consume equal amounts of

TABLE 20.4 PRODUCTION AND CONSUMPTION OF WHEAT AND COTTON AFTER SPECIALIZATION

	PRODUCTION			CONSUMPTION	
	New Zealand	Australia		New Zealand	Australia
Wheat	100 acres × 6 bu/acre 600 bushels	0 acres 0	Wheat	300 bushels	300 bushels
Cotton	0 acres 0	100 acres × 6 bales/acre 600 bales	Cotton	300 bales	300 bales

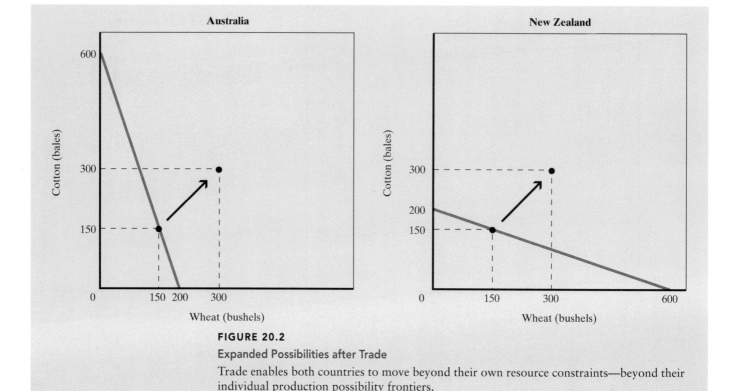

FIGURE 20.2

Expanded Possibilities after Trade

Trade enables both countries to move beyond their own resource constraints—beyond their individual production possibility frontiers.

cotton and wheat.) Again, before any trade takes place each country is constrained by its own domestic production possibilities curve.

Imagine we are at a meeting of trade representatives of both countries. As a special adviser, David Ricardo is asked to demonstrate that trade can benefit both countries. He divides his demonstration into three stages, which you can follow in Table 20.7.

In stage 1, Australia transfers all its land into cotton production. It will have no wheat and 300 bales of cotton. New Zealand cannot completely specialize in wheat because it needs 300 bales of cotton and will not be able to get enough cotton from Australia. This is because we are assuming that each country wants to consume equal amounts of cotton and wheat.

In stage 2, New Zealand transfers 25 acres out of cotton and into wheat. Now New Zealand has 25 acres in cotton that produce 150 bales and 75 acres in wheat that produce 450 bushels.

Finally, the two countries trade. We assume New Zealand ships 100 bushels of wheat to Australia in exchange for 200 bales of cotton. After the trade, New Zealand has 350 bales of cotton and 350 bushels of wheat; Australia has 100 bales of cotton and 100 bushels of wheat. Both countries are better off than they were before the trade (Table 20.6), and both have moved beyond their own production possibility frontiers.

TABLE 20.5   YIELD PER ACRE OF WHEAT AND COTTON

	NEW ZEALAND	AUSTRALIA
Wheat	6 bushels	1 bushel
Cotton	6 bales	3 bales

TABLE 20.6 TOTAL PRODUCTION OF WHEAT AND COTTON ASSUMING NO TRADE AND 100 AVAILABLE ACRES

	NEW ZEALAND	AUSTRALIA
Wheat	50 acres × 6 bushels/acre 300 bushels	75 acres × 1 bushels/acre 75 bushels
Cotton	50 acres × 6 bales/acre 300 bales	25 acres × 3 bales/acre 75 bales

➤ **Why Does Ricardo's Plan Work?** To understand why Ricardo's scheme works, let us return to the definition of comparative advantage.

The real cost of producing cotton is the wheat that must be sacrificed to produce it. *When we think of cost this way, it is less costly to produce cotton in Australia than to produce it in New Zealand, even though an acre of land produces more cotton in New Zealand.* Consider the "cost" of three bales of cotton in the two countries. In terms of opportunity cost, three bales of cotton in New Zealand cost three bushels of wheat; in Australia, three bales of cotton cost only one bushel of wheat. Because three bales are produced by one acre of Australian land, to get three bales an Australian must transfer one acre of land from wheat to cotton production. And because an acre of land produces a bushel of wheat, losing one acre to cotton implies the loss of one bushel of wheat. *Australia has a comparative advantage in cotton production* because its opportunity cost, in terms of wheat, is lower than New Zealand's. This is illustrated in Figure 20.3.

Conversely, New Zealand has a comparative advantage in wheat production. A unit of wheat in New Zealand costs one unit of cotton; a unit of wheat in Australia costs three units of cotton.

> When countries specialize in producing goods in which they have a comparative advantage, they maximize their combined output and allocate their resources more efficiently.

TABLE 20.7 REALIZING A GAIN FROM TRADE WHEN ONE COUNTRY HAS A DOUBLE ABSOLUTE ADVANTAGE

	STAGE 1				STAGE 2	
	NEW ZEALAND	AUSTRALIA			NEW ZEALAND	AUSTRALIA
Wheat	50 acres × 6 bushels/acre	0 acres		Wheat	75 acres × 6 bushels/acre	0 acres
	300 bushels	0			450 bushels	0
Cotton	50 acres × 6 bales/acre	100 acres × 3 bales/acre		Cotton	25 acres × 6 bales/acre	100 acres × 3 bales/acre
	300 bales	300 bales			150 bales	300 bales

	STAGE 3	
	NEW ZEALAND	AUSTRALIA
Wheat	100 bushels (trade) → 350 bushels (after trade)	100 bushels
Cotton	200 bales (trade) ← 350 bales (after trade)	100 bales

FIGURE 20.3

Comparative Advantage Means Lower Opportunity Cost

The real cost of cotton is the wheat sacrificed to obtain it. The cost of three bales of cotton in New Zealand is three bushels of wheat (one-half acre of land must be transferred from wheat to cotton—refer to Table 20.5). But the cost of three bales of cotton in Australia is only one bushel of wheat. Australia has a comparative advantage over New Zealand in cotton production, and New Zealand has a comparative advantage over Australia in wheat production.

terms of trade *The ratio at which a country can trade domestic products for imported products.*

TERMS OF TRADE

Ricardo might suggest a number of options open to the trading partners. The one we just examined benefited both partners; in percentage terms, Australia made out slightly better. Other deals might have been more advantageous to New Zealand.

The ratio at which a country can trade domestic products for imported products is the **terms of trade**. The terms of trade determine how the gains from trade are distributed among trading partners. In the case just considered, the agreed-upon terms of trade were one bushel of wheat for two bales of cotton. Such terms of trade benefit New Zealand, which can get two bales of cotton for each bushel of wheat. If it were to transfer its own land from wheat to cotton, it would get only one. The same terms of trade benefit Australia, which can get one bushel of wheat for two bales of cotton. A direct transfer of its own land would force it to give up three bales of cotton for one bushel of wheat.

If the terms of trade changed to three bales of cotton for every bushel of wheat, only New Zealand would benefit. At those terms of trade *all* the gains from trade would flow to New Zealand. Such terms do not benefit Australia at all because the opportunity cost of producing wheat domestically is *exactly the same* as the trade cost: One bushel of wheat costs three bales of cotton. If the terms of trade went the other way—one bale of cotton for each bushel of wheat—only Australia would benefit. New Zealand gains nothing, because it can already substitute cotton for wheat at that ratio. To get a bushel of wheat domestically, however, Australia must give up three bales of cotton, and one-for-one terms of trade would make wheat much less costly for Australia.

Both parties must have something to gain for trade to take place. In this case, you can see that both Australia and New Zealand will gain when the terms of trade are set between 1:1 and 3:1, cotton to wheat.

EXCHANGE RATES

The examples we have used thus far have shown that trade can result in gains to both parties. We have not yet discussed how trade actually comes about.

When trade is free—unimpeded by government-instituted barriers—patterns of trade and trade flows result from the independent decisions of thousands of importers and exporters and millions of private households and firms.

Private households decide whether to buy Toyotas or Chevrolets, and private firms decide whether to buy machine tools made in the United States or machine tools made in Taiwan, raw steel produced in Germany or raw steel produced in Pittsburgh.

Before a citizen of one country can buy a product made in, or sold by, someone in another country, a currency swap must take place. Consider Shane, who buys a Volkswagen from a dealer in Boston. He pays in dollars, but the German workers who made the car receive their salaries in deutsche marks. Somewhere between the buyer of the car and the producer, a currency exchange must be made. The regional distributor probably takes payment in dollars and converts them into marks before remitting the proceeds to Germany.

To buy a foreign-produced good, then, I in effect have to buy foreign currency. The price of Shane's Volkswagen in dollars depends on both the price of the car stated in deutsche marks and the price of deutsche marks. You probably know the ins and outs of currency exchange very well if you have ever traveled in another country. In December 1987, a dollar exchanged for 5.9 French francs, making each franc worth $0.168. Now suppose that you are in France, and you see a nice bottle of Bordeaux wine for 120 francs. How can you figure out whether you want to buy it? You know what dollars will buy you in the United States, so you have to convert the price into dollars. Each franc will cost you $0.168, so 120 francs is worth 120 × $0.168, or $20.16.

The attractiveness of foreign goods to U.S. buyers, and of U.S. goods to foreign buyers, depends in part on **exchange rates**, the ratio at which two currencies are traded. If the rate at which dollars could be converted into francs jumped to 10 francs for every dollar, that same bottle of wine would cost only $12.

exchange rate *The ratio at which two currencies are traded. The price of one currency in terms of another.*

To understand the patterns of trade that result from the actions of hundreds of thousands of independent buyers and sellers—households and firms—we must know something about the factors that determine exchange rates. Exchange rate determination is very complicated. Here, however, we can demonstrate two things:

> First, for any pair of countries, there is a range of exchange rates that can lead automatically to both countries realizing the gains from specialization and comparative advantage. Second, within that range, the exchange rate will determine which country gains the most from trade. In short, exchange rates determine the terms of trade.

▶ Trade and Exchange Rates in a Two-Country/Two-Good World Consider first a simple two-country/two-good model. Suppose both the United States and Germany produce only two goods—raw timber and rolled steel. Table 20.8 gives the current prices of both goods as domestic buyers see them. In Germany timber is priced at 3 deutsche marks (DM) per foot, and steel is priced at 4 DM per meter. In the United States, timber costs $1 per foot and steel costs $2 per meter.

Suppose U.S. and German buyers have the option of buying at home or importing to meet their needs. The options they choose will depend on the exchange rate. For the time being, we will ignore transportation costs between countries and assume that German and U.S. products are of equal quality.

Let us start with the assumption that the exchange rate is $1 = 1 DM. From the standpoint of U.S. buyers, neither German steel nor German timber is competitive at this exchange rate. A dollar buys a foot of timber in the United States, but if converted into a mark, it will buy only one third of a foot. The price of German timber to an American is $3 because it will take $3 to buy the necessary three DM. Similarly, $2 buys a meter of rolled steel in the United States, but the same $2 buys only half a meter of German steel. The price of German steel to an American is $4, twice the price of domestically produced steel.

At this exchange rate, however, Germans find that U.S.-produced steel and timber are both less expensive than steel and timber produced in Germany. Timber at

	UNITED STATES	GERMANY
Timber	$1	3 DM
Rolled steel	$2	4 DM

home—Germany—costs 3 DM, but 3 DM buys $3, which buys three times as much timber in the United States. Similarly, steel costs 4 DM at home, but 4 DM buys $4, which buys twice as much U.S.-made steel. At an exchange rate of $1 = 1 DM, Germany will import steel and timber and the United States will import nothing.

But now suppose the exchange rate is 1 DM = $0.25. We could say the "price" of a DM is $0.25. This means a dollar buys 4 DM. At this exchange rate, the Germans buy timber and steel at home and the Americans import both goods. At this exchange rate, Americans must pay a dollar for a foot of U.S. timber, but the same amount of timber can be had in Germany for the equivalent of $0.75. (Because 1 DM costs $0.25, 3 DM can be purchased for $0.75.) Similarly, steel that costs $2 per meter in the United States costs an American half as much in Germany, because $2 buys 8 DM, which buys two meters of German steel. At the same time, Germans are not interested in importing, because both goods are cheaper when purchased from a German producer. In this case, the United States imports both goods and Germany imports nothing.

So far, we can see that at exchange rates of $1 = 1 DM and $1 = 4 DM we get trade flowing in only one direction. Let's now try an exchange rate of $1 = 2 DM, or 1 DM = $0.50. First, Germans will buy timber in the United States. German timber costs 3 DM per foot, but 3 DM buys $1.50, which is enough to buy one and one half feet of U.S. timber. Buyers in the United States will find German timber too expensive, but Germany will import timber from the United States. At this same exchange rate, however, both German and U.S. buyers will be indifferent between German and U.S. steel. To U.S. buyers, domestically produced steel costs $2. Because $2 buys 4 DM, a meter of imported German steel also costs $2. German buyers also find that steel costs 4 DM, whether domestically produced or imported. Thus, there is likely to be no trade in steel.

But what happens if the exchange rate changes so that $1 buys 2.1 DM? While U.S. timber is still cheaper to both Germans and Americans, German steel begins to look good to U.S. buyers. Steel produced in the United States costs $2 per meter, but $2 buys 4.2 DM, which buys more than a meter of steel in Germany. When $1 buys more than 2 DM, trade begins to flow in both directions: Germany will import timber and the United States will import steel.

If you examine Table 20.9 carefully, you will see that trade flows in both directions as long as the exchange rate settles between $1 = 2 DM and $1 = 3 DM. Stated the other way around, trade will flow in both directions if the price of a DM is between $0.33 and $0.50.

▶ **Exchange Rates and Comparative Advantage** If the foreign exchange market drives the exchange rate to anywhere between 2 and 3 DM per dollar, the countries will automatically adjust and comparative advantage will be realized. At these exchange rates,

TABLE 20.9 TRADE FLOWS DETERMINED BY EXCHANGE RATES

EXCHANGE RATE	PRICE OF DM	RESULT
$1 = 1 DM	$ 1.00	Germany imports timber and steel.
$1 = 2 DM	$.50	Germany imports timber.
$1 = 2.1 DM	$.48	Germany imports timber; United States imports steel.
$1 = 2.9 DM	$.34	Germany imports timber; United States imports steel.
$1 = 3 DM	$.33	United States imports steel.
$1 = 4 DM	$.25	United States imports timber and steel.

U.S. buyers begin buying all their steel in Germany. The U.S. steel industry finds itself in trouble. Plants close, and U.S. workers begin to lobby for tariff protection against German steel. At the same time, the U.S. timber industry does well, fueled by strong export demand from Germany. The timber-producing sector expands. Resources, including capital and labor, are attracted into timber production.

The opposite occurs in Germany. The German timber industry suffers losses as export demand dries up and Germans turn to cheaper U.S. imports. In Germany, lumber companies turn to the government and ask for protection from cheap U.S. timber. But steel producers in Germany are happy. Not only are they supplying 100 percent of the domestically demanded steel, but they are selling to U.S. buyers as well. The steel industry expands, and the timber industry contracts. Resources, including labor, flow into steel.

With this expansion-and-contraction scenario in mind, let's look again at our original definition of comparative advantage. If we assume that prices reflect resource use and resources can be transferred from sector to sector, we can calculate the opportunity cost of steel/timber in both countries. In the United States, the production of a meter of rolled steel consumes twice the resources that the production of a foot of timber consumes. Assuming that resources can be transferred, the opportunity cost of a meter of steel is two feet of timber (Table 20.8). In Germany, a meter of steel uses resources costing 4 DM, while a unit of timber costs 3 DM. To produce a meter of steel means the sacrifice of only four thirds, or one and one third, feet of timber. Because the opportunity cost of a meter of steel (in terms of timber) is lower in Germany, we say Germany has a comparative advantage in steel production.

Conversely, consider the opportunity cost of timber in the two countries. Increasing timber production in the United States requires the sacrifice of half a meter of steel for every foot of timber—producing a meter of steel uses $2 worth of resources, while producing a foot of timber requires only $1 worth of resources. But each foot of timber production in Germany requires the sacrifice of three fourths of a meter of steel. Because the opportunity cost of timber is lower in the United States, the United States has a comparative advantage in the production of timber.

> If exchange rates end up in the right ranges, the free market will drive each country to shift resources into those sectors in which it enjoys a comparative advantage. Only those products in which a country has a comparative advantage will be competitive in world markets.

THE SOURCES OF COMPARATIVE ADVANTAGE

Specialization and trade can benefit all trading partners, even those that may be inefficient producers in an absolute sense. If markets are competitive, and if foreign exchange markets are linked to goods-and-services exchange, countries will specialize in producing products in which they have a comparative advantage.

So far, we have said nothing about the sources of comparative advantage. What determines whether a country has a comparative advantage in heavy manufacturing or in agriculture? What explains the actual trade flows observed around the world? Various theories and empirical work on international trade have provided some answers. Most economists look to **factor endowments**—the quantity and quality of labor, land, and natural resources—as the principal sources of comparative advantage. Factor endowments seem to explain a significant portion of actual world trade patterns.

THE HECKSCHER-OHLIN THEOREM

Eli Heckscher and Bertil Ohlin, two Swedish economists who wrote in the first half of this century, expanded and elaborated on Ricardo's theory of comparative advantage. The **Heckscher-Ohlin theorem** ties the theory of comparative advantage to factor

factor endowments *The quantity and quality of labor, land, and natural resources of a country.*

Heckscher-Ohlin theorem *A theory that explains the existence of a country's comparative advantage by its factor endowments: A country has a comparative advantage in the production of a product if that country is relatively well endowed with inputs used intensively in the production of that product.*

endowments. It assumes that products can be produced using differing proportions of inputs and that inputs are mobile between sectors in each economy, but that factors are not mobile *between* economies. According to this theorem:

> A country has a comparative advantage in the production of a product if that country is relatively well endowed with inputs used intensively in the production of that product.

This idea is simple. A country with a lot of good fertile land is likely to have a comparative advantage in agriculture. A country with a large amount of accumulated capital is likely to have a comparative advantage in heavy manufacturing. A country with a lot of human capital is likely to have a comparative advantage in highly technical goods.

After an extensive study, Edward Leamer of UCLA has concluded that a short list of factors accounts for a large portion of world trade patterns. Natural resources, knowledge capital, physical capital, land, and skilled and unskilled labor, Leamer believes, explain "a large amount of the variability of net exports across countries."[1]

OTHER EXPLANATIONS FOR OBSERVED TRADE FLOWS

Comparative advantage is not the only reason countries trade. It does not explain why many countries both import and export the same kinds of goods. The United States, for example, both exports and imports automobiles.

And, just as industries within a country differentiate their products to capture a domestic market, so too do they differentiate their products to please the wide variety of tastes that exists worldwide. The Japanese automobile industry, for example, began producing small, fuel-efficient cars long before U.S. automobile makers did. In doing so, they developed expertise in creating products that attracted a devoted following and considerable brand loyalty. BMWs, made only in Germany, and Volvos, made only in Sweden, also have their champions in many countries. Just as product differentiation is a natural response to diverse preferences within an economy, it is also a natural response to diverse preferences across economies.

This idea is not inconsistent with the theory of comparative advantage. If the Japanese have developed skills and knowledge that gave them an edge in the production of fuel-efficient cars, that knowledge can be thought of as a very specific kind of capital not currently available to other producers. The Volvo company invested in a form of intangible capital that we call *goodwill*. That goodwill, which may come from establishing a reputation for safety and quality over the years, is one source of the comparative advantage that keeps Volvos selling on the international market. Some economists distinguish between gains from *acquired comparative advantages* and those from *natural comparative advantages*.

Another explanation for international trade is that some economies of scale may be available when producing for a world market that would not be available when producing for a more limited domestic market. But because the evidence suggests that economies of scale are exhausted at relatively small size in most industries, it seems unlikely that they constitute a valid explanation of world trade patterns.

TRADE BARRIERS: TARIFFS, EXPORT SUBSIDIES, AND QUOTAS

protection *The practice of shielding a sector of the economy from foreign competition.*

Trade barriers—also called *obstacles to trade*—take many forms; the three most common are tariffs, export subsidies, and quotas. All are forms of **protection** shielding some sector of the economy from foreign competition.

[1]Edward E. Leamer, *Sources of International Comparative Advantage: Theory and Evidence* (Cambridge, Mass: MIT Press, 1984), p. 187.

A **tariff** is a tax on imports. The average tariff on imports into the United States is about 5 percent. Certain protected items have much higher tariffs. For example, the tariff rate on concentrated orange juice is a flat $0.35 per gallon. On rubber footwear, the tariff ranges from 20 percent to 48 percent, and on canned tuna it is 35 percent.

Export subsidies—government payments made to domestic firms to encourage exports—can also act as a barrier to trade. One of the provisions of the Corn Laws that stimulated Ricardo's musings was an export subsidy automatically paid to farmers by the British government when the price of grain fell below a specified level. The subsidy served to keep domestic prices high, but it flooded the world market with cheap subsidized grain. Foreign farmers who were not subsidized were driven out of the international marketplace by the artificially low prices.

Farm subsidies remain a part of the international trade landscape today. Many countries, especially in Europe, continue to appease their farmers by heavily subsidizing exports of agricultural products. The political power of the farm lobby in many countries has had an important effect on recent international trade negotiations aimed at reducing trade barriers.

Closely related to subsidies is **dumping**. Dumping takes place when a firm or an industry sells products on the world market at prices *below* the cost of production. The charge has been leveled against several specific Japanese industries, including automobiles, consumer electronics, and silicon computer chips.

Generally, a company dumps when it wants to dominate a world market. After the lower prices of the dumped goods have succeeded in driving out all the competition, the dumping company can exploit its position by raising the price of its product. A U.S. firm attempting to monopolize a domestic market violates the Sherman Antitrust Act of 1890, prohibiting predatory pricing.

The current U.S. tariff laws contain several provisions aimed at counteracting the effects of dumping. The 1974 Trade Act contains a clause that qualifies an industry for protection if it has been "injured" by foreign competition. Building on that legislation, more recent trade bills, including the Comprehensive Trade Act of 1988, contain clauses that permit the president to impose trade sanctions when investigations reveal dumping by foreign companies or countries.

A **quota** is a limit on the quantity of imports. Quotas can be mandatory or voluntary, and they may be legislated or negotiated with foreign governments. The best-known voluntary quota, or "voluntary restraint," was negotiated with the Japanese government in 1981. Japan agreed to reduce its automobile exports to the United States by 7.7 percent, from the 1980 level of 1.82 million units to 1.68 million units. In 1985, President Reagan decided not to ask Japan to continue its restraints—auto imports jumped to 2.3 million units, nearly 20 percent of the U.S. market. Quotas currently apply to products like mushrooms, heavy motorcycles, and color TVs.

▶ **U.S. Trade Policies and GATT**   The United States has been a high-tariff nation, with average tariffs of over 50 percent for much of its history. The highest were in effect during the Great Depression following the **Smoot-Hawley tariff**, which pushed the average tariff rate to 60 percent in 1930. The Smoot-Hawley tariff set off an international trade war when U.S. trading partners retaliated with tariffs of their own. Many economists say the decline in trade that followed was one of the causes of the worldwide depression of the 1930s.[2]

In 1947 the United States, with 22 other nations, agreed to reduce barriers to trade. It also established an organization to promote liberalization of foreign trade. This **General Agreement on Tariffs and Trade (GATT)**, at first considered to be an interim arrangement, continues today and has been quite effective. The most recent round of world trade talks sponsored by GATT, the "Uruguay Round," began in

tariff *A tax on imports.*

export subsidies *Government payments made to domestic firms to encourage exports.*

dumping *A firm or industry sells products on the world market at prices below the cost of production.*

quota *A limit on the quantity of imports.*

Smoot-Hawley tariff *The U.S. tariff law of the 1930s, which set the highest tariffs in U.S. history (60 percent). It set off an international trade war and caused the decline in trade that is often considered a cause of the worldwide depression of the 1930s.*

General Agreement on Tariffs and Trade (GATT) *An international agreement signed by the United States and 22 other countries in 1947 to promote the liberalization of foreign trade.*

---

[2]See especially Charles Kindleberger, *The World in Depression 1929–1939* (London: Allen Lane, 1973).

Uruguay in 1986. It was initialed by 116 countries on December 15, 1993, and was formally approved by the U.S. Congress after much debate following the election in 1994. The "Final Act" of the Uruguay Round of negotiations is the most comprehensive and complex multilateral trade agreement in history. See Global Perspective "A New World Trade Agreement: GATT and the Final Act."

Every president who has held office since the first round of the General Agreement was signed has argued for free-trade policies, yet each used his powers to protect one sector or another. Eisenhower and Kennedy restricted U.S. imports of Japanese textiles; Johnson restricted meat imports; Nixon restrained imports of steel and tightened restrictions on textiles; Carter protected steel, textiles, and footwear; Reagan restricted imports of sugar and automobiles. Both Bush and Clinton imposed new tariffs as well.

Nevertheless, the movement in the United States has been away from tariffs and quotas and toward freer trade. The Reciprocal Trade Agreements Act of 1934 authorized the president to negotiate trade agreements on behalf of the United States. As part of trade negotiations, the president can confer *most-favored-nation status* on individual trading partners. Imports from countries with most-favored-nation status are taxed at the lowest negotiated tariff rates. In addition, in recent years several successful rounds of tariff-reduction negotiations have reduced trade barriers to their lowest levels ever.

economic integration *Occurs when two or more nations join to form a free-trade zone.*

European Union (EU) *The European trading bloc composed of Austria, Belgium, Denmark, Finland, France, Germany, Greece, Ireland, Italy, Luxembourg, the Netherlands, Portugal, Spain, Sweden, and the United Kingdom.*

U.S.-Canadian Free-Trade Agreement *An agreement in which the United States and Canada agreed to eliminate all barriers to trade between the two countries by 1998.*

North American Free-Trade Agreement (NAFTA) *An agreement signed by the United States, Mexico, and Canada in which the three countries agreed to establish all of North America as a free-trade zone.*

➤ **Economic Integration** Economic integration occurs when two or more nations join to form a free-trade zone. In 1991, the European Community (EC, or the Common Market) began forming the largest free-trade zone in the world. The economic integration process began that December, when the 12 original members (the United Kingdom, Belgium, France, Germany, Italy, the Netherlands, Luxembourg, Denmark, Greece, Ireland, Spain, and Portugal) signed the Maastricht Treaty. The treaty called for the end of border controls, a common currency, an end to all tariffs, and the coordination of monetary and even political affairs. In 1995, Austria, Finland, and Sweden became members of this **European Union (EU)**, as the EC is now called, bringing the number of member countries to 15.

On January 1, 1993, all tariffs and trade barriers were dropped among the member countries. Border checkpoints were closed in early 1995. Citizens can now travel among member countries without passports. The most difficult step will be a common currency. The goal is to have it in place by 1999. Many economists believe the advantages of free trade within the bloc, a reunited Germany, and the ability to work well as a bloc will make the EU the most powerful player in the international marketplace in the coming decades.

The United States is not a part of the EU. However, in 1988 the United States (under President Reagan) and Canada (under Prime Minister Mulroney) signed the **U.S.-Canadian Free-Trade Agreement**, which will remove all barriers to trade, including tariffs and quotas, between the two countries by 1998.

During the last days of the Bush administration, the United States, Mexico, and Canada signed the **North American Free-Trade Agreement (NAFTA)**, the three countries agreeing to establish all of North America as a free-trade zone. The North American free-trade area will include 360 million people and a total output of over $7 trillion—larger than the output of the European Union. The agreement will eliminate all tariffs over a 10- to 15-year period and remove restrictions on most investments.

During the presidential campaign of 1992, NAFTA was hotly debated. Both Bill Clinton and George Bush supported the agreement. Industrial labor unions that might be affected by increased imports from Mexico (like those in the automobile industry) opposed the agreement, while industries whose exports to Mexico might increase as a result of the agreement (for example, the machine tool industry) supported it. Another concern was that Mexican companies were not subject to the same environmental regulations as U.S. firms, so U.S. firms might move to Mexico for this reason.

NAFTA was ratified by the U.S. Congress in late 1993 and went into effect on the first day of 1994. The U.S. Department of Commerce has estimated that

A NEW WORLD TRADE AGREEMENT: GATT AND THE FINAL ACT

Launched in Punta del Este, Uruguay, in 1986, the Uruguay Round of multinational trade negotiations was concluded in Geneva on December 15, 1993, when 116 nations initialed what was called the "Final Act." In December 1994, a lame-duck U.S. Congress acted to approve the agreement for the United States.

The Final Act is a document of over 26,000 pages—the most comprehensive and complex trade agreement in history. Proponents say its implementation will increase the volume of world merchandise trade by 9 percent to 24 percent over what it would have been without the agreement.*

The provisions of the Final Act are: First, it reduces tariffs and protection for agricultural products. Throughout history, agricultural goods have been the target of high import duties, large domestic subsidies, and outright trade restrictions. In many cases this was due to the farmers' political power. Talk of reducing subsidies going to agriculture in France led, on several occasions in the last decade, to highway blockades and violent demonstrations by French farmers. The agreement calls for an end to many agricultural subsidies, an end to nontariff barriers, such as quantitative restrictions and bans, and an average tariff reduction of 37 percent on agricultural imports. In general, developed countries have agreed to reduce tariffs on 64 percent of their imports by about 40 percent, from an average rate of 6.3 percent to 3.8 percent. The percentage

of industrial imports allowed to enter the developed countries with no duties at all will increase from 20 percent to 44 percent. The developing countries have agreed to lower tariffs on about 33 percent of their imports.

Second, the Uruguay round is the first multilateral negotiation to reach a comprehensive agreement on international trade in services. It outlaws restrictions on the import of services such as banking, legal services, insurance, accounting, and computer consulting.

Third, the Final Act makes provisions for the protection of intellectual property. While existing patent and copyright laws usually protect artists, designers, computer software producers, authors, and the like from "theft" within their own countries, foreign pirating is common. Though it is usually illegal to reproduce and sell pirated CDs, videotapes, books, and computer software packages produced within a country, there were no internationally applicable rules about pirating across borders before the new agreement was signed. The new trade agreement requires all signatory countries to apply copyright and patent laws equally to foreign owners of intellectual property.

In addition, the Final Act established a Dispute Settlement Body designed to ensure compliance and to resolve conflicts between member countries. Some members of the U.S. Congress argued (in vain) that by signing the treaty the United States would be giving up its sovereignty to an international body.

THE NEW TRADE AGREEMENT REQUIRES ALL SIGNATORY COUNTRIES TO APPLY COPYRIGHT AND PATENT LAWS EQUALLY TO FOREIGN OWNERS OF INTELLECTUAL PROPERTY, SUCH AS THE CONTENT OF THE CDS AND VIDEO TAPES SHOWN HERE.

*Source: See Norman S. Fieleke, "The Uruguay Round of Trade Negotiations: An Overview," *New England Economic Review*, May–June 1995.

For more on trade agreements, see the Case and Fair Web page at http://www.prenhall.com/casefair.

as a result of NAFTA trade between the United States and Mexico increased by nearly $16 billion in 1994. In addition, exports from the United States to Mexico outpaced imports from Mexico during 1994. In 1995, however, the agreement fell under the shadow of a dramatic collapse of the value of the peso. U.S. exports to Mexico dropped sharply, and the United States shifted from a trade surplus to a large trade deficit with Mexico. By 1998, a general consensus emerged among economists that NAFTA had led to expanded employment opportunities on both sides of the border.

FREE TRADE OR PROTECTION?

One of the great economic debates of all time revolves around the free-trade-versus-protection controversy. We briefly summarize the arguments in favor of each.

THE CASE FOR FREE TRADE

In one sense, the theory of comparative advantage *is* the case for free trade. Trade has potential benefits for all nations. A good is not imported unless its net price to buyers is below the net price of the domestically produced alternative. When the Germans in our earlier example found U.S. timber less expensive than their own, they bought it, yet they continued to pay the same price for homemade steel. Americans bought less-expensive German steel, but they continued to buy domestic timber at the same lower price. Under these conditions, *both Americans and Germans ended up paying less and consuming more.*

At the same time, resources (including labor) move out of steel production and into timber production in the United States. In Germany, resources (including labor) move out of timber production and into steel production. The resources in both countries are more efficiently used. Tariffs, export subsidies, and quotas, which interfere with the free movement of goods and services around the world, reduce or eliminate the gains of comparative advantage.

We can use supply and demand curves to illustrate this. Suppose Figure 20.4a shows domestic supply and demand for textiles. In the absence of trade, the market clears at a price of $4.20. At equilibrium, 450 million yards of textiles are produced and consumed.

Assume now that textiles are available at a world price of $2. This is the price in dollars that Americans must pay for textiles from foreign sources. If we assume an unlimited amount of textiles is available at $2 and there is no difference in quality between domestic and foreign textiles, no domestic producer will be able to charge more than $2. In the absence of trade barriers, the world price sets the price in the United States. As the price in the United States falls from $4.20 to $2.00, the quantity demanded by consumers increases from 450 million yards to 700 million yards, but the quantity supplied by domestic producers drops from 450 million yards to 200 million yards. The difference, 500 million yards, is the quantity of textiles imported.

The argument for free trade is that each country should specialize in producing the goods and services in which it enjoys a comparative advantage. If foreign producers can produce textiles at a much lower price than domestic producers, they have a comparative advantage. As the world price of textiles falls to $2, domestic (U.S.) supply drops and resources are transferred to other sectors. These other sectors, which may be export industries or domestic industries, are not shown in Figure 20.4a. It is clear that the allocation of resources is more efficient at a price of $2. Why should the United States use domestic resources to produce what foreign producers can produce at a lower cost? U.S. resources should move into the production of the things it produces best.

Now consider what happens to the domestic price of textiles when a trade barrier is imposed. Figure 20.4b shows the effect of a set tariff of $1 per yard imposed on imported textiles. The tariff raises the domestic price of textiles to $2 + $1 = $3. The result is that some of the gains from trade are lost. First, consumers are forced to pay a higher price for the same good; the quantity of textiles demanded drops from 700 million yards under free trade to 600 million yards because some consumers are not willing to pay the higher price.

a. Domestic supply and demand for textiles

b. Effect of $1 tariff per unit

FIGURE 20.4

The Gains from Trade and Losses from the Imposition of a Tariff

A tariff of $1 increases the market price facing consumers from $2 per yard to $3 per yard.
The government collects revenues equal to the gray shaded area. The loss of efficiency has
two components. First, consumers must pay a higher price for goods that could be produced
at lower cost. Second, marginal producers are drawn into textiles and away from other
goods, resulting in inefficient domestic production.

At the same time, the higher price of textiles draws some marginal domestic producers who could not make a profit at $2 into textile production. (Recall, domestic producers do not pay a tariff.) As the price rises to $3, the quantity supplied by producers rises from 200 million yards to 300 million yards. The result is a decrease in imports from 500 million yards to 300 million yards.

Finally, the imposition of the tariff means the government collects revenue equal to the shaded gray area in Figure 20.4b. This shaded area is equal to the tariff rate per unit ($1) times the number of units imported after the tariff is in place (300 million yards). Thus, receipts from the tariff are $300 billion.

What is the final result of the tariff? Domestic producers receiving revenues of only $2 per unit before the tariff was imposed now receive a higher price and earn higher profits. But these higher profits are achieved at a loss of efficiency.

Trade barriers prevent a nation from reaping the benefits of specialization, push it to adopt relatively inefficient production techniques, and force consumers to pay higher prices for protected products than they would otherwise pay.

THE CASE FOR PROTECTION

Arguments can also be made in favor of tariffs and quotas. Over the course of U.S. history, these arguments have been made so many times by so many industries before so many congressional committees that it seems all pleas for protection share the same themes. We describe the most frequently heard pleas next.

> **Protection Saves Jobs**   The main argument for protection is that foreign competition costs Americans their jobs. When Americans buy Toyotas, U.S. cars go unsold. This leads to layoffs in the domestic auto industry. When Americans buy Japanese or German steel, steelworkers in Pittsburgh lose their jobs. When Americans buy shoes or textiles from Korea or Taiwan, the millworkers in Maine and Massachusetts, as well as in South Carolina and Georgia, lose their jobs.

It is true that when we buy goods from foreign producers, domestic producers suffer. But there is no reason to believe that the workers laid off in the contracting sectors will not be ultimately reemployed in other expanding sectors. Foreign competition in textiles, for example, has meant the loss of U.S. jobs in that industry. Thousands of textile workers in New England lost their jobs as the textile mills there closed over the last 35 years. But with the expansion of high-tech industries, the unemployment rate in Massachusetts fell to one of the lowest in the country in the mid-1980s, and New Hampshire, Vermont, and Maine also boomed. By the 1990s, New England had suffered another severe downturn, due partly to high-technology hardware manufacturing that had moved abroad. But in 1994 it became clear that small-to medium-sized companies in such newly developing areas as biotechnology and software were beginning to pick up steam just as hardware manufacturing had done a decade earlier.

The adjustment is far from costless. The knowledge that some other industry, perhaps in some other part of the country, may be expanding is of little comfort to the person whose skills become obsolete or whose pension benefits are lost when his or her company abruptly closes a plant or goes bankrupt. The social and personal problems brought about by industry-specific unemployment, obsolete skills, and bankruptcy as a result of foreign competition are significant.

These problems can be addressed in two ways. We can ban imports and give up the gains from free trade, acknowledging that we are willing to pay premium prices to save domestic jobs in industries that can produce more efficiently abroad. Or we can aid the victims of free trade in a constructive way, helping to retrain them for jobs with a future. In some instances, programs to relocate people in expanding regions may be in order. Some programs deal directly with the transition without forgoing the gains from trade.

> **Some Countries Engage in Unfair Trade Practices**   Attempts by U.S. firms to monopolize an industry are illegal under the Sherman and Clayton acts. If a strong company decides to drive the competition out of the market by setting prices below cost, it would be aggressively prosecuted by the Antitrust Division of the Justice Department. But, the argument goes, if we won't allow a U.S. firm to engage in predatory pricing or monopolize an industry or market, can we stand by and let a German firm or a Japanese firm do so in the name of free trade? This is a legitimate argument and one that has gained significant favor in recent years. How should we respond when a large international company or a country behaves strategically against a domestic firm or industry? Free trade may be the best solution when everybody plays by the rules, but sometimes we have to fight back.

> **Cheap Foreign Labor Makes Competition Unfair**   Let's say that a particular country gained its "comparative advantage" in textiles by paying its workers low wages. How can U.S. textile companies compete with companies that pay wages that are less than a quarter of what U.S. companies pay?

First, remember that wages in a competitive economy reflect productivity. Workers in the United States earn higher wages because they are more productive. The United States has more capital per worker, and its workers are better trained. Second, trade flows not according to *absolute* advantage but according to *comparative* advantage: All countries benefit, even if one country is more efficient at producing everything.

> **Protection Safeguards National Security**   Beyond saving jobs, certain sectors of the economy may appeal for protection for other reasons. The steel industry has argued for years with some success that it is vital to national defense. In the event of a war, the United States would not want to depend on foreign countries for products as vital as steel. Even if we acknowledge another country's comparative advantage, we may want to protect our own resources.

No industry has ever asked for protection without invoking the national defense argument. The testimony on behalf of the scissors and shears industry argued that "in the event of a national emergency and imports cutoff, the United States would be without a source of scissors and shears, basic tools for many industries and trades essential to our national defense." The question, then, lies not in the merit of the argument but in just how seriously it can be taken if *every* industry uses it.

> **Protection Discourages Dependency**   Closely related to the national defense argument is the claim that countries, particularly small or developing countries, may come to rely too heavily on one or more trading partners for many items. If a small country comes to rely on a major power for food or energy or some important raw material in which the large nation has a comparative advantage, it may be difficult for the smaller nation to remain politically neutral. Some critics of free trade argue that the superpowers have consciously engaged in trade with smaller countries to create these kinds of dependencies.

Therefore, should small independent countries consciously avoid trading relationships that might lead to political dependence? This may involve developing domestic industries in areas where a country has a comparative disadvantage. To do so would mean protecting that industry from international competition.

> **Protection Safeguards Infant Industries**   Young industries in a given country may have a difficult time competing with established industries in other countries. And in a dynamic world, a protected **infant industry** might mature into a strong one worldwide because of an acquired, but real, comparative advantage. If such an industry is undercut and driven out of world markets at the beginning of its life, that comparative advantage might never develop.

infant industry *A young industry that may need temporary protection from competition from the established industries of other countries in order to develop an acquired comparative advantage.*

Yet efforts to protect infant industries can backfire. In July 1991, the U.S. government imposed a 62.67 percent tariff on imports of active-matrix liquid crystal display screens (also referred to as "flat-panel displays" and primarily used for laptop computers) from Japan. The Commerce Department and the International Trade Commission agreed that Japanese producers were selling their screens in the U.S. market at a price below cost and that this "dumping" threatened the survival of domestic laptop screen producers. The tariff was meant to protect the infant U.S. industry until it could compete head-on with the Japanese.

Unfortunately for U.S. producers of laptop computers and for consumers who purchase them, the tariff had an unintended (though predictable) effect on the industry. Because U.S. laptop screens were generally recognized to be of lower quality than their Japanese counterparts, imposition of the tariff left U.S. computer manufacturers with three options: (1) They could use the screens available from U.S. producers and watch sales of their final product decline in the face of *higher quality* competition from abroad; (2) they could pay the tariff for the higher quality screens and watch sales of their final product decline in the face of *lower priced* competition from abroad; or (3) they could do what was the most profitable for them to do—move their production facilities abroad to avoid the tariff completely. The last is exactly what both Apple and IBM announced they would do. In the end, not only were the laptop industry and its consumers hurt by the imposition of the tariff (due to higher costs of production and to higher laptop computer prices), but the U.S. screen industry was hurt as well (due to its loss of buyers for its product) by a policy specifically designed to help it.

AN ECONOMIC CONSENSUS

You now know something about how international trade fits into the structure of the economy.

Critical to our study of international economics is the debate between free-traders and protectionists. On one side is the theory of comparative advantage, formalized by David Ricardo in the early part of the nineteenth century. According to this view, all countries benefit from specialization and trade. The gains from trade are real, and they can be large; free international trade raises real incomes and improves the standard of living.

On the other side are the protectionists, who point to the loss of jobs and argue for the protection of workers from foreign competition. But although foreign competition can cause job loss in specific sectors, it is unlikely to cause net job loss in an economy, and workers will over time be absorbed into expanding sectors.

> Foreign trade and full employment can be pursued simultaneously. Although economists disagree about many things, the vast majority of them favor free trade.

SUMMARY

1. All economies, regardless of their size, depend to some extent on other economies and are affected by events outside their borders.

Chapter 20

TRADE SURPLUSES AND DEFICITS

2. Until the 1970s, the United States generally exported more than it imported—it ran a *trade surplus*. In the mid-1970s, the United States began to import more merchandise than it exported—a *trade deficit*.

THE ECONOMIC BASIS FOR TRADE: COMPARATIVE ADVANTAGE

3. The *theory of comparative advantage*, dating to David Ricardo in the nineteenth century, holds that specialization and free trade will benefit all trading partners, even those that may be absolutely less efficient producers.

4. A country enjoys an *absolute advantage* over another country in the production of a product if it uses fewer resources to produce that product than the other country does. A country has a *comparative advantage* in the production of a product if that product can be produced at a lower cost in terms of other goods.

5. Trade enables countries to move beyond their previous resource and productivity constraints. When countries specialize in producing those goods in which they have a comparative advantage, they maximize their combined output and allocate their resources more efficiently.

6. When trade is free, patterns of trade and trade flows result from the independent decisions of thousands of importers and exporters and millions of private households and firms.

7. The relative attractiveness of foreign goods to U.S. buyers and of U.S. goods to foreign buyers depends in part on *exchange rates*, the ratios at which two currencies are traded for each other.

8. For any pair of countries, there is a range of exchange rates that will lead automatically to both countries realizing the gains from specialization and comparative advantage. Within that range, the exchange rate will determine which country gains the most from trade. This leads us to conclude that exchange rates determine the terms of trade.

9. If exchange rates end up in the right range (that is, in a range that facilitates the flow of goods between nations), the free market will drive each country to shift resources into those sectors in which it enjoys a comparative advantage. Only those products in which a country has a comparative advantage will be competitive in world markets.

THE SOURCES OF COMPARATIVE ADVANTAGE

10. The *Heckscher-Ohlin theorem* looks to relative *factor endowments* to explain comparative advantage and trade flows. According to the theorem, a country has a comparative advantage in the production of a product if that country is relatively well endowed with the inputs that are used intensively in the production of that product.

11. A relatively short list of inputs—natural resources, knowledge capital, physical capital, land, and skilled and unskilled labor—explains a surprisingly large portion of world trade patterns. But the simple version of the theory of comparative advantage cannot explain why many countries import and export the same goods.

12. Some theories argue that comparative advantage can be acquired. Just as industries within a country differentiate their products to capture a domestic market, so too do they differentiate their products to please the wide variety of

tastes that exists worldwide. This theory is not inconsistent with the theory of comparative advantage.

TRADE BARRIERS: TARIFFS, EXPORT SUBSIDIES, AND QUOTAS

13. Trade barriers take many forms; the three most common are *tariffs, export subsidies*, and *quotas*. All are forms of *protection* through which some sector of the economy is shielded from foreign competition.

14. Although the United States has historically been a high-tariff nation, the general movement is now away from tariffs and quotas. The *General Agreement on Tariffs and Trade (GATT)*, signed by the United States and 22 other countries in 1947, continues in effect today; its purpose is to reduce barriers to world trade and keep them down. Also important are the *U.S.-Canadian Free Trade Agreement*, signed in 1988, and the *North American Free-Trade Agreement*, signed by the United States, Mexico, and Canada in the last days of the Bush administration, taking effect in 1994.

15. The *European Union (EU)* is a free-trade bloc composed of 15 nations: Austria, Belgium, Denmark, Finland, France, Germany, Greece, Ireland, Italy, Luxembourg, the Netherlands, Portugal, Spain, Sweden, and the United Kingdom.

Many economists believe that the advantages of free trade within the bloc, a reunited Germany, and the ability to work well as a bloc will make the EU the most powerful player in the international marketplace in the coming decades.

FREE TRADE OR PROTECTION?

16. In one sense, the theory of comparative advantage is the case for free trade. Trade barriers prevent a nation from reaping the benefits of specialization, push it to adopt relatively inefficient production techniques, and force consumers to pay higher prices for protected products than they would otherwise pay.

17. The case for protection rests on a number of propositions, one of which is that foreign competition results in a loss of domestic jobs. But there is no reason to believe that the workers laid off in the contracting sectors will not be ultimately reemployed in other expanding sectors. This adjustment process is far from costless, however.

18. Other arguments for protection hold that cheap foreign labor makes competition unfair; that some countries engage in unfair trade practices; that it protects the national security and discourages dependency; and that it protects *infant industries*. Despite these arguments, most economists favor free trade.

REVIEW TERMS AND CONCEPTS

absolute advantage, 429

comparative advantage, 429

Corn Laws, 428

dumping, 439

economic integration, 440

European Union (EU), 440

exchange rate, 435

export subsidies, 439

factor endowments, 437

General Agreement on Tariffs and Trade (GATT), 439

Heckscher-Ohlin theorem, 437

infant industry, 445

North American Free-Trade Agreement (NAFTA), 440

protection, 438

quota, 439

Smoot-Hawley tariff, 439

tariff, 439

terms of trade, 434

theory of comparative advantage, 429

trade deficit, 428

trade surplus, 428

U.S.-Canadian Free-Trade Agreement, 440

PROBLEM SET

1. Suppose Germany and France each produce only two goods, guns and butter. Both are produced using labor alone and the value of a good is equal to the number of labor units required to produce it. Assuming both countries are at full employment, you are given the following information:

Germany: 10 units of labor required to produce 1 gun
5 units of labor required to produce 1 pound of butter
Total labor force: 1,000,000 units

France: 15 units of labor required to produce 1 gun
10 units of labor required to produce 1 pound of butter
Total labor force: 750,000 units

   a. Draw the production possibility frontiers for each country in the absence of trade.

   b. If transportation costs are ignored and trade is allowed, will France and Germany engage in trade? Explain.

   c. If a trade agreement were negotiated, at what rate (number of guns per unit of butter) would they agree to exchange?

2. The United States and Russia each produce only bearskin caps and wheat. Domestic prices are given in the following table:

	RUSSIA	UNITED STATES	
Bearskin Caps	10 Ru	$ 7	Per hat
Wheat	15 Ru	$10	Per quart

On April 1, the Zurich exchange listed an exchange rate of $1 = 1 Ru.

a. Which country has an absolute advantage in the production of bearskin caps? Wheat?

b. Which country has a comparative advantage in the production of bearskin caps? Wheat?

c. If the United States and Russia were the only two countries engaging in trade, what adjustments would you predict, assuming exchange rates are freely determined by the laws of supply and demand?

3. The United States imported $27.9 billion worth of "food, feeds, and beverages" in 1996 and exported $40.7 billion worth.

a. Name some of the imported items that you are aware of in this category. Also name some of the exported items.

b. The United States is said to have a comparative advantage in the production of agricultural goods. How would you go about testing this proposition? What data would you need?

c. Are the foregoing numbers consistent with the theory of comparative advantage? Suppose you had a more detailed breakdown of which items the United States imports and which it exports. What would you look for?

d. What other theories of international trade might explain why the same goods are imported and exported?

4. The following table gives 1990 figures for yield per acre in Illinois and Kansas:

	WHEAT	SOYBEANS
Illinois	48	39
Kansas	40	24

Source: U.S. Dept. of Agriculture, *Crop Production*, 1992.

a. If we assume that farmers in Illinois and Kansas use the same amount of labor, capital, and fertilizer, which state has an absolute advantage in wheat production? Soybean production?

b. If we transfer land out of wheat into soybeans, how many bushels of wheat do we give up in Illinois per additional bushel of soybeans produced? In Kansas?

c. Which state has a comparative advantage in wheat production? In soybean production?

The following table gives the distribution of land planted for each state in millions of acres in 1990:

	TOTAL ACRES UNDER TILL	WHEAT	SOYBEANS
Illinois	22.9	1.9 (8.3%)	9.1 (39.7%)
Kansas	20.7	11.8 (57.0%)	1.9 (9.2%)

Are these data consistent with your answer to part c? Explain.

5. The U.S. Congress ratified the North American Free-Trade Agreement (NAFTA) in September of 1993 by a very slim vote. The agreement took effect on January 1, 1994. The same Congress ratified the Final Act of the Uruguay Round of the General Agreement on Tariffs and Trade (GATT) in December 1994, and that agreement took effect on January 1, 1995. Both were ratified over very strong political opposition from lobby groups. Using newspaper articles and periodicals from the time, write a short report about the opposition to each of these agreements. Who opposed them? Can you offer an explanation for their opposition? What logic did the Congress rely on to vote in favor?

6. You can think of the United States as a set of 50 separate economies with no trade barriers. In such an open environment, each state specializes in the products that it produces best.

a. What product or products does your state specialize in?

b. Can you identify the source of the comparative advantage that lies behind the production of one or more of these products (a natural resource, plentiful cheap labor, a skilled labor force, etc.)?

c. Do you think that the theory of comparative advantage and the Heckscher-Ohlin theorem help to explain why your state specializes in the way that it does?

7. Germany and France produce white and red wines. Current domestic prices for each are given in the following table:

	GERMANY	FRANCE
White wine	5 DM	10 francs
Red wine	10 DM	15 francs

Suppose that the exchange rate is 1 deutsche mark = 1 franc.

a. If the price ratios within each country reflect resource use, which country has a comparative advantage in the production of red wine? White wine?

b. Assume there are no other trading partners and that the only motive for holding foreign currency is to buy foreign goods. Will the current exchange rate lead to trade flows in both directions between the two countries?

c. What adjustments might you expect in the exchange rate? Be specific.

d. What would you predict about trade flows between Germany and France in the long run?

8. The European Union (EU) is scheduled to remove all trade barriers within its member countries in the next 5 years. Its goal is to become one "common market" with one uniform currency. Explain the likely benefits and costs to the EU's member countries. Should the United States be concerned about the new common market? Why or why not?

TAKE IT TO THE NET

We invite you to visit the Case and Fair page on the Prentice Hall Web site:

http://www.prenhall.com/casefair

for this chapter's World Wide Web exercise.

Chapter 21

O PEN-ECONOMY MACROECONOMICS: THE BALANCE OF PAYMENTS AND EXCHANGE RATES

THE ECONOMIES OF THE WORLD have become increasingly interdependent over the last two decades. No economy operates in a vacuum, and economic events in one country can have repercussions on the economies of other countries.

International trade is a major part of today's world economy. U.S. imports now account for over 13 percent of U.S. GDP, and billions of dollars flow through the international capital market each day. In chapter 20 we explored the main reasons why there is international exchange. Countries trade with each other to obtain goods and services they cannot produce themselves or because other nations can produce goods and services at a lower cost than they can. You can see the various connections between the domestic economy and the rest of the world in Figure 6.2. Foreign countries supply goods and services, labor, and capital to the United States, and the United States supplies goods and services, labor, and capital to the rest of the world.

From a macroeconomic point of view, the main difference between an international transaction and a domestic transaction concerns currency exchange:

> When people in different countries buy from and sell to each other, an exchange of currencies must also take place.

French wine exporters cannot spend U.S. dollars in France—they need French francs. Nor can a U.S. wheat exporter use French francs to buy a tractor from a U.S. company or to pay the rent on her warehouse. Somehow, international exchange must be managed in a way that allows each partner in the transaction to wind up with his or her own currency.

REPRESENTATIVES OF THE 44 COUNTRIES THAT MET IN BRETTON WOODS, NEW HAMPSHIRE, IN 1944 TO ALLAY THE IMPENDING CHAOS IN THE INTERNATIONAL MONETARY SYSTEM AS WORLD WAR II WAS ENDING.

exchange rate *The price of one country's currency in terms of another country's currency; the ratio at which two currencies are traded for each other.*

As you know from chapter 20, the direction of trade between two countries depends on **exchange rates**—the price of one country's currency in terms of the other country's currency. If the German deutsche mark were very expensive, (making the dollar cheap), both Germans and Americans would buy from U.S. producers. If the deutsche mark were very cheap (making the U.S. dollar expensive), both Germans and Americans would buy from German producers. Within a certain range of exchange rates, trade flows in both directions, each country specializes in producing the goods in which it enjoys a comparative advantage, and trade is mutually beneficial.

Because exchange rates are a factor in determining the flow of international trade, the way they are determined is very important. Since the turn of the century, the world monetary system has been changed several times by international agreements and events. Early in the century, nearly all currencies were backed by gold. Their values were fixed in terms of a specific number of ounces of gold, which determined their values in international trading—exchange rates.

In 1944, with the international monetary system in chaos as the end of World War II drew near, a large group of experts unofficially representing 44 countries met in Bretton Woods, New Hampshire, and drew up a number of agreements. One of these agreements established a system of essentially fixed exchange rates under which each country agreed to intervene by buying and selling currencies in the foreign exchange market when necessary to maintain the agreed-upon value of its currency.

In 1971, most countries, including the United States, gave up trying to fix exchange rates formally and began allowing them to be determined essentially by supply and demand. For example, without government intervention in the marketplace, the price of British pounds in dollars is determined by the interaction of those who want to exchange dollars for pounds (those who "demand" pounds) and those who want to exchange pounds for dollars (those who "supply" pounds). If the quantity of pounds demanded exceeds the quantity of pounds supplied, the price of pounds will rise, just as the price of peanuts or paper clips would rise under similar circumstances. A more detailed discussion of the various monetary systems that have been in place since 1900 is in the appendix to this chapter.

In this chapter, we explore what has come to be called "open-economy macroeconomics" in more detail. First, we discuss the *balance of payments*—the record of a nation's transactions with the rest of the world. We then go on to consider how the analysis we presented in chapters 9 through 17 changes when we allow for the international exchange of goods, services, and capital.

THE BALANCE OF PAYMENTS

We sometimes lump all foreign currencies—Swiss francs, Japanese yen, Brazilian cruzeiros, and so forth—together as "foreign exchange." **Foreign exchange** is simply all currencies other than the domestic currency of a given country (in the case of the United States, the U.S. dollar). U.S. demand for foreign exchange arises because its citizens want to buy things whose prices are quoted in other currencies, such as Australian jewelry, vacations in France, and bonds or stocks issued by Sony Corporation of Japan. Whenever U.S. citizens make these purchases, Australians, French, and Japanese gain U.S. dollars, which, from their point of view, are foreign exchange.

But where does the *supply* of foreign exchange come from? Simple: The United States (actually, U.S. citizens or firms) earns foreign exchange when it sells products, services, or assets to another country. Just as France earns foreign exchange when U.S. tourists go to visit the Eiffel Tower, the United States earns foreign exchange (in this case, French francs) when French tourists come to the United States to visit the Statue of Liberty. Similarly, Saudi Arabian purchases of stock in General Motors or Colombian purchases of real estate in Miami increase the U.S. supply of foreign exchange.

The record of a country's transactions in goods, services, and assets with the rest of the world is its **balance of payments**. The balance of payments is also the record of a country's sources (supply) and uses (demand) of foreign exchange.[1]

THE CURRENT ACCOUNT

The balance of payments is divided up into two major accounts, the *current account* and the *capital account*. These are shown in Table 21.1, which provides data on the U.S. balance of payments for 1997. We begin with the current account.

The first item in the current account is U.S. trade in goods. This category includes exports of computer chips, potato chips, and Sting records and imports of Scotch whiskey, Japanese calculators, and Mexican oil. United States exports *earn* foreign exchange for the United States and are a credit (+) item on the current account. United States imports *use up* foreign exchange and are a debit (−) item. In 1997, the United States imported $206.2 billion more in goods than it exported.

Next in the current account is services. Like most other countries, the United States buys services from and sells services to other countries. For example, a U.S. firm shipping wheat to England might purchase insurance from a British insurance company. A Dutch flower grower may fly flowers to the United States aboard an American airliner. In the first case, the United States is importing services and therefore using up foreign exchange; in the second, it is selling services to foreigners and earning foreign exchange. In 1997, the United States exported $87.6 billion more in services than it imported.

The difference between a country's exports of goods and services and its imports of goods and services is its **balance of trade**. If exports of goods and services are less than imports of goods and services, a country has a **trade deficit**.

The third item concerns *investment income*. U.S. citizens hold foreign assets (stocks, bonds, and real assets like buildings and factories). Dividends, interest, rent, and profits paid to U.S. asset holders are a source of foreign exchange. Conversely, when foreigners earn dividends, interest, and profits on assets held in the United States,

foreign exchange *All currencies other than the domestic currency of a given country.*

balance of payments *The record of a country's transactions in goods, services, and assets with the rest of the world; also the record of a country's sources (supply) and uses (demand) of foreign exchange.*

balance of trade *A country's exports of goods and services minus its imports of goods and services.*

trade deficit *Occurs when a country's exports of goods and services are less than its imports of goods and services in a given period.*

---

[1] Bear in mind the distinction between the balance of payments and a balance sheet. A *balance sheet* for a firm or a country measures that entity's stock of assets and liabilities at a moment in time. The *balance of payments*, by contrast, measures *flows*, usually over a period of a month, a quarter, or a year. Despite its name, the balance of payments is *not* a balance sheet.

TABLE 21.1 UNITED STATES BALANCE OF PAYMENTS, 1997

ALL TRANSACTIONS THAT BRING FOREIGN EXCHANGE INTO THE UNITED STATES ARE CREDITED (+) TO THE CURRENT ACCOUNT; ALL TRANSACTIONS THAT CAUSE THE UNITED STATES TO LOSE FOREIGN EXCHANGE ARE DEBITED (−) TO THE CURRENT ACCOUNT.

CURRENT ACCOUNT

Goods exports	682.3
Goods imports	−888.5
(1) Net export of goods	−206.2
Exports of services	257.6
Imports of services	−170.0
(2) Net export of services	87.6
Income received on investments	242.4
Income payments on investments	−255.7
(3) Net investment income	−13.3
(4) Net transfer payments and other	−36.8
(5) Balance on current account (1 + 2 + 3 + 4)	−168.7

CAPITAL ACCOUNT

(6) Change in private U.S. assets abroad (increase is −)	−405.3
(7) Change in foreign private assets in the United States	588.2
(8) Change in U.S. government assets abroad (increase is −)	−1.0
(9) Change in foreign government assets in the United States	90.0
(10) Balance on capital account (6 + 7 + 8 + 9)	271.9
(11) Statistical discrepancy	−103.2
(12) Balance of Payments (5 + 10 + 11)	0

Source: U.S. Department of Commerce, *Survey of Current Business*, March 1998. Data are for the third quarter of 1997, seasonally adjusted at annual rates.

foreign exchange is used up. In 1997, investment income paid to foreigners exceeded investment income received from foreigners by $13.3 billion.

The fourth item in Table 21.1 is *net transfer payments and other.* Transfer payments from the United States to foreigners are another use of foreign exchange. Some of these transfer payments are from private U.S. citizens and some are from the U.S. government. You may send a check to your aunt in Spain or the government may send a social security check to a retiree living in Italy. Conversely, some foreigners make transfer payments to the United States. "Net" refers to the difference between payments from the United States to foreigners and payments from foreigners to the United States.

balance on current account
The balance of trade plus net exports of services, plus net investment income, plus the category "net transfer payments and other."

If we add the balance of trade, net export of services, net investment income, and net transfer payments and other,[2] we get the **balance on current account.** The balance on current account shows how much a nation has spent on foreign goods, services, investment income payments, and transfers relative to how much it has earned from other countries. When the balance is negative, which it was for the United States in 1997, a

---

[2]"Other" includes interest paid by the U.S. government to foreigners. Contrary to the treatment of private interest payments, government interest payments are not counted as income payments on investments. (This treatment is similar to that for government interest payments to domestic citizens, as discussed in chapter 7.) These payments are a use of funds, however, so they must be included in computing the balance on current account.

nation has spent more on foreign goods and services (plus investment income and transfers paid) than it has earned through the sales of its goods and services to the rest of the world (plus investment income and transfers received). If a nation has spent more on foreign goods, services, investment income payments, and transfers than it has earned, its net wealth position vis-à-vis the rest of the world must decrease. By "net" we mean a nation's assets abroad minus its liabilities to the rest of the world. The capital account of the balance of payments records the changes in these assets and liabilities. We now turn to the capital account.

THE CAPITAL ACCOUNT

For each transaction recorded in the current account, there is an offsetting transaction recorded in the capital account. Consider the purchase of a Japanese car by a U.S. citizen. Say that the yen/dollar exchange rate is 125 yen to a dollar, and the yen price of the car is 2.5 million yen, which is $20,000. The U.S. citizen (probably an automobile dealer) takes $20,000, buys 2.5 million yen, and then buys the car. In this case, U.S. imports are increased by $20,000 in the current account and foreign assets in the United States (in this case, Japanese holdings of dollars) are increased by $20,000 in the capital account. The net wealth position of the United States vis-à-vis the rest of the world has decreased by $20,000. The key point to realize is that an increase in U.S. imports results in an increase in foreign assets in the United States. The United States must "pay" for the imports, and whatever it pays with (in this example, U.S. dollars) is an increase in foreign assets in the United States. Conversely, an increase in U.S. exports results in an increase in U.S. assets abroad, because foreigners must pay for the U.S. exports.

Table 21.1 shows that U.S. assets abroad are divided into private holdings (line 6) and U.S. government holdings (line 8). Similarily, foreign assets in the United States are divided into foreign private (line 7) and foreign government (line 9). The sum of lines 6, 7, 8, and 9 is the **balance on capital account** (line 10). If there were no errors of measurement in the data collection, the balance on capital account would equal the negative of the balance on current account, because, as mentioned above, for each transaction in the current account there is an offsetting transaction in the capital account. Another way of looking at the balance on capital account is that it is the decrease in the net wealth position of the country vis-à-vis the rest of the world. If the balance on capital account is positive, this means that the change in foreign assets in the country is greater than the change in the country's assets abroad, which is a decrease in the net wealth position of the country.

Table 21.1 shows that in 1997 the U.S. balance on current account was −$168.7 billion, which means that the United States spent considerably more than it made vis-à-vis the rest of the world. If the balance on current account is measured correctly, then the net wealth position of the United States vis-à-vis the rest of the world decreased by $168.7 billion in 1997. In this case, the balance on capital account should be $168.7 billion. The balance on capital account (line 10) is in fact $271.9 billion, and so the error of measurement, called the statistical discrepancy, is $103.2 billion (line 11) in 1997. The balance of payments (line 12) is the sum of the balance on current account, the balance on capital account, and the statistical discrepancy. By construction, it is always zero.

It is important to note from Table 21.1 that even though the net wealth position of the United States decreased in 1997, the change in U.S. assets abroad increased considerably ($405.3 billion private and $1.0 billion government). How can this be? Because there was an even larger increase in foreign assets in the United States ($588.2 billion private and $90.0 billion government). It is the *net* change (i.e., the change in foreign assets in the United States minus the change in U.S. assets abroad)

FAST FACTS

During the second quarter of 1997, U.S. purchases on foreign stock exchanges were $13.9 billion and U.S. purchases of foreign bonds were $7.4 billion. During the same quarter foreign purchases of U.S. Treasury securities were $46 billion. Foreign purchases of U.S. stocks were $21.7 billion in the second quarter, a record.

Source: Survey of Current Business, October 1997.

balance on capital account
In the United States, the sum of the following (measured in a given period): the change in private U.S. assets abroad, the change in foreign private assets in the United States, the change in U.S. government assets abroad, and the change in foreign government assets in the United States.

that is equal to the negative of the balance on current account (aside from the statistical discrepancy), not the change in just U.S. assets abroad.

There are many transactions that get recorded in the capital account that do not pertain to the current account. Consider a purchase of a U.K. security by a U.S. citizen. This is done by the U.S. citizen selling dollars for pounds and using the pounds to buy the U.K. security. After this transaction, U.S. assets abroad have increased (the United States now holds more U.K. securities) and foreign assets in the United States have increased (foreigners now hold more dollars). The purchase of the U.K. security is recorded as a minus item in line 6 in Table 21.1, and the increase in foreign holdings of dollars is recorded as a plus item in line 7. These two balance out. This happens whenever there is a switch of one kind of asset for another vis-à-vis the rest of the world. When a Japanese company bought Rockefeller Center in New York City in 1990, this was an increase in foreign assets in the United States (the Japanese then owned Rockefeller Center) and an increase in U.S. assets abroad (the United States then had the yen that was used to pay for the Center). If the United States then took the yen and bought Japanese securities, this was simply a switch of one kind of U.S. asset abroad (yen) for another (Japanese securities).

THE UNITED STATES AS A DEBTOR NATION

If a country has positive net wealth position vis-à-vis the rest of the world, it can be said to be a creditor nation. Conversely, if it has negative net wealth position, it can be said to be a debtor nation. Remember that a country's net wealth position increases if it has a positive current account balance and decreases if it has a negative current account balance. It is important to realize that the *only* way a country's net wealth position can change is if its current account balance is nonzero. Simply switching one form of asset for another, such as switching Rockefeller Center for Japanese securities in the above example, is not a change in a country's net wealth position. Another way of putting this is that a country's net wealth position is the sum of all of its past current account balances.

Prior to the mid-1970s, the United States had generally run current account surpluses, and thus its net wealth position was positive. It was a creditor nation. This began to turn around in the mid-1970s, and by the mid-1980s, the United States was running large current account deficits. Some time during this period the United States changed from having a positive net wealth position vis-à-vis the rest of the world to having a negative position. In other words, the United States changed from a creditor nation to a debtor nation. The current account deficits persisted into the 1990s, and the United States is now the largest debtor nation in the world. In 1996, foreign assets in the United States totaled $5.1 trillion and U.S. assets abroad totaled $4.3 trillion. The U.S. net wealth position was thus −$0.8 trillion. This large negative position is the result of the United States having spent much more in the 1980s and 1990s on foreign goods and services (plus investment income and transfers paid) than it earned through the sales of its goods and services to the rest of the world (plus investment income and transfers received).

EQUILIBRIUM OUTPUT (INCOME) IN AN OPEN ECONOMY

Everything we have said so far has been descriptive. Now we turn to analysis. How are all these trade and capital flows determined? What impacts do they have on the economies of the countries involved? To simplify our discussion here, we will assume that exchange rates are fixed. We will relax this assumption later.

THE INTERNATIONAL SECTOR AND PLANNED AGGREGATE EXPENDITURE

Our earlier descriptions of the multiplier took into account the consumption behavior of households (C), the planned investment behavior of firms (I), and the spending of the government (G). We defined the sum of these three components as planned aggregate expenditure (AE).

To analyze the international sector, we must include the goods and services a country exports to the rest of the world, as well as what it imports. If we call our exports of goods and services EX, it should be clear that EX is a component of total output and income. A U.S. razor blade sold to a buyer in Mexico is as much a part of U.S. production as a similar blade sold in Pittsburgh. Exports simply represent demand for domestic products not by domestic households and firms and the government but by the rest of the world.

What about imports? Remember, imports are *not a part of domestic output* (Y). By definition, imports are not produced by the country that is importing them. Remember also, when we look at households' total consumption spending, firms' total investment spending, and total government spending, imports are included. Therefore, to calculate domestic output correctly, we must subtract the parts of consumption, investment, and government spending that constitute imports. The definition of planned aggregate expenditure becomes:

> Planned aggregate expenditure in an open economy:
>
> $$AE \equiv C + I + G + EX - IM$$

The last two terms $(EX - IM)$ together are the country's **net exports of goods and services**.

net exports of goods and services (EX − IM) *The difference between a country's total exports and total imports.*

▶ **Determining the Level of Imports** What determines the level of imports and exports in a country? For now, we assume that the level of imports is a function of income (Y). The rationale is simple: When U.S. income increases, U.S. citizens buy more of everything, including U.S. cars and peanut butter, Japanese TV sets, and Korean steel and videocassette recorders. When income rises, imports tend to go up. Algebraically,

$$IM = mY$$

where Y is income and m is some positive number.[3] Recall from chapter 9 that the marginal propensity to consume (MPC) measures the change in consumption that

---

FAST FACTS

Trade was a smaller part of U.S. output in the past. Here are estimates of annual GNP and exports over two historical decades:

Years	GNP	Exports	as % of GNP
	in billions of dollars		
1889–1898	12.73	.91	7.1%
1919–1928	81.20	5.26	6.4%

Source: Historical Statistics of the United States.

---

[3]*m* is assumed to be less than 1. Otherwise, a $1 increase in income generates an increase in imports of more than $1, which does not make sense.

marginal propensity to import (MPM) *The change in imports caused by a $1 change in income.*

results from a $1 change in income. Similarly, the **marginal propensity to import,** abbreviated as *MPM* or *m*, is the change in imports caused by a $1 change in income. If $m = 0.2$, or 20 percent, and income is $1,000, then imports, *IM*, are equal to $0.2 \times \$1,000 = \$200$. If income rises by $100 to $1,100, then the change in imports will equal $m \times$ (the change in income) $= 0.2 \times \$100 = \$20$.

For now we will assume that exports (EX) are given, i.e., that they are not affected, even indirectly, by the state of the economy. This assumption is relaxed later in this chapter.

> **Solving for Equilibrium**   Given the assumption about how imports are determined, we can solve for equilibrium income. This procedure is illustrated in Figure 21.1. Starting from the consumption function (blue line) in Figure 21.1a, we gradually build up the components of planned aggregate expenditure (brown line). Assuming for simplicity that planned investment, government purchases, and exports are all constant and do not depend on income, we move easily from the blue line to the brown line by adding the fixed amounts of *I*, *G*, and *EX* to consumption at every level of income. In this example, we take $I + G + EX$ to equal 80.

$C + I + G + EX$, however, includes spending on imports, which are not part of domestic production. To correct this, we must subtract the amount that is imported at each level of income. In Figure 21.1b, we assume $m = .25$, or 25 percent of total income is spent on goods and services produced in foreign countries. Imports are a constant fraction of total income; therefore at higher levels of income a larger amount is spent on foreign goods and services. For example, at $Y = 200$, $IM = .25Y$, or 50. Similarly, at $Y = 400$, $IM = .25Y$, or 100.

FIGURE 21.1

Determining Equilibrium Output in an Open Economy

In **a,** planned investment spending (*I*), government spending (*G*), and total exports (*EX*) are added to consumption (*C*) to arrive at planned aggregate expenditure. But $C + I + G + EX$ includes spending on imports because imports are part of planned aggregate expenditure. In **b,** the amount imported at every level of income is subtracted from planned aggregate expenditure. Equilibrium output occurs at $Y^* = 200$, the point at which planned domestic aggregate expenditure crosses the 45° line.

Remember that the AE function in Figure 21.1 must be planned aggregate expenditure on *domestically* produced goods and services. As income rises, some of the additional income is saved and the rest is spent. But not all of that added spending is on domestically produced goods and services. As income rises, some is saved and some is spent on imports. The brown dashed line in Figure 21.1b shows imports subtracted out of the AE function.

Equilibrium is reached when planned aggregate expenditure on domestic output equals aggregate domestic output (income). This is true at only one level of aggregate output, $Y^* = 200$, in Figure 21.1b. If Y were below Y^*, planned expenditure would exceed output, inventories would be lower than planned, and output would rise. At levels above Y^*, output would exceed planned expenditure, inventories would be larger than planned, and output would fall.

▶ **The Open-Economy Multiplier**   All of this has implications for the size of the multiplier. Recall the multiplier, introduced in chapter 9, and consider a sustained rise in government purchases (G). Initially, the increase in G will cause planned aggregate expenditure to be greater than aggregate output. Domestic firms will find their inventories to be lower than planned and thus will increase their output. But added output means more income. More workers are hired and profits are higher. Some of the added income is saved, and some is spent. The added consumption spending leads to a second round of inventories being lower than planned and raising output. Equilibrium output rises by a multiple of the initial increase in government purchases. This is the multiplier.

In chapters 9 and 10, we showed that the simple multiplier equals $1/(1 - MPC)$, or ($1/MPS$). That is, a sustained increase in government purchases equal to ΔG will lead to an increase in aggregate output (income) of $\Delta G[1/(1 - MPC)]$. If the MPC were .75 and government purchases rose by $10 billion, equilibrium income would rise by $4 \times \$10$ billion, or $40 billion. The multiplier is $[1/(1 - .75)] = [1/.25] = 4.0$.

In an open economy, some of the increase in income brought about by the increase in G is spent on imports rather than on domestically produced goods and services. The part of income spent on imports does not increase domestic income (Y) because imports are produced by foreigners. To compute the multiplier we need to know how much of the increased income is used to increase domestic consumption. (We are assuming all imports are consumption goods. In practice, some imports are investment goods and some are goods purchased by the government.) In other words, we need to know the marginal propensity to consume *domestic* goods. Domestic consumption is $C - IM$. So the marginal propensity to consume domestic goods is the marginal propensity to consume all goods (the MPC) minus the marginal propensity to import (the MPM). The marginal propensity to consume domestic goods is ($MPC - MPM$). Consequently,

$$\text{Open-economy multiplier} = \frac{1}{1 - (MPC - MPM)}$$

If the MPC is .75 and the MPM is .25, then the multiplier is $1/.5$, or 2.0. This multiplier is smaller than the multiplier in which imports are not taken into account, which is $1/.25$, or 4.0.

The message of the open-economy multiplier model, put succinctly:

The effect of a sustained increase in government spending (or investment) on income—that is, the multiplier—is smaller in an open economy than in a closed economy. The reason: When government spending (or investment) increases and income and consumption rise, some of the extra consumption spending that results is on foreign products and not on domestically produced goods and services.

THE DETERMINANTS OF IMPORTS AND EXPORTS

For simplicity, we have so far assumed that the level of imports depends only on income and that the level of exports is fixed. In reality the amount of spending on imports depends on factors other than income and exports are not fixed. We will now consider the more realistic picture.

▶ **The Determinants of Imports**   The same factors that affect households' consumption behavior and firms' investment behavior are likely to affect the demand for imports because some imported goods are consumption goods and some are investment goods. For example, anything that increases consumption spending is likely to increase the demand for imports. We saw in chapters 9 and 17 that such factors as the after-tax real wage, after-tax nonlabor income, and interest rates affect consumption spending, and so these should also affect spending on imports. Similarly, anything that increases investment spending is likely to increase the demand for imports. A decrease in interest rates, for example, should encourage spending on both domestically produced goods and foreign-produced goods.

There is one additional consideration in determining spending on imports: the *relative prices* of domestically produced and foreign-produced goods. If the prices of foreign goods fall relative to the prices of domestic goods, people will consume more foreign goods relative to domestic goods. When Japanese cars are cheap relative to U.S. cars, consumption of Japanese cars should be high, and vice versa.

▶ **The Determinants of Exports**   We now relax our assumption that exports are fixed. The demand for U.S. exports by other countries is identical to their demand for imports from the United States. Germany imports goods, some are U.S. produced. So do France, Spain, and so on. Total expenditure on imports in Germany is a function of the factors we have just discussed, except that the variables are German variables rather than U.S. variables. This is true for all other countries as well. The demand for U.S. exports depends on economic activity in the rest of the world—rest-of-the-world real wages, wealth, nonlabor income, interest rates, and so on—as well as on the prices of U.S. goods relative to the price of rest-of-the-world goods.

If foreign output increases, U.S. exports tend to increase. U.S. exports also tend to increase when U.S. prices fall relative to those in the rest of the world.

▶ **The Trade Feedback Effect**   We can now combine what we know about the demand for imports and the demand for exports to discuss the **trade feedback effect**. Suppose the United States finds its exports increasing, perhaps because the world suddenly decides it prefers U.S. computers to other computers. This will lead to an increase in U.S. output (income), which leads to an increase in U.S. imports. Here is where the trade feedback begins. Because U.S. imports are somebody else's exports, the extra import demand from the United States raises the exports of the rest of the world. When other countries' exports to the United States go up, their output and incomes also rise, which leads to an increase in the demand for imports from the rest of the world. Some of the extra imports demanded by the rest of the world come from the United States, so U.S. exports increase. The increase in U.S. exports stimulates U.S. economic activity even more, which leads to a further increase in the U.S. demand for imports, and so on.

> An increase in U.S. imports increases other countries' exports, which stimulates those countries' economies and increases their imports, which increases U.S. exports, which stimulates the U.S. economy and increases its imports, and so on. This is the trade feedback effect. In other words, an increase in U.S. economic activity leads to a worldwide increase in economic activity, which then "feeds back" to the United States.

trade feedback effect *The tendency for an increase in the economic activity of one country to lead to a worldwide increase in economic activity, which then feeds back to that country.*

> **Import and Export Prices**   We have talked about the price of imports, but we have not yet discussed the factors that influence import prices. The consideration of import prices is complicated because more than one currency is involved. When we talk about "the price of imports," do we mean the price in dollars, in francs, or in yen? And because the exports of one country are the imports of another, the same question holds for the price of exports. When France exports wine to the United States, French wine growers are interested in the price of wine in terms of francs, because francs are what they use for transactions in France. U.S. consumers are interested in the price of wine in dollars, because dollars are what they use for transactions in the United States. The link between the two prices is the dollar/franc exchange rate.

Suppose France is experiencing an inflation and the price of wine in French francs rises from 20 francs to 30 francs per bottle. France's export price for wine (in terms of francs) will in general go up by the same amount.[4] If the dollar/franc exchange rate remains unchanged at, say, $0.20 per franc, then France's export price for wine in terms of dollars will also rise, from $4 to $6 per bottle. Because France's exports to the United States are by definition U.S. imports from France, an increase in the dollar prices of French exports to the United States means an increase in the prices of U.S. imports from France. Therefore, when France's export prices rise with no change in the dollar/franc exchange rate, U.S. import prices rise. This holds for any country that trades with France.

> Export prices of other countries affect U.S. import prices.

A country's export prices tend to move fairly closely with the general price level in that country. If France is experiencing a general increase in prices, it is likely this change will be reflected in price increases of all domestically produced goods, both exportable and nonexportable.

> The general rate of inflation abroad is likely to affect U.S. import prices. If the inflation rate abroad is high, U.S. import prices are likely to rise.

> **The Price Feedback Effect**   We have just seen that when a country experiences an increase in domestic prices, the prices of its exports will increase. But it is also true that when the prices of a country's *imports* increase, the prices of domestic goods may increase in response. There are at least two ways this can occur.

First, an increase in the prices of imported inputs will shift a country's aggregate supply curve to the left. In chapter 14 we discussed the macroeconomy's response to a cost shock. Recall that a leftward shift in the aggregate supply curve due to a cost increase causes aggregate output to fall and prices to rise (stagflation).

Second, if import prices rise relative to domestic prices, households will tend to substitute domestically produced goods and services for imports. This is equivalent to a rightward shift of the aggregate demand curve. If the domestic economy is operating on the upward-sloping part of the aggregate supply curve, the overall domestic price level will rise in response to an increase in aggregate demand. Perfectly competitive firms will see market-determined prices rise, and imperfectly competitive firms will experience an increase in the demand for their products. Studies have shown, for example, that the price of automobiles produced in the United States moves closely with the price of imported cars.

---

[4]France's wine exporters could raise the export price but keep it less than the domestic price (to try to stay competitive with the rest of the world), but we ignore this possibility here.

Still, this is not the end of the story. Suppose a country—say, Germany—experiences an increase in its domestic price level. This will increase the price of its exports to France (and to all other countries). The increase in the price of French imports from Germany will lead to an increase in domestic prices in France. But France also exports to Germany. The increase in French prices causes an increase in the price of French exports to Germany, which then further increases the German price level.

price feedback effect
The process by which a domestic price increase in one country can "feed back" on itself through export and import prices. An increase in the price level in one country can drive up prices in other countries. This in turn further increases the price level in the first country.

This is called the **price feedback effect**, in the sense that inflation is "exportable." An increase in the price level in one country can drive up prices in other countries, which in turn further increases the price level in the first country. Through export and import prices, a domestic price increase can "feed back" on itself.

It is important to realize that the discussion so far has been based on the assumption of fixed exchange rates. Life is more complicated under flexible exchange rates, to which we now turn.

THE OPEN ECONOMY WITH FLEXIBLE EXCHANGE RATES

To a large extent, the fixed exchange rates set by the Bretton Woods agreements served as international monetary arrangements until 1971. Then, in 1971 the United States and most other countries decided to abandon the fixed exchange rate system in favor of **floating**, or **market-determined, exchange rates**. While governments still intervene to ensure that exchange rate movements are "orderly," exchange rates today are largely determined by the unregulated forces of supply and demand.

floating, or **market-determined, exchange rates** *Exchange rates that are determined by the unregulated forces of supply and demand.*

Understanding how an economy interacts with the rest of the world when exchange rates are not fixed is not as simple as when we assume fixed exchange rates. Exchange rates determine the price of imported goods relative to domestic goods and can have significant effects on the level of imports and exports. Consider a 20 percent drop in the value of the dollar against the deutsche mark. Dollars buy fewer marks and marks buy more dollars. Both Germans, who now get more dollars for marks, and U.S. citizens, who get fewer marks for dollars, find that U.S. goods and services are more attractive. Exchange rate movements have important impacts on imports, exports, and the movement of capital between countries.

THE MARKET FOR FOREIGN EXCHANGE

What determines exchange rates under a floating rate system? To explore this, we assume there are just two countries, the United States and Great Britain. It is easier to understand a world with only two countries, and most of the points we will make can be generalized to a world with many trading partners.

▶ **The Supply of and Demand for Pounds** Governments, private citizens, banks, and corporations exchange pounds for dollars and dollars for pounds every day. In our two-country case, those who *demand* pounds are holders of dollars seeking to exchange them for pounds. Those who *supply* pounds are holders of pounds seeking to exchange them for dollars. It is important not to confuse the supply of dollars (or pounds) on the foreign exchange market with the U.S. (or British) money supply. The latter is the sum of all the money currently in circulation. The supply of dollars on the foreign exchange market is the number of dollars that holders seek to exchange for pounds in a given time period. The demand for, and supply of, dollars on foreign exchange markets determines *exchange* rates; the demand for money balances and the total domestic money supply determine the *interest* rate.

The common reason for exchanging dollars for pounds is to buy something produced in Great Britain. U.S. importers who purchase Jaguar automobiles or

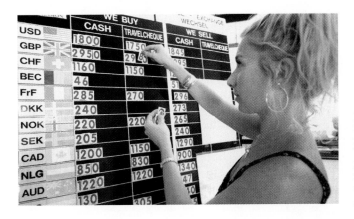

EXCHANGE RATES ARE POSTED DAILY AT BANKS AND OTHER FINANCIAL INSTITUTIONS. THEY ARE ALSO AVAILABLE IN NEWSPAPERS, FROM ELECTRONIC INFORMATION SERVICES, AND ON THE INTERNET.

Scotch whiskey must pay with pounds. U.S. citizens traveling in Great Britain who want to ride the train, stay in a hotel, or eat at a restaurant must acquire pounds for dollars to do so. If a U.S. corporation builds a plant in Great Britain, it must pay for that plant in pounds.

At the same time, some people may want to buy British stocks or bonds. Implicitly, when a U.S. citizen buys a bond issued by the British government or by a British corporation, he or she is making a loan, but the transaction requires a currency exchange. The British bond seller must ultimately be paid in pounds.

On the supply side of the market, the situation is reversed. Here we find people—usually British citizens—holding pounds they want to use to buy dollars. Again, the common reason is to buy things produced in the United States. If a British importer decides to import golf carts made in Georgia, the producer must be paid in dollars. British tourists visiting New York may ride in cabs, eat in restaurants, and tour Ellis Island. Doing these things requires dollars. When a British firm builds an office complex in Los Angeles, it must pay the contractor in dollars.

In addition to buyers and sellers who exchange money to engage in transactions, some people and institutions hold currency balances for speculative reasons. If I think the U.S. dollar is going to decline in value relative to the pound, I may want to hold some of my wealth in the form of pounds. Table 21.2 summarizes some of the major

TABLE 21.2 SOME PRIVATE BUYERS AND SELLERS IN INTERNATIONAL EXCHANGE MARKETS: UNITED STATES AND GREAT BRITAIN

THE DEMAND FOR POUNDS (SUPPLY OF DOLLARS)

1. Firms, households, or governments that import British goods into the United States or wish to buy British-made goods and services
2. U.S. citizens traveling in Great Britain
3. Holders of dollars who want to buy British stocks, bonds, or other financial instruments
4. U.S. companies that want to invest in Great Britain
5. Speculators who anticipate a decline in the value of the dollar relative to the pound

THE SUPPLY OF POUNDS (DEMAND FOR DOLLARS)

1. Firms, households, or governments that import U.S. goods into Great Britain or wish to buy U.S.-made goods and services
2. British citizens traveling in the United States
3. Holders of pounds who want to buy stocks, bonds, or other financial instruments in the United States
4. British companies that want to invest in the United States
5. Speculators who anticipate a rise in the value of the dollar relative to the pound

FIGURE 21.2

The Demand for Pounds in the Foreign Exchange Market

When the price of pounds falls, British-made goods and services appear less expensive to U.S. buyers. If British prices are constant, U.S. buyers will buy more British goods and services, and the quantity of pounds demanded will rise.

Price of pounds, dollars per pound ($/£)

D

0

Quantity of pounds, £

categories of private foreign exchange demanders and suppliers in the two-country case of the United States and Great Britain.

Figure 21.2 shows the demand curve for pounds in the foreign exchange market. When the price of pounds (the exchange rate) is lower, it takes fewer dollars to buy British goods and services, to build a plant in Liverpool, to travel to London, and so forth. Lower net prices (in dollars) should increase the demand for British-made products and encourage investment and travel in Great Britain. If prices (in pounds) in Britain do not change, an increase in the quantity of British goods and services demanded by foreigners will increase the quantity of pounds demanded. The demand-for-pounds curve in the foreign exchange market has a negative slope.

Figure 21.3 shows a supply curve for pounds in the foreign exchange market. At a higher exchange rate, each pound buys more dollars, making the price of U.S.-produced

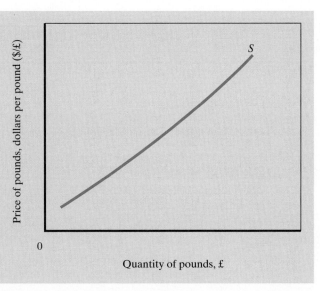

FIGURE 21.3

The Supply of Pounds in the Foreign Exchange Market

When the price of pounds rises, the British can obtain more dollars for each pound. This means that U.S.-made goods and services appear less expensive to British buyers. Thus, the quantity of pounds supplied is likely to rise with the exchange rate.

Price of pounds, dollars per pound ($/£)

S

0

Quantity of pounds, £

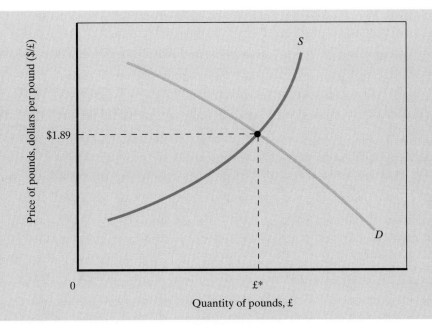

goods and services lower to the British. The British are more apt to buy U.S.-made goods when the price of pounds is high (the value of the dollar is low). An increase in British demand for U.S. goods and services is likely to increase the quantity of pounds supplied. The curve representing the supply of pounds in the foreign exchange market has a positive slope.

> **The Equilibrium Exchange Rate**   When exchange rates are allowed to float, they are determined the same way other prices are determined:

The equilibrium exchange rate occurs at the point at which the quantity demanded of a foreign currency equals the quantity of that currency supplied.

This is illustrated in Figure 21.4. An excess demand for pounds (quantity demanded in excess of quantity supplied) will cause the price of pounds to rise—the pound will **appreciate** with respect to the dollar. An excess supply of pounds will cause the price of pounds to fall—the pound will **depreciate** with respect to the dollar.[5]

appreciation of a currency
The rise in value of one currency relative to another.

depreciation of a currency
The fall in value of one currency relative to another.

---

[5]Although Figure 21.3 shows the supply-of-pounds curve in the foreign exchange market with a positive slope, under certain circumstances the curve may bend back. Suppose the price of a pound rises from $1.50 to $2.00. Consider a British importer who buys 10 Chevrolets each month at $15,000 each, including transportation costs. When a pound exchanges for $1.50, he will supply 100,000 pounds per month to the foreign exchange market—100,000 pounds brings $150,000, enough to buy 10 cars. Now suppose the cheaper dollar causes him to buy 12 cars. Twelve cars will cost a total of $180,000, but at $2.00 = 1 pound, he will spend only 90,000 pounds per month. The supply of pounds on the market falls when the price of pounds rises. The reason for this seeming paradox is simple. The number of pounds a British importer needs to buy U.S. goods depends on both the quantity of goods he buys and the price of those goods in pounds. If demand for imports is inelastic so that the percentage decrease in price resulting from the depreciated currency is greater than the percentage increase in the quantity of imports demanded, importers will spend fewer pounds and the quantity of pounds supplied in the foreign exchange market will fall. The supply of pounds will slope upward as long as the demand for U.S. imports is elastic.

FACTORS THAT AFFECT EXCHANGE RATES

We now know enough to discuss the factors likely to influence exchange rates. Anything that changes the behavior of the people in Table 21.2 can cause demand and supply curves to shift and the exchange rate to adjust accordingly.

> **Purchasing Power Parity: The Law of One Price**   If the costs of transporting goods between two countries are small, we would expect the price of the same good in both countries to be roughly the same. The price of basketballs should be roughly the same in Canada and the United States, for example.

It is not hard to see why. If the price of basketballs is cheaper in Canada, it will pay for someone to buy balls in Canada at a low price and sell them in the United States at a higher price. This decreases the supply and pushes up the price in Canada and increases the supply and pushes down the price in the United States. This process should continue as long as the price differential, and therefore the profit opportunity, persists. For a good with trivial transportation costs, we would expect this **law of one price** to hold. The price of a good should be the same regardless where we buy it.

If the law of one price held for all goods, and if each country consumed the same market basket of goods, the exchange rate between the two currencies would be determined simply by the relative price levels in the two countries. If the price of a basketball were $10 in the United States and $12 in Canada, then the U.S.-Canada exchange rate would have to be $1 U.S. per $1.20 Canadian. If the rate were instead one-to-one, it would pay people to buy the balls in the United States and sell them in Canada. This would increase the demand for U.S. dollars in Canada, thereby driving up their price in terms of Canadian dollars to one U.S. dollar per 1.2 Canadian dollars, at which point no one could make a profit shipping basketballs across international lines, and the process would cease.[6]

The theory that exchange rates are set so that the price of similar goods in different countries is the same is known as the **purchasing-power-parity theory**. According to this theory, if it takes five times as many French francs to buy a pound of salt in France as it takes U.S. dollars to buy a pound of salt in the United States, then the equilibrium exchange rate should be five francs per dollar.

In practice, transportation costs for many goods are quite large, and the law of one price does not hold for these goods. (Haircuts are often cited as a good example. The transportation costs for a U.S. resident to get a French haircut are indeed large unless that person is an airline pilot!) Also, many products that are potential substitutes for each other are not precisely identical. For instance, a Rolls Royce and a Mercedes Benz are both cars, but there is no reason to expect the exchange rate between the British pound and the deutsche mark to be set so that the prices of the two are equalized. In addition, countries consume different market baskets of goods, so we would not expect the aggregate price levels to follow the law of one price. Nevertheless,

> A high rate of inflation in one country relative to another puts pressure on the exchange rate between the two countries, and there is a general tendency for the currencies of relative high-inflation countries to depreciate.

law of one price *If the costs of transportation are small, the price of the same good in different countries should be roughly the same.*

purchasing-power-parity theory *A theory of international exchange holding that exchange rates are set so that the price of similar goods in different countries is the same.*

---

[6]Of course, if the rate were $1 U.S. to $2 Canadian, then it would pay people to buy basketballs in Canada (at $12 Canadian, or $6 U.S.) and sell them in the United States. This would weaken demand for the U.S. dollar, and its price would fall from $2 Canadian until it reached $1.20 Canadian.

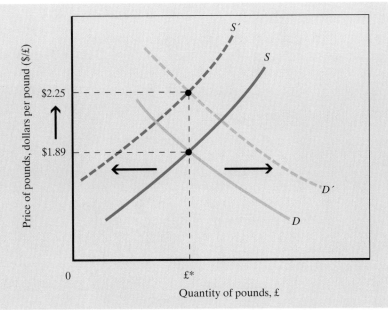

FIGURE 21.5

Exchange Rates Respond to
Changes in Relative Prices

The higher price level in the
United States makes imports
relatively less expensive. U.S.
citizens are likely to increase their
spending on imports from Britain,
shifting the demand for pounds to
the right, from D to D'. At the
same time, the British see U.S.
goods getting more expensive and
reduce their demand for exports
from the United States. The
supply of pounds shifts to the left,
from S to S'. The result is an
increase in the price of pounds.
The pound appreciates and the
dollar is worth less.

Figure 21.5 shows the adjustments likely to occur following an increase in the U.S.
price level relative to the price level in Great Britain. This change in relative prices will
affect citizens of both countries. Higher prices in the United States make imports relatively less expensive. U.S. citizens are likely to increase their spending on imports from
Britain, shifting the demand for pounds to the right, from D to D'. At the same time, the
British see U.S. goods getting more expensive and reduce their demand for exports from
the United States. Consequently, the supply of pounds shifts to the left, from S to S'. The
result is an increase in the price of pounds. Before the change in relative prices, 1 pound
sold for $1.89; after the change, 1 pound costs $2.25. The pound appreciates and the
dollar is worth less.

➤ **Relative Interest Rates**   Another factor that influences a country's exchange rate is
the level of its interest rate relative to other countries' interest rates. If the interest rate
is 7 percent in the United States and 9 percent in Germany, people with money to lend
have an incentive to buy German securities rather than U.S. securities. Although it is
sometimes difficult for individuals in one country to buy securities in another country,
it is easy for international banks and investment companies to do so. If the interest rate
is lower in the United States than in Germany, there will be a movement of funds out of
U.S. securities into German securities as banks and firms move their funds to the
higher-yielding securities.

How does a U.S. bank buy German securities? It takes its dollars, buys German
deutsche marks, and uses the marks to buy the German securities. The bank's purchase
of marks drives up the price of marks in the foreign exchange market. The increased
demand for marks increases the price of the mark (and decreases the price of the dollar). A high interest rate in Germany relative to the interest rate in the United States
tends to depreciate the dollar.

Figure 21.6 shows the effect of rising interest rates in the United States on the
pound-dollar exchange rate. Higher interest rates in the United States attract British investors. To buy U.S. securities, the British need dollars. The supply of pounds (the demand for dollars) shifts to the right, from S to S'. The same relative interest rates affect

If all goes as planned, on January 1, 1999, a number of European countries, including France, Germany and Italy, will shift to a common currency—called the "Euro"—with other countries to follow later. A common currency is yet another step on the long road to a unified European economy, as agreed to in the Maastricht Treaty signed in 1992. Already, steps have been taken to free the movement of goods and workers across borders in Europe. You no longer need a passport to travel from France to Germany, for example. The goal is to achieve the kind of smooth flow of resources that occurs across state lines in the United States. Can you imagine driving across the United States and having to show your passport and change currency at every state line? It certainly would be more difficult to run a multistate business.

One of the stumbling points in the negotiations that led to the European Monetary Union (EMU) was the fact that countries participating in the common currency will no longer be able to exercise independent monetary policy. This argument played a role in Britain's choice not to be among the first group to convert to a common currency. In June of 1998, the countries finally chosen to participate will form a European Central Bank that will regulate the supply of Euros and determine the common monetary policy of the EMU. There will be one common interest rate and bond market.

The fact that countries were giving up the freedom to exercise independent monetary policy continued to be a sensitive issue right into 1998. In February, a large group of economists signed a petition urging German Chancellor Helmut Kohl to delay the implementation of the EMU because of the very high unemployment rate in Germany—close to 12 percent. Kohl, however, the strongest proponent of the EMU in Europe, was unmoved, arguing there was no turning back.

The following was the timetable for the first group of member countries:

TIME LINE FOR INTRODUCING THE EURO

May 1–8, 1998—Participating member states chosen and bilateral exchange rates announced

June 1, 1998—European Central Bank established

Dec. 31, 1998—"Conversion weekend"

Jan. 1, 1999—Economic and monetary union (EMU) begins; irrevocable conversion rates established; the Euro becomes legal currency; single monetary policy starts

Jan. 4, 1999—The markets reopen

1999–2001—National notes and coins remain legal tender

Jan. 1, 2002—Introduction of Euro notes and coins; mass changeover of retail activity to Euro

Jan. 1–June 30, 2002—Maximum dual legal-tender period

June 30, 2002—Latest date for withdrawal of legal-tender status from national currency

Source: From Craig R. Whitney, "Ready or Not, Europe Draws Closer to One Currency," *The New York Times*, January 5, 1998.

For more on this subject matter, see the Case and Fair Web page at
http://www.prenhall.com/casefair.

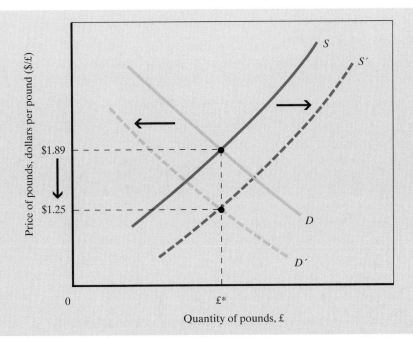

FIGURE 21.6

Exchange Rates Respond to Changes in Relative Interest Rates

If U.S. interest rates rise relative to British interest rates, British citizens holding pounds may be attracted into the U.S. securities market. To buy bonds in the United States, British buyers must exchange pounds for dollars. The supply of pounds shifts to the right, from S to S'. But U.S. citizens are less likely to be interested in British securities, because interest rates are higher at home. The demand for pounds shifts to the left, from D to D'. The result is a depreciated pound and a stronger dollar.

the portfolio choices of U.S. banks, firms, and households. With higher interest rates at home, there is less incentive for U.S. residents to buy British securities. The demand for pounds drops at the same time as the supply increases and the demand curve shifts to the left, from D to D'. The net result is a depreciating pound and an appreciating dollar. The price of pounds falls from $1.89 to $1.25.

THE EFFECTS OF EXCHANGE RATES ON THE ECONOMY

We are now ready to discuss some of the implications of floating exchange rates. Recall, when exchange rates are fixed, households spend some of their incomes on imports and the multiplier is smaller than it would otherwise be. Imports are a "leakage" from the circular flow, much like taxes and saving. Exports, in contrast, are like investment and government purchases; they represent spending on U.S.-produced goods and services ("injections" into the circular flow) and can stimulate output.

The world is far more complicated when exchange rates are allowed to float. First, the level of imports and exports depends on exchange rates as well as on income and other factors. When events cause exchange rates to adjust, the levels of imports and exports will change. Changes in exports and imports can in turn affect the level of real GDP and the price level. Further, exchange rates themselves also adjust to changes in the economy. Suppose the government decides to stimulate the economy with an expansionary monetary policy. This will affect interest rates, which may affect exchange rates.

➤ **Exchange Rate Effects on Imports, Exports, and Real GDP**   As we already know, when a country's currency depreciates (falls in value), its import prices rise and its export prices (in foreign currencies) fall. When the U.S. dollar is cheap, U.S. products are more competitive with products produced in the rest of the world, and foreign-made goods look expensive to U.S. citizens.

FIGURE 21.7

The Effect of a Depreciation on the Balance of Trade (the J Curve)

Initially, a depreciation of a country's currency may worsen its balance of trade. The negative effect on the price of imports may initially dominate the positive effects of an increase in exports and a decrease in imports.

A depreciation of a country's currency can serve as a stimulus to the economy. Suppose the U.S. dollar falls in value, as it did sharply between 1985 and 1988. If foreign buyers increase their spending on U.S. goods, and domestic buyers substitute U.S.-made goods for imports, aggregate expenditure on domestic output will rise, inventories will fall, and real GDP (Y) will increase.

> A depreciation of a country's currency is likely to increase its GDP.[7]

▶ **Exchange Rates and the Balance of Trade: The J Curve** Because a depreciating currency tends to increase exports and decrease imports, you might think it will also reduce a country's trade deficit. In fact, the effect of a depreciation on the balance of trade is ambiguous.

Many economists believe when a currency starts to depreciate, the balance of trade is likely to worsen for the first few quarters (perhaps three to six). After that, the balance of trade may improve. This effect is graphed in Figure 21.7. The curve in this figure resembles the letter J, and the movement in the balance of trade that it describes is sometimes called the **J-curve effect**. The point of the J shape is that the balance of trade gets worse before it gets better following a currency depreciation.

J-curve effect *Following a currency depreciation, a country's balance of trade may get worse before it gets better. The graph showing this effect is shaped like the letter J, hence the name "J-curve effect."*

How does the J curve come about? Recall that the balance of trade is equal to export revenue minus import costs, including exports and imports of services:

$$\text{Balance of trade} = \text{Dollar price of exports} \times \text{Quantity of Exports}$$
$$- \text{Dollar price of imports} \times \text{Quantity of Imports}.$$

---

[7]For this reason, some counties are tempted at times to intervene in foreign exchange markets, depreciate their currencies, and stimulate their economies. If all countries attempted to lower the value of their currencies simultaneously, there will be no gain in income for any of them. Although the exchange rate system at the time was different, such a situation actually occurred during the early years of the Great Depression. So-called *Beggar-thy-neighbor* policies of competitive devaluations were practiced by many countries in a desperate attempt to maintain export sales and employment.

THE IMF'S RESPONSE TO CRISES

In 1997 and 1998, there were severe economic problems in a number of Asian countries including Malaysia, Thailand, the Philippines, South Korea, and Indonesia. In each case, there was eventually a sharp depreciation of the country's currency, just like there was for Mexico in 1994 and 1995. Also, in each case, the International Monetary fund (IMF) stepped in to loan money to the country to help get it through the crisis. In many cases, the conditions imposed by the IMF for these loans were harsh, and a number of economists have criticized the IMF for doing more harm than good. The following article from *The New York Times* summarizes the IMF's response to three cases: Mexico, Indonesia, and South Korea.

MEXICO, 1994–95

SYMPTOMS *Collapse of the peso amid rampant imports, dwindling foreign reserves and high inflation in an overheated economy.*

PRESCRIPTION *Austerity, including a clampdown on credit and wages, in exchange for loans and guarantees led by the United States and backed up by the IMF and other institutions.*

CONSEQUENCES *Widespread bankruptcies. Huge job losses. Increased income inequality, poverty and social strife. But the peso stabilized relatively quickly, and within months Mexico regained the trust of foreign lenders.*

INDONESIA, 1997–98

SYMPTOMS *Collapse of the rupiah amid an explosion of foreign debt and a sharp stock market slide.*

PRESCRIPTION *Austerity and economic restructuring—including an end to special deals for businesses linked to President Suharto's family, the forced breakup of monopolies, the closing of failing banks and tight spending limits—in exchange for billions from the IMF, the United States and other industrial nations.*

CONSEQUENCES *Remain to be seen. Analysts expect inflation, unemployment and bankruptcies to skyrocket. The military stands ready to put down social unrest as political opposition begins to emerge. The IMF projects a stagnant economy this year, but*

renewed growth in 1999. Meanwhile, the rupiah continues to fall.

SOUTH KOREA, 1997–98

SYMPTOMS *Collapse of the won and stock market under staggering foreign debt in a sheltered economy built on crony capitalism.*

PRESCRIPTION *Austerity and economic restructuring—including deep cuts in public spending, tight credit, markets thrown open to imports and foreign investment and the removal of government props for bloated conglomerates—in return for the biggest IMF-led bailout ever.*

CONSEQUENCES *Remain to be seen. Growth in screeching to a halt, and analysts expect a boom in unemployment and bankruptcies. Social unrest remains possible, but the stock market has rebounded and the won has steadied.*

Source: David E. Sanger and Richard W. Stevenson, "Second-Guessing the Economic Doctor," *The New York Times*, February 1, 1998.

For more on this subject matter, see the Case and Fair Web page at
http://www.prenhall.com/casefair.

A currency depreciation affects the items on the right side of this equation as follows. First, the quantity of exports increases and the quantity of imports decreases; both have a *positive* effect on the balance of trade (lowering the trade deficit or raising the trade surplus). Second, the dollar price of exports is not likely to change very much, at least not initially. The dollar price of exports changes when the U.S. price level changes, but the initial effect of a depreciation on the domestic price level is not likely to be large. Third, the dollar price of imports increases. Imports into the United States are more expensive, because one dollar buys fewer French francs and German deutsche marks than before. An increase in the dollar price of imports has a *negative* effect on the balance of trade.

An example to clarify this last point: The dollar price of a Japanese car that costs 2,000,000 yen rises from $10,000 to $15,000 when the exchange rate moves from 200 yen per dollar to 133 yen per dollar. After the currency depreciation, the United States ends up spending more (in dollars) for the Japanese car than it did before. Of course, the United States will end up buying fewer Japanese cars than it did before. But does the number of cars drop enough so the quantity effect is bigger than the price effect, or vice versa? Does the value of imports increase or decrease?

The net effect of a depreciation on the balance of trade could go either way. The depreciation stimulates exports and cuts back imports, but it also increases the dollar price of imports. It seems that the negative effect dominates initially. The impact of a depreciation on the price of imports is generally felt quickly, while it takes time for export and import quantities to respond to price changes. In the short run, the value of imports increases more than the value of exports, so the balance of trade worsens. The initial effect is likely to be negative; but after exports and imports have had time to respond, the net effect turns positive. The more elastic the demand for exports and imports, the larger the eventual improvement in the balance of trade.

▶ **Exchange Rates and Prices**   The depreciation of a country's currency tends to increase its price level. There are two reasons for this. First, when a country's currency is less expensive, its products are more competitive on world markets, so exports rise. In addition, domestic buyers tend to substitute domestic products for the now-more-expensive imports. This means planned aggregate expenditure on domestically produced goods and services rises, and the aggregate demand curve shifts to the right. The result is a higher price level, higher output, or both. (You may want to draw an *AS/AD* diagram to verify this.) If the economy is close to capacity, the result is likely to be higher prices. Second, a depreciation makes imported inputs more expensive. If costs increase, the aggregate supply curve shifts to the left. If aggregate demand remains unchanged, the result is an increase in the price level.

▶ **Monetary Policy with Flexible Exchange Rates**   Let's now put everything in this chapter together and consider what happens when monetary policy is used first to stimulate the economy and then to contract the economy.

Suppose the economy is below full employment and the Fed decides to expand the money supply. The volume of reserves in the system is expanded, perhaps through open market purchases of U.S. government securities by the Fed. This results in a decrease in the interest rate. The lower interest rate stimulates planned investment spending and consumption spending.

This added spending causes inventories to be lower than planned and aggregate output (income) (Y) to rise. But there are two additional effects. One, the lower interest rate has an impact in the foreign exchange market. A lower interest rate means a lower demand for U.S. securities by foreigners, so the demand for dollars drops. Two, U.S. investment managers will be more likely to buy foreign securities (which are now paying relatively higher interest rates), so the supply of dollars rises. Both events push down the value of the dollar.

A cheaper dollar is a good thing if the goal of the monetary expansion is to stimulate the domestic economy, because a cheaper dollar means more U.S. exports and fewer imports. If consumers substitute U.S.-made goods for imports, both the added exports and the decrease in imports mean more spending on domestic products, so the multiplier actually increases.

Now suppose inflation is a problem and the Fed wants to slow it down with tight money. Here again, floating exchange rates help. Tight monetary policy works through a higher interest rate. A higher interest rate lowers investment and consumption spending, reducing aggregate expenditure, reducing output, and lowering the price level. The higher interest rate also attracts foreign buyers into U.S. financial markets, driving up the value of the dollar, which reduces the price of imports. The reduction in the price of imports shifts the aggregate supply curve to the right, which helps fight inflation.

▶ **Fiscal Policy with Flexible Exchange Rates**   The openness of the economy and flexible exchange rates do not always work to the advantage of policy makers. Consider a policy of cutting taxes to stimulate the economy. Suppose Congress enacts a major tax cut designed to raise output. Spending by households rises, but not all of this added spending is on domestic products—some leaks out of the U.S. economy, reducing the multiplier.

As income rises, so does the demand for money (M^d)—not the demand for dollars in the foreign exchange market, but the amount of money people desire to hold for transactions. Unless the Fed is fully accommodating, the interest rate will rise. A higher interest rate tends to attract foreign demand for U.S. securities. This tends to drive the price of the dollar up, which further blunts the effectiveness of the tax cut. If the value of the dollar rises, U.S. exports are less competitive in world markets, and the quantity of exports will decline. Similarly, a strong dollar makes imported goods look cheaper, and U.S. citizens spend more on foreign goods and less on U.S. goods, again reducing the multiplier.

Another caveat to the multiplier story of chapters 9 and 10: Without a fully accommodating Fed, three factors work to reduce the multiplier: (1) A higher interest rate from the increase in money demand may crowd out private investment and consumption; (2) some of the increase in income from the expansion will be spent on imports; and (3) a higher interest rate may cause the dollar to appreciate, discouraging exports and further encouraging imports.

AN INTERDEPENDENT WORLD ECONOMY

The increasing interdependence of countries in the world economy has made the problems facing policy makers more difficult. We used to be able to think of the United States as a relatively self-sufficient region. Thirty years ago, economic events outside U.S. borders had relatively little effect on its economy. This is no longer true. The events of the past three decades have taught us that the United States is a part of a global economy and the performance of the U.S. economy is heavily dependent on events outside its borders.

This chapter and the previous one have provided only the bare bones of open-market macroeconomics. If you continue your study of economics, more will be added to the basic story we have presented.

Keeping us in the international arena, chapter 22 deals with the problems of developing countries, and chapter 23 explores special features of the economies of the former republics of the Soviet Union and some other nations.

SUMMARY

1. The main difference between an international transaction and a domestic transaction concerns currency exchange: When people in different countries buy from and sell to each other, an exchange of currencies must also take place.

2. The *exchange rate* is the price of one country's currency in terms of another country's currency.

THE BALANCE OF PAYMENTS

3. *Foreign exchange* is all currencies other than the domestic currency of a given country. The record of a nation's transactions in goods, services, and assets with the rest of the world is its *balance of payments*. The balance of payments is also the record of a country's sources (supply) and uses (demand) of foreign exchange.

EQUILIBRIUM OUTPUT (INCOME) IN AN OPEN ECONOMY

4. In an open economy, some income is spent on foreign-produced goods rather than domestically produced goods. To measure planned aggregate expenditure in an open economy, we add total exports but subtract total imports: $AE \equiv C + I + G + EX - IM$. The open economy is in equilibrium when aggregate output (income) (Y) equals planned aggregate expenditure (AE).

5. In an open economy, the multiplier equals $1/[1 - (MPC - MPM)]$, where MPC is the marginal propensity to consume and MPM is the marginal propensity to import. The *marginal propensity to import* is the change in imports caused by a \$1 change in income.

6. In addition to income, other factors that affect the level of imports are the after-tax real wage rate, after-tax nonlabor income, interest rates, and the relative prices of domestically produced and foreign-produced goods. The demand for exports is determined by economic activity in the rest of the world and by relative prices.

7. An increase in U.S. economic activity leads to a worldwide increase in economic activity, which then "feeds back" to the United States. An increase in U.S. imports increases other countries' exports, which stimulates economies and increases their imports, which increases U.S. exports, which stimulates the U.S. economy and increases its imports, and so on. This is the *trade feedback effect*.

8. Export prices of other countries affect U.S. import prices. The general rate of inflation abroad is likely to affect U.S. import prices. If the inflation rate abroad is high, U.S. import prices are likely to rise.

9. Because one country's exports are another country's imports, an increase in export prices increases other countries' import prices. An increase in other countries' import prices leads to an increase in their domestic prices—and their export prices. In short, export prices affect import prices, and vice versa. This *price feedback effect* shows that inflation is "exportable"; an increase in the price level in one country can drive up prices in other countries, making inflation in the first country worse.

THE OPEN ECONOMY WITH FLEXIBLE EXCHANGE RATES

10. The equilibrium exchange rate occurs when the quantity demanded of a foreign currency in the foreign exchange market equals the quantity of that currency supplied in the foreign exchange market.

11. *Depreciation of a currency* occurs when a nation's currency falls in value relative to another country's currency. *Appreciation of a currency* occurs when a nation's currency rises in value relative to another country's currency.

12. According to the *law of one price*, if the costs of transportation are small, the price of the same good in different countries should be roughly the same. The theory that exchange rates are set so that the price of similar goods in different countries is the same is known as *purchasing-power-parity theory*. In practice, transportation costs are significant for many goods, and the law of one price does not hold for these goods.

13. A high rate of inflation in one country relative to another puts pressure on the exchange rate between the two countries. There is a general tendency for the currencies of relatively high-inflation countries to depreciate.

14. A depreciation of the dollar tends to increase U.S. GDP by making U.S. exports cheaper (hence more competitive abroad) and by making U.S. imports more expensive (encouraging consumers to switch to domestically produced goods and services).

15. The effect of a depreciation of a nation's currency on its balance of trade is unclear. In the short run, a currency depreciation may increase the balance-of-trade deficit, because it raises the price of imports. Although this price increase causes a decrease in the quantity of imports demanded, the impact of a depreciation on the price of imports is generally felt quickly, but it takes time for export and import quantities to respond to price changes. The initial effect is likely to be negative; but after exports and imports have had time to respond, the net effect turns positive. The tendency for the balance-of-trade deficit to widen and then to decrease as the result of a currency depreciation is known as the *J-curve effect*.

16. The depreciation of a country's currency tends to raise its price level for two reasons. First, a currency depreciation increases planned aggregate expenditure, which shifts the aggregate demand curve to the right. If the economy is close to capacity, the result is likely to be higher prices. Second, a depreciation makes imported inputs more expensive. If costs increase, the aggregate supply curve shifts to the left. If aggregate demand remains unchanged, the result is an increase in the price level.

17. When exchange rates are flexible, a U.S. expansionary monetary policy decreases the interest rate and stimulates planned investment and consumption spending. The lower interest rate leads to a lower demand for U.S. securities by foreigners, and a higher demand for foreign securities by U.S. investment-fund managers. As a result, the dollar depreciates. A U.S. contractionary monetary policy appreciates the dollar.

18. Flexible exchange rates do not always work to the advantage of policy makers. An expansionary fiscal policy can appreciate the dollar and work to reduce the multiplier.

REVIEW TERMS AND CONCEPTS

appreciation of a currency, 463

balance of payments, 451

balance of trade, 451

balance on capital account, 453

balance on current account, 453

depreciation of a currency, 463

exchange rate, 450

floating, or market-determined, exchange rates, 460

foreign exchange, 451

J-curve effect, 469

law of one price, 464

marginal propensity to import (*MPM*), 456

net exports of goods and services (*EX − IM*), 455

price feedback effect, 460

purchasing-power-parity theory, 464

trade deficit, 452

trade feedback effect, 458

Planned aggregate expenditure in an open economy:

$$AE \equiv C + I + G + EX - IM$$

Open-economy multiplier:

$$\frac{1}{1 - (MPC - MPM)}$$

PROBLEM SET

1. During 1997, a series of events rocked the economies of Asia. Describe the effects of each event if they had occurred at separate times on: the exchange rate of the U.S. dollar versus the Japanese yen; and the balance of trade between the United States and Japan.
   a. U.S. holders of Japanese stocks and bonds get spooked and sell their holdings, reinvesting the proceeds in U.S. stock and bond markets.
   b. Japan finds itself in recession with GDP falling sharply.
   c. The Japanese Ministry of Finance decides to balance the budget and to counteract the contractionary effects by expansionary monetary policy, pushing interest rates to under 1 percent.

2. Suppose the following prevailed on the foreign exchange market in 1998 with floating exchange rates:
   a. Name three phenomena that might shift the demand curve to the right.

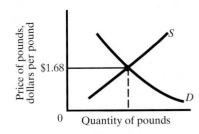

b. Which, if any, of these three might cause a simultaneous shift of the supply curve to the left?
   c. What effects might the three phenomena have on the balance of trade if the exchange rate floats?

3. Explain how each of the following transactions would be treated in the U.S. balance of payments account. (Remember that there are two entries per transaction.)

a. You vacation in Mexico, spending $300 there on a hotel room, food, transportation, and so on.

b. You bring back an Oriental carpet that you bought in the Middle East. The carpet is worth $10,000, but you do not declare it at customs, and no official record of the transaction exists.

c. You buy a new Toyota (made in Japan) for $15,000.

d. You send your cousin in Canada a birthday present worth $50.

e. Volkswagen Inc. of Germany buys a factory in the United States for $100 million.

f. Toyota of Japan buys 10 percent of all the shares in General Motors.

g. You loan your uncle in Canada $5,000.

h. Your uncle pays you $500 in interest on the money you previously loaned him. He also repays $1,000 of the principal.

4. During 1981 and 1982, the president and the Congress were pursuing a very expansionary *fiscal* policy. In 1980 and 1981, the Federal Reserve was pursuing a very restrictive *monetary* policy in an attempt to rid the economy of inflation. Ultimately, the economy went into a deep recession, but before it did interest rates went to record levels with the prime rate topping out at over 21 percent.

a. Explain how this policy mix led to very high interest rates.

b. Show graphically the effect of the high interest rates on the foreign exchange market. What do you think would happen to the value of the dollar under these circumstances?

c. What impact was such a series of events likely to have on the trade balance in countries like Japan? Explain your answer.

5. The exchange rate between the U.S. dollar and the Japanese yen is floating freely—neither government intervenes in the market for either currency. Suppose a large trade deficit with Japan prompts the United States to impose quotas on certain Japanese products imported into the United States and, as a result, the quantity of these imports falls.

a. The decrease in spending on Japanese products increases spending on U.S.-made goods. Why? What effect will this have on U.S. output and employment? On Japanese output and employment?

b. What happens to U.S. imports from Japan when U.S. output (or income) rises? If the quotas initially reduce imports from Japan by $25 billion, why is the final reduction in imports likely to be less than $25 billion? Explain in terms of the trade feedback effect.

c. Suppose the quotas do succeed in reducing imports from Japan by $15 billion. What will happen to the demand for yen? Why?

d. What will happen to the dollar-yen exchange rate, and why? (*Hint:* There is an excess supply of yen, or an excess demand for dollars.) What effects will the change

in the value of each currency have on employment and output in the United States? What about the balance of trade? (Ignore complications such as the J curve.)

e. Considering the macroeconomic effects of a quota on Japanese imports, could a quota actually reduce employment and output in the United States, or have no effect at all? Explain.

6. What effect will each of the following events have on the current account balance and the exchange rate if the exchange rate is fixed? If it is floating?

a. The U.S. government cuts taxes, and income rises.

b. The U.S. inflation rate increases, and prices in the United States rise faster than those in the countries with which the United States trades.

c. The United States adopts an expansionary monetary policy. Interest rates fall (and are now lower than those in other countries), and income rises.

d. Textile companies' "Buy American" campaign is successful, and U.S. consumers switch from purchasing imported products to those made in the United States.

*7. You are given the following model, which describes the economy of Hypothetica.

(1) Consumption function: $C = 100 + .8Y_d$

(2) Planned investment: $I = 38$

(3) Government spending: $G = 75$

(4) Exports: $EX = 25$

(5) Imports: $IM = .05Y_d$

(6) Disposable income: $Y_d \equiv Y - T$

(7) Taxes: $T = 40$

(8) Planned aggregate expenditure:
$AE \equiv C + I + G + (EX - IM)$

(9) Definition of equilibrium income: $Y = AE$.

a. What is equilibrium income in Hypothetica? What is the government deficit? What is the current account balance?

b. If government spending is increased to $G = 80$, what happens to equilibrium income? Explain, using the government spending multiplier. What happens to imports?

Now suppose the amount of imports is limited to $IM = 40$ by a quota on imports. If government spending is again increased from 75 to 80, what happens to equilibrium income? Explain why the same increase in G has a bigger effect on income in the second case. What is it about the presence of imports that changes the value of the multiplier?

c. If exports are fixed at $EX = 25$, what must income be to ensure a current account balance of zero? (*Hint:* Imports depend on income, so what must income be for imports to be equal to exports?) By how much must we cut government spending to balance the current account? (*Hint:* Use your answer to the first part of this question to determine how much of a decrease in income is needed. Then use the multiplier to calculate the decrease in G needed to reduce income by that amount.)

8. The following table shows that over the course of a decade, the U.S. dollar has remained virtually constant against the British pound. In the same time frame, the dollar fell dramatically against the yen; the price of yen rose 160 percent between 1983 and 1995. Explain why this might be so.

	MAY 1983	MARCH 1995
Pound sterling	$1.56	$1.58
Yen	.0042	.0111

TAKE IT TO THE NET

We invite you to visit the Case and Fair page on the Prentice Hall Web site:

http://www.prenhall.com/casefair

for this chapter's World Wide Web exercise.

WORLD MONETARY SYSTEMS SINCE 1900

Since the beginning of the twentieth century, the world has operated under a number of different monetary systems. This appendix provides a brief history of each and a description of how they worked.

THE GOLD STANDARD

The gold standard was the major system of exchange rate determination before 1914. All currencies were priced in terms of gold—an ounce of gold was worth so much in each currency. When all currencies exchanged at fixed ratios to gold, exchange rates could be determined easily. For instance, one ounce of gold was worth $20 U.S.; that same ounce of gold exchanged for 4 British pounds. Because $20 and £4 were each worth one ounce of gold, the exchange rate between dollars and pounds was $20/£4, or $5 to £1.

For the gold standard to be effective it had to be backed up by the country's willingness to buy and sell gold at the determined price. As long as countries maintain their currencies at a fixed value in terms of gold *and* as long as each is willing to buy and sell gold, exchange rates are fixed. If at the given exchange rate the number of U.S. citizens who want to buy things produced in Great Britain is equal to the number of British citizens who want to buy things produced in the United States, the currencies of the two countries will simply be exchanged. But what if U.S. citizens suddenly decide they want to drink imported Scotch instead of domestic bourbon? If the British do not have an increased desire for U.S. goods, they would still accept U.S. dollars because they could be redeemed in gold. This gold could then be immediately turned into pounds.

As long as a country's overall balance of payments remained in balance, no gold would enter or leave the country, and the economy would be in equilibrium. If U.S. citizens bought more from the British than the British bought from the United States, however, the U.S. balance of payments would be in deficit, and the U.S. stock of gold would begin to fall. Conversely, Britain would start to accumulate gold because it would be exporting more than it spent on imports.

But under the gold standard, gold was a big determinant of the money supply.[1] An inflow of gold into a country caused that country's money supply to expand, and an outflow of gold caused that country's money supply to contract. If gold were flowing from the United States to Great Britain, the British money supply would expand and the U.S. money supply would contract.

Now recall from earlier chapters the impacts of a change in the money supply. An expanded money supply in Britain will lower British interest rates and stimulate aggregate demand. As a result, aggregate output (income) and the price level in Britain will increase. Higher British prices will discourage U.S. citizens from buying British goods. At the same time, British citizens will have more income and will face relatively lower import prices, causing them to import more from the States.

On the other side of the Atlantic, U.S. citizens will face a contracting domestic money supply. This will cause higher interest rates, declining aggregate demand, lower prices, and falling output (income). This will lower demand in the United States for British goods. Thus, changes in relative prices and incomes that resulted from the inflow and outflow of gold would automatically bring trade back into balance.

PROBLEMS WITH THE GOLD STANDARD

Two major problems were associated with the gold standard. First, the gold standard implied that a country had little control over its money supply. The reason, as we have just seen, is that the money stock increased when the overall balance of payments was in surplus (gold inflow) and decreased when the overall balance was in deficit (gold outflow). A country that was experiencing a balance-of-payments deficit could correct the problem only by the painful process of allowing its money supply to contract. This brought on a slump in economic activity, a slump that would eventually restore balance-of-payments equilibrium, but only after reductions in income and employment. Countries could (and often did) act to protect their gold reserves, and this prevented the adjustment mechanism from correcting the deficit.

Making the money supply depend on the amount of gold available had another disadvantage. When major new gold fields were discovered (as in California in 1849 or South Africa in 1886), the world's supply of gold (and therefore of money) increased. The price level rose and income increased. When no new gold was discovered, the supply of money remained unchanged and prices and income tended to fall.

When President Reagan took office in 1981, he established a commission to consider returning the nation

---

[1] In the days when currencies were tied to gold, changes in the amount of gold influenced the supply of money in two ways. A change in the quantity of gold coins in circulation had a direct effect on the supply of money; indirectly, gold served as a backing for paper currency. A decrease in the central bank's gold holdings meant a decline in the amount of paper money that could be supported.

to the gold standard. The final commission report recommended against such a move. An important part of the reasoning behind this was that the gold standard puts enormous economic power in the hands of gold-producing nations.

FIXED EXCHANGE RATES AND THE BRETTON WOODS SYSTEM

As World War II drew to a close, a group of economists from the United States and Europe met to formulate a new set of rules for exchange rate determination that they hoped would avoid the difficulties of the gold standard. The rules they designed became known as the **Bretton Woods system**, after the town in New Hampshire where the delegates met. The Bretton Woods system was based on two (not necessarily compatible) premises. First, countries were to maintain fixed exchange rates with each other. Instead of pegging their currencies directly to gold, however, currencies were fixed in terms of the U.S. dollar, which was fixed in value at $35 per ounce of gold. The British pound, for instance, was fixed at roughly $2.40, which meant that an ounce of gold was worth approximately 14.6 pounds. As we shall see, the pure system of fixed exchange rates would work in a manner very similar to the pre-1914 gold standard.

The second aspect of the Bretton Woods system added a new wrinkle to the operation of the international economy. Countries experiencing a "fundamental disequilibrium" in their balance of payments were allowed to change their exchange rates. (The term *fundamental disequilibrium* was necessarily vague, but it came to be interpreted as a large and persistent current account deficit.) Exchange rates were not really fixed under the Bretton Woods system; they were, as someone remarked, only "fixed until further notice."

The point of allowing countries with serious current account problems to alter the value of their currency was to avoid the harsh recessions that the operation of the gold standard would have produced under these circumstances. But the experience of the European economies in the years between World War I and World War II suggested it might not be a good idea to give countries complete freedom to change their exchange rates whenever they wished.

During the Great Depression, many countries undertook so-called competitive devaluations to protect domestic output and employment. That is, countries would try to encourage exports—a source of output growth and employment—by attempting to set as low an exchange rate as possible, thereby making their exports competitive with foreign-produced goods. Unfortunately, such policies had a built-in flaw. A devaluation

of the pound against the French franc may help encourage British exports to France, but if those additional British exports cut into French output and employment, France is likely to respond by devaluing the franc against the pound, which, of course, undoes the effects of the pound's initial devaluation.

To solve this exchange rate rivalry, the Bretton Woods agreement created the International Monetary Fund (IMF). Its job was to assist countries experiencing temporary current account problems.[2] It was also supposed to certify that a "fundamental disequilibrium" existed before a country was allowed to change its exchange rate. The IMF was like an international economic traffic cop whose job is to ensure that all countries are playing the game according to the agreed-upon rules and to provide emergency assistance where needed.

"PURE" FIXED EXCHANGE RATES

Under a pure fixed exchange rate system, governments set a particular *fixed* rate at which their currencies will exchange for each other and then commit themselves to maintaining that rate. A true fixed exchange rate system is like the gold standard in that exchange rates are supposed to stay the same forever.[3] Because currencies are no longer backed by gold, they have no fixed, or standard, value relative to each other. There is therefore no automatic mechanism to keep exchange rates aligned with each other, as with the gold standard.

The result is that under a pure fixed exchange rate system, governments must at times intervene in the foreign exchange market to keep currencies aligned at their established values. Economists define government intervention in the foreign exchange market as the buying or selling of foreign exchange for the purpose of manipulating the exchange rate. What kind of intervention is likely to occur under a fixed exchange rate system, and how does it work?

We can see how intervention works by looking at Figure 21A.1. Initially, the market for Italian lira is in equilibrium. At the fixed exchange rate of $0.02 per lira, the supply of lira is exactly equal to the demand for lira. No government intervention is necessary to maintain the exchange rate at this level. Now suppose Italian wines are found to be contaminated with antifreeze, and U.S.

---

[2]The idea was that the IMF would make short-term loans to a country with a current account deficit. The loans would enable the country to correct the current account problem gradually, without bringing on a deep recession, running out of foreign exchange reserves, or devaluing the currency.

[3]"Forever" is a very long time. Some countries in Central America have maintained fixed exchange rates with the U.S. dollar for almost 30 years, practically forever in the world of international finance!

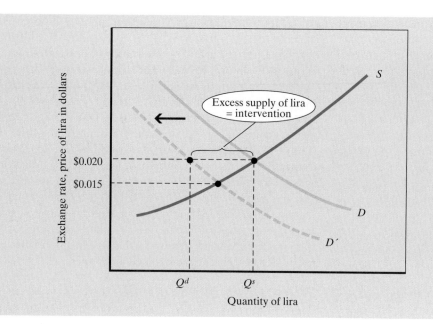

FIGURE 21A.1

Government Intervention in the Foreign Exchange Market

If the price of lira was set by a completely unfettered market, the price of a lira would be .020 when demand is D and .015 when demand is D'. If the government has committed itself to keeping the value of a lira at .020, it must buy up the excess supply of lira ($Q^s - Q^d$).

citizens switch to California wines. This substitution away from the Italian product shifts the U.S. demand curve for lira to the left: The United States demands fewer lira at every exchange rate (cost of a lira) because it is purchasing less from Italy than it did before.

If the price of lira were set by a completely unfettered market, the shift in the demand curve would lead to a fall in the price of lira, just the way the price of wheat would fall if there was an excess supply of wheat. Remember, the Italian and U.S. governments have committed themselves to maintaining the rate at $0.02 per lira. To do this, either the U.S. government or Italian government (or both) must buy up the excess supply of lira to keep the price of the lira from falling. In essence, the fixed exchange rate policy commits governments to making up any difference between the supply of a currency and the demand so as to keep the price of the currency (exchange rate) at the desired level. The government promises to act as the supplier (or demander) of last resort, who will ensure that the amount of foreign exchange demanded by the private sector will equal the supply at the fixed price.

PROBLEMS WITH THE BRETTON WOODS SYSTEM

As it developed after the end of World War II, the system of more-or-less fixed exchange rates had some flaws that led to its abandonment in 1971.

First, there was a basic asymmetry built into the rules of international finance. Countries experiencing large and persistent current account deficits—what the Bretton Woods agreements termed "fundamental disequilibria"—were obliged to devalue their currencies and/or take measures to cut their deficits by contracting their economies. Both of these alternatives were unpleasant, because devaluation meant rising prices and contraction meant rising unemployment. But a country with a current account deficit had no choice, since it was losing its stock of foreign exchange reserves. When its stock of foreign currencies became exhausted, it had to change its exchange rate, because further intervention (selling off some of its foreign exchange reserves) became impossible.

Countries experiencing current account surpluses were in a different position, since they were gaining foreign exchange reserves. Although these countries were supposed to stimulate their economies and/or revalue their currencies to restore balance to their current account, they were not obliged to do so. They could easily maintain their fixed exchange rate by buying up any excess supply of foreign exchange with their own currency, of which they had plentiful supply.

In practice, this meant some countries—especially Germany and Japan—tended to run large and chronic current account surpluses and were under no compulsion to take steps to correct the problem. The U.S. economy, stimulated by expenditures on the Vietnam War, experienced a large and prolonged current account deficit (capital outflow) in the 1960s, which was the counterpart of these surpluses. The United States was, however, in a unique position under the Bretton Woods system. The value of gold was fixed in terms of the U.S. dollar at $35 per ounce of gold. Other countries fixed their exchange rates in terms of U.S. dollars (and therefore only indirectly in terms of gold). This meant the United States could never accomplish anything by devaluing its currency in terms of gold. If the dollar was devalued from $35 to $40 per ounce of gold, the yen, pegged at 200 yen per dollar, would move in parallel with the dollar (from 7,000 yen per ounce of gold to 8,000 yen per ounce), with the dollar-yen exchange rate unaffected. To correct its current account deficits vis-á-vis Japan and Germany, it would be necessary for those two countries to adjust their currencies' exchange rates with the dollar. But these countries were reluctant to do so for a variety of reasons. As a result, the U.S. current account was chronically in deficit throughout the late 1960s.

A second flaw in the Bretton Woods system was that it permitted devaluations only if a country had a "chronic" current account deficit and was in danger of running out of foreign exchange reserves. This meant devaluations could often be predicted quite far in advance, and they usually had to be rather large if they were to correct any serious current account problem. The situation made it tempting for speculators to "attack" the currencies of countries with current account deficits.

Problems like these eventually led the United States to abandon the Bretton Woods rules in 1971. The U.S. government refused to continue pegging the value of the dollar in terms of gold. This meant the prices of all currencies were free to find their own levels.

The alternative to fixed exchange rates is a system that allows exchange rates to move freely or flexibly in response to market forces. Two types of flexible exchange rate systems are usually distinguished. In a *freely floating system*, governments do not intervene at all in the foreign exchange market.[4] They do not buy or sell currencies with the aim of manipulating the rates. In a *managed floating system*, governments intervene if markets are becoming "disorderly"—fluctuating more than a government feels is desirable. Governments may also intervene if they think a currency is increasing or decreasing too much in value, even though the day-to-day fluctuations may be small.

Since the demise of the Bretton Woods system in 1971, the world's exchange rate system can be described as "managed floating." One of the important features of this system has been times of large fluctuations in exchange rates. For example, the yen-dollar rate went from 347 in 1971 to 210 in 1978, to 125 in 1988, to 80 in 1995. These are very large changes, changes that have important effects on the international economy, some of which we have covered in this text.

---

[4]However, governments may from time to time buy or sell foreign exchange for their own needs (rather than to influence the exchange rate). For example, the U.S. government might need British pounds to buy land for a U.S. embassy building in London. For our purposes, we ignore this behavior because it is not "intervention" in the strict sense of the word.

SUMMARY

1. The gold standard was the major system of exchange rate determination before 1914. All currencies were priced in terms of gold. Difficulties with the gold standard led to the *Bretton Woods* agreement following World War II. Under this system, countries maintained fixed exchange rates with each other and fixed the value of their currencies in terms of the U.S. dollar. Countries experiencing a "fundamental disequilibrium" in their current accounts were permitted to change their exchange rates.

2. The Bretton Woods system was abandoned in 1971. Since then, the world's exchange rate system has been one of managed floating rates. Under this system, governments intervene if foreign exchange markets are fluctuating more than the government thinks desirable.

REVIEW TERMS AND CONCEPTS

Bretton Woods The site in New Hampshire where a group of experts from 44 countries met in 1944 and agreed on an international monetary system of fixed exchange rates. 477

1. The currency of Atlantis is the wimp. In 1998, Atlantis developed a balance-of-payments deficit with the United States as a result of an unanticipated decrease in exports; U.S. citizens cut back on the purchase of Atlantean goods. Assume Atlantis is operating under a system of fixed exchange rates.

   a. How does the drop in exports affect the market for wimps? Identify the deficit graphically.

   b. How must the government of Atlantis act (in the short run) to maintain the value of the wimp?

   c. If originally Atlantis was operating at full employment (potential GDP), what impact will these events have on its economy? Explain your answer.

   d. The chief economist of Atlantis suggests expansionary monetary policy to restore full employment; the secretary of commerce suggests a tax cut (expansionary fiscal policy). Given the fixed exchange rate system, describe the effects of these two policy options on Atlantis's current account.

   e. How would your answers to a, b, and c change if the two countries operated under a floating rate system?

Chapter 22

Economic Growth in Developing Nations

OUR PRIMARY FOCUS in this text has been on economic issues facing the United States. Welfare and health-care reform, slow economic growth in recent years, antitrust action against Microsoft, and worries about the deficit are familiar to Americans. But the economics we have been studying also applies to other countries: Welfare reform is a big issue in the Netherlands, Japan is facing major fiscal deficits, and the German central bank has been wrestling with slow economic growth. We can analyze these and other issues in the Netherlands, Japan, and Germany with some confidence because these countries have so much in common with the United States. In spite of differences in languages and cultures, all these countries have modern industrialized economies that rely heavily on markets to allocate resources. But what about the economic problems facing Somalia or Haiti? Can we apply the same economic principles that we have been studying to these less-developed countries (sometimes called LDCs)?

Yes. All economic analysis deals with the problem of making choices under conditions of scarcity, and the problem of satisfying their citizens' wants and needs is as real for Somalia and Haiti as it is for the Netherlands, Germany, and Japan. The universality of scarcity is what makes economic analysis relevant to all nations, regardless of their level of material well-being or ruling political ideology.

The basic tools of supply and demand, theories about consumers and firms, and theories about the structure of markets all contribute to an understanding of the economic problems confronting the world's developing nations. However, these nations often face economic problems quite different from those faced by richer, more developed countries. In the developing nations, the economist may have to worry about chronic food shortages, explosive population growth, and hyperinflations that reach triple, and even quadruple, digits. The United States and other industrialized economies rarely encounter such difficulties.

The instruments of economic management also vary from nation to nation. The United States has well-developed financial market institutions and a strong central bank (the Federal Reserve) through which the government can control the macroeconomy to some extent. But even limited intervention is impossible in some of the developing countries. In the United States, tax laws can be changed to stimulate saving, to encourage particular kinds of investments, or to redistribute income. In most developing countries, there are neither meaningful personal income taxes nor effective tax policies.

But even though economic problems and the policy instruments available to tackle them vary across nations, economic thinking about these problems can be transferred easily from one setting to another. In this chapter we discuss several of the economic problems specific to developing nations in an attempt to capture some of the insights that economic analysis can offer.

LIFE IN THE DEVELOPING NATIONS: POPULATION AND POVERTY

By the year 2000, the population of the world will reach over 6.1 billion people. Most of the world's more than 200 nations belong to the developing world, in which about three-fourths of the world's population lives.

In the early 1960s, the nations of the world could be assigned rather easily to categories: The *developed countries* included most of Europe, North America, Japan, Australia, and New Zealand; the *developing countries* included the rest of the world. The developing nations were often referred to as the "Third World" to distinguish them from the Western industrialized nations (the "First World") and the former Socialist bloc of Eastern European nations (the "Second World").

In the 1990s the world does not divide easily into three neat parts. Rapid economic progress has brought some developing nations closer to developed economies. Countries such as Argentina and Korea, still considered to be "developing," are often referred to as middle-income, or newly industrialized, countries. Other countries, such as much of sub-Saharan Africa and some of South Asia, have stagnated and fallen so far behind the economic advances of the rest of the world that the "Fourth World" has been used to describe them. It is not clear yet where the republics of the former Soviet Union and other formerly Communist countries of Eastern Europe will end up. Production has fallen sharply in many of them. For example, between 1990 and 1997, real GDP fell about 40 percent in the transition economies and by over 50 percent in Russia and Central Asia. One estimate puts current per capita GDP in Russia at around $2,500. Some of the new republics now have more in common with developing countries than with developed countries.

Although the countries of the developing world exhibit considerable diversity, both in their standards of living and in their particular experiences of growth, marked differences continue to separate them from the developed nations. The developed countries have a higher average level of material well-being (the amounts of food, clothing, shelter, and other commodities consumed by the average person). Comparisons of gross domestic product (GDP) per capita—the value of goods and services produced per person in an economy—are often used as a crude index of the level of material well-being across nations. See Table 22.1 where GDP per capita in the industrial market economies significantly exceeds GDP of both the low- and middle-income developing economies.

Other characteristics of economic development include improvements in basic health and education. The degree of political and economic freedom enjoyed by individual citizens might also be part of what it means to be a developed nation. Some of these criteria are easier to quantify; Table 22.1 presents data for different types of economies according to some of the more easily measured indexes of development. As you see, the industrial market economies enjoy higher standards of living according to whatever indicator of development is chosen.

TABLE 22.1 INDICATORS OF ECONOMIC DEVELOPMENT

COUNTRY GROUP	POPULATION (MILLIONS) 1995	GDP PER CAPITA, 1995 (DOLLARS)	LIFE EXPECTANCY, 1995 (YEARS)	INFANT MORTALITY, 1995 (DEATHS BEFORE AGE ONE PER 1,000 BIRTHS)	PERCENTAGE OF POPULATION IN URBAN AREAS, 1995
Low-income (e.g., China, Ethiopia, Haiti, India)	3,180	430	63	69	29
Lower middle-income (e.g., Guatemala, Poland, Philippines, Thailand)	1,153	1,670	67	41	56
Upper middle-income (e.g., Brazil, Malaysia, Mexico)	438	4,260	69	35	73
Industrial market economies (e.g., Japan, Germany, New Zealand, United States)	902	24,930	77	7	75

Source: World Bank, *World Development Report, 1997.* Note that all numbers refer to weighted averages for each country group, where the weights equal the populations of each nation in a specific country group.

Behind these statistics lies the reality of the very difficult life facing the people of the developing world. For most, meager incomes provide only the basic necessities. Most meals are the same, consisting of the region's food staple—rice, wheat, or corn. Shelter is primitive. Many people share a small room, usually with an earthen floor and no sanitary facilities. The great majority of the population lives in rural areas where agricultural work is hard and extremely time-consuming. Productivity (output produced per worker) is low because household plots are small and only the crudest of farm implements are available. Low productivity means farm output per person is barely sufficient to feed a farmer's own family, with nothing left to sell to others. School-age children may receive some formal education, but illiteracy remains chronic for young and old. Infant mortality runs 10 times higher than in the United States. Although parasitic infections are common and debilitating, there is only one physician per 5,000 people. In addition, many developing nations are engaged in civil and external warfare.

Life in the developing nations is a continual struggle against the circumstances of poverty, and prospects for dramatic improvements in living standards for most people are dim. As with all generalizations, there are exceptions. Some nations are better off than others, and in any given nation an elite group always lives in considerable luxury. Income distribution in developing countries is often so skewed that the richest households surpass the living standards of many high-income families in the advanced economies. Table 22.2 presents some data on the distribution of income in some developing countries.

Clearly, poverty—not affluence—dominates the developing world. Recent studies suggest that 40 percent of the population of the developing nations have annual incomes insufficient to provide for adequate nutrition.

In 1995, the poorest country in the world was Mozambique with per capita GDP of $80.

While the developed nations account for only about one-quarter of the world's population, they are estimated to consume three-quarters of the world's output. This leaves the developing countries with about three-fourths of the world's people, but only one-fourth of the world's income. The simple result is that most of our planet's population is poor.

TABLE 22.2   INCOME DISTRIBUTION IN SOME DEVELOPING COUNTRIES

	UNITED STATES	SRI LANKA	BRAZIL	PAKISTAN	INDONESIA	KENYA
Per Capita GDP 1995	$26,980	$700	$3,640	$460	$980	$280
Bottom 20%	4.7	8.9	2.1	8.4	8.7	3.4
Second 20%	11.0	13.1	4.9	12.9	12.3	6.7
Third 20%	17.4	16.9	8.9	16.9	16.3	10.7
Fourth 20%	25.0	21.7	16.8	22.2	21.1	17.0
Top 20%	41.9	39.3	67.5	39.7	40.7	62.1
Top 10%	25.0	25.2	51.3	25.2	25.6	47.7

Source: World Bank, *World Development Report,* 1997.

In the United States, the poorest one-fifth (bottom 20 percent) of the families receives just under 5 percent of total income; the richest one-fifth receives about 42 percent. But the inequality in the world distribution of income is much greater. When we look at the world population, the poorest one-fifth of the families earns about 0.5 percent and the richest one-fifth earn 79 percent of total world income!

ECONOMIC DEVELOPMENT: SOURCES AND STRATEGIES

Economists have been trying to understand economic growth and development since Adam Smith and David Ricardo in the eighteenth and nineteenth centuries, but the study of development economics as it applies to the developing nations has a much shorter history. The geopolitical struggles that followed World War II brought increased attention to the developing nations and their economic problems. During this period, the new field of development economics asked simply: Why are some nations poor and others rich? If economists could understand the barriers to economic growth that prevent nations from developing and the prerequisites that would help them to develop, they could prescribe strategies for achieving economic advancement.

THE SOURCES OF ECONOMIC DEVELOPMENT

Although a general theory of economic development applicable to all nations has not emerged and probably never will, some basic factors that limit a poor nation's economic growth have been suggested. These include insufficient capital formation, a shortage of human resources and entrepreneurial ability, a lack of social overhead capital, and the constraints imposed by dependency on the already developed nations.

➤ **Capital Formation**   One explanation for low levels of output in developing nations is insufficient quantities of necessary inputs. Developing nations have diverse resource endowments—Congo, for instance, is abundant in natural resources, while Bangladesh is resource poor. Almost all developing nations have a scarcity of physical capital relative to other resources, especially labor. The small stock of physical capital (factories, machinery, farm equipment, and other productive capital) constrains labor's productivity and holds back national output.

But citing capital shortages as the cause of low productivity does not explain much. We need to know why capital is in such short supply in developing countries. There are

The following is an excerpt from a speech given by World Bank president James D. Wolfensohn on the challenge facing the world in 1997:

Our goal must be to reduce these disparities across and within countries, to bring more and more people into the economic mainstream, to promote equitable access to the benefits of development regardless of nationality, race, or gender. This—the Challenge of Inclusion—is the key development challenge of our time.

You and I and all of us in this room—the privileged of the developing and the industrial world—can choose to ignore it. We can focus only on the successes. We can live with a little more crime, a few more wars, air that is a little bit dirtier. We can insulate ourselves from whole sections of the world for which crisis is real and daily but which to the rest of us is largely invisible. But we must recognize that we are living with a time bomb, and unless we take action now, it could explode in our children's faces.

If we do not act, in thirty years the inequities will be greater. With population growing at 80 million a year, instead of 3 billion living on under $2 a day, it could be as high as 5 billion. In thirty years, the quality of our environment will be worse. Instead of 4 percent of tropical forests lost since Rio, it could be 24 percent.

In thirty years, the number of conflicts may be higher. Already

we live in a world which last year alone saw twenty-six interstate wars and 23 million refugees. One does not have to spend long in Bosnia or Gaza or the Lakes District in Africa to know that without economic hope we will not have peace. Without equity we will not have global stability. Without a better sense of social justice our cities will not be safe, and our societies will not be stable. Without inclusion, too many of us will be condemned to live separate, armed, and frightened lives.

And economics is fundamentally changing the relationships between the rich and the poor nations. Over the next twenty-five years, growth in China, India, Indonesia, Brazil, and Russia will likely redraw the economic map of the world, as the share in global output of the development and transition economies doubles. Today these countries represent 50 percent of the world's population but only 8 percent of its GDP. Their share in world trade is a quarter that of the European Union. By the year 2020, their share in world trade could be 50 percent more than Europe's.

We share the same world, and we share the same challenge. The fight against poverty is the fight for peace, security, and growth for us all.

How, then, do we proceed? This much we know: No country has been successful in reducing poverty without sustained economic growth. Those countries that have been most successful—

including, most notably, many here in East Asia—have also invested heavily in their people, have put in place the right policy fundamentals, and have not discriminated against their rural sectors. The results have been dramatic: large private capital inflows, rapid growth, and substantial poverty reduction.

The message for countries is clear: Educate your people; ensure their health; give them voice and justice, financial systems that work, and sound economic policies, and they will respond, and they will save, and they will attract the investment, both domestic and foreign, that is needed to raise living standards and fuel development.

But another message is also emerging from recent developments. We have seen in recent months how financial markets are demanding more information disclosure, and how they are making swift judgments about the quality and sustainability of government policies based on that information. We have seen that without sound organization and supervision a financial system can falter, with the poor hurt the most. We have seen how corruption flourishes in the dark, how it prevents growth and social equity, and how it creates the basis for social and political instability.

Source: "The Challenge of Inclusion," address by James D. Wolfensohn, president of the World Bank Group to the Board of Governors, Hong Kong, China, September 23, 1997.

For more on economic development, see the Case and Fair Web page at http://www.prenhall.com/casefair.

vicious-circle-of-poverty hypothesis *Suggests that poverty is self-perpetuating because poor nations are unable to save and invest enough to accumulate the capital stock that would help them grow.*

many explanations. One, the **vicious-circle-of-poverty hypothesis**, suggests that a poor nation must consume most of its income just to maintain its already low standard of living. Consuming most of national income implies limited saving, and this implies low levels of investment. Without investment, the capital stock does not grow, income remains low, and the vicious circle is complete. Poverty becomes self-perpetuating.

The difficulty with the vicious-circle argument is that if it were true, no nation could ever develop. For example, Japanese GDP per capita at the turn of the century was well below that of many of today's developing nations. The vicious-circle argument fails to recognize that every nation has some surplus above consumption needs that is available for investment. Often this surplus is most visible in the conspicuous-consumption habits of the nation's richest families.

> Poverty alone cannot explain capital shortages, nor is poverty necessarily self-perpetuating.

In a developing economy, scarcity of capital may have more to do with a lack of incentives for citizens to save and invest productively than with any absolute scarcity of income available for capital accumulation. Many of the rich in developing countries invest their savings in Europe or in the United States rather than risk holding them in what is often an unstable political climate. Savings transferred to the United States do not lead to physical capital growth in the developing countries. The term **capital flight** refers to the fact that both human capital and financial capital (domestic savings) leave developing countries in search of higher rates of return elsewhere. In addition, government policies in the developing nations—including price ceilings, import controls, and even outright appropriation of private property—tend to discourage investment.

capital flight *The tendency for both human capital and financial capital to leave developing countries in search of higher rates of return elsewhere.*

Whatever the causes of capital shortages, it is clear that the absence of productive capital prevents income from rising in any economy. The availability of capital is a necessary, but not a *sufficient*, condition for economic growth. The Third World landscape is littered with idle factories and abandoned machinery. Clearly, other ingredients are required to achieve economic progress.

> **Human Resources and Entrepreneurial Ability**   Capital is not the only factor of production required to produce output. Labor is equally important. But the quantity of available labor rarely constrains a developing economy. In most developing nations, rapid population growth for several decades has resulted in rapidly expanding labor supplies. The *quality* of available labor, however, may pose a serious constraint on the growth of income. The stock of knowledge and skill embodied in the workforce may act as a barrier to economic growth.

Human capital may be developed in a number of ways. Programs to improve nutrition and health represent one kind of human capital investment that can lead to increased productivity and higher incomes. The more familiar forms of human capital investment, including formal education and on-the-job training, may also play a role. Basic literacy, as well as specialized training in farm management, for example, can yield high returns to both the individual worker and the economy. Education has grown to become the largest category of government expenditure in many developing nations, in part because of the belief that human resources are the ultimate determinant of economic advance.

Just as financial capital seeks the highest and safest return, so does human capital. Thousands of students from developing countries, many of whom were supported by their governments, graduate every year from U.S. colleges and universities as engineers, doctors, scientists, economists, and the like. After graduation, these people face a difficult choice: to remain in the United States and earn a high salary or to return home and accept a job at a much lower salary. Many remain in the United States. This **brain drain** siphons off many of the most talented minds from developing countries.

Innovative entrepreneurs who are willing to take risks are an essential human resource in any economy. In a developing nation, new techniques of production rarely need to be invented, because they can usually be adapted from the technology already developed by the technologically advanced nations. But entrepreneurs who are willing and able to organize and carry out economic activity appear to be in short supply. Family and political ties often seem to be more important than ability when it comes to securing positions of authority. Whatever the explanation:

> Development cannot proceed without human resources capable of initiating and managing economic activity.

> **Social Overhead Capital** Anyone who has spent time in a developing nation knows how difficult it can be to send a letter, make a local phone call, or travel within the country itself. Add to this problems with water supplies, frequent electrical power outages—in the few areas where electricity is available—and often ineffective mosquito and pest control, and you soon realize how deficient even the simplest, most basic government-provided goods and services can be.

In any economy, Third World or otherwise, the government has considerable opportunity and responsibility for involvement where conditions encourage natural monopoly (as in the utilities industries) and where public goods (such as roads and pest control) must be provided. In a developing economy, the government must put emphasis on creating a basic infrastructure—roads, power generation, irrigation systems. There are often good reasons why such projects, referred to as **social overhead capital**, cannot successfully be undertaken by the private sector. First, many of these projects operate with economies of scale, which means they can be efficient only if they are very large. In that case, they may be too large for any private company or group of companies to carry out.

Second, many socially useful projects cannot be undertaken by the private sector because there is no way for private agents to capture enough of the returns to make such projects profitable. This so-called *free-rider problem* is common in the economics of the developed world. Consider national defense: Everyone in a country benefits from national defense, whether they have paid for it or not. Anyone who attempted to go into the private business of providing national defense would go broke. Why should I buy any national defense if your purchase of defense will also protect me? Why should you buy any if my purchase will also protect you?

> The governments of developing countries can do important and useful things to encourage development, but many of their efforts must be concentrated in areas that the private sector would never touch. If government action in these realms is not forthcoming, economic development may be curtailed by a lack of social overhead capital.

brain drain *The tendency for talented people from developing countries to become educated in a developed country and remain there after graduation.*

In 1995, Nepal had a population of 22 million and a per capita GDP of $200. Only 48% of the population had access to safe water and just 6% had access to sanitation.

Source: World Bank, *World Development Report*, 1997.

social overhead capital *Basic infrastructure projects such as roads, power generation, and irrigation systems.*

STRATEGIES FOR ECONOMIC DEVELOPMENT

Just as no single theory appears to explain lack of economic advancement, no one development strategy will likely succeed in all nations. Many alternative development strategies have been proposed over the past 40 years. Although these strategies have been very different, they all recognize that a developing economy faces basic trade-offs. An insufficient amount of both human and physical resources dictates that choices must be made, including those between agriculture and industry, exports and import substitution, and central planning and free markets.

▶ **Agriculture or Industry?**   Most Third World countries began to gain political independence just after World War II. The tradition of promoting industrialization as the solution to the problems of the developing world dates from this time. The early five-year development plans of India called for promoting manufacturing; the current government in Ethiopia (an extremely poor country) has similar intentions.

Industry has several apparent attractions over agriculture. First, if it is true that capital shortages constrain economic growth, then the building of factories is an obvious step toward increasing a nation's stock of capital. Second, and perhaps most important, one of the primary characteristics of more developed economies is their structural transition away from agriculture and toward manufacturing and modern services. As Table 22.3 shows, agriculture's share in GDP declines substantially as per capita incomes increase. The share of services increases correspondingly, especially in the early phases of economic development.

Many economies have pursued industry at the expense of agriculture. In many countries, however, industrialization has been either unsuccessful or disappointing—that is, it has not brought the benefits that were expected. Experience suggests that simply trying to replicate the structure of developed economies does not in itself guarantee, or even promote, successful development.

Since the early 1970s, the agricultural sector has received considerably more attention. Agricultural strategies have had numerous benefits. Although some agricultural projects (such as the building of major dams and irrigation networks) are very capital intensive, many others (such as services to help teach better farming techniques and small-scale fertilizer programs) have low capital and import requirements. Programs like these can affect large numbers of households, and because their benefits are directed at rural areas, they are most likely to help a country's poorest families.

TABLE 22.3   THE STRUCTURE OF PRODUCTION IN SELECTED DEVELOPED AND DEVELOPING ECONOMIES, 1995

COUNTRY	PER CAPITA INCOME	PERCENTAGE OF GROSS DOMESTIC PRODUCT		
		AGRICULTURE	INDUSTRY	SERVICES
Tanzania	$120	58	17	24
Bangladesh	$240	31	18	52
China	$620	21	48	31
Colombia	$1,910	14	32	54
Thailand	$2,740	11	40	49
Brazil	$3,640	14	37	49
Korea (Rep.)	$9,700	7	43	50
Japan	$39,640	2	38	60

Source: World Bank, *World Development Report,* 1997, Tables 1 and 12.

Experience over the last three decades suggests that some balance between these approaches leads to the best outcome—that is, it is important and effective to pay attention to both industry and agriculture. The Chinese have referred to this dual approach to development as "walking on two legs."

▶ **Exports or Import Substitution?** As developing nations expand their industrial activities, they must decide what type of trade strategy to pursue, usually one of two alternatives: import substitution or export promotion.

Import substitution is an industrial trade strategy to develop local industries that can manufacture goods to replace imports. For example, if fertilizer is imported, import substitution calls for a domestic fertilizer industry to produce replacements for fertilizer imports. This strategy gained prominence throughout South America in the 1950s. At that time, most developing nations exported agricultural and mineral products, goods that faced uncertain and often unstable international markets. Furthermore, the *terms of trade* for these nations—the ratio of export to import prices—seemed to be on a long-run decline.[1] A decline in a country's terms of trade means its imports of manufactured goods become relatively expensive in the domestic market, while its exports—mostly primary goods such as rubber and wheat and oil—become relatively inexpensive in the world market.

import substitution *An industrial trade strategy that favors developing local industries that can manufacture goods to replace imports.*

Under these conditions, the call for import-substitution policies was understandable. Special government actions, including tariff and quota protection and subsidized imports of machinery, were set up to encourage new domestic industries. Multinational corporations were also invited into many countries to begin domestic operations.

Most economists believe import-substitution strategies have failed almost everywhere they have been tried. With domestic industries sheltered from international competition by high tariffs (often as high as 200 percent), major economic inefficiencies were created. For example, Peru has a population of just over 24 million, only a tiny fraction of whom could afford to buy an automobile. Yet at one time the country had five or six different automobile manufacturers, each of which produced only a few thousand cars per year. Because there are substantial economies of scale in automobile production, the cost per car was much higher than it needed to be, and valuable resources that could have been devoted to another, more productive, activity were squandered producing cars.

Furthermore, policies designed to promote import substitution often encouraged capital-intensive production methods, which limited the creation of jobs and hurt export activities. A country like Peru could not export automobiles, because it could produce them only at a cost far greater than their price on the world market. Worse still, import-substitution policies encouraged the use of expensive domestic products, such as tractors and fertilizer, instead of lower-cost imports. These policies taxed the sectors that might have successfully competed in world markets. To the extent that the Peruvian sugar industry had to rely on domestically produced, high-cost fertilizer, for example, its ability to compete in international markets was reduced, because its production costs were artificially raised.

As an alternative to import substitution, some nations have pursued strategies of export promotion. **Export promotion** is simply the policy of encouraging exports. As an industrial market economy, Japan is a striking example to the developing world of the economic success that exports can provide. With an average annual per capita real GDP growth rate of roughly 6 percent per year since 1960, Japan's achievements are in part based on industrial production oriented toward foreign consumers.

export promotion *A trade policy designed to encourage exports.*

---

[1] It now appears that the terms of trade for Third World countries as a group were not actually on a long-run decline. Of course, the prices of commodities have changed, with some doing very well and others doing quite poorly. During the 1950s, however, many policy makers believed that the purchasing power of developing-country exports was in a permanent slump.

Several countries in the developing world have attempted to emulate Japan's success. Starting around 1970, Hong Kong, Singapore, Korea, and Taiwan (the "four little dragons" between the two big dragons, China and Japan) all began to pursue export promotion of manufactured goods. Today their growth rates have surpassed Japan's. Other nations, including Brazil, Colombia, and Turkey, have also had some success at pursuing an outward-looking trade policy.

Government support of export promotion has often taken the form of maintaining an exchange rate favorable enough to permit exports to compete with products manufactured in developed economies. For example, many people believe Japan kept the value of the yen artificially low during the 1970s. Because "cheap" yen means inexpensive Japanese goods in the United States, sales of Japanese goods (especially automobiles) increased dramatically. Governments also have provided subsidies to export industries.

In 1997 Japan was in a serious recession. Overall, Japan's performance since 1990 has not been as strong as before 1990. But its recent troubles do not diminish the incredible performance of the Japanese economic machine between 1960 and 1990.

FAST FACTS

According to World Bank statistics, the developing countries most heavily dependent on exports in 1995 were Estonia (75% of GDP) followed by Jamaica (69%), Uzbekistan (63%), and Papua New Guinea (61%).

> **Central Planning or the Market?** As part of its strategy for achieving economic development, a nation must decide how its economy will be directed. Its basic choices lie between a market-oriented economic system and a centrally planned one.

In the 1950s and into the 1960s, development strategies that called for national planning commanded wide support. The rapid economic growth of the Soviet Union, a centrally planned economy, provided an example of how fast a less developed agrarian nation could be transformed into a modern industrial power. (The often appalling costs of this strategy—severe discipline, gross violation of human rights, and environmental damage—were less widely known.) In addition, the underdevelopment of many commodity and asset markets in the Third World led many experts to believe that market forces could not direct an economy reliably and that major government intervention was therefore necessary. Even the United States, with its commitment to free enterprise in the marketplace, supported early central planning efforts in many developing nations.

Today, planning takes many forms in the developing nations. In some, central planning has replaced market-based outcomes with direct, administratively determined controls over such economic variables as prices, output, and employment. In others, national planning amounts to little more than the formulation of general 5- or 10-year goals as rough blueprints for a nation's economic future.

The economic appeal of planning lies theoretically in its ability to channel savings into productive investment and to coordinate economic activities that private actors in the economy might not otherwise undertake. The reality of central planning, however, is that it is technically difficult, highly politicized, and a nightmare to administer. Given the scarcity of human resources and the unstable political environment in many developing nations, planning itself—let alone the execution of the plan—becomes a formidable task.

The failure of many central planning efforts has brought increasing calls for less government intervention and more market orientation in developing economies. The elimination of price controls, privatization of state-run enterprises, and reductions in import restraints are examples of market-oriented reforms recommended by such international agencies as the **International Monetary Fund**, whose primary goals are to stabilize international exchange rates and to lend money to countries that have problems financing their international transactions, and the **World Bank**, which lends money to a country for projects that promote economic development.

Members' contributions to both organizations are determined by the size of their

International Monetary Fund
An international agency whose primary goals are to stabilize international exchange rates and to lend money to countries that have problems financing their international transactions.

World Bank *An international agency that lends money to individual countries for projects that promote economic development.*

economies. Only 20 percent of the World Bank's funding comes from contributions; 80 percent comes from retained earnings and investments in capital markets. The developing world is increasingly recognizing the value of market forces in determining the allocation of scarce resources. Nonetheless, government still has a major role to play. In the decades ahead, the governments of developing nations will need to determine those situations where planning is superior to the market and those where the market is superior to planning.

GROWTH VERSUS DEVELOPMENT: THE POLICY CYCLE

Until now, we have used *growth* and *development* as if they meant the same thing. But this may not always be the case. You can easily imagine instances in which a country has achieved higher levels of income (growth) with little or no benefit accruing to most of its citizens (development). Thus, the question is whether economic growth necessarily brings about economic development.

In the past, most development strategies were aimed at increasing the growth rate of income per capita. Many still are, based on the theory that benefits of economic growth will "trickle down" to all members of society. If this theory is correct, then growth should promote development.

By the early 1970s, the relationship between growth and development was being questioned more and more. A study by the World Bank in 1974 concluded

> it is now clear that more than a decade of rapid growth in underdeveloped countries has been of little or no benefit to perhaps a third of their population. . . . Paradoxically, while growth policies have succeeded beyond the expectations of the first development decade, the very idea of aggregate growth as a social objective has increasingly been called into question.

The World Bank study indicated that increases in GDP per capita did not guarantee significant improvements in such development indicators as nutrition, health, and education. Although GDP per capita did rise, its benefits trickled down to a small minority of the population. This prompted new development strategies that would directly address the problems of poverty. Such new strategies favored agriculture over industry, called for domestic redistribution of income and wealth (especially land), and encouraged programs to satisfy such basic needs as food and shelter.

In the late 1970s and early 1980s, the international macroeconomic crises of high oil prices, worldwide recession, and Third World debt forced attention away from programs designed to eliminate poverty directly. Then, during the 1980s and 1990s, the policy focus turned 180 degrees. The World Bank and the United States began demanding "structural adjustment" in the developing countries as a prerequisite for sending aid to them. **Structural adjustment** programs entail reducing the size of the public sector through privatization and/or expenditure reductions, substantially cutting budget deficits, reining in inflation, and encouraging private saving and investment with tax reforms. These pro-market demands were an attempt to stimulate growth; distributional consequences took a back seat.

In recent years, foreign aid has become a source of controversy. How much foreign aid does the United States provide, and who gets it? For the answers, see the Issues and Debates box "Where Does U.S. Foreign Aid Go?"

structural adjustment *A series of programs in developing nations designed to (1) reduce the size of their public sectors through privatization and/or expenditure reductions, (2) decrease their budget deficits, (3) control inflation, and (4) encourage private saving and investment through tax reform.*

ISSUES IN ECONOMIC DEVELOPMENT

Every developing nation has a cultural, political, and economic history all its own and therefore confronts a unique set of problems. Still, it is possible to discuss common economic issues that each nation must face in its own particular way. These issues

WHERE DOES U.S. FOREIGN AID GO?

Many developed countries provide direct assistance in the form of grants and loans to developing nations. This aid is used to build infrastructure (roads, power plants, and such), drill wells, improve medical care facilities, teach everything from crop management to business development, help rural credit banks grow, and (when necessary) provide food and medical services directly to the people.

Many people think foreign aid is a major part of U.S. government expenditures, and campaign rhetoric is often directed against it because the United States should "help its own people first." In fact, the total amount of direct development assistance in the *world* in 1997 was $55 billion, of which the United States contributed $9.5 billion. This figure amounted to only 6¢ out of every $10 of federal expenditures and only 1.3 percent of domestic transfer payments.

Table 1 shows the top 10 countries that benefit from U.S. economic aid. Israel is the only country that receives more than $1 billion, and most countries receive only a small amount.

TABLE 1	FOREIGN AID, 1997—DESTINATION OF DIRECT U.S. ECONOMIC ASSISTANCE, BY COUNTRY	
COUNTRY		**MILLIONS OF DOLLARS**
Israel		$1,200
Egypt		815
Bosnia		240
Ukraine		227
Peru		99
Russia		99
Haiti		96
South Africa		79
West Bank/Gaza		75
Ethiopia		72

Source: U.S. Agency for International Development.

For more on economic development and foreign aid, see the Case and Fair Web page at
http://www.prenhall.com/casefair.

include rapid population growth, food shortages, agricultural output and pricing policies, and the Third World debt problem.

POPULATION GROWTH

The populations of the developing nations are estimated to be growing at about 1.7 percent per year. (Compare this with a population growth rate of only 0.5 percent per year in the industrial market economies.) If the Third World's population growth rate remains at 1.7 percent, within 41 years the population of the Third World will double from its 1990 level of 4.1 billion to over 8 billion by the year 2031. It will take the industrialized nations 139 years to double their populations. What is so immediately alarming about these numbers is that given the developing nations' current economic problems, it is hard to imagine how they can possibly absorb so many more people in such a relatively short period.

Concern over world population growth is not new. The Reverend Thomas Malthus (who became England's first professor of political economy) expressed his fears about the population increases he observed 200 years ago. Malthus believed populations grow geometrically (at a constant growth rate: thus the absolute size of the increase each year gets larger and larger), but that food supplies grow much more slowly because of the diminishing marginal productivity of land.[2] These two phenomena led Malthus to predict the increasing impoverishment of the world's people unless population growth could be slowed.

Malthus's fears for Europe and America proved unfounded. He neither anticipated the technological changes that revolutionized agricultural productivity nor the eventual decrease in population growth rates in Europe and North America. But Malthus's prediction may have been right, only premature. Do the circumstances in the developing world now fit his predictions? Although some contemporary observers believe the Malthusian view is correct and the earth's population will eventually grow to a level that the world's resources cannot support, others say technological change and demographic transitions (to slower population growth rates) will permit further increases in global welfare.

▶ **The Consequences of Rapid Population Growth** We know far less about the economic consequences of rapid population growth than you might expect. Conventional wisdom warns of dire economic consequences from the developing nations' "population explosion," but these predictions are difficult to substantiate with the available evidence. The rapid economic growth of the United States, for example, was accompanied by relatively rapid population growth by historical standards. Nor has any slowing of population growth been necessary for the economic progress achieved by many of the newly industrialized countries. Nonetheless, population expansion in many of today's poorest nations is of a magnitude unprecedented in world history, as Figure 22.1 clearly shows. From the year A.D. 1 until the mid-1600s, populations grew slowly, at rates of only about 0.04 percent per

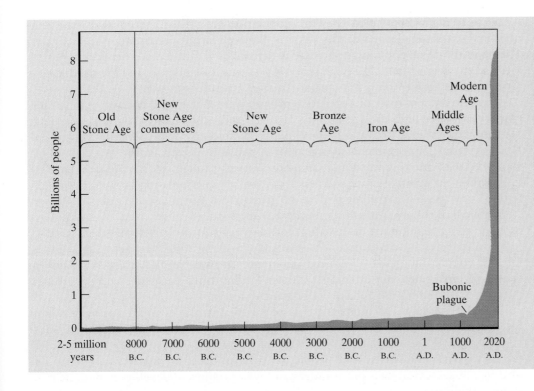

FIGURE 22.1

The Growth of World Population, Projected to 2020 A.D.

For thousands of years, population grew slowly. From A.D. 1 until the mid-1600s, population grew at about .04% per year. Since the Industrial Revolution, population growth has occurred at an unprecedented rate.

---

[2]The law of diminishing marginal productivity says that with a fixed amount of a resource (land), additions of more and more of a variable resource (labor) will produce smaller and smaller gains in output.

CHAPTER TWENTY-TWO
*Economic Growth
in Developing Nations* **493**

year. Since then, and especially since 1950, rates have skyrocketed. Today, populations are growing at rates of 1.5 percent to 4.0 percent per year throughout the developing world.

Because growth rates like these have never occurred before the twentieth century, no one knows what impact they will have on future economic development. But a basic economic concern is that such rapid population growth may limit investment and restrain increases in labor productivity and income. Rapid population growth changes the age composition of a population, generating many dependent children relative to the number of productive working adults. Such a situation may diminish saving rates, and hence investment, as the immediate consumption needs of the young take priority over saving for the future.

Even if low saving rates are not a necessary consequence of rapid population growth, as some authorities contend, other economic problems remain. The ability to improve human capital through a broad range of programs, from infant nutrition to formal secondary education, may be severely limited if the population explosion continues. Such programs are most often the responsibility of the state, and governments that are already weak cannot be expected to improve their services under the burden of population pressures that rapidly increase demands for all kinds of public goods and services.

For example, Mozambique's population growth rate—3.7 percent—is one of the highest in the world. It is likely that its 1997 population of over 17 million people will grow by about 3.4 million in the next five years and by 7.5 million in the next decade. This is a daunting prospect, and it is hard to imagine how in so little time Mozambique, with per capita GNP under $100, will be able to provide its population with the physical and human capital needed to maintain, let alone improve, already low standards of living.

▶ **Causes of Rapid Population Growth** Population growth is determined by the relationship between births and deaths—that is, between **fertility rates** and **mortality rates**. The **natural rate of population increase** is defined as the difference between the birth rate and the death rate. If the birth rate is 4 percent, for example, and the death rate is 3 percent, the population is growing at a rate of 1 percent per year.

Historically, low rates of population growth were maintained because of high mortality rates despite high levels of fertility. That is, families had many children, but average life expectancies were low, and many children (and adults) died young. In Europe and North America, improvements in nutrition, in public health programs (especially those concerned with drinking water and sanitation services), and in medical practices have led to a drop in the mortality rate and hence to more rapid population growth. Eventually fertility rates also fell, returning population growth to a low and stable rate.

Public health programs and improved nutrition over the past 30 years have brought about precipitous declines in mortality rates in the developing nations also. But fertility rates have not declined as quickly, and the result has been high natural rates of population growth. Reduced population growth depends to some extent on decreased birth rates, but attempts to lower fertility rates must take account of how different cultures feel and behave with regard to fertility.

Family planning and modern forms of birth control are important mechanisms for decreasing fertility, but by themselves have had rather limited success in most countries where they have been tried. If family planning strategies are to be successful, they must make sense to the people who are supposed to benefit from them. The planners of such strategies must understand why families in developing nations have so many children.

To a great extent, in developing countries people want large families because they

fertility rate *The birth rate. Equal to (the number of births per year divided by the population) × 100.*

mortality rate *The death rate. Equal to (the number of deaths per year divided by the population) × 100.*

natural rate of population increase *The difference between the birth rate and the death rate. It does not take migration into account.*

believe they need them. Economists have attempted to understand fertility patterns in the developing countries by focusing on the determinants of the demand for children. In agrarian societies, children are sources of farm labor, and they may make significant contributions to household income. In societies without public old-age support social security programs, children may also provide a source of income for parents who are too old to support themselves. With the high value of children enhanced by high rates of infant mortality, it is no wonder that families try to have many children to ensure that a sufficient number will survive into adulthood.

Cultural and religious values also affect the number of children families want to have, but the economic incentives to have large families are extremely powerful. Only when the relationship between the costs and benefits of having children changes will fertility rates decline. Expanding employment opportunities for women in an economy increases the opportunity costs of child rearing (by giving women a more highly valued alternative to raising children) and often leads to lower birth rates. Government incentives for smaller families, such as subsidized education for families with fewer than three children, can have a similar effect. In general, rising incomes appear to decrease fertility rates, indicating that economic development itself reduces population growth rates.

Economic theories of population growth suggest that fertility decisions made by poor families should not be viewed as uninformed and uncontrolled. An individual family may find that having many children is a rational strategy for economic survival given the conditions in which it finds itself. This does not mean, however, that having many children is a net benefit to society as a whole. When a family decides to have a large number of children, it imposes costs on the rest of society; the children must be educated, their health provided for, and so forth. In other words, what makes sense for an individual household may create negative effects for the nation as a whole.

SEVERAL AFRICAN NATIONS HAVE COME TO RELY ON FOREIGN SUPPORT TO HELP PROVIDE FOOD FOR THEIR PEOPLE. HERE, YOU SEE GRAIN RECEIVED FROM THE FRENCH RED CROSS BY PEOPLE IN RWANDA.

> Any nation that wants to slow its rate of population growth will probably find it necessary to have in place economic incentives for fewer children as well as family planning programs.

FOOD SHORTAGES: ACTS OF NATURE OR HUMAN MISTAKES?

Television footage and newspaper photos portraying victims of the famine in Somalia burned indelible images of starving people into the minds of most Americans. No other recent event so forcefully dramatized the ongoing food crisis in many developing nations. The famines that have struck various parts of Africa and Asia in the past 15 years represent the most acute form of the chronic food shortage confronting the developing nations.

Pictures of the parched Somalian countryside might lead an observer to conclude that famines are acts of nature—if the rains do not come or the locusts do, human beings can do little. But this simplistic view of food shortages fails to recognize the extent to which contemporary food crises are the result of human behavior. Even such natural events as severe flooding can often be traced to the overharvesting of firewood, which denudes the landscape, increases soil erosion, and exacerbates spring floods.

Human behavior is a very strong factor in the inadequate distribution of available food to those who need it. India now grows enough grains to feed its vast population, for example, but malnutrition remains widespread because many people cannot afford to feed themselves. Other parts of the distribution problem involve failures to stockpile adequate food reserves in years of good harvests and transportation and communication barriers that prevent supplies from reaching those in need. World and domestic politics also heavily influence where, how, and whether food is available. During the Ethiopian famine in 1988, for example, the Ethiopian government blocked relief agencies from delivering food and medical supplies to the famine area because a civil war was being waged there. Similar events occurred when the United Nations attempted to aid Somalia in 1992. This led to U.S. military intervention in 1992 and 1993. War between the Hutu and the Tutsis in Rwanda in 1994 led to mass exodus into Zaire, loss of crops, and starvation. In 1997, a bitter civil war in the Congo (formerly Zaire) left millions in refugee camps.

Severe food shortages are recognized chronic problems, but developing nations often pursue farm policies that actually discourage agricultural production. Agricultural production in sub-Saharan Africa today is lower than it was 20 years ago, and economists believe that misguided agricultural policies are responsible for much of this decline.

AGRICULTURAL OUTPUT AND PRICING POLICIES

Few governments in either industrialized or developing nations have permitted market forces alone to determine agricultural prices. In the United States and much of Europe, farm subsidies often encourage production that results in food surpluses rather than shortages. Some developing nations follow similar policies, maintaining high farm prices both to increase agricultural production and to maintain farm incomes. However, many developing nations follow a different route, offering farmers low prices for their output.

produce-marketing boards
The channels through which the governments of some developing countries buy domestic farm output and then sell it to urban residents at government-controlled prices.

To appreciate the motives behind different pricing policies, you need to understand several things about the structure of agricultural markets in many developing nations. Often the government is the primary purchaser of both basic foodstuffs and export crops. Through **produce-marketing boards**, the governments of some developing countries buy farm output and sell it to urban residents at government-controlled prices. By setting the prices they pay to farmers at low levels, the government can afford to sell basic foodstuffs to urban consumers at low prices. Governments often find this an attractive course of action because the direct political influence of the relatively small urban population typically far outweighs the influence of the majority who live in the countryside. Because most city dwellers spend about half their incomes on food, low consumer prices bolster the real incomes of the urban residents and help keep them content. Urban food riots have been common in developing nations over the years, and whether a government is allowed to exist may hinge on its food-pricing strategy.

Although we can easily appreciate the political motives behind food pricing, policies that set artificially low prices have significant pitfalls. Farmers react to these prices—often set so low that farmers cannot cover their production costs—by reducing the amount of output they produce. In the city, meanwhile, excess demand for food at the artificially low ceiling prices imposed by the government may promote the emergence of black markets.

Many developing economies that have followed low agricultural pricing policies have experienced exactly these results. Until recently, for example, Mexico kept corn prices low to hold down the price of tortillas, the staple in the diet of much of Mexico's urban population. Corn production fell as farmers switched to crops whose prices the government did not control. Domestic corn shortages became widespread, and corn had to be imported to sustain urban demand.

▶ **Agricultural Output: The Supply Side** In 1998, a single U.S. farmer could provide enough food to feed 80 people. In most developing economies, a single farmer can provide barely enough food to feed his or her own family. Though differences in agricultural pricing policies account for a part of this gap, there are other factors. Low agricultural productivity in the developing world was blamed on the ignorance and laziness of peasant farmers. Today's more enlightened view recognizes a shortage of inputs, including land, fertilizer, irrigation, machinery, new seed varieties, and agricultural extension services (credit and technical advice).

Modern agricultural science has created a so-called **Green Revolution** (not to be confused with the "environmental revolution") based on new, high-yield varieties of wheat, rice, and other crops. Using new, faster-growing varieties instead of the single-crop plants they have relied upon for centuries, some farmers can now grow three crops of rice a year. In Mexico, under ideal conditions, "miracle" wheat has produced 105 bushels of grain per acre, compared with traditional varieties that yield only 11.5 bushels per acre.

Green Revolution *The agricultural breakthroughs of modern science, such as the development of new, high-yield crop varieties.*

If the Green Revolution suggests that science can, in principle, solve world food shortages, the developing countries' experiments with scientific agriculture offers a less optimistic outlook. Economic factors have greatly limited the adoption of Green Revolution techniques in developing countries. New seeds are expensive, and their cultivation requires the presence of many complementary inputs, including fertilizers and irrigation. With poorly developed rural credit markets, farmers often face interest rates so high that new technologies, regardless of their promise of higher crop yields, are out of reach or ultimately unprofitable. Although the reluctance of peasant farmers to adopt new agricultural techniques has often been blamed on superstition or lack of education, such decisions typically reflect a rational choice. Given the costs and benefits of new inputs and the inherent riskiness of any new method of cultivation, it is not surprising that it has been difficult to get farmers in the developing nations to accept the advances of the Green Revolution.

Peasant farmers in developing nations are also constrained by the amount of land they have to work. In some countries, high population density in the rural areas requires highly labor-intensive cultivation. In others, poor distribution of land decreases agricultural output. Throughout Latin America, for example, it is estimated that less than 2 percent of all landowners control almost 75 percent of the land under cultivation. Improved crop yields often follow land reforms that redistribute holdings, because owner households are often more productive than tenant farmers. Land reform has had positive effects on output in countries with economic systems as diverse as those of Korea and the People's Republic of China.

> Although acts of nature will always threaten agricultural production, human actions, especially policies designed to support the agricultural sector, can have a major impact on reducing the food problems of the developing world.

THIRD WORLD DEBT

In the 1970s, development experts worried about many crises facing the developing world, but not the debt crisis. Within a decade, this changed dramatically. The financial plight of nations such as Brazil, Mexico, and the Philippines has become front-page news. What alarmed those familiar with the debt situation was not only its potential impact on the developing nations, but a belief that it threatened the economic welfare of the developed nations as well.

Between 1970 and 1984, developing nations borrowed so much money from other nations that their combined debt increased by 1,000 percent, to almost $700 billion. Three nations alone—Brazil, Mexico, and Venezuela—had outstanding loans to three major U.S. banks (Citibank, Chase-Manhattan, and Manufacturer's Hanover, now part of Chemical) that were more than double the net worth of those financial institutions. As recession took hold in the economically advanced countries during the early 1980s, growth in the exports of the debtor countries slowed, and many found they could no longer pay back the money they owed.

As the situation continued to deteriorate, many feared that debtor nations might repudiate their debts outright and default on their outstanding loans. When *default* (nonpayment) occurs with domestic loans, some collateral is usually available to cover all or part of the remaining debt. For loans to another country, such collateral is virtually impossible to secure. Given their extensive involvement with Third World borrowers, Western banks did not want to set in motion a pattern of international default. Nor did borrowers want to default. Leaders of the developing nations recognized that default might result in the denial of access to developed-country banking facilities and to markets in the industrial countries, posing major obstacles to further development efforts.

debt rescheduling *An agreement between banks and borrowers through which a new schedule of repayments of the debt is negotiated; often some of the debt is written off and the repayment period is extended.*

stabilization program *An agreement between a borrower country and the International Monetary Fund in which the country agrees to revamp its economic policies to provide incentives for higher export earnings and lower imports.*

Various countries rescheduled their debt as an interim solution. Under a **debt rescheduling** agreement, banks and borrowers negotiate a new schedule for the repayment of existing debt, often with some of the debt written off and with repayment periods extended. In return, borrowing countries are expected to sign an agreement with the International Monetary Fund to revamp their economic policies to provide incentives for higher export earnings and lower imports. This kind of agreement, referred to as a **stabilization program**, usually requires austerity measures such as currency devaluations, a reduction in government expenditures, and an increase in tax revenues.

By the early 1990s, the debt crisis was not over but it had lessened, mainly as a result of macroeconomic events that led to reduced interest rates. The international economy has revived somewhat, helping some nations to increase their export earnings. Other nations have benefited from new domestic policies. Still others, including Panama, and many African nations, however, continue to face debt burdens that

COUNTRY	TOTAL EXTERNAL DEBT	TOTAL DEBT AS A PERCENTAGE OF GDP
Mexico	$165.7	69.9
Brazil	159.1	24.0
Russian Federation	120.5	37.6
China	118.1	17.2
Indonesia	107.8	56.9
India	93.8	28.2
Argentina	89.7	33.1
Turkey	73.6	44.1
Thailand	56.8	34.9
Peru	30.8	54.1
Nicaragua	9.3	589.7

TABLE 22.4 TOTAL (PUBLIC AND PRIVATE) EXTERNAL DEBT FOR SELECTED COUNTRIES, 1995 (BILLIONS OF DOLLARS)

Source: World Bank, *World Development Report,* 1997.

are unmanageable in the short run. Table 22.4 presents figures for selected countries in 1995.

Of concern in recent years has been Mexico's monetary and debt situation. Mexico's total external debt in 1995, $166 billion, was highest in the world. Following approval of the North American Free-Trade Agreement (NAFTA), there was great optimism about Mexico, and massive amounts of capital flowed to Mexico to take advantage of the relatively high interest rates available on Mexican debt. As a result, Mexico's total external debt increased dramatically. Though the flow of capital pushed up the value of the peso during 1993 and early 1994, by mid-1994 investors had become nervous about the possibility of a decline in the peso's value and began to pull out of Mexico. The peso's value finally collapsed in early 1995, and the Mexican government's inability to get investors to buy Mexican bonds pushed it to the brink of defaulting on its obligations. A loan guarantee of $37 billion from the United States and the International Monetary Fund at least temporarily restored confidence and may have saved Mexico the embarrassment of a default in 1995.

In 1997, several Asian countries including Korea and Thailand had financial problems that led to loan guarantee funds from the International Monetary Fund. Korea's package totaled over $50 billion.

One economic lesson of the last two decades is that proper management of foreign capital in developing countries is essential. Much foreign borrowing was wasted on projects that had little chance of generating the returns necessary to pay back their initial costs. In other cases, domestic policies that used debt as a substitute for adjusting to new economic circumstances proved to be harmful in the long run. And, overall, much optimism about the prospects of the developing economies was inappropriate. Whatever else we may have learned from these mistakes, the debt crisis underscored the growing interdependence of all economies—rich and poor, large and small.

SUMMARY

1. The economic problems facing the developing countries are often quite different from those confronting industrialized nations. The policy options available to governments may also differ. Nonetheless, the tools of economic analysis are as useful in understanding the economies of less developed countries as in understanding the U.S. economy.

LIFE IN THE DEVELOPING NATIONS: POPULATION AND POVERTY

2. The central reality of life in the developing countries is poverty. Although there is considerable diversity across the developing nations, most of the people in most developing countries are extremely poor by U.S. standards.

ECONOMIC DEVELOPMENT: SOURCES AND STRATEGIES

3. Almost all developing nations have a scarcity of physical capital relative to other resources, especially labor. The *vicious-circle-of-poverty hypothesis* says poor countries cannot escape from poverty because they cannot afford to postpone consumption (that is, to save) to make investments. In its crude form, the hypothesis is wrong inasmuch as some prosperous countries were at one time poorer than many developing countries are today. However, it is often difficult to mobilize savings efficiently in many developing nations.

4. Human capital—the stock of education and skills embodied in the workforce—plays a vital role in economic development.

5. Developing countries are often burdened by inadequate *social overhead capital*, ranging from poor public health and sanitation facilities to inadequate roads, telephones, and court systems. Such social overhead capital is often expensive to provide, and many governments are simply not in a position to undertake many useful projects because they are too costly.

6. Because developed economies are characterized by a large share of output and employment in the industrial sector, many developing countries seem to believe that development and industrialization are synonymous. In many cases, developing countries have pursued industry at the expense of agriculture, with mixed results. Recent evidence suggests that some balance between industry and agriculture leads to the best outcome.

7. *Import substitution* policies, a trade strategy that favors developing local industries that can manufacture goods to replace imports, were once very common in the developing nations. In general, such policies have not succeeded as well as those promoting open, export-oriented economies.

8. The failure of many central planning efforts has brought increasing calls for less government intervention and more market orientation in developing economies.

ISSUES IN ECONOMIC DEVELOPMENT

9. Rapid population growth is characteristic of many developing countries. Large families can be economically rational for parents who need support in their old age, or because children offer an important source of labor. But having many children does not mean a net benefit to society as whole. Rapid population growth can put a strain on already overburdened public services, such as education and health.

10. Food shortages in developing countries are not simply the result of bad weather. Public policies that depress the prices of agricultural goods, thereby lowering farmers' incentives to produce, are common throughout the developing nations, and in such countries, human behavior is very much behind the inadequate distribution of available food to those who need it.

11. Between 1970 and 1984 the debts of the developing countries grew tenfold. As recession took hold in the advanced countries during the early 1980s, growth in the exports of the debtor countries slowed, and many found they could no longer pay back money they owed. The prospect of loan defaults by Third World nations threatened the entire international financial system and transformed the debt crisis into a global problem.

REVIEW TERMS AND CONCEPTS

brain drain, 487
capital flight, 486
debt rescheduling, 498
export promotion, 489
fertility rate, 494
Green Revolution, 497
import substitution, 489
International Monetary Fund, 490

mortality rate, 494
natural rate of population increase, 494
produce-marketing boards, 496
social overhead capital, 487
stabilization program, 498
structural adjustment, 491
vicious-circle-of-poverty hypothesis, 486
World Bank, 490

PROBLEM SET

1. Two developing countries that have been in the news lately are Thailand and Indonesia. Both countries were experiencing excellent growth during the early 1990s but fell on hard times in 1997. Choose either country and, using indexes to the popular press (like the *Wall Street Journal* or the *New York Times*), write a chronology of events starting in 1997. Using what you have learned in economics, what explanations can you offer for what happened? Were the problems that arose problems of mismanagement by governments, or were they the result of the way the markets worked (or failed to work)? What lessons have we learned?

2. For a developing country to grow, it needs capital. The major source of capital in most countries is domestic saving. But the goal of stimulating domestic saving usually is in conflict with government policies aimed at reducing inequality in the distribution of income. Comment on this trade-off between equity and growth. How would you go about resolving the issue if you were the president of a small, poor country?

3. Financial markets have become increasingly international. Savings flows very quickly between countries as investment opportunities arise or expectations change. International investors are reluctant to invest in countries where there is political or economic instability, and domestic investors, faced with uncertainty at home, are likely to protect their wealth by investing it in safe countries. During 1997 and 1998, there was much uncertainty and instability in many parts of the developing world. At the same time, the United States economy was very stable. What effect was this likely to have had on the value of the dollar? Explain. Verify what actually happened to the value of the dollar during 1997 (see, for example, the *Economic Report of the President*). What are the short- and long-term implications for the developing countries?

4. The GDP of any country can be divided into two kinds of goods: capital goods and consumption goods. The proportion of national output devoted to capital goods determines, to some extent, the nation's growth rate.

   a. Explain how capital accumulation leads to economic growth.
   b. Briefly describe how a market economy determines how much investment will be undertaken each period.
   c. "Consumption versus investment is a more painful conflict to resolve for developing countries." Comment on this statement.
   d. If you were the benevolent dictator of a developing country, what plans would you implement to increase per capita GDP?

5. "The main reason developing countries are poor is that they don't have enough capital. If we give them machinery, or build factories for them, we can greatly improve their situation." Comment.

6. "Poor countries are trapped in a vicious circle of poverty. For output to grow, they must accumulate capital. To accumulate capital, they must save (consume less than they produce). But because they are poor, they have little or no extra output available for savings—it must all go to feed and clothe the present generation. Thus they are doomed to stay poor forever." Comment on each step in this argument.

7. If children are an "investment in the future," why do some developing nations offer incentives to households that limit the size of their families? Why are these incentives often ignored?

8. If you were in charge of economic policy for a developing country and wanted to promote rapid economic growth, would you choose to favor industry over agriculture? What about exports versus import substitution? In each case, briefly explain your reasoning. How do you explain the fact that many countries chose industry and a protectionist import-substitution policy?

9. "Famines are acts of God, resulting from bad weather or other natural disasters. There is nothing we can do about them except to send food relief after they occur." Explain why this position is inaccurate. Concentrate on agricultural pricing policies and distributional issues.

TAKE IT TO THE NET

We invite you to visit the Case and Fair page on the Prentice Hall Web site:

http://www.prenhall.com/casefair

for this chapter's World Wide Web exercise.

Chapter 23

ECONOMIES IN TRANSITION AND ALTERNATIVE ECONOMIC SYSTEMS

FOR 40 YEARS, between the end of World War II and the mid-1980s, a powerful rivalry existed between the Soviet Union and the United States. This "cold war" pitted the two superpowers against each other in a struggle for influence and fueled the nuclear arms race. At one time the mutual distrust between them was so strong that the concept of "mutual assured destruction" dominated international relations.

But the world began to change in the mid-1980s as the political and economic structures of the Soviet Union and the Eastern European Communist countries started to crumble. In 1989, relatively peaceful revolutions took place in rapid succession in Poland, Hungary, and Czechoslovakia (now the Czech Republic). A bloody revolution in Romania toppled Nicolae Ceausescu, who had ruled with an iron fist for 24 years. The Berlin Wall, which had separated Berlin since 1961, was knocked down and Germany was reunited. Then, in August 1991, after a failed coup attempt by hard-line Communists, the Soviet Union itself began to come apart. By the end of 1991, the Soviet Union had dissolved into 15 independent states, the largest is the Russian Republic. Ten of these 15 republics formed the Commonwealth of Independent States (CIS) in December 1991. The Cold War was over.

We reflect on historical political rivalries in an economics text for two reasons. First, the 40-year struggle between the United States and the Soviet Union was fundamentally a struggle between two economic systems: market-based capitalism (the U.S. system) and centrally planned socialism (the Soviet system). Second, the Cold War ended so abruptly in the late 1980s because the Soviet and Eastern European economies virtually collapsed during that period. In a sense, we could say 1991 was the year that the market triumphed.

What now? The independent states of the former Soviet Union and the other former Communist economies of Eastern Europe are struggling to make the transition from centrally planned socialism to some form of market-based capitalism. In some countries, such as Serbia and Bosnia-Herzegovina, economic reforms have taken a back seat to bitter and violent ethnic and political rivalries that have been simmering for decades. In other countries, like Poland and Russia, the biggest issue continues to be economic transformation.

The success or failure of this transition from centrally planned socialism to market-based capitalism will determine the course of history. Although many countries have made the transition from a market-based system to a centrally planned system, the opposite has never occurred. The process has been and will continue to be painful and filled with ups and downs. Between 1989 and 1997, industrial production fell more than 40 percent in countries like the former East Germany, Albania, Poland, and Romania. In Russia, production decreased about 30 percent. In all these nations, fairly prosperous people suddenly found themselves with annual real incomes closer to those of people in developing countries. For many people, the issue became survival: how to get enough food and fuel to get through the winter.

By 1995, things had turned around, and though uncertainty and problems remained, output was rising in much of Eastern and Central Europe. A growing optimism seemed to be spreading. The biggest success story was in East Germany, where real output in 1994 grew by over 9 percent, the fastest growth rate of any region of Europe. A construction boom, rapid development of infrastructure, low inflation, and rising exports all contributed to the region's success. But East Germany's situation is unique because it was absorbed by a prosperous, fully developed, and modern West Germany that has made development in the East its primary goal.

Central Europe, including Hungary, Poland, the Czech Republic, Bulgaria, and Romania, also achieved basic macroeconomic stability and began to grow in 1993 and 1994. Poland enjoyed the most rapid economic growth in the group (around 4.5 percent). Fueled by foreign investment, privatization, and entrepreneurship, the Polish private sector by 1992 accounted for well over one-third of the nation's total output, although many problems persist. (See Global Perspective "The Challenges to Private Enterprise in Poland.") Russia and the former countries of the Soviet Union have achieved less through 1997. Nonetheless, conditions have improved and prospects for success are greater than they were only a few years ago.

In this chapter, we focus on the ongoing debate over economic reform. How to make the transition from socialism to capitalism successful? In what sequence should changes be made? How quickly can markets be established? How much help from the United States and the rest of the world will be required?

To understand the transformation process, it is necessary to begin with some history. From what are these countries making a transition? Our chapter starts with a discussion of alternative economic systems, the vision of communism, and a brief description of the economic structure of the former Soviet Union. We then turn to the current debate over the transition process, focusing on the experiences of Poland and Russia. We end the chapter by examining a different kind of economic transformation that has been ongoing for some time in China and discussing the performance of the Japanese economy since World War II.

POLITICAL SYSTEMS AND ECONOMIC SYSTEMS: SOCIALISM, CAPITALISM, AND COMMUNISM

Every society has both a political system and an economic system. Unfortunately, the political and economic dimensions of a society are often confused.

The terms *democracy* and *dictatorship* refer to *political* systems. A *democracy* is a system of government in which ultimate power rests with the people, who make

THE CHALLENGES TO PRIVATE ENTERPRISE IN POLAND

Since 1991 the private sectors of most of the countries of the former Soviet Union and the formerly Communist countries of Central and Eastern Europe have expanded dramatically. Outside of East Germany, Poland's private sector has expanded the most, and it now accounts for well over a third of the economy's production.

This private expansion comes from four sources:

■ FIRST, thousands of entrepreneurs have started new businesses. It is estimated that more than 2 million Polish entrepreneurs have formed businesses, and small business in Poland is growing at about 10 percent per year.

■ SECOND, foreign investment is flowing into the region, although not at the pace once anticipated.

■ THIRD, "spontaneous privatizations," initiated by managers of state-owned enterprises, have converted many firms to private ownership without a great deal of state participation. The earliest forms of spontaneous privatization in Russia took the form of managers setting up parallel private firms opposite or even inside state-owned enterprises. The new private firm would buy the product of the state-owned enterprise at a controlled price and then resell it at the market price.

■ FOURTH, most countries have been selling off state-owned private enterprises directly or indirectly to private shareholders.[a]

Because the process of selling off state-owned assets has been slow, much of the economic action has occurred in entrepreneurial businesses.

Start-ups are the engine of Poland's post-communist boom. A book published this month by the Economist Intelligence Unit, a sister company of The Economist, *calculates that private firms have trebled their share in industrial output since the transition began, from 16% of gross sales at the end of 1989 to 45% in 1995—an annual growth rate of more than a fifth. Since small businesses have every incentive to understate their performance, the real picture is probably even brighter.*

Of course not every post-communist start-up is successful. Mr. Kunsch, at Creditanstalt in Budapest, reckons that the failure rate in Hungary is around 30%—one reason why his own and other banks are so cautious about lending to them. But all the post-communist economies have their quota of success stories, in both manufacturing and service industries. Euronet, a Hungarian operator of bank teller machines, is already listed on Nasdaq, America's small-company stock exchange, PCs, a software developer which started in Prague with
$3,000 in 1990, now has over 100 employees and sales of $30m.

The success of these companies (some of which have annual rates of return on capital of several hundred per cent) is all the more remarkable seen against the uphill struggle of their early years. Premises were cramped, working capital scarce, infrastructure fragile and the bureaucracy tiresome. Many entrepreneurs say that it is only now—with finance becoming easier and their credibility with foreign partners rising—that their businesses can really take off.

The start-ups have done so well for two main reasons. First, they were expanding into a vacuum. The collapse of communism created new markets overnight. Even when competing products or services existed, the locals often turned out to be more knowledgeable, hard-working, flexible and cost-effective.

The second reason has to do with human nature. For Eastern Europeans who had seen large chunks of their working lives wasted by communism, starting a business offered the chance to catch up. . . . Self-employment, therefore, has attracted a large number of Eastern Europe's brightest and best, with impressive results.[b]

Sources: [a]Olivier Jean Blanchard, Kenneth A. Froot, and Jeffrey D. Sachs, eds., *The Transition in Eastern Europe* (Chicago: University of Chicago Press, 1994), [b]*The Economist,* November 22–28, 1997, "Survey: Business in Eastern Europe," p. 10.

For more on economies in transition, see the Case and Fair Web page at
http://www.prenhall.com/casefair.

governmental decisions either directly through voting or indirectly through representatives. A *dictatorship* is a political system in which ultimate power is concentrated in either a small elite group or a single person.

Historically, two major *economic* systems have existed: socialism and capitalism. A **socialist economy** is one in which most capital—factories, equipment, buildings, railroads, and so forth—is owned by the government rather than by private

socialist economy *An economy in which most capital is owned by the government rather than by private citizens. Also called social ownership.*

capitalist economy *An economy in which most capital is privately owned.*

communism *An economic system in which the people control the means of production (capital and land) directly, without the intervention of a government or state.*

citizens. *Social ownership* is another term that is used to describe this kind of system. A **capitalist economy** is one in which most capital is privately owned. Beyond these systems is a purely theoretical economic system called *communism*.

Communism is an economic system in which the people control the means of production (land and capital) directly, without the intervention of a government or state. In the world envisioned by communists, the state would wither away and society would plan the economy in the same way a collective would. Although some countries still consider themselves communist—including China, North Korea, Cuba, and Tanzania—economic planning is done by the government in all of them.

> Comparing economies today, the real distinction is between centrally planned socialism and capitalism, not between capitalism and communism.

No pure socialist economies and no pure capitalist economies exist. Even the Soviet Union, which was basically socialist, had a large private sector. Fully one-fourth of agricultural output in what was the USSR was legally produced on private plots and sold, and in a large "second economy" private citizens provided goods and services to each other, sometimes in violation of the law. Conversely, the strongly capitalistic United States supports many government enterprises, including the postal system. Nonetheless, public ownership is the exception in the United States and private ownership was the exception in the Soviet Union.

Whether particular kinds of political systems tend to be associated with particular kinds of economic systems is debated. The United States and Japan are countries with essentially capitalist economic systems and essentially democratic political institutions. China and North Korea have basically socialist economies with political power highly concentrated in a single political party. These observations do not imply that all capitalist countries have democratic political institutions, nor that all socialist countries are subject to totalitarian party rule.

Many countries—Indonesia, for example—have basically capitalist economies without democratic political systems. Many other countries that are much closer to the socialist end of the economic spectrum also maintain strong democratic traditions. The people of France, for instance, elected the socialist government of François Mitterrand in 1981, and that government promptly nationalized several major industries. Great Britain and Sweden are other examples of democratic countries that support certain strong socialist institutions.

But do certain kinds of economic systems lead to repressive governments? Austrian economist Friedrich Hayek argues yes:

> Economic reforms and government coercion are the road to serfdom. . . . Personal and economic freedoms are inseparable. Once you start down the road to government regulation and planning of the economy, the freedom to speak minds and select political leaders will be jeopardized.[1]

The recent events in Eastern Europe and Russia seem to support Hayek's thesis. There, economic and political reforms are proceeding side by side, and the evidence is mounting that the heart of both the market system *and* democracy is individual freedom.

Nonetheless, some counter Hayek's argument by claiming that social reform and active government involvement in the economy are the only ways to prevent the rise of a totalitarian state. They argue that free and unregulated markets lead to inequality

---

[1]Friedrich Hayek, *The Road to Serfdom* (Chicago: University of Chicago Press, 1944).

and the accumulation of economic power. Accumulated economic power, in turn, leads to political power that is inevitably used in the interests of the wealthy few, not in the interests of all.

CENTRAL PLANNING VERSUS THE MARKET

In addition to ownership of capital, economic systems also differ in the extent to which economic decisions are made through central planning rather than through a market system. In some socialist economies, the allocation of resources, the mix of output, and the distribution of output are determined centrally according to a plan. The former Soviet Union, for example, generated one-year and five-year plans laying out specific production targets in virtually every sector of the economy. In market economies, decisions are made independently by buyers and sellers responding to market signals. Producers produce only what they expect to sell. Labor is attracted into and out of various occupations by wages that are determined by the forces of supply and demand.

Just as there are no pure capitalist and no pure socialist economies, there are no pure market economies and no pure planned economies. Even in the former Soviet Union markets existed and determined, to a large extent, the allocation of resources. Production targets in the United States are set by many agencies, including the Pentagon.

Generally, socialist economies favor central planning over market allocation, while capitalist economies rely to a much greater extent on the market. Nonetheless, some variety exists. The former Yugoslavia was a socialist country that made extensive use of the market. Ownership of capital and land rested with the government, but individual firms determined their own output levels and prices and made their own investment plans. Yugoslavian firms borrowed from banks to finance investments and paid interest on their loans. This type of system, which combines government ownership with market allocation, is referred to as a **market-socialist economy**.

market-socialist economy
An economy that combines government ownership with market allocation.

THE ECONOMIC THEORIES OF KARL MARX

The conflict between economic systems has taken place on two levels. On one, there are alternative economic *theories* that lead to very different conclusions about the relative merits of market-capitalist and planned socialist systems. On the other, the actual *performance* of these different economies must be considered.

The events of the early 1990s in Eastern Europe provide strong evidence that central planning has come up a big loser on the basis of performance. Why, then, should we spend time studying the theoretical underpinnings of communism and socialism? There are at least three reasons. First, for over 70 years in the Soviet Union, and for over 40 years in most parts of Eastern Europe and China, socialist ideology was dominant. Until very recently, about one-third of the world's population lived in countries whose economies were based on socialist and communist philosophies. Second, even though the economies of the republics of the former Soviet Union and the economies of Eastern Europe are moving rapidly toward a market-based system, a number of other countries remain firmly committed to the ideas of centrally planned socialism. Finally, to understand the capitalist system, one must understand the criticisms that have been leveled against it.

➤ **Marxian Economics: An Overview** Perhaps no single modern thinker has had a greater impact on the world in the twentieth century than Karl Marx, whose work is the basis of the communist ideology. Marxian economic analysis concludes that the capitalist system is morally wrong and doomed to ultimate failure.

The most common misconception about Marx's work is that it contains a blueprint for the operation of a socialist or communist economy. In fact, Marx did not write much about socialism; he wrote about capitalism. Published mostly after his death in 1883, his major work, the three-volume *Das Kapital*, is an extensive analysis of how capitalist economies function and how they are likely to develop over time. *The Communist Manifesto* (written with Friedrich Engels and published in 1848) and his other writings contain only a rough sketch of the socialist and communist societies that Marx predicted would ultimately replace capitalism.

Marx's economic theories lie at the root of his interpretation of history. In examining his work, let us begin with what might be called "Marxian microeconomics" and then turn to the macroeconomic conclusions that emerge from it.

labor theory of value *Marx's theory that the value of a commodity depends exclusively upon the amount of labor required to produce it. Commodities are the physical embodiment of the labor that produced them, and capital is the physical embodiment of the past labor used to produce it.*

➤ **The Labor Theory of Value**   The center of Marx's economic theories is the **labor theory of value**. Marx argued that the value of a commodity depends exclusively upon the amount of labor required to produce it. Commodities are thus the physical embodiment of the labor that produced them:

> A commodity has value, because it is a crystallization of social labor. The greatness of its value, of its relative value, depends upon the greater or less amount of that social substance contained in it. . . .The relative values of commodities are, therefore, determined by the respective quantities or amounts of labor, worked up, realized, fixed in them.[2]

The labor theory of value also addresses the nature and uses of capital. Goods can be produced with a variety of combinations of capital and labor. Are goods produced with a lot of capital and little labor worth less than goods produced with a lot of labor and little capital? No. Capital, according to Marx, is the physical embodiment of the *past labor* that was used to produce it. When used in production, capital contributes value by passing that past labor through to the final product. A machine that took 100 hours to build contributes 100 hours of value to final products over its lifetime. The value of a commodity is the sum of the values contributed by present labor and past labor (capital).

means of production *Marx's term for land and capital.*

➤ **The Nature of Profit: The Marxian View**   If, as Marx believed, commodity values depend only on labor's contribution, where does profit come in? The answer: Capitalists own the **means of production**, Marx's term for land and capital. They hire individual workers who have no way to make a living except by selling their labor power. Capitalists make a profit by paying workers a daily wage that is less than the value that workers contribute to final products in a day.

value of labor power *The wage rate, dependent on the amount of clothing, shelter, basic education, medical care, and so on required to produce and sustain labor power.*

The wage rate is the **value of labor power**, and it is determined in the same way as the value of any other commodity. That is, the value of labor power depends on the amount of labor required to "produce" it. To produce and sustain labor power requires food, clothing, shelter, basic education, medical care, and so forth. The value of labor power, then, is determined by the amount of labor it takes to produce those things necessary to sustain a worker and his or her family. In essence, Marx was proposing a *subsistence theory of wages*: Capitalists will pay a wage that is just enough for laborers to live on.

surplus value *The profit a capitalist earns by paying workers less than the value of what they produce.*

Suppose it takes 4 hours to produce everything necessary to sustain a worker for a day. Marx would argue that a day's wage paid by capitalists will be the equivalent of 4 hours' worth of value. If a worker is employed for 12 hours, the capitalist ends up with a final product containing 12 hours of value but needs to give only four hours' worth of value—or wages—to the worker. The difference (8 hours), which Marx called **surplus value**, is profit.

[2]Karl Marx, *Wages, Price and Profit* (Beijing: Foreign Languages Press, 1975), pp. 34–35.

Profit is value created by workers but "expropriated" by capitalists. Capitalists are able to expropriate surplus value because they own the means of production and control access to them. Profit is not a reward for any productive activity; it is extracted solely by virtue of ownership. Marx referred to the ratio of surplus value to the value of labor power as the **rate of exploitation.**

rate of exploitation *The ratio of surplus value to the value of labor power.*

▶ **The Nature of Profit: The Neoclassical View** The bulk of this text has presented mainstream, or neoclassical, economic theory, with its deep roots in nineteenth-century philosophy. At this point we reflect briefly on the nature of profit in that model, because it is so different from the Marxian notion of surplus value.

Neoclassical economics views both capital and labor as productive factors of production. If you have one worker digging a hole and you want a bigger hole faster, you can accomplish your goal by hiring a second worker *or* by giving the first worker a better shovel. Add labor and you get more product; add capital and you also get more product. According to neoclassical theory, every factor of production in a competitive market economy ends up being paid in accordance with the market value of its product. Profit-maximizing firms hire labor and capital as long as both contribute more to the final value of a product than they cost.

Neoclassical theory views profit as the legitimate return to capital. Marx, however, saw profit as value created by labor and unjustly expropriated by nonproductive capitalists, who own the means of production and thus are able to exploit labor.

▶ **Marx's Predictions** The labor theory of value led Marx to conclude that capitalism was doomed. The essence of his argument was that the rate of profit has a natural tendency to fall over time. With the rate of profits falling, capitalists increase the rate of exploitation, pushing workers deeper and deeper into misery. At the same time, the ups and downs of business cycles become more and more extreme. Ultimately, Marx believed, workers would rise up and overthrow the repressive capitalist system.

The theory that capitalism would ultimately collapse was part of Marx's longer view of history. Capitalism had emerged naturally from a previous stage (*feudalism*), which had emerged from an even earlier stage (*ancient slavery*), and so forth. In the economic evolutionary process, Marx believed, capitalism would be replaced by socialism, which ultimately would be replaced by communism.

At each stage of economic evolution, Marx said, a set of rules called the *social relations of production* defines the economic system. Contradictions and conflicts inevitably arise at each stage, and these problems are ultimately resolved in the establishment of a new set of social relations. The conflicts in capitalism include alienation, increasing exploitation, misery (or, as Marx called it, "emiserization"), and deeper and deeper business cycles.

It is clear that Marx was eager for the demise of capitalism. He advocated strong and powerful labor unions for two reasons. First, unions would push wages above subsistence and transfer some surplus value back to workers. Second, unions were a way of raising the consciousness of workers about their condition. Only through class consciousness, Marx believed, would workers be empowered to throw off the shackles of capitalism.

At the heart of Marx's ideas is the argument that private ownership and profit are unfair and unethical. Even if it could be demonstrated that the incentives provided by the institution of private property result in faster economic growth or improved living standards, anyone who accepts Marx's interpretation has to reject capitalism on moral grounds, on ideological grounds, or on both.

TABLE 23.1

PER CAPITA INCOME (RUBLES)

	1861	1913
Russia	71	119
U.K.	323	580
France	150	303
Germany	175	374
U.S.	450	1,033
Netherlands	—	366
Norway	166	659
Sweden	112	340
Italy	183	261
Spain	—	199
Austria-Hungary	—	190

Source: Paul Gregory and Robert Stuart, *Soviet Economic Structure and Performance,* 2nd ed. (New York: Harper & Row, 1981), p. 20.

New Economic Policy *The Soviet economic policy in effect between 1921 and 1928; characterized by decentralization and a retreat to a market orientation.*

five-year plans *Plans developed in the Soviet Union that provided general guidelines and directions for the next five years.*

ECONOMIES IN TRANSITION: EXPERIENCES OF RUSSIA AND EASTERN EUROPE

The Eastern European nations' transitions to market systems were largely the result of the economic failures of centrally planned socialism, which had ultimately failed to "deliver the goods." To understand the failure of the Eastern European socialist economies and the difficult process of transition that lies ahead for them, students of economics must be aware of these countries' economic histories. Here, we briefly describe the Soviet system as it existed for nearly 75 years and the changes taking place today. Although the transformation process is well under way, it will be some time before the process of dismantling the old system is complete.

THE SOVIET UNION: HISTORY AND REFORM

Marx believed that socialist revolution would occur in advanced capitalist states where a repressive industrial society would push workers to unite and rise up against their industrialist masters. The Russian nation in 1913 had experienced the beginnings of modern economic growth, but it could hardly have been called an advanced capitalist system. Table 23.1 shows that its relative position in terms of per capita income had improved in the half century prior to 1913, but that it still lagged far behind the other industrial countries of the world.

When the Bolsheviks took power after the October Revolution in 1917, they found themselves without the advanced industrial base that Marx had envisioned and with no real blueprint for running a socialist or communist state. Marx's writings provided only the broadest guidelines. Undaunted, the new government immediately abolished private land ownership and ordered that the land be distributed to those who worked on it. It also established worker control of industry and nationalized the banks. Sweeping nationalization of industry began in June 1918. Money, private trade, and wage differentials were abolished. All decisions were made centrally.

The rush into uncharted waters was too much too soon. Between 1921 and 1928 Soviet leaders retreated from their initial hard line back toward a market orientation. The **New Economic Policy** of the period was characterized by decentralization. Most smaller industrial enterprises were denationalized, although the peasants remained in control of agriculture. State control of production was replaced by market links between consumers and industry and between industry and agriculture.

The relative merits and demerits of these two periods, 1917 to 1921 and 1921 to 1928, were debated among the Soviet leadership. In 1928, the Soviet Union settled on an economic structure that lasted into the 1980s: comprehensive central planning and collectivization of agriculture. In 1928, under the leadership of Joseph Stalin, the first of many **five-year plans** was approved. The plan emphasized rapid industrialization and the production of industrial capital; the plan called for a doubling of the fixed capital stock of the Soviet Union in five years. Consumer goods were to be produced only when all other needs of the new industrial structure had been met.

The industrialization program depended on a steady flow of food and agricultural raw materials from the countryside, and that did not come easily. As a result, Stalin was forced to rely more and more on coercion. In 1929 the land holdings of the peasants were organized into collective farms that were obligated to deliver state-ordered quotas of farm products. Repression was severe, and millions of peasants perished.[3]

---

[3]George Orwell's novel *Animal Farm* is a parable of this period in Soviet history.

No serious debate about economic matters took place in the Soviet Union until after Stalin's death in 1953. In 1965 official reforms were introduced by the government of Alexei Kosygin. Mikhail Gorbachev announced a series of reforms in 1986 and in 1987, but the structure of the economy was not changed fundamentally.

Since 1991, Boris Yeltsin has been president of the Russian Republic and the champion of reform. Yeltsin has deregulated most prices, begun the privatization process, and attempted to stabilize the macroeconomy. By 1995 progress had been slow but significant. Privatization had made steady progress, reaching a point in 1994 where the private sector was generating 60 percent of personal income. Inflation was down, and a new "economic constitution" in the form of revised laws to establish property rights and stimulate economic activity went into effect in 1995. But things were not going well across the board.

Most observers estimate that Russian GDP began to grow in the spring of 1997, after falling by about 50 percent from its 1989 level. However, problems remained severe into 1998. The biggest problem was attracting investment, and the biggest barrier was crime and corruption. The Russian government was finding it very difficult to enforce the rule of law. The term *cowboy capitalism* is often used to describe the situation in Russia today.

▶ **Economic Performance**   The Stalinist/Soviet strategy to achieve high rates of growth worked for many years. The highest rates of growth in Soviet GNP were during the 1950s. Official Soviet statistics put the real growth rate during that decade at over 10 percent, an extraordinary rate at which real output would double every seven years. Even the CIA's more conservative estimates, shown in Table 23.2, estimated the Soviet growth rate at 5.7 percent, nearly 80 percent above the U.S. average for the decade.

In 1957, the Soviet Union's GNP stood at about 39 percent of the U.S. GNP. A year later, Soviet GNP had jumped to nearly 44 percent of U.S. GNP. The rate at which the Soviet Union was catching up was so remarkable that it prompted Soviet premier Nikita Khrushchev to promise, "We will bury you!" If the Soviet growth rate estimates had been correct, and if both countries had continued to grow at the same rates as during the 1950s, Soviet GNP would have surpassed U.S. GNP by 1970.

TABLE 23.2   ECONOMIC GROWTH AND INVESTMENT IN THE SOVIET UNION AND THE UNITED STATES, 1950–1990

	ANNUAL AVERAGE RATE OF GROWTH				
	USSR NET MATERIAL PRODUCT (USSR, OFFICIAL FIGURES)	USSR REAL GNP (CIA)	USA REAL GNP	USSR CAPITAL STOCK	USA CAPITAL STOCK
1950–1960	10.3	5.7	3.2	9.5	3.6
1960–1970	7.1	5.1	4.0	8.0	4.0
1970–1975	5.7	3.7	2.6	7.9	4.0
1975–1980	4.3	2.7	3.7	6.8	3.9
1980–1984	—	2.6	2.7	6.3*	3.6
1984–1987	—	1.8	2.4	NA	NA
1988–1990	—	0.0	2.4	NA	NA

Note: *1980–1983. NA = not available. GDP data not available.

Sources: Abram Bergson, "Gorbachev Calls for Intensive Growth," *Challenge,* November–December 1985. For the United States, *Statistical Abstract of the United States, 1986* and *1990; Historical Statistics of the United States,* and *Economic Report of the President, 1990.*

The primary force behind Soviet growth was capital accumulation. During the 1950s, the capital stock of the USSR grew at 9.5 percent annually; in the United States, the corresponding figure was only 3.6 percent. Through 1975 Soviet capital stocks grew at twice the rate of capital accumulation in the United States. But these growth rates did not continue, and during the late 1970s they slowed down. Between 1975 and 1985, even the slowly growing U.S. economy outperformed the Soviet Union. In 1975, per capita GNP in the Soviet Union stood at 48.2 percent of per capita GNP in the United States. In 1985 the figure was 48.1 percent.

▶ **Gorbachev and *Perestroika***   In March 1985, Mikhail Gorbachev became general secretary of the Soviet Communist Party and almost immediately began to press for reforms that had an enormous impact on the world. In 1990, Gorbachev won the Nobel Peace Prize for ending the Cold War and was named "Man of the Decade" by *Time* magazine. Despite his enormous popularity around the world and his political successes, one prize continued to elude Gorbachev: improved economic performance in the Soviet Union.

Gorbachev's reforms fell into two categories: *glasnost* ("openness") and *perestroika* ("restructuring"). *Glasnost* led to the almost completely open discussion of every aspect of political and economic reform in the Soviet Union. It also led to a new set of political institutions, including an end to the power monopoly of the Communist party[4] and more free elections. Glasnost was relatively easy to achieve, but the establishment of new economic structures—the key element of Gorbachev's *perestroika*—was more difficult.

The initial goal of *perestroika* was to increase workers' responsibilities and discipline by attacking corruption and alcoholism. In these arenas, Gorbachev met with some success. Numerous bureau chiefs were replaced, alcoholism was reduced through strict law enforcement, absenteeism declined, and productivity increased. Then, in 1986, the focus of reform shifted to the performance of agriculture. In that year, Gorbachev restructured the agricultural sector giving local farm units and the peasantry new freedoms. Local farm units, for example, were allowed to use the market to dispose of any surplus over five-year plan levels. Payments to state and collective farm workers were tied to productivity and profits, and local directors were given more authority over management and investment decisions.

The best was yet to come. In June 1987, Gorbachev announced another series of reforms. The package included some surprising changes. First, price subsidies were to be drastically reduced or eliminated, even on such items as meat, bread, dairy products, and housing. Second, all limits on what workers could earn were to be removed, and salaries were to be tied directly to performance. Third, the decision-making authority of the farms and enterprises was to be greatly expanded. Central plans were to contain far less detail than in previous years. At the same time, Gorbachev called for sharp increases in small-scale family farming and for a "competitive atmosphere" among enterprises to ensure that goods were sold to consumers at the lowest possible prices that would still cover costs of production.

---

[4]For many years, membership in and loyalty to the Communist party were the ticket to the good life in the Soviet Union. Under the *nomenklatura* party patronage system, Communist party leaders received power and privilege in exchange for loyalty to the party. In addition to determining the staffing of government and industrial posts (a practice that led to a good deal of favoritism and nepotism), party members also enjoyed the right to shop at special state-run stores stocking luxury items not available to the general public. Travel privileges, admissions to the best colleges and universities, larger apartments, and bigger cars also went to members of the *nomenklatura*. In 1990, the Central Committee of the Soviet Communist Party approved a proposal by President Gorbachev calling for an end to the party's constitutional guarantee of power, ending the *nomenklatura*. After the failed August 1991 coup, the Communist party was completely dismantled.

Perhaps the most radical of the 1987 reforms was that job security, a sacred tenet of the Soviet system, would be reduced. For the first time, enterprises could fire lazy workers, and unproductive enterprises could be shut down.

➤ **Economic Crisis and Collapse**   Although Gorbachev's ideas seemed promising, the situation in the Soviet Union deteriorated sharply after 1987. The attempted transition from central planning to a partly free-market system caused major problems. Growth of output slowed to a crawl in 1989 and 1990, and in 1991 the economic system collapsed. Industrial production dropped sharply, food shortages grew worse, inflation became serious, and external debt increased rapidly.

Gorbachev ran out of time in August 1991 as the struggle between the hard-liners and the radical reformers came to a head. The hard-liners took Gorbachev prisoner and assumed control of the government. The coup lasted only three days. People took to the streets of Moscow and resisted the tanks, the Soviet army refused to obey orders, and the hard-liners were out.

But the end was near for both Gorbachev and the Soviet Union. In December 1991, the Soviet Union was dissolved, 10 of the former Soviet republics formed the Commonwealth of Independent States (CIS), and Boris Yeltsin became president of the Russian Republic as Gorbachev became part of history. From the beginning, Yeltsin showed himself to be a reformer committed to converting the Russian economy rapidly into a market system while maintaining hard-won political freedoms for the people. His reform plan called for deregulating prices, privatizing public enterprises, and stabilizing the macroeconomy.

FAST FACTS

Gorbachev became a true capitalist in December 1997 when he signed to film a commercial for Pizza Hut.

THE TRANSITION TO A MARKET ECONOMY

The reforms under way in the Russian Republic and in the other formerly Communist countries of Eastern Europe have taken shape very slowly and amid debate about how best to proceed. Remember: there is absolutely no historical precedent to provide lessons. Despite this lack of precedent, however, there is substantial agreement among economists about what needs to be done.

> Economists generally agree on six basic requirements for a successful transition from socialism to a market-based system: (1) macroeconomic stabilization; (2) deregulation of prices and liberalization of trade; (3) privatization of state-owned enterprises and development of new private industry; (4) the establishment of market-supporting institutions, such as property and contract laws, accounting systems, and so forth; (5) a social safety net to deal with unemployment and poverty; and (6) external assistance.

We now discuss each component. Although we focus on the experience of the Russian Republic, these principles apply to all economies in transition.

➤ **Macroeconomic Stabilization**   Virtually every one of the countries in transition has had a problem with inflation, but nowhere has it been worse than in Russia. As economic conditions worsened, the government found itself with serious budget problems. As revenue flows slowed and expenditure commitments increased, large budget deficits resulted. At the same time, each of the new republics established its own central bank. Each central bank began issuing "ruble credits" to keep important enterprises afloat and to pay the government's bills. The issuance of these credits, which were generally accepted as a means of payment throughout the country, led to a dramatic expansion of the money supply.

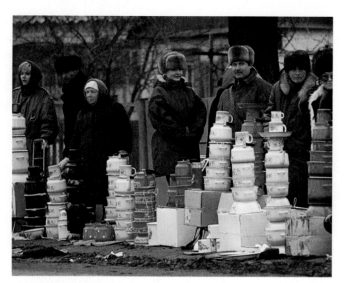

IF THE GOVERNMENT SETS PRICES BELOW MARKET-CLEARING LEVELS, BLACK MARKETS ARE LIKELY TO DEVELOP. IN UKRAINE, IT IS SOMETIMES EASIER TO BUY POTS AND PANS ON THE STREET THAN IT IS TO FIND THEM IN STORES.

Almost from the beginning, the expanded money supply meant too much money was chasing too few goods. This was made worse by government-controlled prices set substantially below market-clearing levels. The combination of monetary expansion and price control was deadly. Government-run shops that sold goods at controlled prices were empty. People waited in line for days and often became violent when their efforts to buy goods at low official prices were thwarted. At the same time, suppliers found that they could charge much higher prices for their products on the black market—which grew bigger by the day, further exacerbating the shortage of goods at government shops. Over time, the ruble became worth less and less as black market prices continued to rise more rapidly. Russia found itself with near hyperinflation in 1992.

To achieve a properly functioning market system, prices must be stabilized. To do so, the government must find a way to move toward a balanced budget and to bring the supply of money under control.

While real GDP in Russia began to grow slowly during 1997, inflation remained at 13% and short-term interest rates were 28%.

> **Deregulation of Prices and Liberalization of Trade**   To move successfully from central planning to a market system, individual prices must be deregulated. A system of freely moving prices forms the backbone of a market system. When people want more of a good than is currently being produced, its price will rise. This higher price increases producers' profits and provides an incentive for existing firms to expand production and for new firms to enter the industry. Conversely, if an industry is producing a good for which there is no market or a good that people no longer want in the same quantity, the result will be excess supply and the price of that good will fall. This reduces profits or creates losses, providing an incentive for some existing firms to cut back on production and for others to go out of business. In short, an unregulated price mechanism ensures an efficient allocation of resources across industries. Until prices are deregulated, this mechanism cannot function.

Trade barriers must also be removed. Reform-minded countries must be able to import capital, technology, and ideas. In addition, it makes no sense to continue to subsidize industries that cannot be competitive on world markets. If it is cheaper to buy steel from an efficient West German steel mill than to produce it in a subsidized antiquated Russian mill, the Russian mill should be modernized or shut down. Ultimately, as the theory of comparative advantage suggests, liberalized trade will push each country to produce the products it produces best.

Deregulating prices and eliminating subsidies can bring serious political problems. Many products in Russia and the rest of the socialist world were priced below market-clearing levels for equity reasons. Housing, food, and clothing were considered by many to be entitlements. Making them more expensive, at least relative to their prices in previous times, is not likely to be popular. In addition, forcing inefficient firms to operate without subsidies will lead many to go out of business, and jobs will be lost. So while price deregulation and trade liberalization are necessary, they are very difficult politically.

➤ **Privatization**   One problem with a system of central ownership is a lack of accountability. Under a system of private ownership, owners reap the rewards of their successes and suffer the consequences of their failures. Private ownership provides a strong incentive for efficient operation, innovation, and hard work that is lacking when ownership is centralized and profits are distributed to the people.

The classic story to illustrate this is called the **tragedy of commons**. Suppose an agricultural community has 10,000 acres of grazing land. If the land were held in common so that all farmers had unlimited rights to graze their animals, each farmer would have an incentive to overgraze. He or she would reap the full benefits from grazing additional calves while the costs of grazing the calves would be borne collectively. The system provides no incentive to manage the land efficiently. Similarly, if the efficiency and benefits of my hard work and managerial skills accrue to others or to the state, what incentive do I have to work hard or to be efficient?

One solution to the tragedy of commons attempted in eighteenth-century Britain was to divide up the land into private holdings. Today, many economists argue, the solution to the incentive problem encountered in state-owned enterprises is to privatize them and let the owners compete.

In addition to increasing accountability, privatization means creating a climate in which new enterprises can flourish. If there is market demand for a product not currently being produced, individual entrepreneurs should be free to set up a business and make a profit. During the last months of the Soviet Union's existence, private enterprises such as taxi services, car repair services, restaurants, and even hotels began to spring up all over the country.

Like deregulation of prices, privatization is difficult politically. Privatization means many protected enterprises will go out of business because they cannot compete at world prices, resulting in a loss of jobs, at least temporarily.

➤ **Market-Supporting Institutions**   Between 1991 and 1997, U.S. firms raced to Eastern Europe in search of markets and investment opportunities and immediately became aware of a major obstacle. The institutions that make the market function relatively smoothly in the United States do not exist in Eastern Europe.

For example, the capital market, which channels private saving into productive capital investment in developed capitalist economies, is made up of hundreds of different institutions. The banking system, venture capital funds, the stock market, the bond market, the commodity exchanges, brokerage houses, investment banks, and the like have all developed in the United States over hundreds of years, and they will not simply be replicated overnight in the formerly Communist world.

Many market-supporting institutions are so basic that Americans take them for granted. The institution of private property, for example, is a set of rights that must be protected by laws that the government must be willing to enforce. Suppose that the French hotel chain Novotel decides to build a new hotel in Moscow. Novotel must first acquire land. Then it will construct a building based on the expectation of renting rooms to customers. These investments are made with the expectation that the owner has a right to use them and a right to the profits that they produce. For such investments to be undertaken, these rights must be guaranteed by a set of property laws. This

tragedy of commons *The idea that collective ownership may not provide the proper private incentives for efficiency because individuals do not bear the full costs of their own decisions but do enjoy the full benefits.*

is equally true for large business firms and for Russian entrepreneurs who want to start their own enterprises.

Similarly, the law must provide for the enforcement of contracts. In the United States, a huge body of law determines what happens to you if you break a formal promise made in good faith. Businesses exist on promises to produce and promises to pay. Without recourse to the law when a contract is breached, contracts will not be entered into, goods will not be manufactured, and services will not be provided.

Another seemingly simple matter that turns out to be quite complex is the establishment of a set of accounting principles. In the United States, the rules of the accounting game are embodied in a set of Generally Accepted Accounting Principles (GAAP) that carry the force of law. Companies are required to keep track of their receipts, expenditures, and liabilities so their performance can be observed and evaluated by shareholders, taxing authorities, and others who have an interest in the company. If you have taken a course in accounting, you know how detailed these rules have become. Imagine trying to do business in a country operating under hundreds of different sets of rules. That's what has been happening in Russia.

Another institution is insurance. Whenever a venture undertakes a high-risk activity, it buys insurance to protect itself. Several years ago, Amnesty International (a nonprofit organization that works to protect civil liberties around the world) sponsored a worldwide concert tour with a number of well-known rock bands and performers. The most difficult part of organizing the tour was obtaining insurance for the artists and their equipment when they played in the then-Communist countries of Eastern Europe.

> **Social Safety Net**   In a centrally planned socialist economy, the labor market does not function freely. Everyone who wants a job is guaranteed one somewhere. The number of jobs is determined by a central plan to match the number of workers. There is essentially no unemployment. This, it has been argued, is one of the great advantages of a planned system. In addition, a central planning system provides basic housing, food, and clothing at very affordable levels for all. With no unemployment and necessities available at very low prices, there is no need for unemployment insurance, welfare, or other social programs.

Transition to a free labor market and liberalization of prices means that some workers will end up unemployed and everyone will pay higher prices for necessities. Indeed, during the early phases of the transition process, unemployment will be high. Inefficient state-owned enterprises will go out of business; some sectors will contract while others expand. As more and more people experience unemployment, popular support for reform is likely to drop unless some sort of social safety net is erected to ease the transition. This social safety net might include unemployment insurance, aid for the poor, and food and housing assistance. The experiences of the developed world have shown that such programs are expensive.

> **External Assistance**   Very few believe the transition to a market system can be achieved without outside support and some outside financing. Knowledge of and experience with capitalist institutions that exist in the United States, Western Europe, and Japan are of vital interest to the Eastern European nations. The basic skills of accounting, management, and enterprise development can be taught to Eastern Europe; many say it is in everyone's best interest to do so. Many also argue that the world's biggest nightmare is an economically weak or desperate Russia armed with nuclear weapons, giving up on reform or falling to a dictator.

There is little agreement about the extent of *financial* support that should be given, however. The United States has pushed for a worldwide effort to provide billions of dollars in aid. This aid, many argue, will help Russia stabilize its macroeconomy and buy desperately needed goods from abroad. But critics in the United States and other potential donor countries say pouring money into Russia now is like pouring it into a black hole—no matter how much we donate, it will have little impact on the ultimate success or failure of the reforms.

SHOCK THERAPY OR GRADUALISM?

Although economists generally agree on what the former socialist economies need to do, they debate the sequence and timing of specific reforms.

The popular press describes the debate as one between those who believe in "shock therapy" (sometimes called the "Big Bang" approach) and those who prefer a more gradual approach. Advocates of **shock therapy** believe that the economies in transition should proceed immediately on all fronts. They should stop printing money, deregulate prices and liberalize trade, privatize, develop market institutions, build a social safety net, and acquire external aid—all as quickly as possible. The pain will be severe, the argument goes, but in the end it will be forgotten as the transition raises living standards. Advocates of a *gradualist* approach believe the best course is to build up market institutions first, gradually decontrol prices, and privatize only the most efficient government enterprises first.

Those who favor moving quickly point to the apparent success of Poland, which moved rapidly through the first phases of reform. Russia's experience during the first years of its transition have demonstrated that, at least in that country, change must be to some extent gradual. In theory, stabilization and price liberalization can be achieved instantaneously. But to enjoy the benefits of liberalization, a good deal of privatization must have taken place—and that will take more time. One analyst has said, privatization means "selling assets with no value to people with no money." Some estimates suggest half of Russian state-owned enterprises are incapable of making a profit at world prices. Simply cutting them loose would create chaos. In a sense, Russia has no choice but to move slowly.

shock therapy *The approach to transition from socialism to market capitalism that advocates rapid deregulation of prices, liberalization of trade, and privatization.*

ALTERNATIVE ECONOMIC SYSTEMS

We now discuss two alternative economic systems: that of China and that of Japan.

THE PEOPLE'S REPUBLIC OF CHINA

Eastward around the globe from the Russian Republic lies China, the world's most populous country. With 1.2 billion people, mainland China accounts for one out of every five people in the world. And China is very poor, with per capita GDP around $850 in 1998.

China remains a country in which political dissent is not tolerated and the economic system remains Communist but in which private enterprise is permitted and even encouraged. This seemingly incongruous system is performing, at least for now, as well as any economy in the world. China, like Russia, is an enormously important power in the world, and understanding its history and the nature of its economic institutions is an essential part of understanding economics.

Compared to the United States, the People's Republic of China is very large and very poor. Per capita income in China is about one-twentieth of per capita income in the United States. The history of the People's Republic, established after the Communist victory in the revolution of 1949, has been marked by wild gyrations of policy and some extraordinary economic experiments.

▶ **Socialization under Mao Zedong**   Soon after gaining power, the Chinese Communists, led by Chairman Mao Zedong, became involved in the Korean War and found themselves heavily dependent on the Soviet Union. That's why the early structure of the Chinese economic system was built on the Soviet-Stalinist model. China's first five-year plan, from 1953 to 1957, focused on developing capital-intensive heavy industries. Agriculture was collectivized, household farming was eliminated, and compulsory output quotas were put in place.

In 1958 China departed sharply from the Soviet model and launched a new economic strategy called the **Great Leap Forward**. The focus of production shifted from large-scale, capital-intensive industry to small-scale, labor-intensive industry scattered across the countryside. In addition, material incentives were reduced and replaced by the motivating power of revolutionary ideology and inspiration. Although initially successful, the strategy ultimately failed. In the early 1960s, output fell below 1958 levels. Between 1961 and 1965, material incentives were restored and a period of relative calm followed.

During the late 1960s and 1970s, economic development in China suffered a blow from the **Great Proletarian Cultural Revolution** that began in 1966. For almost a decade, the rule was ideological purity. The faithful—almost everyone—denounced those who favored material incentives and reform, and scientists, engineers, managers, and scholars whose views were out of favor were sent to the countryside to work in the fields. The universities were essentially closed down. Untrained revolutionary *cadres* (small groups of leaders) replaced trained specialists in almost all jobs, and the economy suffered terribly. Most estimates place per capita income and consumption in the late 1970s at levels only slightly above the levels of 1956 to 1957.[5]

> ▶ **The Reforms of Deng Xiaoping**   When Chairman Mao died in September 1976, the Cultural Revolution formally ended. Meanwhile, China watched as its once poor neighbors—Japan, South Korea, Taiwan, and Singapore—enjoyed extraordinary growth and prosperity.

In December 1978, the Chinese Central Committee, under Deng Xiaoping, announced sweeping reforms. These early reforms focused on agriculture, and they signaled the beginning of profound changes in the Chinese economy that would continue over the next 10 years.

Prior to 1978, each agricultural commune had distributed the harvest equally among its members. Incentives were purely collective, with everything done for the glory of the revolution. Because the cadres often overstated harvests, the state raised local delivery quotas, leaving the peasants with barely enough to go around. The new system begun under Deng Xiaoping gave individual families, through a 15-year family contract, formal rights to the land they worked. Families were also given the rights to dispose of any surpluses and to hire out part of the family labor force to enterprises outside the family plot. Deng gave the Chinese peasants permission to enrich themselves. And they did!

Output of grain and other basic necessities, such as cotton, increased substantially. More importantly, rural industry grew dramatically, employing over 20 percent of the rural labor force by 1985. From 1978 through 1983, wheat production increased at an annual rate of 8.6 percent, rice at 4.3 percent, and cotton at 16.4 percent. From 1981 to 1984, the growth rate of all agricultural output reached 11.0 percent annually. In 1984 China became an exporter of food, despite a population of over one billion. Peasant income more than doubled in less than a decade, and private consumption and housing construction increased sharply.[6]

[5]See Nicholas Lardy, "Agricultural Reform," *Journal of International Affairs*, Winter 1986.

[6]"China: Economic Performance in 1985, A Report to the Subcommittee on Economic Resources, Competitiveness and Security of the Joint Economic Committee," The Central Intelligence Agency, Washington, D.C.: March 17, 1986 (mimeo), p. 2.

Great Leap Forward *The economic strategy in the People's Republic of China that began in 1958 when it departed from the Soviet model and shifted from large-scale, capital-intensive industry to small-scale, labor-intensive industry scattered across the countryside. Material incentives were reduced and replaced by the motivating power of revolutionary ideology and inspiration.*

Great Proletarian Cultural Revolution (1966–1976) *A period of ideological purity in the People's Republic of China: Material incentives and reforms were denounced and highly trained specialists were sent to work in the fields. The effect of the Cultural Revolution on the Chinese economy was catastrophic.*

Similar reforms were implemented in Chinese industry on an experimental basis. Initially, enterprises were able to retain 15 percent to 25 percent of any profits above those specified by the plan. By 1984, Chinese enterprises were retaining over 85 percent of increased profits. As with agricultural reform, the goals of industrial reform were to increase the role of the producing unit, to increase individual incentives, and to reduce the role of the state and the central planners.

The most significant element of these reforms was the Chinese government's support of the expansion of enterprise rights.. In the spirit of the Soviet New Economic Policy of the 1920s, the Chinese are actively encouraging small private trade and manufacturing. Today there is an increasingly important Chinese private sector competing with state stores in style, service, quality, and price. By 1986, 480,000 "new economic associations" were employing 4.2 million people.[7] China is now encouraging foreign investment. Initially only joint ventures with the government were permitted, but now foreigners retain 100 percent ownership in several projects.

➤ **China after Tiananmen Square**   Despite the economic advances that China has made in the last decades, there is a great deal of political unrest in the country. In May 1989, university students openly challenged the authority of the government by occupying Tiananmen Square in Beijing. Many went on hunger strikes to protest China's lack of democracy. The "democracy movement" was crushed on June 3, 1989, when the government cleared the square with troops and tanks as the world watched.

The events of 1989 turned world opinion against the Chinese and at least temporarily slowed the movement toward economic reform. A number of joint ventures were canceled, and the amount of direct aid flowing into China was reduced. But even before Tiananmen Square, Chinese economic reforms were beginning to encounter difficulty.

In 1988, China experienced serious inflation for the first time. By late 1988, prices were rising in historically unprecedented amounts, nearly 30 percent per year. In September, the government began implementing an austerity program that included strict price controls, reduced state investment, and reduced imports. The rate of inflation had dropped by 1989, but output of goods and services in China fell in 1989 and grew only slightly in 1990.

The years 1991 to 1995 saw a dramatic turnaround for China. While the current Communist government has retained power and maintained a hard line on the political front, economic freedoms have been extended into every sphere. Private enterprise continues to be encouraged (see Global Perspective box "China: Free Enterprise in a Communist Country"). A stock market was established and stock prices have boomed. Everyone in China wants a piece of the action. In October 1992, First Boston Corporation, Merrill Lynch and Co., and Salomon Brothers offered five million shares in and raised more than $75 million for the JinBei Vehicle Manufacturing Company in the city of Shenyang. Hundreds of billions of dollars in foreign investment are now flowing into China from the United States, Japan, Singapore, Taiwan, and Korea.

Some problems and challenges remain. Many fear that food shortages are imminent. While the Chinese population has continued to grow, the country's expanding industrial and housing sectors have led to a declining amount of land under cultivation. (China contains 20 percent of the world's population but only 7 percent of the world's arable land.) Also, over 50,000 state-owned enterprises continue to operate, although the process of selling these enterprises to foreign investors and allowing them to go into a form of bankruptcy continues.

FAST FACTS

One of the engines of recent Chinese growth has been exports. But the huge fall in the value of the Korean and Thai currencies in 1997 makes them more competitive with China. Some fear further slowdown for China as its neighbors recover.

---

[7]*Beijing Review*, no. 25, June 23, 1986.

CHINA: FREE ENTERPRISE IN A COMMUNIST COUNTRY

The following excerpt from a recent *New York Times* article summarizes nicely what seems to be happening in a rapidly changing China:

QIAOTOU, China—For a glimpse into China's economic revolution, it is useful to stroll down the main street of this humble little town. . . [which] has propelled itself over the last dozen years into the button capital of the world.

Each year, the privately run factories of Qiaotou produce about 12 billion buttons. . . . This button boom, amounting to two buttons annually per inhabitant on earth, has transformed rice paddies into factory districts, and peasants into tycoons.

One of them is Zhan Yusheng, a 27-year-old who began making buttons in his home 10 years ago. Today he owns a button factory with 100 employees, and last year he had sales of nearly $200,000.

"Now we need to upgrade our quality and produce more high-quality buttons," said Chen Jianlin, Qiaotou's Communist Party secretary. "Then we can expand on the international market.". . . Mr. Chen sees his mission primarily as promoting private enterprise.

"My most important job is building up the economy," Mr. Chen said as he sipped tea at the conference table in his office. "People here say: 'If you push the economy along, you're a good leader. Otherwise, you're not.'"

While his salary is only $20 a month, about a third as much as the 20,000 migrant workers employed in Qiaotou's factories, . . . the party covers most of his expenses, supplies him with a house, a chauffered Audi, a phone with international direct dialing, a beeper, and a Mastercard.

"A lot of people here now carry credit cards when they travel," Mr. Chen said, beaming as he passed around his Mastercard for inspection. "Credit cards are very convenient and you don't have to carry so much cash."

Source: Nicholas D. Kristof, "Free Enterprise Encouraged," *The New York Times*, Jan. 18, 1993. Copyright © 1993 by The New York Times Co. Reprinted by permission.

EACH YEAR, THE PRIVATELY RUN FACTORIES OF QIAOTOU, CHINA, PRODUCE ABOUT 12 BILLION BUTTONS, PRIMARILY OF THE INEXPENSIVE KIND FOUND ON DISCOUNT-PRICED CLOTHING.

For more on what's happening in other economic systems, see the Case and Fair Web page at **http://www.prenhall.com/casefair**.

In July 1997, Hong Kong, previously a British colony, was returned to China with great fanfare. Hong Kong, boasting one of the most successful capitalist economies in the world, would continue to exist as a capitalist enclave albeit under rule of a Communist government. No one knows what the future holds for Hong Kong, although most analysts are optimistic.

At the end of 1997, there were a few signs of potential trouble for the former colony. The Hong Kong stock market fell over 20 percent during the year, and property values, which had been bid up wildly just before the turnover, fell significantly.

In China as a whole, growth cooled to under 8 percent during 1997, but the country seemed to hold its own amid deep troubles around Asia in countries like Korea, Thailand, and Japan. China continues to grow but remains very poor, with per capita GDP around $850 in 1998.

JAPAN

No country in history has accomplished what the Japanese economy has during the post–World War II period. Japan's economic progress over the last several decades is, with good reason, called the "Japanese economic miracle." Between 1951 and 1973, real GNP in Japan grew at an average annual rate of over 10 percent—in just over two decades, a seven-and-a-half-fold increase. Since the mid-1970s, economic growth in Japan has slowed, but until very recently the Japanese economy still significantly outperformed the U.S. economy.

What led to the Japanese "miracle"? Was it culture? Japan is a disciplined society with a strong work ethic and a tradition of cooperation. But although cultural differences may be part of the story, there is far more to it than that.

Structurally, Japan's is essentially a free-market capitalist economy. No industrialized country in the world has a smaller public sector, and none has a more "pro-business" government. To a very large extent, the private decisions of households and firms produced the miracle.

To explain Japan's success more specifically, analysts point to four major factors: (1) very high rates of saving and investment, (2) a highly trained labor force, (3) rapid absorption and effective utilization of technology, much of it imported, and (4) a pro-growth government policy.[8] Of these, perhaps the single most important cause of Japan's growth has been its incredible rate of investment. Between 1951 and 1973, the capital stock of Japan grew by more than 9 percent per year, and for a substantial period investment approached 40 percent of GNP. Between 1960 and 1980, the capital stock in the United States increased at about 4 percent per year, while gross investment fluctuated between 15 percent and 17 percent per year. Virtually all of Japan's investment was financed with domestic saving. Japan's rate of saving by households has been the highest in the world.

Until recent years, rates of return on new investment in Japan were high. But today Japan faces a new problem. Its high rates of investment have virtually exhausted the investment opportunities in the nation and pushed rates of return on saving to very low levels. The saving rate has remained high, however, and this has led many Japanese citizens to look abroad to place their savings. Much of those savings flowed to the United States during the 1980s. Real interest rates are much higher in the United States than in Japan, and a considerable number of new U.S. government bonds are now being sold to the Japanese. The Japanese are also investing billions in U.S. common stocks and real estate.

The second factor contributing to Japan's economic success is the quality of the Japanese labor force. As early as 1950, Japan had an education level comparable to that of the United States, despite a much lower level of economic development. Most Japanese workers were employed in jobs that demanded extremely low productivity relative to the education and training of those holding them. As the country's capital stock grew, workers moved easily into higher-productivity jobs.

Japan also consciously adopted the most advanced industrial technologies in the world. Much of the knowledge necessary to do this was available in technical journals or obtainable in U.S. graduate schools, and some came embodied in machinery and equipment imported into Japan. The Japanese were extremely effective at improving upon and commercializing what they imported. By importing technology, Japan did not have to develop it on its own; and, until recently, Japan devoted a smaller portion of its GNP to research and development than did the United States.

---

[8]This discussion owes much to an excellent paper by Hugh Patrick and Henry Rosovsky, "Japan's Economic Performance: An Overview" in *Asia's New Giant*, eds. Hugh Patrick and Henry Rosovsky (The Brookings Institution, 1976).

Ministry of Trade and Industry (MITI) *The agency of the Japanese government responsible for industrial policy. It uses tariffs and subsidies to protect and subsidize key industries and helps some sectors plan orderly reductions in capacity.*

The role of government in the Japanese economy is certainly different from the role of government in the United States. Economists disagree about the importance of government as an instrument of growth in Japan. It is clear the main source of growth has been the private sector, but the government has played a supportive role. For example, after World War II, the Japanese government, through the **Ministry of Trade and Industry (MITI)**, used tariffs and quotas to protect and subsidize a number of key industries, including coal, steel, electric power, and shipbuilding. During the 1960s, chemicals and machinery were added to the list. In the mid-1980s, the government and the private sector launched a partnership designed to develop and market the next generation of computers. MITI also helps some sectors of the economy plan orderly reductions in capacity. In short, the Japanese government is actively involved in the allocation process and has much to say about which industries will grow and which will not.

➤ **Japan in the 1990s**   The enormous success of the Japanese economy led to seemingly unbounded optimism at the end of the 1980s. Spurred by the profitability of Japanese firms, the market prices of Japanese stocks raced to unprecedented levels. At the same time, Japanese land values boomed. At one point, land in Tokyo was trading for as much as $6,000 per square foot. At that price, a small 100 by 100 foot plot of land (less than a quarter of an acre) was worth $60 million!

Then, in 1992, the Japanese stock market fell dramatically and land prices began to fall. For the first time in the history of modern Japan, confidence in the future was shaken. Beginning in 1992, real growth slowed considerably, and unemployment began to rise. In early 1998, recovery was still not in sight, and the unemployment rate had reached a post–War high.

Despite these setbacks, Japan remains an enormous economic power and a vital U.S. trading partner. As the economy becomes even more globalized in the coming years, it will be essential to understand more fully the successes and failures of Japanese industrial policy.

CONCLUSION

This chapter has introduced very briefly the structure, history, and performance of several different economic systems. It has also discussed the enormous problems of transforming a socialist economy into a market-based economy.

Studying alternative economic systems is a fitting way to conclude an introduction to economics. One of the themes running through this book has been the role of government in a market economy. We have tried to present a balanced description of how economies function, both in theory and in the real world. Throughout, we have focused on the potential benefits and problems associated with public-sector involvement. Eastern Europe, Russia, China, and Japan present very different perspectives on the interaction between the private and public sectors.

Concluding with this chapter is also, we hope, an enticement to further study. This is an exciting time in the world's economic history. Never before have systems changed so dramatically in such a short time. Many believe the reforms in China, Eastern Europe, and Russia have brought the world much closer together and that the time is ripe for a significant reduction in world political tensions. Others believe that the problems of transition are so difficult that the whole process will disintegrate into chaos. Only time will tell.

SUMMARY

POLITICAL SYSTEMS AND ECONOMIC SYSTEMS: SOCIALISM, CAPITALISM, AND COMMUNISM

1. In a *socialist economy* most capital is owned by the government rather than by private citizens. In a *capitalist economy* most capital is privately owned. *Communism* is a theoretical economic system in which the people directly control the means of production (capital and land) without the intervention of a government or state.

2. Economies differ in the extent to which decisions are made through central planning rather than through a market system. Generally, socialist economies favor central planning over market allocation, and capitalist economies rely to a much greater extent on the market. Nonetheless, there are markets in all societies, and planning takes place in all economies.

THE ECONOMIC THEORIES OF KARL MARX

3. According to Marxian thought, private ownership and profit are both unfair and unethical. Profit is value that is created by labor but expropriated by nonproductive capitalists, who are able to exploit labor by virtue of their ownership of the means of production (land and capital).

4. Marx predicted that falling rates of profit, increasing exploitation, and deeper business cycles would eventually cause capitalism to collapse.

5. Neoclassical economics sees profit as a return to a productive factor (capital) just as wages are the return to another productive factor (labor).

ECONOMIES IN TRANSITION: THE EXPERIENCES OF RUSSIA AND EASTERN EUROPE

6. When the Bolsheviks took power in Russia after the October Revolution in 1917, they found themselves without the advanced industrial base that Marx had envisioned and with no real blueprint for running a socialist or communist state. Marx had written mainly about capitalism, not socialism.

7. In 1928, the Soviet Union settled into central planning and collectivization of agriculture, an economic structure that lasted into the 1980s. Virtually all productive assets, including most land and capital, were publicly owned. There was no formal private business sector, no market for capital goods, and no income from property.

8. The Soviet Union grew rapidly through the mid-1970s. During the late 1950s, the Soviet Union's economy was growing much faster than that of the United States. The key to early Soviet success was rapid planned capital accumulation. The late 1970s saw things begin to deteriorate.

Dramatic reforms were finally introduced by Mikhail Gorbachev after his rise to power in 1985. Nonetheless, the Soviet economy collapsed in 1991. The Soviet Union was dissolved, and the new president of the Russian Republic, Boris Yeltsin, was left to start the difficult task of transition to a market system.

9. Economists generally agree on six requirements for a successful transition from socialism to a market-based system: (1) macroeconomic stabilization, (2) deregulation of prices and liberalization of trade, (3) privatization, (4) the establishment of market-supporting institutions, (5) a social safety net, and (6) external assistance.

10. Much debate exists about the sequence and timing of specific reforms. The idea of *shock therapy* is to proceed immediately on all six fronts, including rapid deregulation of prices and privatization. The *gradualist* approach is to build up market institutions first, gradually decontrol prices, and privatize only the most efficient government enterprises first.

ALTERNATIVE ECONOMIC SYSTEMS

11. China, the largest country in the world, became Communist following the revolution of 1949. In its early years under Chairman Mao Zedong, China organized under the Soviet model of central planning and rapid capital accumulation in heavy industry. In 1958, China departed sharply from the Soviet model, shifting instead to emphasis on small-scale, labor-intensive industry scattered around the countryside.

12. In 1978 Deng Xiaoping instituted sweeping reforms in the organization of the Chinese economy, particularly in agriculture. These reforms moved China away from central planning toward a system driven by market incentives.

13. China remains a country in which political dissent is not tolerated and the economic system remains Communist, but in which private enterprise is permitted and even encouraged. In the last several years the country has enjoyed rapid growth and substantial outside investment. However, inflation has been a problem, a fear of food shortages remains, and more than 50,000 state-owned enterprises continue to operate.

14. No country in history has accomplished what the Japanese economy has during the postwar period. Four major factors to explain Japan's success: (1) a very high rate of saving and investment, (2) a highly trained labor force, (3) rapid absorption and effective utilization of technology, much of it imported, and (4) a pro-growth government policy. Despite some setbacks in the 1990s, Japan remains an important economic power.

REVIEW TERMS AND CONCEPTS

PROBLEM SET

1. Choose one of the transitional economies of Central Europe (Poland, Hungary, Bulgaria, the Czech Republic, or Romania) or one of the 10 countries of the Commonwealth of Independent States (Armenia, Azerbaijan, Ukraine, Uzbekistan, Russia, etc.). Write a brief paper on how the transition to a market economy was proceeding in 1998 and 1999. Has the economy (prices, employment, etc.) stabilized? Has there been economic growth? How far has privatization progressed? What problems have been encountered? (A good source of information would be the chronological index to a publication like *The Economist* or the *New York Times*.)

2. In 1997, the Japanese economy was not recovering well from past low growth rates.
   a. What has happened to the Japanese economy since 1997? Has real GDP increased or decreased? At what rate?
   b. What has happened to the value of the yen (the number of yen per dollar at current exchange rates)?
   c. What steps have the Japanese taken to "restructure" their economy?
   Again, good sources for such information include *The Economist,* the *New York Times*, or *The Wall Street Journal.* Another source is the Web site of the Organization for Economic Cooperation and Development (OECD).

3. "The difference between the United States and the Soviet Union is that the United States has a capitalist economic system and the Soviet Union had a totalitarian government." Explain how this comparison confuses the economic and political aspects of the two societies. What words describe the former economic system of the Soviet Union?

4. What is the "tragedy of commons"? Suppose that all workers in a factory are paid the same wage and have no risk of being fired. Use the logic of the "tragedy of commons" to predict the result. How would you expect workers to behave?

5. You are assigned the task of debating the strengths of a socialist economy (regardless of your own viewpoint). Outline the points that you would make in the debate. Be sure to define socialism carefully in your presentation.

6. "The U.S. government should institute a policy of subsidizing those firms that are likely to be successful competitors in the international economic wars! Such an 'industrial policy' should have the authority to override the antitrust laws." Agree or disagree? Explain your answer.

7. Explain why Karl Marx thought profit was unjustified. Be sure to specifically define the labor theory of value. Contrast the Marxian view with the neo-classical view of profit.

8. Do you agree or disagree with each of the following statements? Explain your answers.
   a. Over time, the Chinese have shifted from a decentralized approach to economic development to a more centrally planned system. Since the events of 1989 in Tiananmen Square, there has been a severe crackdown on private businesses.
   b. Both Japan and the Soviet Union grew rapidly during the 1950s and 1960s. Growth in the Soviet Union was based on rapid accumulation of capital forced by the central plan under Stalin and Khrushchev. In Japan, the growth was not due to capital accumulation.
   c. Although economists generally agree that transition from socialism to a market-based system must proceed rapidly, there is little agreement about what must be done to make the transition successful.

9. The distribution of income in a capitalist economy is likely to be more unequal than it is in a socialist economy. Why is this so? Is there a tension between the goal of limiting inequality and the goal of motivating risk taking and hard work? Explain your answer in detail.

10. "There is no doubt that a centrally planned socialist system has the potential to grow faster than a market-oriented capitalist system." Do you agree or disagree? What are some of the trade-offs facing socialist planners who set target growth rates?

11. In the 1990s the world witnessed the rapid decline of several Eastern European governments (East Germany, Poland, and Romania, to name just a few). Poland immediately began moving its socialist economy toward a capitalist economy. Some of the effects of this transition have been increased unemployment and price inflation. Can you explain why? (*Hint:* Focus on differences between socialist and capitalist systems regarding the determination of prices and production levels.)

TAKE IT TO THE NET

We invite you to visit the Case and Fair page on the Prentice Hall Web site:

http://www.prenhall.com/casefair

for this chapter's World Wide Web exercise.

INTERNATIONAL INTEGRATION AND LABOR MARKET CONDITIONS: IS THERE A LINK?

Economies have become increasingly integrated over the past several decades. This increased international economic integration has taken the form of greater movements of goods and services, greater flows of financial capital, and the increased movement of labor (i.e., migration) between countries. Since the early 1970s, the continued international integration has coincided with two disturbing labor market developments. First, despite overall increases in economic activity, unemployment in Europe remains high. Second, the gap between the wages of skilled and unskilled workers has risen in a number of industrial countries (e.g., United States, United Kingdom, and Canada). Some analysts attribute much of the persistent unemployment in Europe and the recent increases in wage inequality to increased international integration. Others believe that the effects of integration on these two labor market trends are small.

The flow of goods and services among countries represents the "main channel of economic integration." The trade of goods and services among countries rose from 23 percent of world gross domestic product (GDP) in 1970 to approximately 40 percent of world GDP in 1990. Both exports and imports of goods and services have also risen significantly for the United States during the past four decades (see Table 1), most of the more recent increases resulting from trade with developing and transition economies.

Some say this increase in trade has caused reductions in the demand for unskilled labor in industrial economies. This decrease in demand can occur as imports of goods produced in low-wage economies compete with domestically produced goods. As the consumption of foreign-produced goods increases, some domestic firms are forced to cut back production and reduce their demand for labor. This reduction, particularly for unskilled labor, can have two effects. In economies where labor markets are not flexible and, therefore, where wages do not adjust quickly to changing labor supply and demand conditions (e.g., Europe), the drop in demand has a smaller effect on wages and wage inequality but has a greater effect on the number of unemployed individuals. In countries where labor markets and wage structures are more flexible, the drop in demand for unskilled labor has a greater effect on wages and on wage inequality and a smaller effect on the number of unemployed individuals. Today, many workers, politicians, and union officials fear that increased international integration (of trade, financial capital, and migration) causes job losses and/or reductions in wages.

Increased trade creates distributional effects as the *relative* demand for goods and services changes between economies. These adjustments can be painful for those workers adversely affected by increased trade. For example, approximately 150,000 U.S. garment workers lost their jobs since the North American Free Trade Agreement went into effect in January 1994. Many of these job losses were attributed to increased competition from Mexican imports. Although these adjustment costs should not be ignored, economists emphasize that increased trade yields benefits that exceed these costs. First, increased trade benefits all consumers as increased competition drives down the prices of goods and services. Second, many workers become more productive as the value of the goods

TABLE 1

YEAR	U.S. EXPORTS AS A PERCENTAGE OF U.S. GDP	U.S. IMPORTS AS A PERCENTAGE OF U.S. GDP	U.S. CIVILIAN EMPLOYMENT
1960	3.6	4.9	65,347,000
1965	3.7	4.6	69,997,000
1970	4.5	6.5	78,780,000
1975	6.1	6.2	85,627,000
1980	7.0	7.4	99,879,000
1985	6.4	8.9	106,302,000
1990	9.0	10.1	119,081,000
1995	11.3	13.0	124,766,000
1997	13.0	14.8	128,580,000

Note: *The percentages represent the first-quarter observations of the variables for each year. The employment data represent the number of civilian individuals employed in January of each year.*

Source: *Federal Reserve Bank of St. Louis.*

and services they produce increases. Third, increased trade increases the income and, therefore, consumption of individuals in developing and transition economies, resulting in an increase in the export of goods and services to those countries. Transition economies are in the process of substituting central planning systems with market systems. Fourth, the larger, global markets might create economies of scale, further depressing the prices of some goods.

Some argue that increased financial flows to developing and transition economies will cause a reduction in the amount of financial capital in (i.e., a "decapitalization" of) industrial economies; financial capital flows to developing and transition economies have increased from $42 billion in 1989 to $175 billion in 1994. This increased demand for financial capital may also cause a "capital shortage" and subsequent increase in world interest rates. Both concerns appear unwarranted. First, the net capital outflows from industrial economies represent a small percentage of their total savings. Second, even if world interest rates increase as the demand for funds rises, the increase in interest rates is a result of firms increasing the demand for funds to finance increasingly more productive activities. Third, the increased capital flows benefit investors and borrowers (i.e., recipients of the funds). Investors can take advantage of possibly higher returns and lower risk through increased portfolio diversification. Fourth, workers in developing and transition economies will also benefit as they obtain additional equipment (financed with these funds).

The flow of migrants to industrial economies has also increased over the past 30 years. The percentage of immigrants in the labor force in Europe increased from 3.5 percent in 1965 to 5.0 percent in 1990; in the United

TRADE BETWEEN QUEBEC AND ANOTHER PROVINCE IS APPROXIMATELY 20 TIMES GREATER THAN TRADE BETWEEN QUEBEC AND A STATE OF SIMILAR SIZE AND DISTANCE IN THE UNITED STATES. PHOTO DEPICTS THE ST. LAWRENCE SEAWAY AT QUEBEC.

States, this percentage increased from 6.0 percent to 8.0 percent during the same period. Increased immigration can have negative effects on workers in the host country as wages in certain sectors fall and unemployment among displaced workers occurs. There are, however, some benefits of increased migration. Migrants are generally more productive in the host country, raising world output. For firms, the increased migration can also cause a reduction in labor costs as wages adjust to the increase in labor supply. More generally, the increased migration can result in a more efficient, global allocation of labor resources.

In addition to changes in the flow of trade, financial capital, and migration, we have also witnessed changes in national borders (e.g. the unification of East and West Germany) and continued debates about the possible separation of the province of Quebec from Canada. Recent research indicates that the effects of national borders on the amount of trade between countries are significant. For example, the trade of goods and services between Quebec and another province

in Canada is approximately 20 times greater than between Quebec and a state of similar economic size and distance in the United States. This suggests that the formation of a European Union that would reduce the importance of national borders might have significant positive effects on trade among its members and on employment in these economies.

A number of policies have been proposed to limit the distributional effects of increased integration. Some argue that trade restrictions are needed to protect workers from the effects of job losses and lower wages, whereas most economists believe that any protectionist policies that restrict trade (e.g. tariffs and quotas) will reduce economic activity and have net negative effects on all workers. Still others argue that trade agreements should be linked to labor standard agreements. For example, because minimum wage legislation exists in the United States, they say all countries should adopt similar minimum wage legislation. There are two problems with linking trade agreements with labor standard issues. Those who favor protectionist policies will use the different labor standards of a country's trading partners as a means of limiting trade and preventing future gains from increased integration. Furthermore, it is the low labor costs in developing and transition economies that provide them with a comparative advantage in global markets. Agreements that force these countries to adopt policies that raise their labor costs will effectively reduce trade.

A more effective approach would be to increase integration among developing, transition, and industrial economies while simultaneously implementing domestic policies like placement services that ease the transition of workers from declining industries to expanding industries. Continued efforts to raise the skill level of unskilled workers will also potentially offset any increases in wage inequality and reductions in employment caused by increased integration.

Questions for Analytical Thinking

1. Suppose restrictions are imposed on the flow of financial capital to developing and transition economies. First, what effect might these restrictions have on economic activity in these countries? Explain. Second, how might these restrictions affect trade between these economies and industrial economies? Explain.

2. The North American Free Trade Agreement reduced tariffs on a number of goods and services. Explain how this reduction in tariffs might have affected consumers, firms, workers, and trade in the United States

3. Explain how the existence of a minimum wage and the extent to which this minimum wage applies to workers in an economy (i.e., the percentage of employed workers paid the minimum wage) can determine the *size* of the effects of increased trade on (1) wage inequality and (2) unemployment.

4. a. Based on your analysis of the data in Table 1, in which year, if any, did the United States experience a trade surplus (exports exceeding imports)? In which year was the trade deficit the largest share of U.S. GDP? Do the data in Table 1 indicate that the United States has become more or less integrated with the rest of the world? Explain.
   b. Between 1960 and 1965, U.S. imports as a percentage of U.S. GDP fell. Does this suggest that the *level* of imports fell during this period? Explain.
   c. U.S. civilian employment increased between each of the years in Table 1. Does this suggest that increases in U.S. trade had no negative effect on wages and employment in the United States during this period? Explain.

Sources: Helen Cooper and Scott Kilman, "Trade Wars Aside, U.S. and Europe Buy More of Each Other's Foods," *The Wall Street Journal*, November 4, 1997; Bob Davis, "At the Heart of the Trade Debate: Inequity," *The Wall Street Journal*, October 31, 1997; Robert S. Greenberger, "As U.S. Exports Rise, More Workers Benefit, and Favor Free Trade," *The Wall Street Journal*, September 10, 1997; John F. Helliwell, "Do National Borders Matter For Quebec's Trade?" *Canadian Journal of Economics*, August 1996, pp. 507–522; John McCallum, "National Borders Matter: Canada–U.S. Regional Trade Patterns," *American Economic Review*, June 1995, pp. 615–623; Ana Ravenga, "The Employment Crisis in Industrial Countries: Is International Integration to Blame?" *Regional Perspectives on World Development Report 1995*, Washington, D.C.: The World Bank.

CONCISE DICTIONARY OF ECONOMIC TERMINOLOGY

ability-to-pay principle   A theory of taxation holding that citizens should bear tax burdens in line with their ability to pay taxes.

absolute advantage   The advantage in the production of a product enjoyed by one country over another when it uses fewer resources to produce that product than the other country does.

accelerator effect   The tendency for investment to increase when aggregate output increases and decrease when aggregate output decreases, accelerating the growth or decline of output.

actual investment   The actual amount of investment that takes place; it includes items such as unplanned changes in inventories.

adjustment costs   The costs that a firm incurs when it changes its production level—for example, the administration costs of laying off employees or the training costs of hiring new workers.

adverse selection   An imperfect-information problem that can occur when a buyer or seller enters into an exchange with another party who has more information.

aggregate behavior   The behavior of all households and firms together.

aggregate demand   The total demand for goods and services in the economy.

aggregate demand (AD) curve   A curve that shows the negative relationship between aggregate output (income) and the price level. Each point on the AD curve is a point at which both the goods market and the money market are in equilibrium.

aggregate income   The total income received by all factors of production in a given period.

aggregate output   The total quantity of goods and services produced (or supplied) in an economy in a given period.

aggregate output (income) (Y)   A combined term used to remind you of the exact equality between aggregate output and aggregate income.

aggregate production function   The mathematical representation of the relationship between inputs and national output, or gross domestic product.

aggregate supply   The total supply of all goods and services in an economy.

aggregate supply (AS) curve   A graph that shows the relationship between the aggregate quantity of output supplied by all firms in an economy and the overall price level.

American Federation of Labor (AFL)   Founded in 1881, the AFL was successfully led by Samuel Gompers from 1886 until 1924. A practical, nonideological union, the AFL existed as a "confederation" of individual craft unions representing skilled workers, each with an independent organization and an exclusive jurisdiction. Now merged with the CIO, the AFL maintains a preeminent position among unions today.

animal spirits of entrepreneurs   A phrase coined by Keynes to describe investors' feelings.

Antitrust Division (of the Department of Justice)   One of two federal agencies empowered to act against those in violation of antitrust laws. It initiates action against those who violate antitrust laws and decides which cases to prosecute and against whom to bring criminal charges.

appreciation of a currency   The rise in value of one currency relative to another.

asymmetric information   A situation in which the participants in an economic transaction have different information about the transaction.

automatic destabilizers   Revenue and expenditure items in the federal budget that automatically change with the economy in such a way as to destabilize GDP.

automatic stabilizers   Revenue and expenditure items in the federal budget that automatically change with the economy in such a way as to stabilize GDP.

autonomous variable   A variable that is assumed not to depend on the state of the economy—that is, it is taken as given.

average fixed cost (AFC)   Total fixed cost divided by the number of units of output; a per-unit measure of fixed costs.

average product   The average amount produced by each unit of a variable factor of production.

average propensity to consume (APC)   The proportion of income households spend on consumption. Determined by dividing consumption (C) by income (Y).

average total cost (ATC)   Total cost divided by the number of units of output.

average variable cost (AVC)   Total variable cost divided by the number of units of output.

Averch-Johnson effect The tendency for regulated monopolies to build more capital than they need. Usually occurs when allowed rates of return are set by a regulatory agency at some percent of fixed capital stocks.

balanced-budget multiplier The ratio of change in the equilibrium level of output to a change in government spending where the change in government spending is balanced by a change in taxes so as not to create any deficit. The balanced-budget multiplier is equal to one: The change in Y resulting from the change in G and the equal change in T is exactly the same size as the initial change in G or T itself.

balance of payments The record of a country's transactions in goods, services, and assets with the rest of the world; also the record of a country's sources (supply) and uses (demand) of foreign exchange.

balance of trade A country's exports of goods and services minus its imports of goods and services.

balance on capital account In the United States, the sum of the following (measured in a given period): the change in private U.S. assets abroad, the change in foreign private assets in the United States, the change in U.S. government assets abroad, and the change in foreign government assets in the United States.

balance on current account The balance of trade plus net exports of services, plus net investment income, plus the category "net transfer payments and other."

barrier to entry Something that prevents new firms from entering and competing in imperfectly competitive industries.

barter The direct exchange of goods and services for other goods and services.

base-year The year chosen for the weights in a fixed-weight procedure.

benefits-received principle A theory of fairness holding that taxpayers should contribute to government (in the form of taxes) in proportion to the benefits that they receive from public expenditures.

black market A market in which illegal trading takes place at market-determined prices.

bond A contract between a borrower and a lender, in which the borrower agrees to pay the loan at some time in the future, along with interest payments along the way.

brain drain The tendency for talented people from developing countries to become educated in a developed country and remain there after graduation.

breaking even The situation in which a firm is earning exactly a normal rate of return.

budget constraint The limits imposed on household choices by income, wealth, and product prices.

budget deficit The difference between what a government spends and what it collects in taxes in a given period: $G - T$.

business cycle The cycle of short-term ups and downs in the economy.

capital Those goods produced by the economic system that are used as inputs to produce other goods and services in the future.

capital flight The tendency for both human capital and financial capital to leave developing countries in search of higher rates of return elsewhere.

capital income Income earned on savings that have been put to use through financial capital markets.

capital-intensive technology A production technique that uses a large amount of capital relative to labor.

capital market The input/factor market in which households supply their savings, for interest or for claims to future profits, to firms that demand funds in order to buy capital goods.

capital stock For a single firm, the current market value of the firm's plant, equipment, inventories, and intangible assets.

capitalist economy An economy in which most capital is privately owned.

cartel A group of firms that gets together and makes joint price and output decisions to maximize joint profits.

Celler-Kefauver Act (1950) Extended the government's authority to ban vertical and conglomerate mergers.

ceteris paribus, or **all else equal** A device used to analyze the relationship between two variables while the values of other variables are held unchanged.

change in business inventories The amount by which firms' inventories change during a period. Inventories are the goods that firms produce now but intend to sell later.

change in inventory Production minus sales.

choice set or **opportunity set** The set of options that is defined and limited by a budget constraint.

circular flow A diagram showing the income received and payments made by each sector of the economy.

Clayton Act Passed by Congress in 1914 to strengthen the Sherman Act and clarify the rule of reason, the act outlawed specific monopolistic behaviors such as tying contracts, price discrimination, and unlimited mergers.

Coase theorem Under certain conditions, when externalities are present, private parties can arrive at the efficient solution without government involvement.

collective bargaining The process by which union leaders bargain with management as the representatives of all union employees.

collusion The act of working with other producers in an effort to limit competition and increase joint profits.

command economy An economy in which a central government either directly or indirectly sets output targets, incomes, and prices.

commodity monies Items used as money that also have intrinsic value in some other use.

communism An economic system in which the people control the means of production (capital and land) directly, without the intervention of a government or state.

community rating A system in which insurance providers must accept all applicants and charge premiums based only on age, location, and perhaps some elements of behavior (such as smoking).

comparative advantage The advantage in the production of a product enjoyed by one country over another when that product can be produced at lower cost in terms of other goods than it could be in the other country.

compensating differentials Differences in wages that result from differences in working conditions. Risky jobs usually pay higher wages, and highly desirable jobs usually pay lower wages.

compensation of employees Includes wages, salaries, and various supplements—employer contributions to social insurance and pension funds, for example—paid to households by firms and by the government.

complements, complementary goods Goods that "go together"; a decrease in the price of one results in an increase in demand for the other, and vice versa.

Congress of Industrial Organizations (CIO) Founded by John L. Lewis, president of the United Mine Workers, after the AFL rejected his plan to organize the steel, rubber, automobile, and chemical industries in 1935. The CIO was the first union to organize semiskilled laborers in the mass production industries. After 20 years of independence, it merged with the AFL in 1955.

consent decrees Formal agreements on remedies between all the parties to an antitrust case that must be approved by the courts. Consent decrees can be signed before, during, or after a trial.

constant returns to scale An increase in a firm's scale of production has no effect on average costs per unit produced.

constrained supply of labor The amount a household actually works in a given period at the current wage rate.

consumer goods Goods produced for present consumption.

consumer price index (CPI) A price index computed each month by the Bureau of Labor Statistics using a bundle that is meant to represent the "market basket" purchased monthly by the typical urban consumer.

consumer sovereignty The notion that people are free to choose, and that things that people do not want will not sell. "The customer rules."

consumer surplus The difference between the maximum amount a person is willing to pay for a good and its current market price.

consumption function The relationship between consumption and income.

contraction, recession, or **slump** The period in the business cycle from a peak down to a trough, during which output and employment fall.

contractionary fiscal policy A decrease in government spending or an increase in net taxes aimed at decreasing aggregate output (income) (Y).

contractionary monetary policy A decrease in the money supply aimed at decreasing aggregate output (income) (Y).

copayment A fixed amount of money that an insured person pays for each visit to a doctor's office.

Corn Laws The tariffs, subsidies, and restrictions enacted by the British Parliament in the early nineteenth century to discourage imports and encourage exports of grain.

corporate bonds Promissory notes issued by corporations when they borrow money.

corporate income taxes Taxes levied on the net incomes of corporations.

corporate profits The income of corporate businesses.

corporation A form of business organization resting on a legal charter that establishes the corporation as an entity separate from its owners. Owners hold shares and are liable for the firm's debts only up to the limit of their investment, or share, in the firm.

cost-benefit analysis The formal technique by which the benefits of a public project are weighed against its costs.

cost-of-living adjustments (COLAs) Contract provisions that tie wages to changes in the cost of living. The greater the inflation rate, the more wages are raised.

cost-push, or supply-side, inflation Inflation caused by an increase in costs.

cost shock, or supply shock A change in costs that shifts the aggregate supply (*AS*) curve.

Cournot model A model of a two-firm industry (duopoly) in which a series of output-adjustment decisions leads to a final level of output between the output that would prevail if the market were organized competitively and the output that would be set by a monopoly.

cross-price elasticity of demand A measure of the response of the quantity of one good demanded to a change in the price of another good.

crowding-out effect The tendency for increases in government spending to cause reductions in private investment spending.

currency debasement The decrease in the value of money that occurs when its supply is increased rapidly.

current dollars The current prices that one pays for goods and services.

cyclical deficit The deficit that occurs because of a downturn in the business cycle.

cyclical unemployment The increase in unemployment that occurs during recessions and depressions.

debt rescheduling An agreement between banks and borrowers through which a new schedule of repayments of the debt is negotiated; often some of the debt is written off and the repayment period is extended.

decreasing returns to scale, or diseconomies of scale An increase in a firm's scale of production leads to higher average costs per unit produced.

deductible An annual out-of-pocket expenditure that an insurance policy holder must make before the insurance plan makes any reimbursement.

defensive medicine Ordering medical tests, procedures, or treatments that are not cost-effective to protect oneself from being sued for malpractice later on.

deficit response index (DRI) The amount by which the deficit changes with a one-dollar change in GDP.

deflation A decrease in the overall price level.

demand curve A graph illustrating how much of a given product a household would be willing to buy at different prices.

demand determined price The price of a good that is in fixed supply; it is determined exclusively by what firms and households are willing to pay for the good.

demand-pull inflation Inflation that is initiated by an increase in aggregate demand.

demand schedule A table showing how much of a given product a household would be willing to buy at different prices.

depreciation The decline in an asset's economic value over time.

depreciation of a currency The fall in value of one currency relative to another.

depression A prolonged and deep recession.

derived demand The demand for resources (inputs) that is dependent on the demand for the outputs those resources can be used to produce.

descriptive economics The compilation of data that describe phenomena and facts.

desired, or optimal, level of inventories The level of inventory at which the extra cost (in lost sales) from lowering inventories by a small amount is just equal to the extra gain (in interest revenue and decreased storage costs).

desired, or planned, investment Those additions to capital stock and inventory that are planned by firms.

diamond/water paradox A paradox stating that (1) the things with the greatest value in use frequently have little or no value in exchange, and (2) the things with the greatest value in exchange frequently have little or no value in use.

discount rate Interest rate that banks pay to the Fed to borrow from it.

discouraged-worker effect The decline in the measured unemployment rate that results when people who want to work but cannot find jobs grow discouraged and stop looking, thus dropping out of the ranks of the unemployed and the labor force.

discretionary fiscal policy Changes in taxes or spending that are the result of deliberate changes in government policy.

disposable, or after-tax, income (Y_d) Total income minus net taxes: $Y - T$.

disposable personal income or after-tax income Personal income minus personal income taxes. The amount that households have to spend or save.

dividends The portion of a corporation's profits that the firm pays out each period to shareholders. Also called *distributed profits*.

dominant strategy In game theory, a strategy that is best no matter what the opposition does.

drop-in-the-bucket problem A problem intrinsic to public goods: The good or service is usually so costly that its provision generally does not depend on whether or not any single person pays.

dumping A firm or industry sells products on the world market at prices below the cost of production.

durable goods Goods that last a relatively long time, such as cars and household appliances.

easy monetary policy Fed policies that expand the money supply in an effort to stimulate the economy.

economic growth An increase in the total output of an economy. It occurs when a society acquires new resources or when it learns to produce more using existing resources.

economic income The amount of money a household can spend during a given period without increasing or decreasing its net assets. Wages, salaries, dividends, interest income, transfer payments, rents, and so forth are sources of economic income.

economic integration Occurs when two or more nations join to form a free-trade zone.

economic problem Given scarce resources, how exactly do large, complex societies go about answering the three basic economic questions?

economics The study of how individuals and societies choose to use the scarce resources that nature and previous generations have provided.

economic theory A statement or set of related statements about cause and effect, action and reaction.

efficiency The condition in which the economy is producing what people want at least possible cost.

efficiency wage theory An explanation for unemployment that holds that the productivity of workers increases with the wage rate. If this is so, firms may have an incentive to pay wages above the market-clearing rate.

efficient market A market in which profit opportunities are eliminated almost instantaneously.

elastic demand A demand relationship in which the percentage change in quantity demanded is larger in absolute value than the percentage change in price (a demand elasticity with an absolute value greater than 1).

elasticity A general concept used to quantify the response in one variable when another variable changes.

elasticity of labor supply A measure of the response of labor supplied to a change in the price of labor.

elasticity of supply A measure of the response of quantity of a good supplied to a change in price of that good. Likely to be positive in output markets.

empirical economics The collection and use of data to test economic theories.

employed Any person 16 years old or older (1) who works for pay, either for someone else or in his or her own business for one or more hours per week, (2) who works without pay for 15 or more hours per week in a family enterprise, or (3) who has a job but has been temporarily absent, with or without pay.

employer mandate A system of health-care insurance provision in which all employers are required to provide health insurance and to pay on average 80 percent of the community-rated premiums.

entrepreneur A person who organizes, manages, and assumes the risks of a firm, taking a new idea or a new product and turning it into a successful business.

equilibrium Occurs when there is no tendency for change. In the macroeconomic goods market, equilibrium occurs when planned aggregate expenditure is equal to aggregate output.

equilibrium price level The point at which the aggregate demand and aggregate supply curves intersect.

equity Fairness.

European Union (EU) The European trading bloc composed of Austria, Belgium, Denmark, Finland, France, Germany, Greece, Ireland, Italy, Luxembourg, the Netherlands, Portugal, Spain, Sweden, and the United Kingdom.

excess burden The amount by which the burden of a tax exceeds the total revenue collected. Also called *dead weight losses*.

excess demand or **shortage** The condition that exists when quantity demanded exceeds quantity supplied at the current price.

excess labor, excess capital Labor and capital that are not needed to produce the firm's current level of output.

excess reserves The difference between a bank's actual reserves and its required reserves.

excess supply or **surplus** The condition that exists when quantity supplied exceeds quantity demanded at the current price.

exchange rate The price of one country's currency in terms of another country's currency; the ratio at which two currencies are traded for each other.

excise taxes Taxes on specific commodities.

expansion or **boom** The period in the business cycle from a trough up to a peak, during which output and employment rise.

expansionary fiscal policy An increase in government spending or a reduction in net taxes aimed at increasing aggregate output (income) (Y).

expansionary monetary policy An increase in the money supply aimed at increasing aggregate output (income) (Y).

expected rate of return The annual rate of return that a firm expects to obtain through a capital investment.

expenditure approach A method of computing GDP that measures the amount spent on all final goods during a given period.

experience rating The insurance-company practice of charging individuals or groups of individuals premiums that are linked to their current state of health or to the probability that they will become sick.

explicit contracts Employment contracts that stipulate workers' wages, usually for a period of one to three years.

export promotion A trade policy designed to encourage exports.

export subsidies Government payments made to domestic firms to encourage exports.

externality A cost or benefit resulting from some activity or transaction that is imposed or bestowed upon parties outside the activity or transaction. Sometimes called *spillovers* or *neighborhood effects*.

factor endowments The quantity and quality of labor, land, and natural resources of a country.

factor substitution effect The tendency of firms to substitute away from a factor whose price has risen and toward a factor whose price has fallen.

factors of production The inputs into the production process. Land, labor, and capital are the three key factors of production.

fallacy of composition The erroneous belief that what is true for a part is necessarily true for the whole.

favored customers Those who receive special treatment from dealers during situations of excess demand.

featherbedding The common union practice of preserving jobs even when it is inefficient to do so.

federal budget The budget of the federal government.

federal debt The total amount owed by the federal government.

federal deficit Federal government expenditures minus receipts.

Federal Open Market Committee (FOMC) A group composed of the seven members of the Fed's Board of Governors, the president of the New York Federal Reserve Bank, and four of the other eleven district bank presidents on a rotating basis; it sets goals regarding the money supply and interest rates and directs the operation of the Open Market Desk in New York.

Federal Reserve System (the Fed) The central bank of the United States.

Federal Trade Commission (FTC) A federal regulatory group created by Congress in 1914 to investigate the structure and behavior of firms engaging in interstate commerce, to determine what constitutes unlawful "unfair" behavior, and to issue cease-and-desist orders to those found in violation of antitrust law.

fee-for-service reimbursement A program in which insurance companies reimburse health-care providers for the services they've rendered.

fertility rate The birth rate. Equal to (the number of births per year divided by the population) $\times$ 100.

fiat, or **token, money** Items designated as money that are intrinsically worthless.

filtering The process whereby the newest and best housing goes to the wealthy, whose former housing passes down to those of middle income, whose former housing passes down to those of low income. Thus housing "filters" down the income-distribution ladder.

final goods and services Goods and services produced for final use.

financial capital market The part of the capital market in which savers and investors interact through intermediaries.

financial intermediaries Banks and other institutions that act as a link between those who have money to lend and those who want to borrow money.

fine tuning The phrase used by Walter Heller to refer to the government's role in regulating inflation and unemployment.

firm An organization that comes into being when a person or a group of people decides to produce a good or service to meet a perceived demand. Most firms exist to make a profit.

fiscal drag The negative effect on the economy that occurs when average tax rates increase because taxpayers have moved into higher income brackets during an expansion.

fiscal policy The government's spending and taxing policies.

five-year plans Plans developed in the Soviet Union that provided general guidelines and directions for the next five years.

fixed cost Any cost that does not depend on the firm's level of output. These costs are incurred even if the firm is producing nothing. There are no fixed costs in the long run.

fixed-weight procedure A procedure that uses weights from a given base year.

floating, or **market-determined, exchange rates** Exchange rates that are determined by the unregulated forces of supply and demand.

food stamps Vouchers that have a face value greater than their cost and that can be used to purchase food at grocery stores.

foreign exchange All currencies other than the domestic currency of a given country.

free-rider problem A problem intrinsic to public goods: Because people can enjoy the benefits of public goods whether they pay for them or not, they are usually unwilling to pay for them.

frictional unemployment The portion of unemployment that is due to the normal working of the labor market; used to denote short-run job/skill matching problems.

full-employment budget What the federal budget would be if the economy were producing at a full-employment level of output.

game theory Analyzes oligopolistic behavior as a complex series of strategic moves and reactive countermoves among rival firms. In game theory, firms are assumed to anticipate rival reactions.

General Agreement on Tariffs and Trade (GATT) An international agreement signed by the United States and 22 other countries in 1947 to promote the liberalization of foreign trade.

general equilibrium The condition that exists when all markets in an economy are in simultaneous equilibrium.

ghetto premiums Evidence suggests that during the 1960s and 1970s housing in sections of U.S. cities inhabited predominantly by African Americans was more expensive than comparable housing in white neighborhoods. The price difference came to be called a ghetto premium.

Gini coefficient A commonly used measure of inequality of income derived from a Lorenz Curve. It can range from zero to a maximum of 1.

goods market The market in which goods and services are exchanged and in which the equilibrium level of aggregate output is determined.

government consumption and investment (G) Expenditures by federal, state, and local governments for final goods and services.

government failure Occurs when the government becomes the tool of the rent seeker and the allocation of resources is made even less efficient by the intervention of government.

government franchise A monopoly by virtue of government directive.

government interest payments Cash payments made by the government to those who own government bonds.

government spending multiplier The ratio of the change in the equilibrium level of output to a change in government spending.

government transfer payments Cash payments made by the government directly to households for which no current services are received in return. They include social security benefits, unemployment compensation, and welfare payments.

Gramm-Rudman-Hollings Bill Passed by the U.S. Congress and signed by President Reagan in 1986, this law set out to reduce the federal deficit by $36 billion per year, with a deficit of zero slated for 1991.

Great Depression The period of severe economic contraction and high unemployment that began in 1929 and continued throughout the 1930s.

Great Leap Forward The economic strategy in the People's Republic of China that began in 1958 when it departed from the Soviet model and shifted from large-scale, capital-intensive industry to small-scale, labor-intensive industry scattered across the countryside. Material incentives were reduced and replaced by the motivating power of revolutionary ideology and inspiration.

Great Proletarian Cultural Revolution (1966–1976) A period of ideological purity in the People's Republic of China: Material incentives and reforms were denounced and highly trained specialists were sent to work in the fields. The effect of the Cultural Revolution on the Chinese economy was catastrophic.

Green Revolution The agricultural breakthroughs of modern science, such as the development of new, high-yield crop varieties.

gross domestic product (GDP) The total market value of all final goods and services produced within a given period by factors of production located within a country.

gross investment The total value of all newly produced capital goods (plant, equipment, housing, and inventory) produced in a given period.

gross national product (GNP) The total market value of all final goods and services produced within a given period by factors of production owned by a country's citizens, regardless of where the output is produced.

gross private investment (*I*) Total investment in capital—that is, the purchase of new housing, plants, equipment, and inventory by the private (or nongovern-ment) sector.

Hart-Scott-Rodino Act The 1980 antitrust legislation that extended the antitrust laws to proprietorships and partnerships and requires that all proposed mergers be reported to the Department of Justice.

health maintenance organization (HMO) A health-care plan that provides comprehensive medical services for employees and their families at a flat fee.

Heckscher-Ohlin theorem A theory that explains the existence of a country's comparative advantage by its factor endowments: A country has a comparative advantage in the production of a product if that country is relatively well endowed with inputs used intensively in the production of that product.

Herfindahl-Hirschman Index (HHI) A mathematical calculation that uses market share figures to determine whether or not a proposed merger will be challenged by the government.

homogeneous products Undifferentiated outputs; products that are identical to, or indistinguishable from, one another.

households The consuming units in an economy.

human capital A form of intangible capital that includes the skills and other knowledge that workers have or acquire through education and training and that yields valuable services to a firm over time.

hyperinflation A period of very rapid increases in the overall price level.

identity Something that is always true.

Immigration Act of 1990 Increased the number of legal immigrants allowed into the United States each year by 150,000.

Immigration Reform and Control Act (1986) Granted amnesty to about 3 million illegal aliens and imposed a strong set of employer sanctions designed to slow the flow of immigrants into the United States.

imperfect competition An industry in which single firms have some control over price and competition. Imperfectly competitive industries give rise to an inefficient allocation of resources.

imperfect information The absence of full knowledge regarding product characteristics, available prices, and so forth.

imperfectly competitive industry An industry in which single firms have some control over the price of their output.

implementation lag The time it takes to put the desired policy into effect once economists and policy makers recognize that the economy is in a boom or a slump.

import substitution An industrial trade strategy that favors developing local industries that can manufacture goods to replace imports.

impossibility theorem A proposition demonstrated by Kenneth Arrow showing that no system of aggregating individual preferences into social decisions will always yield consistent, nonarbitrary results.

income The sum of all a household's wages, salaries, profits, interest payments, rents, and other forms of earnings in a given period of time. It is a flow measure.

income approach A method of computing GDP that measures the income—wages, rents, interest, and profits—received by all factors of production in producing final goods.

income effect of higher wages When wages rise, people are better off. If leisure is a normal good, they may decide to consume more of it and to work less.

income elasticity of demand Measures the responsiveness of demand to changes in income.

increasing returns to scale, or **economies of scale** An increase in a firm's scale of production leads to lower average costs per unit produced.

indirect taxes Taxes like sales taxes, customs duties, and license fees.

Industrial Revolution The period in England during the late eighteenth and early nineteenth centuries in which new manufacturing technologies and improved transportation gave rise to the modern factory system and a massive movement of the population from the countryside to the cities.

industrial policy Government involvement in the allocation of capital across manufacturing sectors.

industry A group of firms that produce a similar product. The boundaries of a "product" can be drawn very widely ("agricultural products"), less widely ("dairy products"), or very narrowly ("cheese"). The term industry can be used interchangeably with the term market.

inelastic demand Demand that responds somewhat, but not a great deal, to changes in price. Inelastic demand always has a numerical value between zero and −1.

infant industry A young industry that may need temporary protection from competition from the established industries of other countries in order to develop an acquired comparative advantage.

inferior goods Goods for which demand tends to fall when income rises.

inflation An increase in the overall price level.

inflation rate The percentage change in the price level.

injunction A court order forbidding the continuation of behavior that leads to damages.

innovation The use of new knowledge to produce a new product or to produce an existing product more efficiently.

input or **factor markets** The markets in which the resources used to produce products are exchanged.

inputs The goods and services that firms purchase and turn into output.

intangible capital Nonmaterial things that contribute to the output of future goods and services.

interest The fee that a borrower pays to a lender for the use of his or her funds.

interest rate The annual interest payment on a loan expressed as a percentage of the loan. Equal to the amount of interest received per year divided by the amount of the loan.

interest sensitivity or **insensitivity of planned investment** The responsiveness of planned investment spending to changes in the interest rate. *Interest sensitivity* means that planned investment spending changes a great deal in response to changes in the interest rate; *interest insensitivity* means little or no change in planned investment as a result of changes in the interest rate.

intermediate goods Goods that are produced by one firm for use in further processing by another firm.

International Monetary Fund An international agency whose primary goals are to stabilize international exchange rates and to lend money to countries that have problems financing their international transactions.

international sector From any one country's perspective, the economies of the rest of the world.

Interstate Commerce Commission (ICC) A federal regulatory group created by Congress in 1887 to oversee and correct abuses in the railroad industry.

invention An advance in knowledge.

inventory investment Occurs when a firm produces more output than it sells within a given period.

investment New capital additions to a firm's capital stock. Although capital is measured at a given point in time (a stock), investment is measured over a period of time (a flow). The flow of investment increases the capital stock.

J-curve effect Following a currency depreciation, a country's balance of trade may get worse before it gets better. The graph showing this effect is shaped like the letter *J*, hence the name "J-curve effect."

job search The process of gathering information about job availability and job characteristics.

kinked demand curve model A model of oligopoly in which the demand curve facing each individual firm has a "kink" in it. The kink follows from the assumption that competitive firms will follow if a single firm cuts price but will not follow if a single firm raises price.

Knights of Labor One of the earliest successful labor organizations in the United States, it recruited both skilled and unskilled laborers. Founded in 1869, the power of the Knights declined after the Chicago Haymarket bombing in 1886.

labor demand curve   A graph that illustrates the amount of labor that firms want to employ at the particular wage rate.

labor force   The number of people employed plus the number of unemployed.

labor-force participation rate   The ratio of the labor force to the total population 16 years old or older.

labor-intensive technology   A production technique that uses a large amount of labor relative to capital.

labor market   The input/factor market in which households supply work for wages to firms that demand labor.

labor market discrimination   Occurs when one group of workers receives inferior treatment from employers because of some characteristic irrelevant to job performance.

labor productivity   Output per worker hour; the amount of output produced by an average worker in one hour.

labor supply curve   A diagram that shows the quantity of labor supplied at different wage rates. Its shape depends on how households react to changes in the wage rate.

labor theory of value   Marx's theory that the value of a commodity depends exclusively upon the amount of labor required to produce it. Commodities are the physical embodiment of the labor that produced them, and capital is the physical embodiment of the past labor used to produce it.

Laffer Curve   With the tax rate measured on the vertical axis and tax revenue measured on the horizontal axis, the Laffer Curve shows there is some tax rate beyond which the supply response is large enough to lead to a decrease in tax revenue for further increases in the tax rate.

laissez-faire economy   Literally from the French: "allow [them] to do." An economy in which individual people and firms pursue their own self-interests without any central direction or regulation.

land market   The input/factor market in which households supply land or other real property in exchange for rent.

law of demand   The negative relationship between price and quantity demanded: As price rises, quantity demanded decreases. As price falls, quantity demanded increases.

law of diminishing marginal utility   The more of any one good consumed in a given period, the less satisfaction (utility) generated by consuming each additional (marginal) unit of the same good.

law of diminishing returns   When additional units of a variable input are added to fixed inputs after a certain point, the marginal product of the variable input declines.

law of one price   If the costs of transportation are small, the price of the same good in different countries should be roughly the same.

law of supply   The positive relationship between price and quantity of a good supplied: An increase in market price will lead to an increase in quantity supplied, and a decrease in market price will lead to a decrease in quantity supplied.

legal tender   Money that a government has required to be accepted in settlement of debts.

lender of last resort   One of the functions of the Fed: It provides funds to troubled banks that cannot find any other sources of funds.

liability rules   Laws that require A to compensate B for damages imposed.

life-cycle theory of consumption   A theory of household consumption: Households make lifetime consumption decisions based on their expectations of lifetime income.

liquidity property of money   The property of money that makes it a good medium of exchange as well as a store of value: It is portable and readily accepted and thus easily exchanged for goods.

logrolling   Occurs when congressional representatives trade votes, agreeing to help each other get certain pieces of legislation passed.

long run   That period of time for which there are no fixed factors of production. Firms can increase or decrease scale of operation, and new firms can enter and existing firms can exit the industry.

long-run average cost curve (*LRAC*)   A graph that shows the different scales on which a firm can choose to operate in the long run.

long-run competitive equilibrium   When P = SRMC = SRAC = LRAC and profits are zero.

Lorenz Curve   A widely used graph of the distribution of income, with cumulative percentage of families plotted along the horizontal axis and cumulative percentage of income plotted along the vertical axis.

Lucas supply function The supply function embodies the idea that output (Y) depends on the difference between the actual price level and the expected price level.

M1, or transactions money Money that can be directly used for transactions.

M2, or broad money M1 plus savings accounts, money market accounts, and other near monies.

macroeconomics The branch of economics that deals with the economy as a whole. Macroeconomics focuses on the determinants of total national income, deals with aggregates such as aggregate consumption and investment, and looks at the overall level of prices rather than individual prices.

marginal cost (MC) The increase in total cost that results from producing one more unit of output. Marginal costs reflect changes in variable costs.

marginal damage cost (MDC) The additional harm done by increasing the level of an externality-producing activity by one unit. If producing product X pollutes the water in a river, MDC is the additional cost imposed by the added pollution that results from increasing output by one unit of X per period.

marginal factor cost (MFC) The additional cost of using one more unit of a given factor of production.

marginal private cost (MPC) The amount that a consumer pays to consume an additional unit of a particular good.

marginal product The additional output that can be produced by adding one more unit of a specific input, *ceteris paribus*.

marginal product of labor (MP_L) The additional output produced by one additional unit of labor.

marginal productivity theory of income distribution At equilibrium, all factors of production end up receiving rewards determined by their productivity as measured by marginal revenue product.

marginal propensity to consume (MPC) That fraction of a change in income that is consumed, or spent.

marginal propensity to import (MPM) The change in imports caused by a $1 change in income.

marginal propensity to save (MPS) That fraction of a change in income that is saved.

marginal revenue (MR) The additional revenue that a firm takes in when it increases output by one additional unit. In perfect competition, $P = MR$.

marginal revenue product (MRP) The additional revenue a firm earns by employing one additional unit of input, *ceteris paribus*.

marginal revenue product of labor (MRP_L) The additional revenue that a firm will take in by hiring one additional unit of labor, *ceteris paribus*. For perfectly competitive firms, the marginal revenue product of labor is equal to the marginal physical product of labor times the price of output.

marginal social cost (MSC) The total cost to society of producing an additional unit of a good or service. MSC is equal to the sum of the marginal costs of producing the product and the correctly measured damage costs involved in the process of production.

marginal utility (MU) The additional satisfaction gained by the consumption or use of *one more* unit of something.

market The institution through which buyers and sellers interact and engage in exchange.

market demand The sum of all the quantities of a good or service demanded per period by all the households buying in the market for that good or service.

market failure Occurs when resources are misallocated, or allocated inefficiently. The result is waste or lost value.

market organization The way an industry is structured. Structure is defined by how many firms there are in an industry, whether products are differentiated or are virtually the same, whether or not firms in the industry can control prices or wages, and whether or not competing firms can enter and leave the industry freely.

market power An imperfectly competitive firm's ability to raise price without losing all demand for its product.

market-socialist economy An economy that combines government ownership with market allocation.

market supply The sum of all that is supplied each period by all producers of a single product.

maximin strategy In game theory, a strategy chosen to maximize the minimum gain that can be earned.

means of production Marx's term for land and capital.

Medicaid and Medicare In-kind government transfer programs that provide health and hospitalization benefits: Medicare to the aged and their survivors and to certain of the disabled, regardless of income, and Medicaid to people with low incomes.

medium of exchange, or **means of payment** What sellers generally accept and buyers generally use to pay for goods and services.

microeconomic foundations of macroeconomics The microeconomic principles underlying macroeconomic analysis.

microeconomics The branch of economics that examines the functioning of individual industries and the behavior of individual decision-making units—that is, business firms and households.

midpoint formula A more precise way of calculating percentages using the value halfway between P_1 and P_2 for the base in calculating the percentage change in price, and the value halfway between Q_1 and Q_2 as the base for calculating the percentage change in quantity demanded.

minimum wage The lowest wage that firms are permitted to pay workers.

minimum wage laws Laws that set a floor for wage rates—that is, a minimum hourly rate for any kind of labor.

Ministry of Trade and Industry (MITI) The agency of the Japanese government responsible for industrial policy. It uses tariffs and subsidies to protect and subsidize key industries and helps some sectors plan orderly reductions in capacity.

model A formal statement of a theory. Usually a mathematical statement of a presumed relationship between two or more variables.

modern economic growth The period of rapid and sustained increase in real output per capita that began in the Western World with the Industrial Revolution.

monetary policy The behavior of the Federal Reserve regarding the nation's money supply.

money income The measure of income used by the Census Bureau. Because it excludes noncash transfer payments and capital gains income, it is less inclusive than "economic income."

money market The market in which financial instruments are exchanged and in which the equilibrium level of the interest rate is determined.

money multiplier The multiple by which deposits can increase for every dollar increase in reserves; equal to one divided by the required reserve ratio.

monocentric models Models of residential location that assume central employment. As people move farther from the center, their costs of commuting increase. Equilibrium in the housing market exists only where land prices just offset the lower transport costs closer to the center.

monopolistic competition A common form of industry (market) structure in the United States, characterized by a large number of firms, none of which can influence market price by virtue of size alone. Some degree of market power is achieved by firms producing differentiated products. New firms can enter and established firms can exit such an industry with ease.

monopoly An industry structure in which there is only one large firm that produces a product for which there are no close substitutes. Monopolists can set prices but are subject to market discipline. For a monopoly to continue to exist, something must prevent potential competitors from entering the industry and competing for profits.

monopsony A market in which there is only one buyer for a good or service.

moral hazard Arises when one party to a contract passes the cost of his or her behavior on to the other party to the contract.

moral suasion The pressure exerted by the Fed on member banks to discourage them from borrowing heavily from the Fed.

mortality rate The death rate. Equal to (the number of deaths per year divided by the population) $\times$ 100.

movement along a demand curve The change in quantity demanded brought about by a change in price.

multiplier The ratio of the change in the equilibrium level of output to a change in some autonomous variable.

NAIRU The non-accelerating inflation rate of unemployment.

Nash equilibrium In game theory, the result of all players playing their best strategy given what their competitors are doing.

national income The total income earned by the factors of production owned by a country's citizens.

national income and product accounts Data collected and published by the government describing the various components of national income and output in the economy.

National Labor Relations Board (NLRB) A watchdog board established by the Wagner Act in 1935. Its duties include ensuring that all workers are guaranteed the right to join unions and that firm managers participate fairly in collective bargaining if so requested by a majority of their employees.

natural monopoly An industry that realizes such large economies of scale in producing its product that single-firm production of that good or service is most efficient.

natural rate of population increase The difference between the birth rate and the death rate. It does not take migration into account.

natural rate of unemployment The unemployment that occurs as a normal part of the functioning of the economy. Sometimes taken as the sum of frictional unemployment and structural unemployment.

near monies Close substitutes for transactions money, such as savings accounts and money market accounts.

negative demand shock Something that causes a negative shift in consumption or investment schedules or that leads to a decrease in U.S. exports.

net exports ($EX - IM$) The difference between exports (sales to foreigners of U.S.-produced goods and services) and imports (U.S. purchases of goods and services from abroad). The figure can be positive or negative.

net exports of goods and services ($EX - IM$) The difference between a country's total exports and total imports.

net factor payments to the rest of the world Payments of factor income to the rest of the world minus the receipt of factor income from the rest of the world.

net income The profits of a firm.

net interest The interest paid by business.

net investment Gross investment minus depreciation.

net national product (**NNP**) Gross national product minus depreciation; a nation's total product minus what is required to maintain the value of its capital stock.

net taxes (T) Taxes paid by firms and households to the government minus transfer payments made to households by the government.

New Economic Policy The Soviet economic policy in effect between 1921 and 1928; characterized by decentralization and a retreat to a market orientation.

nominal GDP Gross domestic product measured in current dollars.

nominal wage rate The wage rate in current dollars.

nondurable goods Goods that are used up fairly quickly, such as food and clothing.

nonexcludable A characteristic of most public goods: Once a good is produced, no one can be excluded from enjoying its benefits.

nonlabor, or nonwage, income Any income received from sources other than working—inheritances, interest, dividends, transfer payments, and so on.

nonresidential investment Expenditures by firms for machines, tools, plants, and so on.

nonrival in consumption A characteristic of public goods: One person's enjoyment of the benefits of a public good does not interfere with another's consumption of it.

nonsynchronization of income and spending The mismatch between the timing of money inflow to the household and the timing of money outflow for household expenses.

normal goods Goods for which demand goes up when income is higher and for which demand goes down when income is lower.

normal rate of return A rate of return on capital that is just sufficient to keep owners and investors satisfied. For relatively risk-free firms, it should be nearly the same as the interest rate on risk-free government bonds.

normative economics An approach to economics that analyzes outcomes of economic behavior, evaluates them as good or bad, and may prescribe courses of action. Also called policy economics.

North American Free-Trade Agreement (**NAFTA**) An agreement signed by the United States, Mexico, and Canada in which the three countries agreed to establish all of North America as a free-trade zone.

not in the labor force People who are not looking for work, either because they do not want a job or because they have given up looking.

Ockham's razor The principle that irrelevant detail should be cut away.

Okun's Law The theory, put forth by Arthur Okun, that the unemployment rate decreases about one percentage point for every 3 percent increase in real GDP. Later research and data have shown that the relationship between output and unemployment is not as stable as Okun's "law" predicts.

oligopoly An industry structure with a small number of (usually) large firms producing products that range from highly differentiated (automobiles) to standardized (copper). In general, entry of new firms into an oligopolistic industry is difficult but possible.

on-the-job training The principal form of human capital investment financed primarily by firms.

Open Market Desk The office in the New York Federal Reserve Bank from which government securities are bought and sold by the Fed.

open market operations The purchase and sale by the Fed of government securities in the open market; a tool used to expand or contract the amount of reserves in the system and thus the money supply.

operating profit (or loss) or **net operating revenue** Total revenue minus total variable cost ($TR - TVC$).

opportunity cost That which we give up, or forgo, when we make a choice or a decision.

optimal level of provision for public goods The level at which resources are drawn from the production of other goods and services only to the extent that people want the public good and are willing to pay for it. At this level, society's willingness to pay per unit is equal to the marginal cost of producing the good.

optimal method of production The production method that minimizes cost.

optimal scale of plant The scale of plant that minimizes average cost.

outputs Usable products.

Pareto efficiency or **Pareto optimality** A condition in which no change is possible that will make some members of society better off without making some other members of society worse off.

partial equilibrium analysis The process of examining the equilibrium conditions in individual markets and for households and firms separately.

partnership A form of business organization in which there is more than one proprietor. The owners are responsible jointly and separately for the firm's obligations.

patent A barrier to entry that grants exclusive use of the patented product or process to the inventor.

per capita GDP or **GNP** A country's GDP or GNP divided by its population.

perfect competition An industry structure in which there are many firms, each small relative to the industry, producing virtually identical products and in which no firm is large enough to have any control over prices. In perfectly competitive industries, new competitors can freely enter and exit the market.

perfect knowledge The assumption that households possess a knowledge of the qualities and prices of everything available in the market, and that firms have all available information regarding wage rates, capital costs, and output prices.

perfectly contestable market A market in which entry and exit are costless.

perfectly elastic demand Demand in which quantity demanded drops to zero at the slightest increase in price.

perfectly inelastic demand Demand in which quantity demanded does not respond at all to a change in price.

perfect substitutes Identical products.

permanent income The average level of one's expected future income stream.

per se rule A rule enunciated by the courts declaring a particular action or outcome to be a per se (intrinsic) violation of antitrust law, whether the result is reasonable or not.

personal consumption expenditures (*C*) A major component of GDP: expenditures by consumers on goods and services.

personal income The total income of households. Equals (national income) minus (corporate profits minus dividends) minus (social insurance payments) plus (interest income received from the government and households) plus (transfer payments to households). The income received by households after paying social insurance taxes but before paying personal income taxes.

personal saving The amount of disposable income that is left after total personal spending in a given period.

personal saving rate The percentage of disposable personal income that is saved. If the personal saving rate is low, households are spending a large amount relative to their incomes; if it is high, households are spending cautiously.

Phillips Curve A graph showing the relationship between the inflation rate and the unemployment rate.

physical or **tangible, capital** Material things used as inputs in the production of future goods and services. The major categories of physical capital are nonresidential structures, durable equipment, residential structures, and inventories.

planned aggregate expenditure (AE) The total amount the economy plans to spend in a given period. Equal to consumption plus planned investment: $AE \equiv C + I$.

plant-and-equipment investment Purchases by firms of additional machines, factories, or buildings within a given period.

policy mix The combination of monetary and fiscal policies in use at a given time.

positive economics An approach to economics that seeks to understand behavior and the operation of systems without making judgments. It describes what exists and how it works.

post hoc, ergo propter hoc Literally, "after this (in time), therefore because of this." A common error made in thinking about causation: If Event A happens before Event B, it is not necessarily true that A caused B.

potential output, or potential GDP The level of aggregate output that can be sustained in the long run without inflation.

poverty line The officially established income level that distinguishes the poor from the nonpoor. It is set at three times the cost of the Department of Agriculture's minimum food budget.

preferred provider organization (PPO) A managed health-care plan in which an employer or insurance company establishes a network of doctors and hospitals to provide a broad set of medical services for a flat fee per participant. In return for the lower fee, the doctors and hospital who join the PPO network expect to receive a larger volume of patients.

price The amount that a product sells for per unit. It reflects what society is willing to pay.

price ceiling A maximum price that sellers may charge for a good, usually set by government.

price discrimination Occurs when a firm charges different buyers different prices for the same product. Such strategies are illegal if they drive out competition.

price elasticity of demand The ratio of the percentage change in quantity demanded to the percentage change in price; measures the responsiveness of demand to changes in price.

price feedback effect The process by which a domestic price increase in one country can "feed back" on itself through export and import prices. An increase in the price level in one country can drive up prices in other countries. This in turn further increases the price level in the first country.

price leadership A form of oligopoly in which one dominant firm sets prices and all the smaller firms in the industry follow its pricing policy.

price rationing The process by which the market system allocates goods and services to consumers when quantity demanded exceeds quantity supplied.

price surprise Actual price level minus expected price level.

principle of neutrality All else equal, taxes that are neutral with respect to economic decisions (that is, taxes that do not distort economic decisions) are generally preferable to taxes that distort economic decisions. Taxes that are not neutral impose excess burdens.

principle of second best The fact that a tax distorts an economic decision does not always imply that such a tax imposes an excess burden. If previously existing distortions exist, such a tax may actually improve efficiency.

private good A product produced by firms for sale to individual households. People can be excluded from the benefits of a private good if they do not pay for it.

private sector Includes all independently owned profit-making firms, nonprofit organizations, and households; all the decision-making units in the economy that are not part of the government.

privately held federal debt The privately held (non-government-owned) debt of the U.S. government.

privatization The transfer of government business to the private sector.

produce-marketing boards The channels through which the governments of some developing countries buy domestic farm output and then sell it to urban residents at government-controlled prices.

producer price indexes (PPIs) Measures of prices that producers receive for products at all stages in the production process.

producers Those people or groups of people, whether private or public, who transform resources into usable products.

product differentiation A strategy that firms use to achieve market power. Accomplished by producing products that have distinct positive identities in consumers' minds.

product, or output, markets The markets in which goods and services are exchanged.

production The process by which inputs are combined, transformed, and turned into outputs.

production function or **total product function** A numerical or mathematical expression of a relationship between inputs and outputs. It shows units of total product as a function of units of inputs.

production possibility frontier (ppf) A graph that shows all the combinations of goods and services that can be produced if all of society's resources are used efficiently.

production technology The quantitative relationship between inputs and outputs.

productivity, or **labor productivity** Output per worker hour; the amount of output produced by an average worker in one hour.

productivity of an input The amount of output produced per unit of an input.

profit The difference between total revenue and total cost.

progressive tax A tax whose burden, expressed as a percentage of income, increases as income increases.

property income Income from the ownership of real property and financial holdings. It takes the form of profits, interest, dividends, and rents.

proportional tax A tax whose burden is the same proportion of income for all households.

proprietorship A form of business organization in which a person simply sets up a business to provide goods or services at a profit. In a proprietorship, the proprietor (or owner) is the firm. The assets and liabilities of the firm are the owner's assets and liabilities.

proprietors' income The income of unincorporated businesses.

protection The practice of shielding a sector of the economy from foreign competition.

public assistance, or **welfare** Government transfer programs that provide cash benefits to (1) families with dependent children whose incomes and assets fall below a very low level and (2) the very poor regardless of whether or not they have children.

public choice theory An economic theory that the public officials who set economic policies and regulate the players act in their own self-interest, just as firms do.

public goods, or **social goods** Goods or services that bestow collective benefits on members of society. Generally, no one can be excluded from enjoying their benefits. The classic example is national defense.

public sector Includes all agencies at all levels of government—federal, state, and local.

purchasing-power-parity theory A theory of international exchange holding that exchange rates are set so that the price of similar goods in different countries is the same.

pure monopoly An industry with a single firm that produces a product for which there are no close substitutes and in which significant barriers to entry prevent other firms from entering the industry to compete for profits.

pure rent The return to any factor of production that is in fixed supply.

quantity demanded The amount (number of units) of a product that a household would buy in a given period if it could buy all it wanted at the current market price.

quantity supplied The amount of a particular product that a firm would be willing and able to offer for sale at a particular price during a given time period.

quantity theory of money The theory based on the identity $M \times V$; $P \times Y$ and the assumption that the velocity of money (V) is constant (or virtually constant).

queuing Waiting in line as a means of distributing goods and services; a nonprice rationing mechanism.

quota A limit on the quantity of imports.

racial covenants Provisions spelled out in property deeds that prohibit sale of that property to members of specific racial or ethnic groups.

rate of exploitation The ratio of surplus value to the value of labor power.

rational-expectations hypothesis The hypothesis that people know the "true model" of the economy and that they use this model to form their expectations of the future.

ration coupons Tickets or coupons that entitle individuals to purchase a certain amount of a given product per month.

Rawlsian justice A theory of distributional justice that concludes that the social contract emerging from the "original position" would call for an income distribution that would maximize the well-being of the worst-off member of society.

real business cycle theory An attempt to explain business cycle fluctuations under the assumptions of complete price and wage flexibility and rational expectations. It emphasizes shocks to technology and other shocks.

real interest rate   The difference between the interest rate on a loan and the inflation rate.

real wage rate   The amount that the nominal wage rate can buy in terms of goods and services.

real wealth, or **real balance, effect**   The change in consumption brought about by a change in real wealth that results from a change in the price level.

recession   A period during which aggregate output declines. Conventionally, a period in which aggregate output declines for two consecutive quarters.

recognition lag   The time it takes for policy makers to recognize the existence of a boom or a slump.

regressive tax   A tax whose burden, expressed as a percentage of income, falls as income increases.

relative-wage explanation of unemployment   An explanation for sticky wages (and therefore unemployment): If workers are concerned about their wages relative to other workers in other firms and industries, they may be unwilling to accept a wage cut unless they know that all other workers are receiving similar cuts.

rental income   The income received by property owners in the form of rent.

rent-seeking behavior   Actions taken by households or firms to preserve positive profits.

required reserve ratio   The percentage of its total deposits that a bank must keep as reserves at the Federal Reserve.

reserves   The deposits that a bank has at the Federal Reserve bank plus its cash on hand.

residential investment   Expenditures by households and firms on new houses and apartment buildings.

resources or **inputs**   Anything provided by nature or previous generations that can be used directly or indirectly to satisfy human wants.

response lag   The time that it takes for the economy to adjust to the new conditions after a new policy is implemented; the lag that occurs because of the operation of the economy itself.

retained earnings   The profits that a corporation keeps, usually for the purchase of capital assets. Also called undistributed profits.

rule of reason   The criterion introduced by the Supreme Court in 1911 to determine whether a particular action was illegal ("unreasonable") or legal ("reasonable") within the terms of the Sherman Act.

run on a bank   Occurs when many of those who have claims on a bank (deposits) present them at the same time.

saving (S)   The part of its income that a household does not consume in a given period. Distinguished from savings, which is the current stock of accumulated saving.

services   The things we buy that do not involve the production of physical things, such as legal and medical services and education.

share of stock   A certificate of partial ownership of a corporation. Entitles the holder to a portion of the corporation's profits.

Sherman Act   Passed by Congress in 1890, the act declared every

contract or conspiracy to restrain trade among states or nations illegal and declared any attempt at monopoly, successful or not, a misdemeanor. Interpretation of which specific behaviors were illegal fell to the courts.

shift of a demand curve   The change that takes place in a demand curve corresponding to a new relationship between quantity demanded of a good and the price of that good. The shift is brought about by a change in the original conditions.

shock therapy   The approach to transition from socialism to market capitalism that advocates rapid deregulation of prices, liberalization of trade, and privatization.

short run   The period of time for which two conditions hold: The firm is operating under a fixed scale (fixed factor) of production, and firms can neither enter nor exit an industry.

short-run industry supply curve   The sum of marginal cost curves (above AVC) of all the firms in an industry.

shut-down point   The lowest point on the average variable cost curve. When price falls below the minimum point on AVC, total revenue is insufficient to cover variable costs and the firm will shut down and bear losses equal to fixed costs.

Smoot-Hawley tariff   The U.S. tariff law of the 1930s, which set the highest tariffs in U.S. history (60 percent). It set off an international trade war and caused the decline in trade that is often considered a cause of the worldwide depression of the 1930s.

social capital, or **infrastructure** Capital that provides services to the public. Most social capital takes the form of public works (roads and bridges) and public services (police and fire protection).

social choice The problem of deciding what society wants. The process of adding up individual preferences to make a choice for society as a whole.

social, or **implicit, contracts** Unspoken agreements between workers and firms that firms will not cut wages.

social insurance, or **payroll, taxes** Taxes levied at a flat rate on wages and salaries. Proceeds support various government-administered social-benefit programs, including the social security system and the unemployment benefits system.

socialist economy An economy in which most capital is owned by the government rather than by private citizens. Also called social ownership.

social overhead capital Basic infrastructure projects such as roads, power generation, and irrigation systems.

social security system The federal system of social insurance programs. It includes three separate programs that are financed through separate trust funds: the Old Age and Survivors Insurance program (OASI), the Disability Insurance program (DI), and the Health Insurance program (HI, or Medicare).

sources side/uses side The impact of a tax may be felt on one or the other or on both sides of the income equation. A tax may cause net income to fall (damage on the sources side), or it may cause prices of goods and services to rise so that income buys less (damage on the uses side).

speculation motive One reason for holding bonds instead of money: Because the market value of interest-bearing bonds is inversely related to the interest rate, investors may wish to hold bonds when interest rates are high with the hope of selling them when interest rates fall.

spreading overhead The process of dividing total fixed costs by more units of output. Average fixed cost declines as quantity rises.

stability A condition in which output is steady or growing, with low inflation and full employment of resources.

stabilization policy Describes both monetary and fiscal policy, the goals of which are to smooth out fluctuations in output and employment and to keep prices as stable as possible.

stabilization program An agreement between a borrower country and the International Monetary Fund in which the country agrees to revamp its economic policies to provide incentives for higher export earnings and lower imports.

stagflation Occurs when the overall price level rises rapidly (inflation) during periods of recession or high and persistent unemployment (stagnation).

sticky prices Prices that do not always adjust rapidly to maintain equality between quantity supplied and quantity demanded.

sticky wages The downward rigidity of wages as an explanation for the existence of unemployment.

store of value An asset that can be used to transport purchasing power from one time period to another.

structural adjustment A series of programs in developing nations designed to (1) reduce the size of their public sectors through privatization and/or expenditure reductions, (2) decrease their budget deficits, (3) control inflation, and (4) encourage private saving and investment through tax reform.

structural deficit The deficit that remains at full employment.

structural unemployment The portion of unemployment that is due to changes in the structure of the economy that result in a significant loss of jobs in certain industries.

subsidies Payments made by the government for which it receives no goods or services in return.

substitutes Goods that can serve as replacements for one another; when the price of one increases, demand for the other goes up.

substitution effect of higher wages Consuming an additional hour of leisure means sacrificing the wages that would be earned by working. When the wage rate rises, leisure becomes more expensive, and households may "buy" less of it. This means working more.

sunk costs Costs that cannot be avoided, regardless of what is done in the future, because they have already been incurred.

supply curve A graph illustrating how much of a product a firm will supply at different prices.

supply schedule A table showing how much of a product firms will supply at different prices.

supply-side policies Government policies that focus on aggregate supply and increasing production rather than stimulating aggregate demand.

surplus value   The profit a capitalist earns by paying workers less than the value of what they produce.

sustained inflation   An increase in the overall price level that continues over a significant period.

tacit collusion   Collusion occurs when price- and quantity-fixing agreements among producers are explicit. *Tacit collusion* occurs when such agreements are implicit.

tariff   A tax on imports.

tax base   The measure or value upon which a tax is levied.

tax incidence   The ultimate distribution of tax's burden.

tax multiplier   The ratio of change in the equilibrium level of output to a change in taxes.

tax rate structure   The percentage of a tax base that must be paid in taxes—25% of income, for example.

tax shifting   Occurs when households can alter their behavior and do something to avoid paying a tax.

technological change   The introduction of new methods of production or new products intended to increase the productivity of existing inputs or to raise marginal products.

terms of trade   The ratio at which a country can trade domestic products for imported products.

theory of comparative advantage   Ricardo's theory that specialization and free trade will benefit all trading partners (real wages will rise), even those that may be absolutely less efficient producers.

three basic questions   The questions that all societies must answer: (1) What will be produced? (2) How will it be produced? (3) Who will get what is produced?

Tiebout hypothesis   An efficient mix of public goods is produced when local land/housing prices and taxes come to reflect consumer preferences just as they do in the market for private goods.

tight monetary policy   Fed policies that contract the money supply in an effort to restrain the economy.

time lags   Delays in the economy's response to stabilization policies.

total cost   The total of (1) out-of-pocket costs, (2) a normal rate of return on capital, and (3) the opportunity cost of each factor of production.

total fixed costs (*TFC*) or **overhead**   The total of all costs that do not change with output, even if output is zero.

total revenue (*TR*)   The total amount that a firm takes in from the sale of its product: The price per unit times the quantity of output the firm decides to produce ($P \times q$).

total utility   The total amount of satisfaction obtained from consumption of a good or service.

total variable cost (*TVC*)   The total of all costs that vary with output in the short run.

total variable cost curve   A graph that shows the relationship between total variable cost and the level of a firm's output.

trade deficit   Occurs when a country's exports of goods and services are less than its imports of goods and services in a given period.

trade feedback effect   The tendency for an increase in the economic activity of one country to lead to a worldwide increase in economic activity, which then feeds back to that country.

trade surplus   The situation when a country exports more than it imports.

tragedy of commons   The idea that collective ownership may not provide the proper private incentives for efficiency because individuals do not bear the full costs of their own decisions but do enjoy the full benefits.

transaction motive   The main reason that people hold money—to buy things.

transfer payments   Cash payments made by the government to people who do not supply goods, services, or labor in exchange for these payments. They include social security benefits, veterans' benefits, and welfare payments.

Treasury bonds, notes, and **bills**   Promissory notes issued by the federal government when it borrows money.

trust   An arrangement in which shareholders of independent firms agree to give up their stock in exchange for trust certificates that entitle them to a share of the trust's common profits. A group of trustees then operates the trust as a monopoly, controlling output and setting price.

unconstrained supply of labor   The amount a household would like to work within a given period at the current wage rate if it could find the work.

underground economy   The part of the economy in which transactions take place and in which income is generated that is unreported and therefore not counted in GDP.

unemployed   A person 16 years old or older who is not working, is available for work, and has made specific efforts to find work during the previous four weeks.

unemployment compensation A state government transfer program that pays cash benefits for a certain period of time to laid-off workers who have worked for a specified period of time for a covered employer.

unemployment rate The ratio of the number of people unemployed to the total number of people in the labor force.

unitary elasticity A demand relationship in which the percentage change in quantity of a product demanded is the same as the percentage change in price in absolute value (a demand elasticity of −1).

unit of account A standard unit that provides a consistent way of quoting prices.

urban decline The deterioration of the private and social capital stock of a city that results from the lack of investment by both private and public sectors.

U.S.-Canadian Free-Trade Agreement An agreement in which the United States and Canada agreed to eliminate all barriers to trade between the two countries by 1998.

utilitarian justice The idea that "a dollar in the hand of a rich person is worth less than a dollar in the hand of a poor person." If the marginal utility of income declines with income, transferring income from the rich to the poor will increase total utility.

utility The satisfaction, or reward, a product yields relative to its alternatives. The basis of choice.

utility possibilities frontier A graphical representation of a two-person world that shows all points at which A's utility can be increased only if B's utility is decreased.

value added The difference between the value of goods as they leave a stage of production and the cost of the goods as they entered that stage.

value of labor power The wage rate, dependent on the amount of clothing, shelter, basic education, medical care, and so on required to produce and sustain labor power.

variable A measure that can change from time to time or from observation to observation.

variable cost A cost that depends on the level of production chosen.

velocity of money The number of times a dollar bill changes hands, on average, during a year; the ratio of nominal *GDP* to the stock of money.

vicious-circle-of-poverty hypothesis Suggests that poverty is self-perpetuating because poor nations are unable to save and invest enough to accumulate the capital stock that would help them grow.

voting paradox A simple demonstration of how majority-rule voting can lead to seemingly contradictory and inconsistent results. A commonly cited illustration of the kind of inconsistency described in the impossibility theorem.

wealth or **net worth** The total value of what a household owns minus what it owes. It is a stock measure.

weight The importance attached to an item within a group of items.

Wheeler-Lea Act (1938) Extended the language of the Federal Trade Commission Act to include "deceptive" as well as "unfair" methods of competition.

Willis-Graham Act (1921) Declared the telephone industry a natural monopoly and exempted telephone mergers from review.

World Bank An international agency that lends money to individual countries for projects that promote economic development.

yellow-dog contracts Contracts in which workers agree not to join unions.

SOLUTIONS TO EVEN-NUMBERED PROBLEMS

CHAPTER 1

2. a. Pos. **b.** Norm. **c.** That Chile should not be allowed to join NAFTA is a normative statement. However, the reasons given are examples of positive economic analysis. **d.** Pos. **e.** Pos. **f.** Norm

4. Answers will vary.

6. a. Shopkeepers would gain by greater access to customers and higher profits. All city residents would gain, because greater access will generate higher sales and greater sales tax revenues. Consumers gain due to the opportunity cost of time not spent waiting in traffic jams.

b. Losers would include shopkeepers closer to the other, older bridge whose customers choose to shop closer to the new bridge. Any taxpayers for whom the extra taxes exceed the added benefit of the new bridge would also lose.

c. The gains/losses could be measured by adding up the value of all the time saved not waiting in line. We might say the bridge is efficient if the value of the time saved were greater than the cost of building the bridge.

8. a. Tuition (which could have been spent on other things), forgone wages, study time, etc.

b. All the money (gas, depreciation of the car, etc.) could have been spent on other items; time spent en route could have been used for other activities.

c. A better grade, no headache, perhaps admission to a better grad school, a higher paying job. He has traded off an investment in human capital (staying in to study) for present consumption (going to the party).

d. The other things that $200 could buy.

e. The $1 million could have been invested in other profit-making ventures or projects or it simply could have been put into the bank or loaned out to someone else at interest.

f. From the standpoint of the store, Alex is free. From Alex's standpoint he gives up other uses of time and wages that could be earned elsewhere.

Appendix

2. a. Negative slope. As price rises, quantity of apples purchased falls.

b. Positive (and declining) slope. As income rises, taxes rise, but the rise in taxes is less at higher incomes than at lower incomes.

c. Negative (and declining slope). As mortgage rates fall, home sales increase, but the increase in home sales is more at lower mortgage rates than at higher mortgage rates.

d. Negative, then positive slope. As young children get older, they run faster, but as adults get older (beyond a certain age), they run slower.

e. Positive slope. Greater sunshine leads to greater corn yield.

f. Positive, then negative slope. Up to a point, more fertilizer increases corn yield, but beyond a certain point, adding more fertilizer actually decreases the yield.

CHAPTER 2

2. Presumably studying means producing human capital, which will be used in the future to produce other things. Studying entails shifting benefits from the present into the future. The yield comes later in the form of higher productivity or a higher-paying job. Similarly, building a boat entails trading present consumption for a higher level of consumption later. The boat, like the knowledge gained while studying, is capital.

4. a. Depends on her state of mind and income. If she will be paying for college, she may have to work more later. In a sense, she is trading future work for present consumption. On the other hand, if she is really stressed out, taking time off may well make her a more productive student and earn her higher grades later on.

b. Sacrificing present consumption for the future benefits of losing weight. For most people, dieting and working out are difficult. The future benefits of feeling well and being healthy make it worthwhile for many.

c. Time and money spent today on maintenance can be thought of as an investment in the future—avoiding costly repair bills and/or the inconvenience of breaking down on the road. ("Pay me now or pay me later.")

d. Present time saved vs. risk of an accident or a ticket, which could be costly.

6. a. A straight-line ppf curve intersecting the Y axis at 1,000 units of luxury goods and intersecting the X axis at 500 units of necessity goods. These are the limits of production if all resources are used to produce only one good.

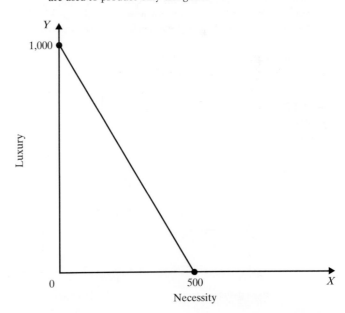

b. Unemployment or underemployment of labor would put the society inside the ppf. Full employment would move the society to some point on the ppf.

c. Answers will vary, but the decision should be based on the relative value of necessities and luxuries, and the degree of concern that all fellow citizens have enough necessities.

d. If left to the free market, prices would (at least ideally) be determined by market forces; incomes would be determined by a combination of ability, effort, and inheritance. It would be up to each individual to find a job and determine how to spend the income.

8. **a.** c **b.** a, d, e, f **c.** clearly d, probably e **d.** e **e.** all but a **f.** b

CHAPTER 3

2. Various. Some obvious examples are telecommunications, television broadcasting, electricity (coming), computer systems and software, etc.

4. Unions were the key opponents of GATT, especially unions in industries vulnerable to foreign competition (for example, sugar producers). Export industries, including the National Association of Manufacturers, favored GATT. Their reason: the theory of comparative advantage. (See chapter 2.)

6. Various.

8. Disagree. Change the word *corporations* to *sole proprietorships* and the statement is true (see Table 3.1).

10. No matter how much the firm produces, it is so small relative to the total market that its output has no effect on the market price. Therefore, the firm must be a "price taker"; it accepts the market-determined price charged by all other firms as a given that it cannot influence.

12. Government spending could increase while taxes are decreasing due to deficit spending (borrowing). Government spending could increase while government employment is decreasing if government is purchasing goods and services from the private sector that it formerly produced itself.

14. Answers will vary.

CHAPTER 4

2. **a.**

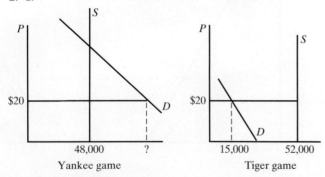

b. It depends on how responsive demand is to lower ticket prices. The way the curves are drawn in the figures, if the tickets were given away *free*, the stadium wouldn't fill up. If demand were

more responsive, the quantity demanded might equal the quantity supplied at a price above zero. Even if the quantity demanded is below the quantity supplied at a price of zero, a *negative* price might fill the stadium! That is, fans might have to be paid to endure such a bad game. This could be done by giving away free prizes to attendees.

c. Some demand was unsatisfied—price was below equilibrium, quantity demanded was below quantity supplied. The most common method of nonprice rationing is first-come, first-served. Sometimes people wait in line. Also, some firms have favored customers. See chapter 5.

4. **a.** Disagree. They are complements. **b.** Agree. **c.** Disagree. A rise in income will cause the demand for inferior goods to fall, pushing prices down. **d.** Disagree. Sure they can. Steak and lobster are both normal goods. **e.** Disagree. Price could go down if the shift of supply is larger than the shift of demand. **f.** Agree.

6.

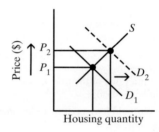

a. A simple demand shift: same diagram for both cities.

b. Rightward shift of supply with new development; leftward shift of demand with falling incomes: same diagram for both cities.

c. Trade-up buyers shift demand in the higher-income towns and supply in the lower-income towns.

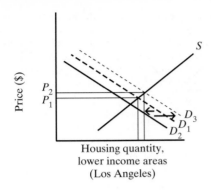

Housing quantity,
lower income areas
(Los Angeles)

d. Falling income pushes demand to the left; more households push demand to the right. The rightward shift is stronger.

8.

a. *P* decreases, *Q* decreases

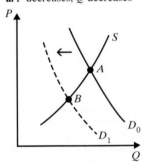

b. and **d.** *P* increases, *Q* increases

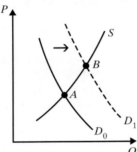

c. *P* increases, *Q* decreases

e. *P* decreases, *Q* increases

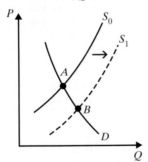

10. a.

PRICE	QUANTITY DEMANDED (IN MILLIONS)	QUANTITY SUPPLIED (IN MILLIONS)
$ .50	90	30
$1.00	80	50
$1.50	70	70
$2.00	60	90
$2.50	50	110

b. Quantity demanded equals quantity supplied at $P = \$1.50$, with quantity = 70 million dozen eggs.

c.

12. a.

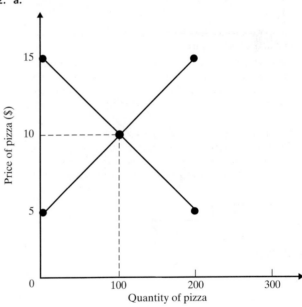

b. $Q_d = Q_s \rightarrow 300 - 20P = 20P - 100 \rightarrow P = \$10$. Substitute $P = \$10$ into either the demand or supply equation to get $Q = 100$.

c. With $P = \$15$, producers would want to supply $20(15) - 100 = 200$ pizzas, but consumers would want to buy $300 - 20(15) = 0$ pizzas. There would be an excess supply of pizzas, which would bring the price down. As the price decreased, quantity supplied would decrease while quantity demanded would increase until both were equal at a price of $10 and quantity of 100.

d. The new market demand for pizzas would be $Q_d = 600 - 40P$.

e. $Q_d = Q_s \rightarrow 600 - 40P = 20P - 100 \rightarrow P = 700/60 = \$11.67$. Substitute $P = \$11.67$ into either the demand or supply equation to get $Q = 133$.

CHAPTER 5

2. Answers will vary. But scalping—regardless of its morality—helps to eliminate shortages by creating a "market" where the price can rise to its equilibrium value. Anyone willing to pay the equilibrium price should be able to obtain a ticket. Also, by allowing price rationing to work somewhat, scalping reduces the need for waiting in line, and so results in less wasted time.

c. Rental housing

d. Plants

4.

a. Wheat market   **b.** Hamburger market

c. Gasoline market

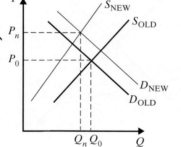

8. a. Using demand and supply data for the United States only, equilibrium price is $22 and equilibrium quantity is 12 million barrels.

b. With a price ceiling of $18, quantity demanded equals 14 million barrels, while quantity supplied equals 8 million barrels. There is an excess demand of 6 million barrels.

c. Quantity supplied will determine the quantity purchased. In a market system, no one can be forced to buy or sell more than he or she wants to. Under conditions of excess demand, suppliers will supply only as much as they want, and some consumer demand will go unsatisfied.

10. The key here is that total revenue is equal to $P \times Q$. When price rises (cab fares go up), quantity demanded goes down, depending on the elasticity of demand. Cab drivers who were expecting a 10% increase in revenues were expecting *no* loss of riders. They expected demand to be perfectly inelastic. But while fares did not go up 10%, they did go up. Thus, the increase in price was *more* than the decrease in riders, thus the percentage decrease in Q was less than the percentage increase in price: Demand in fact was *inelastic*.

12. a. −1.2   **b.** +10%   **c.** +15%   **d.** +12%   **e.** .67

14. a. % $\Delta Q \div$ % $\Delta P = 0.2$
Thus % $\Delta P =$ % $0\Delta Q \div 0.2 = 10\% \div 0.2 = 50\%$.

b. A price ceiling at $1.40 per gallon would create a shortage of gasoline. The result might be long lines at gas stations and perhaps a black market in gasoline.

CHAPTER 6

2. The unemployed are those who are not working for pay or profit but who have made specific efforts to find a job during the week of the employment survey. In simple terms it is the excess of labor supplied over labor demanded in the market. The labor demand curve measures the quantity of labor (workers or hours) demanded by firms at each possible wage rate. Firms' demand for labor is derived from the demand for products. Firms will hire workers as long as the product of their labor sells for a price high enough to produce a profit. Thus, the "productivity" of workers is critical. Labor supply reflects the choices made by households to work and how much to work. The alternative to working is leisure or "home production." Home production can include child rearing, subsistence farming, or other unpaid work. The value of leisure and home production is the opportunity cost of working.

6.

a. Housing   **b.** Beef in Continental Europe

4. The problem was that while output was rising, employment was not. The recovery doesn't really have much of an impact on people in general until new jobs begin to appear, reducing unemployment. The unemployment rate actually did not reach its highest level until the third quarter of 1992, just in time for the election.

6. Macro looks at aggregates in the total economy, while micro looks at individual markets and individual economic agents. It is often helpful (and more accurate) to base macroeconomics theories on the behavior of the individuals who make up the macroeconomy.

8. Wars result in high levels of government spending, which helps to increase total spending in the economy.

10. When demand shifts to the right in a market, prices tend to rise. Higher interest rates make buying a car or a home more expensive to those who must borrow to finance those items. Thus, high interest rates tend to shift demand curves back to the left, taking pressure off prices.

CHAPTER 7

2. Every payment made by a buyer becomes income for the seller. Thus, the dollar value of the purchases of new goods and services in a year must be the dollar value of the income generated in that year.

4. With fixed-weight indexes, the percentage change in the index from year to year depends on the weights chosen and thus on the base year.

   Goods whose output decreases (or increases slowly) because of slowly- or backward-shifting supply curves will have their relative prices increase. If we use the old prices as weights, we will tend to understate the importance of this decrease. Likewise, if we use the new prices as weights, we overstate the importance of the production decline.

   Fixed-weight price indexes that use old quantities as weights are generally taken as overestimates of the increase in the price level, because these indexes ignore consumers' opportunities to find substitutes for goods whose relative prices rise. Those that use current-year quantities as weights are taken to underestimate changes in the price level because they implicitly assume that the substitutes people chose for the goods whose relative prices rose are considered just as good as the "real thing."

   The use of fixed-weight indexes poses special problems when used to make measurements over long periods of time, because the use of, say, 1950 weights for 1995's economy is not desirable.

   The BEA's new approach does two things: First, it takes the (geometric) average of fixed-weight indexes, to deal with the overestimation and underestimation issues. Second, it "updates" the base years for the fixed-weight indexes every time it makes a new calculation, to ensure that the weights remain appropriate. That is, the indexes whose average it takes are those whose base years are the previous year and the current year.

6. You can't tell how much inflation is forecast. If you knew the forecast for "nominal" GDP (for GDP in current dollars) in addition to the forecast for real GDP, you could figure out how much of the forecast change was due to inflation. The 1998 per capita GDP: $26,943; 1999 per capita GDP: $27,355. Forecast for real GDP: +2.39%. Forecast for per capita real GDP: +1.53%.

8. Consumption as measured by retail sales is just part of GDP. Using the expenditure approach, real GDP is made up of consumption plus investment plus net exports plus government purchases. If the sum of I, G, and $(X - M)$ grows more rapidly than C, real GDP will rise more rapidly than retail sales.

10. The pizza is entirely consumed in the year it was produced, while the car will last many years. To correct for this, we could count just the value of the services provided by the car *each year*. For example, if the car lasts 5 years, then 20% of its value could be counted in each year's GDP.

12. There is no right or wrong answer here. But counting environmental damage requires a dollar estimate of this damage, about which there will be little consensus.

CHAPTER 8

2. *Full employment* is another term for the natural rate of unemployment. The idea behind this terminology is that if the only unemployment in the economy is the unemployment that comes about as the result of the normal working of the labor market, then there is no "unnecessary" unemployment. Labor is being "fully" utilized because the only unemployment that exists is the natural consequence of an efficiently working market. Thus the economy can be at full employment with a 4.9% unemployment rate, provided that the 4.9% unemployment is frictional and structural only.

4. This is structural unemployment, which can sometimes exist for long periods, especially when workers must learn new skills to find jobs. The social costs of this unemployment might be greater than the costs of retraining these workers, providing some justification for government assistance.

6. Yes, inflation would still be a problem. There are other costs of inflation besides the redistribution of income that occurs when incomes are not indexed. One example is the waste of time and resources spent coping with inflation. See the section on "Administrative Costs and Inefficiencies" under the heading "Costs of Inflation."

8. Yes, both statements can be true. The labor force of Tappania may have grown faster than the number of employed, implying an increase in the number who are looking for work but not working, and an increase in the unemployment rate.

10. Answers will vary.

CHAPTER 9

2. We know that $C = .75Y = 150$ billion. $C + I = 150 + 75 = 225$ billion. Thus, $C + I > Y$ ... aggregate spending is greater than aggregate output. Inventories will fall and in the coming months Y (real GDP) will rise. GDP will stop rising when $C + I = Y$. That is when $.75Y + 75 = Y$ or $75 = .25Y$ or $Y = 300$ billion Yuck dollars.

4. Think of the adjustment that occurs when, with the economy at the equilibrium level of output, an increase in planned investment occurs. Inventories are drawn down, and output increases. If firms increase output by the amount of the increase in planned investment, equilibrium will not be reestablished. The increased output (income) will also increase consumption. Thus there will have been an increase in Y of ΔI, but an increase in aggregate expenditure of more than ΔI. Y must increase further to establish equilibrium. The multiplier is finite because a fraction of income is saved. Thus, as Y grows, S grows; so we will eventually reach a level of Y at which the new planned investment just offsets the leakage into savings. This will be a new equilibrium. At this point, $\Delta S = \Delta I$. Because $\Delta S = MPS \times \Delta Y$, we can solve for ΔY:

$$\Delta Y = \frac{1}{MPS} \times \Delta I.$$

6. a. $MPC = .8$; $MPS = .2$.

b.

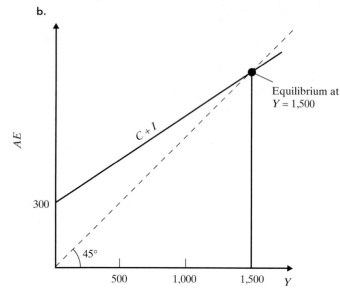

Equilibrium at $Y = 1,500$

$C + I$

AE

300

$45°$

500 $1,000$ $1,500$ Y

c. $\Delta Y = (1/MPS)\Delta I$. Multiplier $= 1/MPS = 1/.2 = 5$. In this case, with the multiplier equal to 5 and an increase in investment of 10, $\Delta Y = (5)(10) = 50$. Equilibrium Y increases from 1,500 to 1,550.

d. $S = Y - C$
$= Y - (200 + .8Y)$
$= -200 + .2Y$

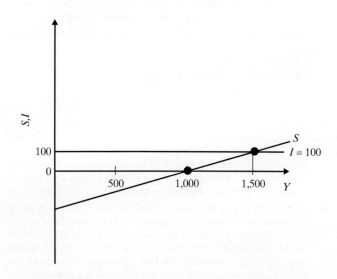

S,I

100

0

S

$I = 100$

500 $1,000$ $1,500$ Y

The equilibrium must be the same in both graphs because $Y = C + I$ and $S = I$ are the same condition. To see this, remember that $Y = C + S$ always. Substitute $C + S$ for Y in the equilibrium condition $Y = C + I$ to obtain $C + S = C + I$, which simplifies to $S = I$.

8. No. AE is *planned* aggregate expenditure. If you add unplanned changes in inventory to it, the sum equals aggregate output (income).

CHAPTER 10

2. $Y = 1,000$, $Y_d = 800$, $C = 600$, $S = 200$, $I = 100$, $G = 200$. Because total spending $= C + I + G = 600 + 100 + 200 = 900$ is less than total output of 1,000, one would predict that inventories will pile up, and firms will decide to reduce output.

b. Y would settle at 600. At this level of output, we would have $C = 300$, $I = 100$, and $G = 200$ so that $Y = C + I + G = 600$.

c. Cutting government purchases would make the fall in output worse! In particular, a cut of 25 would cause equilibrium Y to decline by $25(1/MPS) = (25)(4) = 100$. This would mean Y would decline to 500 instead of 600.

4. The statement is true if one only cares about the budget deficit. But there are also political controversies about the efficiency and appropriate size of the government sector that would lead some to favor the tax cut even though it raises the deficit by more.

6. If G goes up and T does not, the equilibrium level of Y rises. $C + I + G > Y$, inventories fall, and Y increases! In 1946 gross federal debt was 127.5% of GDP. Recent figures put the figure at just under 70%.

8. a. Govt. spending multiplier $= 1/.4 = 2.5$.

b. Govt. spending multiplier $= 1/(1 - .9) = 10$.

c. Govt. spending multiplier $= 1/(1 - .5) = 2$.

d. Tax multiplier $= -.75/(1 - .75) = -3$.

e. Tax multiplier $= -.9/(1 - .9) = -9$.

f. MPC must be .833. Tax multiplier $= -.833/(1 - .833) = -5.0$.

g. MPC must be .666. Government spending multiplier $= 1/(1 - .666) = 3.0$.

h. Output will increase by $100 billion (use the balanced-budget multiplier, which has a value of 1).

CHAPTER 11

2. *Cash:* Asset—Bank has it on hand.
Demand Deposits: Liability—claims by depositors can be withdrawn at any time.
Savings deposits: Liability—same logic.
Reserves: Assets—They are in the vault as cash or on deposit with the Fed.
Loans: Assets—They represent claims of the *bank* on borrowers.
Deposits at the Fed: Assets—They can be withdrawn at any time; they are owned by the bank.

4. Before the change, the banks are holding $67.2 billion (10% of demand deposits) in reserve assets against demand deposits. Changing the reserve requirement does not increase or decrease the quantity of reserves. Rather, it changes the volume of deposits that can be held for each dollar of reserves. At an 11% reserve requirement, $61 billion can support only about $611 billion in demand deposits. Thus, the money supply would have to shrink by $61 billion ($672 billion - $611 billion) to restore banks to compliance with the reserve requirement.

6. M2 includes everything in M1, plus savings accounts, money market accounts, and some other categories. A shift of funds between, say, savings accounts and checking accounts will affect M1 but not M2, because both savings accounts and checking accounts are part of M2.

8. Money injected through open market operations results in a multiple expansion of the money supply only if it leads to loans, and loans can be made only if the new money ends up in banks as reserves. If the Fed buys a bond from James Q. Public, who immediately deposits the proceeds into a dollar-denominated Swiss bank account, the U.S. money supply won't expand at all. If the money ends up in his pockets or in his mattress, the expansion of the money supply will stop right there. If he had deposited the proceeds in a U.S. bank, excess reserves would have been created, stimulating lending and further money creation.

10. In addition to controlling the money supply, the Fed clears interbank payments, is responsible for many of the regulations governing banking practices and standards, and is the lender of last resort for the banking system. It is also responsible for managing exchange rates and the nation's foreign exchange reserves.

Answers to the second part of the question will vary.

CHAPTER 12

2. If households believe that interest rates will rise, why should they lend money now? They will desire to hold more of their wealth as money for the time being, betting that they can get a higher interest rate if they wait. If they buy bonds now, they risk a capital loss (a decrease in the value of their assets), because bond prices fall when interest rates rise. When households hold money to speculate in this way, we call their motive for holding money the "speculation motive."

4.

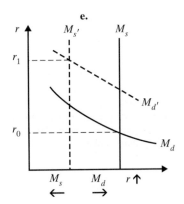

6. *Ceteris paribus*, an expansionary fiscal policy at a time when the Fed want to hold the rate of growth of the money supply steady will drive up interest rates. First, the added expenditure will push up the growth of real GDP. The increased spending and GDP would increase the demand for money, M_d. If the Fed holds the line, $M_d > M_s$ and rates will rise. At the same time these policies hit taxpayers, the Asia crisis of 1998 hit the U.S. economy and slowed down the growth of real GDP as exports to Asia fell. By early 1998, the Fed was even thinking of expanding M_s to push r down to restore GDP growth.

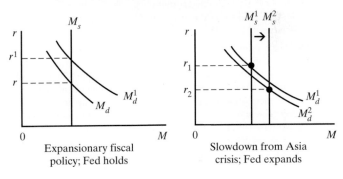

Expansionary fiscal policy; Fed holds

Slowdown from Asia crisis; Fed expands

CHAPTER 13

2. Taxes (T) rise, causing disposable income (Y_d) to fall. When Y_d falls, C falls, causing $AE < Y$. When $AE < Y$, inventories rise and firms cut back on output/income: Y falls and unemployment rises. If I were the central bank and I wanted to counteract these effects, I might lower interest rates to try to stimulate investment with expansionary monetary policy.

4. a. In 1998, the tax cuts cause disposable income to rise. When Y_d rises, C increases and $C + I + G > Y$. Inventories contract, causing Y to rise. Higher Y causes money demand M_d to rise. If M^s is fixed, that will cause r to rise. In 1999–2000 the story is reversed. The expenditure cuts kick in, causing G to fall. $C + I + G < Y$, inventories rise, Y falls. That causes money demand to fall and with M^s constant, r will fall.

b. The tax increase reduced disposable income and thus consumption $C + I + G < Y$, so inventories build and output falls. A lower Y means lower money demand. At the same time that the Fed is increasing the money supply, interest rates will fall sharply, causing I to rise, perhaps offsetting the effects of the initial tax increase on Y. (Final result: ambiguous Y, lower r.)

c. The drop in consumption cuts aggregate expenditure: $C + I + G < Y$, so inventories rise and Y falls. As Y falls, money demand drops. If the Fed holds M^s constant, r will fall. Here again, the lower r may stimulate I, causing I to rise, partially offsetting the initial decline in Y. (Final result: lower Y, lower r.)

d. The Fed expands the money supply. $M^s > M^d$, so r falls. Normally, the lower r might be expected to cause I to rise, but gloomy expectations and no need for new plant and equipment keep I low. Thus the link to the goods market is broken, and the monetary policy doesn't have much impact. (Final result: lower r, little or no change in Y.)

6. a. The decline in investment would be a reduction in aggregate expenditure, causing equilibrium output (income) to decrease in the goods market. In the money market, the drop in income would decrease the demand for money (shift the M^d curve to the left), causing the interest rate to fall and investment spending to rise back up somewhat. But the net effect would be a decline in output (income) and the interest rate.

b. Option 3 is the most expansionary, because the increase in the money supply works to offset the crowding-out effect. Option 2 would come next, but would involve some crowding out. Option 1 would be least expansionary, because the tax increase would decrease consumption spending. (Option 1 relies on the balanced-budget multiplier, which has a value of 1. Option 2 relies on the government spending multiplier, which is larger than 1.)

8. The Fed's tight monetary policy would drive up interest rates, discouraging investment and causing aggregate output to fall. The simultaneous expansionary fiscal policy would increase the government spending and consumption components of aggregate output, increasing money demand and driving up interest rates further. The policies have opposing effects on aggregate output, so the ultimate effect on Y depends on which effect is stronger. But both policies drive interest rates higher. (In 1981, as a result of this policy, the prime interest rate rose to 21.5%!)

CHAPTER 14

2. a.

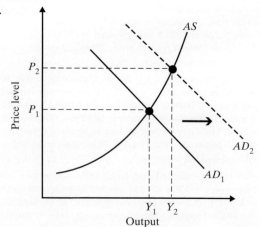

The price level will rise considerably; equilibrium GDP will rise only a little.

b.

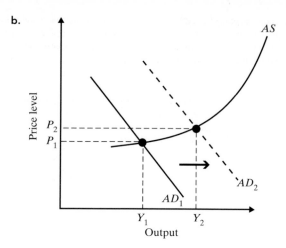

GDP will rise considerably; prices will rise only a little.

c.

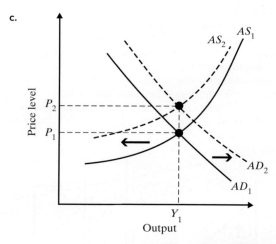

The price level will rise considerably. Equilibrium GDP may fall, but by less than it would if the Fed did not accommodate.

d.

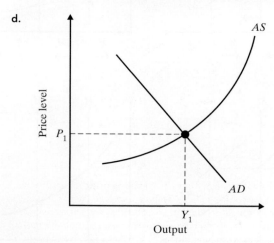

Neither the price level nor output would change. The fiscal and monetary policies have opposing effects on the AD curve. If they are of equal strength, there will be no shift in the curve.

4. a. Expansionary fiscal policy shifts the *AD* curve to the right if the Fed expands the money supply to accommodate the expansion and prevent crowding out. If it pushes us beyond potential GDP, inflation could be the result.

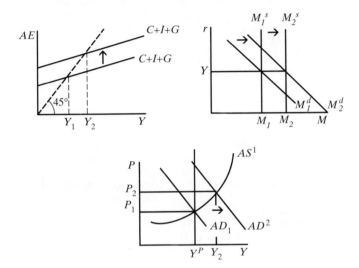

b. Contractionary monetary policy shifts the *AD* curve to the left.

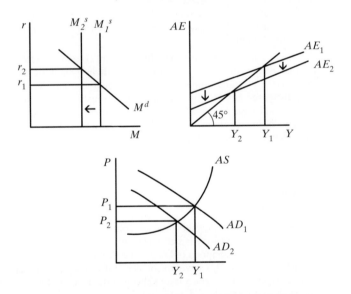

6. The actual physical capacity of existing plants represents the maximum output level the economy could produce in the short run. It is where the short-run *AS* curve becomes vertical. Potential GDP is the maximum output the economy could maintain in the long run without exacerbating inflation. It is less than full-capacity output because the bottlenecks and labor shortages that would exist at full-capacity output would cause wages and input prices to rise, leading to worsening inflation.

8.

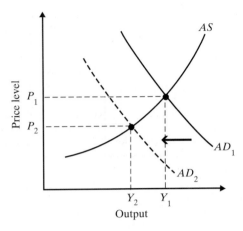

The government expected the decrease in the money supply to shift the aggregate demand curve to the left by raising interest rates and reducing planned investment. The shift should have caused aggregate output to fall from Y_1 to Y_2 and the price level to fall from P_1 to P_2.

Prices could have continued to increase because (a) there were expectations of continuing inflation, causing input prices to rise despite the fall in output; (b) OPEC increased the cost of oil to the United States during this period. Both explanations would be represented by a leftward shift in the *AS* curve.

CHAPTER 15

2. a. If the minimum wage is 9 slugs per hour, then:

$$Q_D = 100 - 5(9) = 55 \text{ million workers;}$$
$$Q_S = 10(9) - 20 = 70 \text{ million workers.}$$

The excess supply of labor (number of unemployed) would be $70 - 55 = 15$ million workers. The unemployment rate would be $15/70 = .214$ or 21.4%.

b. With no minimum wage, the equilibrium wage is found by setting labor demand equal to labor supply:

$$100 - 5W = 10W - 20 \rightarrow 120 = 15W \rightarrow W = 8 \text{ slugs per hour.}$$

Equilibrium employment is found by substituting $W = 8$ into either the labor-demand or labor-supply equation:

$$Q_D = 100 - 5(8) = 60 \text{ million workers;}$$
$$Q_S = 10(8) - 20 = 60 \text{ million workers.}$$

The labor force shrinks from 70 million to 60 million workers. Total employment rises from 55 million to 60 million workers. The unemployment rate shrinks from 21.4% to zero. (The model assumes no frictional unemployment.)

c. The labor market might not adjust so quickly due to wage rigidity, which has a number of possible causes, including implicit and explicit contracts, worker concerns over their relative wages, and firms' concerns over the decline in productivity that might follow a wage cut.

4. The point here is simple: If inflation is running at more than 10%, your real wage will decrease, and you will be less well off in terms of purchasing power.

6. a.

b.

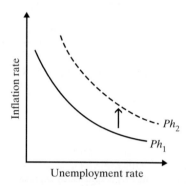

Here, it is assumed that inflationary expectations have increased.

c.

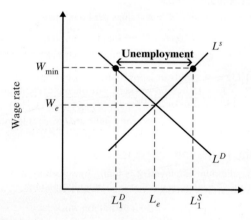

Number of workers

8. The trade-offs might be different for the two countries because social contracts and long-term explicit and implicit contracts may keep Japanese firms from laying off workers. Because the labor force in the United States is more transient, layoffs may be more likely. In Japan, a given reduction in inflation would probably require a smaller increase in unemployment.

CHAPTER 16

2. Fine-tuning means using monetary and fiscal policy to make adjustments to keep growth from going too fast (inflation) or drifting into recession. Many economists are skeptical of the government's ability

to do this. Nevertheless, the 1990s were a very stable period, and the Fed made a number of seemingly effective monetary policy changes then. During the spring of 1994, the Fed tightened credit and drove up interest rates. The economy responded just as chapter 28 would suggest, and the growth of GDP slowed markedly. Then when things got too slow in 1995, the Fed expanded the money supply, dropping rates, and the economy seemed to respond by growing more rapidly a few months later.

4. When the economy contracts, both taxable income and corporate profits fall, causing a decrease in tax revenues. In addition, some government expenditure categories, such as unemployment insurance benefits, tend to rise. With decreased tax revenues and increased government expenditures, the government deficit typically rises when the economy contracts.

6. The Federal Reserve increased short-term interest rates seven times during 1994 by directly raising the discount rate and by using open-market operations to raise the federal funds rate. With a lag, such moves have an effect on aggregate expen-diture (investment spending and consumption spending). The purpose was to prevent inflation. As unemployment fell below 6% in 1994, the Fed's Board of Governors decided that the United States was getting close to the natural rate of unemployment, or to "potential GDP." As GDP expands above potential GDP, inflation occurs. Inflation was not in fact a problem after 1994, and so it is not clear with hindsight that the Fed needed to tighten.

8. The Fed "leans against the wind" when it increases the money supply to lower interest rates to counteract contraction of the economy, and decreases the money supply to raise interest rates to counteract rapid expansion. These policies are designed to sta-bilize the economy.

10. It takes a full year for the spending multiplier to take effect because neither individuals nor firms alter their spending plans immediately. It takes time for the additional income derived from increased government spending to be translated into additional purchases, and when taxes are cut there are also decisions to be made about what portion of the tax cut to spend and what to spend it on. This makes correct timing of fiscal policy more difficult.

CHAPTER 17

2. Answers will vary.

4. When taxes increase (net wages decrease), one of the impacts is a reduction in income. If leisure is a normal good, the decrease in income will lead to less consumption of leisure, and therefore an increase in desired work hours. This serves to counteract the substitution effect of a decrease in wages, which lowers the opportunity cost of leisure and tends to decrease desired work hours.

6. The value of homes is an important component of household wealth. When home prices rise, household wealth rises and consumption tends to increase. When home prices fall, household wealth falls and consumption decreases. Because changes in consumption are changes in aggregate expenditure, they lead to changes in output and employment in the same direction.

8. A given consumption path requires a given amount of lifetime income to pay for it. But, given initial wealth, lifetime income is determined by working hours. This implies that income is not really an "independent" variable in the consumption function. Rather, the desire to consume and the desire to enjoy leisure together will determine how much income one will earn.

10. Maintaining inventory stocks helps a firm maintain a smooth production level. When sales unexpectedly increase, goods can be sold out of inventory. When sales unexpectedly decrease, goods can be added to inventories. By smoothing production, a firm can save on the adjustment costs associated with frequent changes in capital stock and employment levels. The cost of this policy is the forgone interest from investing funds in inventory stocks instead of lending out the money in financial markets.

CHAPTER 18

2. **a.** Graph I: Supply-side economics; it focuses on the supply-side effects of a tax cut and tends to ignore the demand-side impacts. Tax cuts should increase the incentive to work, save, and invest. If work effort, saving, and investment all increase, the AS curve will shift to the right, increasing output and reducing the price level. The extent to which the supply curve is likely to shift depends on the responsiveness of behavior to the tax cuts. This is the subject of much controversy.

   Graph II: Monetarism/New classical economics. Both schools believe that fiscal policy cannot have an impact on the level of real output. Monetarism believes that nominal GDP cannot change as long as the money supply and the velocity of money remain constant. Thus real GDP will not respond to a tax cut. New classical theories predict that "anticipated" fiscal policies will have no effect on real GDP, which remains at the potential output level determined in the long run in markets such as the labor market.

   Graph III: Keynesian economics. As long as the economy is not operating at capacity, and as long as the Fed accommodates somewhat by increasing the money supply, a permanent tax cut can increase the level of real GDP and is likely to be inflationary. The impact on the price level is determined by how close to capacity the economy is operating.

   b. Individual response.

4. Individual response.

6. **a.** Clinton's tax increases and spending cuts would be a fiscal contraction. With no change in Fed policy, output would decrease and unemployment would increase. If the Fed matches the fiscal contraction with a monetary expansion, lowering interest rates to stimulate investment, the decline in output could be avoided.

   b. Monetarists would worry about imperfect policy timing. Fed stimulation might take effect at the wrong time (e.g., after the economy has recovered from the impact of the fiscal contraction). Supply-siders would worry that higher tax rates would decrease the incentive to work and invest. Extreme supply-siders might worry that an increase in tax rates would decrease tax revenue and result in an even larger budget deficit.

   c. To evaluate the supply-side argument, you would need to see what happened to tax revenues and labor supply after the tax rate increases. An increase in tax revenues, *ceteris paribus*, would contradict the view of extreme supply-siders. If labor supply did not decrease much, general supply-side arguments would be weakened. To evaluate the monetarist argument, you

would need to see if investment spending increased as consumption spending declined (proper policy timing), or only after consumption began to recover (poor timing).

8. Reagan believed that the lower tax rates would provide incentives for households to work more hours and to save more and for firms to invest more. These actions would expand the supply of goods and services and, thus, expand aggregate income and the tax base. The tax base would rise by so much that tax revenues would actually rise despite the lower tax rates. Bush believed that incentives were important, but that the effects would not be large enough to raise revenues and reduce the deficit.

CHAPTER 19

2. **TABLE 1**

Y/L	GROWTH RATE
4.28	—
4.23	3.7
4.17	3.6
4.12	3.7

TABLE 2

Y/L	GROWTH RATE
4.28	—
4.41	3.9
4.53	3.9
4.66	3.9

TABLE 3

Y/L	GROWTH RATE
4.28	—
4.45	5.0
4.63	5.0
4.81	5.0

In Table 1, L is growing rapidly while K is growing slowly. It is likely that much of the growth in Y is due to growth in L. Because of diminishing returns to L, it is not surprising that Y/L is declining.

In Table 2, L is growing slowly while K is growing rapidly. In this case it seems that the growth in Y is caused mainly by growth in K. The ratio Y/L is increasing because each worker has more capital with which to work.

Finally, in Table 3, both L and K are growing slowly relative to Y. Technology must be the cause of most of the growth in Y in this case. This technological improvement also has the effect of increasing the amount of output per worker (Y/L).

4. Households would receive a higher after-tax rate of return on their stock portfolios. It could lead to higher saving. It could

also lead households to shift their portfolios toward stocks and away from bonds. Some argue it could lead to more frequent trading among stockholders, leading to a more efficient stock market. Firms would be more likely to retain earnings for investment purposes because paid-out dividends would be taxed at a higher rate than capital gains. Some argue that it would lead to more start-up companies. When a small firm goes "public," successful entrepreneurs who cash in have to pay capital gains rates on the proceeds of their stock sale; lower CG rates increase the incentive to start a firm. Empirical research suggests that these effects are small.

6. Assuming that the economy stays at full employment, the bill would cause the economy to produce more capital goods and fewer consumption goods. This would lead to a higher growth rate over time. The trade-off is less consumption today. There are also distributional consequences. Capital income earners (who have higher incomes on average) would benefit. The members of the higher-income households (who spend a smaller fraction of their incomes) would bear relatively less of the consumption-tax burden, while the members of the low-income households (who spend a higher fraction of their incomes) would bear relatively more of the consumption-tax burden.

8. High budget deficits are financed with private saving. That saving otherwise would have found its way through financial markets into private capital production. If the deficit is used to finance current expenditures like paying judges and congresspeople, it is not contributing to an expansion of output in the long run. The same is true of a tax cut, which is used to increase current consumption expenditures. But if the government used the money to build capital such as roads and bridges or to increase human capital through better education and job training, it would at least offset part of the reduction in private investment spending. Whether the net result for output growth is positive or negative depends on whether private capital or public capital has a higher rate of return. This is a subject of much debate, and would depend on the specific capital expenditures undertaken by the government.

CHAPTER 20

2. a. You cannot tell from the information given which country has an absolute advantage because you are not given any information that would indicate the actual quantities of inputs used in production in either country.

   b. If resources are fully mobile between sectors the opportunity cost of a cap is 2/3 of a quart of wheat in Russia; the opportunity cost of a cap is 7/10 of a quart of wheat in the United States. Russia has a comparative advantage in cap production. The opportunity cost of a quart of wheat in Russia is 1.5 caps. The opportunity cost of a quart of wheat in the United States is 10/7 or 1.43 caps. The United States has a comparative advantage in wheat.

   c. At $1 = 1 Ru, both goods in the United States are cheaper to everyone. That would mean that there was a big demand for dollars and no supply on foreign exchange markets. The price of the dollar would rise. When a dollar was valued at between 1.43 and 1.50 Ru, caps would be cheaper in Russia and wheat would be cheaper in the United States. If the price of a dollar rises to more than 1.50 Ru, everyone would buy both goods in Russia.

4. a. Illinois would have an absolute advantage in both wheat and soybeans.

   b. In Illinois, taking 1 acre out of wheat and moving it into soybeans sacrifices 48 bushels of wheat for 39 bushes of soybeans. This is 48/39 = 1.23 bushels of wheat for each bushel of soybeans. In Kansas, the sacrifice is 40/24 = 1.67 bushels of wheat for each bushel of soybeans.

   c. Based on the calculations in b. above, Kansas has a comparative advantage in wheat, and Illinois has a comparative advantage in soybeans.

   d. Yes, the data are consistent with the conclusions in c. above. Kansas has more acreage devoted to wheat than soybeans, while in Illinois there is more acreage devoted to soybeans than to wheat. Although neither state completely "specializes," each state seems to be devoting more of its resources to producing the good in which it has a comparative advantage.

6. Answers will vary.

8. EC members will clearly benefit, because the volume of trade will increase, and the pattern of production in each country will conform more closely to comparative advantage. Initially, the EC will be a powerful trading bloc concerned with improvements of trade within its own unified area. This may mean it will conduct less trade with the United States, especially if trade barriers between the United States and the EC remain in place. Eventually, however, we would expect comparative advantage to bring about efficient trade flows between the United States and the new unified Europe.

CHAPTER 21

2. a. Answers can include an increase in U.S. incomes, an increase in British interest rates, a decrease in U.S. interest rates, a decrease in the British price level, and an increase in the U.S. price level.

   b. All of the above, except for the increase in U.S. incomes, would also cause the supply curve to shift to the left.

   c. The two changes in interest rates listed in a. and b. above—which would raise the value of the pound without any other simultaneous change in import or export demand—would make British goods relatively more expensive and decrease Britain's trade balance (shrink the surplus, or increase the deficit).

4. a. The expansionary fiscal policy increased incomes and the demand for money. This in itself would cause U.S. interest rates to rise. In addition, the contractionary monetary policy caused interest rates to rise further.

   b. The supply curve for dollars would shift to the left, and the demand curve would shift to the right. The value of the dollar would rise.

   c. The rise in the value of the dollar—with no other change in the desire to buy imports or exports—would make U.S. goods relatively more expensive. The U.S. trade deficit would worsen, and the trade balance of other countries with the United States would rise.

6. a. Under fixed rates, higher U.S. income would increase the demand for imports. The U.S. current account balance would decrease (i.e., the trade surplus would decrease or the trade deficit would increase). Under floating rates, there would be

two forces acting on the exchange rate. Higher U.S. income would increase the demand for imports, increasing the supply of dollars on foreign exchange markets and causing the dollar to depreciate. However, with higher income, assuming the Fed is not fully accommodating, the interest rate in the United States would rise due to the higher demand for money. This increase in the interest rate would increase the demand for (and decrease the supply of) dollars in foreign exchange markets, causing an appreciation of the dollar. The net effect on the value of the dollar is ambiguous. However, because of the increased U.S. income, the demand for imports would increase and the current account balance would decrease, although this change in the current account balance may be partially offset if the dollar depreciated.

b. Under fixed rates, higher U.S. prices would make U.S. goods less attractive. U.S. imports would increase, and exports would decrease, causing a decrease in the current account balance. Under floating rates, the dollar would depreciate, with no effect on the current account balance.

c. Because U.S. interest rates fall, foreigners will take their money out of U.S. financial markets and the demand for dollars will decrease. U.S. citizens will find foreign financial markets more attractive, so the supply of dollars will increase. At the same time, U.S. income increases so the demand for foreign goods also increases, further increasing the supply of dollars. Under fixed rates, all this would decrease the current account balance. Under floating rates, the dollar would depreciate, causing a decrease in imports and increase in exports. Since imports would increase due to the higher U.S. income, the net effect on the current account balance is ambiguous.

d. Imports will decrease and consumers will buy more domestic goods, so the demand for foreign currency decreases. Under fixed rates, this would increase the current account balance. Under floating rates, this would cause the dollar to appreciate, and the impact on the current account balance would be ambiguous.

8. Possible reasons are lower Japanese inflation rates and higher interest rates during much of the period.

CHAPTER 22

2. Answers will vary. There is no clearly "right answer" to this problem, only trade-offs. Capital accumulation requires saving (reduced consumption), and when most citizens are earning subsistence wages, reducing consumption is not an option for many.

4. a. Capital increases the productivity of labor. A given-sized labor force can produce more output, and output per capita rises.

b. In a market economy, individual household savings decisions determine the pool of aggregate savings. Aggregate savings, in turn, is the amount made available for firms to purchase capital. Savings are matched to investment projects in financial markets, where the interest rate adjusts to equate total desired investment with total desired savings.

c. In developing countries, a greater fraction of output is needed just to ensure the current population's survival. An increase in investment—which requires a decrease in current consumption—cuts dangerously close to this survival level of consumption, and at a minimum causes more discomfort than it would in developed countries.

d. Answers will vary. Market-oriented economists would stress increased incentives for private investment (political stability, lower government budget deficit, and perhaps loans from abroad). Planning-oriented economists might stress government-directed projects, taxes on luxury goods, and capital controls designed to prevent capital flight to developed countries.

6. It is true that poor countries must accumulate capital in order to grow, but many poor countries do indeed have extra output available for savings. The problem is often that the available savings goes abroad (capital flight). Increased political stability and a more stable investment climate would help investment in the domestic economy. In addition, poor countries can get loans and other assistance from developed countries to help them accumulate capital.

8. A country should work to develop both its agricultural and its industrial sectors. Development of the agricultural sector can have high payoffs because it often requires little capital investment and directly benefits the poorest (rural) segment of society. Experience has shown that import substitution is a poor development policy. Its disadvantages include lessened competition in the domestic market, fewer jobs created, and expensive inputs for domestic industries.

Many countries favor industry as a more direct route to growth in the capital stock, and also to emulate the production pattern of already developed countries. Import substitution is attractive because it lessens dependence on unstable foreign demand for exports.

CHAPTER 23

2. It depends on what happened. As of February 6, 1998, the yen had regained some of its value, closing at 123 yen = \$1. There were signs that real growth, albeit slow, was returning to Japanese GDP.

4. The "tragedy of the commons" occurs when the costs or benefits of individual action are widely dispersed, rather than concentrated on the individual taking the action. In the case of a guaranteed job at a guaranteed wage, the benefits of doing one's job are dispersed widely among the other workers, and so are the costs of shirking. If workers follow narrow self-interest, we would expect productive behavior to decrease, and all workers would suffer.

6. There are arguments on both sides. Firms that acquire market power tend to overprice and underproduce relative to the efficient price and output levels. Market power, it is argued, stifles both price and quality competition. Microsoft was charged with anticompetitive behavior by packaging its web browser with its dominant operating system, Windows. After knocking out the competition, the story goes, they can raise prices without competitive pressure. But what about foreign competition? Isn't it a bigger, tougher game when the competition is a foreign firm receiving government support? The real problem is that the government is likely to be lousy at picking winners. What makes us think that the government can pick winners better than the market? Even recent Japanese attempts to subsidize a winner (fifth-generation computer) have failed.

8. a. Disagree. Exactly the opposite has occurred. Since 1958, China has moved toward a decentralized industrial base. Since Tiananmen Square, China has cracked down on political dissent but it has encouraged private enterprise.

b. The first two sentences are correct, the third is not. Japan's growth was primarily due to very high rates of saving and investment—capital accumulation.

c. Disagree. The opposite is true. Economists agree about the six components of transition, but disagree about the sequencing and speed.

10. Disagree. Though it is true that central planners can command a higher rate of national saving and capital accumulation, central planning requires keen and virtuous planners to ensure that scarce capital flows to where it is needed most. In a capitalist market economy, the self-interest of capital owners steers capital to those sectors where it is needed most—that is, those sectors offering the highest rate of return. Thus, although under central planning there might be more capital accumulation, it will not necessarily be the right kind of capital and will not necessarily find its way to the right places. Empirically, the United States grew faster than the USSR in the 1970s and 1980s.

INDEX

PHOTO CREDITS

Chapters

Case Studies